INDIAN EPIGRAPHICAL GLOSSARY

INDIAN EPIGRAPHICAL GLOSSARY

D. C. Sircar

Carmichael Professor and Head of the Department of Ancient Indian History and Culture, University of Calcutta

MOTILAL BANARSIDASS

DELHI :: VARANASI :: PATNA

First Edition 1966

ISBN: 978-81-2080-562-0

Also available at:

MOTILAL BANARSIDASS
41 U.A. Bungalow Road, Jawahar Nagar, Delhi 110 007
8 Mahalaxmi Chamber, Warden Road, Mumbai 400 026
120 Royapettah High Road, Mylapore, Chennai 600 004
Sanas Plaza, Subhash Nagar, Pune 411 002
16 St. Mark's Road, Bangalore 560 001
8 Camac Street, Calcutta 700 017
Ashok Rajpath, Patna 800 004
Chowk, Varanasi 221 0011

PRINTED IN INDIA
BY JAINENDRA PRAKASH JAIN AT SHRI JAINENDRA PRESS,
A-45 NARAINA, PHASE I, NEW DELHI 110 028
AND PUBLISHED BY NARENDRA PRAKASH JAIN FOR
MOTILAL BANARSIDASS PUBLISHERS PRIVATE LIMITED,
BUNGALOW ROAD, DELHI 110 007

*Dedicated to the Memory of James Prinsep
and Other Savants who deciphered our
Forgotten Scripts and reconstructed
the History of our Past.*

CONTENTS

PREFACE

It is with a sense of diffidence that I am placing my *Indian Epigraphical Glossary* in the hands of the students of Indian epigraphy and lexicography. Originally it was my intention to insert it in my *Indian Epigraphy* as an Appendix to the Chapter on 'Technical Expressions'. But, as my collection of the material progressed, I felt that it would be rather too big for an Appendix. At the same time, I also realised that it was not possible for a single man to collect all interesting words and expressions from all published epigraphic records in the various Indian languages in a short period of time. But I was eager to do as much as it was possible for me in the limited time I could devote to the work, and the result of the attempt is this nucleus now placed in the hands of readers interested in inscriptions. I am fully conscious of my own limitations as well as of the possibility of errors of judgment and of omission and commission creeping into the work. There may be cases wherein I have been misled by earlier writers, or accepted their doubtful suggestion as correct, or misunderstood them. It is hoped, nevertheless, that the work may be of some help to the students and to the future compiler of a fuller Glossary of this type.

The majority of words collected in this Glossary occur in inscriptions in Sanskrit or in the Sanskritic and Dravidian languages. My aim has primarily been to collect Sanskrit words, and generally the Prakrit and *tadbhava* words have been given in their Sanskrit forms, although some Dravidian or Deśī words have also been included. Sanskrit words used in Tamil with *n* and *m* suffixed to them have been ususally quoted without the suffixes; e.g., *varāhaṉ* and *liṅgam* have been recognised as *varāha* and *liṅga*. Likewise, the suffix *mu* in Sanskrit words used in Telugu has been generally omitted. Feminine words ending in *a* and *i*, as used in the Dravidian languages, have often been quoted with the vowels lengthened. In Tamil words, intervocalic *k*, *c*, *ṭ*, *t* and *p* have sometimes been represented by *g*, *j*, *d*, *d* and *b* respectivly. It is felt that, while weeding out words without special significance from my original collection, some were left over. There are also some words collected from sources other than epigraphic records.

There are three Appendices at the end of the volume, the first of which contains passages indicating the privileges, etc., enjoyed by the donees of rent-free (or partially rent-free) holdings. Appendix II contains a list of various levies that are known from inscriptions in Dravidian languages, especially Tamil. These Appendices are expected to throw light on the rights and obligations of the tenants of ancient and medieval India and on the meanings of some of the Sanskritic words in the Glossary. The third Appendix contains words of numismatic interest.

The words have been mostly taken from my *Indian Epigraphy* and the Indices and Glossaries appended to various epigraphical publications, and references to these have been indicated in short. Full references with the indication of pages, etc., have, however, been provided in certain cases especially when the words occur in the epigraphic texts, but are not noticed in the Indices, etc., pertaining to the Volumes in question. A key to the shortened references is supplied below separately. The references cited under a word are of course not exhaustive in all cases. The Index has been prepared by Sri Dipak Ranjan Das, Lecturer, Sanskrit College, Calcutta, to whom my sincere thanks are due.

While it is a matter of satisfaction that I have probably succeeded in explaining a number of expressions, which were previously unintelligible or misunderstood, and in grouping together connected items by cross-references in numerous cases, I am sorry to feel that it is difficult to compile a work of this type without errors, and even more difficult is to print it without technical blemishes including misprints. I therefore crave the indulgence of sympathic readers for all kind of mistakes that might have crept into the book and request them to be so kind as to draw my attention to the defects they may notice in it.

Pramāṇa-siddhānta-viruddham=atra
yat=kiñcid=uktaṁ mati-māndya-doṣāt ।
mātsaryam=utsārya tad=ārya-cittāḥ
prasādam=ādhāya viśodhayantu ॥

645, New Alipore, Calcutta-53, D. C. Sircar
November 15, 1965.

SPECIAL ABBREVIATIONS TO THE SECTIONS OF *INDIAN EPIGRAPHY* AND TO OTHER GLOSSARIES AND INDICES

ASLV =*Administration and Social Life under Vijayanagara* by T. V. Mahalingam, pp. 418-76 (Index).

BL =Bhandarkar's List=*A List of Inscriptions of Northern India in Brāhmī and its Derivative Scripts from about 200 A. C.* by D. R. Bhandarkar, Appendix to the *Epigraphia Indica*, Volumes XIX-XXIII, pp. 297-365 (Index).

Chamba=*Antiquities of Chamba State*, Part II, by B. Ch. Chhabra, pp. 180-93 (Index).

CII =*Corpus Inscriptionum Indicarum*; e. g., CII 2-1= *Corpus Inscriptionum Indicarum*, Volume II, Part i, pp. 181-85 (Index) ; CII 3, 4=Indices to *Corpus Inscriptionum Indicarum*, Volumes III and IV.

CITD =*Corpus of Inscriptions in the Telingana Districts of H. E. H. the Nizam's Dominions* by P. Sreenivasachar, Part II, pp. 201-12 (Glossary).

EI =*Epigraphia Indica*; e. g., EI 1=*Epigraphia Indica*, Volume I, pp. 461-78 (Index) ; EI 2, 6, 12= Indices to *Epigraphia Indica*, Volumes II, VI and XII.

HA =*Holy Abu* by Muni Jayantavijaya, translated by U.P. Shah, pp. 198-204 (Glossary).

HD =*History of Dharmaśāstra* by P. V. Kane, Volume III, pp. 975-1007 (Glossary styled 'Appendix—Note 191').

HRS =*Hindu Revenue System* by U. N. Ghoshal, pp. 289 ff. (Glossary and Index).

IA =*Indian Antiquary*; e.g., IA 5=*Indian Antiquary*, Volume V, pp. 363-71 (Index) ; IA 8, 15, 20=Indices to *Indian Antiquary*, Volumes VIII, XV and XX.

IE =*Indian Epigraphy* by D.C. Sircar; e.g., IE 8-2= *Indian Epigraphy*, Chapter VIII, Section ii; IE 7-1-2=*Indian Epigraphy*, Chapter VII, Section i, Subsection 2.

LL =Lüders' List=*A List of Brāhmī Inscriptions* by H. Lüders, Appendix to the *Epigraphia Indica*, Volume X, pp. 213-24 (Index).

LP =*Lekhapaddhati*, G. O. S., No. XXI, pp. 97-128 (Glossary).

ML =Majumdar's List=*A List of Kharoṣṭhī Inscriptions* by N. G. Majumdar in the *Journal of the Asiatic Society of Bengal*, New Series, Vol. XX, 1924, pp. 35-39 (Index).

PJS =*Prācīna Jaina-lekha Sandoha* by Muni Jayantavijaya, p. 61 (Glossary).

SII =*South Indian Inscriptions*; e.g., SII 1=*South Indian Inscriptions*, Volume I, pp. 171-83 (Index); SII 11-2=*South Indian Inscriptions*, Volume XI, Part ii, pp. 267-72 (Index) ; SII 1, 3, 12-2=Indices to *South Indian Inscriptions*, Volumes I, III, and XII, Part ii.

SITI =*South Indian Temple Inscriptions* by T. N. Subramanian, Volume III, Part ii, pp. i-civ (Glossary in an 'Annexure' at the end of the volume).

GENERAL ABBREVIATIONS

Ag. Syst. or *Ag. Syst.*	
Anc. Ind.	=*Agrarian System of Ancient India* by U. N. Ghoshal.
Ant. Ch. St.	=*Antiquities of Chamba State*, Vol. I, by J. Ph. Vogel.
Arch. Rev.	=*Indian Archaeology—A Review* published by the Archaeological Survey of India.
A. R. Ep.	=*Annual Report on* [*Indian* or *South Indian*] *Epigraphy*.
Bhandarkar's List	—see *BL* under *Special Abbreviations*.
Bhār. Vid.	=*Bhāratīya Vidyā*, Bombay.
Bomb. Gaz.	=*Bombay Gazetteer*.
Bul. Dec. Col. Res. Inst.	=*Bulletin of the Deccan College Post-Graduate and Research Institute*, Poona.
Carm. Lect.	=*The Carmichael Lecturers* delivered by D. R. Bhandarkar in 1918, 1921 and 1923.
CII	—see *CII* under *Special Abbreviations*.
DHNI	=*Dynastic History of Northern India* by H. C. Ray.
Dh. S.	=*Dharmasūtra*.
Dict.	=*Dictionary*.
Ep. Ind.	—see *EI* under *Special Abbreviations*.
G. O. S.	=Gaekwad Oriental Series.
Hist. Asp. Ins. Beng.	=*Historical Aspects of the Inscriptions of Bengal* by B. C. Sen.
Hist. Dharm.	—see *HD* under *Special Abbreviations*.
H. Rev. Syst.	—see *HRS* under *Special Abbreviations*.
I.E.	—see *IE* under *Special Abbreviations*.
IHQ	=*Indian Historical Quarterly*, Calcutta.
Imp. Ins. Bar. St.	=*Important Inscriptions from the Baroda State* edited by A. S. Gadre and others.
Ind. Ant.	—see *IA* under *Special Abbreviations*.
Ind. Cult.	=*Indian Culture*.
Ind. Ep.	—see *IE* under *Special Abbreviations*.
JAHRS	=*Journal of the Andhra Historical Research Society*, Rajahmundry.
JAS	=*Journal of the Asiatic Society*, Calcutta.

JBBRAS	=*Journal of the Bombay Branch of the Royal Asiatic Society*, Bombay.
JBORS	=*Journal of the Bihar and Orissa Research Society*, Patna.
JNSI	=*Journal of the Numismatic Society of India*, Varanasi.
Journ. As. Soc.	=*Journal of the Asiatic Society*, Calcutta.
Journ. As. Soc. Pak.	=*Journal of the Asiatic Society of Pakistan*, Dacca.
Journ. Mad. Univ.	=*Journal of the Madras University*, Madras.
Journ. Or. Inst.	=*Journal of the Oriental Institute*, Baroda.
Mathura Ins.	=*Mathura Inscriptions* by H. Lüders, edited by K. L. Janert.
Nach. Akad. Wissen. Goetting.	=*Nachrichten der Akademie der Wissenschaften in Goettingen.*
Naik's List	=*Inscriptions of the Deccan* by A. V. Naik, published in the *Bulletin of the Deccan College Post-Graduate and Research Institute*, Poona, Vol. IX, 1947-48.
Pāli-Eng. Dict.	=*Pāli-English Dictionary* published by the Pali Texts Society, London.
Proc. IHC	=*Proceedings of the Indian History Congress.*
Proc. IHRC	=*Proceedings of the Indian Historical Records Commission.*
Prog. Rep. ASI, WC	=*Progress Report of the Archaeological Survey of India, Western Circle.*
Select Inscriptions or *Sel. Ins.*	—see *SI* under *Special Abbreviations.*
S.I.I.	—see *SII* under *Special Abbreviations.*
Stud. Geog. Anc. Med. Ind.	=*Studies in the Geography of Ancient and Medieval India* by D. C. Sircar.
Suc. Sāt. or *Suc. Sāt. L. Dec.*	=*The Successors of the Sātavāhanas in the Lower Deccan* by D. C. Sircar.
Univ. Cey. Rev.	=*University of Ceylon Review.*
Viṣṇu Dh. S.	=*Viṣṇu Dharmasūtra.*
Wilson's Glossary	=*Glossary of Judiciat and Revenue Terms* by H. H. Wilson.
Z. D. M. G.	=*Zeitschrift der Morgenlaendischen Geselschaft.*

SYSTEM OF TRANSLITERATION

आ=ā,	ई=ī,	ऊ=ū,
ऋ=ṛ,	ॠ=ṝ,	ऌ=ḷ,
ॡ=ḹ,	ए (long)=e,	ए (short)=ĕ,
ओ (long)=o,	ओ (short)=ŏ,	ङ=ṅ,
च=c,	ञ=ñ,	ट=ṭ,
ड=ḍ,	ण=ṇ,	श=ś,
ष=ṣ,	ड़=ḍ̤	ळ=ḷ,

Dravidian palatal alveolar *n*=n̤,

Dravidian palatal alveolar *r*=r̤,

Dravidian cerebral voiced fricative (i.e. voiced *ṣ*)=ḷ̥,

anusvāra	=ṁ,	visarga	=ḥ,
upadhmānīya	=h̤,	jihvāmūlīya	=ḣ

A

ābādha (CII 1), illness.

ābādhā (EI 15), same as *bādhā* or *vādhā*; obstacle.

abātamāla, abātamālā, Prakrit; meaning doubtful (cf. *Ep. Ind.*, Vol. XV, p. 272; *ZDMG*, Vol. XL, pp. 345-46); explained as a kind of sculptured slab (LL).

abdapa (IA 16), the entrance of the sun into the Aries (*Meṣa*).

abda-pūjā (EI 32), a rite.

ābdārkhānah (IE 8-3; EI 31), Persian; 'water-house'; cf. *Pānīy-āgārika*.

abdhi (IE 7-1-2), 'four'; see *sāgara*.

ābdika-śrāddha (CII 4), an annual rite in honour of a dead person.

ābhāvya (EI 11, 16), income or proceeds; cf. *rāja-rāja-puruṣ ādibhiḥ svaṁ svam=ābhāvyaṁ parihartavyam*; see also *rāja-bhāvya*, etc. Cf. 'the income (*ābhāvya*) derived from the loads on bullocks going on their way or coming to Nāḍlāi' (*Ep. Ind.*, Vol. XI, p. 36).

abhaya (EI 24), pose of hand (*mudrā*); see *abhaya-mudrā*. (*SITI*), place of security to persons in distress; called *añjinānpugal-idam* in Tamil. Cf. *abhaya-śāsana*.

abhaya-hasta (SII 2), pose of hand known as *abhaya-mudrā* (q. v.).

abhaya-mudrā (HA), pose of hand offering protection, in which the palm of the right hand, facing the devotee, is held with fingers upwards. Cf. *abhaya-hasta*.

abhaya-śāsana (EI 12, 27; SITI), 'grant of shelter', 'charter of security'; a deed offering protection; a grant recording the provision of shelter.

ābhigāmika-guṇa (CII 3, 4), certain attractive qualities.

abhighāta (LP), an injury.

abhihāra (CII 1), a reward.

abhijñāna (LP), a token by which the identity of a person is recognised.

abhikāra, cf. *kṛt-ābhikāra* (CII 1), probably, one who has committed an offence under the instigation of another.

abhilekhitaka (IE 8-8), probably, a written complaint.

abhinava (EI 5; IA 18), name of a tax; cf. *abhinava-mārgaṇaka-prabhṛti-sarv-ādāyair=upetaḥ*, epithet of the gift village. It may also mean 'new' and the reference may be to the new *mārgaṇaka* tax. See *abhinava-mārgaṇaka*.

abhinava-mārgaṇaka (*Ep. Ind.*, Vol. III, p. 264, note 1), name of a tax. See *mārgaṇaka*, *mārg-ādāya*, etc.

abhipreta (CII 1), intention.

Ābhīra (IE 8-3), member of the cowherd community.

abhirakta (CII 1), beloved one.

abhiṣeka (EI 4), coronation; cf. *abhiṣeka-kkāṇi*, *abhiṣeka-kkāṇikkai* (SITI), Sanskrit-Tamil; presents offered to the king at the time of his coronation.

abhiṣeka-maṇḍapa (SITI), a hall where ceremonial baths are taken; the coronation hall; also called *tiru-mañjana-śālai* and *kuḻikkum-iḍam* in Tamil.

abhiṣeka-nāman (SITI), the name or title assumed by a king at the time of his coronation.

abhiṣikta (CII 1), cf. *dvādaśa-varṣ-ābhiṣikta*, 'when one has been anointed twelve years', 'when twelve years have elapsed from one's coronation'. See *Ep. Ind.*, Vol. XXXIII, pp. 333 ff.

abhīṣṭa-devatā (IA 18), same as *iṣṭa-devatā*; the favourite deity; the tulelary deity.

abhisthāna, correctly *abhiṣṭhāna*; used in the sense of *adhiṣṭhāna*, 'the residence', 'a city', or 'the headquarters'. Cf. *Ep. Ind.*, Vol. XXXIV, p. 219.

Abhitvaramāṇa, *Abhitvaramāṇaka* (IE 8-3; EI 31; HD), the letter-carrier or a special kind of messenger. Cf *Ep. Ind.*, Vol. XVII, p. 321 (*dūta-praiṣaṇika-gamāgamik-ābhitvaramāṇaka*); Vogel, *Ant. Ch. St.*, pp. 125-26.

ābhoga (IE 8-4), a territorial unit; similar to *bhoga*; cf. *Gorajj-ābhoga*.

abhra (IE 7-1-2), 'cypher'.

abhyaṅga (IA 22), smearing the body with oil.

Ābhyantara (HD), an officer specially intimate or in close contact with the king. Cf. *Antaraṅga*. See *Rājataraṅgiṇī*, VIII. 426. But cf. also *Ābhyantarika*, *Abhyantar-opasthāyaka*.

Abhyantara-bhāṇḍār-ādhikārin, cf. *Bhītara-bhaṇḍār-ādhikārin* (IE 8-3; EI 28).

ābhyantar-ādāya, cf. *bāhy-ābhyantar-ādāya* (IE 8-5); internal revenue income of a village; probably, taxes payable to the village authorities as against those payable to the king. Cf. *antar-āya*, *abhyantara-siddhi*, *antaḥ-kara*, etc. See *bāhya*.

abhyantara-siddhi, *abhyantara-siddhika* (IE 8-5; EI 20, 22), same as *ābhyantara-siddhi*; internal income or revenue, or taxes payable to the village authorities as against those payable to the king; cf. *tribhog-ābhyantara-siddhi*, *bāhy-ābhyantara-siddhi*, *bāhy-ābhyantar-ādāya*; also *sarv-ābhyantara-siddhi* (EI 20), and *antaḥ-siddhika* (CII 4), a privilege of the donee of rent-free land. According to some (CII 4), it refers to the privilege of the donee offering full power of adjudication in law-suits. But expressions like *tribhog-ābhyantara-siddhi* (q. v.) render it doubtful. See *bāhya*, *siddhi*, *siddh-āya*.

ābhyantara-siddhi (CII 4), same as *abhyantara-siddhi*; explained by some as 'the powers of adjudication'; probably, taxes payable to the village authorities as against those payable to the king. See *abhyantara-siddhi*, etc.

Ābhyantarika (IE 8-3), a guard of the inner apartments of the palace; cf. *Ābhyantarikā*. See *Ābhyantara*, *Abhyantar-opasthāyaka*.

Ābhyantarikā, a female guard of the inner apartment of the palace; probably also a concubine (*Ep. Ind.*, Vol. XXXV,p.3).

Abhyantar-opasthāyaka (LL), a servant.

Abhyāsin (SII 13), a student.

abhyavahāra-maṇḍapa (EI 3), dining hall.

abhyupāgama (IE 8-8), arrival.

abhyūṣa (EI 7), a cake.

abhyutsarpita (CII 2-1), same as *utsarpita*; erected.

abhyutthita, cf. *abbhuṭṭhio khāmavo* (HA), obeisance to one's teacher (i.e. a Jain monk) with formal query about the his health and confession of one's own weakness.

abja (IE 7-1-2), 'one'.

abja-dala (IE 7-1-2), 'one hundred'.

Āboṭī (EI 11), an inferior class of Brāhmaṇas in Rajasthan.

ā-candr-ārkkam (SITI), 'so long as the moon and the sun last'; 'in perpetuity'.

acala-pravṛtti (SII 11-1), cf. 'was administering Pandigoḷa as *acala-pravṛtti*'; a kind of tenure; probably, a permanent holding. See *vṛtti*, the same as *pravṛtti*.

ācāra (IE 8-5; EI 30), a custom or customary law.

(*EI* 20), religious practice, being regarded as five in number.

Cf. navanavaty-ācāreṇa (LP), '99 per cent', i.e. 'certainly'.

ācāra-pātra (EI 30), same as *sthiti-pātra*, *ācāra-sthiti-pātra*, etc.; a document relating to customary laws.

ācāra-sthiti-pātra (IE 8-5), same as *ācāra-pātra*, etc.; regulation regarding customary laws; cf. *sthiti-pātra*, a charter relating to customary laws (*Ep. Ind.*, Vol. XXX, p. 169).

Ācārya (EI 33; BL), title of a religious teacher; used commonly by the Buddhists and Jains (LL; SII 1).

(*CII* 3 ; EI 32 ; ML), a spiritual guide or teacher; a preceptor.

Same as *Sthān-ācārya* (EI 17), a temple priest.

(*EI* 8; IA 14), an architect; used in the sense of 'a master', i.e. 'a master-mason'; cf. *Ācāri* (EI 17), an artisan. Pāli *Ācariya* is explained as 'a master goldsmith' in the *P.T.S. Pāli-Eng. Dict.*

(*LL*), title of a sculptor.

(*HA*; IA 19), Jain; a *Sādhu* who has the right of both reading the sacred texts publicly and explaining them authoritatively.

ācāryakula (LL), a Buddhist temple; cf. *devakula*.

ācārya-pīṭha (EI 16), a holy site; a site sanctified by a religious teacher.

ācārya-pūjanā (SITI), honorarium payable to priests.

ācchanna (EI 30), a word of doubtful import.

accu (IE 8-8; SITI), Tamil; name of a coin; cf. *ānai-accu*, *nall-ānai-accu*, *paḻamudal-ānai-accu*, *paḻañjalāgai-accu*, *paducca-lāgai-accu*, *amudan-accu*, *uṇḍi-accu*, etc. Cf. also *pañcālav-accu* (SITI), name of a coin probably struck by the body called *pañcālattār* or *pañcakarmāra*; *uṇḍiy-accu* (SITI); *vaḻudiy-accu-varggam* (SITI), a group of taxes payable in Pāṇḍya coins; *yakki-accu* (SITI), from Sanskrit *Yakṣī*; name of a coin current in the Koṅgu country.

(*EI* 24), name of a tax.

accu-pannāya (EI 16), department of taxation or coining.

Accupannāyadadhiṣṭhāyaka (IE 8-3), Kannaḍa; superintendent of the revenue from mints; sometimes also called *Mahā-sāmantādhipati*, *Mahāpradhāna*, *Bhānasavĕrgaḍĕ*, etc., additionally.

accuvari (SITI), Tamil; probably the same as *pŏnvari*; the duty payable for minting gold into coins.

āchu (CII 4), same as *āsu*, the name of a coin; cf. Tamil *accu*.

acita (SITI), damage; injury.

āḍa, *aḍḍa* (CITD), Telugu; a measure of capacity equal to 2 *mānikas* or one-eighth of a *tūm*; half, especially half of a *fanam* or a certain measure called *kuñcamu*; a weight representing the eighteenth portion of a *varāha* (q. v.).

ādāna (IE 8-5; EI 12; CII 4), a levy or impost; same as *ādāya*.

āḍāṇaka (LP), same as *aḍḍāṇaka*; cf. *āḍāṇake muktā*, mortgaged; *valitāya āḍāṇake muktam*, Gujarātī *vaḷat dāṇ mukyuṁ*, 'something morgaged, the produce of which will pay off the debt in course of time'.

ādatta (IE 8-5), *adattā* (EI 33), *ādattā* (EI 28), a tax of uncertain import; probably, interest or fine on arrears of tax.

ādāya (EI 33), income or impost; cf. *bhūta-bhaviṣyad-vartamāna-niḥśeṣ-ādāya-sahita* (IE 8-5); cf. also *viseṇim-ādāya* (EI 21), name of a tax.

adbhuta (EI 33), same as *utpāta* (q. v.).

adbhuta-dharma, cf. *abbhuta-dhamma* (EI 33), Buddhist. Cf. Childers, *Pāli-Eng. Dict.*, s.v.

adbhuta-śānti (EI 33), a ceremony to avert evil.

aḍḍa-cinna (EI 18), name of a coin.

aḍḍaga, *aḍḍuga* (CITD), Telugu; half a *fanam*.

aḍḍāṇaka (LP), a morgaged thing; cf. *gṛh-āḍḍāṇaka-patra* (LP), deed for mortgaging a house.

Ādeśakārin (EI 10), an officer or agent, or a representative.

Ādeśa-naibandhika (EI 7; CII 4), official designation indicating the recorder of orders.

ādeya (EI 7, 12, 15; CII 3), 'what is to be taken or levied'; a fiscal term meaning the same thing as *ādāya*, i.e. income or impost; dues (*Ep. Ind.*, Vol. XXV, p. 237).

āḍha (IE 8-6), same as *āḍhika* or *āḍhaka*; a measure of capacity; a land measure also called *āḍhavāpa*.

āḍhā (IE 8-6), Bengali form of *āḍhaka* and *āḍhavāpa*.

adhaḥ, cf. *s-ādha-ūrdhva* (IE 8-5); what is below the surface of the ground; root-crops.

āḍhaka (IE 8-6; EI 27), a measure of capacity; often

regarded as equal to 264 handfuls and to one-fourth of a *droṇa*; 16 to 20 seers according to Bengali authors; also used as a shortened form of *āḍhavāpa* or *āḍhakavāpa*.

ādhāna, cf. *dān-ādhāna-vikraya* (IE 8-5); mortgaging. Cf. *n=ādheyaṁ na ca vikreyam* (*Ep. Ind.*, Vol. XXV, p. 218).

āḍhavāpa, also called *āḍhakavāpa* (IE 8-6), 'an area of land requiring one *āḍhaka* measure of seed grains for being sown'; a land measure which was not the same in all ages and localities.

Adhi (LP), contraction of *Adhikārin*, regarded by some as 'a revenue officer like the Māmlatdār'.

Adhi, *Ādhi* (IE 8-1; 8-8), shortened forms of *Adhikaraṇika* or *Ādhikaraṇika*.

ādhi (SII 2; LP), a mortgage or deposit; *ādhau kṛtam*, 'mortgaged'; cf. *ādhau muktam*, *ādhau dattam*. Cf. *vinaṣṭ-ādhi-sakta* (LP), used in connection with a lost thing which had been given in mortgage.

adhika (EI 3), intercalary [month].

adhik-ākṣara (LP), 'with words in excess'.

adhika-paḍi (CITD), Sanskrit-Telugu; an extra allowance in food (grain, salt, vegetables and all that is required to prepare a meal, including firewood), sometimes also in money, granted to servants, friends or poor people.

Adhikāra, cf. Tamil *Adigāram* (EI 25); same as *Adhikārin* (SII 1), explained as 'a magistrate'.

adhikāra-mel-eḻuttu (SITI), Sanskrit-Tamil; revisional order.

adhikaraṇa (IE 8-1, 8-8; EI 28), an office; cf. *rājakule='dhikaraṇasya*, apparently referring to an office. See *adhikaraṇ-āvadhāraṇā*, 'official investigation' (*Ep. Ind.*, Vol. XXXI, p. 267).

(*EI* 24), a court or department.

(*EI* 30), a law-court.

(*SITI*), a class of law courts; probably, the chief court.

(*EI* 30, 31), an administrative office or a board of administration.

(*EI* 31), a district.

(*SII* 2), same as *Adhikārin*, a magistrate.

adhikaraṇa-daṇḍa (SITI), fine imposed by the *adhikaraṇa* or law-court.

Adhikaraṇa-lekhaka (EI 30), a scribe pertaining to a law-court or office.

(*HD*), the official recorder or scribe [who drew up deeds of sale and the like after having measured the land to be sold]. Cf. *Rājataraṅgiṇī*, VI. 38; *Viṣṇu Dh. S.*, VII, 3.

Adhikaraṇika, *Ādhikaraṇika* (IE 8-1; EI 28), an officer belonging to or in charge of an *adhikaraṇa* or office.

adhikāra-varttanā (SITI), customary payments made to an officer at stipulated periods; probably the same as Sanskrit-Tamil *adhikāra-ppeṟu*, *adhikāra-ppŏn*, etc.

Adhikārika, *Ādhikārika* (IE 8-3; EI 2, 23, 28; CII 4; BL; HD), 'an officer'; same as *Adhikārin*, *Niyogika*, *Adhyakṣa*, etc., regarded as meaning a minister, magistrate, superintendent, governor or director. See *Ep. Ind.*, Vol. XXIV, p. 184.

Adhikāri-mukhya (EI 33), explained as 'the chief minister'.

Adhikārin (IE 8-3; EI 28; BL), 'an officer'; same as *Ādhikārika*; cf. Kannaḍa *Vĕrgaḍĕ*, etc., and Sanskrit *Adhyakṣa*, meaning a superintendent, governor or director.

(*ASLV*), explained as 'a special officer or royal agent'.

(*EI* 7), explained as 'a minister'.

(*SII* 2), explained as 'a magistrate'.

Cf. Viḍaiy-adhikāri, *Viḍaiyil-adhikāri* (SITI), an officer issuing royal orders.

Adhikṛta (EI 23, 24), 'an officer'; cf. *Adhikārin*.

Adhimahārāja (EI 15), royal title. Cf. *Adhirāja*.

Adhipati (LL), a king; cf. *pati*.

ādhi-patra (LP), a mortgage bond.

Adhirāja (IE 8-2), sometimes used as an imperial title, but sometimes as the title of a feudatory. Cf. *Adhimahārāja*.

(*BL*), title of a subordinate ruler.

(*LL*), designation of a supreme king.

Adhirājarāja (EI 9), royal title. Cf. *Rājarāja*, *Rājādhirāja*, etc.

adhirājya (EI 24), a realm or kingdom.

ādhirājya (CII 3), a derivative from the title *Adhirāja*; supreme sovereignty.

adhisthāna, *adhiṣṭhāna* (CII 1), cf. *dharm-ādhisthāna*, *dharm-ādhiṣṭhāna*, 'the establishment of morality'.

adhiṣṭhāna (IE 8-3; EI 24, 28, 31; LL), the capital or headquarters of an administrative unit; a city or town; the chief city. See *abhisthāna*.

(*EI* 9), probably, residence.

(*EI* 8), same as *sthāna*.

(*EI* 24), cf. *adhiṣṭhānam*, 'under the supervision of'.

(*SITI*), the base of the *vimāna* in a temple; a seat.

adhiṣṭhān-ādhikaraṇa (IE 8-3; EI 23; BL), administrative office or board at the headquarters of a territorial unit; office of the administrators of a city; the city office.

Adhiṣṭhāyaka (EI 16), official designation; same as *Adhyakṣa* (q.v.).

adhivāsa, cf. *adhivāsa-sakta-cāturvarṇya-samakṣam* (LP), 'in the presence of the people of the four castes living in the vicinity'; cf. *adhivāsa-saktīya* (LP); neighbours.

Adhvapa (EI 20), official designation; same as *Mārgapati*, etc.

Adhyakṣa (EI 24; CII 4), the head of a department; the superintendent of a department; a superintendent or director; sometimes mentioned in the list of officials (*Ep. Ind.*, Vol. XXXI, p. 80). Cf. *Mahādhyakṣa*.

(*IA* 20), explained as the *Dūtaka* or *Ājñapti*, i.e. executor of grants.

Adhyakṣa-pracāra (EI 12, 15), a list of superintendents of departments; probably also a notice setting forth the distribution of the *Adhyakṣas* in various departments and stations.

Adhyāpaka (EI 32), a teacher.

a-dhyātam, 'without any consideration or hesitation' (*Select Inscriptions*, p. 239).

adhyayana (SII 1), study of the Vedas.

Adhyayana-bhaṭṭa (IA 12), assistant officiating priest (also called *Sādhācārya*) at the temple at Rāmeśvaram.

adhyayan-āṅga (SITI), same as *adhyayana-vṛtti* (q. v.).

adhyayana-vṛtti (SITI), tax-free land endowed for reciting the Vedas in temples.

adhyetṛ (EI 32), a student.

ādi (IE 7-1-2), 'one'.

ādikāra (CII 1), an initiator; one who starts a practice or to do a particular deed.

Ādikartṛ (CII 3), 'an originator'; epithet of the Jain *Tīrthaṅkaras*.

Ādirāja (EI 12), an ancient king, e.g., Bharata, Nala, Nahuṣa, etc.; founder of a royal family (*Select Inscriptions*, pp. 412, 415).

āditya (IE 8-2; EI 33), ending of royal titles like *Vikramā-*

ditya, *Kramāditya*, *Mahendrāditya*, etc., probably popularised by the Imperial Guptas in the fourth century A.D.

(*IE* 7-1-2), 'twelve'.

āditya-kāca (EI 32), probably, the jewel called *sūryakānta*.

ādivarāha-dramma (EI 30; CII 4), name of a coin (*dramma*) styled after Ādivarāha, i.e. Pratīhāra Bhoja I (c. 836-85 A.D.).

adri (IE 7-1-2; EI 25), 'seven'.

ādvaliśa (IA 17), or *dvaliśa*; regarded as a word of doubtful meaning; but really, a geographical name.

ādya māṣa, the original *māṣa* 5 *ratis* in weight, later its weight being regarded as 6, 7 or 10 *ratis* (*JNSI*, Vol. XV, p. 139). See *māṣa*.

aga (IE 7-1-2), 'seven'.

(*SII* 3), earth or land.

āgama (SII 1), a doctrine; cf. *Lākul-āgama* (EI 32), the doctrine of Lakula (Lakulīśa). Cf. *āgama-samaya*.

Cf. *s-āgama-nirgama-praveśa* (IE 8-5), 'together with approaches, ingress and egress'.

āgama-nigama-dāna (LP), tax for importing and exporting.

agamārga (SITI), a variety of dance performed in the presence of the gods in temples.

āgama-samaya, cf. *Lākul-āgama-samaya* (EI 32), the tenets of Lakula's doctrine.

āgāmin (IE 8-5; EI 19; SITI), future income, future benefits; one of the 8 kinds of rights in the property; cf. *aṣṭa-bhoga*.

agara (EI 19), a corrupt form of *agrahāra*, often noticed in Tamil inscriptions.

agara-brahmadeya (SITI), village granted to Brāhmaṇas; also called *agara* (*agrahāra*) and *brahmadeya*. See *agara*.

agara-ppaṟṟu (SITI), Tamil; same as *agara* or *agrahāra*; land granted to Brāhmaṇas.

Agosāli (EI 28), a goldsmith; same as *Akṣaśālin*.

āghāṭa (EI 16), boundary; cf. *āghāṭana*, *āghāṭī*.

āghāṭana (*Ep. Ind.*, Vol. XII, p. 264, text line 42), same as *āghāṭa*, boundary; see also *āghāṭī*.

āghāṭī (EI 23), same as *āghāṭa*; boundary; see also *āghāṭana*.

aghoṣa (IE 7-1-2), 'thirteen' [being the number of surds in the Sanskrit alphabet].

agni (IE 7-1-2), 'three'.

agni-cayana (EI 32; IA 19), a sacrificial rite.

Agnicit (SII 2), title of a Brāhmaṇa. cf. *agni-cayana.*

agnihotra (EI 22; CII 3, 4), offerings to fire; a particular sacrifice, often mentioned as one of the five sacrificial rites (*mahāyajña*) which are the daily duties of a Brāhmaṇa.

Agnihotrin (CII 4), epithet of a Brāhmaṇa performing the *agnihotra* sacrifice.

agni-kārya (EI 33; SII 3), fire-oblation.

Agni-kula, 'a family, the progenitor of which was born from the fire pit of a sage'. See *Ep. Ind.*, Vol. XXXV, p. 162, for a 12th century 'Fire family' in the Nanded District, Maharashtra.

agni-kuṇḍa (CII 4), fire-pit; an emblem of the worship of the Fire or Sun.

agni-skandha (CII 1), masses of fire.

agniṣṭhā (SITI), firewood.

agni-sthitikā, fire-place (*Ep. Ind.*, Vol. XXXV, p. 107).

agniṣṭoma (CII 3), a particular sacrifice.

Agnyāhita (EI 15), same as *Āhitāgni*, 'a Brāhmaṇa perpetually maintaining and consecrating the sacred fire in his house'.

agra (EI 24), same as *agra-bhāga*; the king's share.

(*CII* 1), cf. *anyatra agreṇa parākrameṇa*, 'without a great effort'.

agra-bhāga (CII 2-1; ML), the principal share; same as *agra*, *agra-pratyāya*, the king's share.

agrabhāga-pratyaṁśa (CII 2-1), same as *agra-bhāga*, *agra-pratyaṁśa*.

agra-bhṛti (CII 1), a superior personage.

agra-dharmarājikā (ML), the chief Dharmarājikā (a *stūpa* enshrining the relics of the Dharmarāja or Buddha).

agahara, *agāhara*, *āgahara* (Chamba), corruptions of *agrahāra*.

Agrahara (EI 24), a collector of the king's share. See *agra*.

agrahāra (IE 8-4; EI 30; CII 4; SII 1; HRS; Chamba), rent-free land given to Brāhmaṇas; a rent-free village; a Brāhmaṇa village; sometimes suffixed to names of localities especially in South India. It was primarily, 'a rent-free village in the possession of Brāhmaṇas'; but there are occasional references to *dev-āgrahāra* (rent-free holding in the possession of a deity), *vaiśy-āgrahāra* (rent-free holding in the possession of the Vaiśyas), etc.; sometimes spelt *agrāhāra* (CII 3). See *mah-āgrahāra, brahmapurī, caturvedi-maṅgala,* etc.; also *aṅga-bhoga.*

agrahāra-pradey-āṁśa (EI 33), a small rent payable for land granted to Brāhmaṇas and declared rent-free.

Agrahārika, Āgrahārika (IE 3-8; EI 23; HD; CII 3; etc.), the owner of an *agrahāra*; sometimes probably, the superintendent of *agrahāras*; same as *Agrahārin.* Cf. *Ep. Ind.,* Vol. XXIV, p. 127.

Agrahārin, Agrahārīṇa (EI 23, 24), the holder of an *agrahāra*; headman or owner of an *agrahāra* village. Cf. *Agrahārika.*

Agrahārīṇa-mahattara (EI 24), headman among the *Agrahārīṇas,* i.e. owners of an *agrahāra* (rent-free village in the possession of Brāhmaṇas).

āgrahāyaṇī (EI 8), Mārgaśīrṣa su-di 15.

agraja (EI 23), the elder brother (or cousin); rarely used wrongly in the sense of 'the eldest son' (EI 9).

agrajanman (EI 9), same as *agraja* (q.v.); wrongly used to mean 'the eldest son' instead of 'the elder brother' (cf. *agraja*).

(*El* 24), a Brāhmaṇa.

Agra-mahādevī (SITI), chief queen of a king.

Agra-mahāmahiṣī (IE 8-2), title of a chief queen; cf. *Mahiṣī, Agra-mahiṣī, Mahāmahiṣī, Agra-mahādevī.*

Agra-mahiṣī (IE 8-2; EI 22; LL; ML), designation of the chief queen; cf. *Mahiṣī, Agra-mahādevī,* etc.

agra-maṇḍapa (SITI), front hall of a temple.

agra-pra.āda, same as *tala-vṛtti* (*Ep. Ind.,* Vol. XXXI, p. 166, note 2).

agra-pratyaṁśa (EI 23; CII 2-1; ML), principal share; same as *agra-bhāga.*

agra-pratyāya (EI 23), principal share or income; same as *agra-bhāga.*

agra-śālā (SII 3), a temple-kitchen.

āgrayaṇa (EI 7), the first Soma libation at the *agniṣṭoma* sacrifice; oblation consisting of first-fruits at the end of the rainy season.

agrika (LP), 'the previous one'.

agrika-pāyā (LP), original foundation; cf. Gujarātī *pāyā*, foundation.

Agronomoi (IE 8-3), Greek; probably the same as *Rajjuka*.

āhāḍa (EI 1), probably, a quarry.

Ahaṁvīra, see *Amīra*. Cf. *Ep. Ind.*, Vol. XXXIV, p. 178.

ahan (CII 3), 'a day'; used to denote the solar, or more properly civil, day.

āhāra (IE 8-4; EI 27; CII 1, 3, 4), a district; cf. *āharaṇī*.

Cf. grām-āhāra (IE 8-4), a group of villages.

(*IA* 17), cf. *s-āhāra* in Buddhist literature explained as *sa-janapada*. *Āhāra*= [land for] food; cf. *bhoga*.

āharaṇī (IE 8-4; EI 16), a district or its subdivision; cf. *Hastakavapr-āharaṇī* (*Ep. Ind.*, Vol. XI, p. 109); also cf. *āhāra*.

āhāra-viṣaya (IE 8-4), originally an *āhāra*, but later a *viṣaya*; cf. *Kheṭak-āhāra-viṣaya*.

āhavanīya (EI 32), the sacred fire.

ahi (IE 7-1-2), 'eight'.

ahi-daṇḍa (IE 8-5; EI 12, 28, 33), professional tax levied from snake-charmers or levy for their maintenance.

aiḍūka, same as *eḍūka* (q.v.).

airāvata (IE 7-1-2), 'one'; sometimes *hastin*, etc., are used in this sense though they really mean 'seven'.

aiśvary-āṣṭaka (EI 33), same as *aṣṭa-bhoga* (q. v.).

aitada (EI 28), derived from *etad*.

ājīvaka-kāsu (SITI), same as Tamil *āśuva-kkāśu*, *āśuvikaḻ-kāśu*, *āśuva-kkaḍamai*; tax payable by Ājīvakas or for the maintainance of Ājīvaka monks.

Ājñā (IE 8-3; EI 27; BL; CII 3), an order or command; same as *ājñapti* or *ājñāpti* supposed to be connected with giving the order for the drawing up of a charter; person receiving a king's order regarding the preparation of a charter; usually translated as 'executor of a grant'; standing alone, the word is supposed to indicate the office of the *Dūtaka*, though the latter seems to have been additionally responsible for giving the donee the possession of the gift land. Cf. *Ep. Ind.*, Vol. XIV, p. 362 (of the Gaṅga year 149) where the words are *ājñā mahāmahattara-Śivavarmā*; also *svayam=ājñā* (*CII*, Vol. III, p. 115; *Ep. Ind.*, Vol. XVI, p. 19) taken to mean that the king employed no *Dūtaka* to convey the details of his grant to the local officers, but that he gave the details in person.

The expression *sva-mukh-ājñā* (literally, the oral order of the king) is also explained in the same way. The suggestion that *Ājñādāpaka* sometimes occurs as a synonym of *Dūtaka* is wrong. See *Ājñapti*, *Ājñā-sañcārin*, etc. Cf. *Ind. Ep.*, pp. 143-44.

Cf. Tamil *āṇai* (EI 23), sign; the insignia.

Ājñā-bhogika (EI 21; BL), *Ājñā* and *Bhogika* wrongly made into a single official designation. See *Ājñā* and *Bhogika*.

Ājñā-dāpaka (BL; HD), wrongly taken as a compound expression meaning an officer (*Ind. Ant.*, Vol. XIV, p. 161). See *Ājñā* and *Dāpaka*.

Ājñādhāraka (ASLV), an executor of the royal order; cf. *Ājñā-paripālaka*.

Ājñā-paripālaka (ASLV), an executor of the royal order; cf. *Ājñā-dhāraka*.

Ājñapti, *Ājñāpti* (IE 8-3; EI 24, 27, 30; SII 1; HD), 'the agency that obtains the command'; the executor of a grant; one who communicates, at the order of the king, the details about a land grant to local officers; probably the same as *Dūtaka*. Cf. *Ājñā*; also Tamil *Vāy-kkeḻvi*, *Vāy-kkeḻviyār*. See *Ind.Ep.*, pp. 143-44; *Ep. Ind.*, Vol. VII, p. 184; Vol. VIII, p. 146. Cf. *Ājñā-sañcārin*.

Ājñā-sañcārin (EI 23, 24, 27), same as *Ājñapti*, etc.

Ājñā-śata-prāpayitṛ (EI 12), official designation.

ājñāta (IA 18), 'an order'; *sañcaritaṁ c=ājñātam*, 'and the command has been communicated or carried into effect.'

a-kālika (CII 1), 'not restricted to time'.

ākāra (CII 1), same as *prakāra*, a way or kind.

ākarṣaka (EI 5), probably, the extent [of a piece of land].

ākāśa (IE 7-1-2), 'cypher'.

Ākāśamukhin (ASLV), epithet of certain Śaiva ascetics, also called *Ākāśavāsin*.

ākāśa-pātāl-otpatti (EI 30), fruits and roots produced in a piece of land. Cf. *ākāś-otpatti*.

ākāśa-vāṇī (IA 11), an unearthly voice.

Ākāśa-vāsin (ASLV), same as *Ākāśamukhin* (q.v.).

ākāś-otpatti (HRS), 'produce of the sky'; fruits; wrongly regarded by some as the same as *bhūta-vāta-pratyāya* (q.v.). See *ākāśa-pātāl-otpatti*.

akhaṇḍa-dīpa (EI 30), a lamp to be perpetually burnt before a deity in a temple, the installation of which was regarded as a meritorious act; same as *nandā-dīpa*, etc.

Akhasāli (EI 7), same as *Akṣaśālin.*

akiñcid-grāhya (HRS), same as *akiñcit-kara*, 'free from tax'.

akiñcit-kara (HRS), same as *akiñcit-grāhya*, 'free from tax'.

akkam (SII 3; SITI), Tamil; name of a coin; one-twelfth of a *kāśu*; a mint (cf. *akka-śālā*).

akka-śālā (SITI), Tamil-Sanskrit; a mint; cf. *akkaśālai-vari* (SITI), charges payable to the mint for minting coins.

akkasālavaru (CITD), cf. Telugu *agasāli*, *akkasāla*, *akasālĕ*; also Kannaḍa *agasālavāḍu*; a goldsmith or his workshop.

Akkasāliga (EI 7), a goldsmith; same as *Akṣaśālika.*

akṛti (IE 7-1-2), 'twentytwo'.

akṣa, same as *suvarṇa* (q.v.).

akṣapaṭala (BL), the department of records and accounts. See *Akṣapaṭalika*, etc. Cf. *Mahāsāndhivigrah-ākṣapaṭal-ādhipati.*

akṣapaṭal-ādāya (IA 18), levy for the maintenance of the *akṣapaṭala* department or the *Paṭvārī*. Cf. *akṣapaṭala-prastha.*

Akṣapaṭal-ādhikṛta (CII 3; HD; BL), an officer of the *akṣapaṭala* department or the officer in charge of it; same as *Akṣapaṭalika*, etc. See *CII*, Vol. III, p. 257; *Rājataraṅgiṇī*, V. 301, 397-98.

Akṣapaṭal-ādhipati (BL), the head of the *akṣapaṭala* department; same as *Akṣapaṭalin*, etc.; also called *Akṣapāla* (cf. *karaṇa*).

Akṣapaṭal-ādhyakṣa (HD), the superintendent of records and accounts. Cf. *Arthaśāstra*, II. 7; *Hist. Dharm.*, Vol. III, p. 143.

akṣapaṭala-prastha (IA 18; HRS), contributions paid by the villagers at the rate of a *prastha* of grain (probably, per standard measure) for the expenses of the *akṣapaṭala* department (probably for the maintenance of the *Paṭvārī*). Cf. *akṣapaṭal-ādāya.*

Akṣapaṭalika (EI 30; CII 4; HD; BL), same as *Akṣapaṭal-ādhipati*, officer in charge of accounts and records. *Akṣapaṭala* means 'accounts office' (Stein) or 'records office' (Bühler).There is *Grām-ākṣapaṭalika* in the *Harṣacarita* (VII,para. 2) probably meaning the *Paṭvārī*, and a section on the superintendent of the *akṣapaṭala* in the *Arthaśāstra* (II. 7). See *Ep. Ind.*, Vol. XX, p. 128; Vol. IX, p. 305. Cf. *Mahākṣapaṭalika.*

Ākṣapaṭalika (HD), same as *Akṣapaṭalika*; officer in charge of the accounts and records office. Cf. *Ep. Ind.*, Vol. I, pp. 316, 318.

Akṣapaṭalin (EI 19; BL), same as *Akṣapaṭal-ādhipati*, *Akṣapaṭalika*, etc.

akṣara, cf. *hast-ākṣarāṇi* (LP), a deed for borrowing money; also *kṛṣṇ-ākṣarāṇi* (LP), the record containing a censure; also *ujjval-ākṣarāṇi* (LP), a certificate of good conduct; also *viśuddh-ākṣarāṇi* (LP), an acknowledgement. Cf. *uttar-ākṣarāṇi* (LP), same as Marāṭhī *utarāi*; probably, a deed by which land is given at a favourable rent to merchants, etc., who helped the government with money.

Cf. guṇ-ākṣara, also called *guṇa-patra*; see also *gupt-ākṣara*.

akṣarapalli (IA 11), the system of writing numbers by syllables; name applied to the system of writing numbers as found in inscriptions before the popularisation of the decimal system, though the symbols employed in the Brāhmī inscriptions do not appear to be *akṣaras* in all cases.

Akṣaśālika (EI 29), same as *Akṣaśālin*, etc.; a goldsmith.

(*HD*), explained as 'an officer in charge of the gambling-hall'.

Akṣaśālin (EI 29; BL), same as *Akṣaśālika*, etc.; a goldsmith; from Telugu-Kannaḍa *Akkasālĕ* (EI 3), *Agasāli*, etc. Cf. *Ep. Ind.*, Vol. XXIV, p. 173.

(*HD*), explained as 'an officer in charge of the gambling hall'.

akṣatā (IA 11), probably, rice grains mixed with red powder.

akṣata-tṛtīyā (EI 24), same as *akṣaya-tṛtīyā*.

akṣauhiṇī (IE 7-1-2), 'eleven'.

Akṣāvāpa (HD), superintendent of gambling. Cf. *Hist. Dharm.*, Vol. II, p. 1216; Vol. III, p. 112.

akṣayanī, *akṣayaṇī* (EI 32), modified forms of *akṣaya-nīvī*.

akṣayanidhi-dharma (EI 12), same as *akṣayanīvī-dharma* (q.v.).

akṣayanīkā (EI 30), corrupt form of *akṣaya-nīvikā*, a perpetual endowment.

akṣaya-nīvi, *akṣaya-nīvī* (CII 3, 4; HRS), a permanent endowment.

akṣayanīvī-dharma (EI 29), the nature of a permanent endowment; also called *akṣayanidhi-dharma* (EI 12).

akṣaya-nīvikā (EI 24, 30), same as *akṣaya-nīvī*; a perpetual endowment.

akṣaya-pūrṇamāsī (EI 23), probably, the same as Māgha su-di 15.

akṣaya-tṛtīyā (EI 4, 23; CII 4; IA 18; BL), same as Vaiśākha su-di 3; see *akṣata-tṛtīyā*.

akṣi (IE 7-1-2), 'two'; cf. *netra*.

akṣiṇin (IE 8-5; EI 19; SITI), actual or fixed income; regarded as one of the eight rights of ownership. Cf. *aṣṭa-bhoga*.

akṣoṭa-bhaṅga (HRS), same as *khoṭa-bhaṅga* and *ukkoṭa-bhaṅga* (*Abhidhānarājendra*, s.v. *parihāra*). Cf. *utkoṭa* and *bhaṅga*.

aḻag-accu (SITI), Tamil; name of a coin.

alam (CII 1), 'capable'.

ālambana (LL), the base stone.

alavaṇa (IA 19), probably a Sanskritised form of *aṟuvaṇa* (q. v.).

ālaya, cf. *ālai* (SII 3), a temple; a contraction of *dev-ālaya*. Cf. *āyatana*, *bhavana*, *pura*, etc.

ālepana (SITI), anointing; coating the image with unguent.

āli (Chamba), wet land, irrigable land; also called *kohlī*.

alinī (EI 26), 'a swarm of bees'; female Jain devotees.

alīpaka, also read as *alīyaka* (EI 32), a fiscal expression of uncertain import; see *nidhān-ālīpaka*. The word *alipaka* means 'a bee'. Thus *ālipaka* may refer to the right over wax, bee-hives, and honey. *Alīyaka*, from *ali*, 'a bee', would mean the samething.

Aḻiya (EI 15), an official title. Cf. *alīpaka*.

alīyaka, cf. *alīpaka*.

allavāṭa (IE 8-8; EI 30), meaning uncertain.

alpa-bhāṇḍatā (CII 1), moderation in the hoarding of wealth.

alpam-irai (SITI) Sanskrit-Tamil; a minor tax payable in grains.

amā (EI 24), abbreviation of *amāvāsyā*.

Amaca (HD), Prakrit *Amacca*=Sanskrit *Amātya* (q.v.). Cf. *Ep. Ind.*, Vol VIII, pp. 71, 73.

amalasāraka (CII 4), the circular fluted disc on the spire of a temple.

amaliman (EI 12), purity.

amānta (CII 3), the technical name for the scheme of the lunar months in Southern India, according to which a month ends with the new-moon day, and the bright fortnight precedes the dark. According to Fleet, it is always this arrangement that is taken for calculation in astronomical works, though, even in Southern India, the arrangement was not applied to the Śaka years, for the civil reckoning, till between 804 and 866 A.D.; on the other hand, according to him, even in Northern India, this arrangement was used in Nepal with the years of the Newār era, though it was abandoned there when the Newār era was followed by the Vikrama era in its northern variety. For its prevalence in Indonesia, see *Sel. Ins.*, p. 470.

amara (IE 7-1-2), 'thirtythree' [being the original number of the gods].

(*SITI*; ASLV), land or revenue granted by a ruler to his retainers for military service; land assigned to military officers who were entitled to collect only certain revenues with the obligation to raise a contingent of army ready for service whenever called upon and also to pay tribute to the king; same as *amara-māgaṇi*. Cf. *Amara-nāyaka*.

amara-māgaṇi (SITI; ASLV), same as *amara*; estate given to an *Amara-nāyaka*.

Amara-nāyaka (EI 16; SITI; ASLV), a retainer chief enjoying *amara*, i.e. land or its revenue, for military service to be rendered to his master.

amāri-rūḍhi (EI 11), Jain; an edict for the non-slaughter [of animals].

Amātya (IE 8-3; EI 28, 30; CII 3, 4; BL; HD; LL), a minister; sometimes, officer in charge of a district; explained as *deś-ādi-kārya-nirvāhaka*; in some cases, called *Sarvādhikārin*, etc., additionally. Cf. *Hist. Dharm.*, Vol. III, p. 114, note 150. See *Mahāmātya*.

amātya-sabhā (EI 32), same as *mantri-pariṣad*.

amāvāsyā, cf. *ṣaṣṭhī amāvāsyā*, *caturthī-amāvāsyā*, *nava-rātri-amāvāsyā*, *mahānavamī-amāvāsyā*, etc.

amboka (IE 7-1-2), 'two'; cf. *netra*.

ambā-kapīlikā, same as *āmra-pipīlikā* (q. v.).

ambara (IE 7-1-2), 'cypher'.

ambhonidhi (IE 7-1-2), 'four'; cf. *sāgara*.

ambikā-janika (CII 1), 'mothers and wives'; women in general.

ambudhi (IE 7-1-2), 'four'; see *sāgara*.

amburāśi (IE 7-1-2), 'four'; see *sāgara*.

aṁhati, also spelt *aṁhiti* (EI 4), a gift.

āmi (EI 28), same as Arabic *amīn*; an officer of the revenue or judicial department.

Amīra (IA 11), Indianised form of Arabic *Amīr*; often found in the form *Hammīra* in Indian records and rarely as *Hambīra*, *Haṁvīra* and *Ahaṁvīra* (*Ep. Ind.*, Vol. XXXIV, p. 178).

amma (EI 24), literally 'the mother'; a village goddess.

Ammanagandhavāraṇa (IE 8-2), Kannaḍa-Sanskrit; 'the musk-elephant of the father'; subordinate title; also found in the form *Appanagandhavāraṇa*.

āmnāta (EI 12), cf. *śrī-Mālava-gaṇ-āmnāte praśaste Kṛta-saṁjñite*; explained as 'authoritatively laid down' or 'constantly used'; cf. *sthiti*.

āmnāya (CII 4), a Jain sub-sect.

(*IA* 20), same as *kula* or *kula-krama*; generations, successions.

āmra-pipīlikā, cf. *aṁbā-kapilikā* (EI 2; CII 1), usually interpreted as 'the mother-ant'; but really, big red ants generally living in large numbers on mango trees. See *Ep. Ind.*, Vol. XXXV, pp. 99-100.

āmreḍana (EI 12), repetition.

amṛta-gaṇa (SII 12), same as Tamil *amirta-gaṇattār* (SITI), members of the committee for the management of village affairs; members in charge of the cash-receipts of a temple.

amṛta-paḍi, cf. Tamil *amuda-ppaḍi* (SII 1; SITI), raw rice; food offering to a deity; (CITD), *paḍi* is an allowance in food (i.e. all the necessary commodities to prepare a meal) and sometimes also in money and *amuda-paḍi* is an endowment often made in favour of a deity for daily offering of food as *bhoga*, etc.

amṛta-yoga (EI 9), a particular time regarded as auspicious.

aṁśa, a small territorial unit (*Ep. Ind.*, Vol. XV, p. 297, text line 26).

Aṁśa-bṛhadbhogika (IE 8-3; EI 28), probably, the shareholder of a big *jāgīr*. See *Bhāgika*.

aṁśa-gaṇa (EI 33); a class of metres; cf. *mātrā-gaṇa*.

Aṁśapati (EI 30), co-sharer of a gift land.

aṁśuka-bhāṇḍāra-karaṇa, cf. *karaṇa* (LP); the department of clothes.

amukāka-sakta (LP), 'belonging to a certain man', *sakta* being often used for *satka*.

anācchedya (IE 8-5), 'uncurtailable'; 'not to be resumed'; epithet of gift land. Cf. *Ep. Ind.*, Vol. XII, p. 267, note 4.

anādeśya (EI 12), 'not to be pointed out (or, ordered)'; epithet of gift land; same as *anirdeśya*.

anāhārya (IE 8-5), 'unresumbale'; epithet of gift land.

āṇaka, see *anna*.

anaka, *anikā* (EI 20), Prakrit suffixes to male and female names respectively, known from early South Indian inscriptions; same as *annaka*, *annikā*.

anala (IE 7-1-2), 'three'.

ānanda-nidhi (EI 24), a gift.

ānandathu (EI 12), joy.

ananta (IE 7-1-2), 'cypher'.

ananta-nidhi (EI 24), mistake for *ānanda-nidhi*.

ānantarya (CII 1), quickness.

anāsedhya (*Ep. Ind.*, Vol. XII, p. 267, note 4), free from legal restraints (e.g. *kāl-āsedha*, 'limitation of time'; *sthān-āsedha* 'confinement to a place'; *pravās-āsedha*, 'prohibition of removal or departure'; and *karm-āsedha* 'restriction from employment'); epithet of gift land.

anātha-saṁrakṣaṇa (EI 23), 'protection of the helpless', mentioned as the purpose of a donation.

āṇatti (SITI), Tamil; Sanskrit *ājñapti*; an executor of order; royal order.

anāvāsa (CII 1), 'habitation which is quite unsuitable for one'.

andhāruvā, *āndhāruvā* (IE 8-5; EI 12), variant readings of *arthāruvā* or *ārthāruvā* (q.v.); Oḍiyā name of a tax.

Āndhra-daṇḍa (IE 8-5), a tax; cf. *Turuṣka-daṇḍa* and *Tiguḷa-daṇḍa*. There is also reference to 'an assembly of *Āndhra-daṇḍa*', the meaning of which is doubtful unless *daṇḍa* is taken here in the sense of 'an army'.

aṇḍikā, weight equal to $\frac{1}{4}$ of a *māṣa* (*JNSI*, Vol. XVI, p. 48); same as the copper *paṇa* (ibid., Vol. II, p. 7); also called *dhānaka* and regarded as equal to 4 *kārṣāpaṇas* or to $\frac{1}{12}$th *suvarṇa* (ibid., p. 8).

anekānta-mata (SII 1), same as *syādvāda-mata* (q. v.).

Anĕsāhiṇi-vĕrgaḍa (*A. R. Ep.*, 1958-59, p. 12), Kannaḍa; official designation; same as Sanskrit *Gaja-sādhanik-ādhyakṣa*.

aṅga (IE 7-1-2), 'six'.

(*EI* 15), an abbreviation of *aṅga-bhoga*; cf. *gātra* (IA 11).

aṅga-bhoga (EI 17; CITD), often associated with *raṅga-bhoga* as *aṅga-raṅga-bhoga*, usually explained as 'decorations and illuminations of a deity'. That *aṅga-bhoga* means decoration of the image of a deity is clear from the fact that a queen is known to have received a village as an *agrahāra* for her *aṅga-bhoga*, i.e. as her pin-money (*Bomb. Gaz.*, Vol. I, Part ii, p. 448). Sometimes the land granted for the *aṅga-bhoga* of a deity came to be known as the deity's *aṅga-bhoga* (*Ep. Ind.*, Vol. XXXIII, p. 182); cf. *aṅga*, same as *gātra* (IA 11).

aṅgaḍa-siddhāya (CITD), Telugu-Sanskrit; fixed revenue from shops.

aṅga-devatā (SITI), attendant deity of a superior god; same as *parivāra-devatā*.

Aṅgaja (EI 16), same as the god Kāma.

aṅga-maṇi (SITI), property owned by a woman; cf. *aṅga-maṇi-dravya* (SITI), dowry.

Aṅga-nigūhaka (BL), an official designation of uncertain import; probably, a kind of spies.

aṅgāra, aṅgāraka, cf. *a-carm-āṅgāraka* (IE 8-5; EI 15); charcoal for cooking, which the villagers were obliged to supply to the king or landlord on occasions or to the touring officers.

aṅga-racanā (HA), adorning of the various limbs of an image of the Jina with marks of sandal paste or leaves of gold, silver, etc., and with additional ornaments.

Aṅgaraka (SII 11-1), corruption of *Aṅgarakṣa* (q.v.).

aṅgārakī (IA 26), same as *ba-di* 4.

Aṅgarakṣa, Aṅgarakṣaka (IE 8-3; EI 15, 29; SITI), body-guard; the king's body-guard, or the head of the body guards.

aṅga-raṅga-bhoga (EI 23; SII 1), decorations and illuminations of a deity; various kinds of enjoyment provided for a deity; sometimes explained as 'worship to include all kinds of enjoyments' (SITI). Cf. *aṅga-bhoga-raṅga-bhoga, raṅg-āṅga-bhoga*, etc.

aṅga-raṅga-bhoga-vaibhava (EI 3; SII 1; SITI), enjoyments of all kinds provided for a deity; same as *aṅga-raṅga-bhoga*.

aṅga-raṅga-vaibhoga (EI 3; SII 1; SITI), same as *aṅga-raṅga-bhoga*, i.e. *aṅga-bhoga* and *raṅga-bhoga*.

aṅga-śālā (SITI), same as *aṅka-śālā*.

Aṅga-vaidya (SITI), same as Tamil *Aṅga-vavicciyar*; a physician.

Āṅgīkaraṇika (IE 8-3), officer in charge of administering oaths in a court of law.

aṅgula, aṅguli (IE 8-6), a linear measure equal to the breadth of the middle finger.

aṅguli (IE 7-1-2), 'ten'; sometimes used to indicate 'twenty'.

Aniketŏs (IE 8-2), Greek; royal title; 'unopposed'; translated into Prakrit as *Apadihata* (Sanskrit *Apratihata*).

animeṣ-ānokaha (EI 4), same as *sura-druma*, i.e. *kalpa-vṛkṣa*.

Anivartaka-nivartayitṛ (CII 4), 'repeller of the unrepellable'; title of a ruler.

anivṛtti (LP), anxiety.

aniyata, cf. *niyat-āniyata* (IE 8-5); occasional taxes.

aniyukta (IA 9), cf. *niyukt-āniyukta-rājapuruṣa*; probably refers to officials of the king, who were not actually appointed by the government, but occupied posts by virtue of heredity or election.

añjaṣṭa-sabhā, añjaṣṭa-śattu-sabhai (SITI), Tamil-Sanskrit; village committee of five or eight members. Cf. *pañca-kula* and *aṣṭa-kula*.

añjuvaṇṇam (SITI; EI 35), Tamil; Sanskrit *pañca-varṇa*; the five artisan classes; called *hañjamāna* in Kannaḍa inscriptions; sometimes regarded as a form of Persian *anjuman*.

aṅka (IA 19), a name, appelation or *biruda*.

(*IE* 7-1-12; CII 4), 'nine'.

Cf. aṅke, aṅkena, aṅkataḥ (IA 15), 'in figures'.

Cf. aṅka, abbreviation of Telugu-Kannaḍa *aṅkakāṟa*; same as Sanskrit *gaṇḍa* (*Ep. Ind.*, Vol. XXXIV, p. 270), 'a hero, champion or warrior'. See *aṅkakāra*.

aṅka-daṇḍa-khaṇḍana, translated as 'faults, fines and divisions'; cf. *pañch-āṅga-prasāda*.

aṅkakāra (EI 3, 4), a champion; same as Telugu-Kannaḍa *aṅkakāṟa*, sometimes explained as 'a soldier or warrior who took a vow to defend his master and fight in the latter's cause to death' (*Hyderabad Archaeological Series*, No. 18, p. 34). See *aṅka*.

aṅka-śālā (SITI), probably, the place where duels were fought; cf. *aṅga-śālā*.

anna, Anglicised form of *āṇaka*; $\frac{1}{16}$th of a *rupee* (*JNSI*, Vol. XV, p. 142).

annaka, *annikā*, cf. *anaka*, *anikā*.

Aṇṇanasiṁha (IE 8-2), Kannaḍa; 'the lion of the brother'; a subordinate title. Cf. *Ayyanasiṁha*.

anta (IE 8-4; CII 1), a state beyond the borders of one's territories, or a bordering district; also its people; cf. *pratyanta*.

(*CII* 1), cf. *Anta-mahāmātra*, officer employed in districts bordering on the frontiers of one's kingdom.

(*EI* 3), a neighbour.

antaḥ-kara (CII 4), explained as 'excise duty'; probably, 'internal revenue' or revenue income; same as *antar-āya*, *antar-ādāya*, *abhyantar-ādāya*, etc.; cf. *antaḥ-kara-viṣṭika* (EI 6), *antara* (EI 15), etc.

Antaḥ-pratīhāra (IE 8-3), officer in charge of defending the back gate of the palace or of the palace-gates as distinguished from the gates of the capital city.

antaḥpura, cf. *karaṇa* (LP); the royal harem.

(*ML*), the household; same as *avarodhana* in Aśoka's edicts.

Antaḥpur-ādhyakṣa (IE 8-3; EI 13; SII 11-2), superintendent of the royal harem; same as *Āntaḥpurika*, *Stryadhyakṣa*, etc., and Sanskrit-Kannaḍa *Antaḥpura-vĕrgaḍĕ* (IE 8-3); sometimes also called *Mahāpradhāna*, *Mahāpasāyita*, *Hĕri-Lāḷa-Kannaḍa-sandhivigrahin*, *Manĕ-vĕrgaḍĕ*, etc., additionally.

Āntaḥpurika (EI 13, 14, 18, 19, 23; HD), officer in charge of the royal harem; cf. *Antaḥpur-ādhyakṣa*, etc. Cf. *Ep. Ind.*, Vol. IX, p. 305.

Antaḥpura-mahāmātra (HD), officer in charge of the royal harem, mentioned in the Masulipatam plates of Amma II (*Ep. Ind.*, Vol. XXIV, p. 276). Cf. *Stryadhyakṣa-mahāmātra* of Rock Edict XII of Aśoka (CII 1).

antaḥ-siddhika (CII 4), same as *abhyantara-siddhika*.

Anta mahāmātra (IE 8-3; CII 1), executive officers in charge of the bordering districts of an empire and probably not ambassadors at the courts of neighbouring kings. Cf. *Antapāla*.

Antapāla (EI 9), frontier guard; explained by some as 'an officer in charge of the boundaries' (HD). Cf. *Arthaśāstra*, I. 12 (one of the 18 *tīrthas*); II. 21; V, 1; Kāmandaka, XII. 5; *Mālavikāgnimitra*, Act I. See *Anta-mahāmātra*.

antara (CII 1), a period of time.

(*EI* 15), name of a tax; cf. *antar-ādāya*, *antaḥ-kara*, etc.

antarā (CII 1), 'in the interval'.

antar-ādāya (CII 4), explained as 'excise duty'; but same as *antaḥ-kara*, *abhyantar-ādāya*, etc.

antarāla (EI 1), part of a temple; cf. *antarāla-maṇḍapa*.

antarāla-maṇḍapa (SITI), portion of a temple connecting the *garbha-gṛha* and the *mukha-maṇḍapa*; also called *ardha-maṇḍapa*.

Antaraṅga (IE 8-3; BL), explained as 'a privy councillor or a physician', though the same person is known to be called *Rāja-vaidya* (i.e. the royal physician) and *Antaraṅga*; probably a private secretary; but mentioned along with *Vaiśvāsika* (EI 3); regarded by some as a class of royal servants very intimate with the king, probably the same as *Ābhyantara* (HD). Cf. *Ep. Ind.*, Vol. XI, p. 286; Vol. XII, p. 99.

āntarāvaḍḍi (IE 8-5; EI 12; 33), a variant reading of *āturāvaḍḍi* (q.v.); name of a tax; cf. *rintakābaḍḍi*.

antara-viniyoga (SITI), individual share to make up the shortage in the total revenue occasioned by the grant of exemption of *antar-āya* or *uḻvari*.

antar-āya (EI 22, 23; SII 1, 2), explained as 'a tax', 'revenue' or 'a kind of revenue'; same as *antar-ādāya*; also explained as internal revenue or taxes levied by local bodies, called *uḻvari* in Tamil (SITI).

antarāya-kkāśu, *antarāya-ppāṭṭam* (SITI), Sanskrit-Tamil; explained as 'internal taxes or minor taxes like the profession tax, etc., payable to the village assembly'.

antarikā (CII 1), a period of time passed.

antarikṣa (IE 7-1-2), 'cypher'.

antarīpa (EI 12), an island.

Antarvaṁśika (HD), officer in charge of the inner apartments or harem. See *Arthaśāstra*, I. 12 (mentioned among the 18 *tīrthas*); *Kādambarī* (para. 88); *Daśakumāracarita*, III; cf. *Antarveśika* in the *Amarakośa*, Kṣatriya-varga, 8.

Antevāsin (LL), a male pupil.

Antevāsinī (EI 25; LL), a female pupil.

anubandha (CII 1), same as *krama*, order.

(*SITI*), help.

anubhavana (IA 18), 'the time or period of office [of a person]'.

anubhoga-ppaṟṟ-ōḻugu (SITI), Sanskrit-Tamil; renewal of title deeds.

anucita (SITI), evil; damage.

anudhyai (IE 8-2), 'to meditate', etc.; 'to favour', etc.; cf. *anudhyāya* (IE 8-2), 'having favoured'; also *Svāmi-Mahāsena-Mātṛgaṇ-ānudhyāt-ābhiṣikta* (IE 8-2), 'favoured and anointed [as king] by the lord Mahāsena and the Mothers'; also *anudadhyuḥ* (IE 8-2), same as *anujagṛhuḥ*, '[they] favoured'. See *anudhyāna*; also *pād-ānudhyāta.*

anudhyāna (IE 8-2), same as *anugraha*; favour.

anudhyāna-rata (IE 8-2), see *pād-ānudhyāna-rata*, 'engaged in meditating on the feet of'.

anudhyāta (IE 8-2), see *pād-ānudhyāta.*

anudhyeya (IE 8-2), same as *anugrāhya*; 'to be favoured'.

anudivasam (CII 1), daily.

anudṛiś, cf. *anudarśayanti* (EI 15), 'inform [as follows]'.

anuga-jīvita, spelt in Kannaḍa as *aṇuga-jīvita* or *aṇuṁga-jīvita* (SII 11-1), a fief held by a king's subordinate for his maintenance; similar to *biḻa-vṛtti, bīḻ-ānuvṛtti.*

anugraha (IE 8-2), same as *anudhyāna*; favour.

anugraha-sthiti-pātra (IE 8-5), same as *sthiti-pātra* or *ācāra-sthiti-pātra* (*Ep. Ind.*, Vol. XXX, p. 169).

anugrāhya (IE 8-2), same as *anudhyeya*, 'to be favoured'.

anuja (*Ep. Ind.*, Vol XXXIII, p. 271), a younger cousin.

anuloma (CII 4), name of a kind of marriage, in which the bride belongs to a lower social order than the bridegroom.

anunidhyāpti, cf. *anunijhapayati* (CII 1); explanation or exhortation; cf. *nidhyāpti.*

anupratipatti, cf. *dharm-ānupratipatti* (CII 1), practice of morality.

anupūrvī, cf. *saṁvatsaraḥ dvitīyaḥ hemanta-pakṣaḥ caturthaḥ tithir=daśamī anay=ānupūrvyā.* Cf. *pūrvā.*

anurūpa (CII 1), adequate.

anusaṁyāna (CII 1), a ṭour.

anusandhāna, recitation (*A.R.Ep.*, 1959-60, No. B 335).

anuśās (CII 1), 'to inculate'.

anuśāsana, anuśāsanā (CII 1), same as *anuśasti*, inculcation.

anuśasti (CII 1), inculcation, instruction; same as *anuśāsana.*

Anusenāpati (EI 18), probably, a subordinate of the *Senāpati* (q.v.).

anuṣṭubh (IE 7-1-2), 'eight'.

anutāra (SITI), protection, guardianship.

Anutpanna-dāna-samudgrāhaka, an official title (Ghoshal, *H. Rev. Syst.*, pp. 221-22); officer engaged in the forcible collection of unrealised *dāna* (q. v.).

anuttara (EI 18), penance.

anuvah, cf. *anuvahamānaka* (EI 15), literally, 'flowing on'; but actually, 'ever-prospering'.

anuvarttanā (SITI), a class of contingent dues which come under the head *varttanā* (q.v.).

anuvidhā (CII 1), 'to conform to'.

anuvṛtti, same as *vṛtti*; cf. *bīḻa-vṛtti*, *bīḻ-ānuvṛtti* (SII 11-1).

anvaya (EI 33; SII 1), a [spiritual] race; a Jain sect.

anya-jāta (HRS), accidental revenue; one of the three kinds of revenue specified in the *Arthaśāstra*.

anyat, 'another thing' (*Ind. Ep.*, p. 133, note 2).

anyathā (LP), 'quite changed'.

anyatra (CII 1), 'excluding'.

apabhāra (EI 8), a burden.

apacāra (IE 8-5), same as *aparādha*; cf. *daś-āpacāra* (EI 15), same as *daś-āparādha*.

apadāna, cf. *dharm-āpadāna* (CII 1); a noble deed.

apagratha (CII 1), same as *upaghāta*; injury.

apakṛṣṭa (CII 1), distant.

āpaṇa (IE 8-5), a shop.

(*CII* 4), a market.

āpāna (EI 2; CII 1), a watering station or shed.

aparādha, see *daś-āparādha* (IE 8-5).

apara-pakṣa (IA 16), used to indicate 'the dark fortnight'.

aparigodha (CII 1), same as *aparibodha*.

aparipanthya (IE 8-5), 'not to be troubled'; an epithet of gift land.

apasaraka (EI 1), probably, a porch or portico.

apatya (CII 1), descendants.

apavāha (CII 1), the act of carrying away [as a prisoner].

apavaraka, cf. Prakrit *ovaraka* (EI 20; LL), a cell.

apaviñch, cf. *apaviñchya* (EI 15), 'having separated'.

apohana (SITI), waste or uncultivated; cf. Tamil *agovana*, waste land.

Apracarāja (IE 8-2, 8-3), Prakrit; Sanskrit *Apratyagrāja* (q. v.).

apradā (EI 15) '[gift land] not to be alienated'; same as *nīvī* ; sometimes used as an epithet of *akṣaya-nīvī*

apradā-dharma (EI 15), custom regarding inalienable gift land; same as *nīvī-dharma.*

aprahata (EI 15), uncultivated; same as *khila.*

apraharṭṛ (CII 1), 'one who observes or maintains'.

Apratihata, see *Aniketos*.

apratikara (HRS), explained as 'without the right of alienation'; 'without yield of revenue'; but cf. *pratikara.*

apratiṣṭhāpita (ML), non-interred.

Apratyagrāja, 'having no rival among kings'; feudatory title.

āptakriya (IA 18), a trusty agent.

āptoryāma (CII 3), name of a sacrifice.

apūrva, cf. *apūrva-Brāhmaṇa* (IA 18), a new Brāhmaṇa who was not fed on a previous occasion and is not to be fed again.

apūrvin, *apūri* (SITI), a Brāhmaṇa well-versed in the Vedas on a visit to holy shrines.

aputra-dhana (IE 8-5; EI 25; CII 4), confiscation of the property of one dying without leaving a son or an heir.

aputrikā-dhana (EI 3; CII 4; HRS), same as *aputra-dhana*; the property of persons who died sonless, which the king could confiscate; escheat of the property of females.

aputrika-dravya (EI 20), escheat property.

ārādh (CII 1), 'to attain'; cf. *svargam=ārādhayantu*; also *ārāddha* (CII 1), 'obtained'.

Ārādhya (EI 15), 'the worshipful one'; title of certain Śaivite Brāhmaṇas of Karṇāṭaka.

araghaṭṭa (EI 10, 14, 22), a water-drawing machine; a well with a water-wheel.

Ārakṣ-ādhikṛta (IE 8-3); cf. Prakrit *Ārakh-ādhikata* (EI 2), a police officer; a magistrate looking after the maintenance of law and order, or the chief of the king's body-guards; same as *Ārakṣika.*

Ārakṣika (EI 10), cf. Prakrit *Ārakhiya* (EI 2), a police officer; same as *Arakṣ-ādhikṛta*, and also *Talāra* (q. v.) and *Daṇḍapāśika* (q. v.); cf. *IHQ*, December 1960, p. 266.

ārāma (LL), a park.

(*ML*), a grove or monastery.

ārāmika (LL), a gardener.

araṇya (IE 8-5), a jungle.

Āraṇyaka (LL), a Buddhist hermit.

ārati, ārti (EI 1), a lamp; same as *ārātrika.*

ārātrika (SII 1), same as *nīrājana*; cf. *maṅgal-ārātrika* (EI 4), 'a lamp used in waving before an idol' ; also the rite.

ārcā (EI 24), the image of a god; cf. *arcā*, adoration.

arcā-deśa (EI 24), an object of adoration.

arcanā-bhoga (EI 23), offerings to be made to a deity at the time of worship.

(*SII* 3, 12; SITI), land set apart for meeting the expenses of worship (*arcanā*) in the temple; an endowment created for conducting worship; same as *arcanā-vṛtti.*

arcanā-vibhava-kāṇi (SITI), Sanskrit-Tamil; rent-free land granted to temple priests.

arcanā-vṛtti (SII 3; SITI); see *arcanā-bhoga.*

ardha-candra (SITI), literally, 'half-moon'; a part of the *tiruvāśi*; a variety of ornament.

(*SII* 2), the arch of an aureola.

ardha-jā(yā)ma (SII 13), midnight; midnight service in a temple; cf. *ardhajāma-ppuṟam* (SITI), Sanskrit-Tamil; land set apart for conducting the midnight worship in temples.

ardha-kākiṇī (CII 4), the half of a *kākiṇī*; name of a coin.

ardha-namasya-vṛtti (IE 8-5); see *namasya-vṛtti*; a gift land, taxed at half of the normal rate; cf. *pannāsa.*

Ardhanārīśvara (CII 4), a form of Śiva, in which the bodies of Śiva and Pārvatī are combined into one.

Ardha-nauvāṭaka (EI 28), official designation; mentioned together with *Nauvāṭaka* probably in the sense of an officer in command of half of a fleet.

ardhāṅgī (SITI), wife.

ardha-puruṣārika (CII 4), name of a tax.

ardha-sīrika (EI 9), same as *ārdhika.*

ardha-srotikā (EI 4), probably, a small stream or half of a river bed.

ardha-tṛtīya (CII 1), two and a half.

ārdhika (EI 9), a cultivator who tills other's lands and gets half the crop as his share.

Cf. Prakrit *addhika* (EI 1), a slave.

ardhodaya (EI 5), the new-moon *tithi* falling on a

Sunday when, during day time, the *nakṣatra* is Śravaṇā and the *yoga* Vyatīpāta.

ārdrā (SITI), Tamil *ātrai*; probably, the expenses for the *ārdrā* festival in the month of Mārgaḷi.

argala (IA 19), a check; used in certain dates and translated as 'checked by'; cf. *dvy-argala-catvāriṁśat-samadhika-vatsara-sahasra*, 'one thousand years, increased by forty [which have run into and are] checked by two', i.e. the year 1042.

argha-vañcana (EI 30), probably, fraud committed in respect of the price of articles.

Arhad-ācārya (EI 29), a Buddhist or Jain teacher.

Ardhad-āyatana (LL), a Jain temple.

Arhad-dāsa, a Jain monk; cf. *Arhad-dāsī*.

Arhad-dāsī (EI 10), a Jain nun.

Arhat (IE 7-1-2), 'twentyfour'.

(*CII* 3; LL), Buddhist and Jain; a class of saints.

ari (IE 7-1-2), 'six'; cf. *ari-ṣaḍ-varga*.

ari-ṣaḍ-varga, also called *ari-ṣaṭka* (CII 3), the group of six enemies, viz. *kāma*, *krodha*, *lobha*, etc.

Arjuna-kara A (IE 7-1-2), 'one thousand'.

Arka (IE 7-1-2; EI 25), 'twelve'.

(*EI* 7), explained as 'metal' in relation to *Arkaśālika*.

Arkaśālika (EI 7), same as *Akkasāliga*, *Akṣaśālika*; a goldsmith.

Arkaśālin (BL), same as *Akṣaśālin*; a goldsmith.

Arkasālin (EI 29), same as *Akṣaśālin*; a goldsmith.

arṇava (IE 7-1-2), 'four'.

arṇikā, weight equal to 2 *māṣas* (*JNSI*, Vol. VI, p. 46).

ārogya-dakṣiṇā (ML), the gift of health.

ārogya-śālā (EI 24; ASLV), hospital; cf. *Raṅgādhip-ārogyaśālā* (EI 24), 'the hospital of [the god] Raṅganātha [at Śrīraṅgam]'.

Ārohaka (EI 27), official designation; possibly, same as *Aśvāroha*.

artha (IE 7-1-2), 'five',

(*CII* 1), a cause or matter.

(*CII* 1), business.

Arth-ābhiyukta (IE 8-8), an accused.

artha-karman (CII 1), performance of duty.

Arthalekhin (CII 4), a secretary.

arthāruvā (IE 8-5; EI 28), a tax of uncertain import; probably, Sanskrit *artha-rūpyaka* in the sense of a levy from the money-lenders on the amounts loaned out; also read as *andhāruvā*; see *pratyarthāruvā*.

artiga, a lover (*Ep. Ind.*, Vol. XVI, p. 58).

aruhaṇa (EI 27), probably, the tax also called *āruvaṇa*.

āruvaṇa (EI 27), same as Tamil *aṟuvaṇa* (IA 19), the tax of six *paṇas* levied on *mānya* lands.

Arya (CII 1), same as *Vaiśya*.

ārya, cf. Tamil *ayyar* (EI 25), the father.

Cf. bhadatasa aya-Isipālitasa, 'of the Reverend Lord Ṛṣipālita' (*Ind. Ant.*, Vol. XI, p. 29).

(*SII* 1), a [Jain] saint.

āryā, cf. *āī* (EI 9), the mother.

ārya-guru, cf. *ajja-guru* (EI 5), 'a grandfather preceptor'; preceptor's preceptor.

āryaka, Prakrit *ajjaka*, *ayyaka* (EI 20, 28; CII 3; IA 15), the grandfather; father's father. Cf. *prārya*, *āryikā*.

Cf. Prakrit *ajjaka* (EI 24), an ascetic.

āryakā, cf. Prakrit *ajjakā* (EI 24), Sanskrit *āryikā*; a female ascetic of the Jain order.

Ārya-putra, Prakrit *Aya-puta* (IE 8-2; EI 3; HD), probably, title of a son of the ruling king. Cf. *CII*, Vol. I, p. 175.

ārya-saṁgha (CII 3), 'the community of the faithful (i.e. the Buddhist monks)'.

ārya-satya, cf. Pali *ariya-sacca* (EI 5), Buddhist; four in number.

āryikā, cf. Prakrit *āyikā* (EI 20, 28), the grandmother; 'father's mother'; mentioned side by side with *mahāmātṛkā*, 'mother's mother' (*Select Inscriptions*, p. 225).

āśā (IE 7-1-2), 'ten'.

Asamīyā, see *Assamese*.

asaṁpratipatti (CII 1), unseemly behaviour.

āsana (IE 8-8), a seat.

Cf. a-cār-āsana-carm-āṅgāra (IE 8-5; EI 15), probably, camping [of the royal officers in a village]; *āsana-carma* is sometimes taken as one expression meaning 'a hide seat'.

āsana-paṭṭa (EI 23, 24), a seat; a slab used as a seat.

āsana-pīṭhikā (LL), a bench for sitting.

ā-ṣāṇmāsika (CII 1), 'less than six months in age'.

Āśāpāla (HD), 'the guardian of the quarters'; a chief ruling over 10,000 villages, according to the *Śukranītisāra*, I. 192.

aśātanā (HA), Jain; disrespect or disobedience.

Āsedhabhaṅg-ādhikṛta (IE 8-3; EI 31), a police officer to check people's escape from prison or legal restraint.

aśeṣa-mahāśabda (IE 8-2), same as *pañca-mahāśabda*.

aśeṣa-vidya (SII 1), belonging to all the branches of sacred studies.

asi-daṇḍa-prahāra (LP), war.

asidhārā-vrata (EI 16), name of a vow.

āsīhāra, cf. *udak-āsīhāra-kullaka*; probably, a kind of channel.

āsīna (*JAHRS*, Vol. IX, Part i, p. 31, text line 12), literally 'seated'; downcast, dejected. Cf. *Ep. Ind.*, Vol. XXXV, pp. 264-65.

āsnava (CII 1), sin.

āsphoṭana (SII 1), a challenge.

āśrama (EI 13) a stage of life; a religious establishment (*Ep. Ind.*, Vol. XXX, p. 67); cf. *Caṇḍik-āśrama-guru* (IA 11), 'the Superior of the hermitage of *Caṇḍikā*'.

(*IE* 7-1-2), 'four'.

āśraya (IA 20), subdivision of a *viṣaya*.

Cf. āśiriyam, āśiriya-kkal, āśiriya-ppramāṇam (SITI), a document by which a person submits to another's protection.

Assamese, same as *Asamīyā*; language and alphabet of Assam, the alphabet being sometimes called Bengali-Assamese.

aṣṭa, cf. *aṣṭa-bhoga*, probably 'all kinds of enjoyment' (and not merely 'eight' kinds) ensuring *tejaḥ-svāmya* or ownership endowed with complete authority. Cf. *aṣṭādaśa*, etc.

āṣṭa-bhāgika (CII 1), '[a village] paying one-eighth of the produce [instead of the usual rate of one-sixth or so]'.

aṣṭa-bhoga (IE 8-5; EI 14, 17), privileges of the donee of a rent-free holding, believed to be grouped into eight classes which are sometimes enumerated as *nidhi*, *nikṣepa*, *jala*, *pāṣāṇa*, *akṣīṇin*, *āgāmin*, *siddha* and *sādhya*. Cf. *aiśvary-āṣṭaka* and *aṣṭa-bhūti* (EI 33); also *aṣṭabhoga-tejaḥsvāmya*.

(*CITD*), the eight privileges associated with the enjoyment of rent-free land, also enumerated as (1) *nidhi* (a treasure or a hoard, i.e. a natural hoard such as a mine),

(2) *nikṣepa* (a treasure hidden or stored up by some one), (3) *akṣīṇa* (permanent or lasting benefits), (4) *āgāmin* (future benefits); (5) *sañcita* (benefits already stored up), (6) *jala* (waters); (7) *taru* (trees) and (8) *pāṣāṇa* (stones). See *JAHRS*, Vol. X, p. 124. *Pāṣāṇa* seems to mean 'hilly area'.

(*SITI*), eight kinds of rights in enjoying landed property; mentioned sometimes as *vikraya*, *dāna*, *vinimaya*, *jala*, *taru*, *pāṣāṇa*, *nidhi* and *nikṣepa*, and also as *nidhi*, *nikṣepa*, *jalāmṛta*, *pāṣāṇa*, *akṣiṇin*, *āgāmin*, *siddha* and *sādhya*.

aṣṭabhoga-tejaḥsvāmya (IA 8), unbridled ownership endowed with all the rights associated with the enjoyment of property; translated as 'with the eight rights of full possession' though *aṣṭa* probably means 'all' and not merely 'eight' (cf. *aṣṭādaśa*, etc.); cf. *aṣṭabhoga-tejaḥsvāmyaṁ ca krayeṇ=ādāya* (EI 23), 'having secured the *aṣṭabhoga-tejaḥsvāmya* rights by purchase'; (IA 19), translated as 'the proprietorship of all the glory of the *aṣṭa-bhoga*', and *aṣṭa-bhoga* explained as 'the deposits of buried treasure (*nidhi-nikṣepa*), water, stones, the *akṣiṇī*, that which may accrue, that which has been made property, that which may be made property, and augmentation'. But there is probably no justification for taking *nidhi-nikṣepa* as a single unit.

Cf. *aṣṭabhoga-tejassvāmya-daṇḍaśulka-yukta* (*Ind. Ant.*, Vol. XIX, p. 247, text line 102), mentioned along with *nidhi-nikṣepa-pāṣāṇ-ārām-ādi-catuṣ-prakāra-bīravaṇa-pārikh-āya-sahita*. The separate mention of these two groups shows that *aṣṭa-bhoga* vaguely indicated all kinds of proprietary rights.

aṣṭa-bhūti (EI 33), same as *aṣṭa-bhoga*.

aṣṭādaśa, cf. *aṣṭādaśa-jāti-parihāra* (IE 8-5); literally, 'eighteen'; actually, 'all' (*Ep. Ind.*, Vol. XXX, p. 115). Cf. Oḍiyā *aṭhara-gaḍajāta* (EI 26). See *aṣṭa*, *ṣaṭtriṁśat*, *ṣaṭpañcāśat*, *bāhattara*, etc.

aṣṭādaśa-doṣa (SII 1), the eighteen or all sins.

aṣṭādaśa-jāti (CITD), same as *aṣṭādaśa-prajā*; the 18 castes. Kittel enumerates the 18 castes of the Kannaḍa-speaking area as the Brāhmaṇa, Kṣatriya, Vaiśya, Liṅgavanta, Baṇajige, Gaṅgaḍikāra-vokkaliga, Maḍivāli, Kelasiga, Kuṟuba, Kumbāṟa, Kaṭuka, Baḍagi, Akkasālĕ, Toreya, Uppāra, Besta, Holeya and Mādiga. But really the number 18 means 'all' in such cases. The number 36 has the same meaning in the

Bengali expression *chatriś-jāti*, '36 castes'. See *Ep. Ind.*, Vol. XXX, p. 115.

aṣṭādaśa-prajā (CITD), same as *aṣṭādaśa-jāti*, *aṣṭādaśa-prakṛti*.

aṣṭādaśa-prakṛti, cf. *s-āṣṭādaśa-prakṛty=opeta* (EI 2); all classes of tenants; tenants belonging to all cummunities.

(*IA* 17), 'the eighteen (i.e. all) officials (i.e. classes of officials)'.

aṣṭa-diggaja (EI 33), eight poets at king Kṛsṇadevarāya's court at Vijayanagara..

asta-giri (IA 22), the mythical Sun-set mountain.

āṣṭ-āhikā (EI 8), Jain festival; same as *aṣṭ-āhnika* (q. v.).

aṣṭ-āhnika, *aṣṭ-āhnikā* (EI 8, 33), Jain festival held in the months of Phālguna, Āṣāḍha and Kārttika; also called *aṣṭ-āhnika-parvan*; same as *aṭṭhāi-mahotsava*. See the Halsi plates of Kadamba Ravivarman (c. 490-538 A.D.) in *Ind. Ant.*, Vol. VI, pp. 25-26. Cf *The Successors of the Sātavāhanas*, p. 271; *Ep. Ind.*, Vol. XXXIII, p. 47 and note; cf. p. xvi.

aṣṭaka (EI 7), same as *ba-ḍi* 8; worship of the manes with oblations to them.

Cf. *aṭṭagam* (SII 13), division of land, and *aṭṭagattār* (SII 13), share-holders in a land. See *dvādaśaka*.

aṣṭa-kula, cf. Tamil *ūr-ĕṭṭu* (SITI); the committee of eight members of the village assembly (*ūr*); taxes payable for the expenses of the committee (cf. *eṇ-per-āyam* which may also refer to the eight major items of revenue). See *añjaṣṭa-sabhā*.

Cf. *aṣṭakul-ādhikaraṇa* (IE 8-3; EI 31), an administrative board (like the *Pañcāyat*) consisting of eight (or more) members representing various classes or communities of people; cf. *grām-āṣṭa-kul-ādhikaraṇa*; *mahattar-ādy-aṣṭakul-ādhikaraṇa*.

aṣṭamī-pakṣa (CII 1), used to indicate *pakṣ-āṣṭamī*, i.e. the eighth *tithi* of each fortnight.

astamba, cf. *samudaya-bāhy-ādy-astamba* (EI 23), 'land originally devoid of vegetation which does not yield any revenue to the State'.

aṣṭamikā, same as *śatamāna* (q. v.).

aṣṭāṅga (CITD), the eight constituents of *yoga* consisting of (1) *niyama* (restraint of the mind), (2) *āsana* (a particular posture or mode of sitting), (3) *prāṇāyāma* (restraining or suspending the breath during the mental recitation of the names or attributes of a deity), (4) *yama* (self-control), (5) *pratyāhāra* (restraining the organs), (6) *dhāraṇa* (the faculty of retaining in the mind, steady abstraction of mind), (7) *dhyāna* (abstract contemplation, religious meditation), and (8) *samādhi* (perfect absorption of thought in the one object of meditation, i.e. the Supreme Spirit); mentioned in connection with obeisance, it means the 8 parts of the body, viz., the two hands, chest, forehead, two knees and two feet (cf. *aṣṭāṅga-namaskāra*).

aṣṭāṅga-bhakti-krama (EI 19), eight forms of worship; same as *aṣṭa-vidh-ārcana*, etc.

aṣṭāṅga-namaskāra (HA), obeisance with the eight limbs (viz. forehead, chest, two hands, two knees and two feet) done by lying straight on the ground, face downwards. See *pañc-āṅga-namaskāra*.

aṣṭa-paripālana (SITI), deities of the eight cardinal points; same as *aṣṭa-dikpāla*.

Aṣṭaprahārika (IA 17), probably an official designation; may be derived from *aṣṭa-prahara*; probably 'a watchman'. The correct form would, in that case, be *āṣṭaprāharika*, etc.

aṣṭaprāharikā, *aṣṭapraharikyā* (LP), 'within 24 hours'.

aṣṭa-puṣpikā (EI 15), 'eightfold offering of flowers'.

Aṣṭāvadhāna (IA 11), one who has the power of listening and grasping eight things at a time; epithet of a poet.

Āṣṭavargika (IE 8-3; EI 7), probably, the superintendent of eight departments; mentioned as a *Pātra*.

aṣṭa-vidha-bhakti-kriyā (SITI), eight aspects of worship including *arcanā*, *vandana*, *smaraṇa*, *pāda-sevana*, *stava*, *pradakṣiṇa*, *sakhya* and *ātma-nivedana* or *ātm-ārpaṇa*.

aṣṭa-vidh-ārcana, *aṣṭa-vidh-ārcanā* (EI 19), same as *aṣṭāṅga-bhakti-krama*, the eight forms of worship.

(*IA* 14; SITI), explained as 'worship with eight materials, e. g., *jala* (water), *gandha* (scent), *puṣpa* (flower), *akṣatā* (grains), *dhūpa* (incense), *dīpa* (lamps), *naivedya* (food) and *tāmbula* (betel)'.

āsthāna-maṇḍapa (EI 4), an assembly hall.

Āsthāyika-puruṣa (IA 8), official designation; probably the same as *Sthāyin*; may be 'hereditary village officials'.

asti (*Ep. Ind.*, Vol XXVIII, p. 302, note 2), a mere particle used to introduce the narration of a grant.

aṣṭi (IE 7-1-2), 'sixteen'.

āśu (SII 2), probably, a hilt.

āsu (CII 4), name of a coin; cf. *āchu* and *accu*.

a-śuddha-pakṣa (IA 16), used to indicate the dark fortnight.

Āśu-kavi (EI 5), epithet of a poet; cf. *Sukara-kavi*, *Śīghra-kavi*.

a-śukla (IA 15), also called *a-śukla-pakṣa* (IA 16), the dark fortnight.

āśulopa (CII 1), hurry.

āsura-kriyā (IA 23), the worship of spirits.

Asura-vijayin (CII 4), 'a devilish conqueror'; epithet of a conqueror.

aśva (IE 7-1-2), 'seven'.

aśv-āḍḍāṇaka-patra (LP), deed for mortgaging a horse.

Aśv-ādhyakṣa (EI 18), superintendent of stables or cavalry officer; cf. *Aśva-sādhanika*, *Aśvapati*.

Aśva-ghāsa-kāyastha (HD), a petty officer in charge of the fodder for horses. Cf. *Rājataraṅgiṇī*, III. 489.

aśvamedha (CII 3, 4), a sacrificial ceremony centering in a horse, generally performed by independent monarchs. Kings celebrating the sacrifice sometimes assumed suitable titles (cf. *Aśvamedha-parākrama* and *Aśvamedha-Mahendra* claimed respectively by Samudragupta and Kumāragupta I on their coins). Some kings performed two, four or more horse-sacrifices. For a list of the performers of *aśvamedha* known form epigraphic and numismatic records, see *Sundaram Pillai Com. Vol.*, pp. 93 ff.

āśvamedha (EI 12), same as *āśvamedhika*.

asvāmika (EI 19), anarchy.

Aśvapati (IE 8-2; CII 4)), cf. *Aśvapati-Gajapati-Narapati-rāja-tray-ādhipati*; royal title; the king as 'the leader of the cavalry'; title of the Vijayanagara kings on account of their strength in horses (ASLV); title assumed by the rulers of some royal families.

(*EI* 9, 21; CII 3; HD), an official title meaning either the master of the stables or the commander of the cavalry; cavalry officer; cf. *Aśv-ādhyakṣa* (EI 18). See *CII*, Vol. III, p. 259.

Aśvapati-Gajapati-Narapati-mūvaru-rāyara-gaṇḍa (IE 8-2),

title of the Vijayanagara kings; Kannaḍa translation of the title *Aśvapati-Gajapati-Narapati-rāja-tray-ādhipati.*

Aśvapati-Gajapati-Narapati-rāja-tray-ādhipati (IE 8-2; CII 4), holder (or, lord of the holders) of the three royal titles, viz., leader of the cavalry, leader of the elephant corps and leader of infantry; title assumed by the rulers of certain dynasties. Cf. *Aśvapati-Gajapati-Narapati-muvaru-rāyara-gaṇḍa.*

Aśvāroha (EI 18), a trooper.

Aśva-sādhanika (EI 21; CII 4), a cavalry officer.

Aśva-saṁstha (EI 8), a horseman.

aśvaśālā-karaṇa, cf. *karaṇa* (LP); the department of horses.

Aśvati (EI 9), Tamil; same as *Aśvinī.*

Aśvavāra, cf. *Asavāra* (EI 2), a horseman.

Aśvavāraka, Àśvavārika (LL), a trooper; same as *Aśvavāra.*

Aśvin (IE 7-1-2), 'two'; sometimes *Āśvina* is also used in this sense.

Āśvina (IE 7-1-2), 'two'; cf. *Aśvin.* See *IHQ*, Vol. XXXIII, p. 101.

aśvīya (EI 12), a number of horses.

Atapika (LL), a Jain monk.

aṭavī (CII 1), the forest-folk.

(*SITI*), troops.

āṭavika (*Ep. Ind.*, Vol. XIV, p. 303, text line 50), a kind of grains.

(*EI* 20; HD), an officer in charge of forest tracts. See *Arthaśāstra*, I 12 (mentioned among the 18 *tīrthas*).

aṭha-gānī, a coin equal to a *ṭaṅka*; there are *do-gānī* ($\frac{1}{4}$ *ṭaṅka*), *cau-gānī* ($\frac{1}{2}$ *ṭaṅka*), *cha-gānī* ($\frac{3}{4}$ *ṭaṅka*), *bārah-gānī* (1$\frac{1}{2}$ *ṭaṅkas*), *caubīs-gānī* (3 *ṭaṅkas*), *aḍotālīs-gānī* (6 *taṅkas*). See *JNSI*, Vol. XXII, pp. 198-99.

Atharva-veda (CII 3; etc.), one of the four Vedas. See *Veda.*

Ati-brahmaṇya (CII 3), probably meaning 'extremely friendly to the Brāhmaṇas' and not 'a devout worshipper of the god Brahman'. See *Parama-brahmaṇya.*

atidhṛti (IE 7-1-2), 'nineteen'.

atijagatī (IE 7-1-2), 'thirteen'.

atipara (EI 24), an inveterate foe.

atiprasaṅga (*Ep. Ind.*, Vol. IV, p. 347, note 5), a case in which a grammatical rule exceeds its sphere.

atirātra (CII 3), name of a particular sacrifice.

atireka (CII 1), excess; cf. *mano-'tireka*, 'enthusiasm'.

atisattra (EI 27), name of a sacrifice.

atīta (IA 17), 'expired'; cf. *Śaka-nṛpa-kāl-ātīta-saṁvatsareṣu*. The word *gateṣu*, sometimes additionally used, refers to the expiry of the expired years.

atīta-rājya (IA 19), indicates that so many years 'since [the commencement of] the reign have [now] passed'; used in connection with the regnal reckoning of Govindapāla and Lakṣmaṇasena and rarely with the years of an era (e.g. the Vikrama-saṁvat associated with the reign of a legendary king named Vikramāditya). See also *gata-rājya* and *vinaṣṭa-rājya*. Cf. *JAS*, Letters, Vol. XX, 1954, pp. 43 ff.

atithi (EI 10; CII 3, 4), reception of guests; one of the five daily rites (*mahāyajñas*) of a Brāhmaṇa. See *sattra*.

ātithya (HRS), land assigned to government officers for public charities, as indicated by the *Arthaśāstra*.

ātivāhika (HRS), escorting fee paid by the merchants, as indicated by the *Arthaśāstra*. See Ghoshal, *H. Rev. Syst.*, pp. 77.

atiyātra (EI 30), same as *atiyātrika*; exit tax.

atiyātrika (IE 8-8), tax for crosssing the boundary; see *śulk-ātiyātrika*, 'the boundary-crossing fee' ; also *atiyātra*.

ātmaka, cf. *apaṇaga* (ML), 'one's own'.

ātman (IE 7-1-2), 'one'.

ātma-patika (CII 1), independent.

ātodya (EI 23), music.

Atri (IE 7-1-2), 'seven'.

Atrinayanaja (IE 7-1-2), 'one'.

Aṭṭapati (HD), the market-master. Cf. *Rājataraṅgiṇī*, V.167.

aṭṭapati-bhāga (HRS), office entrusted with the collection of the share of the lord of the market, as indicated by the *Rāja-taraṅgiṇī*; literally, 'share of the market-master'.

aṭṭhāi-mahotsava (HA), an eight-day festival celebrated by the Jains especially in the months of Āśvina and Caitra according to some but Phālguna, Āṣāḍha and Kārttika according to others; same as *aṣṭāhnika-parvan* (q.v.).

aṭu (Chamba), a land measure. Cf. *jilo*, etc.

ātura-śālā, cf. *ātula-śālai* (EI 24; SITI), a hospital.

āturāvaḍḍi (IE 8-5; EI 28), tax of uncertain import; probably, a levy related to the treatment of the king when sick; also read as *āntarāvaḍḍi*.

atyagniṣṭoma (EI 26), name of a sacrifice. cf. *agniṣṭoma.*

Atyanta-bhagavad-bhakta (IE 8-2; CII 3), 'extremely devoted to the Bhagavat (Viṣṇu)'; epithet of a pious Vaiṣṇava.

Atyanta-māheśvara (EI 23; CII 3), epithet of a pious Śaiva.

Atyanta-svāmi-mahābhairava-bhakta (EI 23; CII 3), epithet of a pious Śaiva.

atyaṣṭi (IE 7-1-2), 'seventeen'.

atyaya (HRS), prescribed fine, as indicated in the *Artha-śāstra*. See Ghoshal, *H.Rev. Syst.*, pp. 26, 108. Cf. *ātyayika.*

ātyayika (CII 1; EI 22), a matter for urgent disposal; derived from *atyaya*, emergency, distress.

Audayantrika (LL), cf. Prakrit *Odayantrika* (EI 8); the maker of hydraulic machines or the person owning or working on such a machine.

Audraṅgika (IE 8-3; EI 23), collector of the *udraṅga* tax meaning 'tax on permanent tenants or the principal tax'; sometimes mentioned side by side with the *Hiraṇyasāmudāyika* or the collector of tax in cash. See *Ṣaṣṭh-ādhikṛta*, *Dhruvasthān-ādhikaraṇika*, etc.

aukapiṇḍa, cf. *okapiṇḍa* (CII 1), probably, household vermin.

aulikara, cf. *aulikara-lāñchana* (EI 26; CII 3), the *lāñchana* or crest of the kings of the Aulikara dynasty of Mandasor. The real meaning of *auli* is uncertain; sometimes *aulikara* is interpreted as *himakara* or the moon.

Auparika (EI 8-3), same as *Uparika* (q.v.).

Aupaśatiko, cf. Prakrit *Opasati* (EI 16), name of a *gotra*.

aupāyanika (HRS), earnings from presents, as indicated by the *Arthaśāstra*. See Ghoshal, *H. Rev. Syst.*, pp. 28, 38.

aupāyika (EI 25), probably, an adopted [son].

aureus (IE 8-8), name of the Roman gold coin, also called *denarius* (q.v.).

Aurṇasthānika (IE 8-3; EI 23), officer in charge of an *ūrṇā-sthāna* (wool factory) or of all the *ūrṇā-sthānas*. Cf. *ūrṇā-sthāna*.

auṣadha (EI 24), medicine.

Autkheṭika (HRS), officer in charge of the collection of the impost called *utkheṭana* (q. v.).

Auttarāha (EI 8), a northerner.

Autthitāsanika (IE 8-3), same as *Utthitāsanin*; probably, courtier of a special rank provided with a special seat; perhaps, the chief nobleman at the royal court.

avabhṛtha (EI 9; CII 4), name of the ceremonial bath at the end of a sacrifice.

avacaṭita (EI 13), a crack; cf. *khaṇḍa-sphuṭit-āvacaṭita-patita-saṁskār-ārtham*, 'for the repairs of dilapidated, broken, cracked and fallen [parts]'.

avacchinna, cf. *sva-sīm-āvacchinna* (IE 8-5), demarcated.

avadāna, also spelt *āvadāna* (EI 28, 29, 33), Oḍiyā; a present; a tax; tax in general; also called *āvedana*.

(*SITI*), same as Sanskrit *avasāna*; termination, end.

avadāra (EI 13), cf. *paśukul-āvadāra-karmānta-koṇakalikā-gaṅgāgrāme*; meaning uncertain; possibly 'a pound' or 'a pen'.

Avadhānin (EI 16), title of Brāhmaṇas; cf. *Śatāvadhāna*.

avadhāraṇā, cf. *adhikaraṇ-āvadhāraṇā*, 'official investigation' (*Ep. Ind.*, Vol. XXXI, p. 267).

avadhi, cf. *avadher=anantaram* (LP), 'after the time limit is over'.

Avadhī, language of Avadh (Oudh).

āvāha (CII 1), marriage of a son; cf. *vivāha*, 'marriage of a daughter'.

avakara (EI 32), sweepings, a mound. Cf. *avaṣkara*; also *niravakara*, remainder after deduction (*Ep. Ind.*, Vol. XXVIII, p. 188).

avakāśa (*Ep. Ind.*, Vol. IV, p. 347, note 5), 'opportunity for a grammatical rule taking effect'.

avalagā (LP), same as Gujarātī *oḷaga*; cf. *avalagā sad=aiv=āvalokyā* (LP), 'care should be constantly taken'.

avalagaka (EI 2; HRS), same as *avalagā* (q.v.); sometimes regarded as presents or supplies.

avalagana (EI 2; HRS), same as *avalagaka* and *avalagā*.

avalambaka (EI 30), probably, a rod from which loops are suspended for carrying bundles.

avalokya (IE 8-8), detection.

āvaṇa (SITI), Tamil; a document; generally, a sale-deed; also called *vilaiy-āvaṇam*; cf. *āvaṇa-kkaḷari* (SITI), a place where documents like sale-deeds, etc., are registered; registration office.

avanī (EI 7-1-2), 'one'.

(EI 3), a district.

avani-maṇḍala, cf. *Kon-āvani-maṇḍala* (EI 32), also called *Kona-maṇḍala*, *Kona-sīma*, etc.

avani-randhra-nyāya (CII 4), same as *bhūmi-cchidra-nyāya* (q.v.), 'the maxim of the fallow land.'

avani-vetana (SITI), police duties of a village; contribution for such duties; the same as Tamil *pā ḷikāval*.

āvara (CII 4), a stall. Cf. *āvāra*.

āvāra ((IE 8-5), cf. *āpaṇeṣu āvāraḥ*, 'collections to be made from the shops in a market'. Cf. *āvara*.

avar-ādhika (CII 1), 'more or less'.

avaraja (ML), a younger brother or cousin.

āvaraṇa (EI 17), a shield.

(*SITI*), shelter, covering; same as *prākāra* or wall around the temple.

āvarjanīya (LP), 'to be received'.

avarodhana (CII 1), household; cf. *antaḥpura*.

avarodha-jana (EI 23), inmates of the royal harem or the king's wives and concubines; wrongly interpreted as 'a watchman'.

āvarta, cf. *sarv-āvarta-yutā*, 'assigned as the date of payment as it falls annually' (*Ep. Ind.*, Vol. XIV, p. 310, note 1).

āvāsa, cf. *a-kūra-cullaka-vināśi-khaṭv-āvāsa* (IE 8-5), shelter or accommodation [which the villagers were obliged to provide for the touring officers of the king]; cf. *saṁvāsa*, etc.

āvāsaka (IE 8-5; EI 25), same as *āvāsa* or *saṁvāsa*, i.e. accommodation [which the villagers were obliged to provide to the royal officers on tour].

āvāsanikā (EI 1), a house.

Avasara (SITI), an officer of the royal household having

the duty of bringing to the notice of the king anything that demanded his immediate attention. Cf. *Kārtākṛti'ka*.

avasara (*Ep. Ind.*, Vol. XVI, p. 347), one of the periods when the worship is performed and offerings are made to the deity in a temple.

Avasara-varttanā (SITI), presents payable to an *Avasara* (q.v.).

avasatha (IE 8-3), explained as 'a college or a *dharma-śālā*'. But see *Āvasathika*.

Āvasathika (IE 8-3), variously explained as 'the superintendent of *avasathas*, i.e. colleges or *dharma-śālās*', 'the supervisor of the royal palace and other government buildings' (*Hist. Beng.*, I, ed. Majumdar, p. 284); 'one who keeps the domestic fire (*āvasathya*) burning with daily offerings' (D. Bhattacharya, *Halāyudha's Brāhmaṇasarvasva*, p. xx); etc.

(*EI* 9, 11, 24), title or family name of Brāhmaṇas. Cf. *Āvasathin*.

Āvasathin (EI 23), explained as 'one who keeps the sacred fire called *āvasathya*'; cf. *Āvasathika*.

avaṣkara, sweepings, a mound; cf. *s-oṣar-āvaṣkara-sthāha-nivīta-lavaṇākara* (EI 22); also *sa-gart-āvaṣkara* (*Ep. Ind.*, Vol. XXXV, p. 135, text line 21). See *avakara*.

avaṣṭabdhi (LP), detention.

avasthā (IA 16), a territorial unit.

Āvasthika (EI 23), corruption of *Āvasathika*; same as *Āvasathin*.

āvāta (IE 8-5), same as *vāta*, storm; cf. *udvāta*.

(*EI* 32; CII 3; etc.), a fiscal term referring to the income from lands as a result of changes caused by natural agencies; an income probably resulting from storms. See *vāta*, probably meaning 'a storm or tempest'; also *āvāt-āya*.

avatāra (IE 7-1-2), 'ten'.

avataraṇa, cf. *gṛh-āvataraṇa* (IE 8-5), probably the same as *umbara-bheda* (q.v.).

avatāri-amāvāsyā (IA 18), Kannaḍa name for the new-moon of Pauṣa.

āvāt-āya (HRS), 'the income derived from storms'; cf. *āvāta* and *bhūta-vāta-pratyāya*.

avatrap (CII 1), 'to be disinclined'.

āvedana (EI 28), same as *avadāna* or *āvadāna* of Oḍiyā records; tax in general. Cf. *Ep. Ind.*, Vol. XXX, p. 115.

āvedanaka (IE 8-8), a written complaint or application.

avaṇḍ-āya (*Ep. Ind.*, Vol. V, p. 96), Telugu; name of a tax.

Āveśanin, cf. Prakrit *Āvesani* (EI 2; LL), the chief artisan; the foreman of artisans.

avimanas (CII 1), pleased.

aviprahīna (CII 1), used in the sense of *ahīna*, 'not lost'; undiminished.

avirodha (SITI), not inimical; amicability.

āvṛti (CII 1), order; cf. *sakala-deś-āvṛtika* (CII 1), 'one whose order has reached all parts of the country'.

Cf. anāvṛti (CII 1), 'want of practice'.

āvṛtti (IE 8-4; EI 26), an administrative unit like a Pargana (*JAS*, Letters, Vol. XX, p. 205).

aya (IE 7-1-2), 'four'.

āya (IE 7-1-2), 'four'.

(*EI* 33; CII 3; SII 1, 2), a fiscal term meaning 'revenue', 'tax'.

(*SITI*), literally, income; a general term denoting 'taxes'; cf. *vaḻiy-āyam* (SITI), tolls on the roadway.

(*HRS*), revenue in general according to the *Arthaśāstra* and other authorities; a special branch of revenue according to the inscriptions of the Uccakalpa kings and later epigraphs.

(*CITD*), profit, income, receipt; tribute; corn given by the well-to-do villagers to the hereditary servants of the village as their established fees of office.

āyāga (EI 1), an object of homage; cf. *āyāga-paṭṭa*.

āyāga-paṭa, āyāga-paṭṭa (EI 24; LL), Jain; tablet for worship.

āyāga-sabhā (LL), Jain; a hall of homage.

(*SITI*), administration of a village by a group of officers called *āyāgār* (village officers and servants).

āyaka (EI 21; LL), the entrance pavilion of a Buddhist monastery; a pavilion in front of the door of a Buddhist monastery.

āya-mukha, 'sources of income'; cf. *āya-śarīra*. See Ghoshal, *H. Rev. Syst.*, p. 26.

ayana (IE 7-1-2), 'two'.

ayan-āṁśa (CII 3), the degree of procession of the equinoxes.

āya-pada (LP), income; property (*Ep. Ind.*, Vol. XXXIV, p. 145).

āya-śarīra, 'body of income' separated from *āya-mukha*, 'source of income'. See Ghoshal, *H. Rev. Syst.*, pp. 25-26.

āya-śulka (EI 33), taxes and tolls.

āyata (CII 1), engaged or appointed.

āyatana (EI 30), a temple or shrine. Cf. *bhavana*, *ālaya*, *pura*, etc.

Cf. *ṣaḍ-āyatana*; an organ.

Cf. *tuṣṭy-āyatana* (CII 1), same as *tuṣṭi-pātra*.

āyati (EI 14), future prosperity.

āyudhīya (HRS), land granted for supplying troops in lieu of tax, as indicated by the *Arthaśāstra*. See *amara*.

Āyukta (CII 4; HD), literally 'an officer'. Same as *Āyuktaka*. Pāṇini (II, 3. 40) knows the word in the sense of a servant or office. Cf. *Āyukta-puruṣa* (*CII*, Vol. III, p. 8).

Āyuktaka (IE 8-3; CII 3, 4; EI 30; BL; HD), same as *Āyukta*; often the governor of a district or subdivision. See *Kāmasūtra*, V. 5. 5; Kāmandaka, V. 82.

Āyukta-puruṣa (CII 3), the same as *Āyukta*.

āyuṣa, used in the sense of *āyus* in the Junagadh inscription of Rudradāman, text line 10 (*Sel. Ins.*, p. 171).

āyuṣya (EI 10), Jain; a variety of *karman*.

Ayyanagandhavāraṇa (IE 8-2), Kannaḍa-Sanskrit; 'the musk-elephant of the grandfather'; a subordinate title.

Ayyanasiṁha (IE 8-2), Kannaḍa-Sanskrit; 'the lion of the grandfather'; a subordinate title. Cf. *Aṇṇanasiṁha*.

B

ba (IE 8-1; CII 3, etc.); an abbreviation of *bahula* or of *bahula-pakṣa*, i.e. the dark fortnight; used in connection with *di* or *ti* (see *ba-di*, *la-ti*) and also by itself. Cf. *va*.

Bā° (PJS), contraction of the honorific *Bāi* (q.v.) applied to ladies (especially in medieval Jain inscriptions of Western India).

bābū (*Ep. Ind.*, Vol. IX, p. 316), meaning uncertain.

bācaka (LP), handful; cf. Gujarātī *bācko*.

bācha, bāchī (Chamba), a tax in cash. See *vākṣa*.

bāḍa (EI 5), Kannaḍa; a town or village.

(*IE* 8-4), Kannaḍa; a small territorial unit like a Pargana.

bāḍaba (SII 1), the submarine fire.

badalā (Chamba), return, exchange; same as *parata*.

badara, same as *tolaka* (q. v.) or *tolā*.

badhā (LP), obstacle; cf. Sanskrit *bādhā*.

bādhā (EI 15), obstacle; also spelt *vādhā*.

bāḍhataram (CII 1), 'more excessively'.

ba-di (IE 8-1; CII 3; etc.), contraction of *bahula-pakṣa-dina* or °*divasa*; also spelt *va-di*, cf. *śu-di*; abbreviations of separate words (see *ba, di, śu* and *va*) and not words in themselves, *ba-di* or *va-di* referring to the dark fortnight and *śu-di* the bright fortnight; they denote the fortnight and the solar or civil day, with reference to the lunar *tithi*, in the fortnight.

baḍi-māḍuvulu (CITD) Telugu; a coin of unknown value. *Baḍi* means 'petty' or 'a tax' and *māḍuvu* may be the same as *māḍa* meaning half a *dīnār* or the tenth of a *paṇa*.

Bāguli, cf. *Vārgulika*.

bāhattara (IE 8-3), literally, 'seventytwo', but actually 'all' (cf. *aṣṭādaśa*, etc.); see *Bāhattaraniyogādhipati*, *Bāhattara-niyogin*, *Senādibāhattaraniyogādhiṣṭhāyaka*.

Bāhattaraniyogādhipati (IE 8-3; EI 23, 30), the highest executive officer under South Indian kings like the Yādavas of Devagiri; same as *Bāhattaraniyogin*, etc.

Bāhattaraniyogin (EI 19), official designation; same as *Bāhattaraniyogādhipati*.

bahir-gṛha, cf. *vāra-gṛha*.

bāhirikā (EI 20), a suburb.

bahis, 'excluding'; same as Bengali *baï* (*JAS*, Letters, Vol. XX, p. 215).

bāhu (IE 7-1-2; EI 25), 'two'.

bāhuleya (CII 3; IA 1), a bull.

bahuśruta (CII 1), well informed in various doctrines.

bahusuvarṇa, bahusuvarṇaka (EI 4; IA 19; CII 4), name of a sacrifice.

bahutāvatka (CII 1), 'many times that number'.

bāhu-valaya, cf. *pāku-valayam* (SITI), an armlet.

bāhya, cf. *bāhy-ābhyantar-ādāya* (IE 8-5; *Ep. Ind.*, Vol.

XVI, p. 276, text line 14); 'income from the sale of things imported in a village', same as Tamil *puṟav-āyam* (SITI), 'revenue from external sources (collected mainly in cash)' or Tamil *puṟa-kaḍamai* (SITI), 'external taxes', explained as taxes and fees payable to the State. But *puṟa-kaḍamai* is the same as *puṟav-āyam*. *Bāhya* and *ābhyantatra* may thus mean respectively taxes payable to the king and those payable to the village authorities. See *ābhyantara*. Cf. *samudaya-bāhy-ādya-stamba* (EI 23), 'land covered with original shrubs, i.e. waste which does not yield any revenue to the State'.

(*HD*), a class of royal servants distinguished from *Antaraṅga*. See *Rājataraṅgiṇī*, VIII. 426, 680, 1542.

bāhyāli (CII 4), the outskirt of a town.

Bāi, *Bāī* (EI 8), honorific epithet or name-ending of ladies in Western India; cf. *Bāyi*, *Bā*.°

bala, an escort; cf. *pañcāṅga-prasāda*.

Balādhi (LP), abbreviation of *Balādhikṛta*.

Balādhikṛta (CII 3, 4; BL; HD), 'the commander of an army'. See *JBBRAS*, Vol. XVI, p. 108 (*Balādhikṛta* following *Senāpati*); *Kādambarī*, para. 74. According to some (cf. *Balādhi* in LP), the *Balādhikṛta* was probably the head of a territorial unit like the present *Māmlatdār*. See *Balādhipa*.

Balādhipa (BL), a leader of the army; cf. *Balādhikṛta*.

Balādhīra (CII 4), official designation; probably, mistake for *Balādhīśa*, same as *Balādhipa*.

Balādhyakṣa (IE 8-3), officer in charge of the army; mentioned along with the *Senāpati* who was probably a subordinate officer.

baladī, see *valadī*.

balaharaṇa, cf. *balaharaṇena* (LP), same as Gujarātī *lāine*.

Bālaka-mahārājakumāra (EI), a young prince.

Balakauṣṭhika, cf. *Valatkauṣan*.

bāl-ālaya (SITI) temporary shrine to lodge the images of gods when repairing a temple; small shrine probably consisting of a single room wherein the images of all the gods are lodged; same as Tamil *iḷaṅ-koyil*.

balānaka (HA), a *maṇḍapa* above the entrance of a Jain shrine or the courtyard of a shrine, later known as *ṭhākorkhānā*.

(*BL*), a stone seat.

(*EI* 8), same as Marāṭhī *balāṇī*, 'a raised seat along the walls of the *gābhāra* or *sabhā-maṇḍapa* of a temple.'

bala-yaṣṭi (EI 33; CII 4), a stout memorial pillar.

Balharā (IE 8-2), Arabic corruption of *Vallabha-rāja* through Prakrit *Ballaha-rāa*.

bali (IE 8-5; HRS), voluntary gift (afterwards, compulsory contribution) and tribute from the subjects as indicated by Vedic literature; later, tax in general as suggested by the standard lexicons; king's grain share, identical with *bhāga* but different from *kara* according to the *Arthaśāstra*, but not the Junagadh inscription of Rudradāman (cf. *bali-śulka-bhāga* in line 14). The Rummindei inscription of Aśoka also distinguishes between *bali* and *bhāga* and seems to identify *bali* with *kara* (or with pilgrims' tax). See *Select Inscriptions*, pp. 71, 173.

(*EI* 10, 23, 32; CII 3, 4), an offering to creatures; one of the five *mahāyajñas* or sacrificial rites. Cf. *bali-caru-vaiśvadev-āgnihotra-kratu* (EI 26), the five rites of a Brāhmaṇa.

(*SITI*), offering of flowers, fruits, uncooked rice, etc., to the gods; same as *śrībali*. Cf *Nārāyaṇa-baly-upahāra* in the sense of *Nārayaṇa-pūjā* (*Ind. Ant.*, Vol. VI, p. 363).

Cf. varāha-bali, 'pig sacrifice' (*Ep Ind.*, Vol. XXXVI, p. 39). Cf. *śrī-bali*, *havir-bali*.

balīvarda, cf. *a-paramparā-balīvarda*, etc. (IE 8-5); a pair of bullocks (which the villagers were obliged to provide for the cart of the royal officers when they camped or toured in their villages). See also *vara-balīvarda*.

bāṇa (IE 7-1-2; EI 25), 'five'.

Bānasa-vĕrgaḍĕ (599-11-2), variant spelling of Kannaḍa *Bhānasa-vĕrgaḍĕ* (q.v.).

bandha (EI 31), a dam or highway.

bandha-daṇḍa (IE 8-5; EI 12, 33), probably, ransom or fine in lieu of imprisonment.

bandhāṇa (Chamba), a settlement, an agreement.

bandhāṇa-paṭṭa (Chamba), an agreement, a deed.

bandhanīya (LP), 'to be fixed', i.e. to be served to one; cf. Gujarātī *bāndhī āpavāṁ*.

bandheja (Chamba), a settlement, an agreement.

bandhu (IE 7-1-2), 'four'.

bappa (EI 29, 30; CII 3; etc.), a Prakrit word meaning

'the father', often used in Sanskrit inscriptions. Cf. *bappa-bhaṭṭāraka-pāda-parigṛhīta* (EI 31), epithet of certain rulers.

bappa-bhaṭṭāraka (EI 4), 'the father, the lord'. Cf. *bappa.*

bāra (EI 13), Telugu; the distance between the ends of out-stretched arms.

bārāḍ, derived from Sanskrit *varāṭa* or *varāṭaka*, 'a cowrie-shell (used as money)' (*JNSI*, Vol. XVI, p. 18). Cf. *varāṭikā.*

baraṭa (CII 4), a plant grown for fencing.

bārhaspatya (IA 11), name of a reckoning.

Barkandāz, Persian; same as *Pāik* (q.v.).

bartanā (IE 3-5), Rājasthānī; a blunt stick for writing on a wooden slate; same as *barthā.*

barthā (IE 3-5), same as *bartanā.*

Basilĕos Basilĕon Mĕgalŏu (IE 8-2), Greek; 'of the great king of kings;' used in the legend on the coins of the Scytho-Parthian kings; adapted from old Persian *Khshyāthiya Khshāyathiyānām*, 'the king of kings'; translated into Prakrit as *Maharajasa Rajarajasa* (or *Rajadirajasa*) *mahatasa* (Sanskrit *Mahārājasya Rājarājasya mahataḥ* or *Rājātirājasya mahataḥ*).

Basilĕos Mĕgalŏu (IE 8-2), Greek; 'of the great king', found in the legend on the coins of Indo-Greek kings at first translated in Prakrit as *Rajasa mahatakasa* (Sanskrit *Rājñaḥ mahataḥ*) and later as *Maharajasa* (Sanskrit *Mahārājasya*); adapted from old Persian *Kshāyathiya vazrka.*

ba-ti (*IE* 8-1), abbreviation of *bahula-pakṣa-tithi*. See *ba-di.*

bāva (*CII* 3, etc.), a Prakrit word denoting 'a relative of the same generation with the father'; generally, 'an uncle'; used in Sanskrit inscriptions.

Bāyi (*Hyderabad Archaeological Series*, No. 18, p. 35), suffix to the name of respectable women; same as *Bāi*; wrongly regarded as derived from the Kannaḍa words *abbĕ* (Sanskrit *ambā*) and *āyi* (Sanskrit *āryā*).

Beharā-mahāpātra (EI 28), Oḍiyā; official designation; probably, Sanskrit *Vyavahārika-mahāpātra*. See *Vyavahārika*, etc.

Bengali, Anglicised spelling of *Vaṅgālī*; the name of the people, language and alphabet of Bengal.

Beṇṭakāra (CITD), same as *Beṭakāra, beṭa* (Telugu-Kannaḍa) meaning 'the separation of lovers'. As an epithet of a ruler, *Beṇṭakāra* means 'one who causes the separation of his enemies' wives from their husbands'; cf. *ripu-nārī-vaidhavya-vidhāyak-ācārya*, 'one who renders the wives of his enemies widows'.

bha (IE 7-1-2), 'twentyseven'.

Bha° (PJS), abbreviation of *Bhagavān* (especially in medieval Jain inscriptions).

bhā° (PJS), abbreviation of *bhāryā* (especially in medieval Jain inscriptions).

bhāḍaka (LP), same as Sanskrit *bhāṭaka*.

Bhadanta (IA 11; LL), a title of monks (Buddhist, Jain and Ājīvika); cf. *Bhadatasa aya-Isipālitasa*, 'of the Reverend Lord Ṛṣipālita'; also cf. *Bhadantī*.

Bhadantī (LL), used as the title of a Buddhist nun; cf. *Bhadanta*.

bhadra (SII 2), probably, an auspicious mark.

bhadrā (IA 26), same as *ba-di* 7.

Bhādra (IE 8-1), same as *Bhādrapada*.

bhadra-bhoga, cf. 'according to *bhadra-bhoga*' (Ghoshal, *H.Rev. Syst.*, p. 215); principle of proper enjoyment.

bhadra-ghaṭa, cf. Tamil *pattira-kaḍam* (SITI), a pot filled with water and sanctified by rites.

bhadra-mukha (EI 16), an honorific used with personal names.

bhadra-nigama (LL), a righteous hamlet.

bhadr-āsana (EI 25), a throne.

bhāga (IE 8-5; CII 3, 4; EI 30; HRS), the king's share of the produce, distinguished from *bali* in the Rummindei inscription and the Junagadh inscription of Rudradāman and from *kara* in many other records; later, tax in general, identical with *bali* and *kara* (according to lexicons); cf. references in the *Arthaśāstra* to (1) *lavaṇa-bhāga* (king's share of salt sold by private merchants), (2) *udaka-bhāga* (king's grain share levied as water-tax upon irrigated fields), (3) king's share of the produce of mines leased out to private persons; (4) share paid to the king by merchants for selling the royal merchandise.

(*IE* 8-5), dues (see *kara*); generally, the king's share of grains, which was originally one-sixth.

(*IE* 8-4), a subdivision of a district or a territory.

(*EI* 23, 33), an allotment; a share.

bhāga-bhoga (CII 3; etc.), a fiscal expression in which

bhāga means the king's share of the produce and *bhoga* the periodical supplies made by tenants to the king; cf. *bhāga-bhog-ādika*, *bhāga-bhoga-kara-hiraṇy-ādika* (*EI* 23), meaning 'royal dues'; see *bhāga*, etc.

bhāga-bhoga-kara (HRS), taken by some as a single levy and explained as the king's grain-share, identical with *bhāga* of the *Arthaśāstra* and *bali* of the Smṛtis, though distinguished from *dhānya* in a Maitraka record, where it has been supposed to mean a fixed contribution in kind as distinguished from the contribution consisting of a share of the produce. If *bhāgabhogakara* was a single levy (and did not indicate *bhāga*, *bhoga* and *kara*), it may have really been a tax collected in lieu of *bhāga* (grain share) and *bhoga* (periodical offerings).

Bhāgadugha (HD), an official title; probably the same as *Bhāgahāra*. See Ghoshal, *H. Rev. Syst.*, p. 9.

Bhāgahara (EI 24), same as *Bhāgin*; a collector of the king's grain share. Cf. *Bhāgahāra*.

Bhāgahāra (HD), 'he who recovers the [king's] share [of the procuce of land]'; one of the six officers of each village, according to Śukra, II. 120. Cf. *Bhāgahara*.

bhāgalāga, cf. *bhāgalāg-ādika* (LP), payments in kind or taxes.

bhāga-karṣaṇa (LP), taking away the portion allotted to someone else.

bhagaṇa (IA 19), a bangle.

Bhagavad-bhakta (CII 3, etc.), a Vaiṣṇava sectarian title indicating 'a follower of the Bhagavat (Viṣṇu)'.

Bhagavat (ML; CII 3, 4), 'the lord' or 'the divine'; an epithet of divinities such as Viṣṇu, Buddha, Jinendra, Nārāyaṇa, Śiva, the Sun-god, Kārttikeya, etc; also applied to sages, etc. in the sense of 'venerable', e.g. to Vyāsa, the arranger of the Vedas; rarely applied to kings apparently on account of their saintliness (cf. *Ep. Ind.*, Vol. XXX, p. 19).

Bhāgavata (LL), a votary of the Bhagavat (Viṣṇu). (*CII* 3; etc.), a Vaiṣṇava sect.

Bhagavatī (CII 3, 4; etc.), feminine form of *Bhagavat* (q.v.); often applied to goddesses, etc.

Bhagavatpād-ācārya (EI 6), epithet of a Vaiṣṇava religious teacher.

Bhagavatpāda-karmakara (CII 4), 'a servant of the feet of the Bhagavat'; epithet of a temple official.

Bhāgika (*IE* 8-3; HD), probably, the collector of the king's grain share; same as *Bhāgahāra*. See Vogel, *Ant. Ch. St.*, p. 166. Cf. *Bhāgin*.

(*EI* 13), mentioned along with *Bhogika*; probably, one getting a share [in a free-holding]. See *Aṁśa-bṛhadbhogika*.

Bhāgin (EI 24), same as *Bhāgika*, a collector of the king's grain share.

bhagna (CII 1), 'departed', 'lost', i.e. 'inferior'; cf. the Hindī verb *bhāgnā*, Bengali *bhāgā*.

Cf. bhagna-viśīrṇa-samāracana, repairs to the rents in and the wornout parts of a building (*Ep. Ind.*, Vol. XXXIV, p. 144).

bhagna-kriyā (IA 7), same as *bhagna-saṁskāra*, repairs.

bhāgya-rekhā (EI 3), line of fortune on the palm.

bhamāti (EI 7), corruption of *brahma-hatyā*.

bhaikṣaka (EI 21), land set apart for charity.

bhaitra (IA 14), corruption of *vahitra*.

bhakṣaṇa, Tamil *pakkiṇam* (SITI), confection.

bhakt-ādāya (SII 1), same as Tamil *pakt-ātāyam* (SITI), revenue in rice or paddy. Cf. *bhakt-āya*.

bhakt-āya, cf. Kannaḍa *bhatt-āya* (SII 11-1); same as *bhakt-ādāya*.

bhakta-grāma, cf. *bhatta-grāma*, provision-village; village granted for maintenance (*Ep. Ind.*, Vol. XV, pp. 8, 92; cf. Vol. XVIII, pp. 191, 193).

bhakti (CII 4), devotion to a god.

bhaktī (EI 8), name of a land measure.

bhakt-oddeśaka (LL), Buddhist; distributor of food.

Bhaṁ° (PJS), abbreviation of *Bhaṇḍārin* (especially in medieval Jain inscriptions). See *Bhīṇḍārin*, etc.

bhā-maṇḍala (HA), halo, aureole; same as *prabhā-maṇḍala*.

bhamatī (*HA*), same as *jagatī* (q.v.).

bhaṁḍi (CITD), same as Telugu *baṁḍi*, 'a cart'; really 'a cart load'.

Bhānasa-vĕrgaḍĕ (IE 8-3), Kannaḍa; same as *Mahānas-ādhyakṣa*; superintendent of the royal kitchen. Cf. *Sūpakāra-pati*, *Khādyaṭapākika*, *Mahānasika*.

Bhāṇaka (LL), Buddhist; a preacher.

bhāṇḍa, cf. *bhaṇḍa* (EI 5), a bale of goods.

bhāṇḍa-bhṛta-vahitra (IE 8-8), 'a wagonfull of pots or jars'.

Bhāṇḍ-ādhyakṣa (EI 28), officer in charge of the store-house. Cf. *Bhāṇḍāgār-ādhikṛta*, etc.

bhāṇd-āgāra (EI 23, 30), a treasury or store-house.

Bhāṇḍāgār-ādhikṛta (EI 12; BL; HRS), an officer employed in the treasury or store-house or the officer in charge of it. Cf. *Bhāṇḍāgārika*.

Bhāṇdāgāra-prathama (HD), the chief of the royal store-house or treasury. See *JBBRAS*, Vol. IX, p. 219.

Bhāṇḍāgārika (IE 8-3; CII 4; HD; BL), officer in charge of the treasury or the royal store-house. See *Ep. Ind.*, Vol. IX, p. 305.

bhaṇḍāra, same as Sanskrit *bhāṇḍāra*; cf. *Bhaṇḍārin*, etc.

bhāṇḍāra, cf. Tamil *paṇḍāra-kkal* (SITI), stone of standard weight used in the treasury; also cf. *paṇḍāra-kkaṇkāṇi*, treasury officer, supervisor of the treasury.

(*IA* 23), the five images used in the worship of *Bhūtas*, e.g., Jārandāya, etc.

Cf. paṇḍāram (SII 1), a treasury; a Śaiva mendicant.

Bhāṇḍāra-pustaka, cf. Tamil *baṇḍāra-ppottagam* (EI 25), literally, 'account book of the treasury'; a treasury accountant.

Bhaṇḍārin, *Bhāṇḍārin* (EI 9; SITI), officer in charge of the treasury; same as *Bhāṇḍāgārika*. Cf. *Sejjeya-bhaṇḍārī* (EI 13), 'officer in charge of the stores in the king's bed-chamber'.

bhaṅga (Chamba), a land measure; a share or portion.

(*IA* 23), hemp.

Bhānu (IE 7-1-2; EI 25), 'twelve'.

bhāra (EI 10), a weight equal to 2000 *palas*.

(*LP*), probably, a load or bundle.

bharaka (CII 4), name of a measure or weight; one load (*Ep. Ind.*, Vol. XIV, p. 309).

Cf. mahiṣ-oṣṭra-bharaka (IE 8-8), 'a load on a buffalo or a camel'; cf. *bhāṇḍa-bhṛta-vahitra*.

bharaṇa (CII 4), name of a measure.

(*EI* 1), probably, a load [of stones].

Bhāratavar (SITI), Tamil; fishermen.

Bharata-kalā (EI 33), the art of dancing.

Bhāratī-vṛtti (SITI), land set apart for expounding the *Mahābhārata*.

Bharga (IE 7-1-2), 'eleven'.

bhārikā (IE 8-5; EI 25), cf. *bhārikāyāṁ vaṇik-putrasy=āṣṭottara-śataṁ rūpakāṇām*; a crime, the nature of which is uncertain.

bhāṣā (IE 8-8; EI 30), probably, a written declaration.

bhāṣā-bheda (LP), breach of words.

Bhāṣya-vṛtti (SITI), land set apart for meeting the expenses of expounding the *Śrī-Bhāṣya* of Rāmānuja.

Bhaṭa (IE 8-3; CII 3, 4; EI 30; HD), same as *Bhaṭa-manuṣya*; probably derived from *bhṛta* which is sometimes used in its place. Generally used along with *cāṭa* or *chātra*; literally, 'a soldier'; but really a *Pāik, Barkandāz* or *Piāda*, i.e. a constable. It is spelt as *bhaṭṭa* in the medieval inscriptions of Eastern India, though rarely the two are distinguished. See *Bhaṭṭa*.

(*SITI*), a personal servant or soldier.

bhāṭaka (EI 30), same as *prabhāṭaka*; rent or hiring charges; cf. *naukā-bhāṭaka* (EI 14).

Bhaṭa-manuṣya (IE 8-3; EI 31; LL), explained as 'a soldier, policeman or warden'; a *Barkandāz, Pāik* or *Piāda*.

Bhaṭāra (IE 8-2), Kannaḍa corruption of *Bhaṭṭāraka*; also spelt *Bhaḍāra* and *Bhaḷāra*.

Bhaṭṭa (IE 8-3), cf *a-caṭṭa-bhaṭṭa-praveśa* (IE 8-5); same as *Bhaṭa* of earlier records; but rarely distinguished from *Bhaṭa, Bhaṭṭa* in that ease meaning 'a minstrel'.

(*CII* 3, 4; etc.), a title of respect attached to the names of learned Brāhmaṇas.

(*IE* 8-3), a minstrel.

Bhaṭṭā° (PJS), abbreviation of *Bhaṭṭāraka* (in medieval Jain inscriptions); an epithet of Jain teachers.

Bhaṭṭa-bhāga (EI 15), same as *bhaṭṭa-vṛtti*.

Bhaṭṭa-grāma (EI 15, 25), a village owned by learned Brāhmaṇas as a rent-free holding; same as an *agrahāra* village.

Bhaṭṭāmākutika (EI 7), an official designation of uncertain import.

Bhaṭṭa-mahattara (EI 30), a *Bhaṭṭa* who was a *Mahattara*, or a leading *Bhaṭṭa*. *Bhaṭṭa* may not be a corruption of *paṭṭa* (cf. *Bhaṭṭa-nāyaka*).

Bhaṭṭa-nāyaka (EI 9), see *Bhaṭṭa* and *Nāyaka* (chief of a district) as well as *Bhaṭṭa-mahattara*. Cf. also *Paṭṭa-nāyaka* of medieval Orissan epigraphs.

Bhaṭṭaputra (EI 4; LP; BL), title of Brāhmaṇas; epithet of a Brāhmaṇa whose father was famous for learning.

(*LP*), explained as 'sepoys or soldiers'.

(*EI* 11), explained as 'a panegyrist'.

Bhaṭṭāraka (IE 8-2; CII 3; EI 30), title used in Sanskrit but really Prakrit derived from Sanskrit *bhartṛ* through the plural form *bhartāraḥ*=Prakrit *bhaṭṭāra* (see *Svāmin*); often suffixed to the personal names of paramount sovereigns as well as of feudatory *Mahārājas*, or *Yuvarājas* (crown-princes); applied to gods and priests in the sense of 'worthy of worship or sacred'. Cf. *bappa-bhaṭṭāraka-pāda-parigṛhīta*, *bhaṭṭāraka-Mahāsena-parigṛhīta*, etc.

(*EI* 33), the king.

(*SII* 1), title of Jain religious teachers.

(*CII* 4), title of Śaiva ascetics, etc.

(*LP*), a respected man.

(*EI* 11), probably, epithet of the chief priest of a temple.

(*SITI*), a deity; a spiritual preceptor.

Bhaṭṭāraka-pād-ānudhyāta (CII 4), 'meditating on (or, favoured by) the feet of the lord paramount'; epithet of the feudatories and officers of the Gupta emperors and later imperial rulers. See *Paramabhaṭṭāraka-pād-ānudhyāta*.

Bhaṭṭārakaprabha (CII 4), a title.

Bhaṭṭa-rāṇaka (EI 9) see *Bhaṭṭa*, *Rāṇaka*, *Bhaṭṭa-mahattara*.

Bhaṭṭa-vṛtti (EI 25; SII 1), a grant for the maintenance of the Bhaṭṭas or learned Brāhmaṇas.

Bhaṭṭavṛtti-mānya (SITI), tax-free land (*inām*) given for the support of Brāhmaṇas; same as *bhaṭṭa-vṛtti*.

Bhaṭṭārikā (EI 23; CII 3; etc.), feminine form of *Bhaṭṭāraka* (q.v.); a title of the wives of independent and feudatory rulers; often suffixed to personal names.

Cf. Tamil *paṭṭārikai* (SITI), name of the goddess Durgā.

Bhaṭṭ-opādhyāya (EI 23), title of a Brāhmaṇa teacher.

bhauli, *bhaulī* (Chamba), a share, portion or allotment.

bhauma-yantra (IA 14), a particular mystic diagram.

Bhava (IE 7-1-2), 'eleven'.

bhāva (EI 26), a brother-in-law.

bhavana (LL), a temple. Cf. *pura*, *āyatana*, *ālaya*, etc.

bhāvanā (CII 4), sentiment, e.g., *maitrī*, etc.

(*EI* 3), Jain; a method of *kāy-otsarga*.

Bhavasṛj (CII 3), 'the creator of existence'; an epithet of the god Śiva.

bhāva-śuddhi (CII 1), purity of mind.

bhavat, cf. *sa bhavān* (EI 3), same as *tatrabhavān*.

Bhāvinī (IA 10), same as *Devadāsī*; a dancing girl attached to a temple.

bhaviṣya-kkiḍai-ppuṟam (SITI), Sanskrit-Tamil; tax-free land set apart to enable a teacher to reside permanently in a village for teaching.

bhavya (EI 3, 8), the Jain community.

bhāvya, cf. *rāja-bhāvya-sarva-pratyāya-sameta* (EI 23), income, levies; same as *ābhāvya*. According to some, *bhāvya* and *ābhāvya* mean *pāghḍī*. Cf. *talār-ābhāvya*.

(*LP*), probably the same as *bhāvyapada-paṭṭa*.

bherī (SITI, ASLV), a musical instrument.

bheruṇḍa (EI 31), a shortened form of *gaṇḍabheruṇḍa* (q.v.).

bhet (IA 11), Pañjābī; low lands inundated by rivers.

bheṭa (IE 8-5; EI 29), presents to be offered by a subject or subordinate to a ruler on occasions; occasional offering of money or presents; same as *vandāpanā*. See *bheṭana*.

bheṭana (LP), a present or gift; cf. *bheṭa*.

bhīdā (LP), 'straitened circumstances'; cf. Gujarātī *bhīd*.

bhikṣā (IE 8-4), a grant or endowment; cf. *ekādaśa-Rudra-bhikṣā* (EI 32), an endowment in the gods' name.

Bhikṣu (EI 7, 21; CII 3; ML), Buddhist monk, also called *Śākya-bhikṣu*.

Bhikṣu-hala (*LL*), 'the monks' land'; rent-free land in the possession of Buddhist monks.

Bhikṣuhala-parihāra, cf. Prakrit *Bhikhuhala-parihāra* (HRS), known from Śātavāhana records as a number of privileges relating to rent-free land belonging to the community of Buddhist monks.

Bhikṣuṇī (EI 25; CII 3; LL), feminine form of *Bhikṣu*; 'a Buddhist nun'; also called *Śākya-bhikṣuṇī*.

Bhikṣuṇy-upāśraya (LL), Buddhist; a nunnery.

Bhikṣuṇī-saṅgha, cf. *bhikkhuṇī-saṁgha* (EI 23), a community of nuns.

Bhikṣurāja (LL), title of a pious [Jain] king.

Bhikṣu-saṅgha (EI 26; CII 4), community of Buddhist monks.

Bhīmapriya (EI 11), name of a coin (*dramma*).

bhīmasenī-karpūra (SII 13), a kind of camphor.

Bhiṣak (HD), the king's medical advisor. See *Ep. Ind.*, Vol. IX, p. 305.

(*EI* 24), a physician.

Bhīṣmāṣṭamī (IA 17), Māgha su-di 8 or *amānta* Māgha (i.e. *pūrṇimānta* Phālguna) va-di 8.

bhīṭ (IA 15), see *bhīṭī* and *bhṛṣṭī*.

Bhitara-bhaṇḍāra-adhikārin (IE 8-3; EI 28), Oḍiyā; Sanskrit *Abhyantara-bhāṇḍār-ādhikārin*, 'officer in charge of the inner store-house or treasury (i.e. one within the palace or the harem)'.

bhītara-navara (EI 28), Oḍiyā=Sanskrit *abhyantara-nagara*; the palace.

bhīṭha (EI 31), probably, a mound.

bhīṭī (IA 15), see *bhṛṣṭī*.

bhitti-citra, wall-painting (*Journ. Mad. Univ.*, Vol. XXXII, p. 141).

Bhitvaramānya (IA 17), probably, a mistake for *Abhitvaramāṇa* (q.v.).

bhoga (IE 8-4; CII 3; EI 23, 33), literally, 'enjoyment' (cf. *bhukti*); a *jāgīr* (cf. *Mahārāja-Sarvanātha-bhoga*, *Mahāsāmantādhipati-Śrīdhara-bhoga*, etc.); possession (cf. *bhog-ādhīnā gṛhītā*). Originally 'enjoyment'; then 'property', 'a *jāgīr*'; then also a territorial unit which was generally the subdivision of a district (IE 8-4; EI 25; 28; CII 4). See *bhukti*, *āhāra*.

Cf. Kaivarta-bhoga (IE 8-4; EI 2; CII 1), the fishermen's preserve.

(*IE* 8-5; EI 29, 30; HRS), periodical supplies of fruits, firewood, flowers and the like which the villagers had to supply to the king; sometimes explained as 'tax in kind' (CII 4).

(*EI* 1), [an object of] enjoyment.

(*SITI*), tax-free land set apart for the enjoyment of a person for the performance of specified services; same as *mānya*. See *bhogottara*, *Bhogin*, etc.

Cf. bhoge (LP), 'for the right of enjoyment'.

Cf. sa-bhoga (IA 9), privilege of the donee of rent-free land; probably refers to *aṣṭabhoga-tejaḥsvāmya* (q.v.).

bhoga-bhāga (CII 3, etc.,), the same as *bhāga-bhoga*. Cf. *bhoga-bhāga-kara-hiraṇy-ādi* (EI 23), royal dues; see *bhoga*, etc.

bhoga-janapada (EI 12), probably, a free-holding in the country-side, or a rent-free area.

bhoga-lābha (EI 33), usufruct in lieu of interest.

Bhogapati (IE 8-3; EI 25, 27; HD), an *Ināmdār* or *Jāgīrdār*, or an officer in charge of *inām* lands or *jāgīrs*, or the officer in charge of a territorial unit called *bhoga*. The last alternative is more probable; cf. *Bhogika*, etc. See also *Mitākṣarā* on the *Yājñavalkyasmṛti*, I. 320; *Ep. Ind.*, Vol. IX, p. 298. See *Bhuktipati*, *Bhogikapāla*, etc.

Bhogapatika (IE 8-3; EI 23), same as *Bhogapati*.

bhoga-patra (ASLV, SITI), a deed recording conveyance of land; a lease deed; the deed of re-conveyance of land.

bhoga-strī, a concubine (*Ep. Ind.*, Vol. XXXIII, p. 272).

bhogatrā (IE 8-5), same as *bhogottara*.

bhogāvanīya (LP), 'should be enjoyed'.

bhog-āyaka (ASLV, SITI), land held as the result of a mortgage.

Bhogi-jana (EI 33), explained as 'a village headman'. Cf. *Bhogika*,

Bhogika (IE 8-3; CII 3; HD; BL), the owner of a *bhoga* or *jāgīr*; a *Jāgīrdār* or *Ināmdār*; same as *Bhogin*. See *Bhoktṛ*. Explained by some as the head of a district, or the collector of the State's share of the produce of lands taken in kind (*Bomb. Gaz.*, Vol. I, Part i, p. 82). See *CII*, Vol. III, pp. 96, 104.

(*IE* 8-3); EI 18; 23), a groom or horse-keeper, according to lexicons; cf. its Telugu modification *Bhoi*, 'a palanquin-bearer'. But these meanings may have been derived from the first as the people appear to have enjoyed rent-free land for their services.

(*EI* 33), same as *Bhojaka* meaning a *Jāgīrdār* or *Ināmdār*.

(*CII* 4), explained as 'the head of a *bhoga*'.

(*EI* 5), explained as 'a village proprietor'.

Bhogikapāla, Bhogikapālaka (EI 5; CII 4; BL), superintendent of the *jāgīrs* and cesscollector; cf. *Bhogapati*.

Bhogin (IE 8-3; EI 12, 28, 29, 30; BL), one in possession of a *bhoga* or *jāgīr*; a *Jāgīrdār*; same as *Bhogika* (q.v.).

bhogīna (EI 13), cf. *dattidāyaka-sādhupratipādita-prāg-*

bhujyamān-āvicchinna-bhogīna-bhuvām translated rather loosely as 'of the pieces of land in all the places that have been obtained in good manner from liberal donors'; probably, '[land] under possession'.

bhoginī, cf. *bogi* (EI 7), a concubine.

bhogi-rūpa (EI 12, 28), one who enjoys a free-holding as a representative of the real free-holder, or a title-holder who is not in actual possession of the land.

bhogiyār (SITI), Tamil; mistress, concubine; cf. *bhogyār*.

Bhog-oddharaṇika (HD), explained as 'the collector of the king's share of the grains'; cf. *bhoga*, *caur-oddharaṇika*.

bhogottara (IE 8-5; EI 33), corrupt form of *bhogatrā*; land granted to the family priest for his services; grant for the enjoyment of a Brāhmaṇa or deity.

bhogyā, cf. *pokiyār* (SITI), a concubine; see *bhogiyār*.

bhogya-tithi (CII 3), the portion of a *tithi* that is still to run.

Bhoi, Telugu modification of Sanskrit *Bhogin* (q.v.); palanquin-bearer (*Ep. Ind.*, Vol. XVIII, p. 308, note 8).

Bhoja, *Bhojaka* (IE 8-2; EI 1; 27; HD; LL), a *Jāgīrdār*; title of a feudatory; cf. the feminine form *Bhojikī*; also *Mahā-bhoja*. See *Ep. Ind.*, Vol. I, p. 5.

(*EI* 3; CII 3), a priest; title of a class of priests.

Cf. Tamil *pośar* (SITI), one who enjoys a thing; the possessor.

bhojana-catuḥśāla (LL), Buddhist; a dining hall.

bhojana-ākṣayanī, *bhojan-ākṣayaṇī* (EI 32), a permanent endowment created for the maintenance of the donee; cf. *akṣayanīvī*, *grāmagrāsa*, etc.

bhojana-maṇḍapa (LL), Buddhist; a refectory.

bhojana-śālā (EI 23), an almshouse; a free-feeding house. Cf. *sattra*.

Bhojikī (LL), wife of a *Bhojaka* (q.v.). cf. *Mahābhojī*.

Bhojpurī, language and people of the Bhojpur Pargana of the Shahabad District of Bihar and the adjoining regions.

Bhoktṛ (*Ep. Ind.*, Vol. XXXIII, p. 193), same as *Bhogin*, *Bhogika*; an *Ināmdār* or *Jāgīrdar*; cf. *Sammāṇaka-bhoktā*; also *Bhoktāri* (EI 11), a free-holder.

(*BL*), a proprietor.

Bhoṭṭa-viṣṭi (HRS), known from Nepal records; forced labour for carrying loads for officers sent to Tibet. See *H. Rev. Syst.*, p. 233.

bhrama-jala-gati (*Ep. Ind.*, Vol. XIV, p. 98), probably, a sluice.

bhṛṣṭī (IA 15), 'raised ground [near a tank] for planting piper betel'; cf. *bhiṭī*.

bhṛta (LP), loaded.

(*IE* 8-8), cf. *bhāṇḍa-bhṛta-vahitra*, 'a wagonful of pots or jars'. See *bharaka*.

Cf. *a-bhṛta-prāvesya* for *a-bhaṭa-prāveśya*, *bhṛta* being used for *bhaṭa* in the sense of a *Pāik*, *Barkandāz* or *Piāda*.

bhū (IA 17), a land measure; equal to four *bhū-māṣakas*. See *bhūmi*.

(*EI* 9), a land measure or a plot of land.

(*IE* 7-1-2; EI 15, 25), 'one'.

bhūbhṛt (IE 7-1-2), 'seven'.

bhūdhara (IE 7-1-2), 'seven'.

bhūcchidra-nyāya (EI 22), same as *bhūmicchidra-nyāya* (q.v.).

Bhujabalan-māḍai (SITI), name of a coin of the *māḍai* (*māḍha*) type. See *māḍa*, etc.

Bhujabalapratāpacakravartin (IE 8-2), see *Cakravartin*.

Bhujabalaprauḍhapratāpacakravartin (IE 8-2), see *Cakravartin*.

bhujaṅga (IA 20), an ogre. The word *bhujaṅga* was adopted in Javanese in the sense of a 'pupil, disciple, scholar; a philologist, poet, literary councillor; an officially appointed professional usually residing at or near the court'. It has been suggested on this basis that Bhavadeva-bhaṭṭa's title *Bālavalabhī-bhujaṅga* may really mean 'the pupil of the Bālavalabhī school'. See *IHQ*, Vol. XXVII, pp. 80-82.

bhujiṣya-patra (EI 24), a document granting maintenance.

bhujyamāna (IA 18), also *prabhujyamāna*; 'being enjoyed'.

bhukta-tithi (CII 3), the elapsed portion of a *tithi*.

bhukti (IE 8-4; EI 28, 33), a province including a group of districts called *viṣaya* or *maṇḍala*; small territorial unit like a Pargana in South India; cf. *bhoga*.

(*IE* 8-3; 8-4; CII 3), literally, 'enjoyment'; same as *bhoga*; a *jāgīr*; originally meaning 'enjoyment'; then 'property' or 'a *jāgīr*'; then 'a province'. See *bhoga*.

(*BL*), personal property.

Cf. putti, pukti (SITI), the enjoyment of a property.

bhukti-maṇḍala (IE 8-4), originally a *bhukti* but later on a *maṇḍala*; cf. *Daṇḍabhukti-maṇḍala, āhāra-viṣaya.*

Bhuktipati (IE 8-3), a *Jāgīrdār*; or, the officer in charge of a territorial unit called *bhukti.* See *Bhogapati.*

bhūmāṣaka (IA 17), a land measure, four *bhūmāṣakas* making one *bhū* (q.v.)

bhumbhuka (EI 13), Kannaḍa; cf. *bhuvana-bhumbhuka,* probably, 'an ornament of the world'.

bhūmi, bhūmī (EI 3; CII 3), a particular land measure; sometimes also called *bhū* and regarded as equal to four *bhūmāṣakas* (cf. *bhū*).

(*CII* 4), a territorial divison.

(*EI* 7-1-2), 'one'.

bhūmicchidra (*IE* 8-5), sometimes explained as 'uncultivable land'. See *bhūmicchidra-nyāya.*

bhūmicchidra-nyāya (IE 8-5; EI 30; CII 3, 4; HRS), literally, 'the maxim of the fallow land'; the principle of the rent-free enjoyment of land by one who brings it under cultivation for the first time. See *Ep. Ind.*, Vol XXIX, p. 86. The maxim is based on the old custom of allowing a person, who first brings a plot of fallow or jungle land under cultivation for the first time, to enjoy it without paying rent. *Bhūmicchidra* gradually came to mean 'uncultivable land'. See *bhūmicchidrapidhāna-nyāya, avanirandhra-nyāya.*

bhūmicchidrapidhāna-nyāya (IE 8-5; EI 11), the same as *bhūmicchidra-nyāya*; but it means 'the maxim of covering up the hole in the land' referring probably to the reclamation of fallow land for the first time; cf. *bhūmicchidra* understood in the sense of *kṛṣy-ayogyā bhū*, 'land unfit for cultivation'. See *Ep. Ind.*, Vol. XXIX, p. 86.

bhūmicchidravidhāna-nyāya (EI 24); same as *bhūmicchidra-nyāya, bhumicchidrapidhāna-nyāya. Chidra-vidhāna=furrowing.*

bhūmipeṇḍe (ASLV), a mark of honour.

bhūmi-putra. cf. *pūmi-puttirar* (SITI), husbandmen regarded as the sons of Mother Earth.

bhūpa (IA 7-1-2), 'sixteen'.

bhurja (IE 3-2), really 'the birch'; but same as *lekhana*; a written document.

bhūsphoṭa (EI 9), a mushroom.

bhūta (CII 1), a living being.

(*IE* 8-5), the element or nature.

(*IE* 7-1-2), 'five'.

(*CII* 3, etc.), a fiscal term; cf. *sa-bhūta-pāta-pratyāya*, in which we have sometimes *pātta* (mistake for *upātta*), *upātta*, *āvāta* or *vāta*. See *bhūta-pāta*, etc.

bhūta-bali (EI 11; SII 13), explained as 'offering of boiled rice to the ghosts'.

bhūta-koṭya (IA 23), the place of residence of the family ghost.

bhūta-pāta, cf. *sa-bhūta-pāta-pratyāya* (IE 8-5); often written as *bhūta-vāta* and *bhūt-opātta*; probably, an event relating to the elements, such as an earthquake. See *bhūta-pāta-pratyāya.*

bhūta-pāta-pratyāya (CII 4), explained by some as 'excise and octroi duties'; but really, 'the income resulting from storms, earthquakes, changes in the course of a river, etc'. See *bhūta-vāta-pratyāya*, etc. *Pāta* may be a mistake for *upātta* or *vāta.*

bhūta-pratyāya (CII 3), an income derived from natural changes in the land. See *bhūta-vāta-pratyāya*, etc.

bhūtapūrva (CII 1), 'existing in the past'.

bhūta-vāta-pratyāya (EI 23; CII 4; HRS), 'the income derived from the elements and the winds'; explained by some as 'excise and octori duties'; but really, 'the income resulting from storms, earthquakes, changes in the course of a river, etc.' See *bhūt-opātta-pratyāya*, etc.

bhūt-opātta-pratyāya (EI 32), income brought about by elemental or natural changes (e.g. storms, earthquakes, etc.).

Bhūvara (*Ep. Ind.*, Vol. XIV, p. 98), 'a king'.

bighā, *bīghā* (IE 8-6), a land measure.

bījaka, cf. *bījak* (EI 9), an inscribed stone or an inscription.

bīja-saṁskāra (CII 4), an astronomical term.

bīḻ-ānuvṛtti, also called *bīḻa-vṛtti* (599 11-1), Kannaḍa-Sanskrit; fief held by a king's subordinate for his maintenance; cf. *anuga-jīvita.*

bilkoḍe (EI 28), Kannaḍa; tolls.

biṁ° (PJS), abbreviation of *bimba*, 'an image' (especiacially in medieval Jain inscriptions).

bimba (IA 3; HA), same as *pratimā*; an image.

binduka, same as *suvarṇa* (q.v.).

birāḍa (EI 24), name of a tax.

bīravaṇa-pārikhāya (IA 19), levy stated to have been of four kinds; cf. *nidhi-nikṣepa-jala-pāṣāṇ-ārām-ādi-chatuṣ-prakāra-bīravaṇa-pārikhāya-sahitaṁ* which is mentioned along with *aṣṭabhoga-tejassvāmya-daṇḍa-śulka-yuktam* ; Sanskrit *vīra-paṇa* (tax for the maintenance of constables) and *pārīkṣ-āya* (*pārīkṣika*).

biruda (SII 1), also spelt *viruda*; 'a surname'.

Biśī (EI 24), derived from *Viṣayin* (*Viṣayapati*), the governor of a district.

bīsva (EI 28), a land measure equal to $\frac{1}{20}$ of a *bīghā*; derived from Sanskrit *viṁśopaka*.

bīṭaka (*Ep. Ind.*, Vol. I, p. 279), modern *bīḍā* (i.e. a betel *bīḍā*).

bittuvaṭṭa (*A.R.Ep.*, 1958-59, p. 10), Kannaḍa; probably also called *bittukaṭṭe* ; explained as 'a portion of the produce derived from the lands irrigated by tanks, or wet land irrigated by a tank, granted to the person who built the tank or repaired it.'

bodhi (LL), Buddhist; supreme knowledege attained by the Buddha; the tree of enlightenment; cf. *mahābodhi*, *saṁbodhi*.

bodhi-cakra (LL), Buddhist; the wheel of enlightenment.

Bodhisattva (CII 2-1; LL), Buddhist; a would-be Buddha in a previous birth. Cf. *Chadmastha*.

bodhyaṅga, cf. *bojjhaṅga* (EI 5), Buddhist; seven in number.

Boḍiyā, local name of the Gujarātī alphabet (*Ind. Ep.*, p. 55).

bommalāṭa (ASLV), a puppet show.

boppa (CII 3), a Prakrit word meaning 'the father'; see *bappa*.

boṭa, also spelt *voṭa* (CII 3), a termination of geographical names; meaning uncertain.

botkaṭa (IA 19), a goat; cf. Deśī *bokkaḍa*; also *varkara* (IA 19).

Brā, abbreviation of *Brāhmaṇa* (*Ep. Ind.*, Vol. XXX, p. 55).

brahmacārin (SII 2; LL), a Brāhmaṇa student; an unmarried student of the Vedas.

(*BL*), epithet of one who takes a vow of celebacy.

(*SII* 2), a temple servant.

brahma-dāna, cf. *pirama-dānam* (SITI), gift to Brāhmaṇas; same as *brahmadāya*, etc.

brahmadāya (EI 23; CII 4), gift to a Brāhmaṇa; the rent-free holding of Brāhmaṇas; same as *brahmadeya*. See *brahmatrā*, etc.

brahmadeya (EI 30; ASLV; HRS; SITI), land or village given as gift (generally tax-free) to Brāhmaṇas; land to be granted to or in the possession of Brāhmaṇas.

brahmadeya-kkiḻavar (SITI), Sanskrit-Tamil; sole owner of a Brahmadeya village; sometimes supposed to be the headman or chief of a Brahmadeya village.

Brahm-ādhirāja (SITI), title of distinguished Brāhmaṇa military commanders; also spelt *Brahmādarāya* in Tamil. See *Brahma-mahārāja, Brahma-rāja*.

brahma-hatyā (CITD), killing a Brāhmaṇa, considered to be a great sin.

brahma-kalpa (CITD), the *kalpa* or age of the god Brahman, extending to many thousands of years.

Brahma-kṣatra, Brahma-kṣatriya (EI 5, 12, 24), a Kṣatriya family claiming descent from a Brāhmaṇa parent; a family in which the blood of the Brāhmaṇas and Kṣatriyas has been mixed. See *Vishveshvaranand Ind. Journ.*, Vol. I, pp. 87 ff., etc. In one record (*Journ. Karnatak Univ.*, Vol. II, No 2, January 1959, p. 47), the Nāgavaṁśa, to which a Kadamba king's minister Māyideva belonged, is called *Brahma-kṣatra* because it originated from the intercouse of its progenitor Nāgarāja with a Brāhmaṇa girl. *Brahma-vaiśya* should be likewise explained.

Brahma-mahārāja, cf. *pirama-mārāyaṉ* (SITI), title of Brāhmaṇa ministers. See *Brahm-ādhirāja, Brahmarāja*.

brahma-mantra (IA 12), five in number.

brahma-medha, cf. *pirama-metam* (SITI), special funeral rite for a saintly person.

Brahman (IE 7-1-2), 'nine'.

brāhmaṇa-rāśa(*rāja*)*-kkāṇam* (SITI), Sanskrit-Tamil; tax payable by the Brāhmaṇa (*Purohita*) to the king.

brāhmaṇa-viṁśati (HRS), tithe upon villagers for the maintenance of the Brāhmaṇas.

brahmāṇḍa (EI 16, 21), name of a *mahādāna*.

brahmaṇya (EI 22) 'hospitable to the Brāhmaṇas'; see *Paramabrahmaṇya, Atibrahmaṇya*.

brāhmaṇya (SII 1), the community of Brāhmaṇas.

brahmapura (EI 2), same as *brahmapurī*; a rent-free village in the possession of Brāhmaṇas; same as *agrahāra*, etc.

brahmapurī (EI 4, 28; SITI), also called *agara-brahmadeya* (Sanskrit *agrahāra-brahmadeya*); a Brāhmaṇa settlement. See *brahmapura.*

Brahmarāja (SITI), title of a Brāhmaṇa minister.

Brahmarākṣasa (EI 3, 16), a Brāhmaṇa defeated in disputations.

Brahmarāya (SITI), same as *Brahmarāja*. Cf. *Brahm-ādhirāja.*

Brahmarṣi (EI 22), a Brāhmaṇa sage.

brahma-stamba (CII 4), a settlement of Brāhmaṇas.

brahma-sthāna (SII 13; SITI), explained as 'an assembly hall'; the Brāhmaṇa quarters of a village; cf. Tamil *pirummastānam* (SITI), the quarters of the Brāhmaṇas where the village assembly (*sabhā*) used to meet.

Brahmāsya (IE 7-1-2), 'four'.

brahmatrā (IE 8-5), same as *brahmadāya*, etc.

Brahma-vaiśya (*A. R. Ep.*, 1919, No. 208); cf. *Brahma-kṣatra.*

brahma-yajña (EI 22; CII 4), study of the Vedas; name of a *mahāyajña.*

Brāhmī, name of an early Indian alphabet, from which a large number of alphabets of India and some other countries have derived.

brahmottara (IE 8-5), Bengali; corrupt form of *brahmatrā.* (*IA* 15), explained as 'the sanctuary of a temple'.

Bṛha, abbreviation of *Bṛhatpuruṣa* (q. v.). See *Ep. Ind.*, Vol. XXXIV, p. 143.

bṛhac-chulka, cf. Kannaḍa *perjuṅka*, *perujuṅka*, *pejjuṅka*, *hejjuṅka.*

Bṛhad-bhogika (IE 8-3), same as *Bṛhad-bhogin*; see *Bhogika* and *Aṁśa-bṛhadbhogika.*

Bṛhad-bhogin (IE 8-3; EI 28, 29; BL), same as *Bṛhad-bhogika*; a chief *jāgīrdār*; see *Bhogin.*

Bṛhaddeva, cf. Tamil *Periya-devar* (SITI), literally, 'the great king'; the predecessor or predecessors of the ruling monarch; also called *Periya-perumāḷ* sometimes indicating the paramount sovereign or emperor. Cf. *Bṛhan-nṛpati.*

bṛhaddhala (EI 7), 'the big plough'; name of a land measure (*Ep. Ind.*, Vol. II, p. 125); cf. *hala.*

Bṛhad-rājñī (EI 4), same as *Paṭṭa-rājñī* (q.v.).

Bṛhad-uparika (EI 15, 26; HD), 'the great governor of a province'; a viceroy. See *Ep. Ind.*, Vol. XII, p. 9. Cf. *Uparika.*

Bṛhad-vāchaka (LL), a Jain preacher.

Bṛhad-vājika (LP), probably, a police officer.

bṛhan-māna (EI 23; CII 4), a measure larger than the standard one; cf. *viṣaya-māna.*

Bṛhan-nṛpati (IE 8-2), predecessor of the ruling monarch; called *Periya-devar* in Tamil; cf. Oḍiyā *Baḍa-Narasiṁha* and Telugu *Pedda-Narasiṁha.* See *Bṛhaddeva.* Cf. *Ep. Ind.*, Vol. XXXII, p. 231 and note 2; *JAS*, Letters, Vol. XX, p. 212.

bṛhaspatisava (EI 22; CII 3), name of a sacrifice.

bṛhatī (IE 7-1-2), 'nine'.

Bṛhat-kumāramahāpātra (EI 28), cf. *Kumāra-mahāpātra* which is similar to *Kumārāmātya.*

Bṛhat-purohita, cf. *Baḍā-purohit* (EI 24), 'the high priest'.

Bṛhatpuruṣa, probably the same as *Mahājana* (*Ep. Ind.*, Vol. XXXIV, pp. 143-44).

Bṛhat-sandhivigrahi-mahāpātra (EI 28), same as *Mahā-sandhivigrahin.*

Bṛhat-tantrapati (IE 8-3; EI 33), explained by a Kashmirian commentator as the *Dharmādhikārin* who was a judge also in charge of charities; cf. the Muslim official designation *Ṣadruṣ-Ṣudūr*, etc., explained as 'the chief judge and grand almoner, or the custodian of the king's bequests and charities' (*Journ. As. Soc. Pak.*, Vol. IV, pp. 53-54).

bṛha-vāra, (EI 31; cf. *Ep. Ind.*, Vol. XXXIII, p. 125 and note), Saturday or Thurdsday (A. Venkatasubbiah, *Some Śaka Dates in Inscriptions*, pp. 57ff.); same as *Vaḍḍa-vāra* (q. v.).

bṛndāvana (EI 12), a tomb.

Buddha (LL), Buddhist; a class of saints. See *Bodhisattva.*

buddha-caitya (EI 28), a Buddhist shrine.

buddh-ādhiṣṭhāna (EI 22), a city or locality in the possession of a Buddhist monastery.

Buḍhāleṅkā (IE 8-3), Oḍiyā; same as *Mahāpādamūlika*, 'chief attendant.'

budh-āṣṭamī (IA 26), the eighth *tithi* on a Wednesday.

bullaga-kara (HRS), tax relating to the supervision of meals according to the *Abhidhānarājendra*, s.v. *kara.*

būreḍu (CITD), Telugu; an unknown quantity.

busa (IE 8-5), chaff.

busi-bhaṁḍālu (CITD), Telugu; probably, stores of unhusked grain. Cf. *kola-bhaṁḍālu.*

būṭīya (EI 32), a mound.

C

caba (Chamba), wet land, marshy land.

cabūtarā (EI 32), Hindī; a platform.

Cāḍa (IE 8-3), same as *Cāṭa* (q. v.) and the modern *Cāḍ* of Chamba, the latter being the designation of the head of a Parganā.

cāḍḍā (LP), a camp; an attacking party.

caitra-pavitra, *caitra-pavitraka* (EI 7, 18), name of a rite (*Ind. Ant.*, Vol. XXXVIII, p. 52); *caitra* is the *daman-āropaṇa* ceremony which takes place in the month of Caitra and *pavitra* is the *pavitr-āropaṇa* ceremony which occurs in Śrāvaṇa (*Ind. Ant.*, Vol. XI, p. 274, notes 12-13); cf. Kannaḍa *caitra-pavitr-ābhyāgat-ādi pūje gaḷgaṁ*, translated as 'for the *caitra* and *pavitra* and the entertainment of guests and other rites' (IA 30).

caitya (EI 22, 33; BL), a prayer hall; usually, a place of worship in a Buddhist monastery; same as *caitya-gṛha*.

(*EI* 6, CII 4), same as *stūpa*.

caity-āgāra (SII 1), a Jain temple; same as *caity-ālaya*.

caitya-gṛha (EI 8, 33, LL), Buddhist; cf. Prakrit *cetiya-ghara*. (EI 24), the hall for worship or prayer; hall in a monastery.

caityaka-śaila, a stone pillar raised in memory of a dead person on his cremation ground (*Ep. Ind.*, Vol. XXVIII, p. 133). See *yaṣṭi*.

caity-ālaya (EI 7), same as *caitya*.

(*EI* 3; SII 1), a Jain temple; same as *caity-āgāra*.

caitya-paṭṭa (LL), Buddhist; a slab bearing the representation of a *caitya*. See *cakra-paṭṭa*.

Caitya-śaila (EI 24), a Buddhist school.

caitya-vandana (HA), obeissance to and worship of the Jina with recitation of hymns, etc., and meditating on the qualities of a Jina.

Caityika (EI 24), same as *Caitya-śaila*.

cakalī, a small coin, smaller than the *ṭaṁka* regarded as $\frac{1}{62}$ of a rupee.

cākāntara (EI 3), a village institution of uncertain meaning.

cakra, cf. *Cakrin* (EI 4); a district; same as *maṇḍala*.

Cf. sakkaram (SITI), wheel of authority; the king's order; an officer entrusted with the execution of the king's order.

(*CII* 3), 'the discus'; an emblem on seals.

Cf. śakkara-kāṇikkai (SITI), Sanskrit-Tamil; tax paid by potters; also called *tirigai-āyam.*

cakra-paṭṭa (LL), Buddhist; a slab bearing the representation of a wheel. See *caitya-paṭṭa.*

Cakravāla-giri (SITI), same as Tamil *Śakkaravāḷam*; a mythical mountain encircling the earth; the horizon.

cakravarti-kṣetra (IE 8-2; EI 33), the sphere of influence of an Indian imperial ruler lying between the Himalayas and the three seas, viz. Bay of Bengal, Indian Ocean and Arabian Sea; sometimes regarded as conterminous with *Āryāvarta* or *Dākṣiṇātya.* See Sircar, *Stud. Geog. Anc. Med. Ind.*, pp. 1 ff.

Cakravartin (IE 8-2; EI 21, 28; CII 3, 4), a title of paramount sovereignty; the title of an emperor. See *Saptama-cakravartin*; also *Cakreśvara, Cakrin.*

(*IE* 8-2), often suffixed to expressions like *Pratāpa, Prauḍhapratāpa, Bhujabalapratāpa, Niḥśaṅkapratāpa*, etc., and sometimes also to dynastic names like *Yādava.*

(*EI* 31), epithet of the Buddha.

(*IE* 8-2), cf. *cakravarti-kṣetra.*

Cakreśvara (*EI* 3), same as *Cakravartin.*

Cakrin (EI 9), same as *Cakravartin.*

(*EI* 4, 19), 'the ruler of a *cakra* (circle) or district'; title of a provincial ruler.

cakṣus (IE 7-1-2), 'two'; cf. *netra.*

Cf. Pali *cakkhu* (EI 5), Buddhist; vision, five in number.

Cf. cakṣur-vadha, 'killing at sight', 'killing instantaneously'; or probably 'blinding of the eyes'. See *Ep. Ind.*, Vol. XXXIII, p. 307 and note 1.

Calamartigaṇḍa (CITD), Telugu-Kannaḍa; a title of the Kākatīya kings; from Kannaḍa *gaṇḍa* meaning 'the husband, lord, master,' i.e. 'one who can control or punish', and Telugu *calam* meaning 'obstinacy, rudeness, overbearing'; transalated as 'one who is the controller or punisher of spiteful men or men of overbearing conduct'.

cālī (IA 15), a system of land revenue.

calivaṁdili, caliveṁdala, caliveṁdra, calipaṁdili (CITD), Telugu-Kannaḍa; halting place for travellers, where they are supplied gratis with milk and whoey or with water.

cāmara (IE 8-8), name of a coin; cf. *cāmara-māda.*

(*SII* 3), a fly-whisk. See *cauri, cavarālu.*

Cāmara-kumāra, cf. *Cavari-kumāra* (EI 10), probably, a prince in charge of the fly-whisk which was one of the royal insignia.

cāmara-māḍa (EI 7), name of a coin; cf. *cāmara.*

campā-ṣaṣṭhī (EI 5), name of a *tithi.*

Camūnāyaka (EI 27), a general; cf. *Senāpati,* etc.

Camūpa (IA 10), a general; same as *Camūpati,* etc.

Camūpati (*EI* 8-3); a general, same as *Senāpati,* etc.

Caṇḍa-pracaṇḍa (SITI), divinities guarding the inner shrine of a Viṣṇu temple.

Caṇḍeśvara (SITI), traditional executive of Śiva temples; also called *Ādi-dāsa.*

Caṇdeśvara-pperuvilai (SITI), Sanskrit-Tamil; literally, the sale-price of Caṇḍeśvara, the traditional executive of Śiva temples; actually, sale-price of land purchased from a Śiva temple.

candra (IE 7-1-2; EI 25), 'one'.

candrādityavat (SITI), same as Tamil *candrādittaval, candrādittavar*; 'as long as the moon and the sun last'; 'in perpetuity'.

candra-grahaṇa (SII 1), lunar eclipse.

candrahāsa (EI 25), name of Rāma's sword.

candraka (EI 2), the young moon.

candra-kālikam (LP), permanently.

candramas (*IE* 7-1-2), 'one'.

candr-ārka-yoga-parvan (EI 19), same as *amāvāsyā.*

candra-viśada (LP), 'as white as the moon', i.e. guiltless.

candy (IA 26), Anglicised form of *khaṇḍī,* a weight of different value in different parts. See *khaṇḍikā.*

caṅga, see *chaṅga.*

caṅkrama (LL), Prakrit *caṁkama* (EI 24); a promenade, a walk.

capalaṁ (CII 1), quickly.

Cara (CII 4), a spy.

Cāra (IE 8-3; EI 26), a spy; same as *Cara*; sometimes used in place of *Cāṭa.*

(*EI* 15), cf. *a-cār-āsana-carm-āṅgāra* (IE 8-5), probably, passage [of royal officers through a village]; cf. also *a-pār-*

āsana-carm-āṅgāra with *pāra* (probably, ferrying) instead of *cāra*.

cara-balīvarda (IE 8-5), cf. *vara-balīvarda*.

caraṇa (CII 4; IA 18, 20), a Vedic school; a sect or school studying a particular *śākhā* of the Vedas; e. g. *Taittirīya-caraṇa*.

(*CII* 1), same as *ācaraṇa*; cf. *dharma-caraṇa* for *dharm-ācaraṇa*.

Cāraṇa (EI 3), same as *Vidyā-cāraṇa*, a Jain monk endowed with magical powers.

Cf. *harita-pakva-sasy-ekṣu-cāraṇa-lavaṇ-opamardana* (IE 8-5); grazing of cattle.

caraṇḍi (EI 31), Gujarātī; a narrow passage of water.

carī (EI 33), pasture land; same as *carī-kṣetra*.

(*EI* 21), grazing tax; grazing land. Cf. *cārī*.

cārī (LP), Gujarātī *cāro*, grass; probably, pasture land; cf. *carī*.

(*CII* 4), grazing tax.

Carmakāra (EI 32), a shoe-maker.

carman (EI 15), cf. *a-carm-āṅgāraka* (IE 8-5); hide-seat which the villagers were obliged to supply to the touring officers of the king.

caru (EI 10, 22, 23; CII 3, 4), an offering to the manes; one of the five *mahāyajñas*.

caruka (EI 1), same as *caru*, one of the five *mahāyajñas*.

caryā (CII 4), discipline in Śaivite practices.

cash (IE 8-8), Anglicised form of Tamil *kāśu*; name of a small copper coin.

caṭ, cf. *alīkaṁ caṭāpitam* (LP), 'circulated a false rumour'.

Cf. *caṭanti* (LP); 'to accumulate'; also cf. Gujarātī *caḍhśe*.

Cāṭa (HD), irregular soldiers according to Fleet and Bühler. Vogel (*Ant. Ch. St.*, pp. 130-32) points out that Chamba is the only place where the ancient word *Cāṭa* is still extant in the modern form *Cāḍ* meaning 'the head of a Parganā'. An important privilege of a gift village was 'not to be entered by *Cāṭas* and *Bhaṭas*'. Inscriptions (*Ep. Ind.*, Vol. XI, p. 221) often specify that the granted land was not to be entered by *Cāṭas* and *Bhaṭas* except for seizing robbers and those guilty of harm or treason to the king (cf. *a-cāṭa-bhaṭa-praveśyaṁ cora-drohaka-varjam* in op. cit., Vol. VIII, p. 287). Sometimes we have *bhaṭa-cāṭa-sevak-ādīn* (*Ep. Ind.*, Vol. IV, p. 211) and *caṭṭa-bhaṭṭa-jātīyān janapadān* (ibid., Vol. XIV, p. 160).

(*IE* 8-3; CII 3, 4), generally mentioned along with *bhaṭa*; sometimes replaced by *cāra* (spy) and *chātra* (literally, 'umbrella-bearer', but really, a constable, i.e. a *Pāik* or *Piāda*); probably indicates the leader of a group of *Bhaṭas*, i.e. *Pāiks* and *Piādas*; a policeman leading a group of *Pāiks*. See *caṭṭa*. Yājñavalkya, I. 336, speaks of the duty of the king to protect people from the harassment caused by *cāṭas*, robbers and *Kāyasthas* and the *Mitākṣarā* explains *cāṭa* as persons who deprive people of their wealth after creating false confidence in them. According to Bṛhaspati quoted by Aparārka, 'dangers common to all are those arising from the *cāṭas* and thieves'. The word *cāṭa* in the passage *tārkika-cāṭa-bhaṭa-rāj-āpraveśya* in Śaṅkara's *Bhāṣya* on the *Bṛhadāraṇyaka Upaniṣad* is explained by Ānandagiri by saying that the *cāṭas* are those that transgress the rules of conduct for decent people and that *bhaṭas* are servants telling falsehood (*Ep. Ind.*, Vol. IX, p. 296). But *cāṭa* is used in inscriptions in the sense of a royal official.

caṭāpaka (LP), 'increasing [the rent already fixed]'; cf. Gujarātī *caḍhāvo*.

caṭāpya (LP), 'to be entered [on the back of the bond]'; cf. Gujarātī *caḍhāvavā*.

ca-ṭī abbreviation of an expression probably meaning 'a mound suitable for planting fruit trees'. See *Ep. Ind.*, Vol. XXX, p. 56. Cf. *ṭī*.

caṭita (LP), one who makes an attack.

(*LP*), accumulated.

Cf. khaṇḍa-sphuṭita-caṭita-pratiṣaṁskāra; a crack.

Caṭṭa (*EI* 25), Tamil corruption of Sanskrit *Chātra*; a student.

(*IE* 8-3), cf. *a-caṭṭa-bhaṭṭa-praveśa* (*IE* 8-5); same as *Cāṭa* of earlier records.

caṭṭanā (LP), food; sauce; cf. Gujarātī *cāṭvuṁ*, licking.

cāṭu (IA 15), probably, a spoon.

(*EI* 32), a eulogistic stanza.

catuḥ-śāla, catuḥ-śālā (EI 20; SITI), a cloister.

(*SITI*), a meeting hall; see *catuś-śālā*.

(*EI* 24), same as *catur-ālaya*.

cātu-paḍi (CITD), Telugu; an offering of food to the deity.

catura, cf. *caturaka*; a square.

caturaka (LP), same as Sanskrit *catvara*; Gujarātī *coro*;

a public place in a village, or a police station; probably, a tax for the maintenance of a police station.

(*IE* 8-4), a small territorial unit.

catur-ālaya (EI 24), known, especially from Tamil inscriptions, in the sense of 'a hall or pavilion attached to a temple'; also called *catuḥ-śālā*.

Caturānana-vadana (IE 7-1-2), 'four'.

caturaṅga (EI 2), a complete army.

caturaśīti (*IE* 8-4), a territorial unit like a Parganā; see *caurāsī*.

caturdanta-samara, *cāturdanta-samara*, a war of elephants; cf. *ghoṭaka-vigraha*. See *Ep. Ind.*, Vol. XXXVI, p. 8.

caturdaśa-vidyā-sthāna (CII 3), the fourteen sections of science.

Caturdhara-pratīhāra, cf. Kannaḍa *Sodare-vadiyara* (*Hyderabad Archaeological Series*, No. 18, p. 34); explained as 'the chief of the royal guards'. *Caturdhara* is modern *Caudhari*, written in Kannaḍa as *Saudore*, *Saudare*, *Caudore*, *Cavudore* and *Cavudari* and explained as 'an officer of the royal guard'.

cāturdiśa (*EI* 23; ML), 'belonging to all the quarters'; cf. *cāturdiś-ārya-bhikṣu-saṅgha*, 'Buddhist monks of all places'; 'all monks coming from different places'.

catur-garbha (LL), a four-celled building.

caturjātaka (*IE* 8-3), same as *cauthiā*, an administrative board of four members known from the *Pañcāyat* system of Western India; cf. *pañcakula* or *pañcāyat*. See *Ep. Ind.*, Vol. XXXIII, p. 193. See *caukaḍikā*.

(*EI* 20), four fragrant articles, viz. *tvak*, *elā*, *patraka* and *nāgakesara*.

Cāturjātaka (*EI* 1), a member of the *caturjātaka* or *cauthiā* (q.v.). Cf. *Pañcakulika*. See *Ep. Ind.*, Vol. XXXIII, p. 193.

Caturjātakīya, same as *Cāturjātaka* (EI 1); a member of the *caturjātaka* (q.v.); cf. *Pañcakulika*. See *Ep. Ind.*, Vol. XXXIII, p. 193.

cāturmāsī (EI 2; CII 1), the full-moon *tithis* of Phālguna, Āṣāḍha and Kārttika.

cāturmāsī-pakṣa (IA 18), the fortnight ending in a *cāturmāsī* (i.e. the full-moon of Phālguna, Āṣāḍha and Kārttika).

cāturmāsya (SII 11-1, CITD), the season consisting of 4 months, viz. *grīṣma* consisting of the *pūrṇimānta* months of Caitra,

Vaiśākha, Jyeṣṭha and Āṣāḍha, *varṣā* consisting of Śrāvana, Bhādrapada, Āśvina and Kārttika; and *hemanta* consisting of Mārgaśīrṣa, Pauṣa, Māgha and Phālguna. This was the official division of the year which was popularly divided into six seasons, viz. *grīṣma* (Jyeṣṭha-Āṣāḍha), *varṣā* (Śrāvaṇa-Bhādrapada), *śarad* (Āśvina-Kārttika), *hemanta* (Mārgaśīrṣa-Pauṣa), *śīta* (Māgha-Phālguna) and *vasanta* (Caitra-Vaiśākha). Some times, the word *cāturmāsya* specially means the four months of the year, containing the two seasons of *varṣā* and *śarad*, i.e. from Śrāvaṇa to Kārttika. During this period, Viṣṇu is supposed to sleep, so that religious celebrations are avoided. During the period, religious mendicants desisted from roving.

(*EI* 7; BL), related to the *cāturmāsī* or the full-moon day of Phālguna, Āshāḍha and Kārttika; a rite; same as *cāturmāsya-vrata*.

cāturmāsya-vrata (EI 32), a rite. See *cāturmāsya*.

caturmukha-bimba (EI 2), Jain; a four-sided slab with images on all the sides.

caturtha (IE 8-8), one-fourth of the standard measure [of liquids like liqour].

caturtha-kula (EI 29), the Śūdra community.

caturthī-amāvāsyā, cf. *cauti-amāvāse* (EI 5), the new-moon following the Gaṇeśa-caturthī.

cāturvaidya-maryādā (EI 27), custom relating to rent-free land granted to learned Brāhmaṇas.

caturvarṇin (LL), Jain; 'consisting of four classes'; an epithet of the Jain community.

caturvedi-bhaṭṭa-ttāna-pperumakkaḻ (SITI), Sanskrit-Tamil; general assembly of the Vedic scholars in a Brāhmaṇa village.

caturvedi-maṅgala (IE 8-4; SITI), same as *agrahāra*; a village owned by Brāhmaṇas, generally tax-free; also called *maṅgala*; written as *śaruppeṭi-maṅgalam* in Tamil; sometimes suffixed to names of localities especially in the Tamil-speaking area.

Caturvedin (EI 23, 24; CII 3, 4; SII 1), a Brāhmaṇa versed in the four Vedas; one who has studied the four Vedas; later stereotyped as a family name among Brāhmaṇas.

cāturvidya (EI 23, 32), cf. *Caturvedin*; 'relating to the *Caturvedin*', a community of Brāhmaṇas; cf. *cāturvidya-grāma*, *cāturvidy-āgrahāra*, *cāturvidya-sāmānya* (EI 22).

catur-upāya (SII 1), the four expedients. Cf. *upāya*.

caturviṁśati-tīrthaṅkara-paṭṭa (EI 2), a slab with the images o all the 24 Jain *Tīrthaṅkaras*. See *covīsī*.

catuṣkikā (EI 19; CII 4), a hall; a hall resting on four pillars (*Ep. Ind.*, Vol. XIX, p. 75).

catuṣpatha (LP), a place where four roads meet.

catuś-śālā (SITI), a meeting hall; see *catuḥ-śālā*.

catvāraka (IA 17), used in the sense of *catuṣṭaya*.

Chau° (PJS), contraction of *Caudharī* (*Caturdhara*) especially in medieval Jain inscriptions.

caukaḍikā (EI 11), a variety of the *Pañcāyat* system; cf. *caturjātaka* or *cauthiā*.

(*BL*), explained as 'a method of recovering stolen property'.

caumukha (HA), Sanskrit *caturmukha* (cf. *caturmukha-bimba*); a quadruple image called *pratimā sarvatobhadrikā* (LL) in the Mathurā inscriptions of the Kuṣāṇa period, showing one Jina or several Jinas on each of the four faces; also seen on the top or in the centre of representations of the *samavasaraṇa* (q.v.).

Caura-caraṭa (LP), cf. Marāṭhī *Cor-cilaṭāṁcā upadrav*.

caurāsī (IE 8-4; EI 3, 4), literally, 'eightyfour'; same as *caturaśīti* (q.v.); a group of eightyfour villages; a Parganā consisting of eightyfour villages; simetimes the name of a Parganā and often suffixed to its name.

caura-varjam (CII 3; HRS), cf. *cora-varjam*, *coradaṇḍa-varjam*, *cora-rājāpathyakāri-varjam*; 'with immunity from the police tax' according to some; may really mean 'without any right to inflict punishment on thieves and persons committing the crime of treason or to levy fines from them'; may also be connected with *a-bhaṭa-praveśa* so as to indicate that the *bhaṭas* should not enter except for catching thieves and persons committing the crime of treason; cf. *Cāṭa*.

cauri (ASLV), spelt *chowrie* in English; a flywhisk; sometimes the right of its use was granted to persons as a mark of honour. See *cāmara*, *cavarālu*.

Caurika (*Ep. Ind.*, Vol. XIX, p. 71), official designation. Cf. *Cāmara-kumāra*, *Caur-oddharaṇika*.

caurikā, cf. *carma-caurikā* (LP), 'theft of skin'.

caur-oddharaṇa (EI 33; HRS), according to some, the right to punish or levy fines from thieves; probably, the right to recover stolen property; recovery of stolen property; cf. *sa-chauroddharaṇa* (IE 8-5; EI 23).

Caur-oddharaṇika (IE 8-3; EI 23; CII 3), an official designation indicating an officer in charge of the recovery of stolen property; a police officer; same as *Cor-oddharaṇika*, *Caur-oddhartṛ*.

(*HD*; *CII*, Vol. III, p. 216), explained as 'the thief-catcher or one who exterminates thieves'. But cf. *Daṇḍ-odddharaṇika*.

Caur-oddhartṛ (HD), same as *Caur-oddharaṇika* (cf. *Yājñavalkyasmṛti*, II. 271; also Kātyāyana quoted by Aparārka).

cauthiā (IE 8-3; EI 33), an administrative board consisting of four members headed by the *Nagarseṭh* (*Nagaraśreṣṭhin*) as known from the *Pañcāyat* system of Western India; cf. *caturjātaka*, *caukaḍikā*.

cāvaḍi (IE 8-4; SITI; ASLV), same as *śāvaḍi* or *uśāvaḍi*; an administrative unit or a territorial division.

(*EI* 16), same as *rājya*; a district or subdivision.

cavala (EI 6), name of a coin, $\frac{1}{8}$ of a *pagoda*; cf. *cāmara*, *cavela*.

cavarālu (CITD), Telugu; also called *savarālu*, *savaramulu*; the hair of the *camarī-mṛga*, used by women as queue; also *cavara*, *camara* or *cāmara*, the chowrie (*cauri*) or long brush or fan usually made of the tail of the yak, which was one of the insignia of royalty.

cavaraṅga (EI 28), a Śaiva altar.

cavathe, a levy of one-fourth; see *chavathā*.

cavela (EI 6), same as *cavala*; name of a coin, $\frac{1}{8}$ of a *pagoda*. Cf. *cāmara*.

ceṭaka (*Ep. Ind.*, Vol. XXXI, p. 78), an attendant; sometimes mentioned in the list of officials.

cha (PJS) written as a mark indicating the end of a section of a record or of the whole of it. Cf. *Ep. Ind.*, Vol. XXX, p. 218.

cha-cokī (HA), Sanskrit *ṣaṭ-catuṣkikā*; a hall adjacent to and in front of the *gūḍha-maṇḍapa*, with its ceiling divided into six sections by the pillars supporting it.

Chadmastha (HA), a would-be Jina [living a monk's life] before attainment of *kevala-jñāna*. Cf. *Bodhisattva*.

chādya, cf. *tṛṇa-cchādya*, thatch-covering (*Ep. Ind.*, XXXIV, p. 145); same as Gujarātī *chāj*, thatch.

chala (IE 8-8), meaning uncertain; probably, a pretext.

(*EI* 30), probably, a plea, or persecution, prosecution.

chālī (LP), sheep.

chandas (IE 7-1-2), 'seven'.

chaṅga (*Ep. Ind.*, Vol. XIV, p. 310), a measure of grain.

chandovicita, the metrical science (*Ep. Ind.*, Vol. XXXV, p. 146).

chappanna, cf. *ṣaṭpañcāśat*.

chatra, an umbrella; cf. *pañcāṅga-prasāda*.

(*EI* 27), an attendant or *Piāda*; cf. *Chātra*.

Cf. Varāha-kṣetra = *Barāh-chatra* (Sircar, *Studies in the Geography of Ancient and Medieval India*, p. 221); corruption of Sanskrit *kṣetra*.

Chātra (IE 8-3, 8-8; EI 23, 30), cf. *a-bhaṭa-cchātra-prāveśya* (IE 8-5); literally, 'one bearing an umbrella' or 'the king's umbrella-bearer'; but probably the same as the *Cāṭa* or the leader of a group of *Bhaṭas* (*Pāiks* or *Piādas*) as in *a-cāṭa-bhaṭa-prāveśya*; a peon of the law-court. See *Chatracchāyika*.

(*CII* 3), used in composition with *bhaṭa* and also singly; literally, 'an umbrella-bearer'; but actually, a constable like a *Pāik* or *Piāda*.

(*SITI*), celebate (*Brahmacārin*) in charge of a temple and the *śālai* attached to it; also called *Śaṭṭar*, *Śāttirar*.

chatra-bhaṅga (IA 8), 'the breaking of the umbrella [of sovereignty]'; sometimes interpreted as 'an interregnum'.

chatr-ābhoga (IA 17), corrected from *ṣatr-ābhoga* and explained as 'the expanse of the royal umbrella'; but really, 'the *ābhoga* (a territorial unit) called Ṣa(Kha)tra'.

Chatracchāyika (IE 8-3; HD), an umbrella-bearer; the king's umbrella-bearer. See Vogel, *Ant. Ch. St.*, p. 128. Cf. *Chātra*.

chatra-yaṣṭi (LL), an umbrella on a post.

chavathā (IA 18), cf. *viṁśati-chavathā*, a levy of doubtful implication; may be a levy of 6 out of a unit of 20; cf. *cavathe*.

chāyā (EI 1), an image.

chāyā-dīpa (EI 33), a lamp held by an image, often arranged to burn continuously in front of a deity in a temple; cf. *akhaṇḍa-dīpa*.

chāyā-stambha (EI 33, 35), memorial pillar bearing image of the deceased.

cheda (EI 13), a quarter, area or subdivision; cf. *Brahma-cāri-ccheda*.

cheṇḍikā (EI 1), meaning doubtful.

chidra (7-1-2), 'nine'; cf. *randhra*.

Chimpaka (IE 8-8; EI 30), a dyer of clothes; same as Prakrit *Chimpaya.*

choha, same as Gujarātī *cho*, mortar (*Ep. Ind.*, Vol. XXXIV, p. 144).

chotyamāna, cf. *chotyamāna-gṛhe* (LP), 'when the house is being vacated'.

choultry, Anglicised form of a Dravidian word; a *dharma-śālā.*

churi-prabandha (BL), name of a grant made in favour of a *Churikāra*, 'a maker of *churis*'. The word *churi* may be the same as *kṣurikā*, 'a knife', and a *Churikāra* may have been an officer in charge of the production of knives and swords.

chuṭ (LP), cf. *choṭanīya*; Gujarātī *choḍāvavuṁ*; also cf. *granthi-baddhair=api drammaiḥ kṣetraṁ choṭayituṁ dhāraṇiko na labhate*, '[when the date is already over], the debtor will not get his farm liberated by the ready money tied in a piece of cloth'.

Cf. patra-grahāt chuṭanti (LP), 'will be free from the bond'; also Gujarātī *chaṭśe.*

cihna (EI 33), flag; cf. *Cihna-dhara* (BL), standard-bearer.

ci-khi, abbreviation of *cira-khila*, '[land] never brought under cultivation' (*Ep. Ind.*, Vol. XXX, p. 56).

cikitsā (CII 1), medical treatment.

Cīna-kkanakam (IE 8-8), Tamil; 'the Chinese gold coin'.

Cīna-pagoda (SII 12), 'Chinese shrine'; name of a Buddhist temple at Nāgapaṭṭanam.

cinna (EI 3; SITI), name of a coin; sometimes regarded as a *fanam* (CITD); also spelt *sinna* in Telugu; a weight equal to $\frac{1}{30}$ of a *tola* and called a *Canteroy fanam*; one-eighth part of a coin called *pagoda*; the weight of 4 *guri-giñjas.*

cintriṇī (EI 33), the tamarind tree.

cira-khila (EI 30), land which was never cultivated.

cira-khila-śūnya (EI 23), epithet of gift land; fallow land.

cirañjīva (EI 30), 'long-lived'; epithet of living (not dead) persons.

cirantana-loka (LP), old men.

ciravida (CITD), Telugu; name of a coin; probably a special kind of *gadyāṇa.*

cīrikā (EI 26), a document; cf. *kraya-cīrikā*, 'a deed of purchase', i.e. a sale-deed.

cīrṇa-vrat-opāyanaka (LP), the gift (*upāyana*) for the vows practised. Cf. *Sel. Ins.*, p. 210, text line 14.

ciṭalā (IE 8-5), a tax; cf. *coṭāla*, *ciṭola*.

cīṭhikā (LP), a chit; cf. Gujarātī *ciṭṭhī*.

ciṭola (IE 8-5), a tax or obligation of uncertain import.

citra (ASLV), a kind of poetry.

citrajarta (LP), various kinds of armour.

Citraka (IA 8), 'a painter'; epithet of the engraver of an inscription.

Citrakāra, cf. *Cittirakārar* (EI 22), a painter.

citrakārya, cf. *cittirakāri* (EI 22), painting.

citra-bhāsa (ASLV), paintings on the walls and ceilings of temples.

citrameḻi (SITI), also spelt *śittirameḻi*, an organisation of the agriculturists; agricultural corporation of the Vĕḷḷāḷas; the plough which was the emblem of this organisation; the boundary stone with the representation of the plough emblem planted to mark the limits of their land.

cīvara, cf. *cīvarika* (EI 8); garments of Buddhist monks.

cīvarika (EI 8), expenses of *cīvara*; Sanskrit *caivarika*.

cīvarikā (EI 20), a Buddhist monk's robe.

cokhā (EI 11), rice.

cola (Chamba), rice.

collika (EI 3), *collikā* (EI 10), a load [of leaves]; a quantity of betel leaves.

cora (IE 8-5), same as *caura* and *cora-daṇḍa*; probably, the power of punishing thieves and realising fines from them; cf. *cora-varja*; also *Cāṭa*.

coradaṇḍa-varjam (HRS), same as *caura-varjam* (q. v.).

cora-daṇḍa-varjya (CII 3), a fiscal term which means either that no fines for theft should be collected from the gift village or, more probably, that the donee was not entitled to fines realisable on theives in the gift villages. But see also *caura-varjam*.

cora-drohaka-varja (CII 3, etc.), a fiscal term which is similar to *coradaṇḍa-varja*. The word *drohaka* means one committing a crime against the king. See *caura-varjam*, *Cāṭa*.

Cora-grāha (HD), a thief-catcher (cf. Nārada, Pariśiṣṭa, verse 18; also Kātyāyana quoted by Aparārka).

cora-rājāpathyakāri-varjam (HRS), 'with immunity from the police tax', according to some; seems to mean 'without any right to inflict punishment on or levy fines from thieves and rebels'. But see *caura-varjam*; also *Cāṭa*.

cora-rajjū (HRS), 'the rope for binding thieves'; supposed to be the dues collected by the superintendent of the boundaries of villages.

Corarajjuka (HD), probably the same as *Dāṇḍapāśika*, an officer whose duty it was to secure robbers with ropes (cf. *Arthaśāstra*, IV. 13; II. 6 referring to *cora-rajjū* as a constituent of the *rāṣṭra*).

corāsī (IE 8-4), same as *caurāsī* (q. v.).

cora-varja, also spelt *cora-varjya* (CII 3; HRS); a fiscal term which is the same as *coradaṇḍa-varjya* (q. v.). See also *caura-varja*.

cora-varjita (CII 3), same as *coradaṇḍa- varjya* (q.v.).

cora-varjya, see *cora-varja*.

Cor-oddharaṇika (EI 28, 30), same as *Caur-oddharaṇika*; a police officer in charge of the recovery of stolen goods; explained by some as 'the eradicator of thieves' (CII 4). But cf. *Daṇḍoddharaṇika*.

coska (EI 4), a horse.

coṭāla (IE 8-5), a tax of uncertain import; cf. *ciṭola*, *ciṭalā*.

covīsī (HA); Sanskrit *caturviṁśati* or *caturviṁśati-paṭṭa*; a group of the 24 Jinas carved on one stone slab or cast in bronze together.

cūḍā (IA 11), the top knot of hair; cf. *cūḷā*.

cūḍāmaṇi (IA 26), an eclipse on certain days.

cukka, error, fault (*Ep. Ind.*, Vol. XXXI, p. 7, note 4).

cūḷā (IA 11), tresses; cf. *cūḍā*.

cullaka, cf. *a-kūra-cullaka-vināśi-khaṭv-āvāsa* (IE 8-5), explained as 'a pot', i.e. cooking pot. The villagers were obliged to supply it to the touring officers of the king.

cūmā (EI 1), meaning doubtful.

cumbaka (EI 13), the balance.

cūnā, same as Sanskrit *cūrṇa*, lime (*Ep. Ind.*, Vol. XXXIV, p. 144).

Cūṇakara, same as Sanskrit *Cūrṇakāra*, a lime-burner or white-washer (*Ep. Ind.*, Vol. XXXIV, p. 145).

Cūrakāra, cf. *Cūṟakāra* (CITD), from Telugu-Kannaḍa *cūṟa* and Sanskrit *kāra*; 'one who has plundered'.

cūrṇi (EI 3), an appended note. Cf. *cūrṇī*.

cūrṇi, cūrṇī (EI 29, 33), one hundred cowrie-shells; cowrie-shells of the value of a *purāṇa* or *kārṣāpaṇa* (*kāhaṇ*).

D

dabhra-sabhā (SII 3), the golden hall in the Chhidambaram temple.

dāḍhā (CII 4), a canine tooth; derived from Sanskrit *daṁṣṭrā*.

dadhi (IE 7-12), confused with *udadhi* and used to indicate 'four'.

Cf. a-dugdha-dadhi-grahaṇa (IE 8-5); curds which the villagers (probably, the milkmen) were obliged to supply to the king or landlord on occasions and to the touring officers.

dahana (IE 7-1-2), 'three'.

dahara-bhikṣu (LL), a young Buddhist monk.

dairgh-āyuṣa (CII 1), 'conducive to long life'.

Daivāgārika (EI 7), the priest in charge of a temple or an officer in charge of temples.

(*IE* 8-3), probably, a priest of the shrine of the king's tutelary deity; sometimes mentioned as a *Pātra*.

Daivajña (IE 8-3; EI 7), an astrologer; sometimes mentioned as a *Pātra*.

Daivaputra (IE 8-2; EI 30), same as *Devaputra*; title of certain kings of the Kuṣāṇa dynasty; derived from a Chinese title meaning 'the Son of Heaven'.

daivya (SITI), an act of the gods.

dakṣa, used in the late Tantra literature in the sense of *dakṣiṇa*, 'the south' (cf. Sircar, *Studies in the Georgraphy of Ancient and Medieval India*, p. 76, note 19).

dakṣiṇa (EI 32), the sacred fire.

dakṣiṇā (EI 32), perquisite.

(*BL*), a present or gift to a Brāhmaṇa for a service.

(*CII* 1), cf. *prāṇa-dakṣinā*, same as *prāṇa-dāna*.

Dakṣiṇa-bhuja (SITI), 'the right hand'; a trusted lieutenant.

Dakṣiṇāmūrti (SII 12), an aspect of Śiva.

Dakṣiṇāpatha (CII 3), 'the region of the south'; a name for Southern India.

Dakṣiṇāpatha-sādhāra (CII 3), 'the Pillar of Dakṣiṇāpatha'; title of a ruler. *Sādhāra* may be a mistake for *sv-ādhāra*.

dakṣiṇāvarta-śaṅkha (SII 1), a conch-shell with convolutions from left to right.

dakṣiṇ-āyana (IA 19), the period during which the sun moves from south to north; cf. *uttar-āyaṇa* (IA 17).

dakṣiṇī, dākṣiṇya, cf. Prakrit *dachini* (ML); same as *dakṣiṇā*.

dākṣiṇya, cf. *dakṣiṇya* (EI 23); same as *dakṣiṇā*.

Dala-adhikāri (IE 8-3; SITI; ASLV), Dravidian-Sanskrit; same as *Sainyādhikārin* or *Senāpati*, *Dalada-adhikāri* or *Dalavāy*, a commander of forces.

Dalada-adhikāri (ASLV), same as *Dala-adhikāri* or *Dalavāy*, the commander of forces.

Dalavāy (IE 8-3; ASLV; SITI), same as *Dala-adhikāri*, *Dalada-adhikāri* or *Senāpati*; the commander of forces; sometimes also enjoying the title *Daṇdanāyaka*.

Dalavāy-agrahāra (ASLV), village granted for military service.

Dalavāyi (CITD), Telugu-Kannaḍa; a general, a chieftain, or the minister of state; same as *Dalavāy*.

Dala-vṛtti (CITD), from Telugu-Kannaḍa *dala*, 'army', and Sanskrit *vṛtti*; probably, a grant for the maintenance of the army.

dama, cf. *dāma* (EI 23); same as *dramma* (q. v.).

dāma (EI 27; CII 4), name of a coin; derived from *dramma*.

(*EI* 19), abbreviation of the name *Dāmodara*.

damanaka (SITI), a fragrant plant.

damanaka-caturdaśī (EI 23), same as Caitra su-di 14; also called *damanaka-parvan*.

damanaka-parvan (EI 23, 31), same as *damanaka-caturdaśī*.

ḍāmara (EI 12), tumultuous, terrible; a landlord or wealthy cultivator possessing much land [in ancient Kashmir], according to the *Rājataraṅgiṇī*.

damma (SITI), same as *dramma*; name of a coin; derived from Greek *drachma*.

dāna, dānā (ML), a gift.

(*HRS*), known from Maitraka records to mean the so-called voluntary gifts of subjects.

Cf. dānā-sambandhe (LP), 'as regards the sale-tax'.

dāṇa (IE 8-5; LP), same as *dāna*, road-cess; customs duties; cf. the official designation *Dāṇī* (Sanskrit *Dānin*).

dāṇa-cori (EI 32), smuggling.

dānādāya-dānībhoga (LP), explained as 'local cess or road-cess'; *dāya* is explained as 'a gift to Brāhmaṇas or temples', *dānī* as 'land tax' and *bhoga* as 'right of enjoyment'; but probably, *dāṇ-ādāya* means excise or customs duties and *dāni-bhoga* a tax for the maintenance of the tax-collector.

Dān-ādhikārin (EI 12), officer in charge of gifts, mentioned along with the *Śāsan-ādhikārika*, 'officer in charge of grants (or their writing)'. See *Dharm-ādhikārin*. It may also mean 'a tolls-collector' (cf. *dāna*, *Dānin*).

Daṇāik (ASLV), corrupt form of *Daṇḍanāyaka*.

dāna-mukha (EI 7; ML), a gift; the principal gift; same as *deya-dharma*.

dāna-palaṁ (IA 11), actually *dāna(ṁ*) palaṁ*, i.e. 'the *dāna* (levy) is one *pala*'.

Dānapati (EI 28, 30; HD), one who gives a gift; one who dedicates the image of a deity (especially as the result of a previous vow); probably, also an official designation; see *Horamurta* (CII 2-1), *Dānādhikārin*.

dāna-ppuṟam (SITI), Sanskrit-Tamil; land set apart for the purpose of charity.

dāna-pradānaka (CII 4), all kinds of gifts.

dāna-śālā (IA 11), a hall for the distribution of gifts.

dāna-volāpana (LP), *dāna* (road-cess) and *volāpana* (tax; cf. Gujarātī *valāvaṇuṁ*). See *Volāpika*.

Danāyaka (IA 20), corrupt from of *Daṇḍanāyaka*.

daṇda (IE 8-5; EI 12), fine or tax, mentioned along with *suṅka* (*śulka*); a levy or free service (cf. *prayāṇa-daṇda*).

(*EI* 24), fines; authority.

(*HRS*), fines; distinguished from *atyaya* in the *Artha-śāstra*.

(*CII* 1), punishment.

(*ASLV*), judicial punishment; sometimes possibly also 'administration'.

(*EI* 25), 'five'.

(*EI* 30; LP), contraction of *Daṇdanāyaka*.

(*EI* 28), Oḍiyā; a path (cf. *daṇḍā*).

Cf. *taṇḍu* (*SITI*), a palanquin; a pole for carrying the vehicle on which the image of a deity is set up.

Cf. *daṇḍu*, *taṇḍu* (SITI), an army; going on a military expedition.

Cf. *taṇdam* (SII 1; CITD); fine, penalty or punishment; a punitive tax; a fine or tax payable as penalty.

daṇḍā (EI 31), Oḍiyā ; a boundary line or road. See *daṇḍa*.

Dāṇḍabhogika (HD), same as *Dāṇḍapāśika* (q.v.), or the police magistrate. See *Ep. Ind.*, Vol XIII, p. 339.

daṇḍa-daś-āparādha (CII 4), fines including those imposed for the ten offences; same as *daś-āparādha*. See *daṇḍadoṣa-daś-āparādha*, *daṇḍa-śulka*, etc.

daṇḍ-ādāya (EI 20), fines; see Ghoshal, *H. Rev. Syst.*, pp. 253-54.

Daṇḍādhinātha (EI 16; SII 1; HD), same as *Daṇḍapāla*, *Daṇḍanāyaka*, etc. See *Ind. Ant.*, Vol. XIV, p. 55.

Daṇḍādhināyaka (SII 1), a general; same as *Daṇḍādhinātha*.

Daṇḍādhipa (BL; HD), the commander of forces; same as *Daṇḍapāla*, *Daṇḍādhipati*, etc. See the commentary on the *Yaśastilaka*, I, p. 91; *Ep. Ind.*, Vol. IX, p. 151.

Daṇḍādhipati (EI 26), cf. *Daṇḍanāyaka*, etc.

(LP), explained as 'a governor'.

Daṇḍādhīśvara (EI 5), same as *Daṇḍādhipati*, etc.

daṇḍa-doṣa, cf. *sa-daṇḍadoṣa* (EI 23); fines. See *daṇḍa*.

daṇḍadoṣa-daśāparādha (HRS), same as *daṇḍa-daśāparādha*; cf. *sahya-daś-āparādha*; *sa-daśāparādha* means 'with the privilege of remission for the ten offences', according to some; seems to mean 'with the right to enjoy fines for the ten offences'; cf. *daś-āparādha*.

daṇḍaka (EI 30), probably, a regulation.

(*IE* 8-8), meaning uncertain; probably, fines.

Cf. daṇḍaku (IA 16), a boundary mark or land-mark.

daṇḍa-kkāṇam (SITI), Sanskrit-Tamil; amount imposed as fine; cf. *daṇḍam kuṟṟam* (EI 30; SITI), a levy of fines; fine and penalty imposed.

daṇḍa-mārga (ASLV), military route.

Daṇḍanātha (EI 16; CII 4; SII 1), commander of an army. See *Ep. Ind.*, Vol. V, p. 31. Cf. *Daṇḍanāyaka*, etc.

Daṇḍanāyaka (IE 8-3; EI 30; CII 4; BL), probably a translation of Greek *Strategos*; a general; a leader of forces, an army officer; a military commander; also called *Daṇḍanātha*, *Daṇḍanetṛ*, etc.; sometimes also called *Mahāsāmanta*, *Senādibāhattaraniyogādhiṣṭhāyaka*, *Mahāpradhāna*, *Sarvādhikārin*, *Mahāpasāyita*, etc., additionally; see *Mahādaṇḍanāyaka*, *Sarvadaṇḍanāyaka*, *Mahāsarvadaṇḍanāyaka*.

(*LP*), generally, the viceroy or governor of a province; representative of the king.

(*ASLV*), the commander of forces and officer in charge of administration; title of the provincial governors; similar to the *Mansabdār* of the Mughal period.

(*HD*), a prefect of the police, according to Stein (*Rājataraṅgiṇī*, VII. 951); 'a General or Magistrate', according to some (cf. Kielhorn's Southern List, Nos. 291, 292, 296). In the *Bṛhatsaṁhitā* (7. 2-4), the queen, *Yuvarāja*, *Senāpati* and *Daṇḍanāyaka* are placed on the same level in the matter of the staff (*daṇḍa*) to be prepared for them.

Cf. Taḍeya-daṇḍanāyaka, explained as 'the general in charge of reserves', from Kannaḍa, *taḍĕ*, 'far, restraint'.

Dāṇḍanāyaka (EI 23; HD), same as *Daṇḍanāyaka*. See *Ep. Ind.*, Vol. XIX, p. 269.

Daṇḍanetṛ (*Ep. Ind.*, Vol. XXVIII, p. 233), designation of a leader of forces; cf. *Daṇḍanāyaka*, etc.

Daṇḍapāla (HD), an officer in charge of all branches of the army (*Arthaśāstra*, I. 12); cf. *Daṇḍanāyaka*.

(*IE* 8-3), cf. *Dāṇḍika*.

Daṇḍapāṇika (IE 8-3), same as *Daṇḍapāśika*.

Daṇḍaparīkṣā (*Ep. Ind.*, Vol. XXIX, p. 101); Oḍiyā; a governor; same as Sanskrit *Daṇḍaparīkṣaka* as well as *Daṇḍanāyaka* of other inscriptions; governor of a *daṇḍapāṭa* or province.

Daṇḍapāśika (IE 8-3; CII 3, 4; BL; HD), a policeman; an official who was probably the leader of a group of *Dāṇḍikas*; officer in charge of punishment (i.e. criminal justice), according to some; a policeman (same as Oḍiyā *Daṇḍuāsi* meaning 'a village watchman'); called *Talāra* and *Ārakṣika* (*IHQ*), December 1960, p. 266). See *Yaśastilaka*, I, p. 50; *Ep. Ind.*, Vol. XI, p. 83; Vol. XII, p. 9. Cf. *Dāṇḍabhogika*.

Dāṇḍapāśika (IE 8-3; EI 23; CII 3, 4; HD), same as *Daṇḍapāśika* or *Daṇḍapāṇika*, 'an officer entrusted with the punishment of criminals'; see *Pañcatantra* II, Kathā 4 (spelt *Daṇḍapāśaka* meaning 'a watchman'); *Ep. Ind.*, Vol. XI, p. 94.

daṇḍapāṭa (*Ep. Ind.*, Vol. XXIX, p. 107); Oḍiyā; the province of a kingdom; an administrative unit under a *Daṇḍaparīkṣā*; cf. *Daṇḍa* or *Daṇḍanāyaka* called *Daṇḍaparīkṣā* in the Orissan records; also *paṭṭa* in the sense of 'a district'.

Daṇḍapati (BL; HD), a commander of forces, or a governor;

same as *Daṇḍanātha*, etc. See *Ep. Ind.*, Vol. IX, pp. 148, 156.

Daṇḍaśakti (IE 8-3; HD), a police officer; possibly the same as *Dāṇḍika* or *Daṇḍapāśika*. See *Ep. Ind.*, Vol. IV, p. 250.

daṇḍa-śulka, cf. *daṇḍa-śulk-ādi-vividh-āya-samanvita* (EI 23); income from fines and tolls.

daṇḍavāṇi (SII 2), standard gold.

Daṇḍavāsika (HD), Prakrit form of *Daṇḍapāśika*. See Vogel, *Ant. Ch. St.*, p. 129.

Dāṇḍavāsika (EI 23), same as *Daṇḍavāsika*, *Dāṇḍapāśika*.

daṇḍ-āya (IA 29; SII 11-1), income from fines; explained as 'a tax'; cf. 'the whole of the levy called *daṇḍ-āya* as much as accrued in the village'.

Daṇḍeśa (EI 5; SII 1; HD), official designation; same as *Daṇḍanātha*. See *JBBRAS*, Vol. XV, p. 386.

Daṇḍika (HD), same as *Daṇḍapāśika*. See Vogel, *Ant. Ch. St.*, p. 166. (CII 4), explained by some as a magistrate. Cf. *Dāṇḍika*.

Dāṇḍika (CII 3; HD), a police officer. See *Ind. Ant.*, Vol. XV, p. 306; *CII*, Vol. III, p. 216; *Ep. Ind.*, Vol. XVII, p. 321. Generally *Dāṇḍika* and *Dāṇḍapāśika* are mentioned side by side (*Ep. Ind.*, Vol. XVII, p. 231); probably the *Dāṇḍika* was the head of a group or outpost of the *Dāṇḍapāśikas*. Cf. *Daṇḍika*, *Daṇḍ-oddharaṇika* (collector of fines).

daṇḍikā (SITI), also called *daṇḍu*; a palanquin.

daṇḍikā-jīvita (SITI), tax-free land given to palanquin-bearers for enjoyment during their life-time.

daṇḍinadāri (ASLV), military route. See *daṇḍudova*.

Daṇḍ-oddharaṇika (EI 9), literally, 'collector of fines'; mentioned along with *Daṇḍapāśika*; may be the same as *Dāṇḍika*. Cf. *Caur-oddharaṇika*.

daṇḍ-opajātaka (EI 28), money exacted as fines.

Daṇḍoparika (EI 13), probably *Daṇḍa* (i.e. *Daṇḍanāyaka*) and *Uparika*; otherwise *Daṇḍoparika* may mean a judge.

daṇḍu (ASLV), a palanquin; its use was a privilege sometimes specially granted to favourites or distinguished persons by the king.

Daṇḍuāsi (IE 8-3), Oḍiyā; village watchman; derived from Sanskrit *Dāṇḍapāśika*.

daṇḍudova (ASLV), a military route. See *daṇḍinadāri*.

ḍāṅg (IA 26), also spelt *dāṅk*, corrupt form of *ṭaṅka*.

dāṇi (HRS), known from Caulukya records and explained by some as 'the king's dues'; perquisite of the collector of the duties called *dāṇa* or *dāna*.

Dānī (IE 8-5; EI 26), i.e. *Dānin*, officer collecting tax or corn; officer storing the corn collected as tax from the farmers.

dāni-bhāga, same as *dāṇi-bhoga* (q.v.). See Ghoshal, *H. Rev. Syst.*, p. 256.

dāṇi-bhoga (HRS), periodical supplies of fruits, firewood and the like by the villagers, according to some; tax for maintaining the collectors of the tax called *dāna*; same as *dāṇi-bhoga-bhāga*.

dāṇi-bhoga-bhāga (HRS), same as *dāṇi-bhoga*.

Dānī-volāpika (LP), explained as 'the collector of *dānī* (land cess) and *volāpanā* (tax, relating to Gujarātī *vaḻāvaṇuṁ*).' See *Volāpika*.

ḍāṅk (IA 26), corrupt form of *ṭaṅka*.

Ḍaṇṇāik (ASLV), corrupt form of *Daṇḍanāyaka*; sometimes the designation of a judge at the capital of the Vijayanagara kings.

Daṇṇāyaka (IE 8-3; ASLV), corrupt form of *Daṇḍanāyaka*; a designation sometimes enjoyed by the *Dala-adhikāri* or commander of forces.

danta (EI 7), a pin.

(*IE* 7-1-2), 'thirtytwo'.

Dantakāra (LL), a worker in ivory; here *danta* means *hasti-danta*.

dantin (IE 8-1-2), 'eight'.

Dāpaka (EI 3; BL; HD), usually regarded as the same as *Dūtaka*; but really 'one who causes another to give', i.e. the creator of a rent-free holding which was ratified by the king. Cf. *Ep. Ind.*, Vol. XIX, pp. 177, 243.

(*CII* 1), a matter relating to giving gifts.

dāpana, cf. *dāpanāya* (LP), 'for making one pay'. See *dāvāpana*.

dāpita (LP), 'caused to be paid'.

dāradraṇaka (CII 3), a fiscal term of uncertain implication; an agricultural cess or marriage tax, according to some. See Ghoshal, *H. Rev. Syst.*, p. 242.

Dāraka (IA 18; CII 1), explained as 'the son of a king, whose mother's rank does not assure him an official title'.

darśa (IA 17), the new-moon; cf. *darśa-tithi.*

darśana (IE 8-5; EI 32, 33), a levy; same as Persian *nazrāna*. Cf. Tamil *tariśana-kāṇikkai* (SITI), presents offered to a king or a chief when one meets him.

(*CII* 1), used in the sense of *pradarśana*, 'showing'.

(*IE* 7-1-2), 'six'; cf. *dṛṣṭi*, 'two'.

(*IA* 14), used in the sense of 'a religious procession for the purpose of visiting a deity'.

darśapūrṇamāsa (CII 4), name of a Vedic sacrifice.

darśa-tithi (EI 13), name of a *tithi*. Cf. *darśa.*

Darvīkarman (EI 21), measurer of land.

Daśabala-mahābala (EI 20), epithet of the Buddha.

daśabandha (SITI), variously explained as (1) one-tenth of the revenue set apart for repairs to the tanks and wells for irrigation purposes; (2) land, the income from which would be equal to the amount thus set apart; (3) the right of collecting one-tenth of the produce of lands irrigated from the waters of a tank or well by the person who repairs the water source; also explained as tax equal to one-tenth of the income of the subject (Ray, *DHNI*, Vol. II, p. 1113). See *daśavandha.*

(*SITI*) tax or cess levied to keep the source of water supply like the tanks, etc., in good repair.

(*EI* 4), rent-free land or probably land paying only one-tenth of the actual rent.

(*EI* 20), one-tenth share.

Cf. daśa-bandhe (LP), 'at 10 per cent'.

Cf. daśavandha (SII 3), a tax.

dāśabandha-visatia (*viṁśatika*) *ttriprastha* (HRS), kinds of tax.

dāsa-bhṛtaka (CII 1), slaves and servants.

Dāśagrāmika (IE 8-3; EI 24), the headman of a group of ten villages or the chairman of the council of a group of ten villages.

Daśaharā-vrata (EI 27), a religious ceremony.

daśa-kriyā (SITI), work of the architects who were to look after the repairs of temples.

Daśamūlika (CII 4), official designation; same as *Daśamūlin* (q.v.).

Daśamūlin (EI 21; CII 4; BL), an official designation; probably, a physician; same as *Daśamūlika.*

daś-āpacāra (IE 8-5; EI 29), same as *daś-āparādha.*

daś-āparādha (CII 3, 4), literally, 'the ten offences'; but really, the fines for the ten offences; cf. *sa-daś-āparādha* (IE 8-5); power to punish and realise fines for the ten offences; also called *daś-āpacāra.* According to the Buddhists, the ten sins were murder, theft, adultery, lying, calumny, insult, idle talk, hatred, covetousness and dogmatic error (A. Getty, *The Gods of Northern Buddhism*, p. xxv, note). For a Brahmanical list, see *Dāśāparādhika*; cf. *pañca-mahāpātaka, pañc-āparādha.*

Dāśāparādhika (IE 8-3; EI 29; HD), a judge dealing with the ten offences (viz. theft, murder of women, adultery, use of abusive language, violation of order, mixing of castes, illegal pregnancy, obscenity, assault and abortion, according to some). It has been said that the ten offences or *aparādhas* are those of which the king could take cognisance *suo moto.* For the ten *aparādhas*, see Kane, *Hist. Dharm.*, Vol. III, p. 264; cf. *Ep. Ind.*, Vol. XVII, p. 321.

Dasarā (EI 5), Āśvina su-di 10.

Daśaratha-strī (IE 7-1-2), 'three'.

Dāśari (ASLV; SITI), a class of subordinates of the headman of particular communities in the Vijayanagara empire; same as *Samayācāra* or *Samayācārya.*

daśavandha, cf. *daśavanna* (IA 30), explained as 'land granted to a person for repairing or building a tank on condition of paying in money or kind one-tenth or some small share of the produce' and as 'land granted at one-tenth of the usual rates to a person in consideration of his constructing or repairing a tank'. See *daśabandha.*

dāsī (CITD), a handmaid, slave, concubine, dancing girl.

dasra (IE 7-1-2), 'two'.

dāsūri-paṭṭu (CITD), Telugu; probably, silk of the Tusser variety; cf. Hobson-Jabson, s.v. *tussah, tusser.*

daṭita (LP), well-founded.

datti (EI 23; CII 4; CITD), a gift; cf. *Sarvasiddhi-datti* (EI 19).

Dauḥsādhasādhanika (EI 30; HD), explained as 'those who catch dangerous robbers whom it is difficult to secure'. See *Ep. Ind.*, Vol. IV, p. 211. Cf. *Duḥsādhasādhanika* (ibid., Vol. XI, p. 310), *Dussādhyasādhaka, Duṣṭasāhanī, Mahādauḥsādhanika*, etc.

Dauḥsādhika (IE 8-3; HD), same as *Dauḥsādhasādhanika*,

Duḥsādhyasādhanika, Dussādhyasādhaka, Duṣṭasāhani, etc. See *Ep. Ind.*, Vol. XII, p. 9. Lexicons explain it as 'gate-keeper'.

dautya, see *dūtya* and *Dūtaka.*

Dauvārika (EI 28; SII 1; ASLV; BL; HD), a door-keeper; a gate-keeper. See *Arthaśāstra*, I. 12; *Lalitavistara*, p. 136; *Viṣṇudharmottara*, II. 24. 30.

dāvāpana, cf. *dāvāpanāya* (LP), 'for making one pay'; cf. *dāpana*.

dāvāpita (LP), caused to be paid.

dāya (EI 23), a gift.

dāyāda (CII 4), an agnate.

(LL), Buddhist; an heir of the faith.

denarius (IE 8-3), name of the Roman silver coin and also of the Roman gold coin usually called *aureus*; cf. *dīnāra.*

deśa (IE 8-4; CII 3, 4), a territorial term meaning a small area or a group of villages in some cases but a kingdom, district, tract or country in others.

(*IE* 8-4), a country of which there were seventytwo in Bhārata or Bhāratavarṣa.

(*CII* 1), a part of anything.

(*EI* 24), a synonym of *āspada.*

(*ASLV*), a school of music.

Cf. Kona-deśa (EI 32), also called a *maṇḍala, rāṣṭra, sīma, sthala*, etc.

Cf. deśa-bhāṣā (*EI* 17), 'vernacular of a province'.

Cf. teśa-kālam (SITI), locality and time; also *teśa-vāḻi*, officer in charge of a village or district.

Deś-ādhikṛta (IE 8-3; HD), same as *Deśādhipati*; governor of a *deśa* or a province, district or sub-division. See *Ep. Ind.*, Vol. I, p. 5 (Prakrit *Desādhikata*). See *Sarva-deś-ādhikṛta.*

(LL), explained as 'a local prefect'.

Deś-ādhipati (EI 26, 30), same as *Deśādhikṛta*; ruler of the territorial or administrative unit called *deśa.*

Deś-ākṣapaṭalādhikṛta (EI 28), officer of the records and accounts office pertaining to a territorial unit.

Deśakūṭa (AI 7), official designation; cf. *Rāṣṭrakūṭa, Grāmakūṭa, Deś-ādhipati.*

deśa-maryādā, custom prevalent in a locality; cf. *deśa-maryād-āṟuvaṇa-ānvita* (*Ind. Ant.*, Vol. XIX, p. 247, text line 103), *aṟuvaṇa* being a tax of six *paṇas* levied on rent-free lands.

deśanā, Prakrit *desanā* (EI 21), exposition of the Buddhist doctrine.

deśa-rīta (Chamba), customary taxes of a locality.

Deśa-talāra (LP), probably, a police superintendent. Cf. *Talāra*.

Deśa-ṭhakkura (LP), probably, a small chieftain.

Deśavāḻi (EI 18), official designation. Cf. *deśa*.

Deśāyi (ASLV), same as Sanskrit *Deśādhipati* or *Deśādhikṛta*.

deśī (EI 11), a guild of local merchants. This is also the name of Prakrit words which are neither Sanskrit (*tat-sama*) nor derived from Sanskrit (*tad-bhava*).

Deśika (SII 1), a [Jain] teacher.

Deśilaka, official designation (*Ep. Ind.*, Vol. XIX, p. 71); same as *Deśillaka*.

Deśillaka (EI 28), official designation as in *rāṣṭra-grāma-kūṭa-deśillaka-mahattar-ādhikārik-ādīn*; same as *Desilaka*, *Deśakūṭa*; cf. *Purillaka*.

Deśi-mukhya (EI 31), same as modern *Deśmukh*.

deś-ottāra (LP), permission for allowing the cargo to go from one place to another.

deva, a god; cf. *te-aḍimai* (SITI), a dancing woman as the servant of a god; maid servant attached to a temple; cf. *teva-kuḍimai*, tenancy under the control of a temple; *tevakulam* (*deva-kula*), a temple.

(*EI* 7), the king.

(*EI* 3), a saint.

(*EI* 7-1-2), 'thirtythree'.

deva-bhoga (EI 23, 31; SITI), rent-free property of a temple; land given for the enjoyment of temples; same as *deva-dāya*, etc.. Cf. *devabhoga-hala*.

devabhoga-hala (EI 7, 8, 15, 24), rent-free land in the possession of temples.

deva-cchanda (SII 2), name of a jewel.

deva-dāna (EI 5, 23, 25, 30; SITI; ASLV), gift made to a god; rent-free land in the possession of a temple; same as *deva-bhoga*, *deva-deya*, *deva-dāya*, *dev-āgrahāra*.

Cf. devadāna-iṟaiyili (SITI), village or land granted to a temple.

deva-dāsī (EI 22, 33; LL), a dancing girl attached to a temple; a female temple-servant. See *vilāsinī*, *gaṇikā*, *mahārī*.

deva-dāya (IE 8-5; EI 23; CII 4; SITI), a rent-free holding in the possession of a temple; a gift made in honour of a god; same as *deva-deya*, etc.

deva-deya (IE 8-5; HRS), grant made in favour of temples; same as *deva-dāya*, etc.

deva-dharma (*Ep. Ind.*, Vol. XXVIII, p. 144), same as *deya-dharma* when the gift was the image of a god.

Dev-ādhyakṣa, superintendent of religious foundations. See Ghoshal, *H. Rev. Syst.*, p. 99.

devadi (IA 19), 'the establishment of a temple'.

deva-droṇī (IE 8-3; EI 10), usually taken to mean 'a procession of the images of gods', or 'procession or ablution of images'; but probably, 'rent-free property of a temple' (*Ep. Ind.*, Vol. XXXIV pp. 143-44); cf. *deva-droṇī-sambaddha* (EI 23). A Prakrit inscription (*A.R.Ep.*, 1959-60, No. B 173) has *deva-doṇi data*=Sanskrit *deva-droṇī dattā*.

Devadroṇī-sambaddha (IE 8-3), same as *Devadroṇy-adhikṛta*; officer in charge of temple property (*devadroṇī*, usually taken in the sense of 'a procession of the images of gods).'

Devadroṇy-adhikṛta (IE 8-3; BL), explained as 'the superintendent of the procession of idols'; but probably, the superintendent of the property of a temple or of temple property in general; same as *Devadroṇī-sambaddha*; cf. *deva-droṇī* (EI 13).

dev-āgāra, cf. *tevāram*, *devāram* (SITI), a temple.

dev-āgrahāra (IE 8-5; EI 23, 25, 30; SITI), rent-free village granted to a temple; same as *deva-bhoga*, etc.; see *agrahāra*.

deva-gṛha (EI 24), a temple.

devagṛha-jagatī (IA 14), explained as 'a temple and its ground' or 'a temple with the buildings attached to it.' But cf. *jagatī*.

devaka (IA 23), the guardian spirit or a god.

deva-karaṇa, cf. *karaṇa* (LP); explained as the *deva-sthāna* department.

devakarman (SII 1), divine rites.

Devakarmin (EI 30; SII 1, 3, 12); cf. *tevar-kaṇmi*, *devar-kaṇmi* (EI 3; SITI); a *Pūjāri* or temple priest, a temple servant; servant of a god; an officer in charge of the affairs of a temple.

deva-kriyā (IA 23), worship of gods.

devakula (EI 9, 23), a temple; cf. *ācāryakula* (LL).

(*EI* 21), a gallery of portrait statues of deified or semi-deified ancestors.

devakula-puṣkariṇī (IE 8-5), temples and tanks [the construction of the former and the excavation of the latter requiring the permission of the king or landlord].

devakulī (CII 4), a small shrine.

devakulika (LL), a temple-servant.

devakulikā (EI 8; HA), a shrine; a cell; a supplementary or smaller shrine.

devakuṭī-kāṣṭha (EI 7), a measuring rod.

dev-ālaya (EI 23), a temple; same as *devakula.*

Devānāṁpriya (EI 21; CII 1; LL), a royal title; title assumed by the Maurya kings.

Devāṇḍaja (EI 32), same as *Garuḍa.*

deva-nikāya (*Ep. Ind.*, Vol. XIII, p. 115), probably, temple authorities.

Devaputra (IE 8-2; EI 8, 21, 30), royal title of foreign origin; 'the Son of Heaven'; title of certain Kuṣāṇa kings; same as *Daivaputra.*

(LL), Buddhist; an angel.

devaraḍiyāḻ (ASLV), Tamil; a dancing girl attached to a temple.

devāram (SITI), Tamil corruption of Sanskrit *devāgāra*; a temple.

Devātideva (EI 1), epithet of the Buddha and gods.

devaṭisalam (EI 12), a ceremony indicative of royalty.

devatrā (IE 8-5), same as *deva-dāya.*

Deva-vārika (EI 33), superintendent of a temple; cf. *Vārika.* See *Ep. Ind.*, Vol. XXVII, p. 142, text line 35.

devaveśma-karaṇa, cf. *karaṇa* (LP); the department of temples.

deva-vihāra, land in the possession of temples. See Ghoshal, *H. Rev. Syst.*, p. 217.

deva-vṛtti (SITI), land set apart for the maintenance of temples.

deva-yajña (CII 4), offerings to gods; one of the five *mahāyajñas.*

dev-āyatana (EI 23), a temple; same as *devakula.*

Devī (IE 8-2; CII 1, 3; LL), a title originally of wives

of independent monarchs and later also of feudatory rulers; often used as a termination of the names of wives of rulers of all classes; cf. *Mahādevī*; also means the Mother-goddess.

Devī-karmāntika (EI 16), a temple officer.

Devī-kumāra (IA 18; CII 1), explained as 'the son of a king, who has the rank of a prince'; the king's son born of a queen and not of a concubine.

devottara (IE 8-5), Bengali corruption of *devatrā*; same as *deva-dāya*, etc.

deya (IE 8-5), periodical offerings to be presented to the king or landlord; cf. *ādeya*, *deya-meya*.

deya-dharma (EI 1; CII 3; ML), a pious gift; an appropriate religious gift; an expression used in numerous donative inscriptions. A deity installed for worship was also called *deya-dharma* (sometimes *deva-dharma*) in medieval records. Same as *dharma-deya*, *dharma-dāya*, *dharma-dāna*.

deyadharma-parityāga (*Ep. Ind.*, Vol. XXXIV, p. 10, text line 2), donation of a religious gift.

deya-meya (HRS), known from a Śātavāhana record; king's share in kind and in cash; same as *dhānya-hiraṇya* of later records. See *deya*, *meya*.

deyya-dharma (EI 32), Pali-Prakrit form of *deya-dharma*.

dhaḍā, *dhaḍī*, a small measure of capacity (*Ind. Ant.*, Vol. XLI, p. 20).

ḍhakkā (CII 3), a war drum; used in the *Rājataraṅgiṇī* in the sense of a watch-station (cf. Sircar, *Geog. Anc. Med. Ind.*, p. 238).

dhaḷa-vādi, *dhala-vali* (CITD), Telugu-Kannaḍa; a tax probably connected with *dala-vṛtti*, or at least with *dala* or the army.

dhānaka, see *hema-dhānyaka*; also called *aṇḍikā*; equal to 4 *kārṣāpaṇas* or to 4 *suvarṇas* or *dīnāras* (*JNSI*, Vol. II, p. 7).

dhanika, *dhanin* (LP), the owner; cf. Gujarātī *dhaṇī*; used in the sense of 'one who is spending or lending money' in the Maithilī documents (*Proc. IHRC*, Vol. XVIII, p. 90).

dhānika, a coin equal to 4 *kārṣāpaṇas* or 64 *paṇas* according to the *Kṛtyakalpataru* (Vyavahāra-kāṇḍa, ed. K.V. Rangaswami Aiyanger, p. 125); cf. *dhānaka*.

dhanikatva, cf. *dhanikatvaṁ vidhāya* (LP), 'having claimed ownership'.

dhānya, cf. *sa-hiranya-dhānya-praṇaya-pradeya* (IE 8-5); produce of the fields, a share of which was payable to the king or landlord; cf. *dhāny-ādāya*.

dhāny-ādāya (SITI), tax payable in grains; cf. *dhāny-āya*.

dhāny-ādhivāsa (EI 32), a rite.

dhānya-hiraṇya (HRS), revenue in kind and in cash; same as *dhānya-hiraṇy-ādeya*.

dhānya-hiraṇy-ādeya (EI 32), tax in crops and cash. See *dhānya-hiraṇya*.

dhānya-māṣa, weight eaual to 1 *yava* or 2 *taṇdulas* (*JNSI*, Vol. XVI, p. 48).

dhānya-varga (SITI), literally, 'the grain group'; actually, a class of taxes payable in grains.

dhāny-āya (EI 7), tax in grains; cf. *dhāny-ādāya*; called *nĕll-āyam* (SII 12) in Tamil.

Dhānyika (LL), a dealer in paddy.

dhara, cf. *Vinaya-dhara* (EI 33), 'one who has committed the [Buddhist] *Vinaya* texts by heart'.

dharā (IE 7-1-2), 'one'.

dhārā-datta, cf. *tārā-tattam* (SITI), a gift made with the ceremony of libation of water.

dharā-maṇḍala (SII 1), a country.

dharaṇa (CII 4), name of a coin.

(IE 8-8), a silver coin weighing 24 *ratis* (cf. *JNSI*, Vol. II, pp. 28-29) or the half of a *gadyāṇaka* according to the *Līlāvatī*; silver coin of 32 *ratis* according Manu, etc.

(*IE* 8-8), same as *kārṣāpaṇa* or *purāṇa*.

(*EI* 3), a gold coin or weight (320 *ratis*).

(*JNSI*, Vol. XVI, p. 44), sometimes called *śāna* and *ṭaṅka*.

dharaṇī (IE 7-1-2), 'one'.

dhāraṇī (IA 9; BL), a magic litany usually of the Buddhists; an occult Indian charm, especially Buddhistic; a short formula intended to represent a particular Tantra text, the recitation of the *dhāraṇī* being regarded as equally meritorious as that of the Tantra itself (*Univ. Cey. Rev.*, January-April, 1960, p. 62, note 42).

dhāraṇika (LP), a debtor.

dhārā-pūrvakam, cf. *udaka-pūrvam*, etc. See *dhātrā-datta*.

dharma (SII 1), the sacred law; religious merit; a meritorious gift, a pious work, a charity; moral precept.

(EI 24), law or law and order.

(*Ep. Ind.*, Vol. XXXV, p. 116) virtue or religious merit.

(*IE* 8-2), sometimes prefixed to the titles of kings and crown-princes; cf. *Dharma-mahārāja*, etc.

dharma-baddha, cf. *tarma-pattar* (SITI), persons bound by the law; judicial officers.

dharma-bāndhava, 'one whose only friend is his religious faith' or 'a person who has become the friend of another on an oath in the name of his religious faith' (*Ep. Ind.*, Vol. XXXIV, p. 144).

dharma-cakra (CII 3; LL), Buddhist; the wheel of Dharma which was .the symbol representing the Buddha on early Buddhist sculptures, on stone inscriptions and on seals attached to copperplate grants.

(*HA*) Jain; the wheel of law supposed to move in the sky in front of a Jina when he goes on his wanderings from place to place; one of the members of the *parikara* of a Jina image.

dharmacakra-mudrā (EI 29), seal bearing the emblem of the Buddhist wheel of law.

dharma-dāna (ML; SITI), a religious gift; a gift for religious merit; grant of tax-free land; same as *deya-dharma*.

dharma-deya (IA 9; HRS), same as *deya-dharma*, *dharma-dāya*, etc.; a religious grant in general.

dharma-deśanā (SII 1), a discourse on the sacred law.

dharm-ādhikāra (EI 15; IA 9), court of law; an office relating to the civil and criminal courts as well as to religious and charitable institutions. See *Dharmādhikārin*.

dharm-ādhikaraṇa (EI 18, 23, 25; CII 4; LP), a law-court; a court of justice. See *Dharm-ādhikaraṇin*.

Cf. karaṇa (LP); the department of justice.

(*HD*), a judge. See *Viṣṇudharmottara*, II. 24. 24-25.

Dharm-ādhikaraṇika (IE 8-3), a judge; mentioned as a *Pātra*.

Dharm-ādhikaraṇin (HD), a judge. See *Matsya Purāṇa*, 215. 24. The reading is *Dharm-ādhikaraṇa* in some manuscripts.

Dharm-ādhikārin (IE 8-3; EI 33), cf. *dharm-ādhikāra* (IA 9); an officer in charge of civil and criminal justice as well as charitable and religious institutions; same as *Bṛhat-tantra-*

pati, according to a Kashmirian commentator; usually explained as 'a judge'; same as *Dharmakarm-ādhikārin* and *Dharm-ādhyakṣa*. Cf. the Muslim official designations *Ṣadruṣ-ṣudūr*, *Dādbak*, etc., explained as 'the chief judge and grand almoner, or custodian of the king's bequests and charities' (*Journ. As. Soc. Pak.*, Vol. IV, pp. 53-54).

Dharm-ādhyakṣa (EI 15; HD), generally explained as 'a judge'; but he was probably also the superintendent of charities, etc.; cf. *Dharm-ādhikārin*.

dharma-hala (EI 7), a rent-free holding. See *hala*.

dharma-jaya-stambha (IA 19), 'a pillar of the victory of religion'.

Dharmakarm-ādhikārin (EI 21; CII 4), officer in charge of charities and other religious works; probably the same as *Dharm-ādhyakṣa*; cf. *Dharm-ādhikārin*, *Dharma-Pradhāna*.

Dharma-kartṛ (EI 19; IA 12), a temple superintendent.

Dharma-kathika (LL), cf. Prakrit *dhamma-kadhika* (EI 15), a [Buddhist] preacher; a preacher of the [Buddhist] religious system; same as *Dharma-kathin*; also spelt *Dharma-kathaka*.

Dharma-kathin (CII 2-1; ML), Buddhist; the preacher of the [Buddhist] religious system; same as *Dharma-kathika*.

dharma-lābha (LP), expression uttered by the Jain monks [of the Śvetāmbara sect] when they bless a householder saluting them.

Dharma-lekhin (EI 4; CII 4; BL), a writer of charters or religious documents.

dharma-lipi (EI 2, 33; CII 1), an edict on the subject of *dharma* (religion or moral precepts).

Dharma-mahādhirāja (EI 12, 28), royal title; cf. *Mahādhirāja* and *Dharma-mahārāja*, etc.

Dharma-mahāmātra (IE 8-3; EI 26; CII 1; HD), superintendent of morality; a *Mahāmātra* (high executive officer) of the department of religion; an executive officer superintending matters relating to religious affairs.

Dharma-mahārāja (IE 8-2; EI 15, 28), royal title; supposed to mean 'a *Mahārāja* who, at the particular time of issuing a record, was engaged in an act of religious merit.'

Dharma-māhārājādhirāja (IE 8-2; EI 5, 15, 28), imperial title; title assumed by certain rulers. Cf. *Dharma-mahārāja*.

dharma-nigama (LL), probably, a pious hamlet or its administrative council.

Dharma-pradhāna (EI 21; CII 4), head of the religious department; cf. *Dharm-ādhyakṣa* and *Dharmakarm-ādhikārin*.

dharma-putra (EI 32), 'one theoretically accepted as a son'.

Dharmarāja (EI 28), royal title; title of a pious king; cf. *Dharma-mahārāja*, etc.; also *dharmarājikā*.

Dharma-rājaguru (EI 11), designation of the king's preceptor.

dharmarājikā (IA 14; ML), Buddhist; a *stūpa* built on the relics of the Buddha called *Dharmarāja*; a Buddhist *stūpa*.

dharma-śālā (IE 8-3; IA 9), a house for accommodating pilgrims free of cost; cf. *śrī-Vāgmatī-jal-āvatāra-sopān-ārāma-ghaṇṭā-dharmaśālā-pratiṣṭhā-karma*. See *choultry*.

dharm-āsana (EI 26; SII 3, 13; SITI), a court of justice; cf. Tamil *daṉm-āsanam* (EI 22), the seat of justice; a law-court.

Dharmāsana-bhaṭṭa (SITI) a Brāhmaṇa versed in law assisting in a *dharm-āsana* or law-court.

dharma-śāsana (EI 18, 22, 33; SII 1), an edict relating to *dharma*; a religious edict.

(*EI* 22; SITI), same as *tāmra-śāsana*; a document recording a gift made for charitable purposes.

dharmaśāsana-paṭṭa (EI 3), a slab containing a religious edict.

dharma-śāstra (BL), scriptures.

dharma-sthāna (EI 24, 26, 32), a temple; a holy place; a place of religious worship. Cf. a *mijigiti* or mosque referred to as a *dharma-sthāna* (*Ep. Ind.*, Vol. XXXIV, p. 144); see also *dharmasthāna-goṣṭhika*.

(*Ep. Ind.*, Vol. I, p. 279, note 52), land or money assigned for a religious purpose.

(*EI* 23), the office of justice.

dharmasthāna-goṣṭhika (EI 33), member of a committee managing the affairs of a temple.

Dharma-sthita (IE 8-2), 'steadfast in religion'; epithet of a Kuṣāṇa king who may have been a convert to Buddhism. See *Satyadharma-sthita*.

dharma-vāriyam (SITI), Sanskrit-Tamil; committee looking after charitable endowments and institutions.

dharmavijaya-śāsana (EI 33), same as *dharma-śāsana*; a royal record relating to one of the king's meritorious acts; cf. *vijaya-śāsana*.

Dharma-vijayin (CII 4), a righteous conqueror; epithet of certain rulers.

dharma-vṛtti-iṟaiyili (SITI), Sanskrit-Tamil; tax-free land for the maintenance of some charity.

dharma-yātrā, cf. *dhaṁma-yātā* (EI 5; CII 1), pilgrimage; a tour of pilgrimage.

Dharma-yuvamahārāja (IE 8-2; EI 24, 32), designation of a crown-prince engaged in a pious activity; cf. *Dharma-mahārāja* and *Yuvamahārāja*.

dhārmika (IE 8-8; EI 30), probably, a cess collected in the name of a religious institution cr festival.

(*IE* 8-2), royal title; same as Prakrit *Dhramika*, translated from Greek *Dikaios*.

Dharmin, cf. *dharmikaḻ* (SITI), a body or commission managing endowments.

Dhārtarāṣṭra (IE 7-1-2), 'one hundred'.

dhāṭī (LP), campaign; cf. *para-rāṣṭr-opari datta-dhāṭyām*, 'in the course of an expedition led against a foreign country'.

dhāṭivāha (*Ep. Ind.*, Vol. I, p. 277, note 24), meaning doubtful.

dhātrī (IE 7-1-2), 'one'.

dhātu (ML), Buddhist; corporeal relics [of the Buddha].

(*IE* 7-1-2; EI 25), 'seven'.

Cf. Dhātu-parigṛhīta, an epithet of the Buddha; probably, salvation (*Select Inscriptions*, p. 228).

dhātu-garbha, 'containing the corporeal relics of the Buddha' (*Journ. Mad. Univ.*, Vol. XXXII, p. 136).

dhātu-vara (*Ep. Ind.*, Vol. XXVII, p. 16, text line 13), a Buddhist *stūpa* containing the Buddha's relics.

Dhātuvara-parigṛhīta (EI 20), 'one who has attained *nirvāṇa*'; epithet of the Buddha. Cf. *dhātu*.

dhaukaṇa-patra (LP), permission of divorce; cf. Gujarātī *chuṭāchedā meḻvavā*.

ḍhaura (LP), cattle.

Dhāvaka (EI 18), the fore-runner.

dhavala-cchatra (SII 2), a white parasol which was one of the royal insignia.

dhaval-āgāra, cf. *dhavalāra* (IA 14), 'a mansion'.

ḍheṅku (EI 30), a machine for extracting juice.

ḍheṅku-kaḍḍhaka (IE 8-8), probably, one whose profession was to draw water from a well by means of a machinery.

dhī (IE 7-1-2), 'seven'.

ḍhiṁka (EI 13), a well.

dhīrmara (CII 4), probably, 'a fish-basket', according to some.

dhiṣṇi (EI 5), a house.

dhṛti (LP), consolation or encouragement.

(*IE* 7-1-2), 'eighteen'.

Dhruva (EI 16, 32; HD), [a collector of] the fixed royal share of grains; contraction of *Dhruv-ādhikaraṇika*; cf. the Gujarātī family name *Dhruva*; same as *dhruva-sthāna*. See *Bomb. Gaz.*, Vol. I, Part i, p. 477.

(*IE* 7-1-2), 'one'.

(*CII* 1), regular.

dhruvā (CII 1), certainty.

Dhruv-ādhikaraṇa (EI 30), office of [the collector of] the king's share of the produce of the fields from the farmers. Cf. *Dhruva*, *Dhruvapati*, *Dhruv-ādhikaraṇika.*

Dhruv-ādhikaraṇika (IE 8-3; CII 3; HD; HRS), known from Maitraka records; according to some, the officer in charge of persons entrusted with the superintendence of the collection of the king's grain-share from the farmers; an official title of the Kathiawar region indicating an officer collecting the king's share of grains; sometimes called *Dhruvasthān-ādhikaraṇika*; the same as *Dhruva* or an employee of the *dhruva-sthāna* or *Dhruva's* office. Cf. *Ep. Ind.*, Vol. VII, p. 339.

Dhruvapati (EI 32), cf. *Dhruv-ādhikaraṇika.*

dhruva-sthāna (IE 8-3), a station for the collection of the king's fixed grain share; cf. *Dhruva.*

Dhruvasthān-ādhikaraṇa (IE 8-3; EI 30), the station for collecting the king's share or the office in its charge; cf. *Dhruv-ādhikaraṇa* and *Dhruv-ādhikaraṇika.*

dhvaja (CII 3), banner or standard as distinguished from *lāñchana* or crest. Cf. *cihna* (*Ep. Ind.*, Vol. XXXIV, pp. 135 ff.).

dhvaj-ārohaṇa (EI 31), a ceremony; cf. *dhvaj-āvarohaṇa*

dhvaja-stambha (CII 3, 4), a flag-staff.

dhvaj-āvarohaṇa (SITI), function at the conclusion of a festival.

dhvaṁśī, same as *vaṁśya*; a theoretical unit of measurement (*JNSI*, Vol. XVI, p. 48).

di (IE 8-1; CII 3), abbreviation of *dina*, *dine*, *divasa* or *divase*; used in connection with *śu* or *su* and *ba* in the case of lunar months and by itself in the case of solar months.

Dibira, same as *Divira* (q.v.).

Digambara (IA 7), a Jain sect.

diggaja (IE 7-1-2), 'eight'. Eight poets patronised by Kṛṣṇadevarāya were called the *aṣṭa-diggaja*.

dig-vijaya, used in Kannaḍa inscriptions in the sense of 'going in state; going in a triumpal procession; making a state progress through one's dominions' (*Ep. Ind.*, Vol. V, p. 223, note 5; Vol. VI, p. 51, note 5). See *vijaya*.

Dikaios (IE 8-2) Greek; royal title; 'pious'; translated in Prakrit as *Dhramika* (Sanskrit *Dhārmika*).

dikolā (LP), same as *dāsī*.

Dikpāla (HD), probably, officers in charge of the borders of a kingdom. See Nārada, Jolly's ed., Pariśiṣṭa, verse 17; *Mitākṣarā* on *Yājñavalkyasmṛti*, II. 271; Kātyāyana (v. 813) quoted by Aparārka. (IE 7-1-2), 'eight'.

dīkṣā (HA), initiation as a monk or recluse; initiation into any doctrine.

dīkṣā-guru (EI 32, 33), preceptor.

Dīkṣita (EI 22; CII 3, 4), same as *Yajña-dīkṣita*; epithet of Brāhmaṇas; later stereotyped as a Brahmanical family name.

dina (CII 3), a day; used to denote the solar, or more properly civil, day. See also *di* and *divasa*.

(*IE* 7-1-2), 'fifteen'.

dināra (SITI), name of a coin; same as *dīnāra*; derived from the Roman coin name *denarius*; a cowrie-shell according to the *Rājataraṅgiṇī* (Stein's trans., Vol. II, pp. 308 ff.).

dīnāra (IE 8-8; EI 9, 23, 30; CII 3; SITI), a gold coin, the name being derived from the Roman *denarius*; gold coin equal to 16 silver *rūpakas* in the Gupta age (*JNSI*, Vol. II, p. 5); sometimes called *kāśu* in Tamil records; sometimes regarded as half of a *satera* or *sateraka* (Greek *stater*); mentioned as a silver coin (K. V. Rangaswami Aiyanger, *Kṛtya-kalpataru*, Vyavahāra-kāṇḍa, p. 125); also spelt *dīnnāra*, etc.

dināri (IE 8-8), name of a coin probably modified from the Roman *denarius*; cf. *dīnāra* and *dināri-māṣaka*.

dināri-māṣaka (IE 8-8), name of a coin; cf. *dināri.*

dīpa-mālā, cf. *tīpa-mālai* (SITI), the string of lights hung in temples; same as *śara-viḻakku.*

dīpanā (CII 1), glorification.

dīpa-pūjā (EI 9), *dīpa* and *pūjā* wrongly taken as a compound word of special significance.

dīpa-skambha (LL), a lamp-post.

dīpāvalī (EI 5; CII 4), name of a festival; the festival of lights; cf. *dīp-otsava.*

dīp-otsava (EI 11, 32), same as *dīpāvalī*, the fesival of lights.

diramam (IE 8-8), Tamil form of *dramma.*

dīrgha-mānya (SITI), land set apart for the supply of water for the holy bath of idols.

dīrghā (CII 1), distance or the distant future.

dīrghanāsiky-ārcā (EI 24), the image of a deity with long nose.

dīrghikā (SITI), bath; a long or oval pond.

diś, diśā (IE 7-1-2), 'ten'; rarely used to indicate 'four' also.

diśā (IA 7), precepts.

diśaḥ (EI 2), the nymphs of the quarters.

Diśāmpati (EI 29), a provincial governor. A *Cakravartin* was sometimes conceived as a *Dig-vijayin* or a *Diśāmpati.*

Diśāpaṭa (EI 16), Kannaḍa; 'causing one's enemies to be scattered in all directions'; same as *Diśāpaṭṭa.*

Diśāpaṭṭa (EI 5, 16), Kannaḍa; 'causing one's enemies to be scattered in all directions'; same as *Diśāpaṭa.*

diṣṭa (IA 18), same as *kāla*, time.

ditya (EI 9, 12, 28; CII 4; HRS), known from Maitraka records; name of a tax, according to some; probably, the same as *datti*, i.e. a gift or occasional present to be offered to the landlord; cf. *sarva-ditya-viṣṭi-prātibhedikā-parihīna* or °*parihṛta* (*Ep. Ind.*, Vol. VI, p. 298, text line 20); also cf. *sa-ditya-dāna-karaṇa* (*Ep. Ind.*, Vol. XXXI, p.301, text line 14), an epithet of the gift land. *Ditya* is probably derived from Prakrit *dijja*=Sanskrit *deya*, 'to be given', 'an object that has been given away' in the sense of 'customary presents'. For *ditta*, cf. *Bhār. Vid.*, Vol. XVII, Nos. 3-4 pp. 125-26. See *Dity-odgrāhaka.*

Dity-odgrāhaka (CII 4), probably, 'an officer in charge of collecting customary presents'; cf. *ditya*.

diva (CII 3, etc.), abbreviation of *divasa* or *divase*; used to denote the solar or, more properly, civil day.

divā(CII 3), 'by day'; an indeclinable used in some of the Nepal inscriptions in composition with words denoting *tithis* or lunar days.

divākara (IE 7-1-2), 'twelve'.

Dīvān (BL), the chief administrator or finance minister; see *Dīwān, Dīwānjī*.

divasa (CII 3, etc.), a day; sometimes used for the week-day, instead of the usual term *vāra*; generally used to denote the solar or, more properly, civil day; sometimes used in connection with words denoting *tithis* or lunar days. See also *di*, *dina*, *diva*.

Divira (HD), same as Persian *Dabīr*, 'a clerk'. See *Rājataraṅgiṇī*, VIII. 131, mentioning *Divira* as distinct from *Kāyastha*; also *CII*, Vol. III, p. 122. Cf. *Divirapati*.

Divirapati, Divīrapati (IE 8-3; EI 5, 28; BL; HD); chief secretary or the chief of the clerks; cf. *Divira*. See *Ep. Ind.*, Vol. XI, p. 180 (*Sandhivigrahādhikṛta-Divirapati*); Vol. XXII, p. 117 (*Divirapati* also called *Sandhivigrahika*, *Mahā-pratīhāra* and *Sāmanta*).

divya (IA 10; LP), an ordeal; same as *parīkṣā*.

divya-prabandha, see *prabandha*.

Dīwān, Dīwānjī (BL), the chief administrator or finance minister. See *Dīvān*.

doḍḍi (EI 4), a yard.

ḍohalikā (EI 13), explained as 'a piece of land granted to Brāhmaṇas, Svāmins, Sādhus and others' (*Prog. Rep. A. S. I., W. C.*, 1908-09, p. 53); cf. *dohalikā dattā*. See *dohalikā-bhūmi*.

ḍohalikā-bhūmi (LP), explained as 'land, of which the ownership is doubted and hence taken by government'; cf. Gujarātī *ḍūlā*, *dulavuṁ*, *ḍohalavum*; also *lupta-ḍohalikā* (LP), eplained as 'the *ḍohalikā* which is lost to the owner'. But see *ḍohalikā*.

dokārā (LP), an old man.

dola-yātrā (IA 9), the festival of the swinging of the image of Kṛṣṇa on Phālguna su-di 15.

doṇ (IE 8-6), Bengali form of *droṇavāpa*.

doṅgaka (EI 24), a variety of resin or aloe.

doṣa (LP), doing anything wrongly.

(*IE* 7-1-2), 'three'.

(*EI* 9), black or red spots on the tongue supposed to be a foreboding of death.

Cf. daṇḍa-doṣa; fines; see also *pradhān-āpradhāna-doṣa-samanvita* used as an epithet of the gift village (*Ep. Ind.*, Vol. III, p. 274). Here *doṣa* apparently means *daṇḍa-doṣa.*

dosya (IE 8-8; EI 30), meaning uncertain.

doyaraka (EI 33), probably, 'the singer who repeats part of a song after it has been once sung'; cf. Hindī *dohrānā.*

dra (EI 33; LP), abbreviation of *dramma.*

drachma (IE 8-8; CII 4), name of an old Greek coin; Indian *dramma.*

drahyitavya (CII 1), 'should be firm'.

drakṣaṇa, see *draṁkṣaṇa.*

drakṣuṇa, see *draṁkṣaṇa.*

drama (EI 23), same as *dramma.*

draṁkṣaṇa, same as *tolaka* (q.v.); a weight of 8 *māṣas,* also spelt *drakṣaṇa, drakṣuṇa,* etc.; cf. *maṁkṣūṇa,* equal to 7 *māṣas.*

dramma (EI 25, 30; CII 4; SITI; BL), name of a coin; originally derived from Greek *drachma.*

(IE 8-8), a silver coin, equal to one-sixteenth of a gold *niṣka* according to the *Līlāvatī.*

Cf. pañciyaka-dramma (EI 30), *Śrīmadādivarāha-dramma, Vigraha-dramma, Vigrahapāla-dramma, Vigrahapāla-satka-dramma, Vigrahapālīya-dramma, Vigrahatuṅgīya-dramma* (IE 8-8; EI 1); *Bhīmapriya-dramma* (IE 8-8); *poruttha-dramma* (EI 23).—(IE 8-8), cf. *gara-dramma, dāya-dramma, belliya-dramma* (i.e. silver *dramma*), etc., of Kannaḍa inscriptions; the name *dramma* was also applied to the silver coin called *purāṇa, dharaṇa* or *kārṣāpaṇa,* though it was often used as the name of copper coins; money. For gold and ordinary (copper) *dramma,* cf. *Ep. Ind.*, Vol. XXX, p. 111.

Cf. vāśal-tiramam (SITI), door tax.

dramm-ārdha (CII 4), 'half of a dramma'; name of a coin.

dramma-tribhāga (CII 4), 'three-fourths of a dramma'; name of a coin.

draṅga (EI 32), used to indicate *dramma*; name of a coin.

(*EI* 10), cf. *Navagrāma-draṅga,* 'the *draṅga* of Navagrāma'; possibly 'a station for the collection of revenue'.

(*EI* 8-3), a town or watch-station; possibly also a station for the collection of revenue; also called *udraṅga* which may thus indicate both revenue and the station for its collection.

Draṅgapāla (EI 28), same as *Drāṅgika* official designation. See *draṅga*.

Drāṅgeśa (EI 20; HD), supposed to be the designation of a guardian of the frontiers (cf. Stein, *Rājataraṅgiṇī*, Vol. II, pp. 291-92 for *draṅga* or *draṅgā*); cf. *Draṅgapāla* and *Drāṅgika*.

Drāṅgika (IE 8-3; EI 10, 30; CII 3, 4; HD), probably, an officer in charge of a city-station or watch-tower for collection of customs duties. *Draṅga* means either 'a town' (Bhandarkar's List, No. 810) or 'a watch-station' (*Rājataraṅgiṇī*, VIII. 2010). *Drāṅgika* was an officer in charge of a *draṅga* probably meaning a watch station or a station for revenue collection; similar to *Audraṇgika* in the latter sense; mentioned along with the *Dhruvasthān-ādhikaraṇa* or 'the collector of the king's grain-share'. Cf. *draṅga*, *Draṅgapāla*, etc. See *CII*, Vol. III, p. 169.

drava (EI 20), a kind of dancing.

Drāviḍī, name applied to the South Indian variety of the Brāhmī alphabet.

dravyabhāṇḍāra-karaṇa, cf. *karaṇa* (LP); the department of stores.

droṇa (IE 8-6; Chamba), a grain measure; often regarded as equal to four *āḍhakas*; between one maund fourteen seers and two maunds, according to Bengali authors.

(*IE* 8-1; EI 24, 29, 30), name of a land measure derived from that of a measure of capacity; shortened form of *droṇavāpa*.

Droṇāgīka (EI 33), official disignation; possibly a mistake for *Droṇāgraka*.

Droṇāgraka (EI 27), official disignation; probably an officer in charge of a *droṇamukha* or an important city,or one who collected the king's grain-share fixed per *droṇa* measure.

Droṇamāpaka, measurer of the king's grain-share (Ghoshal, *Ag. Syst. Anc. Ind.*, pp. 26-27).

droṇavāpa (IE 8-6; EI 30), 'an area of land requiring one *droṇa* measure of seed grains to be sown'; a land measure which was not the same in different ages and localities.

droṇi, *droṇī* (CII 4; IA 11), treasury; property (cf. *Ep. Ind.*, Vol. XXXIV, p. 144—'the *droṇī* of Śrī-Somanāthadeva' to which a piece of land was attached); see *devadroṇī* probably meaning 'rent-free property of a temple'.

droṇī-kara, cf. Tamil *toṇi-kkaḍamai* (SITI), tax on boats.

dṛś, cf. *peṭaṁ* (Sanskrit *udaraṁ*) *darśayitum* (EI 11), literally, 'to show one's belley'; but actually 'to ask for the means of livelihood'.

Dṛśidhārikā (EI 32), a female torch-bearer.

dṛṣṭa (EI 3, 23; CII 3; etc.), Prakrit *diṭṭham*, 'has been seen', i.e. 'found correct and approved', found on some copper-plate grants indicating the approval of the proper authorities endorsed on the original document later engraved on the plates. Cf. *ni* (an abbreviation of *nibaddha* or *nirīkṣiṭa*) in certain medieval copper-plate grants of Eastern India. In *dṛṣṭa-pañcāśat-padāti* (LP), *dṛṣṭa-ghoṭaka* (LP), etc., the word *dṛṣṭa* indicates that money should be paid after actually seeing the foot-soldiers and horses in question.

dṛṣṭ-ādṛṣṭa (IA 20), dimly seen.

dṛṣṭi (IE 7-1-2), 'two'; cf. *netra*; also *darśana*, 'six'.

(*IA* 19), Buddhist; theory or doctrine; a peculiar or heretical doctrine.

Dū (IE 8-1; LP), abbreviation of *Dūtaka*.

dugdha, cf. *a-dugdha-dadhi-grahaṇa* (IE 8-5); milk which the villagers (probably, the milkmen) were obliged to supply to the king or landlord on occasions and to the touring officers.

duḥkhana (CII 1), causing pain.

Duḥsādha-sādhanika (IE 8-3; HD), the leader of policemen engaged in apprehending robbers, etc., or of expeditionery forces requisitioned on occasions of emergency; cf. *Sādhanika*, *Duṣṭa-sādhaka*, *Dauḥsādhanika*, *Dussādhya-sādhaka*, etc.

Duḥsādhya (EI 2), abbreviation of *Duḥsādhya-sādhanika*, etc., or a criminal; cf. *dussādhya*.

duḥsādhy-ādāya (EI 21), a tax probably levied from habitually criminal people or for the maintenance of certain police or military officers called *Duḥsādhya*, etc. See *duṣṭasādhy-ādāya*.

Duḥsādhya-sādhanika (IE 8-3), same as *Dauhsādha-sādhanika*, etc. Cf. *Dussādhya-sādhaka*, *Duṣṭa-sāhaṇi*, etc.

duḥśamya (ML), unpreventable.

ḍulita (LP), '[land, etc.,] that has become *ḍohalikā* (q.v.)'.

ḍumphaka (IE 8-8; EI 30), probably the same as Sanskrit *dṛmphaka*, 'one who presses'; see *nīla-ḍumphaka*.

dundubhi (ASLV), a musical instrument.

durga (ASLV), a fort.

Durga-daṇḍanāyaka (ASLV), the ruler of a fort; cf. *Daṇḍanāyaka.*

Durgapāla (HD), superintendent of a fort.

Durgapati (EI 27), governor of a fortress.

Durgā-putra (EI 33), epithet of one devoted to the goddess Durgā; used along with such similar epithets as *Rudra-putra* and *Puruṣottama-putra.*

durita (SITI), famine; disturbance.

Durlabha (EI 23), an official designation of uncertain import.

dur-vāchaka, cf. *tur-vāyakam* (SITI), abusive language.

duṣkṛta (CII 1), a bad deed.

dussādhya (CII 4), 'a criminal'; abbreviation of *Duḥsādhya-sādhaka*, etc.

Dussādhya-sādhanika, same as *Duṣṭa-sāhaṇi* (EI 33), etc.

Duṣṭa-sādhaka (EI 7; CII 4; HD), official designation; 'the mentor of criminals'; same as *Duḥsādhya-sādhanika*, *Dauḥsādhanika*, etc. See *Ep. Ind.*, Vol. VII, p. 91.

Duṣṭa-sādhya (EI 21; CII 4), same as *dus-sādhya* or a criminal; abbreviation of the official designation *Duṣṭa-sādhya-sādhanika*; same as *Duṣṭa-sādhaka*, etc.

duṣṭasādhy-ādāya, probably, a tax levied for maintaining the police engaged in suppressing dacoits. Cf. Ghoshal, *H. Rev. Syst.*, p. 254, note. See *duḥsādhy-ādāya.*

Duṣṭasādhya-sādhanika (*Ep. Ind.*, Vol. XXXV, p. 132), same as *Duṣṭa-sādhaka*, etc.

Duṣṭa-sāhaṇi (EI 33), same as *Duṣṭa-sādhaka*, *Duṣṭasādhya-sādhanika*, etc.

dūṣya (CII 1), robe or clothes.

Dūta (IE 8-3; EI 23, 30; CII 1; HD), a messenger or envoy. See *Viṣṇudharmottara*, II. 24. 13-14, 28; *CII*, Vol. I, p. 67.

(*EI* 23; CII 3, 4), an occasional substitute for *Dūtaka*, the executor of a grant.

Dūtaka (IE 8-3; HD), messenger; conveyor of a request or message; cf. the Khalimpur plate of Dharmapāla (*Ep. Ind.*, Vol. IV, p. 250), according to which the king was requested to make a grant by a *Mahāsāmantādhipati* through prince

Tribhuvanapāla as the *Dūtaka*. His function is called *dūtya* in the Nalanda plate of Devapāla (*Ep. Ind.*, Vol. XVII, 318 ff., text line 51).

(*IE* 8-3; EI 23, 30; CII 3, 4), according to some, the technical title of an officer connected with royal charters, whose duty it was to carry the king's orders to the local officials by whom the charter was then drawn up and delivered. But the *Dūtaka* seems to have been responsible for putting the document and also perhaps the gift land in the donee's possession. There are instances of more *Dūtakas* than one (IA 19). See also *Ājñā*, *Dūta*, and *sva-mukh-ājñā*. Cf. *Ind. Ep.*, pp. 143-44.

Dūta-praiṣaṇika (HD), officer in charge of sending envoys; same as *Dūta-preṣaṇika*. See *Ep. Ind.*, Vol. XVII, p. 321; *Ind. Ant.*, Vol. XV, p. 306. Cf. *Preṣaṇika*.

Dūta-preṣaṇika (CII 4), also called *Duta-saṁpreṣaṇika* and *Dūta-praiṣaṇika*; the officer who despatched *Dūtas*.

dūtya, same as *dautya*; function of the *Dūtaka* (q.v.).

Dūyaka (LP), Sanskrit *Dūtaka*; a messenger.

dvādaśa-bhāga (*Rājataraṅgiṇī*, VII. 203); name of an additional levy which was $\frac{1}{12}$ of the fixed tax.

dvādaśaka (SII 13), partnership in a land; cf. *aṣṭaka*.

Dvādaśasthān-ādhipati, the head of twelve departments (*Ep. Ind.*, Vol. XXIV, p. 276).

dvandva (IE 7-1-2), 'two'.

dvāra (CII 1), a way or means.

(*IE* 7-1-2), 'nine'.

(*EI* 4), the mouth of a river.

(*IE* 8-3), cf. 'the lord of the *dvāra*' which was the designation of a commander of forces in Kashmir; possibly, a pass [leading into the Kashmir valley].

Cf. Tamil *vāśal-paṇam*, 'door-tax'; periodical payment due to the palace. Cf. *dvār-ādeya*.

Cf. *dvāra-koṣṭhaka*.

dvār-ādeya (HRS), 'gate-dues'; explained as a surcharge over and above the tolls on goods imported into a city. See Ghoshal, *H. Rev. Syst.*, p. 60, note. But cf. Tamil *vāśal-paṇam* explained as 'door-tax', i.e. the periodical payment due to the palace.'

Dvār-ādhipa (IE 8-3; HD), same as *Dvāranātha*, *Dvārapati*, etc.; 'the lord of the pass'; cf. *dvāra*.

dvāra-koṣṭhaka (Lüders, *Mathurā Inscriptions*, p. 135, text line 4), translated as 'gateway'; gate-chamber.

dvāra-maṇḍapa (HA), a hall or pavilion on the entrance or door of a shrine.

Dvāranātha (IE 8-3; HD), superintendent of the passes leading into the kingdom, according to Stein (*Rājataraṅgiṇī*, V. 214); same as *Dvār-ādhipa*, *Dvārapati*, etc.

Dvārapāla (EI 22), a door-keeper.

Dvāra-parīkṣā (IE 8-3; EI 28), Oḍiyā; Sanskrit *Dvāra-parīkṣaka*; same as *Pratīhāra*. Cf. *Parīkṣā*.

Dvārapati (IE 8-3; HD), 'lord of the gate'; a commander of forces under the *Kampanāpati* [in Kashmir]; the guardian of a pass [leading into the Kashmir valley]; same as *Dvāranātha*, *Dvār-ādhipa*, etc.

dvāroṣṭha (EI 1), meaning doubtful; probably a mistake for *dvāra-koṣṭha*, a gate-chamber.

dvaya (IE 7-1-2), 'two'.

Dveda (EI 24, 29), contracted form of *Dviveda*.

dvesa (CII 3), an epithet applied to land; a term of uncertain significance.

Dvi (EI 11), abbreviation of *Dviveda*.

(*IE* 8-1), abbreviation of *dvitīya*.

dvi-bhūmika (LP), two-storied.

dvi-garbha (LL), a two-celled building.

dvijāti-dāya (EI 22), same as *brahma-dāya*.

dvikā, double measure (*Ep. Ind.*, Vol. XXXVI, p. 52, note 5).

dvipa (*EI* (7-1-2), 'eight'.

dvīpa (IE 7-12), 'seven'.

dvi-vallakya (LP), [coins] in which there is a mixture of two *vāls* (6 *ratis*) of a base metal. Cf. *JNSI*, Vol. XXII, p. 197.

Dviveda (CII 4), also called *Dvivedin*; epithet of Brāhmaṇas; later stereotyped as a Brahmanical family name.

dvyardha (CII 1), one and a half.

dyu (IE 7-1-2), 'cypher'

dyu-maṇi (IE 7-1-2; EI 25), 'twelve'.

dyūta (HRS), gambling; the king's dues collected by the superintendent of gambling.

Dyūtasabhāpati (BL), superintendent of the gambling hall.

E

eḍūka, cf. *eḍuo* (CII 2-1), supposed to be 'a wall into which bones (meaning planks and other hard substances) have been inserted in order to strengthen the structure', because it is explained in a commentary as *asthy-aṅkita kuḍya*; but *asthy-aṅkita-kuḍya* seems to mean a Buddhist *stūpa* raised on corporeal relics which were an object of worship. Although the word *kuḍya* is reckoned in the lexicons in the sense of a wall, it seems to mean 'a mound' in this case. The word *aidūka* derived from *eḍūka* is used in Buddhist Sanskrit in the sense of a Buddhist *stūpa*. See *IHQ*, Vol. XXIX, pp. 302-03.

eka-bhoga (EI 16; SITI; ASLV), a tenure indicating exclusive ownership of a property invested in a single individual; sole possession and enjoyment of a village by a single person (without any joint owner); cf. *ekabhoga-iṟaiyili*, tax-free land or village in the sole enjoyment of a single owner. Same as *eka-bhogya*. Cf. *gaṇa-bhoga*.

(*SITI*), single crop; same as Tamil *oru-pū*.

eka-bhogya (EI 13, 14), a tenure; same as *eka-bhoga*.

ekadā (CII 1), sometimes.

ekādaśa-prasūti (LP), probably, eleven births.

ekādaśa-Rudra-bhikṣā (EI 32), arrangement of free supply of food to Śaiva ascetics in the name of the eleven Rudras; land granted for such an arrangement.

ekādaśa-śata (ML), same as *ekādaś-ottara-śata*, one hudred and eleven.

ekādaśī-vrata (EI 31; CII 4), name of a *vrata* rite.

eka-dhana (LP), joint family.

ekala-mūrti (HA), a single Jina image without any ornamental *parikara*.

eka-muṣṭi, cf. *eka-muṣṭyā* (LP), 'collectively'.

Ekāṅga (HD), probably, an officer belonging to a body organized in military fashion for collecting revenue or performing police duties. See *Rājataraṅgiṇī*, V. 249; VII. 1604.

Ekāṅgin (SITI), a single person; one who has no family, especially the Vaiṣṇava devotee in charge of temples.

Ekapātra (EI 27), probably, *Yāvadeka-pātra* (q.v.); official designion; cf. *Pātra* and *Mahāpātra*.

Eka-śāṭa (EI 29), same as *Eka-cīvara*; epithet of a monk who has taken a vow to wear only one piece of cloth.

eka-tīrthī (HA), a sculpture showing only one Jina (Tīrthaṅkara) together with his *parikara*.

ekatya (CII 1), 'of one kind'.

ekāvalī, ekāvallī (SITI), necklace of a single string.

eradu-bilkode (IE 8-5), Kannaḍa; name of a tax.

Erjhuna (ML), a title of foreign origin; 'a prince'.

etatka cf. *etaka* (CII 1); same as *etat*.

evaṁpariṇā (LP), 'in this way'; cf. Gujarātī *evī-pere*.

F

fanam, English spelling of Tamil *paṇam*; see *paṇa*. It was sometimes regarded as a gold coin equal to $\frac{1}{10}$ of a *partāb* and $\frac{1}{20}$ of a *varāha* (*SII*, Vol. I, p. 161).

farmān, also spelt *firmān*; Persian; cf. *phuramāṇa*.

fīl, Arabic-Persian; cf. *pīlu, Pīlupati*.

firmān, cf. *farmān*.

G

ga (IE 8-1), used for *gā* (in Kharoṣṭhī) as an abbreviation of *gāthā*; also abbreviation of *gadyāṇa* (q.v.).

gabhāro (HA), Sanskrit *gorbha-gṛha*; the sanctum of a temple.

gaccha (IA 11; BL), name of particular communities of Jain monks; cf. the eightyfour *gacchas* of the Jains.

gaddī (EI 8), a throne; cf. *pañcāṅga-prasāda*.

gadhaiyā, also called *gadhaiyā paisā*; same as *gadhiyā*; a copper coin modified from old Sasanian types.

gadhiyā, same as *gadhaiyā* (q. v.).

gadiāṇaka, cf. *Kumāra-gadiāṇaka* (EI 8); same as *gadyāṇaka*.

(*EI* 27), also called *gadyāṇa*; name of a coin.

gadiyāṇa (EI 27; CII 4), same as *gadyāṇa, gadyāṇaka*; name of a coin called *suvarṇa-gadiyāṇa*, 'gold *gadiyāṇa*'.

gadyā, abbreviation of *gadyāṇa* (q.v.).

gadyāna (EI 3), a gold coin or weight; also spelt *gadyāṇa*. generally regarded as 48 *ratis* in weight (*JNSI*, Vol. XVI, p. 42).

gadyāṇa (IE 8-8; EI 27, 30), also called *gadyāṇaka*, often contracted as *ga* or *gadyā*; sometimes called *pon-gadyāṇa* or *gadyāṇa-ponnu* indicating that it was a gold coin; sometimes called *suvarṇa*; cf. *bhairava-gadyāṇa*, *lokki-gadyāṇa* (SII 11-2), *aṅka-gadyāṇa*, *gāva-gadyāṇa*, *komarina-gadyāṇa*, *priyaśrāha-gaja-malla-gadyāṇa*, *ambili-gadyāṇa*, *jagadalaṁ-gadyāṇa*, etc. Cf. also *aṟu-gadyāṇa* (IA 12) and *kula-gadyāṇa* (EI 17), names of coins. Cf. *parameṣṭhi-gadyāṇa-ponnu* (*Ep. Ind.*, Vol. XXXVI, p. 61).

(*SITI*), name of a coin, probably equal to a *varāha* or *pagoda*; cf. *bṛhad-bhairava-gadyāṇa* (EI 30); also *kaṭhāri-aṅkuśa-gadyāṇa* (EI 8), name of a coin with the representation of a dagger and a goad; *varāha-gadyāṇa* (EI 8), name of the gold coin called both *varāha* and *gadyāṇa*.

gadyāṇa (CITD), same as *gadyāṇa*; a coin like a farthing equal to $\frac{1}{4}$ or $\frac{1}{5}$ of the *paikamu*; also a *dināra* or *varāha*; a weight used in weighing silver; equal in some places to 20 *vals*, 8 *māṣas*, or half a *tola*.

gadyānaka (EI 28), *gadyāṇaka* (IE 8-8; EI 27), same as *gadyāna* or *gadyāṇa*; name of a coin; a coin weighing 48 *ratis* according to the *Līlāvatī*.

gagana (IE 7-1-2; EI 52), 'cypher'.

gāhṇa (Chamba), threshing floor; from Sanskrit *gāhana*.

gairāṭa, cf. *gelāṭa* (CII 1); probably, a hill bird.

gaja (IE 7-1-2), 'eight'.

Gajadhara (EI 4), same as *Sūtradhara* or *Sūtradhāra*, 'mason'.

Gajādhīśa (CII 4), 'the lord of elephants'; official designation; title of certain rulers. Cf. *Gajapati*, etc.

Gajalakṣmī (EI 32), representation of Lakṣmī receiving water on the head from a jar held in the trunk of an elephant on either side; found on the seals of certain rulers.

gajamāla (HA), row of elephants in the plinth of shrines; also called *gajathara*.

Gaja-mṛgayā-vihāra (ASLV), 'sportful hunting of elephants'; a title of the Vijayanagara kings.

Gajapati (IE 8-2; EI 9, 30; CII 4; HD), 'the lord of elephants'; officer in charge of the elephant arm in an army; title of certain rulers; dynastic name of the Sūryavaṁśīs of Orissa. Cf. *Ind. Ant.*, Vol. XV, p. 7. See *Mahāgajapati*, etc.

Gaja-sāhaṇī (EI 32), a leader of the elephant force; same as *Gaja-sāhiṇi*, *Gaja-sādhanika*.

Gaja-sāhiṇi (IE 8-3; EI 27), same as *Gaja-sāhaṇi*, *Gaja-sādhanika*; leader of the elephant corps; cf. *Sāhiṇi* or *Sāhaṇī*, derived from *Sādhanika*.

gajathara (HA), same as *gajamāla*.

Gajavāha-rāuta (EI 31), title of a subordinate chief.

gal-puṭṭi (CITD), Telugu; an unknown measure of land; a variation of *puṭṭi*.

gāṇṭhi (LP), a package; cf. Gujarātī *gāṇṭhḍī*.

Gamāgamika (IE 8-3; EI 4, 23; CII 4; HD), same as *Gamāgamin*; official designation; probably, an officer in charge of regulating the people's entrance and departure into cities; explained by some as 'a kind of messenger' (*Ind. Ant.*, Vol. XV, p. 306). *Utpala* on the *Bṛhatsaṁhitā*, 85. 34, explains *Dūta* as *Gamāgamika*, though some Pāla inscriptions have *dūta-khola-gamāgamik-ābhitvaramāṇa* (*Ep. Ind.*, Vol. IV, pp. 250, text line 45).

Gamāgamin (EI 31), same as *Gamāgamika*.

gampaṇa (EI 27), same as *kampaṇa*; an administrative and territorial unit.

Gāmuṇḍa (EI 15), Kannaḍa; same as *Gāvuṇḍa*; a village headman; probably derived from *Grāmakūṭa*, 'headman of a village', through *Gāmauḍa* >*Gāmuḍa* under the influence of *muṇḍa*, 'head'. Cf. *Nāḍa-gāmuṇḍa Nāṟ-gāmuṇḍa*, 'headman of a district (*nāḍu*)'.

gaṇa (LL), a section of the Jains.

(*SITI*), a group of persons; a community or religious guild.

(*EI* 26; CII 4), a guild or corporation.

(*EI* 3), wrongly explained as a share.

(*SII* 12), managing committee.

(*SII* 2), the attendants of Śiva; also the fourteen divisions of learning.

gaṇa-bhoga (SITI, ASLV), a tenure in which land is held in common by a group of persons; joint ownership of a village or villages by a number of persons; same as *gaṇa-bhogya*, *gaṇa-bhojya*. Cf. *eka-bhoga*, etc.

gaṇa-bhogya (EI 13, 15), see *gaṇa-bhoga* or *gaṇa-bhojya*. Cf. *eka-bhoga* or *eka-bhojya*.

gaṇa-bhojya (EI 16), same as *gaṇa-bhoga* or *gaṇa-bhogya*.

Gaṇabhṛt (EI 3; SII I), the head of a [Jain] school; same as *Gaṇin*, *Gaṇa-dhara*.

Gaṇ-ācārya (LL), the teacher of a Buddhist community.

Gaṇadaṇḍa (EI 30), epithet of a hero; probably, an abbreviation of *Gaṇa-daṇḍanāyaka*.

Gaṇa-daṇḍanāyaka, also called *Gaṇa-daṇḍapāla* (EI 18); official designation; probably, a *Daṇḍanāyaka* serving under a *gaṇa* or corporation or commanding several *gaṇas* or contingents.

Gaṇa-daṇḍapāla, same as *Gaṇa-daṇḍanāyaka*.

Gaṇadhara (HA), chief disciple of a Jina.

Gaṇaka (EI 18), official designation; cf. Tamil *kaṇakaṉ* (SITI), a village accountant; also *vāśal-kaṇakkaṉ* (SITI), accountant at the *vāśal* (palace or palace-gate); *ūrkkaṇakkar-jīvitam* (SITI), land assigned in lieu of salary to the village accountant or perquisites of the office of the village accountant (i.e. the *Paṭvārī* as he is called in many parts of India).

gaṇanā (EI 20), accountancy.

(CII 1), 'taking into account'.

Gaṇapaka (CII 4), official designation; probably the same as Sanskrit *Gaṇaka*.

gaṇa-paṇa (EI 20), communal and professional guilds.

Gaṇa-pperumakkaḷ (SII 12; SITI), Sanskrit-Tamil; the elders of a *gaṇa* managing its affairs.

Gaṇa-śreṣṭha (CII 3), probably, the head of a corporation.

Gaṇastha (EI 15), probably, the member of a corporation; same as Tamil *Gaṇattār*; see *Mahāgaṇastha*.

gaṇa-sthiti (IA 19), cf. *Mālavānāṁ gaṇa-sthityā*, *Mālava-gaṇa-sthiti-vaśāt*, explained as 'by, or according to, the reckoning of the Mālavas', *gaṇa* being taken to mean *gaṇanā*. But see *sthiti*.

Gaṇattār (SITI), Tamil; Sanskrit *Gaṇastha*; people belonging to a *gaṇa*.

gaṇa-vāriyam (SITI), Sanskrit-Tamil; committee managing the affairs of a *gaṇa*.

Gaṇa-vāriya-pperumakkaḷ (SITI), Sanskrit-Tamil; elders of the committee called *gaṇa-vāriyam* (q.v.).

Gaṇḍa (EI 12), cf. Tamil *Gaṇḍaṉ*; a hero, probably from the meaning 'rhinoceros'; cf. similar use of *vyāghra*, *siṁha*, etc.; also cf. *Paragaṇḍabhairava* (*EI* 29). See *Gaṇḍaṉ* and *Gaṇḍa-peṇḍāra*; also *Calamartigaṇḍa*.

gaṇḍā (IE 8-6; EI 19; IA 27), in the monetary system of some areas of medieval and modern India, regarded as equal to four cowrie-shells and $\frac{1}{20}$ of a *paṇa*; also a small area of land, twenty of which make one *kāṇī*.

gaṇḍabheruṇḍa (EI 3), a mythical double-headed eagle.

Gaṇḍagopāla (EI 30), title.

gaṇḍaka (EI 21), name of a coin; cf. *gaṇḍā*.

(*EI* 27), an official designation.

Gaṇḍakānāyaka (EI 33), official designation.

gaṇḍa-māḍa (EI 5), name of a coin; sometimes specified as 'small'; also called *kārṣāpaṇa*, *niṣka* or *gaṇḍa-niṣka*; cf. *māḍa*. See *JNSI*, Vol. XVI, p. 43.

Gaṇḍaṉ (SITI), Tamil; a warrior.

gaṇḍa-peṇḍāra (ASLV), Tamil; 'the anklet of a hero' which was worn by men of distinction.

gaṇḍa-śaila (EI 12), a boulder.

gandhakuṭī (EIA9, 18; IA 14), originally, 'a chamber for the Buddha's use'; later 'the chamber enshrining the Buddha image in a monastery'; a shrine where the image of the Buddha is worshipped; a Buddhist temple.

gāndharva (EI 28), dance and music.

gandha-śāli (EI 5), a kind of rice or paddy.

Gāndhika (EI 28; LL), a perfumer.

Gaṇeśa-caturthī (EI 5; IA 17; CII 4), name of a *tithi* and festival; same as Bhādrapada su-di 4.

Ganeśa-homa (EI 26), a rite; same as *Vināyaka-homa*.

Gaṅgaikoṇḍa (IE 8-2), title of a Coḻa king meaning 'the conqueror of the Gaṅgā'.

gaṅgā-mārga (IE 7-1-2), 'three'.

gaṅgāpupuṭaka (IA 18; CII 1), probably *gaṅgā-puppuṭaka*; a particular fish of the Ganges.

Gaṅgā-yamunā (EI 24, 29), royal insignia probably consisting of the representation of the Gaṅgā and Yamunā on the flags or at the gate.

gāṅgeya (*Ep. Ind.*, Vol. XIV, p. 38), gold.

Gaṅgā-snāna (LP), 'absence of sin'.

gaṅginikā (EI 18), a stream.

(*EI* 12), a dried up river bed.

gāṇī, cf. *aṭha-gāṇī*, a coin equal to a *ṭaṅka* (*JNSI*, Vol. XII, p. 198); cf. *jītal*.

gaṇikā (EI 33), same as *devadāsī*.

(*EI* 7), a female elephant.

gaṇikā-karaṇa, cf. *karaṇa* (LP); explained as 'the amusement department.'

Gaṇin (SII 2), an astrologer.

(*EI* 3), head of a school.

(*IA* 19; LL), Jain; a Jain eclesiastic; an *ācārya* who has disciples but has not risen to be the head of his *gaccha* or *śākhā*.

gañja (*EI* 30), Persian *ganj*; a treasury or store-house. *Utpala* on the *Bṛhatsaṁhitā*, 52. 13, explains *gañja* as *kośa-bhavana*, i.e. treasury. See *Gañjavara*.

(*IE* 8-8), a store-housc of liquor.

Gañj-ādhikārin (HRS), a treasury-officer according to the *Rājataraṅgiṇī*. See *Gañjapati*, etc.

Gañjapati (EI 13; HRS; HD), same as Persian *Ganjwar*, treasurer (*Ep. Ind.*, Vol. XIII, p. 115). See *gañja*.

Gañjavara (IE 8-3; EI 9; HD), Persian *Ganjwar*; a treasurer or store-keeper (*Ep. Ind.*, Vol. IX, p. 247; *Rājataraṅgiṇī*, V. 177). See *Gañjapati*, etc.

Ganjwar, Persian; see *Gañjavara*.

garbha (LL), a cell; cf. *pañca-garbha* (LL), 'a five-celled building'; *nava-garbha* (LL), 'a nine-celled building'; *sapta-garbha* (LL), 'seven-celled building'.

garbha-dvāra (LL), the hall-front.

garbh-āgāra (CII 1), the inner apartment of a temple or palace; same as *garbha-gṛha*.

garbha-gṛha (SITI), the innermost sanctuary of a temple; inner part of palace; same as *garbh-āgāra*.

garcā (Chamba), same as *gocara*.

Garga-yavana (EI 33), name applied to the Turkish Muslim invaders of North India, *Garga* probably being *Ghaznī*.

Garjanak-ādhirāja, *Garjanik-ādhirāja* (LP), 'the emperor of Ghaznī'.

garta, *gartā* (EI 3, 27; CII 3), a trench or pit; a boundary trench; a pit or valley; cf. *sa-gart-oṣara* (IE 8-5); also found as the termination of names of villages.

garuḍa (IA 20), the royal eagle; the white kite (in areas like Bihar and Madras).

Garuḍadhvaja (CII 4), title of a ruler.

gata-rājya, same as *vinaṣṭa-rājya* or *atīta-rājya* (q.v.).

gati (IE 7-1-2; EI 25), 'four'; also explained as five in number (EI 19).

gātra (IA 14), same as *aṅga-bhoga*.

(EI 33), same as *gotra* or *gotra-śailikā*, i.e. a memorial pillar for the dead members of one's family. See *yaṣṭi*.

gātrī (LP), cf. Gujarātī *gāḍa*, a cart.

Gauda (EI 5; ASLV), Kannaḍa; same as *Gāvuṇḍa*; a village headman; the chief farmer of a village. See *Gavuḍa*.

(*EI* 1), a temple priest.

(*IE* 8-5; EI 28), Oḍiyā; same as *gokuṭa*; a cowherd or milkman.

Gauḍo-mahāsāndhivigrahika (IE 8-3), 'the *Mahāsāndhivigrahika* of the Gauḍa country'; cf. *Mahāsāndhivigrahika*.

Gauḍī, name applied to the East Indian alphabet, language and style of composition.

Gauḍika (EI 28), maker and seller of sugar; see *Guḍika*.

Gauggulika (EI 13), a dealer in *guggulu*.

Gaulmika (IE 8-3; EI 30; CII 3, 4; HD), same as *Gulmapati* (q.v.); 'chief of a troop'; officer in charge of a *gulma* or outpost or group of guards, soldiers or policemen; 'superintendent of woods and forests' according to Fleet (*CII*, Vol. III, p. 50). See Ghoshal, *H. Rev. Syst.*, p. 246.

gaurī, a virgin; cf. *gaurī-varāṭikā*.

gaurī-paṭṭa, same as the *yoni-paṭṭa* of a *Śiva-liṅga*.

gaurī-varāṭikā, 'virgin-money'. *Gaurī* means 'a virgin' and *varāṭikā* is used primarily in the sense of *varāṭa* or *varāṭaka*, 'a cowrie-shell', and secondarily in that of 'money'. In the records of Mithilā, *gaurī-varāṭikā* means 'money to be paid to the master of a slave girl of marriageable age by the master of her bridegroom'. See *JNSI*, Vol. XVI, pp. 264 ff.

Gautamī-putra (IE 2-8), metronynic meaning 'the son of a lady born in a family belonging to the Gautama *gotra*'. Such metronymics refer to the absence of *gotr-āntara* (i.e. the change of the bride's paternal *gotra* to that of her husband at the time of marriage) in a popular form of ancient Indian marriage.

Gavuḍa (EI 5; ASLV), Kannaḍa; same as *Grāmakūṭa*, *Gauḍa*, *Gāvuṇḍa*; village headman.

Gāvuṇḍa, *Gavuṇḍu* (HD), same as *Grāmakūṭa*, *Gavuḍa*, *Gauḍa*. Cf. *Ep. Ind.*, Vol. XVI, p. 74; *JBBRAS*, Vol. X, p. 208.

gavya (*IE* 7-1-2), 'five'.

gavyūta (EI 22), a distance of about 4 miles; same as *gavyūti*.

gavyūti (EI 27), a linear measure; same as *gavyūta* (q.v.).

gayāḍa, cf. *guyāda* (EI 22), courtyard. Cf. the royal names *Gayāḍa* and *Gayāḍatuṅga*.

Gayā-mukta (EI 33), one whose *śrāddha* ceremony has been performed at Gayā.

gāyatrī (IE 7-1-2), 'twentyfour'.

gelāṭa (IA 18; CII 1), probably Sanskrit *gairāṭa*, 'a hill bird'.

geṇu (IE 8-6), Kannaḍa; 'one span'; a unit of measurment.

gevaka (CII 1), inferior.

ghāḍḍā (Chamba), a system by which the tiller receives one half of the produce. See *ghāḍḍotā*.

ghāḍḍaka, also called *ghāḍḍī* (Chamba); land cultivated on the *ghāḍḍā* system.

ghada-maṟuturu (CITD), Telugu; an unknown measure of land; a variation of *maṟuturu* (q.v.). Cf. *kāl-maṟuturu*.

ghaḍa-puṭṭi (CITD), Telugu; a variation of *puṭṭi*. Cf. *gāl-puṭṭi*.

ghāḍḍī, cf. *ghāḍḍaka*.

ghaḍiyāramu (CITD), Telugu-Kannaḍa; a gong, a watch, a clock, an hour glass; a cup with a hole at the bottom placed on water for measuring time, an hour being counted when it sinks. Cf. *ghaṭikā-gṛha*.

ghāḍḍotā (Chamba), spoken of a land tilled on the condition that one half of the produce should go to the owner. See *ghāḍḍā*, etc.

ghale (IE 8-6), Kannaḍa; measuring rod; cf. *Gaṅgana ghale*, 'the rod [measured by the length of the forearm] of a person named Gaṅga'; cf. *hasta* in *Śivacandra-hasta*, etc.

ghāṇaka (EI 2, 32), an oil-mill.

gharahaṇa (Chamba), same as *gorathā*, etc.

ghora-kṣetra (SITI), *gṛha-kṣetra*; a building site.

gharaṭhā (Chamba), also called *gharahana*, *gharaṭhāi*, *gharṭhāi*; a house site; homestead; from Sanskrit *gṛha-sthāna*.

Ghāñcika, maker of or dealer in oil (*Ep. Ind.*, Vol. XXXIV, pp. 145-46); same as Gujarātī *Ghāṁci*.

ghasra (IE 7-1-2), 'fifteen'.

ghāṭa (EI 21), name of a tax. Cf. *ghaṭṭa*.

ghaṭaka, a jar (*Ep. Ind.*, Vol. XIV, p. 309).

Ghaṭaśāsulu (CITD), Telugu; logicians. See *Ghaṭikāsāhasa*.

ghaṭi, *ghaṭī* (CII 3), same as *ghaṭikā*, the sixtieth division of a day (i.e. day and night); equal to twentyfour English minutes. Cf. *ghaḍīyāramu*.

ghaṭī (CII 4), name of a measure of capacity.

ghaṭika (CII 2-1), used in the sense of *ghaṭikā*, an hour equal to twentyfour English minutes.

ghaṭikā (CII 3; ML), an hour; time equal to twentyfour English minutes; same as *ghaṭi*, *ghaṭī*.

(*Ep. Ind.*, Vol. VIII, p. 34, note 6), an establishment oi holy and learned men. Cf. Tamil *ghaṭikai* (SII 12).

Cf. ghaṭige (SII 3), an assembly.

(*SITI*), an educational institution for advanced studies; a university; probably the same as *śālā* and *mahāśālā*. Cf. Prakrit *ghaḍia-ghaḍā* (EI 8), same as *goṣṭhī*.

ghaṭikāgṛha-karaṇa, cf. *karaṇa* (LP); the deparment oi time-keeping. Cf. *ghaḍiyāramu*.

Ghaṭikaiyār (SII 12; SITI), Tamil; members of a *ghaṭikā* managing its affairs; officials who declare to the public, by beat of tomtom, the orders of kings and other officers.

ghaṭik-ālaya (EI 1), a water-clock.

Ghaṭikā-madhyastha (SITI), an intermediary officer having the authority of the *ghaṭikā* or recognised by the *ghaṭikā*.

Ghaṭikāsāhasa (EI 8), same as the Brahmanical family name *Ghaisāsa*, also called *Ghaṭaśāsin*, etc. See *Ghaṭaśāsulu*.

ghaṭikā-śālā (EI 25), same as *ghāṭikā-sthāna*; an establishment of holy and learned men.

ghaṭikā-sthāna (EI 14, 16) 'a religious centre'; the official meeting place of learned and godly men; cf. *ghaṭikā-śālā*.

ghaṭita (CII 1), 'put together'.

(*Ind. Ant.*, Vol. XII, p. 121, text line 55), engraved.

ghaṭita-hīna-drammā (LP), '*drammas* that are wanting'.

ghaṭi-yantra (EI 14), a clock. Cf. *ghaḍiyāramu*.

ghaṭṭa (BL), bathing or landing place on the bank of a river.

(*IE* 8-5), a harbour or a mountain pass.

(*ASLV*), a contingent of elephants, the number being ten according to some authorities.

Ghaṭṭapāla (IE 8-3); EI 31), the superintendent of landing places on the river banks or of passes.

Ghaṭṭapati (EI 7; CII 4; HD), same as *Ghaṭṭapāla*; generally explained as 'an officer in charge of quays or landing places (*ghāṭs*)'; may also be an officer in charge of a pass (cf. the Orissan royal title *Aṣṭādaśa-ghaṭṭa-gondram-ādhipati*);

see *Ep. Ind.*, Vol. VII, p. 91; *JBORS*, Vol. V, pp. 582, 588.

ghoṣa (CII 4), a settlement of the milkmen.

ghoṭaka-vigraha (CII 4; BL), 'a battle of horses'; probably, an encounter of horsemen; cf. *caturdanta-samara*.

ghoṭikā (EI 31), a boundary post bearing the representation of a mare.

ghṛṇi (EI 12), a ray.

ghṛṣṭa-mūrdhaka (LP), 'with hairs of one's head fallen off.'

ghṛta-pradīpa (LL), a lamp to be burnt with ghee instead of oil.

ghumara (EI 23), used in Bastar in the sense of 'waterfalls'.

gi (IE 8-1), abbreviation of Prakrit *gimha*=Sanskrit *grīṣma* (q.v.).

gidda (CITD), Telugu-Kannaḍa; a gill, or a liquid ounce; a quarter especially of a *sola* weighing 16 *dubbus*.

gimha (CII 4), Prakrit; same as Sanskrit *grīṣma*; name of a season consisting of eight fortnights or four months.

giri (IE 7-1-2), 'seven'.

giri-durga (ASLV), hill fort.

girīndra (SII 2), 'a hill-chief'.

go (IE 7-1-2), 'one'; rarely used in the sense of 'nine' (cf. *graha*).

Cf. a-paramparā-go-balīvarda (IE 8-5) ; a cow. See *balīvarda*.

gocara (EI 15; Chamba), pasture land.

(*LP*), a tax for allowing cattle to graze in the pasture land.

gocaraka (Chamba), pasture land; same as *gocara*.

gocarman (IE 8-6; EI 28; CITD), an area of land often regarded as equal to ten *nivartanas* although the exact area varied in different ages and localities.

Gocchakapati (EI 28), official designation of uncertain import. Cf. the Bengali family name *Guchāita* < *Gochāyati* < *Gocchakapati*.

go-dvādaśī (*Ep. Ind.*, Vol. XVIII, pp. 161, 163-64), name of a *tithi*; Āśvina su-di 12; regarded doubtfully also as Mārgaśīrṣa su-di 12.

go-gauḍa (EI 12, 28), name of a tax probably levied on the cowherds; *gauḍa* is the same as *gokuṭa* meaning a cowherd or milkman.

go-grāsa, troughful of fodder for the cattle (*Ep. Ind.*, Vol. XXXV, p. 108).

gohara, *gohārā* (Chamba), a path.

gohari (EI 31), Oḍiyā; cattle track or pasture land; or probably, a road (cf. *gohara*, *gohārā*).

goja, the moon (*Ep. Ind.*, Vol. XVI, p. 58).

gojha (Chamba), pocket; pocket money; personal property.

gokara (IE 8-5; EI 4, 8, 13), probably, grazing tax.

gokarṇa (EI 9), *gokarṇa-kuśa-kusuma-karatal-odaka-pūrṇa* (EI 23), *gokarṇa-kuśalatā-pūta-hast-odakena* (*Ind. Ant.*, Vol. XV, p. 10, note 57), referring to an elaborate form of the ritual relating to donation generally indicated by the expression *udak-ātisargeṇa*; same as *gaṇḍūṣa* (in Bengali); palm hollowed to hold water and resembling a cow's ear.

gokula (EI 9), cf. 'officer in charge of the *gokulas*'; cf. *Gokul-ādhikārin*, *Gokulika*, *Gomaṇḍalika*.

(*SITI*), a temple of Kṛṣṇa; also called *āyappāḍi* in Tamil.

Gokul-ādhikārin (EI 24), superintendent of cattle; officer in charge of the royal cattle and cowpens (*Ep. Ind.*, Vol. XIV, p. 194). See *Gokulika*, *Gomaṇḍalika*. Cf. *Vivīt-ādhyakṣa*, *Vrajabhūmika*, *Gomahiṣāj-ādhyakṣa*.

Gokulika (*Ep. Ind.*, Vol. XIX, p. 71), same as *Gokul-ādhikārin*, *Gomaṇḍalika*.

Gokuṭa (IE 8-5; EI 28), same as Oḍiyā *Gauḍa*; a milkman or cowherd.

golā (IA 21), a district.

(*EI* 31), a granary.

golakā (SITI), also called *gulikā*, *goḷakkai*, *koḷakkai*, *kuḷigai*; name of a coin, probably circular in shape.

Golla (EI 3), a cowherd.

(*IE* 8-4), a small territorial unit.

Golla-vāru (CITD), Telugu; a caste of watchmen [employed as treasure-guards], generally herdsmen.

Go-mahiṣ-āj-āvikā-vaḍav-ādhyakṣa (IE 8-3), cf. *Kiśora-vaḍavā-go-mahiṣ-āj-āvik-ādhyakṣa*, etc.

Go-mahiṣy-aj-ādhyakṣa (EI 28), official designation; cf. *Go-mahiṣ-āj-āvikā-vaḍav-ādhyakṣa*.

Gomaṇḍalika (EI 18), officer in charge of the royal cattle. See *Gokulika*, *Gokul-ādhikarin*, etc.

gomaṭha (EI 12), name of a *sattra*-like institution built by a Musalman chief together with a step-well and a garden.

Gomin (IA 13), epithet of a Buddhist priest hailing from Gauḍa-viṣaya; supposed to denote a learned lay brother who held some high office on the establishment of a monastery.

gomūtrikā-bandha (CITD), the style of composition of a stanza, the second half of which repeats nearly all the syllables of the first.

gondrama (EI 30), Oḍiyā; probably, a hill fort or a state having its headquarters on a hill.

goṇī (CII 4), name of a measure of capacity; cf. *goṇī-prasṛti*.

goṇī-prasṛti (EI 1), a measure of uncertain weight; probably, a handful.

Gopa (EI 24), a watchman.

(*HD*), officer in charge of the royal cattle; officer over five or ten villages according to the *Arthaśāstra*, II. 35.

(*HRS*), according to the *Arthaśāstra*, (1) officer in charge of five or ten villages with revenue and police functions; (2) officer in charge of ten, twenty or forty families in the city; similar to the *Paṭel*, or *Paṭwārī* (*H. Rev. Syst.*, pp. 146-47).

Gopāla (IE 8-8), a milkman or cowherd.

go-patha (EI 31), a cattle-track.

gopathaśara (CII 3), perhaps 'a cattle-path'.

gopīcandana (IA 16), a kind of coloured earth.

gopracāra (EI 24, 31, 32; CII 4), pasture land.

(*EI* 30), right of grazing cattle.

go-pracāra-bhūmi (SITI), grazing-ground; same as Tamil *kaṉṟu-meypāḻ*.

gopura (EI 3, 19, 24) a gateway; the gateway of a temple; a tower.

gopura-vāśal (SII 1), Sanskrit-Tamil; the gate of a *gopura*.

goracara (Chamba), same as Sanskrit *gocara*.

goracarakā (Chamba), same as Sanskrit *gocara*.

Gorava (EI 7), a Śaiva priest; same as *Gurava*, etc.

go-sahasra (EI 16, 24), name of a gift (*mahādāna*).

go-stana (IE 7-1-2), 'four'.

goṣṭhī (EI 24; SII 3; BL), an assembly; a corporate body; cf. Tamil *goṣṭhiśeydāṉ*, convener of a *pariṣad*.

(LL), Buddhist; a committee; cf. *Bauddha-goṣṭhī*, *Goṣṭhī-śramaṇa*.

Goṣṭhika (EI 4, 24, 33; CII 4), member of a committee or assembly; member of a managing committee; member of a committee like that of the trustees.

gotra (CII 3; IA 19; CITD), a family or clan, a tribe or lineage; a caste. No Hindu can marry a girl of his own *gotra* or stock, though some forms of ancient Indian marriages did not involve the *gotr-āntara*, i.e. the change of the wife's *gotra* to that of the husband at the time of marriage (*Proc. IHC*, Annamalainagar, 1945, pp. 48 ff.). Cf *Gautamī-putra*, etc.

(*EI* 33), abbreviation of *gotra-śailikā*, a memorial pillar raised for the dead members of one's family.

gotr-āntara (IE 8-2), the change of the wife's paternal *gotra* to that of her husband, which was absent in some popular forms of marriage in ancient India (*Proc. IHC*, Annamalainagar, 1945, pp. 48 ff.).

gotra-śailikā (EI 33), a pillar raised in memory of the dead members of one's family.

Gouḍ (*ASLV*), Anglicised spelling of *Gauḍa* or *Gavuḍa* (q.v.).

Go-vallabha, cf. Prakrit *Go-vallava* (EI 24; II), a cowherd; keeper of the royal cattle; see *Mahāgovallabha* (EI 24).

Go-vallava (IE 8-3), a cowherd; Sanskrit *Go-vallabha*.

go-yūthī, cf. *sva-sīmā-tṛṇagoyūthī-gocara-paryanta* (EI 8-5); *yuthī* is the same as *yūti* (or *pūti*) used in the same context in many other records in the compound *tṛṇa-yūti* (or *tṛṇa-pūti*). *Goyūthī-gocara* may be 'the enclosure for cattle and pasture ground'.

go-yūti, same as *ga-yuthī*; cf. *yūti*.

graha (IE 7-1-2), 'nine'.

(*IA* 21), seizure; cf. *go-graha*, cattle-lifting.

Cf. sūrya-graha (EI 24), an eclipse of the sun.

grahaṇa (IE 7-1-2), 'two'.

grahaṇaka (IE 8-8; EI 30), probably, the custody or mortgage of an object.

(*LP*), an ornament; cf. Gujarātī *ghareṇuṁ*.

grāhya (IE 8-8), 'to be apprehended or recruited'.

Cf. a-kiñcid-grāhya; 'to be levied'.

grāma (IE 8-4), 'a village'; often suffixed to the names of localities.

(*EI* 24), a village assembly.

(*IE* 8-4), sometimes used to indicate the number of villages in a territory or geographical unit; but the number was often either exaggerated or traditional without relation to reality; sometimes wrongly interpreted as 'a unit of revenue assessment'. Cf. *navanavati-sahasra-grāma-bhāj* (IE 8-4), epithet of a territory. See Sircar, *Stud. Geog. Anc. Med. Ind.*, pp. 200 ff.

(*Ep. Ind.*, Vol. XXXV, pp. 146-47), a villager; same as *Grāmeyaka*.

Grāmabhartṛ (HD), same as *Grāmapati* (*Yājñavalkyasmṛti*, II. 271).

Grāma-bhogika (EI 24, 29; CII 4), probably the *Jāgīrdār* of a village or one who enjoys a village as a free-holding. Cf. *rāja-sāmanta-viṣayapati-grāmabhogika-purillaka-cāṭa-bhaṭa-sevak-ādīn* (*Ep. Ind.*, Vol. XXIX, pp. 114-15).

grāma-deva (IA 14), a village god; cf. *grāma-devatā*.

grāma-devatā (EI 3; SII 2), a village divinity; cf. *grāma-deva*.

grām-ādhipati (IE 8-4), 'headquarters of a Parganā' (cf. *triṁśad-grām-ādhipati-śrī-Kukkunūru*); also called *modala-vāḍa* or *rājadhāni* in Kannaḍa inscriptions.

(*HD*), same as *Grāmapati* (*Kāmasūtra*, V. 5. 5).

Grāma-drohin (SITI), traitor to the village; cf. *Grāmakaṇṭaka*.

Grāmāgrāma-bhojaka (IE 8-3; LL), free-holders or *Jāgīrdārs* of various villages.

grāma-grāsa (EI 5, 6, 31), a village granted for the maintenance of the donee; cf. *grām-opahāra* (EI 5).

grām-āhāra (IE 8-4; LL), 'a village-district'; a group of villages; a small territorial unit; cf. *mahāgrāma* and *āhāra*.

grāmaka (EI 8), a small village.

Grāma-kaṇṭaka (EI 24; SII 13; SITI), a traitor to the village; enemy of the security of a village; annoyance to a village. Cf. *Grāma-drohin*.

grāma-kārya (IA 8), explained as 'village rites'; probably, 'the various functions of the village'; village business (SITI); administration; committee of administration (SII 13).

Grāma-kāyastha (HD), a village scribe or *Paṭvārī*. See *Rājataraṅgiṇī*, V. 175.

Grāmakūṭa (EI 8-3); EI 30; CII 4; HD), cf. *Grāmamahattara*; the headman of a village (or probably, a member of the village council). Paiṭhīnasi and Kauṭilya (IV 5) use the word, and the commentary on the *Kāmasūtra* (V. 55) explains *Grāmakūṭa* as *halottha-vṛtti*. Cf. *Ep. Ind.*, Vol. IV, p. 285; *Ind. Ant.*, Vol. XVI, p. 24. See *Rāṣṭrakūṭa*, *Deśakūṭa*.

Grāmakūṭaka (EI 7, 12; HD), same as *Grāmakūṭa*.

Grāma-mahattara (IE 8-3; EI 12, 28), same as *Grāmakūṭa* and *Mahattara*; the village headman and a member of the village council.

Grāmamahattar-ādhikārin (EI 25), official designation; probably, *Grāma-mahattara* and *Adhikārin*.

grāma-maryādā (EI 32), fixed local usage.

Grāma-netṛ (HD), a village headman. See Śukra, II. 120.

Grāmaṇī (EI 27; LL; HD), a village headman; same as *Grāmakūṭa*. See *Hist. Dharm.*, pp. 153-54; Pāṇini, V. 2. 78.

grāma-parihāra (SITI), obligatory dues of a village.

Grāmapati (EI 24, 26, 29; IA 9; HD), cf. *Grāmakūṭa*; the headman, owner or *Jāgīrdār* of a village (*Mitākṣarā* on *Yājñavalkyasmṛti*, II. 281). See *Grāma-svāmika*, etc.

Cf. Kuḍipati (EI 18), the headman of a village.

grāma-patra (EI 9), a document indicating the revenue fixed for a village.

Grāma-pradhāna (EI 2), a village headman.

grāma-saṁsthā (LP), a village institution.

grām-āṣṭakul-ādhikaraṇa (EI 31), the administrative board (e.g. *Pañcāyat*) of a village; see *aṣṭakul-ādhikaraṇa*.

Grāma-svāmika, cf. *Gāma-sāmika* (EI 24); same as *Grāmapati*.

Grāmaṭaka (*Ep. Ind.*, Vol. XIX, p.71), official designation; probably a mistake for *Grāmakūṭaka*.

Grāma-talāra (LP), probably, something like a *Faujdār*. See *Talāra*.

grāmaṭikā (EI 9, 19; SII 1), a hamlet; a small village.

Grāmeyaka (EI 31; LL), a villager; inhabitant of a village; probably also the village headman, the same as *Grāmika* (*Ep. Ind.*, Vol. XVII, p. 327); cf. *Vaṭṭa-grāmeyaka* (EI 27); also *Grāmeyika*.

Grāmeyika (LL), a villager; same as *Grāmeyaka*.

Grāmika (IE 8-5; EI 15; CII 3; LL; HD), a village headman (*Manusmṛti*, VII. 116; *Arthaśāstra*, III. 10; *CII*, Vol. III, p. 112); same as *Grāmaṇī*, etc.

Cf. grāmika-jana-samūha (EI 24), 'an assembly of the villagers'.

grāmīya-kula (EI 24), an assembly of the village.

grām-opahāra (EI 5), same as *grāma-grāsa*.

granthavāri (IA 24), household histories in Travancore.

grāsa (EI 11; LP), food; land granted for maintenance; cf. *grāsa-lopana* (LP), confiscation of the lands given for maintenance; also cf. *grāma-grāsa*.

grāsagraha, same as *suvarṇa* (q.v.).

grāsa-vāsas (CITD), food and raiment.

gṛ (IE 8-1), also spelt *gri*; wrong abbreviation of *grīṣma* in Prakrit records.

Cf. gṛ-ṭī; abbreviation of *gṛha*.

gṛ-ca-ṭī, abbreviation of an expression probably meaning 'a mound on which houses can be (or, have been) built and fruit trees can be (or, have been) planted'. Cf. *Ep. Ind.*, Vol. XXX, p. 56.

gṛha, cf. *ghara* (EI 7), a *caitya*; a cave. Cf. *gṛha-mukha*.

gṛha-kara, cf. *ilvari*, *manai-iṟai*, *manai-ppaṇam* (SITI), house-tax.

gṛha-kṛtya (HRS), an office concerned with domestic affairs of the kingdom as indicated by the *Rājataraṅgiṇī*. See Ghoshal, *H. Rev. Syst.*, p. 250.

gṛha-mukha, cf. *ghara-mugha* (LL), the door of a cave.

Gṛhapati (EI 25; CII 3; LL), a householder; same as *Gṛhastha*.

Gṛhastha (LL), a householder; same as *Gṛhapati*.

gṛha-sthāna (EI 24), a house-site.

gṛha-vārtā (LP), household articles.

Gṛha-veṭaka (EI 9), possibly a mistake for *Gṛha-ceṭaka*, 'a servant'.

Gṛhīta-sāhasra (EI 33), probably, 'one from whom one thousand coins have been realised'.

grīṣma (EI 24; CII 4), one of the three seasons constituting the ancient Indian official year; the four months from Caitra ba-di 1 to Āṣāḍha su-di 15.

gṛ-ṭī, abbreviation of *gṛha-ṭikkara* (*ṭīkara*) or *gṛha-vāstu-ṭīkara*, 'a mound suitable for building houses'. Cf. *Ep. Ind*, Vol. XXX, p. 56.

guḍa, cf. *a-lavaṇa-guḍa-kṣobha* (IE 8-5); sugar, the production of which was the monopoly of the king or landlord.

guḍānta-patra (*Journal of the Bihar Research Society*, Vol. XL, Part 2, pp. 96-97), name of a type of document, the exact nature of which is doubtful; probably, a kind of lease deed. Cf. *guṇa-patra*.

guḍḍa, *guḍḍa-dhvaja* (IA 10), Kannaḍa; the meaning of *guḍḍa* is doubtful; probably, a disciple.

gūḍha-jāla-bandha (CITD), probably, the style of a verse with an artificial arrangement of the letters.

gūḍha-maṇḍapa (HA), an adjacent hall; hall in front of the sanctum, where devotees carry on worship, etc.

Gūḍha-puruṣa (HD), an officer of the secret service. See *Ep. Ind.*, Vol. XXII, p. 156.

Guḍika (EI 28, 31), maker or seller of sugar; see *Gauḍika*.

guggula (CII 4), bdellium.

guhā (SITI), literally, 'a cave'; a monastery.

guhā-vihāra (CII 2-1), a cave-monastery.

Gujarātī, the people, language and alphabet of Gujarat. See *Boḍiyā*.

gulikā , cf. *pudu-kkuḻigai* (SITI), name of a coin; also *śeṇapaka-kkuḻigai* (SITI), name of a coin probably struck by the Śambuvarāyas; *puḻḻi-guḻikai-varāhaṉ* (SITI), name of a gold coin; *vīracampaṉ-kuḻigai* (SITI), a coin struck and issued by the Śambuvarāya king Vīracampa; *vāḻāl-vaḻitiṟantāṉ guḻikai* (SITI), a Pāṇḍya coin supposed to have been issued by Jaṭā-varman Sundara-pāṇḍya I who had the title *Vāḻāl-vaḻi-tiṟantāṉ*.

gulma (EI 8, 12), a battalion, squadron or outpost. Cf. *Gaulmika*. (IE 8-5), a bush; cf. *sa-gulma-latāka* as an epithet of a gift village.

gulma-deya (HRS), dues paid at the military or police station as indicated in the *Arthaśāstra*. See Ghoshal, *H. Rev. Syst.*, pp. 78, 227.

Gulmapati (HD), officer in charge of a *gulma* which means a group or outpost of guards, soldiers or policemen; same as *Gaulmika*. Cf. *JBORS*, Vol. V, p. 588.

gulpha (IE 7-1-2), 'two'.

guṇa (IE 7-1-2; EI 15, 17, 25), 'three'; rarely in late records, 'six'.

(*EI* 8), six in number.

Guṇacarita (BL), supposed to be an epithet of a Pratīhāra king.

guṇ-ākṣara (LP), a document for a lease of land by the proprietors to cultivators; see *guṇa-patra*.

Cf. guṇ-ākṣarāṇi (LP), a concession letter.

guṇa-patra (LP), a lease of land granted by propriteors to tenants or cultivators for the purpose of cultivating or improving it; cf. *Pañcāladeśīya-kulānāṁ guṇa-patra-vidhiḥ*, 'an order of royal favour concerning the farmers of the Pañcāla country'; also cf. Gujarātī *gaṇotnāmuṁ*. See *guṇākṣara*, *guḍāntapatra*.

guṇḍa (EI 8), probably, a niche.

guñjā (IE 8-8; IA 26), same as *raktikā* or *rati*.

(*EI* 12), a kettle-drum.

guṇṭha (IE 8-6; EI 28, 31), a land measure of Orissa; equal to one-twentififth of a Māṇa.

(*Ep. Ind.*, Vol. XII, p.62), Telugu; a pond; cf. *silā-guṇṭha*.

gupta, cf. *gupt-ākṣarāṇi* (LP), same as *gupta-paṭṭaka*, a deed of permanent lease. See Tamil *guttagai*=Sanskrit *guptakā*.

guptakā, see *guttagai*.

gupta-paṭṭaka (LP), a deed of permanent lease; called *gupta* probably because it reserved the right of use to a particular man; cf. *gupt-ākṣara* (also *gupta*).

gupti (EI 4), three in number.

guracarakā (Chamba), same as *gocara*.

Gurava, same as *Gorava*; epithet of a Śaiva priest (*Ind. Ant.*, Vol. XIV, p. 140, note 4); also supposed to be a Jain priest.

(*EI* 4), a teacher; cf. *Gorava*.

Gurāva (IA 11), same as *Gorava*; a Śaiva priest.

guru (SII 1), a preceptor; also 'the head' as in *Caṇḍikāśrama-guru*.

guru-dakṣiṇā (EI 32), money paid to the preceptor for initiation.

Gurumukhī, also spelt *Gurmukhī*; alphabet in which the Punjabi language is written by the Sikhs.

gurv-āyatana (EI 21, 28) a temple where one's deceased *guru* (preceptor) is worshipped.

guttagai (ASLV), Sanskrit *guptakā*; a contract or lease.

guttige (ASLV), a contract; cf. *guttagai*.

guvāka, cf. *sa-guvāka-nārikela* (IE 8-5); arecanut palms, the enjoyment of which was not allowed to the ordinary tenants.

H

hāda (IE 8-6), Kannaḍa; same as Sanskrit *pāda*; a land measure equal to one-fourth of the standard measure which was the *mattaru* or *nivartana*.

Haḍapada (EI 11), the bearer of the king's betel-bag (cf. Oḍiyā *Vāguli*, etc.); also explained as 'a courtier'.

hāga (IE 8-8, EI 5), Kannaḍa; same as *pāga*, or Sanskrit *bhāga*; name of a coin.

Hairaṇyaka (LL), *Hairaṇyika*; a treasurer; also a goldsmith or mint-master. Cf. *Hiraṇyakāra*, *Sauvarṇika*.

hala (IE 8-6), literally 'a plough'; a free-holding (cf. *bhikṣu-hala*); an area of land, which was not exactly the same in different ages and localities (EI 7,24,29,30,31; CII 4).

(*IA* 18), a land measure equal to one-fourth of a *sīrā* (cf. *halavāhā*); half of a *kula*; one plough-measure.

(*EI* 3), probably, 'arable land'; cf. *sītā*.

hāla (EI 19), a land measure; same as *hala*.

haladagāṅga (IA 19), explained as 'the portion having (*ga*) water (*da*) and arable land (*hala*)'; meaning doubtful; probably the name of a locality.

hala-daṇḍa (EI 33), tax on ploughs.

hala-kalita, 'cultivated [land]' (*Ep. Ind.*, Vol. XV, p. 297, text line 25).

Hālakiya (LL), a ploughman.

halavāhā (IA 18), a land measure; cf. *hala*.

hali (EI 24), a land measure; same as *hala*.

Hālika (LL), a ploughman (*Ep. Ind.*, Vol. XV, p. 274 and note).

Hālikā (EI 15), feminine form of *Hālika*, 'an agriculturist or ploughman'.

halikā-kara, cf. *halirākara*.

halirākara (CII 3), a fiscal term of uncertain implication; probably a mistake for *halikā-kara*, 'plough-tax'.

Hammīra (EI 2l, 33,34), derived from Arabic *Amīr*, often adopted by Hindu princes as a personal name; sometimes written as *Hambīra* and *Ahaṁvīra* (EI 34). Cf. *Suratrāṇa*.

Haṁsa (EI 15), an ascetic; cf. *Paramahaṁsa*.

haṁsapada, same as *suvarṇa* (q.v.); same as *kākapada* (q.v.).

haṁyamana (EI 32,35), same as *hañjamana*; regarded by some as derived from Persian *anjumān*; cf. *haṁyamana-paura*, explained as 'the assembly of the Parsees'. But see *añjuvaṇṇam*.

haṇa (IE 8-8; EI 8), Kannaḍa; same as Sanskrit *paṇa*; name of a coin.

Haṇḍikāpati (EI 5), epithet of a Brāhmaṇa donee; meaning uncertain. *Haṇḍikā* means 'an earthern pot [for cooking]', and the expression may mean 'the head of a joint family (i.e one responsible for feeding the family)'.

hañjamaṇa, hañjamana (EI 25, 32), regarded by some as 'a Parsee colony', same as Persian *anjumān* (cf. *haṁyamana*), though really it is the same as Tamil *añjuvaṇṇam*=Sanskrit *pañca-varṇa*.

hara (IE 7-1-2), 'eleven'.

hāraka, cf. 'one *hāraka* of barley corn' (cf. *Ep. Ind.*, Vol. XI, p. 30, text line 2); possibly *bhāraka*, a load or measure.

hara-nayana (IE 7-1-2), 'three'.

haraṇī, cf. *Hastavapra-haraṇī* (EI 17), a district; probably a mistake for *āharaṇī*.

haribāhu (IE 7-1-2), 'four'.

haricandana (CITD), a sort of yellow sandal-wood; one of the five trees of *svarga*; a title of nobility in medieval Orissa (*Ep. Ind.*, Vol. XXXIII, p. 4); cf. *Śrīcandana*.

hari-dina (SITI), 'the day of Hari'; Saturday; the *ekādaśī* day.

hārita (CII 1), 'caused to be imported'.

harītaka, cf. *a-harītaka-śāka-puṣpa-grahaṇa* (IE 8-5); myrobalan [which the villagers were obliged to supply to the king or landlord on occasions or to the touring officers].

Hārītī-putra (IE 8-2), originally a metronymic (cf. *Gautamī-putra*), but later sometimes adopted by members of a royal family like a dynastic usage.

harmikā (EI 28), a pavilion.

harmya (LL), a temple or pavilion.

hasantikā (IA 15), a brazier or portable heater; also called *kaṅgār* in Kashmiri.

hasta (IE 8-6), a cubit (24 *aṅgulas*); sometimes regarded as 36 *aṅgulas* (27 inches), 20$\frac{3}{4}$ inches, 34 inches, etc., in length; cf. *Śivacandra-hasta*, 'the cubit measured according to the length of the forearm of Śivacandra' (cf. *ghaḻe*).

(*EI* 23; SII 2), a square cubit; a land measure.

(*Ep. Ind.*, Vol XIV, p. 366 and note), probably the same as *pakṣa*, 'a fortnight'.

hasta-bhāṁ (LP), abbreviation of *hastaka-bhāṇḍārin*; 'by the hand of (i.e. through) the *Bhāṇḍārin*'.

hastaka (EI 31), same as *hasta*.

hasta-prakṣepa (EI 23), obstruction.

hasti-bandha (EI 32), name of a tax; cf. *hasti-daṇḍa*.

hasti-daṇḍa (IE 8-5; EI 33), name of the tax for keeping elephants. Cf. *hasti-bandha*.

hasti-danta (IE 8-5, EI 1), 'ivory', referring to the right to keep elephants' tusks without surrendering them to the king.

Hastikośa, official designation (cf. *The Successors of the Sātavāhanas*, p. 110, note 2), mentioned along with *Vīrakośa* as an officer related to a district; probably, an officer in charge of elephants or the elephant corps.

hastin (IE 7-1-2), 'eight'.

Hastipaka, cf. *Hāthivaka* (EI 18), keeper of elephants.

Hasti-sādhanika (EI 30), leader of the elephant corps; cf. *Gajasāhanī*, etc.

hastiśālā-karaṇa, cf. *karaṇa* (LP); the department of elephants.

Hasti-vaidya (EI 38), the physician for elephants.

hast-odaka, cf. *hatha-paṁni*, etc.

Hasty-adhyakṣa (BL; EI 18), keeper of elephants; officer in charge of the elephant corps. Cf. *Hasti-sādhanika*, etc.

Hasty-āroha (*Sel. Ins.*, p. 54), elephant-rider or elephant-driver; cf. *Hāthāroha* (EI 18).

Hasty-aśva-go-mahiṣ-āj-āvik-ādhyakṣa (IE 8-3), officer or officers in charge of elephants, etc.; *Nauk-ādhyakṣa*, *Bal-ādhyakṣa*, etc., are often mentioned separately in the same context.

Hasty-aśva-jana-vyāpṛta, *Hasty-aśva-jana-vyāpṛtaka* (EI 33), leader or leaders of the elephant corps, cavalry and infantry. Cf. *Hasty-aśv-oṣṭra-bala-vyāpṛta*, *Karī-turagapaṭṭasāhaṇi*, etc.

Hasty-aśv-oṣṭra-bala-vyāpṛta (EI 33), *Hasty-aśv-oṣṭra-bala-vyāpṛtaka* (EI 23, HD), military officer or officers in charge of the elephant, horse and camel corps.

Hasty-aśv-oṣṭra-go-mahiṣ-āj-āvik-ādhyakṣa (IE 8-3), cf. *Kiśoravaḍavā-go-mahiṣ-āj-āvik-ādhyakṣa*.

Hasty-aśv-oṣṭra-nau-bala-vyāpṛtaka (IE 8-3; EI 24, 29; HD), military officer or officers in charge of the elephant force, cavalry, camel corps and navy. See Vogel, *Ant. Ch. St.*, p. 166; *Ep. Ind.* Vol. XVII, p. 321. Cf. *Hasty-aśv-oṣṭra-go-mahiṣ-āj-āvik-ādhyakṣa*. It has to be noted that these two are never mentioned together while, on the other hand, one is used in place of the other. See *Naubala-hasty-aśva-go-mahiṣ-ājāvik-ādi-vyāpṛtaka*, etc.

hatha-paṁṇi, hatha-pāṇi, hatha-pāṇī (Chamba), libation of water; from Sanskrit *hasta-pānīya*. See *hast-odaka*.

haṭṭa (EI 1, 30, LP), a market or market-place.

haṭṭa-dāna (EI 3), name of a tax; tolls collected at the market place. Cf. *aṭṭapati-bhāga*.

haṭṭa-mārga (EI 19), the main bazar.

haṭṭa-rathyā (EI 30), passage between rows of stalls in the market.

haṭṭa-vyavaharamāṇa (LP), probably, 'current in the market (*haṭṭa*)'.

haṭṭikā (LP), a market.

(*EI* 4) probably 'market-dues', mentioned along with *talapāṭaka* or *talavāṭaka*.

havana (SII 3), a burnt oblation.

havir-bali (SITI), same as *śrī-bali*; *bali* offered with cooked food; same as Tamil *ti-yeṟiśoṟu*; tax payable for meeting the expenses of the same in a temple.

Hayapati (EI 1, 24, 29; BL; CII 4), same as *Aśvapati*; 'the lord of horses'; keeper of horses' or a leader of horsemen.

he (IE 8-1), abbreviation of *hemanta* (q. v.).

heḍa, cf. *heḍāu, heḍavālā* (LP), a man who wanders along with a herd of cattle (*heḍa*) for selling them.

heḍāvika (EI 12), also called *heḍāvuka*; a horse-dealer. See *heḍa*.

Hĕggaḍĕ (IE 8-3; EI 28; ASLV) Kannaḍa; official designation indicating a chief, superintendent or director; same as *Vĕrgaḍĕ, Pĕrgaḍĕ, Adhyakṣa*, etc.

hĕjjuṅka (EI 21), Kannaḍa; name of a tax; also called *pĕrjuṅka*; Sanskrit *mahāśulka* or *bṛhac-chulka*.

hema (IE 8-1), abbreviation of *hemanta*. See also *hema-dhānyaka*.

hemadhānyaka, same as *māṣa* (*JNSI*, Vol. XVI, p. 45); sometimes *hema* or *dhānaka* is used in the same sense (ibid., p. 44).

hema-garbha (EI 12, 16; SII 3), name of a *mahādāna*; same as *hiraṇya-garbha*.

hem-āśva (EI 16), name of a *mahādāna*.

hemāśva-ratha (EI 12), name of a *mahādāna*.

hema-ṭaṅka, 'a gold *ṭaṅka* (q.v.)'. See *JNSI*, Vol. XXII, p. 197.

hemidrachma (IE 8-8), name of a Greek coin.

Hĕri-Lāḷa-Kannaḍa-sandhivigrahin (IE 8-3), same as Sanskrit *Mahā-Lāṭa-Karṇāṭa-sandhivigrahin*; the same officer is sometimes also called *Mahāpradhāna*, *Antaḥpur-ādhyakṣa*, *Manĕ-vĕrgaḍĕ*, etc., additionally. Cf. *Sandhivigrahin*.

Hĕri-Lāḷa-sandhivigrahin (IE 8-3), 'the great *Sandhivigrahin* of Lāṭa'; cf. *Sandhivigrahin*.

Hĕri-Lāṭa-Karṇāṭa-sandhivigrahin (IE 8-3), 'the great *Sandhivigrahin* of Lāṭa and Karṇāṭa'; cf. *Sandhivigrahin*.

Hĕri-sandhivigrahin (IE 8-3), Kannaḍa-Sanskrit; same as *Mahāsandhivigrahin*.

hevaka (IA 18), love or desire; same as Arabic *hawwa*.

hi (IE 8-1), abbreviation of *hiraṇya*, 'cash' or 'revenue income in cash'. Cf. *sāṁ-hi*.

hīn-ākṣara (LP), 'with some words wanting'.

hīnavādin (LP), the defeated party.

Hiṇḍipaka (LP), explained as 'a touring revenue officer'.

hīṇḍolī (LP), a swing.

Hindurāja-suratrāṇa (IE 8-2), title assumed by some of the Vijayanagara kings, adopted from the Muslim royal title *Sulṭān*. See *Suratrāṇa*, *Hindurāya-suratrāṇa*.

Hindurāya-suratrāṇa (*Ep. Ind.*, Vol. I, p. 363), title of the Vijayanagara kings, *Suratrāṇa* being the same as Arabic *Sulṭān*. See *Hindurāja-suratrāṇa*.

hīni (CII 1), same as Sanskrit *hāni*; loss or diminution.

hiraṇya (IE 8-5; EI 12,28,29), same as *hirany-āya*, *hiraṇya-deya*; tax payable to the king in cash; dues payable in coins; cash; sometimes abbreviated as *hi* as in *sāṁ-hi*=*sāṁvatsarika-hiraṇya*, annual revenue income in cash; cf. *a-hiraṇya-dhānya-praṇaya-pradeya* (IE 8-5); it may be in addition to the tax in grain or in lieu of the latter. Cf. Tamil *kāś-āya*, etc.

(*HRS*), king's share of certain crops paid in cash. (*CII* 1), probably, 'money'.

hiraṇyagarbha (EI 16; IA 10; SII 3), name of a *mahādāna.*

Hiraṇyakāra (LL), a treasurer; also a goldsmith or mint-master. Cf. *Hairaṇyika.*

Hiraṇyasāmudāyika (IE 8-3), a collector of revenue in cash; sometimes mentioned along with the *Audraṅgika* or the collector of the *udraṅga* tax probably levied in grains.

hiraṇyāśva (EI 24), name of a *mahādāna.*

hiraṇyāśvaratha (EI 12), name of a *mahādāna*; same as *hemāśvaratha.*

hiraṇy-āya (EI 7), tax in cash; cf. *hiraṇya-deya*, *kāś-āya.*

Hiriya-bhāṇḍāgārin (IE 8-3), Kannaḍa-Sanskrit; same as *Mahābhāṇḍāgārin.*

hiraṇya-deya (EI 17), tax in cash; cf. *hiraṇy-āya*, *kāś-āya.*

hobaḻi, also spelt *hobḻi* (IE 8-4; ASLV), Kannaḍa; a small territorial unit like a Parganā.

hobḻi, cf. *hobaḻi.*

holī (EI 3, 5), the spring festival.

homa (BL; SII 3), an oblation; name of a ceremony.

hon, same as *hūn.*

hora, *horaka* (EI 9), probably, a foreign word meaning 'a lady''

Horamurta (CII 2-1), a foreign word explained as 'donation-master [of someone else]'; cf. *Dānapati.*

hotṛ (IE 7-1-2), 'three'.

hrada (LL), a tank.

hrasita (IE 8-3), cf. *svayaṁ hrasite karṇe*; partly cut off.

Hṛtapragrāh-āmātya (EI 31), officer in charge of the recovery of stolen property. See *Ep. Ind.*, Vol. XXXIV, p. 29.

hūhūkānta (IA 18), the moon.

hūn (IE 8-8), same as *varāha*; name of a gold coin of about 50 grains, called *pagoda* or 'star *pagoda*' in English.

huṇḍikā (LP), a bill of exchange (*Rājataraṅgiṇī*, V. 266).

hutāśana (IE 7-1-2), 'three'.

I

ibha (EI 25), 'eight'.

Ibhya (CII 1), same as *Rājanya* or *Kṣatriya.*

iḍaṅgaḻi (EI 28), Tamil; a measure of capacity.

īḍara-vāru, *īḍige-vāḍu* (CITD), Telugu; a toddy-man or arrack-drawer; from *īḍa*, 'a date tree', *ilā* (IE 7-1-2), 'one'.

Īḻam (SII 1), Tamil name of Ceylon.

Iḷaiya-nāyanār (SITI), the same as the god Subrahmaṇya.

īḻa-kkāśu, also called *īḻa-kkaruṅ-kāśu* and *karuṅ-kāśu* (SITI); the Ceylonese coin.

Immaḍi (IE 8-2), Kannaḍa; literally, 'double' or 'twice'; prefixed to the names of certain kings in order to distinguish them from their predecessors bearing the same name; cf. *Nūrmaḍi, Mummuḍi.*

indra (IE 7-1-2), 'fourteen'.

(*EI* 7), a Jain priest.

indracchanda (SII 2), name of a jewel.

indra-daṇḍa (CII 4), a pole raised in honour of Indra; also called *indra-dhvaja, śakra-dhvaja,* etc.

indra-dṛṣṭi (IE 7-1-2), 'one thousand'.

iindr-āsana (IA 23), hemp.

indriya (IE 7-1-2; EI 5), five in number; 'five'.

indu (IE 7-12), 'one'.

Īśa (EI 23), the god Śiva; the king.

(*IE* 7-1-2), 'eleven'.

īśa-dṛś (IE 7-1-2), 'three'.

iṣṭāpūrtta (EI 4; SII 3), a charitable deed; performance of charitable deeds.

iṣṭi, used in the sense of *viṣṭi*; cf. *sarv-eṣṭi-parihāra-parihṛta.*

iṣu (IE 7-1-2), 'five'.

īśvara (IE 7-1-2), 'eleven'; name-ending of Śiva-liṅgas.

īśvar-ālaya (SII 11-1), a temple; a Śiva temple.

itihāsa (EI 13), legendary lore.

J

jadiākṣetra (IA 16), explained as 'a kind of land', but may be 'land of a person named Jadiā'.

jagat (IE 7-1-2), 'three'.

jagati, jagatī (EI 11), explained variously as 'ground'; (EI 3), 'lower ground or compound'; (EI 1), 'a kind of building'; also as 'railed parapet' (R. Narsimhachar, *The Keśava Temple at Somanāthapura,* p. 2). Cf. *devagṛha-jagatī* (IA 14); also *jagati-ppaḍai* (SII 2), the upper tier of the basement. See *jagatī* below.

jagatī (HA), same as *bhamatī*; the corridor of a shrine

on the four sides of its open court, used for circumambulation of the main shrine.

(*IE* 7-1-2), 'twelve'; sometimes also 'fortyeight'; rarely used in the sense of 'the earth' to indicate 'one'.

jagatīpura (EI 3), supposed to be the same as *brahmapurī* or Kannaḍa *jagati-kaṭṭĕ* which is 'the raised square seat around a tree before a village'.

jāgīr (EI 33; BL), Persian; a fief; a tenure under Muhammadan rule, in which the public revenues of a given tract of land were made over, either conditionally or unconditionally, to persons like a servant of the State together with the powers required to enable them to collect and appropriate such revenues and administer the general government of the tract. Cf. Wilson's Glossary. See *Jāgīrdār*.

Jāgīrdār (EI 33), Persian; a fief-holder. Cf. *jāgīr*.

jāgṛ (CII 1), cf. [*yūyaṁ*] *jāgṛta sampratipādayitum*, 'you would succeed in accomplishing [your duty]'.

jāhnavī-vaktra (IE 7-1-2), 'one thousand'.

jala, cf. *sa-jala-sthala* (IE 8-5); the waters [in a village].

(*IE* 7-1-2), used in the sense of *jaladhi* to indicate 'four'.

jāla (*Ep. Ind.*, Vol. XIV, p. 309), cf. Sanskrit *jālaka*, 'a bunch of buds'; a load.

jaladhi (IE 7-1-2), 'four'; see *sāgara*.

jala-durga (ASLV), a fort surrounded by water.

jalajakaraṇḍa (CITD), probably, some sort of drum which was either made of conch or shell or was shaped like a lotus.

jala-kara (IE 8-5; EI 4), 'water-tax' paid for fishing rights, etc., in tanks, lakes and rivers; sometimes wrongly read as *jāta-kara* (*Ep. Ind.*, Vol. VIII, p. 157, note 1).

jala-karaṇa, cf. *karaṇa* (LP); explained as 'navy'.

jala-krīḍā (ASLV), water sports.

jalanidhi (IE 7-1-2), 'four'; see *sāgara*.

jala-pavitra (SII 3), a ceremony.

jal-āśaya (IE 7-1-2), 'four'; see *sāgara*.

jala-yantra (SII 2, 3), a water-lever.

jala-yātrā (IA 13), Jain; the festival of bathing a Tīrthaṅkara on the occasion of the consecration of an image or of the erection of a *dhvaja-stambha* or of the prevalence of a plague.

jālī (EI 5), a trellis window.

jamalikāmbali (IA 18), also spelt *yamalikāmbali* (q. v.).

jamātha (IA 11), Indianised form of Arabic *jamā'at*; the congregation of a community. See *Ep. Ind.*, Vol. XXXIV, p. 144.

jambu-dvīpa, jambū-dvīpa (CII 1), used in the sense of 'the earth' or the dominions of the Maurya emperor Aśoka; cf. *pṛthivī*.

jana (IE 7-1-2), 'one'.

janapada, jānapada (IE 8-3; EI 23, 33), people of the countryside; regarded by some as an official designation (EI 26), and by others as a corporate body (EI 21).

Jana-pradhānin (SITI), probably, a minister governing a district.

Janendra (CII 3; IA 15), wrongly interpreted as 'the lord of a people or tribe, a tribal ruler'; really, the same as *Narendra*, 'a king'.

jāṅgala (IA 18), cf. *s-ānūpa-jāṅgala*, an epithet of the gift land; either 'arid' or 'covered with jungle'.

jaṅgama, cf. *sa-sthāvara jaṅgama* (IE 8-5); the moveable belongings of a village.

(*SITI*), a priest of the Liṅgāyat or Vīraśaiva sect.

jaṅghā (HRS), forced service as messenger, as indicated by the Jātakas; also same as *Jaṅghākarika*.

Jaṅghākarika (HRS), 'one who pays the royal dues by means of his legs'; 'one who is liable to compulsory service as a messenger', according to the *Amarakośa*. Same as *Jaṅghā* (q.v.).

jaṅghāla, an embankment (*JAS*, Letters, Vol. XX, p.204).

Jāṅghika (HRS), same as *Jaṅghā* or *Jaṅghākarika*.

Jānī (EI 22), a corruption of *Yājñika*.

janīno (IA 17), 'kind to people'.

janitha (EI 13), cf. *sudhā-janitha-niḥsyandad-vapuḥ*, 'its body welling forth from nectarous sources'.

janma-bhūmi, called *janma-kkāṇi* in Tamil (SITI), gift of land, probably made for the lifetime of a person.

janma-patra (EI 1), a document recording the birth of a child prepared by an astrologer on payment.

jānu (IE 7-1-2), 'two'.

jāta (EI 2; CII 1), a living being.

jātaka (LL), Buddhist; birth-story [of one who is to be a Buddha in a future life]; story of a previous birth of Gautama Buddha.

jātaka-kkuḍi (SITI), Sanskrit-Tamil; persons who have undertaken to serve for their lifetime in a temple, etc.

jāta-kara (IA 15), explained as 'a tax on things grown'; a mistake for or misreading of *jala-kara* (q.v.).

jāta-karman (EI 4), a ceremony performed at the birth of a child.

jāti (IE 7-1-2), 'twentytwo'.

jāti-siddh-āya (SITI), communal tax payable in coin; cf. *inavari* or *inavari-kkāśu* of Tamil inscriptions.

Jaṭila (LL), an ascetic.

jāti-smaraṇa-jñāna (HA), knowledge of previous births.

jātīya, cf. *jñātīya*.

jatuka (EI 2), a bat.

jauhar (IA 29), *javhar* (IA 6), Rājasthānī; funeral pile; commitment of suicide *en masse*; same as *sākā* or *śākā*.

jayā (IA 23), hemp.

(*EI* 12), name of a *tithi*.

Jayadhara (IE8-2), royal title; translated from Greek *Nikephoros*.

jaya-ghaṇṭā (EI 15; IA 12), a gong.

jāyāmya (IA 19), a kind of charm.

Jayanapati (EI 13), probably, an officer in charge of armour or the armoury. Cf. *jayanaśālā-karaṇa*.

jayanaśālā-karaṇa, cf. *karaṇa* (LP), explained as 'the armour department'. Cf. *Jayanapati*.

jayantapura (EI 4), probably, the same as *brahmapurī*.

jayantī (EI 9, IA 26), the twelfth *tithi*; the 12th *tithi* of a lunar month joined with the Punarvasu *nakṣatra*.

jayantī-vrata (IA 6), a festival in which *maṇḍapanirmāṇa-jāgaraṇa-pratimādān-ādi* (erection of a shed, watching through the night, distribution of images, etc.) take place.

Jayapāla (SITI), a class of merchants.

Jāyāpara (LL), probably, a householder.

jaya-patra, jayarekha-patra (SITI), a certificate of victory in a dispute; a copy of the judgement. See *jayarekha-patrikā*.

(*EI* 5), a cetificate of success.

jayarekha-patrikā (ASLV), a certificate of victory. See *jayapatra, jayarekha-patra*.

jaya-skandhāvāra (EI 30, 33; CII 3; BL) 'camp of victory'; the royal camp or capital; epithet of royal camps or residences; same as *skandhāvāra*.

jaya-stambha (EI 23, 30, 33; CII 4; SII 1, 11-1), a pillar of victory; cf. *dharma-jaya-stambha* (IA 19).

jayika (IE 8-8), the party that comes off victorious in a dispute.

jemaka (IE 8-5; EI 25, 28), meals or food which the villagers were obliged to provide to the royal officers on tour; the obligation of the villagers to provide food to such officers; wrongly explained by some as 'a tax for the boarding of touring royal officers' (CII 4). Cf. Marāṭhī *jevā*, 'a feed, a meal; subsistence which the villagers were bound to provide for the subordinate servants or Peons when sent to receive the collections' (Wilson's Glossary, s.v.).

jena (CITD), Telugu; a span (about 7 inches).

Jenā (*Ep. Ind.*, Vol. XXVIII, p. 304), Oḍiyā; 'a prince'; a title of nobility; later stereotyped as a family name in Orissa.

jhampin (EI 12), 'excelling'.

jhāṭa (*Ep. Ind.*, Vol. V, p. 183), a shrub, wood or thicket; Bengali *jhāḍ*; a bush; used in *sa-jhāṭa-viṭapa* (EI 27).

jhāṭa-viṭapa (EI 8-5), bushes and shrubs.

jilo, jiḷo, jīlo (Chamba), a land measure. Cf. *aṭu*.

Jina, same as *Tīrthaṅkara*.

(*IE* 7-1-2), 'twentyfour'.

(*LL*), an epithet of the Buddha.

jina-bhavana (EI 24), a Jain temple.

Jina-kalpin (HA), a Jain monk practising rigorous austerities like those practised by the Jinas before their attainment of *kevala-jñāna*.

Jina-mātṛ (HA), the mother of a Jina.

jina-nagara, cf. Tamil *śinakaram* (SITI), a Jaina temple.

jina-nigama (EI 24), a township in the possession of a Jain temple or, more probably, a Jain temple (cf. *jina-nagara*).

Jina-yugma (HA), an image showing two Tīrthaṅkaras; a pair of Jina images.

jīrṇa-śreṣṭhi-śrīmalla-priya (LP), name of a coin struck by the old *Śreṣṭhin* named Śrīmalla. Cf. *śreṣṭhijīrṇa-viśvamalla-priya*.

jīrṇa-viśvamalla-priya (LP), literally, 'the favourite (coin) of old Viśvamalla'; name of a coin. Cf. *jīrṇa-śreṣṭhi-śrīmalla-priya* and *śreṣṭhi-jīrṇa-viśvamalla-priya*; also cf. *vīsalapriya-dramma*.

jīrṇ-oddhāra (EI 23, 26; HA), repairs or renovation and conservation.

jita, jīta (EI 28, 29), income or wages; revenue income; derived from Sanskrit *jīvita* in the same sense.

jītal (SII 1), a copper coin; Indianised as *jithala*; $\frac{1}{48}$th of a silver *ṭaṅka* of the Delhi Sulṭāns (*JNSI*, Vol. XVI, p. 44); sometimes regarded as a copper coin equal to $\frac{1}{3}$ of a silver *tār* which was itself equal to $\frac{1}{6}$ of a gold *fanam* (*SII*, Vol. I, p. 161); also called *dehlīwāl* (*Num. Supl.*, No. 38, p. 33).

jitaṁ bhagavatā, also quoted as *jitaṁ Viṣṇunā* (CII 3, etc.); 'victory has been achieved by the Divine One, i. e. Viṣṇu'; an invocation used at the commencement of certain inscriptions.

jīthala, same as *jītal*. See *JNSI*, Vol. XXII, p. 197.

jīva-loka (EI 3), a village institution of uncertain meaning.

jīvana (SITI), maintenance; cf. *jīvaṇa-śeṣa*. See also *bhṛtyebhyo jīvanaṁ kartuṁ* (*Ep. Ind.*, Vol. XXXV, pp. 109-10).

jīvana-śeṣa (SITI), maintenance. Cf. *jīvana*.

Jīva-putrā, Prakrit *Jīva-putā* (EI 24), a lady whose son is (or, sons are) still living.

jīvita (EI 28; SII 13; ASLV; SITI), maintenance; income or wages; also called *jīvita-ppaṟṟu*, *jita* and *jīta*.

Jīvita-kkārar (SITI), persons in enjoyment of lands in the *jīvita* (maintenance) tenure; a class of officials enjoying *jīvita*.

Jīyar (EI 25; SITI), an ascetic (*sannyāsin*) looking after the affairs of a temple; same as *Maṭh-ādhipati*.

jñāna-dīkṣā (EI 32), a kind of initiation.

jñāpaka (SITI; ASLV), remembrancer; memorandum of events and happenings.

jñātīya (*Ep. Ind.*, Vol. VIII, pp. 208, 229), used in the sense of *jātīya*; e.g. *Prāgvāṭa-jñātīya*=*Prāgvāṭa-jātīya* (i.e. 'belonging to the Prāgvāṭa community).

Jo (EI 30), an abbreviation of *Joṣī*, same as *Jyotiṣin*, an astrologer or astronomer.

joḍa (*Ep. Ind.*, Vol. XXXI, p. 19), used in some East Indian records in the sense of 'a canal'. Cf. *joṭī*, *jolaka*.

jolaka (EI 4), a canal; same as Bengali *jolā*; cf. *joḍa*.

Joṣī (EI 30), modification of Sanskrit *Jyotiṣin*.

joṭī, same as *joṭikā* (EI 28), a stream.

joṭikā (*Ep. Ind.*, Vol. IV, p. 253, text iine 37), a canal; same as *joḍa* and *joṭī* or *joḍī*.

jūhaka (EI 3), a village institution of uncertain meaning.

jvalana (IE 7-1-2), 'three'.

Jyeṣṭh-ādhikaraṇika (EI 18, 31), explained as 'the chief judge'; senior officer, chief officer of a class, or officer in charge.

Jyeṣṭha-devara (LP), elder brother of the husband.

Jyeṣṭha-kāyastha (IE 8-3; EI 4, 24), the chief scribe, or the foreman of the Kāyastha class, or the scribe-member of the board of administration; explained as 'the senior registrar' (EI 31). Cf. *Prathama-kāyastha*, *Paṭvārī*.

Jyeṣṭha-pitā, elder brother of one's father.

jyeṣṭhikā-grāma (CII 4), 'the chief village'.

jyoti-skandha (CII 1), masses of light; cf. *agni-skandha*.

jyotiṣṭoma (EI 4), name of a sacrifice.

K

ka (IE 8-1), for *kā* (in Kharoṣṭhī), abbreviation of *kāla*.

kā (PJS), abbreviation of *kārita* and *kāritā* (especially in medieval Jain inscriptions); also of *Kāyastha*; also of *kāṇḍa*, 'a cluster' (*JAS*, Letters, Vol. XX, p. 204).

kacakadā (LP), Gujarātī; tortoise-shell.

kaccha (*Ep. Ind.*, Vol. XIV, p. 177), a field bordering on a stream; land near a well (*Ep.Ind.*, Vol XXXIV, p. 175, line 15).

(*EI* 22), a resolution.

kacchaka (EI 19), a low hill.

(*IA* 18), wrongly read also as *kasthaka*; cf. *khalaka-kacchaka-bhūmī-sahitā* as an epithet of the gift land; probably, 'land around a well'. See *kūpaṁ khalakaṁ kacchakaṁ* (*Ind. Ant.*, Vol. XVIII, p. 114, text line 55, cf. line 43); also *kūpa-kaccha* (*Ep. Ind.*, Vol. XXXIV, p. 175, text line 15).

kacchapa, cf. *sa-matsya-kacchapa* (IE 8-5); tortoise; see *jala-kara*.

kaḍā (IE 8-6; EI 19), Bengali; the cowrie-shell regarded as a coin; a small area of land; one-fourth of a *gaṇḍā* and one-eightieth of a *paṇa*.

kadaru (CII 4), same as *kṛdara*; a granary.

kaḍḍhaka (IE 8-8; EI 30), probably the same as Sanskrit *karṣaka*; see *ḍheṅku-kaḍḍhaka*.

kādi (EI 28), a grain measure.

Kaḍit-āmātya (EI 23), Kannaḍa-Sanskrit; official designation; same as *Kaḍita-vĕrgaḍĕ* (q.v.).

Kaḍita-vĕrgaḍĕ (IE 8-3), Kannaḍa; superintendent of accounts and records; same as *Akṣapaṭalika*; sometimes also called *Mahāpradhāna*, *Hĕrisandhivigrahin*, *Senādhipati*, etc., additionally. See *Kaḍit-āmātya*.

Kaḍīya (LP), a bricklayer or mason; cf. Gujarātī *Kaḍīyā*.

kāhala, *kāhalā* (EI 24; IA 15), a musical instrument; a trumpet. See *kākala*.

kāhaṇa, *kāhāṇa* (IE 8-8; EI 29), Bengali-Oḍiyā; modified forms of *kārṣāpaṇa*.

kai (IE 8-6), Dravidian; same as *hasta*, 'cubit'; a unit of measurement.

Kaïsara (EI 26), title of a Kuṣāna king; derived from Roman *Caesar*.

kaiṭāla (IA 12), a castanet.

kaivarta-bhoga (IE 8-5), fishermens' preserve.

kāka (IE 8-6), same as *kākinī*.

(*EI* 14), name of a land measure.

kāka-bindu (SII 2), name of a flaw in diamonds.

(*SITI*), a black dot.

kākala (IA 12), a trumpet. See *kāhala*, *kāhalā*.

kakali (IE 3-4), paper; same as *kakari*.

kākaṇī, *kākaṇikā* (EI 15), same as *kākinī*.

kākapada, *kākapāda* (SII 2), name of a flaw in diamonds; a mark indicating omission of letters written outside the line.

kakari (IE 3-4), paper; same as *kakali*.

kāka-vṛnta (SII 2), a variety of diamond.

kākinī (IE 8-6), also called *kāka*.

(*IE* 8-6), a small land measure; cf. *kānī*.

(*IE* 8-8; EI 1; CII 4), name of a small coin; equal to 20 cowrie-shells according to the *Līlāvatī*; ¼ of a *paṇa* according to the *Kṛtyakalpataru* (Vyavahāra-kāṇḍa, ed. K. V. Rangaswāmi Aiyangar, p. 125).

kakubha (IE 7-1-2), 'ten'.

kalā (IE 7-1-2), 'sixteen'.

kāla (IE 7-1-2), 'three'.

(*CII* 3, etc.), time, a period of time; used in the sense of 'an era'; cf. *kāl-ānuvartamāna-saṁvatsara* (*Select Inscriptions*, p. 270, text lines 3-4), etc. See *prakāla*.

kalabhaśālā-karaṇa, cf. *karaṇa* (LP); explained as 'the camel department'.

kāla-cakra, a mechanical weapon placed at the gate of forts according to the *Vasudevahiṇḍī* (*Journ. Or. Inst.*, Vol. X, No. 1, p. 15). See *śataghnī*.

kāl-ākṣarita (LP), probably, 'a word of censure passed'.

kalam (EI 28), a grain measure.

kalamba (EI 12), an arrow; 'five'.

kalana, a betelnut plantation (*JAS*, Letters, Vol. XX, p. 205).

kaḷañju (IE 8-8; EI 28, 30; SITI), Tamil; name of a gold coin; also of the equivalent weight; about 32 *ratis* (*JNSI*, Vol. XV, p. 141).

Cf. ūr-kaḷañju (EI 28), name of a coin.

(*SII* 13), same as *suvarṇa*.

kalāpacchanda (SII 2), name of an ornament.

kalasa (CITD), a vase, flagon or water-pot; an ornamental piece of painted wood, stone, brass, etc., fixed on the spires of temples, carts, etc.; a rounded pinnacle or ball on the top of a temple; a dome.

(*EI* 5), the pinnacle of a temple; same as *kumbha*.

(*EI* 11, 33), a measure; cf. *droṇa*.

(*SII* 3), a pot.

(*EI* 33), also called *kalasikā*; probably, the same as *droṇa*; a measure of capacity.

kāla-sandhi (SII 1), same as *trikāla*.

kalasī (LP), a measure of capacity equal to sixteen maunds; cf. *kalasikā*, *kalasikāvāpa*.

kalasikā (EI 33), same as *kalasī* or *kalasa*; probably the same as *droṇa*; cf. *kalasikāvāpa*.

kalasikāvāpa (EI 33), a land measure; originally, a plot of land on which one *kalasī* measure of seed could be sown; cf. *droṇavāpa*.

kalatra (IE 7-1-2), 'seven'.

Kalavāḍa, *Kalavāḍā*, *Kālavāḍa*, *Kālavāḍā* (EI 24), same as *Kālavāḷa*, *Kālavāḷā*.

Kālavāḷa, *Kālavāḷā* (EI 24), designation of uncertain meaning if it is not the same as Sanskrit *Kalyapāla*, a vintner.

kāḷi-gaṇattār (SITI), Tamil; a committee for the temple of Kāḷi (Kālī).

kalikā (LP), quarrel; cf. Gujarātī *kali*.

kalikāvalika (LP), a quarrel; cf. *kalikā*.

kaliṅga-vāriyam (SITI), Tamil; committee looking after the sluice; derived from *kaliṅgu*, 'a sluice'.

kāl-maṟuturu (CITD), Telugu; an unknown measure of land. Cf. *maṟuturu*, *ghaḍa-maṟuturu*, etc.

kal-nāḍu (SITI), Tamil; a hero-stone; setting up of a hero-stone.

kalpa (CII 1), same as *saṁvarta-kalpa*, the aeon of destruction.

(*CII* 3, etc.), name of a fabulous tree in Indra's paradise, supposed to grant all desires.

kalpādi (EI 5; IA 18), name applied to certain *tithis*.

Kalpāla (EI 30), also called *Kalvapāla*, *Kalyapāla*, *Kalyāpāla*; a distiller of liquor.

kālu (IE 8-6), Kannaḍa; 'one foot'; a unit of measurement.

Kalvapāla (EI 30), same as *Kalpāla*, etc.; a vintner.

Kalvapāla-vārika (IE 8-8), official designation indicating a spirit-distiller.

kalyāṇa (CII 1), a good deed which is beneficial to the people; a ceremony to bring health and prosperity to a person (*Ep. Ind.*, Vol. XXXV, p. 147); cf. *maṅgala* in the same senses.

(EI 19), a festival (especially, marriage); cf. *kalyāṇa-maṇḍapa*.

kalyāṇ-āgama (CII 1), 'having pure knowledge'.

kalyāṇa-dhana (HRS), tax levied for the expenses of festivals or for the performance of rites to avert evil. Cf. *prathama-kalyāṇa* (*Ep. Ind.*, Vol. XXXV, p. 147).

kalyāṇaka (HA), a chief auspicious event in the life of a Tīrthaṅkara, there being five such events, viz. *cyavana* or descent from heaven, *janma* or birth, *dīkṣā* or initiation as monk, *jñāna* or attainment of *kevala-jñāna*, and *mokṣa* or *nirvāṇa*, i.e. death which means freedom from the last bondage in the life of a Jina. See *kalyāṇikā*.

Kalyāṇasundara, Śiva represented as marrying Umā Haiṁavatī.

kalyāṇī (EI 8), a square pond.

kalyāṇikā (EI 8), a festival.

(EI 11), certain auspicious days with the Jains. Cf. *kalyāṇaka.*

Kalyapāla, Kalyāpāla (EI 30), same as *Kalpāla,* etc.; a vintner.

Kalya-śreṣṭhin (IA 18), a dealer in liquors, *Kalya* being an abbreviation of *Kalyapāla,* or a word meaning 'distillery'.

kāma (IE 7-1-2), 'thirteen'.

kāma-dhenu (EI 16), name of a *mahādāna.*

kāma-koṣṭha, cf. *kāma-kkoṭṭam* (SITI), a shrine of the goddess Pārvatī as an adjunct of the Śiva temple in the same compound.

kamala-pūjā (BL), probably, worship of a deity with lotuses or flowers of gold or silver.

kāmali (EI 24), often written as *kambalin,* which means 'a bull'; a levy probably on prize bullocks (cf. *vara-balīvarda*). Cf. *yamali-kambali.*

kāmata (EI 21; CII 4), name of a tax.

kām-āvacara (IA 10), Buddhist; belonging to the domain of sensual pleasure.

kamba, kambha (IE 8-6), Kannaḍa; name of a land measure; see *kamma* and *stambha.*

kambala (IA 23), an agricultural ceremony.

kambalin (EI 24), 'a bull'; a levy probably on prize bullocks (cf. *vara-balīvarda*); see *kāmali* and *yamali-kambali.*

kaṁdāsaghūṭa (EI 1), meaning doubtful.

Kāmgār (BL), an official designation meaning a servant, a manager, a public officer; a person employed on public works. Cf. Wilson's Glossary.

kamma (IE 8-6; EI 12, 19), Kannaḍa; same as *stambha*=*skambha*; a land measure equal to one-hundredth of a *mattaru* or *nivartana.*

kammāḻar (SITI), Tamil; the five artisan classes; also called *añju pañcālattār.*

kampala (ASLV), same as *kampaṇa*; name of an administrative division.

kampana, kampanā (IE 8-3), the army [in ancient Kashmir]; cf. *Kampanapati,* etc.

kampaṇa (IE 8-4), a small territorial unit like a Parganā.

Kampan-ādhipati (HD), commander-in-chief [in ancient Kashmir]; same as *Kampanapati,* etc. See *Rājataraṅgiṇī,* V. 447; VII. 1362, 1366.

Kampanapati (IE 8-3), same as *Kampan-ādhipati*, etc.; commander-in-chief [in ancient Kashmir].

Kampanāpati (HD), same as *Kampan-ādhipati*, etc.

Kampaneśa (HD), same as *Kampan-ādhipati*, etc.

Kampan-odgrāhaka (HD), probably, collector of levies for the army. Cf. *Rājataraṅgiṇī*, VIII. 1430.

Kaṁsakāra (EI 1, 19, 23), also called *Kaṁsāra, Kāṁsāra*; same as *Kāṁsyakāra*, 'a brazier'.

Kaṁsāra, Kāṁsāra (EI 23), same as *Kāṁsyakāra*. See *Kāṁsāraka*.

Kāṁsāraka (BL), a worker in bell metal; a brazier. See *Kaṁsāra*, etc.

Kāṁsyakāra (EI 19, 32), a worker in bell-metal; a brazier. See *Kaṁsāra*, etc.

kan (EI 12), to glitter.

kaṇa-bhaktaka (LP), undressed provisions.

kaṇaka (LP), grains.

kanaka-haya (EI 24), same as *hiraṇy-āśva*; name of a *mahādāna*.

kanakamaṇi-tulāpuruṣa (EI 16), name of a *mahādāna*.

Kanakasabhāpati (EI 3), 'the god worshipped in the Kanakasabhā', i.e. Naṭarāja Śiva in the Chidambaram temple.

kanaka-tulāpuruṣa (EI 16; BL), name of a *mahādāna*.

kaṇakka-kkāṇi (SITI), Tamil; cf. *kaṇakka-ppeṟu*; land set apart for the village accountant, *Kaṇakka* being the same as Sanskrit *Gaṇaka*.

kaṇakka-ppeṟu (SITI), Tamil; cf. *kaṇakka-kkāṇi*; tax, payable in grains, for the maintenance of the village accountant.

kāṇam (EI 21, 28; SII 3; SITI), Tamil; name of a coin; a gold coin; a weight; a share.

Kanarese, see *Kannaḍa*.

kāñcana-medinī (EI 24), name of a *mahādāna*.

kāñcana-tulā (EI 23), name of a *mahādāna*.

kañcola (IA 15), same as *kañcūla*; a bodice or waistcoat.

kañcūla, same as *kañcola* (IA 15), a bodice or waist-coat.

kanda (CITI), name of a metre common in Telugu and Kannaḍa.

kandācāra (ASLV), the military department.

kandala (LP), controversy; beating (from Sanskrit *kand*, to strike).

Kāṇḍapati (IE 8-3); EI 31), an official designation of uncertain import; probably 'the custodian of the arrows or the armoury'.

kāṇḍapaṭika (EI 9), probably, a quiver.

kaṇḍāra, Prakrit; cf. *utkṛ*, 'to engrave'. See *kaṇḍāraṇa*.

kaṇḍāraṇa, Kannaḍa; carving or engraving; see *Ep. Ind.*, Vol. XVI, p. 36.

kāndiśīka (EI 13; LP), frightened; eager to flee.

kanduka (EI 1), probably, a sugar-boiler.

kaṇḍūla (EI 14), 'itching'.

kānī (IE 8-6), Bengali; a land measure equal to one-sixteenth of a *Doṇ*; cf. *kākinī*.

kāṇi (IE 8-6; EI 24, 28, 30; SII 3) Tamil; a land measure equal to one-eightieth of a *veli*.

(*SITI*), Tamil; a weight.

kānika (IE 8-5), Tamil; also spelt *kānuka*; same as *kāṇika*. (EI 33), also called *kānikĕ* or *kānikĕ-kappa* in Kannaḍa; tolls.

kāṇika (IE 8-5), same as Kannaḍa *kāṇika-kānĕ*, *kāṇikĕ-kappa* or *kappa-kānikĕ*, 'presents from an inferior to a superior', etc.

kānikĕ, *kānikĕ-kappa* (EI 33), Kannaḍa; same as *kānika*; tolls.

kāṇikĕ, *kāṇiki* (CITD), Telugu-Kannaḍa; a land measure of 57000 square feet; sixty-fourth part [especially of any coin]; also $\frac{1}{8}$ or $\frac{1}{34}$ part; a visit; a present or gift. See *kānuka*.

kaṇikkā (IE 8-8), same as Sanskrit *kaṇikā*, commin seed.

kaṇikkai (EI 17), *kāṇikkai* (EI 21; SITI), a voluntary offering; a present offered like *nazarāna*; presents or customary payments to the king and other high officials.

Kaṇkāṇi (EI 25; SII 2), Tamil; overseer; cf. *Māheśvara-Kaṇkāṇi*.

kaṅkaṭa (EI 9; IA 18), boundary.

Kannaḍa, written in English as *Kanarese*; language and alphabet of the Kannaḍigas, i.e. the people of Karṇāta (Sanskrit form of *Kannada*).

Kannaḍa-sandhivigrahin (IE 8-3), 'the *Sandhivigrahin* of the Kannaḍa (Karṇāṭa) country'; cf. *Sandhivigrahin*.

Kannadiga, see *Kannada*.

kaṇṭaka, cf. *catuṣ-kaṇṭaka-viśuddha* (EI 23), same as *catur-āghāṭa-viśuddha*; probably, 'the boundary demarcated by planting thorny shrubs'.

kaṇṭaka-śodhanā (SITI), criminal justice; cf. the Madras Museum plates of Jaṭilavarman Parāntaka-pāṇḍya and the *Arthaśāstra* of Kauṭilya.

kaṇṭhikā (EI 4, 25, 31; SII 1), a necklace; the emblem of heir-apparency.

kaṇṭhikā-paṭṭa-bandha (IA 11), the ceremony of anointing the *Yuvarāja* with a necklace which was his sign.

kānuka (CITD), Telugu; an offering or courtesy made in homage to a superior or a god. See *kāṇikĕ*, etc.

(*EI* 33), same as *kānika*, tolls.

kanyā-dāna (SII 1), giving a daughter in marriage.

(EI 29; ASLV), a form of marriage in which bride-price was not demanded or paid; offering one's daughter in marriage without demanding bride-price.

kanyā-dharma (EI 25), same as *kanyā-dāna-dharma*, the gift of a girl in marriage without demanding bride-price.

kapahaḍ̤ī (Chamba), field meant for growing cotton only. Cf. *kaphāḍ̤ī*.

kapāla-sandhi (CII 4), a peace treaty.

kāpālikā (EI 3), a cloud [of dust].

kaparda (CII 4), also called *kapardī*, *kapardaka*, etc.; cowrie-shell used as coin.

kapardaka (EI 1), a cowrie-shell used as coin.

kapardaka-purāṇa (IE 8-8; EI 14, 21), 'a *purāṇa* [of silver] counted in cowrie-shells'. Cf. *paṇa-purāṇa*.

kapardaka-voḍ̤i (EI 23), a cowrie-shell used as coin.

kapardī, *kapardikā* (EI 9; CII 4), a cowrie-shell used as coin.

kaphāḍ̤ī (Chamba), same as *kapahaḍ̤ī*.

kapilā (BL), a kind of cow.

Kapila-ṣaṣṭhī (EI 25), cf. *Kapila-caṭṭi* (EI 5), name of a *tithi*.

kappa (EI 33), Kannaḍa; same as Sanskrit *śulka* or *kara*.

(*SITI*), Tamil-Telugu-Kannaḍa; periodical and customary payments by persons engaged in some professions.

kara (IE 8-5), explained by a commentator as 'the dues

(*bhāga*) to be realised by the king for the enjoyment of royal land by using it for cultivation and for grazing cattle'; tax in general.

(*IE* 8-5) rent or tax to be paid in grains when mentioned side by side with *hiranya.*

(*HRS*), tax in general, according to the lexicons; according to the *Arthaśāstra*, (1) periodical tax over and above the king's customary grain-share; (2) emergecy tax levied upon the villagers over and above the normal grain-share; (3) tax upon merchants' profits.

(*EI* 29; Chamba; CITD), a tax or impost; royal revenue; rent, dues; toll, tribute.

(*IE* 7-1-2), 'two'.

karaghaṭikā (EI 2), meaning uncertain.

kara-grāma (ASLV; SITI), a revenue-paying or ryotwari village.

karaiyīdu (ASLV), system of periodical redistribution of lands.

kāraka (IE 7-1-2), 'six'.

Cf. Prakrit *Karavaka* (EI 12), same as Prakrit *Kārāpaka*; superintendent of the construction of a building.

karakaca (LP), 'talk that may annoy the hearer'; cf. Gujarātī *kackac.*

karākara-karaṇa, cf. *karaṇa* (LP); the department of revenue.

Karaṇa (EI 4), an accountant.

(*EI* 28; HD), a clerk; a scribe. Cf. *Ep. Ind.*, Vol. XXII, p. 155.

(*EI* 19), same as Marāṭhī *Kulkarṇī.*

(*SITI*), a type of law-court lower in rank than an *adhikaraṇa.*

(*IE* 8-1, 8-8; EI 28, 30), same as or a shortened form of *adhikaraṇa*; a court of law.

(*IE* 8-3), an office or department.

(*CII* 4), a committee.

(*LP*), a department, according to the editors of the *Lekhapaddhati*, the thirtytwo *karaṇas* or departments being the following : *śrī-karaṇa*, *vyaya-karaṇa*, *dharm-ādhikaraṇa*, *maṇḍapikā-karaṇa*, *velākula-karaṇa*, *jala-karaṇa*, [*sthala*]*patha-karaṇa*, *ghaṭikāgṛha-karaṇa*, *ṭaṅkaśālā-karaṇa*, *dravya-bhāṇḍāra-karaṇa*, *aṁśuka-bhāṇḍāra-karaṇa*, *vārigṛha-karaṇa*, *devaveśma-karaṇa*, *gaṇikā-karaṇa*,

karaṇa, *hastiśālā-karaṇa*, *aśvaśālā-karaṇa*, *kalabhaśālā-karaṇa*, *śreṇi-karaṇa*, *vyāpāra-karaṇa*, *tantra-karaṇa*, *koṣṭhāgāra-karaṇa*, *upakrama-karaṇa*, *karākara-karaṇa*, *sthāna-karaṇa*, *deva-karaṇa*, *sandhi* [*vigraha*]-*karaṇa*, *mahākṣapāla-karaṇa*, *mahārasa-karaṇa*, *jayanaśālā-karaṇa*., *sattrāgāra-karaṇa*, *antaḥpura-* [*karaṇa*] and *koṣṭhikā-* [*karaṇa*].

(*CII* 3, 4), a document.

Cf. *Karaṇam* (SII 1; SITI), Tamil; also spelt *Karṇam*; a document; an accountant, also called *Kaṇakkaṉ* or *Karaṇikka*.

(*IA* 17), name of the half of a *tithi*.

kāraṇa, cf. *ahaṁ kāraṇaṁ karomi* (LP), 'I shall prove'.

karaṇa-daṇḍa (SITI), fine imposed by the *karaṇa* (court).

Kāraṇaka (EI 32), a scribe.

karaṇa-karman (EI 30), the profession of the scribe.

Karaṇa-kāyastha (EI 7; HD; BL), official designation of a scribe; a writer of legal documents. Cf. Vogel, *Ant. Ch. St.*, p. 133.

(*IE* 8-3), mentioned as a *Pātra*.

kāraṇa-pūjā (IA 9), translated as 'occasional worship'.

Karaṇattār (*SII* 12), same as *Kāraṇavan*.

Kāraṇavan (SITI), Tamil; an accountant; also called *Kāraṇika* and *Karaṇattār*.

Karaṇika (CII 4; BL), official designation of a scribe; the writer of legal documents; explained by some as 'an officer in charge of a State department or office' (HD); but really, a scribe. Cf. *Karaṇika-ṭhakkura* (i.e. a *Karaṇika* who enjoyed the dignity of a *Ṭhakkura*) in *Ep. Ind.*, Vol. XX, p. 44; Vol. VIII, p. 158; and *Karaṇika-Brāhmaṇa* (i.e. a *Karaṇika* who belonged to the Brāhmaṇa community) in Bhandarkar's List, No. 350. See *Mahākaraṇika*.

(*EI* 6; ASLV), same as *Karṇam* or *Senabova*; a village accountant.

Cf. *Vāśal-karaṇikam* (SITI), same as *Vāśal-kaṇakkam* (°*gaṇaka*).

Kāraṇika (EI 31), same as *Karaṇika*.

Karaṇikka-joḍi (SII 2; SITI), the quit-rent of the *Karaṇam* or *Karṇam*.

Karaṇika-ṭhakkura (EI 33), see *Karaṇika* and *Ṭhakkura*.

Karaṇin (*HD*), same as *Karaṇika*. Cf. *karaṇi-parikara* (*Harṣacarita*, VII, para. 2).

karaṅka (EI 30), a cup made of coconut shell, used in

measuring liquids; a *karaṅka* measure; also the same as *tāmbūla-karaṅka* (the king's betel-box). Cf. *Karaṅkika.*

Karaṅkika (EI 13), officer in charge of the *karaṅka* (i.e. *tāmbūla-karaṅka* or the king's betel-box).

Kārāpaka (EI 19; IA 19), Prakrit; same as Sanskrit *Kāraka*; an agent.

kara-śāsana (EI 29, 33), charter recording a grant of land for which the donee had to pay rent; a grant for which revenue (either in full or at a concessional rate) was fixed; land granted in the said way.

karaṭikā, cf. *karaḍigai* (SII 13), a musical instrument.

karavṛnda (SITI), a variety of diamond.

Karika (*Ep. Ind.*, Vol XIII, p. 119, text line 8), official designation; probably a mistake for *Tarika.*

kariṇī-bhramaṇa (EI 24, 25), 'taking the she-elephant around'; a ceremony in fixing the boundaries; cf. *piḍi-śūḷndu* (SITI), walking around by a female elephant to mark the boundary of the gift land, etc.

kariṇī-paribhramaṇa (EI 15), same as *kariṇī-bhramaṇa.*

karīṣa (IA 9), name of a land measure.

Kari-turaga-pattan-ākarasthāna-gokul-ādhikārin (EI 18, 24, 33), designation of an officer (or designations of several officers) in charge of elephants, horses, townships, mines and cowpens.

Kari-turaga-paṭṭasāhaṇi (EI 5), military officer (or officers) in charge of the elephant force and cavalry. *Sāhaṇi* is the same as *Sādhanika* (q.v.).

Kari-turag-oṣṭra-nau-sādhanika (EI 23), military officer (or officers) in charge of the elephant force, cavalry, navy and camel corps. See *Hasty-aśv-oṣṭra-bala-vyāpṛta*, etc.

Karivāhinīśa (EI 30), leader of the elephant force. Cf. *Hasty-adhyakṣa*, etc.

Karivṛndanātha (EI 30), leader of the elephant corps. cf. *Hasty-adhyakṣa*, etc.

kārkhānā (HA), office of the managing body of a Jain shrine or of a group of Jain shrines.

karman (IE 7-1-2), 'ten'.

(*EI* 3), eight in kind.

karmānta (EI 13), cf. *paśukul-āvadāra-karmānta-konakalika-gaṅgā-grāme.* The reference seems to the *karmānta*, etc., at Gaṅgā-grāma. Cf. *Karmāntika*, *Kārmāntika*, etc.

(*EI* 31), also called *karmānta-sthalikā*, a barn.

karmāntaka (EI 15), cf. *Khaliṣa-karmāntaka-prabhu-Bhaṭṭa-Jayasomasvāmin* in the description of a donee Brāhmaṇa who was the master of a *karmānta* at Khaliṣa.

Karmāntika (IA 14; LL), 'the superintendent of a work'. Cf. *Kārmāntika.*

Kārmāntika (HD), superintendent of the mines and state manufactories. See *Arthaśāstra*, I. 12 (mentioned among the 18 *tīrthas*); II. 12 (section called *ākara-karmānta-pravartanam*, 'the working of mining operations and manufactories'). Cf. *Karmāntika.*

Karmāra (LL), a blacksmith.

Karma-saciva (IE 8-3; HD), an administrative officer; an executive minister; cf. *Mati-saciva*, a counsellor or minister. See *Ep. Ind.*, Vol. VIII, p. 36.

karma-sthāna (IA 18), a public building.

karma-sthāya (LP), building operation.

Karmika (LL), a labourer.

Karmin, cf. Tamil *Kaṇmi* (SITI), an official; 'an officer' as distinct from 'a servant'.

karṇa (IE 7-1-2), 'two'.

Karṇam, also spelt *Karaṇam*. See *Karaṇa.*

Karṇaprāvṛta (SII 2), same as *Karṇaprāvaraṇa*, 'a people whose ears are so large that they use them as a cloak'. Cf. Sircar, *Stud. Geog. Anc. Med. Ind.*, pp. 36, 67.

karṇapūra (EI 17), an ear-ornament.

karṇa-troḍanikā, see *karṇa-troṭana* (EI 30).

karṇa-troṭana (IE 8-8), cutting off a bit from somebody's ears.

karpaṭa, cf. *karpaṭa-pade* (LP), supposed to be something like *nazarāna*; literally, '[payment] on account of clothes' (same as *karpaṭa-bhāvena*).

karpaṭa-bhāva (LP), explained as *Pāghḍī*, i.e. a present, bribe or *inām*; but cf. also *aśana-karpaṭā(ṭa)-bhāvena* (*Ep. Ind.*, Vol. XXVIII, p. 50 , text lines 16-17 and note 4).

Kārpaṭika (BL), probably, a hermit or mendicant; cf. *karpaṭi-vrata.*

(*EI* 11), explained as 'a pilgrim'.

karpaṭī(ṭi)-vrata (EI 31), observance of the life of a hermit.

karpūra-mūlya, cf. *kappūra-vilai* (SITI), the sale-price

paid for temple lands; the price paid for cultivation rights of temple lands and in commutation of the taxes thereon.

karṣa (IE 8-8; CII 4), name of a weight equal to 80 *ratis*; same as *tolā*; sometimes regarded as 100 or 120 *ratis* in weight (*JNSI*, Vol. II, p. 3).

(*Ep. Ind.*, Vol. XV, p. 309), a measure of capacity for liquids.

(*CII* 4), name of a coin; cf. *kārṣāpaṇa*.

kārṣāpaṇa (IE 8-8; EI 29; CII 4), name of a gold, silver or copper coin one *karṣa* (80 *ratis*) in weight; name of a silver coin of 32 *ratis*, same as *purāṇa* or *dharaṇa*; name applied to the gold *gaṇḍa-māḍa* also called *niṣka* or *gaṇḍa-niṣka* (*JNSI*, Vol. XVI, p. 43). The weight of a copper or gold *kārṣāpaṇa* was 80 or 100 *ratis* (*JNSI*, Vol XV, p. 143); copper *kārṣāpaṇa* was also called *paṇa*. Cf. *kāhāpaṇa* (EI 8), Prakrit for Sanskrit *kārṣāpaṇa*; see *kāhāṇa*, *kāhaṇa*.

karṣ-ārdha, 'half *karṣa* (q.v.)'.

kartavya (LP), derived from *kṛt*; 'to be cut'.

Kārtākṛtika (IE 8-3), probably, an officer who reported to the king about the progress of important undertakings; cf. *kṛt-ākṛta-jño bhṛtyānām* (*Matsya Purāṇa*, CCXV, 17). See *Mahākārtākṛtika*.

Kartṛ (CII 3, etc.), the maker; a technical term for the composer of a record, as opposed to the person who reduced it to writing.

Cf. Karttār (EI 33), Tamil; an officer.

kārttika (CITD), crops reaped in the month of Kārttika.

kārttikeya-mukha, cf. *kumār-āsya* (IE 7-1-2), 'six'.

kārttik-odyāpana (IA 18), also called *kārttik-odyāpana-parvan* (BL), a festival in honour of Viṣṇu, connected with Kārttika su-di 11.

kāru-deya, cf. *sarva-parihāra-kāru-deya* (EI 24); tax realised from the artisans; same as *kāruka*.

Kāruka (LB), an artisan. The five classes of artisans may be the carpenter, the blacksmith, the potter, the barber and the washerman.

(*IE* 8-5; EI 25, 32), tax on artisans and craftsmen; same as *kāru-deya*.

kārukara (HRS), traced by some in the Prakrit passage *sa-karukara* in a Śātavāhana record and indentified with *udraṅga* and *uparikara*; but may be Sanskrit *kar-otkara*, i.e. *kara* and *utkara* (probably the same as *upakara* or *uparikara*), or *kāru-kara*=*kāru-deya* (q.v.).

karuṇā (CII 4), one of the *bhāvanās*.

kāru-śilpi-gaṇa, various types of artisans. Cf. Ghoshal, *H. Rev. Syst.*, p. 98.

karvaṭaka (EI 13), a market town; cf. Sanskrit *kharvaṭa*.

kārya, cf. Tamil *kāriyavārāycci* (EI 24), name of a tax.

Cf. Vāśal-kāriyam (SITI), the officer in charge of the palace gate; also known as *Vāśal-mudali* or *Vāśal-nirvāham*.

Kārya-cintaka (CII 4), a member of the executive committee of a corporation.

Kārya-darśin (EI 22), a secretary or manager.

Kārya-kartṛ (SITI), an agent; also called *Kāriyattukku-kkaḍavar*, a designation sometimes enjoyed by the *Pradhāni* or the provincial governor (ASLV).

kārya-vārāycci (SITI), Tamil; also spelt *ārāycci*; cess paid for the superintendence of transactions.

Kāsāra (EI 4), a brazier; same as *Kāṁsyakāra*.

kaṣāya (CII 4), a spirituous liquor.

kāś-āya (SITI), same as *kāśu-āyam*; taxes and dues payable in coin; also called *kāś-āya-vargam*, *kāśu-vargam* and *kāśu-kaḍamai*. Cf. *hiraṇy-āya*, *dhānya-varga*.

kāṣṭha, cf. *a-tṛṇa-kāṣṭha-grahaṇa* (IE 8-5), fuel or wood which the villagers were obliged to supply to the king or landlord on occasions or to the touring officers. See also *devakuṭī-kāṣṭha*.

kāṣṭh-āgāra, cf. *kaṭṭāgara* (SII 3), a wooden house.

Kāṣṭhakāra (SII 3), a carpenter.

kāṣṭha-yūti, cf. *yūti*; 'a wood for preserving fuel'.

kāśu (SII 1), Tamil; money; a coin; 'a tax'; cf. *kāśu-kaḍamai*, tax payable in cash.

(*IE* 8-8), name of a coin; sometimes called *dīnāra* (q.v.); cf. *ūr-kāśu* (EI 28), *vīrapañcālaṅ-kāśu* (SITI), *sambiraṇippalaṅ-gāśu*; also *īḻa-kkāśu* (EI 28), 'the Ceylonese coin'; *śoḻiya-kkāśu* (SITI), name of a copper coin believed to have been introduced by the Coḻas; *palaṅ-kāśu*, *nat-kāśa*, *nal-kāśu* (SII 12); generally regarded as $\frac{1}{100}$ of a *paṇam*; cf. *triśūla-kāśu* (SII 3).

Cf. āśuva-kkāśu (SITI), or *ājīvaka-kāśu*, tax payable by the Ājīvakas.

Cf. aḍimai-kkāśu (SITI), fees collected from the temple

servants; also *adi-kkāśu*, tax collected from stall-keepers in the markets.

Cf. uppu-kkāśu (SITI), salt-tax.

Cf. vagainda-kāśu (SITI), tax payable in cash for marking details of land, etc.; fees for the division of land; also the fee for settlement of a dispute, etc.

Cf. *veli-kkāśu*, *veli-ppayaṟu* (SITI), Tamil; tax payable in cash, the exact nature of which is not clear. Cf *veli-kkuḻi-ppaṇam*.

Cf. inavari-kkāśu (SITI), communal tax payable in coin; cf. *jāti-siddh-āya* of Telugu inscriptions.

(*SITI*), Tamil; a measure of weight equal to $\frac{1}{4}$ *palam.*

kaṭaka (EI 8, 17), the camp or capital.

(*SITI*), a fortified place; a cantonment; a military camp.

Cf. kaṭakaṁ kartavyam (LP), 'an army should be sent [against one]'.

Kaṭak-ādhirāja (EI 4), same as *Kaṭakarāja*, etc.; a military officer in charge of the royal camp.

Kaṭakādhīśa (HD), same as *Kaṭakarāja*, etc.

Kaṭaka-nāyaka (EI 23), same as *Kaṭakarāja*, etc.

Kaṭakarāja (EI 9; HD), officer in charge of the royal camp; same as *Kaṭakādhīśa*, etc. Cf. *Ep. Ind.*, Vol. IV, p. 309, note 1.

Kaṭaka-vārika (EI 30), probably, officials serving under the superintendent of the royal camp (*Kaṭakarāja*, etc.).

Kaṭakeśa (EI 29; HD), superintendent of the royal camp; same as *Kaṭakarāja*, etc. Cf. *Ep. Ind.*, Vol. VII, p. 185.

ka-ṭa-pa-y-ādi (IE 7-1-3; EI 33; IA 19, 24), a system of recording numbers.

kaṭhāri (ASLV), same as Sanskrit *kartarī*, a sword.

kaṭha (LP), cf. Gujarātī *kāṭmāl.*

kathita, drawn up or dictated (*Ep. Ind.*, Vol. XXXIV, p. 179). Cf. *cintita*, 'composed' (ibid., Vol. XXXV, p. 58).

kaṭī-sūtra (EI 16), an ornament.

kaṭṭaṇa (SITI), periodical presents made to superiors by their subordinates.

kaṭṭu-guttagai (ASLV), Tamil; a contract.

Kaṭuka (EI 13; HD), an official designation of uncertain import; cf. *Mahākaṭuka*. See *Ep. Ind.*, Vol XIII, p. 117.

kaṭumukha (EI 5), name given to a musical instrument.

kauberacchanda (CII 3), a particular kind of pearl-necklace.

kaulika-nikāya (LL), the weaver's guild.

kaumāra-saudha (EI 34), a prince's palace.

Kauptika (EI 1, 23), official designation of uncertain import; pobably, a collector of tolls.

kā-usaggiyā (HA), Sanskrit *kāyotsargikā*; the image of a Tīrthaṅkara standing in the *kāy-otsarga* posture. See *kā-ussagga.*

kā-ussagga (HA), Sanskrit *kāy-otsarga* (q.v.); a posture of meditation in which one stands erect with arms hanging and the soles of the feet kept four inches apart.

kauṣṭheyaka (HRS), occurring in the *Arthaśāstra* and understood by some in the sense of earnings from the king's store-houses.

kaustubha (CII 3, etc.), a jewel worn on the breast of Viṣṇu.

Kauṭumbika, cf. Prakrit *Koṭubika* (EI 24), a householder.

kavaca (SITI), same as Tamil *tiru-kkŏḻgai*, the metallic cover exactly fitting the image of a deity; same as *kholī*, *kholikā.*

kavale, also called *kavaleḍu*, *kavaligĕ* (CITD), Telugu-Kannaḍa; a pack of written leaves; palm leaves prepared for writing accounts.

kaveluka, *kāveluka* (LP), tile; cf. *kivelu*, Marāṭhī *kaul*, etc. See *Ep. Ind.*, Vol. XXXIV, pp. 144-45.

Kavirāja (IA 26), title; sometimes found also among the Musalmans.

kāya (IE 7-1-2), 'six'.

Kāyastha (EI 24; ASLV; HD), a clerk; explained by some as 'a registrar' (EI 31); a scribe or writer in the king's revenue department according to some. See *Yājñavalkyasmṛti*, I. 322; *Viṣṇu Dharma Sūtra*, VII. 3; etc. Cf. *Aśvaghāsa-kāyastha* and *Grāma-kāyastha* (*Rājataraṅgiṇī*, V. 175; *IHQ*, Vol. IX, p. 12). See also *Hist. Dharm.*, Vol. II, pp. 75-77. For derivation, cf. *Bhār. Vid.*, Vol. X, pp. 280 ff.

kāya-vrata (EI 11), self-immolation.

kāy-otsarga (EI 3), a kind of obeisance.

Cf. Prākrit *kā-ussagga* (HA), a posture of meditation in which one stands erect with arms hanging and the soles of feet kept four inches apart. Cf. *kāusaggiyā*.

kedāra (EI 28), a corn-field.

(*EI* 32), low land.

Cf. bhū-kedāra (EI 19); a land measure; cf. the land measure called *keyār* in the Sylhet region of East Pakistan.

kedārikā (IA 15), a small field; cf. *kedāra*.

kelā (IE 8-8; EI 30), meaning uncertain; probably, a doll or toy.

keli (EI 9), the earth.

kendra (IE 7-1-2), 'four'.

(*CII* 3), anomaly of the moon, taken to be her distance from apogee, from which point it is always reckoned by Hindu astronomers; the annual variation in the moon's *kendra* is 3 signs 2 degrees and 6.2 minutes, or 7 *tithis* 9 *ghaṭīs* and 42 *palas*. See also *nīcocca-māsa*, *tithi-kendra*, *tithi-madhyama-kendra* and *tithi-spaṣṭa-kendra*.

ketu (EI 24), the shape or form.

kevala-jñāna (HA), Jain; omniscience; a technical term for the highest knowledge; the Jain doctrine of unity (IA 18).

kha (IE 7-1-2), 'cypher'.

khada (LP), grass.

Khadgadhara, cf. *Mahākhaḍgadhara*, *Khaḍagrāhin*, etc.

Khaḍgagrāha (IE 8-3; EI 30), probably the same as *Khāḍgika*; swordsman; sometimes distinguished from *Khaṇḍapāla*.

Khaḍgagrāhi-mahāpātra (EI 28, 31), official designation in which *Khaḍgagrāhin* seems to indicate an officer in charge of swordsmen (as opposed to the clubmen); see *Mahāpātra*.

Khaḍga-grāhin (EI 28), same as the *Khaṇḍāita* (originally, swordsmen of the kings of Orissa); cf. *Khaḍgagrāha*.

Khaḍga-rakṣa (EI 30), same as *Khaḍga-grāha*; used in place of *Aṅgarakṣa* and *Khaṇḍarakṣa* of some records (*Ind. Ant.*, Vol. XVII, p. 11, text line 14); probably, the king's bodyguards.

Khāḍgika (IE 8-3), 'swordsman'; probably 'a palace-guard'; mentioned separately from *Khaṇḍarakṣa* which is also spelt *Khaḍgarakṣa*.

Khāḍgin (EI 23), same as *Khāḍgika*.

khāḍī (EI 31), a canal.

khāḍūrikā (EI 9), a military exercise ground.

Khādyakūṭapākika, see *Khādyaṭapākika*.

Khādyaṭapākika (IE 8-3), propbably a mistake for *Khādyakūṭa-pākika* (cf. *anna-kūṭa*, 'a heap of food'); same as *Mahānas-ādhyakṣa*; called *Sandhivigrahika*, *Kumārāmātya*, *Mahā-daṇḍanāyaka*, etc., additionally. See *Bhānasa-vĕrgaḍĕ*, *Mahānas-ādhyakṣa*, *Sūpakārapati*, *Mahānasika*.

khājaṇ (IE 8-8), Marāṭhī, etc.; see *khajjana*, etc.

khajjana, khajjaṇa, khajjāna, khajjaṇaka (IE 8-8; EI 33), same as Marāṭhī and Koṅkaṇī *khājaṇ*; an area near the sea shore, on which a thin layer of sand accumulates after the ebbtide coming through inlets; a rice field created out of such an area near a hillock by erecting embankments on the three other sides; a field created by reclaiming a river bed; cultivable land created from the bed of a river which carries the flood-water from the sea; a salty marsh or meadow; a rice field created near the bed of a nullah on the sea shore by putting embankments. See *Ep. Ind.*, Vol. XXXIII, pp. 53-54. It is sometimes called *pukkoli-khajjana*, *pukkoli* probably meaning a similar kind of land.

khala (Chamba, etc.), threshing floor.

khala-bhikṣā (EI 3, 25; HRS), a levy; cess payable at the threshing floor; portion of crop over and above the usual grainshare, collected from grains heaped upon the threshing floor.

khalaka (IA 18), a threshing floor [probably situated near a well]; cf. *khala*.

Cf. khalak-ānte (LP), 'at the end of the threshing season'.

khalakīya (LP), tax payable at or for using the threshing floor; cf. *khala-bhikṣā*.

Khala-rakṣaka, cf. *Mahā-khalarakṣaka*.

khalla (IE 8-5), same as Oḍiyā *khāl*; low land; cf. *sa-khall-onnata* (EI 12), 'with low land and high land'.

(*IE* 8-8), a hide.

(*EI* 30), leather vessel for carrying wine.

khallara (IA 13), probably, a pond.

khaṁ, abbreviation of *khaṇḍa*, 'a piece' (*JAS*, Letters, Vol. XX, p. 204).

khampaṇa (EI 23), a territorial division; same as *kampaṇa*.

khampaṇaka (IE 8-4), a small territorial unit; same as *khampaṇa* or *kampaṇa*.

khānaka (EI 15), same as *khātaka* in the sense of *khanana*.

khaṇḍa (IE 8-4; EI 23), a territorial division; the subdivision of a *deśa*.

(*IE* 7-1-2), 'nine'.

Cf. nava-khaṇḍa (IE 8-4), 'having nine divisions' ; an epithet of Bhārata or Bhārata-varṣa.

(*EI* 30), a habitation.

(*EI* 3, 24), also called *khaṇḍi*; a land measure. See *khaṇḍaka.*

Cf. Tamil *kaṇḍam* (SITI), a portion of the *mukha-maṇḍapa* of a temple.

khaṇḍa, khaṇḍā (IA 15), a sword.

Khaṇḍāit (IE 8-3), a community in Orissa; probably the swordsmen maintained by kings as opposed to their *Pāiks* or clubmen; cf. *Khaṇḍarakṣa* and *Khaṇḍapāla.*

khaṇḍaka (SITI), cf. Tamil *kaṇḍakam*, a land measure. See *khaṇḍa.*

khaṇḍa-kṣetra (EI 3, 16, 23), a plot of land.

khaṇḍala (IE 8-4; EI 12, 18), a territorial unit; a district or its subdivision.

khaṇḍala, khaṇḍalaka, same as *khaṇḍa*; cf. *kṣetra-khaṇḍala* or °*khaṇḍalaka* (*Ep. Ind.*, Vol. XXXV, p. 135, text time 22; p. 139, text line 22).

Khaṇḍapāla (IE 8-3; EI 28), official designation; same as *Khaṇḍapati* or *Khaṇḍarakṣa* (q.v.). See *Khaṇḍavāla.*

khaṇḍapāla, also called *khaṇḍapāliya* (IE 8-3; EI 24, 28), tax for the maintenance of swordsmen; tax for the maintenance of the *Khaṇḍapāla* or *Khaṇḍapālas.*

Khaṇḍapati (EI 12, 28), official designation; same as *Khaṇḍapāla.*

Khaṇḍarakṣa (IE 8-3; HD), sometimes spelt as *Khaḍga-rakṣa,* 'swordsman'; probably the king's bodyguard; mentioned separately from *Khāḍgika*; cf. *Khaṇḍapāla*; also *Khaṇḍāit*; sometimes regarded as the same as *Khaṇḍapāla* meaning the ruler of a small territorial unit. See *Ep. Ind.*, Vol. XVII, p. 321. Cf. *Khaḍgarakṣa* (Vogel, *Ant. Ch. St.*, pp. 127-28).

khaṇḍa-sphuṭita-jīrṇ-oddhāra (EI 23), also called *khaṇḍa-sphuṭita-navakarman, khaṇḍa-sphuṭita-prakaraṇa*; repairs.

Khaṇḍavāla (EI 7; HD), modification of *Khaṇḍapāla.* See *Ep. Ind.*, Vol. VII, p. 91; *JBORS*, Vol. V, p. 588.

khaṇḍi (EI 3), also called *khaṇḍa,* a land measure. Cf. *khaṇḍī* spelt in English as *candy.*

khaṇḍī (CII 4), a measure of capacity; cf. *khaṇḍikā.* See *candy.*

(*IA* 15), a land-measure.

khaṇḍika, khaṇḍikā (EI 22; CII 4; IA 20), measure of capacity; same as *khaṇḍī* or candy; often regarded as equal to between 800 and 1000 seers. See *puṭṭi*.

Cf. Ṛgveda-khaṇḍikā, a school for teaching the *Ṛgveda* (*Ep. Ind.*, Vol. XXXIV, p. 37 and notes).

khaṇḍuga (IE 8-6; EI 4; CITD), Telugu-Kannaḍa; a weight of 192,000 *tolās* for silk, sugar, drugs and cotton; a land measure; a land measure of 64,000 square yards of dry and 10,000 square yards of wet land [in Mysore]; a dry measure of 409,6000 or 134,400 or 128,000 *tolās* in different places. Cf. *khaṇḍuka*.

khaṇḍuka (IE 8-6), a measure of capacity; cf. *khaṇḍukavāpa*.

khaṇḍukavāpa (IE 8-6), an area of land requiring one *khaṇḍuka* measure of seed grains for sowing.

khanika, cf. Prakrit *khaniya* (EI 20), a pillar. Cf. *khāṇu*.

khāṇu (EI 24), a pillar; cf. *khanika*.

khāri (EI 17), a land measure; cf. *khārī, khārīvāpa*.

khārī (IE 8-6; CII 4), a measure of capacity equal to sixteen *droṇas*.

(*IE* 8-6), shortened form of *khārīvāpa* or *khārikāvāpa*.

khārikā (IE 8-6), shortened form of *khārikāvāpa* or *khārī-vāpa*; also same as *khārī*.

khārikāvāpa (IE 8-6), same as *khārīvāpa*.

khārīvāpa (IE 8-6), an area of land requiring a *khārī* measure of seed grains for sowing; a land measure equal to sixteen *droṇavāpas* or two *kulyavāpas*.

Kharoṣṭhī, an early Indian alphabet which was an Indian modification of the Aramaic alphabet; called *Kharoṣṭrī* by some.

kharvaḍa (EI 5), Sanskrit *kharvaṭa*; a market town.

kharvaṭa (ASLV), an administrative unit. See also *kharvaḍa*.

khaścā (LP), also spelt *ṣaścā*; teasing; cf. *khāṁc-khuṁc* in Gujarātī. See *khaśrā*.

khaśrā (EI 1), loss or injury. Cf. *khaścā*.

khāta (EI 19), a well.

khātaka (*Ep. Ind.*, Vol. IV, p. 253, text line 33, note 4), probably, a canal; same as Bengali *khāt*.

Khatiba, same as Arabic *Khatīb*, preacher (*Ep. Ind.*, Vol. XXXIV, p. 145).

khāṭikā (*Ep. Ind.*, Vol. IV, p. 253); the mouth of a river; same as Bengali *khāḍī*.

khattaka (EI 8), Kannaḍa; a pedestal or seat.

(*EI* 11; HA), a niche; a term found in Jain inscriptions in the said sense.

khaṭvā, cf. *a-kūra-chullaka-vināśi-khaṭv-āvāsa* (IE 8-5); a cot which the villagers were obliged to provide for a touring officer of the king.

khaṭvāṅga (EI 5; SII 2), a club with a skull fixed at the top; a Śaiva emblem.

khaṭvāpāda (EI 7-1-2), 'four'.

kheḍanīya (LP), same as *pātanīya*.

kheṭa (IE 8-5), a village or hamlet.

khila (EI 15; Chamba), unclultivated land; fallow land; cf. *sa-khila-nāla* (IE 8-5).

khila-kṣetra (EI 23), fallow land.

Khoja (EI 6), a merchant. Cf. *Khwāja*, the Muslim title of distinction.

Khola (IE 8-3); HD), an official designation of uncertain meaning (*Ep. Ind.*, Vol. IV, pp. 250, 253); probably a kind of messenger. Utpala on the *Bṛhatsaṁhitā*, 85. 34, explains *Dūta* as *Gamāgamika* while some Pāla inscriptions place *Khola* between the two; probably the same as *Preṣaṇika* or *Dūta-preṣaṇika*, a dispatcher of messengers.

Kholī, *kholikā*, same as *kavaca* (q.v.).

khoṭa (HRS), what is payable to the king in the shape of *hiraṇya*, etc., and of compulsory labour and the provision of food for the *Cāṭas* and *Bhaṭas*, according to the *Abhidhāna-rājendra*, s.v. *parihāra*. See *khoṭa-bhaṅga*, *ukkoṭa-bhaṅga*.

khoṭa-bhaṅga (HRS), applies to a person residing for one, two or three years, or as long as the king's favour extends, without contributing the *hiraṇya*, etc., and without providing food for the *Cāṭas* and *Bhaṭas*, according to the *Abhidhānarā-jendra*, s.v. *parihāra*; also called *ukkoṭa-bhaṅga*, *akṣoṭa-bhaṅga*.

khovā (IE 8-8), cf. *khovādāna*; meaning uncertain.

Khshathrapāvan (IE 8-2, 8-3), Old Persian; 'a provincial governor.' See *Kṣatrapa*.

Khshāyathiya Khshāyathiyānām (IE 8-2), Old Persian; 'king of kings'; same as Modern Persian *Shāhān Shāh*. See *Basilĕos Basilĕon*, *Ṣāhānuṣāhi*.

Khshāyathiya vazrka (IE 8-2), Old Persian; 'the great king'; royal title. It was translated by the Indo-Greek kings in Greek and Prakrit in the legend of their coins and was the original of the Indian royal title *Mahārāja*. See *Basilĕos Mĕgalŏu*.

kila, cf. *Paṭṭakila, Veṭakila*.

kīlaka (EI 23), a peg [for marking boundaries].

kīla-mudrā, letter written on wedge-shaped wooden tablets (*Select Inscriptions*, pp. 236-37).

kiṁ-chandaḥ (CII 1), cf. *kiṁ-chandaḥ svit rājā asmāsu*, 'of what attitude is the king towards ourselves ?'

kiṇva-kreṇi (EI 15), mistake for *kliṇva-kreṇi* meaning such articles as sugar, liquor, etc.

kīrtana (EI 24, 28, 33; SII 1; CII 4), same as *kīrti*; a temple or any other thing that renders famous the name of the person responsible for it; often interpreted as 'a building or temple'; but really, 'any fame-producing work'; 'a monument of fame'; a pious work like a temple. See *kīrtanā*.

kīrtanā (EI 33), same as *kīrtana* and *kīrti*; cf. *kīrtita*.

kīrti (EI 20, 24; CII 3, 4), literally, 'the thing that speaks of or glorifies one'; used in the special meaning of 'any work which renders the constructor of it famous'; a meritorious work; a pious deed; same as *kīrtana, kīrtanā*; often interpreted as 'a building or temple'; but actually, 'any fame-producing work'. See *kīrti-sthāna*.

(CII 1), fame of a dead person; cf. *yaśo vā kīrtir=vā*. See *yaśas*.

kīrti-mukha (CII 4), a decorative motif.

kīrti-stambha, cf. *mahāmeru-śrī-kīrtistambha* (BL); 'the pillar of fame'.

kīrti-sthāna (EI 1), same as *kīrti* or *kīrtana*; a temple or some such object calculated to render famous the name of the person responsible for it.

kīrtita (EI 24), 'built'; cf. *prakīrtita*.

Kiśoravaḍavā-go-mahiṣ-āj-āvik-ādhyakṣa (IE 8-3), cf. *Go-mahiṣ-āj-āvikā-vaḍav-ādhyakṣa*, *Hasty-aśv-oṣṭra-go-mahiṣ-āj-āvik-ādhyakṣa*, *Kari-turaga-pattan-ākarasthāna-gokul-ādhikārin*, etc.

Kiśoravaḍavā-go-mahiṣy-adhikṛta (IE 8-3; EI 17, 23), cf. *Go-mahiṣy-aj-ādhyakṣa*, *Kiśoravaḍavā-go-mahiṣ-āj-āvik-ādhyakṣa*, etc.

Kiśoravaḍavā-go-mahiṣy-aj-āvik-ādhyakṣa (EI 29), cf. *Go-*

mahiṣy-aj-ādhyakṣa, *Kiśora-vaḍavā-go-mahiṣ-āj-āvik-ādhyakṣa*, etc.

kiṭikā (EI 14), Sanskritised form of *kiḍi* or *kiḍā*, 'a matting screen'.

kivelu (LP), 'tile'; cf. Marāṭhī *kaul*. See *kaveluka*.

kliṇva, cf. *a-lavaṇa-kliṇva-khātaka* (IE 8-5); probably, such things as sugar and liquor; same as *kliṇva-kreṇi*; cf. also *a-lavaṇa-guḍa-kṣobha* (IE 8-5), etc.

kliṇva-kreṇi, cf. *a-lavaṇa-kliṇva-kreṇi-khanaka* (IE 8-5); same as *kliṇva* meaning articles like sugar, liquor, etc.

kḷpta (CII 3, 4; HRS), cf. *sa-kḷpt-opakḷpta* (IE 8-5); probably, the tax on permanent tenants or the fixed revenue; fixed tax which is one of the seven sources of revenue specified in the *Arthaśāstra*; cf. *upakḷpta*, *kḷpta-kara*, *udraṅga*, *kḷpta-śluka*, etc.

kḷpta-kara (IE 8-5), fixed tax; same as *kḷpta-śulka*; cf. *sa-kḷpt-opakḷpta*.

kḷpta-śulka (IE 8-5), fixed duty; same as *kḷpta*, *kḷpta-kara*; cf. *sa-kḷpt-opakḷpta*.

koḍe (CITD), Telugu; an unknown measure of capacity. Cf. Kannaḍa *koda-visa*, an allowance of a *visa* of grain, etc., for every bullock-load that comes into a town, paid to a person employed to check the demands of the toll-collector.

koḍevaṇa (EI 27), name of a tax.

kodrava (EI 5, 12), name of a grain.

kohlī (Chamba), wet land, irrigable land; same as *āli*; opposed to *otaḍa*.

kol (IE 8-6), Tamil; a measuring rod; cf. *śrīpāda-kkol*, 'rod measured according to the length of the king's foot'; *māliga-kkol*, 'the measuring rod of the palace'; etc.

(*EI* 25), a land measure.

kola, same as *tolaka* (q.v.).

kolaga (IE 8-6), Kannaḍa; a land measure.

koḷaga (CITD), Telugu-Kannaḍa; measure of capacity equal to 4 *baḷas*; a dry measure of 768 or 384 or 72 *tolas* in different places.

kola-bhaṇḍālu, also called *kolla-baṇḍi* (CITD), Telugu; a bullock-cart load. Cf. *busi-baṇḍi* or *busi-bhaṇḍālu*.

Kolika (IE 8-8; EI 30), same as Sanskrit *Kaulika*, a weaver.

kolika-nikāya (CII 4), a guild of the *Kaulikas* or weavers.

kolla-baṇḍi, see *kola-bhaṇḍālu*.

kolu (IE 8-6), a measuring rod.

Komaṭi (CITD), Telugu-Kannaḍa; a Vaiśya shop-keeper; a member of the mercantile caste.

kommu-maṟturu (CITD), Telugu; see *maṟuturu.*

koñjalla, cf. *a-kara-viṣṭi-koñjalla* (IE 8-5); a fiscal term of doubtful import.

koraṭa (CII 3), a fiscal term of uncertain import.

koṣa, treasure, see Ghoshal, *H. Rev. Syst.*, pp. 15-16.

Koś-ādhipa (EI 32, 33), a treasurer; same as *Koś-ādhyakṣa.*

koṣa-gṛha (HRS), treasury.

Kośajā (EI 9), a cocoon-producer.

koṣavāha (EI 14), name of a land measure; as much land as can be irrigated by one *koṣa* or leather bucket.

koṣṭha (IE 7-1-2), 'four'. Cf. *koṣṭhaka.*

koṣṭh-āgāra (HRS), the royal granary.

(EI 29), cf. Tamil *koṭṭagāram*, *koṭṭāram* (EI 22; SITI), treasury or store-house.

Cf. Tamil *koṭṭagāram*, etc. (SII 2), stables.

koṣṭhāgāra-karaṇa, cf. *karaṇa* (LP); department of the collection of the king's share of grains.

Koṣṭhāgārin, officer in charge of the treasury or store-house; cf. *Mahākoṣṭhāgārin.*

koṣṭhaka (BL; LP), a granary or store-house.

Koṣṭha-karaṇa (EI 29), a treasury accountant; also the revenue department (cf. *koṣṭha-vyāpāra*).

koṣṭha-vyāpāra (EI 29), the revenue department (cf. *koṣṭha-karaṇa*).

koṣṭhī, cf. Prakrit *koḍhi* (LL), a hall.

koṣṭhikā (EI 15), same as *koṣṭha.*

koṣṭhikā-karaṇa (LP), the royal treasury.

koṭa (LP), also called *koṭaḍi*; 'wall of the compound'.

Koṭ-ādhikaraṇika (BL), officer in charge of or related to the government of a *koṭa* or *koṭṭa* (fort).

koṭaḍi, *kotaḍī*; cf. *koṭaḍi-sahita* (LP), 'together with walls of the compound'.

koṭaka (*Ep. Ind.*, Vol. XIV, p. 313), 'a district'; same as *koṭṭaka*; cf. *koṭṭa-viṣaya.*

Koṭapāla (EI 17), same as *Koṭṭapāla.*

koṭha-vyāpāra (EI 28), same as *koṣṭha-vyāpāra*; the revenue department.

koṭi-homa (EI 12, 33), name of a rite.

koṭikā, a load [of cloth] (*Ep. Ind.*, Vol. XIV, p. 309).

(*EI* 14), a measure.

koṭṭa (EI 24), a fort. See *koṭṭai* and *koṭṭam* of the South Indian inscriptions.

koṭṭai (ASLV), a fort.

koṭṭaka, see *koṭaka*.

koṭṭam (IE 8-4; EI 27), Tamil; a district; a district within a *maṇḍala* or province.

(*ASLV*), a division of the *rājya*; sometimes subdivided into *nāḍus*.

Koṭṭa-nigraha (EI 8; IA 30; BL), commander of a fort; same as *Koṭṭapāla*. Cf. *Koṭṭanigrahin*.

Koṭṭanigrahin (IA 30), probably, the commander of a fort; same as *Koṭṭanigraha*.

Koṭṭapāla (IE 8-3; EI 12, 18, 25, 30; BL), officer in charge of a fort; governor of a fort. Cf. the Bhagalpur plate of Nārāyaṇapāla (*Ind. Ant.*, Vol. XV, p. 306); sometimes spelt *Koṭapāla* (cf. the Nalanda plate of Devapāla in *Ep. Ind.*, Vol. XVII, p. 321). Same as *Koṭṭapati*.

(*EI* 25), the city prefect; same as *Kotwāl*.

Koṭṭapati (IE 8-3), same as *Koṭṭapāla*.

koṭṭa-viṣaya (IE 8-4; CII 1), a *viṣaya* or district around a fortress; a district with its headquarters in a fort. See *koṭaka*.

Kotwāl (IE 8-2, 8-3), same as *Talāra* or the prefect of the city police; the chief police officer of a city or town.

kovai (SITI), Tamil; name of a gold coin.

kovera (IE 8-5), cf. *karaṇe koveram*; probably, some levy at the court of law.

Koyil-nāyakam (EI 25), Tamil; temple officer.

Koyil-śrīkāryam (EI 25), Tamil; a temple officer.

Kramāditya (IE 8-2), see *āditya*. The word *krama* here seems to mean *vikrama*.

Kramaka (EI 5), also called *Kramavid*, *Kramayuta*; epithet of Brāhmaṇas. Cf. *Krama-vitta*.

Kramavid (EI 5), epithet of Brāhmaṇas; same as *Kramaka*, *Kramayuta*. Cf. *Krama-vitta*.

Krama-vitta (SITTI), a Brāhmaṇa well-versed in the method of reciting the Vedas according to the *krama* order. Cf. *Kramaka*, etc.

Kramayuta (EI 5), epithet of Brāhmaṇas; same as *Kramaka*, *Kramavid*. Cf. *Krama-vitta*.

kraya-cīrikā (EI 26), a deed of purchase or sale-deed.

kṛdara (CII 4), a granary.

krīḍāyita (EI 12), sporting.

kṛś-ānna, 'minor food'; cf. *kṛśānna-mūlya* which is the money to meet expenses of light food (*Select Inscriptions*, p. 159). See *mukh-āhāra*.

kriyā (CII 4), Śaiva ceremonies.

kriyaṇakā (LP), cf. Gujarātī *kariyāṇuṁ*.

kroḍa, same as *suvarṇa* (q.v.).

krośa (CII 1), a distance of about two miles and a quarter.

kṛpaṇa (CII 1), poor.

kṛśānu (IE 7-1-2), 'three'.

kṛṣṇala (IA 26), same as *rati* or *guñjā*. One *kṛṣṇala* is regarded by the *Kṛtyakalpataru* (Vyavahāra-kāṇḍa, ed. K. V. Rangaswami Aiyangar, p. 125) as equal to three *guñjās* or *raktikās* apparently through confusion.

kṛṣṇarāja-rūpaka (EI 30), name of a silver coin issues by the Kalacuri king Kṛṣṇarāja.

kṛta (EI 12, 14, 23; BL; CII 3), literally 'accomplished'. i.e. 'completed'; used in earlier records in connection with the era later associated with Vikramāditya. Often spelt *krita*, possibly standing for *krīta* meaning 'purschased', which was a name sometimes applied to certain foreign rulers of North-Western Bhāratavarṣa (*Ep. Ind.*, Vol. XXXIII, p. 152).

(*IE* 7-1-2), 'four'.

(*CII* 1), 'arranged for', 'made arrangements for'.

(*EI* 23), fruit, booty, reward.

(*Sel. Ins.*, p. 202), 'engraved'.

(*Ep. Ind.*, Vol. XXXIV, p. 41, verse 13), written, drafted or composed.

kṛtānta (EI 3), same as *siddhānta*.

kṛta-prānta, cf. *sa-kṛta-prānta* (IE 8-5), Prakrit *sa-kuta-ppanto*; probably, demarcated boundaries.

kṛti (*IE* 7-1-2), 'twenty'; cf. *kṛtin*, 'twentytwo'.

(*Ep. Ind.*, Vol. XIV, p. 98), a composition or performance.

kṛtin (EI 7-1-2,, 'twentytwo'; cf. *kṛti*, 'twenty'.

kṛt-opasanna (EI 30), an expression of doubtful import; epithet of a house.

kṛttidāra (IA 15), an ornament.

krūra-dṛiś (EI 12), designation of Mars and Saturn.

kṣānti (CII 1), forgiveness.

kṣapeśvara (IE 7-1-2), 'one'.

kṣāra (IE 7-1-2), 'five'.

kṣata (EI 23), engraved; cf. *utkīrṇa*, *udghāṭita*, etc.

Cf. Prakrit *chata* (EI 7), 'written' (*Select Inscriptions*, p. 202).

Kṣatrapa (IE 8-2, 8-3; ML; HD), feudatory title of foreign origin; Old Persian *Khshathrapāvan*, 'a provincial governor'; a Satrap. See *CII*, Vol. II, pp. xxxiv, 23, 28; Vogel, *Ant. Ch. St.*, p. 166. See *Mahākṣatrapa*.

Kṣattṛ (HD), a chamberlain. See *Hist. Dharm.*, Vol. III, p. 111. According to Manu (X. 16) and Yājñavalkya (I. 94), the offspring of a Kṣatriya woman from a Śūdra male was called *Kṣattṛ*. This apparently refers to a tribe or community.

kṣauṇī (IE 7-1-2), 'one'.

Kṣemarāja (LL), title of a pious king.

kṣetra (EI 24), a department or committee.

(*SII* 1), a sacred place. Cf. *Varāha-kṣetra*.

Kṣetrakara (EI 12, 15), a cultivator.

Kṣetrapa (IE 8-3; HD), same as *Kṣetrapāla*; supreintendent of the king's *Khās Mahāl*. See *Ind. Ant.*, Vol. XV, p. 306.

Kṣetrapāla (IE 8-3; EI 17; HD), same as *Kṣetrapa*. Cf. *Ep. Ind.*, Vol. XVII, p. 321.

kṣetra-sīman (SII 1), explained as 'a hamlet'.

kṣīra, cf. *a-puṣpa-kṣīra-grahaṇīya* (IE 8-5); milk which the villagers (probably, the milkmen) were obliged to supply to the king or landlord on occasions and to the touring officials.

kṣiti (IE 7-1-2), 'one'.

kṣiti-dāna (EI 23), same as *bhūmi-dāna*; name of a gift.

kṣmā (I 7-1-2; E 25), 'one'.

kṣobha, cf. *a-lavaṇa-guḍa-kṣobha* (IE 8-5; EI 1); obligation or trouble.

kṣoṇī (IE 7-1-2), 'one'.

kṣudra, cf. Prakrit *cūla*=*culla* 'small'; prefixed to the names of persons, localities, etc., in order to distinguish them from others; e.g., *Kṣudra-Mūla*, *Mahā-Mūla*; *Kṣudra-Dharmagiri*, *Mahā-Dharmagiri*.

Kṣudraka (CII 1), a person of a low position; a poor man.

(*JNSI*, Vol. XVI, p. 44), same as *tolaka* or *draṁkṣaṇa*; also spelt *kṣudrama*.

kṣudrama, see *kṣudraka*; same as *tolaka*.

kṣuṇa (CII 2-1), corruption of *kṣaṇa*.

kṣūṇa (EI 3), fault or defect.

Cf. *kṣūṇāni* (LP), probably, 'expenses'; *kṣūṇ-ādika*, 'expenses, etc.'

Cf. *mānak-aikaṁ yāvat kṣūṇaṁ na hi* (LP), 'it matters not if there is a loss of one maund only', i.e. such a case should not be considered a loss.

ku (IE 7-1-2), 'one'.

(*CITD*), a contraction of Telugu *kuṇṭalu* or *kuccelu*, a certain measure of land.

kuca (IE 7-1-2), 'two'.

kucaṭa (LP), disturbance of the peace of mind; cf. Gujarātī *kacvāṭ*.

kuḍya, probably, 'a mound'; see *eḍuka*.

kula (LL), Jain; a particular section of the Jains.

Cf. *udhaḍīyā-jhumpaḍīya-kula* (LP), 'farmers on whom revenue is fixed in a lump sum and who live in huts'.

Cf. *kulam* (EI 25), a land measure; equal to 2 *halas*.

kūla (SITI), tax on grains and pulses; cf. Tamil *kiru-kūlam*.

Cf. Tamil *kūlam* (SII 1), a market.

Kula-brāhmaṇa (SII 1), a family priest.

Kulacārika (*Ep. Ind.*, Vol. XIII, p. 119, text line 8), wrong reading of *Kulavārika*=*Kulavāra* (q.v.).

Kulakaraṇi (EI 15; SII 11-1), a hereditary clerk or officer; a clerk; cf. the modern family name *Kulkarṇī*. The word occurs in the Sūdi inscription of Śaka 981 (*Ep. Ind.*, Vol. XV, p. 91).

kul-ākhyā (CII 3), a family appellation.

Kula-kuṭumbika (LP), farmers who are permanently settled.

kula-pañjikā, cf. *vaṁśāvalī* (IA 30).

Kulapati (EI 9), probably, the head of a school or institution.

Kulaputra (EI 22; CII 8), literally, 'high-born'; epithet of a nobleman. See *Kulaputraka*.

(*Ep. Ind.*, Vol. XVIII, p. 156); explained as 'the chief architect'.

Kulaputraka (EI 22, 23), a nobleman. See *Kulaputra.*

Kularika (CII 4), a potter.

Kulavāra (EI 23), arbitrator; also called *Kulavārika.*

Kulvārika, see *Kulacārika.*

kulavāy (IE 8-6), Bengali form of *kulyavāpa.*

kuli (IE 8-6; EI 28), Tamil; a small land measure equal to $\frac{1}{240}$ of a *pāḍagam.*

kūli (SII 1), Tamil; hire.

Kulika (EI 15, 35), 'the head of a guild'; but cf. *Prathama-kulika,* 'the foremost among the Kulikas', who was the member of a board of administration like the *Pañcāyat* Board. Some inscriptions of the Gupta age mention a board of administration consisting of the *Nagara-śreṣṭhin Sārthavāha, Prathama-Kulika* and *Prathama-Kāyastha* (*Ep. Ind.*, Vol. XV, p. 130), where *Kulika* seems to mean 'an artisan'. *Kulika* is also mentioned as a people probably meaning mercenary soldiers of the Kullu valley (ibid., Vol. XVII, p. 321); cf. Vogel, *Ant. Ch. St.*, pp. 126-27.

(*HD*), an officer in charge of ten villages who was granted a *kula* of land for his salary (Manu, VII. 119, and Kullūka thereon); also 'an arbitrator as a tribunal' (*IHQ*, Vol. XIX, p. 14).

kullaka, cf. *udak-āsihāra-kullaka*; probably, a kind of channel.

kulya (IE 8-6), a measure of capacity equal to 8 *droṇas.*

(*IE* 8-6; EI 29), a land measure; shortened form of *kulyavāpa.*

kulyavāpa (IE 8-6; EI 28), 'an area of land requiring one *kulya* measure of seed grains to be sown'; a land measure which was not the same in different ages and localities.

kulyā (EI 13), a channel for irrigation.

Kumāra (IE 8-2; EI 28, 30; BL; HD), designation of a prince or the king's heir-apparent; usually a prince younger than the *Yuvarāja* (heir-apparent). See *CII*, Vol. I, pp. 93, 97; Vol. II, pp. 40, 48.

Cf. Devī-kumāra (IA 18; CII 1).

Kumārādhirāja (EI 12, 28), title of a ruler.

Kumāra-Divāna (BL), possibly, a *Divāna* or minister enjoying the status of a *Kumāra* or a *Kumāra* who was the *Divāna.* Cf. *Kumār-āmātya, Kumāra-mahāpātra.*

kumāra-gadiāṇaka (CII 4), taken to be the name of a coin by some scholars; but probably, a tax. Same as *kumāra-gadyāṇa.*

kumāra-gadyāṇa (IE 8-5; EI 4; HRS), probably, a tax of one *gadyāṇa* (i.e. the coin of that name) payable on the occasion of a prince's birth. See *kumāra-gadiāṇaka*, *komarina-gadyāṇa*, etc. Cf. Tamil *kumara-kaccāṇam* (EI 21), supposed to be a tax payable in coin for the maintenance of the temple of Kumāra or Subrahmaṇya (SITI). But *kumāra-gadyāṇa* is found in the records of the Gāhaḍavālas of Vārāṇasī, in whose dominions the god in question was not as popular as in the South.

Kumāra-guru (BL), probably, the royal preceptor enjoying the status of a *Kumāra.*

kumara-kaccāṇam (EI 21), a tax; cf. *kumāra-gadyāṇa.*

Kumāra-mahāpātra (IE 8-3; EI 28), a *Mahāpātra* enjoying the status of a *Kumāra* or a *Kumāra* who was the *Mahāpātra*; cf. *Kumār-āmātya.*

Kumār-āmātya (IE 8-3; CII 3, 4; BL; HD), probably 'an *Amātya* enjoying the status of a *Kumāra*'. Cf. Tamil *piḻḻaigaḻ-tanam* (SITI), 'the status of a *Piḻḻai* (prince)', an officers' cadre mainly composed of the junior members of the royal family. See *Proc. 6th AIOC*, pp. 211 ff.; Vogel, *Ant. Ch. St.*, p. 123.

(*IE* 8-3), in one case, a *Kumār-āmātya* was at first a *Mantrin*, but later became a *Mahābalādhikṛta*; in another case, a *Kumārāmātya* was also a *Mantrin*. Cf. *Kumāra-mahāpātra*, etc.

Cf. Kumāra-varga=piḻḻaigaḻ-tanam (SITI), literally, 'the status of the *Piḻḻai* or prince'; supposed to be an officers' cadre composed mainly of the junior members of the royal family.

(*IE* 8-3), also called *Khādya*(*kū**)*ṭapākika*, *Sāndhivigrahika*, *Mahādaṇḍanāyaka*, etc., additionally.

Kumārāmāty-ādhikaraṇa (BL), office of the *Kumār-āmātya*

Kumārapādīya-āmātya (BL), an *Amātya* serving a *Kumāra* or enjoying the status of a *Kumāra.* Cf. *Kumār-āmātya.*

kumār-āsya (IE 7-1-2), 'six'.

Kumāra-varga (SITI), subordinate chieftains who considered themselves as sons of the king or members of the royal family.

kumāra-vṛtti, cf. Tamil *piḻḻai-vari* (SITI), tax for the upkeep of the order of *Piḻḻais* or *Kumāras* (princes). *Kumāra-vṛtti* occury in the inscriptions of the Western Cālukyas of Kalyāṇa.

kumārī-sāhasa (IE 8-5; EI 3, 25; CII 4), 'offence against an unmarried girl'; fine for abducting an unmarried girl; same as *kumārīsāhasa-doṣa.*

humārīsāhasa-doṣa (EI 32), fine for abducting an unmarried girl.

kumbha (EI 5), the pinnacle of a temple; same as *kalaśa.* See also *kumbhaka.*

kumb-ābhiṣeka (SII 3), same as Tamil *tiru-kkalaśa-muḍittal* (SITI), the consecration ceremony of a temple.

kumbhaka (LL), the base of a pillar.

kumosa (Chamba), forced labour.

Kuṁvara (BL), regional modification of *Kumāra.*

kāṇam (EI 16), name of a gold coin.

kuñci (IE 8-6), a measure of capacity usually regarded as equal to eight handfuls.

kuṇḍa (EI 23), a spring.

(*EI* 31), a pond.

kūṇḍi (EI 23), a land measure.

kuṇḍikā (LP), a reservoir of water.

kuñjara (IE 7-1-2), 'eight'.

kuṅkuma-vastra (ASLV), 'saffron-coloured cloth'; sometimes the privilege to wear it was granted to particular persons.

kunnu (Chamba), also called *kunu*; a land meausre.

kunta (Chamba), name of a tax.

kuṇṭa (EI 21), a land measure; cf. *guṇṭha.*

kuntala (EI 24), 'one who wields the spear'.

kunu (Chamba), also called *kunnu*; a land measure.

kūpa (*Ep. Ind.*, Vol. VII, p. 46, note 8), an ordinary well; cf. *vāpī* which is a well with a flight of stairs.

Kūpadarśaka (EI 24), a water-diviner; an inspector of wells.

kupya-gṛha (HRS), a store-house for forest produce as indicated by the *Arthaśāstra.*

kūra, cf. *a-kūra-chullaka-vināśi-khaṭvā-vāsa* (IE 8-5); explained as 'boiled rice'; but probably 'unboiled rice'. The villagers were obliged to supply it to the touring officers of the king. See *vodā, siddh-ānna.*

kuraṅga-mada (IA 18), musk.

kūrma (EI 14), see *madhya-kūrma*, 'a plot of land elevated in the middle.'

kuṟṟam (IE 8-4), Tamil; a district or its subdivision; sometimes the same as *nāḍu*, but sometimes only the part of a *nāḍu*.

kuruvinda, cf. *kuṟuvindam* (SII 2), an inferior ruby.

kuśa, cf. *kuśa-kkāṇam* (SITI), Tamil, tax on the potters.

kuśala (IA 17), used in the sense of *puṇya*, religious merit; cf. *kuśala-mūla*.

kuśala-mūla (CII 2-1; ML), 'the root of merit'; used to indicate 'a pious deed'.

Kuśalin (CII 3; SII 3; IA 9), 'being in good health', used in the preamble of charters to indicate the genuineness and validity of the grant made by the donors when they were in a healthy state of body and mind; epithet of a donor of copper-plate grants to indicate that the charters were issued when the donor was not subject to any disease like madness.

kusūtra, (LP), wrong.

Kūṭa (IA 7), cf. *Rāṣṭrakūṭa*, *Deśakūṭa*, *Grāmakūṭa*.

Kūṭaka (EI 5), probably, headman of the cultivators; same as *Grāmakūṭaka*.

(*IE* 8-5; EI 4, 26), tax for the maintenance of the *Kūṭaka*; see *pravaṇikara-kūṭaka-prabhṛti-samast-ādāya* (*Ep.Ind.*, Vol. IV, p. 101).

(*CII* 4), a measure of capacity.

(*EI* 2), a load or measure of salt.

Kūṭakolasa (*IE* 8-3; EI 29), known from the Bhauma-Kara records of Orissa; official designation of uncertain import; cf. *Kūṭa* or *Kūṭaka*.

ku-tāmra (IA 30), a fraudulent charter.

kūṭa-śāsana (EI 7; IA 30; BL), a forged charter.

Kūṭāyukta (EI 22), official designation; probably *Kūṭa* (*Kūṭaka*) and *Āyukta*.

kuṭī (IE 8-8), a factory; cf. *nīla-kuṭī*.

(*LL*), a Buddhist temple; an abbreviation of *gandhakuṭī*.

Kuṭila, cf. *Siddhamātṛkā*.

Kuṭum (EI 33; LP), abbreviation of *Kuṭumbika*.

kuṭumba (IE 7-1-2), 'two'.

kuṭumba-kṣetra (CII 4), an ancestral field.

kuṭumba-vṛtti, cf. Kannaḍa *kuttumbitti* (EI 18), gift of land for the maintenance of the donee's family.

kuṭumba-yātrā (EI 12; BL), name of a religious ceremony;

a procession of the royal family to the temple of the family deity on the occasion of the king's coronation or a marriage in the palace.

Kuṭumbin (EI 12, 17, 23; SII 1), a cultivator; an agriculturist householder; a householder or ryot.

kuṭumbinī (EI 19; CII 2-1; ML), originally, 'the wife of a householder'; later, 'wife' in general (cf. *Sel. Ins.*, p. 164).

kuttumbitti, Kannaḍa; cf. grant of certain towns and *kuttumbittis* as *aṇuga-jīvita* or fief (*Ep. Ind.*, Vol. XVI, pp. 81-83); mentioned along with *bhatta-grāma* (Sanskrit *bhakta-grāma*), 'provision village' (ibid., Vol. XVIII, p. 193); probably, Sanskrit *kuṭumba-vṛtti*, grant made for the maintenance of the donee's family.

Kuvara (BL), regional modification of *Kumāra*. Cf. *Kuṁvar* (*Kuñar*), *Kunwar*, etc.

L

labdhi, 'nine' (*Ep. Ind.*, Vol. XV, p. 345).

lābha (IE 7-1-2), 'eleven'.

lāḥhārikā, lābhālikā (Chamba), Sanskritised form of the land measure called *lāhaḍī*.

lag, cf. *lagitvā* (EI 9), 'commencing from, beginning with'.

lāga (EI 11), a cess.

lagaḍā (*Ep. Ind.*, Vol. XIV, p. 309), a load; a bar of metal.

lagaṇa (Chamba), fines.

lāga-sambandha, lāga-bhāga (LP), 'any connection.'

laggāvayitvā(IE 8-5), 'having planted'; cf. Bengali *lāgāiyā*. See *JAS*, Letters, Vol. XX, p. 202.

lāgi-drammāḥ (LP), 'expenses incurred'.

lagna (IA 17; SII 1), an astronomical term; the rising of a sign of the zodiac or its passing the meridian. See *Ind. Ant.*, Vol. XVIII, pp. 16 ff.

lagna-devī (IA 30), Jain; a stone-cow.

lāhaḍi, lāhaḍī (Chamba), a land measure. See *lābhārikā, lābhālikā*.

lakāra (IE 7-1-2), 'ten'.

lakaṭā (IE 8-8), meaning uncertain. Cf. *ārdraka-lakaṭā*, probably, dried ginger stick or undried fire-wood.

lakṣa-dāna (EI 12), name of a gift.

lakṣa-homa (SII 11-1), name of a rite.

lakṣaṇa (IA 18), the sexual parts; the male organ; cf. *nirlakṣitavya*, to be castrated.

(*CII* 1), branding.

(*SII* 3; SITI), a document or deed; an inscription.

Lakṣaṇ-ādhyakṣa (HRS), according to the *Arthaśāstra*, the superintendent of the mint, or royal dues received by the superintendent of the mint.

Lākula, also called *Lākuleśvara*(EI 15), a Śaiva sect following Lakulīśa.

Lakuleśvar-āgama (CITD), a form of Śaivism associated with Lakulīśa.

Lāḷa-khaṇḍeya-kāṟar-adhiṣṭhāyaka (IE 8-3), Kannaḍa-Sanskrit; 'superintendent of the revenue from Lāṭa'.

lambā-paṭaha (EI 12), a kind of drum.

lāñchana (EI 28), an emblem. Cf. *cihna*.

(*EI* 9), the [royal] emblem; cf. Tamil *lāñjanai-ppeṟu*, *lāñjinai-ppeṟu*, *ilāñjai-ppeṟu* (SITI), the royal seal.

(*CII* 3, etc.), a crest as distinguished from *dhvaja* or a banner. Cf. *cihna*.

(*HA*), the distinguishing mark or symbol of a Jina image, which helps one to identify the diffrerent Jinas.

lāñchita (EI 29), 'registered with a seal (*lāñchana*)'.

lāṅgaḍi (LP), a cart or carriage; cf. *uchālaka-bhṛta-lāṅgaḍi*, 'a cartful of household furniture'.

Laṅka (EI 19), a carpenter; cf. *Leṅka*, *Leṅkā*, *Buḍhāleṅkā*.

lapita (CII 1), used in the sense of *ukta*.

la-saṁ (IA 18), abbreviation of *lakṣmaṇasena-saṁvatsara*, 'the era of Lakṣmaṇasena'.

laṣṭi (CII 4), same as Sanskrit *yaṣṭi*; a memorial pillar.

Lattalūrapura-parameśvara (IE 8-2), a typical title of the Rāṣṭrakūṭas claiming the city of Lattalūra to have been their original home. Similar titles are quite common in the early medieval records especially of the Kannaḍa-speaking area.

lauki°, *laukika*° (IA 18), abbreviation of *laukika-gaṇanayā*. *Laukika-saṁvatsara* is a year of the Laukika era.

lavalikā (LP), loquacity; cf. Gujarātī *lavlav* or *lavāro*.

lavaṇa, cf. *a-lavaṇa-khātaka* (IE 8-5); salt [the production of which was the monopoly of the king or landlord].

(*IE* 7-1-2), 'five'; also 'cutting [of plants]'.

lavaṇ-ākara (EI 24, EI 30), a salt pit or mine.

layana (LL, EI 22), Prakrit *leṇa*; an excavated cave; a cave; the residence of monks.

lekha (LP), official letter; cf. *likhita*, a private letter.

Lekh-ādhikārin (HD), secretary. See *Rājataraṅgiṇī*, III. 206.

Lekhahāra, *Lekhahāraka* (EI 21; HD), the carrier of letters (see *Rājataraṅgiṇī*, VI. 319).

Lekhaka (CII 3, etc.), a writer; a technical term for one who wrote a record [on copper plates, stone slabs, etc., in order to facilitate its correct engraving by an artisan], as opposed to the composer of the document (see also *likhita*).

(*IE* 8-3; EI 28, 30; LL; HD), a writer, scribe or clerk (see *Bomb. Gaz.*, Vol. XVI, pp. 582 and 605; *Viṣṇudharmottara*, II. 24. 26-28; *Śukranītisāra*, II. 120).

(*LP*), a record or document; mistake for *lekhana*.

Lekhan-ādhyakṣa (CII 3), the superintendent of the writing of documents.

Lekhayitṛ (EI 12), one who is responsible for getting a grant recorded; mentioned together with *Śāsayitṛ*; cf. *Ājñapti*.

Lekhita, *Lekhitṛ* (EI 24), same as *Lekhaka*; a writer.

Leṅka (EI 3; SII 11-1), *Leṅkā* (EI 28), a servant; a Śūdra servant; a writer, according to some.

Lepyakāra, model-maker (*Journ. Or. Inst.*, Vol. X, No. 1, p. 13).

likhita (CII 3, 4, etc.), 'written'; a technical term indicating the manual drafting or writing of a record, as opposed to the composition and engraving of it; see also *lekhaka*.

(*LP*), a private letter; cf. *lekha*, an official letter.

liṅga (BL; SII 1; CII 3, etc.), same as *śiva-liṅga*; the phallic emlem of Śiva; the emblem connected with the worship of Śiva; generally named after the founder with the suffix *īśvara*.

liṅgoraṇa (IA 11), conjecturally translated as 'the festival of rams [to be sacrificed] to the *liṅgas*'.

lipi (SII 3), a letter.

Lipikara (IE 8-3; EI 3; HD), a scribe or writer. See *CII*, Vol. I, p. 176; Pāṇini, III. 2. 21.

Lipikṛt-kula (EI 33), the community of scribes; the Kāyastha community.

Lobha-vijayin (CII 4), 'an avaricious conqueror'.

locana (IE 7-1-2), 'two'.

loha, cf. *so-loha-lavaṇ-ākara* (IE 8-5), 'together with mines of metals and salt pits [the right of which normally belonged to the king]'.

Loha-carma-kāra (EI 24), workers in metal and leather.

lohaḍiyā, name of a coin equal to 20 *pāvīsās* and 100 cowrie-shells; cf. *Ep. Ind.*, Vol. XXXIII, p. 238.

Lohāra (EI 4; BL), modification of *Lohakāra*; a blacksmith.

Loha-vāṇija (LL) an iron-monger.

Lohika-kāruka (LL), a worker in metal.

Lohita (ML), a blood relation.

lohitaka, weight equal to 3 *māṣas* (*JNSI,* Vol. XVI, p. 46).

loka (IE 7-1-2), 'fourteen'; sometimes also 'three'; rarely used to indicate 'seven'.

Lokapāla (CII 3, etc.), a guardian of one of the quarters of the world, originally conceived as four in number and later as eight.

(*EI* 15), cf. the king called 'the fifth *Lokapāla*', the four *Lokapālas* (guardians of the four quarters) being originally Yama of the south, Varuṇa of the west, Kubera of the north and Vāsava of the east. In the same sense, the king was also called *madhyama-loka-pāla,* though *madhyama-loka* may also mean 'the earth' standing midway between the heavens and the netherworld. See *Suc. Sāt.*, pp. 196, 202; *Ep. Ind.*, Vol. XXXII, p. 93. Cf. *Pañcama-lokapāla.*

M

Ma (IE 8-1), abbreviation of *Maṅgala-vāra,* Tuesday.

(PJS), abbreviation of *Mahattama, Mantrin, Mahetā* (meaning 'a clerk' or 'a teacher' in Gujarātī), etc. (especially in medieval Jain inscriptions).

mā (IE 8-6; SII 12; SITI), Tamil; a land measure equal to one-twentieth of a *veli*; also the name of a weight.

māḍa (IE 8-8; EI 7), Telugu; same as Oḍiyā *māḍha* or *māḍhā* and Tamil *māḍai*; a coin of gold or silver; 40 *ratis* in weight; cf. *biruda-māḍa, malla-māḍa, mallanandi-māḍa, surabhi-*

māḍa, gaṇḍa-māḍa, kulottuṅga-māḍa (EI 29), *gandhavāraṇamāḍa* (or *gandhahasti-māḍa*), *cāmara-māḍa, uttama-gaṇḍamāḍa, padmanidhi-malla-māḍa, rājarāja-māḍa, rājendracoḻa-māḍa,* etc. The *gaṇḍa-māḍa* is sometimes called *kārṣāpaṇa, niṣka* and *gaṇḍaniṣka* and is also characterised in a few cases with the epithet 'small'. See *māḍai, māḍha.* Note names like *kulottuṅga-māḍa,* a coin issued by the Coḻa king Kulottuṅga. See *JNSI,* Vol. XVI, p. 43.

(*CITD*), Telugu; half a *pagoda*; half of a *dīnār* or the tenth of a *paṇa* (cf. *badi-māḍuvulu*); half or 50 per cent of revenue, etc.; a weight of gold; money in general. Four *māḍas* are equal to one *carṣam* (*karṣa* ?).

(*IE* 8-5), probably, payment of 50 per cent; see *māḍalu.*

māḍa-baḍi-pātuka (CITD), Telugu; an unknown coin with a fraction of the value of a *māḍa. Baḍi* means 'petty' and *pātika* 'a quarter'.

Madahastipādarakṣā-pālaka (IA 30), explained as 'the captain of the guards of elephants'.

māḍai (IE 8-8; EI 7), Tamil; same as *māḍha, māḍhā* and *māḍa*; cf. *rājarājaṉ-māḍai, madhurāntakaṉ-māḍai, bhujabala-māḍai* (EI 7), etc.; often a gold coin (SII 12). Tamil *māḍai* is the same as *māṣā* derived from Sanskrit *māṣaka.*

(*SITI*), name of a gold coin; a half *pagoda*; cf. *nellūr-māḍai* (SITI), a coin current in olden days and issued from Nellore; also known as *nellūr-ppudu-māḍai*; also cf. *gaṇḍagopālaṉ-māḍai.*

māḍalu (IE 8-5; EI 33), same as *māḍa,* a levy; probably, 'payment of 50 per cent'; cf. Kannaḍa *pannasa* or *pannāsa.*

maḍamba (EI 24), a territorial division.

Madana-tithi (IA 17), Caitra ba-di 13.

māḍāsyāta (CII 3), usually taken to be a word of uncertain import, but may really be the name of a locality.

maddala (SII 3), a musical instrument.

māḍha, māḍhā (IE 8-8; EI 28, 29, 30, 33), Oḍiyā; a silver coin; also a gold coin; 40 ratis in weight; same as *māḍa* or *māḍai.*

madhya (CII 1), middle course.

madhya-divasa (ML), mid-day.

madhya-kūrma (*Ep. Ind.,* Vol. XIV p. 98), probably, a plot of land elevated in the middle.

madhyama (CII 1), a class between the upper and the lower.

Madhyamalokapāla, epithet of kings; cf. *Lokapāla*.

madhyastha (EI 8, 25; SII 2; ASLV; SITI), a neutral person, generally the village headman; a mediator or arbitrator; secretary of the village assembly (SII 13).

madya-pāna (SII 3), intoxicating drinks.

madya-vahanaka (IE 8-8), a carrier of wine.

Maga (EI 9; BL), the same as *Śākadvīpīya*; a community of Brāhmaṇas; name of the members of the Persian priestly community (Magi) settled in India and absorbed in the Brāhmaṇa class.

māgāṇi (ASLV), an administrative unit.

māgāṇi-sthāna (EI 13), epithet of a locality.

Mahā (*PJS*), abbreviation of *Mahājana* (especially in medieval Jain inscriptions).

Cf. Mahā-Mūla (i.e. the elder Mūla) distinguished from *Kṣudra-Mūla* (i.e. the younger Mūla); also *Mahā-Dharmagiri* and *Kṣudra-Dharmagiri*, etc.

Mahābalādhikaraṇika (IE 8-3), superintendent of the office of the *Mahābalādhikṛta*.

Mahābalādhikṛta (HD), 'the great commander'; designation of a military officer who was, in one case, originally a *Muntrin* (IE 8-3); see *Balādhikṛta* and *Mahābalādhyakṣa*.

Mahābalādhyakṣa (CII 3), military title. See *Balādhyakṣa* and *Mahābalādhikṛta*.

Mahābalakoṣṭhika (IE 8-3), treasurer of the military department. Cf. *raṇabhāṇḍāgār-ādhikaraṇa* (Raychaudhuri, *PHAI*, 1950, p. 563).

mahābhāṇḍāgāra (EI 12), treasury; cf. *bhāṇḍāgāra*.

Mahābhāṇḍāgārika (IE 8-2; HD) treasurer; one of the designations often included in the *pañca-mahāśabda* as indicated by the *Rājataraṅgiṇī*. Cf. *Ep. Ind.*, Vol. II, p. 39; *Rājataraṅgiṇī*, IV. 142. Cf. *Bhāṇḍāgārika*.

(*CII* 4), explained as 'the Chancellor of the Exchequer'.

Mahābhāṇḍāgārin (IE 8-3), Kannaḍa *Hiriyabhaṇḍāgārin*; sometimes also called *Mahāpradhāna*, *Sarvādhikārin*, etc., additionally.

Mahābhārata-vṛtti (SITI), land endowed to persons for expounding the *Mahābhārata*.

Mahābhogapati (EI 26), official designation; probably, the superintendent of rent-free holdings; cf. *Mahābhogika*, *Bhogapati*.

Mahābhogika (EI 26; HD), a big *Jāgīrdār*; cf. *Ep. Ind.*,

Vol. XII, p. 9; also cf. *Bhogika* and *Mahābhogapati.*

Mahābhoja (IE 8-2; EI 7, 22, 28; LL), a big *Jāgīrdār*; title of a feudatory ruler; see *Bhojaka.*

Mahābhojī (LL), wife of a *Mahābhoja.*

mahābhūta (IE 7-1-2), 'five'.

mahābhūtaghaṭa-dāna (SITI), name of a *mahādāna.*

mahābhūtaka (EI 14), name of a *mahādāna*; same as *mahābhūtaghaṭa-dāna.*

mahācaturdaśī-parvan (EI 9), 14th *tithi* of the bright half of a month.

mahācaitya (LL), a great *caitya* (q. v.).

mahādāha (SITI), name of a hell which one is supposed to pass through after death on the way to the other world.

mahādāna (EI 7, 16; CII 4), a great gift, 16 of which are enumerated in the Purāṇas (see *Hist. Dharm.*, Vol. II, pp. 869-70; *Suc. Sāt. L. Dec.*, pp. 50f.).

Mahādān-ākṣapaṭal-ādhikṛta (EI 31), officer in charge of the accounts section of the gift department.

Mahādānapati (EI 23; ML; HD), 'the great gift-lord', designation of one who gives a gift. Cf. *CII*, Vol. II, Pt. i., p. 28. Cf. *Dānapati* (EI 28), dedicator of an image of a god on the fulfilment of a desire.

Mahādānapatnī (EI 20), feminine form of *Mahādānapati*; a female bestower of gifts.

Mahādaṇḍanāyaka (IE 8-2, 8-3; EI 30; CII 3,4; BL.; HD); commander of forces; also called *Khādya(kū*) ṭapākika*, *Sāndhivigrahika*, *Kumārāmātya*, etc., additionally; one of the designations sometimes included in the *pañca-mahāśabda*; cf. the case of Maitraka Dhruvasena I (*Ep. Ind.*, Vol. XX, p. 7; *Ind. Ant.*, Vol. IV, p. 105). The five *mahāśabdas* applied to Dhruvasena are *Mahādaṇḍanāyaka*, *Mahāsāmanta*, *Mahāpratīhāra*, *Mahākārtākṛtika* and *Mahārāja*. See *Daṇḍanāyaka*, *Sarvadaṇḍanāyaka*, *Mahāsarvadaṇḍanāyaka*, *Daṇḍapati.*

Mahādānika (CII 4), head of the department of charity; officer in charge of donations; somtimes explained as 'the officer superintending the performance of the *mahādāna* ceremonies' (HD). See *Ep. Ind.*, Vol. VII, p. 91. Cf. *Dharmādhyakṣa.*

Mahādauḥsādhasādhanika (HD), cf. *Dauḥsādhasādhanika.* See *Ep. Ind.*, Vol. XVII, p. 321.

mahādeva (IE 7-1-2), 'eleven'.

Mahādevī (IE 8-2; EI 7; CII 3, 4; HD), a queen; often wrongly taken as the first wife of a king or his chief queen (SITI); a title of the wives originally of paramount sovereigns and later also of feudatory rulers; cf. *Devī*, *Agramahādevī*, *Mahāmahādevī*.

Mahādharmādhikaraṇika (CII 4), explained as the chief justice (HD). Cf. *Ep. Ind.*, Vol. II, p. 309. See *Dharmādhikaraṇika* and *Mahādharmādhyakṣa*, head of the department of religious; affairs.

Mahādharm-ādhyakṣa (IE 8-3; EI 12, 21, 26, 33; HD), explained as 'the chief judge'; but really 'officer in charge of charities, etc.'; cf. *Dharmādhyakṣa* and *Mahādharmādhikaraṇika*.

Mahādhirāja (IE 8-2; EI 12), royal title; cf. *Adhirāja*; also cf. *Dharmamahādhirāja* (EI 12).

(*CII* 3), a feudatory title.

Mahādhyakṣa (EI 12; CII 4), 'the chief superintendent'; cf. *Adhyakṣa*.

Mahādīkṣita (EI 4), cf. *Dīkṣita*.

mahā-doṣa, cf. *mahādoṣa-vivarjita* (EI 23) as an epithet of the gift village; probably, fines for great crimes.

mahā-dvādaśaka (IE 8-4), 'the great twelve'; suffixed to the name of a district probably consisting of twelve Parganās or sub-districts.

mahā-dvādaśī (EI 9; IA 26), also called *pāpanāśinī*; name of a *tithi*; eight kinds of the twelfth *tithi*.

Mahādvār-ādhipati (BL), possibly the same as 'the lord (i.e. the guard) of the *Dvāra* (a pass)' of the *Rājataraṅgiṇī*; mentioned along with the *Mahāsainyapati* and *Mahāpratihāra*.

Mahāgajapati (EI 30), 'the great lord of elephants'; cf. *Gajapati*, etc.

Mahāgaṇastha (IE 8-3; EI 26; HD), probably, the chairman of a guild or superintendent of guilds; cf. *Gaṇastha* and *Gaṇattār*. Cf. *Ep. Ind.*, Vol. XIV, p. 160.

mahā-gandhakūṭī (LL), a Buddhist temple; cf. *gandhakuṭī* and *kūṭī*.

Mahāgovallabha (EI 24), the superintendent of cattle; see *Govallabha*.

mahāgrahāra (SII 11-1), see *agrahāra*.

mahāgrāma (IE 8-4), a small territorial unit; a group of villages; cf. *grām-āhāra*.

Mahāgrāmika (IE 8-3), ruler of a *mahāgrāma* (subdivision of a district or a group of villages).

Mahājana (SITI; ASLV), Brāhmaṇa residents of the entire village; all the members of the village assembly; general body of the *sabhā* or village assembly.

(*IE* 8-3), a member of village council.

(*EI* 8), a merchant.

(*LP*), generally, the merchants, magnates, grandees.

mahājana-sabhā (IE-3), village council.

mahājaya, mahājayā (EI 7; IA 26), name of a *tithi*; same as *su-di* 7.

mahākaraṇa, cf. *sa-mañca-mahākaraṇa* (IE 8-5), an expression of doubtful import; probably, 'official records'.

Mahākaraṇādhyakṣa (IE 8-3), head of the department of records.

Mahākaraṇika (CII 4; HD), the chief secretary; the chief scribe. Cf. *Ep. Ind.*, Vol. II, p. 309. Cf. *Karaṇika.*

Mahākartaka (LL), epithet of an artisan.

Mahākārtākṛtika (IE 8-2; EI 29, 30; CII 3; HD), official designation of uncertain import; probably, a reporter who informed the king about the progress of big undertakings; sometimes explained as 'the royal agent or judge'; one of the designations sometimes included in the *pañca-mahāśabda*; cf. the case of Maitraka Dhruvasena I. Cf. *Ind. Ant.*, Vol. XV, p. 306. See *Kārtākṛtika.*

Mahākārttikī (EI 11; CII 4), full-moon day of the month of Kārttika.

Mahākaṭuka (IE 8-3), official designation of uncertain import.

Mahākavi (CII 4), 'great poet'; title.

Mahākavicakravartin (EI 30; BL), title of a poet.

Mahākhaḍgadhara (EI 30), official designation. See *Khaḍgadhara, Khaḍgagrāha,* etc.

Mahākhalarakṣaka (LP), superintendent of the king's threshing floors.

mah-ākheṭa (EI 5), a great hunting expedition.

Mahākoṣṭhāgārin (SII 2), 'great treasurer'; cf. *Koṣṭhāgārin.*

Mahākoṭṭapāla (CII 4), chief guardian of a frot or the forts; cf. *Koṭṭapāla.*

Mahākṣa (EI 33), abbreviation of *Mahākṣapaṭalika*.

mahākṣa-ni (IE 8-1), abbreviation of *mahākṣapaṭalika-nirīkṣita*, 'examined by the *Mahākṣapaṭalika*' ; *ni* may not be an abbreviation of *nibaddha* (registered) in this case since *mahākṣa-ni* is often used along with serveral other expressions of the kind. See *ni*.

mahākṣapāla-karaṇa, cf. *karaṇa* (LP); explained as 'the depository of legal documents'.

Mahākṣapaṭal-ādhikaraṇ-ādhikṛta (BL) superintendent of the office of the *akṣapaṭala* or *mahākṣapaṭala* department; sometimes regarded as the same as *Mahākṣapaṭalika* (HD). Cf. *Mahākṣapaṭal-ādhikṛta*, etc.

Mahākṣapaṭal-ādhikṛta (BL), same as *Mahākṣapaṭalādhi-karaṇ-ādhikṛta* or *Mahākṣapaṭalādhyakṣa*; also called *Mahā-kṣapāla* (cf. *karaṇa*).

Mahākṣapaṭal-ādhyakṣa (BL), see *Akṣapaṭal-ādhyakṣa*.

Mahākṣapaṭalika (IE 8-3; CII 3; EI 30; BL; HD), record-keeper and accountant; same as *Mahākṣapaṭal-ādhyakṣa*; see *Akṣapaṭalika*, sometimes explained as 'the chief keeper of records' (CII 4). Cf. *CII*, Vol. III, p. 120.

(*IE* 8-3), mentioned as a *Pātra*.

Mahākṣapaṭalin (EI 33), same as *Mahākṣapaṭalika*.

Mahākṣatrapa (IE 8-2, 8-3; EI 16, 27; CII 4; BL; ML; HD), the great *Satrap* or provincial governor; feudatory title of foreign origin; originally, title of a provincial governor; later the Śakas of Western India continued to use it even when they were practically independent. Cf. *CII*, Vol. II, p. 48. See *Kṣatrapa*.

Mahākulapati (EI 29), epithet of a priest.

Mahākumāra (CII 4), title of a prince or the crown-prince.

(*IE* 8-2; EI 28; BL), title of certain rulers; title of some semi-independent Paramāra rulers.

Mahākumārāmātya (EI 29; CII 3; HD), see *Kumārāmātya*. Cf. *Ep. Ind.*, Vol. XVII, p. 321.

mahālayā (EI33), name of a *tithi*; *pūrṇimānta* Āśvina-badi 15.

Mahale, Mahaleka (IA 9), Ceylonese; official designation.

Mahallaka (IE 8-5; EI 25), probably, a member of the *Pañcāyat*; explained as 'city elders'; cf. *yat......nagara-mahallakā vicārya vadante*, etc.

(*Ep*. *Ind*., Vol. XXXI, p. 20) ; also called *Mahallāka*, *Mahallika*.

(*CII* 4), same as *Mahattara*.

(*EI* 2; CII 1), an old man. In Oḍiyā, it means a guard of the royal harem.

(*CII* 1), big, vast.

(*EI* 23), a landlord.'

Mahaṁ (BL), abbreviation of *Mahattama*.

(*LP*), abbreviation of *Mahantaka*.

Maha, *Mahaṁ* (IA 18), abbreviations of *Mahattara* or *Mahattama*.

Mahāmahādevī (BL), designation of a queen or the chief queen; cf. *Mahādevī*.

Mahāmahantaka (EI 7; CII 4; HD), same as *Mahāmahattaka*. Cf. *Ep*. *Ind*., Vol. VII, p. 91.

Mahāmahattaka (EI 25, 33; CII 4; HD; BL), head of a group of villages or of the village council; chief among the village headmen; same as *Mahāmahattara*, *Mahāmahattama*. Cf. *Ep*. *Ind*., Vol. XIV, p. 362. See *Mahattaka*.

Mahāmahattama (BL), same as *Mahāmahattaka*, *Mahāmahattara*.

Mahāmahattara (IE 8-3; EI 26, 29; BL), mentioned along with the *Mahattara*; probably, the chairman of the council of *Mahattaras*; same as *Mahāmahattaka*, *Mahāmahattama*; see *Mahattara*.

mahāmahāvāruṇī (EI 4), name of a *tithi*; same as *vāruṇī* and *mahā-vāruṇī*; *amānta* Caitra-badi 13 with Śatabhiṣā-nakṣatra.

Mahāmahiṣī (IE 8-2), cf. *Piriya-arasi* (IE 8-2), Kannaḍa; title of a chief queen; see *Mahiṣī*.

Mahāmahopādhyāya, title of certain scholars like Jīvadeva of Orissa.

mahamai (EI 17), Tamil *magamai*; name of a tax.

mahāmakha (EI 25), a festival.

Mahāmaṇḍala-cakravartin (EI 9), royal title.

Mahāmaṇḍal-ācārya (EI 26), title of a Buddhist teacher.

Mahāmaṇḍal-ādhipati (EI 29), same as *Mahāmaṇḍaleśvara*.

Mahāmaṇḍala-nātha (HD), same as *Mahāmaṇḍaleśvara*. Cf. *Ep*. *Ind*., Vol. II, p. 227.

Mahāmaṇḍaleśvara (IE 8-2; EI 30; CII 4; HD; BL; SITI; CITD), according to the lexicons, a sovereign ruler who is the lord of 40 *yojanas* of land and a lakh of villages; but, in insciriptions, generally, the governor of a district or province; title of a feudatory ruler or governor (see *Bomb. Gaz.*, Vol. XXI, p. 354); see *Maṇḍaleśvara* essentially meaning 'the ruler of a *maṇḍala* or district'; also called *Mahāmaṇḍalika*, etc.,. cf. *Mahāmaṇḍaleśvar-ādhipati*. The status of a *Mahāmaṇḍaleśvara* seems to have been superior to that of a *Maṇḍaleśvara*, while *Mahāmaṇḍaleśvarādhipati* apparently enjoyed a still higher rank.

Mahāmaṇḍaleśvar-ādhipati (IE 8-2; EI 23), title of a feudatory higher in rank than a *Mahāmaṇḍaleśvara* (cf. *Mahāsāmantādhipati*); a feudatory who had some subordinate chiefs under him; cf. *Mahāmaṇḍaleśvara, Maṇḍaleśvara.*

Mahāmaṇḍalika (IE 8-3), feudatory title; see *Mahāmaṇḍalīka.*

Mahāmaṇḍalīka (HD), same as *Mahāmaṇḍaleśvara.* Cf. *Ind. Ant.*, Vol. IX, p. 35. See *Mahāmaṇḍalika, Mahāmaṇḍaleśvar-ādhipati, Māṇḍalika* etc.

mahāmaṇḍapa (SITI), a large pillared hall next to the *ardha-maṇḍapa* in a temple; also called *mukha-maṇḍapa.*

Mahāmantrin (EI 12, 30; CII 4; IA 19; BL; HD), 'the chief minister or counsellor'. See *Mantrin.* Cf. *Ep. Ind.*, Vol. II, p. 309.

Mahāmanuṣya (IE 8-3), probably, a landlord; mentioned in the list of a king's subordinates. cf. *Mahājana.*

Mahāmātra (IE 8-3), cf. Prakrit *Mahāmāta* (EI 3); a high executive officer employed in various capacities; cf. *Nagaravyavahārika-mahāmātra, Stryadhyakṣa-mahāmātra, Dharma-mahāmātra,* etc.; adopted in Greek as *Mamdtrai.* See *CII*, Vol. I, p. 92, etc.; *Arthaśāstra*, I. 12, V. 1; etc.; *Kāmasūtra*, V. 5. 17. 33 and 35. The word *Mahāmātra* in Manu, IX. 259, is explained by Medhātithi as 'the *Mantrin, Purohita* and others' and by Kullūka as meaning 'the professional tamers of elephants'. (SITI) explained as 'a senior minister.' See *Mātra* in a similar sense.

Cf. Antaḥpura-mahāmātra in the Masulipatnam plates of Amma II (*Ep. Ind.*, Vol. XXIV, p. 276).

(*EI* 28; CII 4), 'an elephant-driver'.

Mahāmātra-gaṇa (CII 4), corporation of elephant-drivers.

Mahāmātra-nagaravyavahārika (CII 1), an executive officer who is the judge or administrator of a city.

mahāmātṛkā, 'mother's mother'; used side by side with *āryikā*, 'father's mother' (*Select Inscriptions*, p. 225).

Mahāmātya (IE 8-3; EI 25; CII 4; BL), the chief minister or executive officer; the prime minister or a viceroy (HD); see *Amātya*; sometimes also called a *Mahāpradhāna* additionally. Cf. Vogel, *Ant. Ch. St.*, p. 122; *Ind. Ant.*, Vol. XI, p. 242.

Mahāmātya-vara (EI 30), chief minister; cf. *Amātya* and *Mahāmātya*.

mahāmeru-śrī-kīrtistambha (BL), name of *Mahārāṇā* Kumbhā's tower at Chitor.

Mahāmudr-ādhikṛta (IE 8-3; EI 12, 14, 15; HD), the keeper of the royal seal; officer in charge of the royal seal; cf. *Mahāmudr-āmātya*. See *Ep. Ind.*, Vol. XII, p. 9.

Mahāmudr-āmātya (IA 11), same as *Mahāmudr-ādhikṛta*; cf. *Mudr-ādhikārin*, etc.

mahā-muraja (ASLV), a musical instrument.

Mahāna (Chamba), a writer; possibly from Sanskrit *Mahantaka*.

Mahānāḍ-prabhu (ASLV), the *Paṭṭanasvāmin* (q.v.) of the rural areas.

mahā-nāḍu (SITI), general assembly of the mercantile community of a district.

mahā-nagara (SITI), merchants' guild of a city; cf. *nagara*.

mahaṇaloka, possibly the same as Sanskrit *mahalloka*= *mahājana* (*Ep. Ind.*, Vol. XXXIV, p. 143).

Mahānas-ādhyakṣa (IE 8-3), Kannaḍa *Bhānasa-vĕrgaḍĕ* (EI 5); superintendent of the royal kitchen; sometimes also called *Mahāsāmantādhipati*, *Mahāpradhāna*, *Accupannāyadadhiṣṭhāyaka*, etc., additionally; cf. *Mahānasika*, *Sūpakārapati*, *Khādya-(kū*)ṭapākika*, etc.

Mahānasika, 'the kitchen-officer' (*Ep. Ind.*, Vol. XVIII, p. 156); cf. *Mahanas-ādhyakaṣa*.

mahānavamī-amāvāsyā (EI 5; IA 18), Kannaḍa name for the new-moon of Bhādrapada; new-moon preceding the *mahānavamī*.

Mahānāvika (EI 27), the captain of a ship.

Mahānāyaka (EI 4; BL), official designation probably indicating a class of feudatories; a subordinate title.

mahā-ni (IE 8-1), abbreviation of some such expression

as *Mahāsāndhivigrahika-nirīkṣita*, 'approved by the *Mahāsāndhivigrahika*'. See *ni*.

mahā-niyoga (SITI), king's order; royal command; an officer bearing the same.

Mahant (EI 4), variant spelling of *Mahanta*; the same as *Mahantaka*.

Mahanta (EI 8; BL), head of a monastery; title of a pontiff.

(*ML*), Prakrit form of Sanskrit *mahat*; 'the great'; a title.

Mahantaka (LP), an accountant; a clerk. It is a term of respect among the Baniyās of Gujarat.

Mahāpādamūlika (IE 8-3), the king's chief personal attendant.

Mahāpalupati (*Ep. Ind.*, Vol. II, p. 22), same as *Mahāpīlupati*.

mahāpaṇa, cf. *māppaṇam* (SITI), name of a coin.

Mahāpañcakulika (CII 4; HD), 'head of the department of *Pañcāyats*' or 'the chairman of a *Pāñcāyat* board'; see *pañcakula*. Cf. *JBORS*, Vol. V, p. 588.

Mahāpāndhākulika (*Ep. Ind.*, Vol. VII, p. 87), a mistake for or wrong reading of *Mahāpāñcakulika*.

mahā-pāpa (IE 7-1-2), 'five'.

Mahāpaṇḍita (EI 9; BL), title of a learned man, generally a learned Brāhmaṇa.

Mahāparamaviśvāsin (IE 8-3; EI 5), probably, a private secretary or privy councillor; same as *Rahasyādhikṛta*, etc.; sometimes called *Mahāpradhāna*, *Sarvādhikārin*, etc., additionally. See *Paramaviśvāsin*, *Vaiśvāsika*, etc.

mahāparinirvāṇa (CII 4), the passing away of the Buddha.

mahāparṣad (EI 32), an assembly or committee.

mahāpārṣika (EI 32), used in the sense of 'a member of the *mahāparṣad*'.

mahā-parvan (EI 12), auspicious time.

Mahāpātra (IE 8-3; EI 19, 30), a minister; a minister higher in rank than the *Pātra*; cf. *Pātra* and *Ekapātra*.

Mahāpasāyita (IE 8-3; EI 5, 27), probably from Sanskrit *Prasādita*, 'favoured', meaning a *Jāgīrdār* of a particular type; sometimes also called *Mahāpradhāna*, *Antaḥpuravĕrgaḍĕ*, *Daṇḍanāyaka*, *Sarvādhikārin*, *Mahāsāmanta*, *Senādibāhattaraniyogādhiṣṭhāyaka*, etc., additionally; cf. *Pasāita*, *Pasāyita*.

Mahāpěriyapradhāna (EI 24), Sanskrit *Mahābṛhatpradhāna*; see *Mahāpradhāna*.

Mahāpīlupati (IE 8-3; EI 28), 'the great superintendent of elephants'; chief of the elephant corps; the master of elephants; sometimes also called *Mahārāja*, *Mahāsāmanta*, *Pañcādhikaraṇ-oparika*, *Mahāpratīhāra*, *Pāṭy-uparika*, *Purapāl-oparika*, etc., additionally. Cf. *Ep. Ind.*, Vol. IX, p. 298. The word *pīlu* is the same as Perso-Arabic *fīl*. See *Mahāpalupati* and *Pīlupati*.

Mahāprabhu (EI 21, 32), sometimes used in respect of subordinate rulers; (HD), a governor; cf. *Ep. Ind.*, Vol. XII, p. 335. (*SITI*) 'the great banker'; the senior merchant; the title by which the leader of the *nānādeśi* merchant community was designated.

(*IA* 30), a village official; see *Prabhu*.

(*EI* 19), explained as 'the high sheriff'.

Mahāpracaṇḍa (EI 12), either a separate official designation or an epithet prefixed to the designation *Nāyaka* or *Daṇḍanāyaka*.

Mahāpracaṇḍa-daṇdanāyaka (EI 20), official designation; cf. *Mahāpracaṇḍa* and *Daṇḍanāyaka*.

Mahāpracaṇḍa-nāyaka (EI 29), official designation; cf. *Mahāpracaṇḍa-daṇḍanāyaka*.

Mahāpradhāna (IE 8-3; EI 30; CII 4; BL; HD), 'the great minister'; 'the chief minister or administrator'; sometimes also called *Mahāsāmant-ādhipati*, *Antaḥpura-vĕrgaḍĕ* (°*ādhyakṣa*), *Mahāpasāyita*, *Senāpati*, *Hĕri*(*Mahā*)*sandhivigrahika*, *Manĕ-vĕrgaḍĕ*, *Kaḍitavĕrgaḍĕ*, *Senādhipati*, *Antaḥpur-ādhyakṣa*, *Hĕri-Lāḷa-Kannaḍa-sandhivigrahin*, *Bhānasa-vĕrgaḍĕ*, *Accupanāyadadhiṣṭhāyaka*, *Sarvādhikārin*, *Hĕri*(*Mahā*)*bhāṇḍāgārin*, *Bāhattaraniyogādhipati*, *Paṭṭasāhaṇ-ādhiṣṭhāyaka*, *Senāpati*, *Daṇḍanāyaka*, *Mahāsāmanta*, *Senādibhāhattaraniyog-ādhiṣṭhāyaka*, *Mahāmātya*, *Paramaviśvāsin*, *Mahāparamaviśvāsin*, etc., additionally. Cf. *Ep.Ind.*, Vol.V, p. 28.

(*SITI*), senior councillor of the king, usually a military officer; same as *Mahāpradhāni*. See *Pradhāna*.

Mahāpradhāna-nāyaka (IA 12), regarded as a single official designation; but probably *Mahāpradhāna* and *Nāyaka*.

Mahāpradhāni (CITD; ASLV), often, the chief minister or administrator; same as *Mahāradhāna*; a high executive officer.

Mahāpramātāra (BL; MD), same as *Mahāpramātṛ*, *Mahāpramātra* or *Mahāpramattavāra*. Cf. *Ep. Ind.*, Vol. IV, p. 280;

Mahāpramātṛ (CII 4), explained as 'the chief surveyor'; same as *Mahāpramātāra*, etc.

Mahāpramātra (EI 12), same as *Mahāpramātṛ*, *Mahāpramātāra*, etc.

Mahāpramattavāra (HD), probably, the same as *Mahāpramātāra*, etc.; explained wrongly as 'the chief of the elephant corps' (CII 4); cf. *Ep. Ind.*, Vol. XI, p. 141.

Mahā-prati (IA 18), abbreviation of *Mahāmātya-Pratihāra*.

Mahāpratihāra, *Mahāpratīhāra* (IE 8-2; EI 30; CII 3; BL), head of the door-keepers of the palace or the king's chamber, or of the capital city; sometimes explained as 'the chief usher' (CII 4). See *Pratihāra*.

(*HD*), the superior officer above all door-keepers, the great chamberlain. See *Kādambarī*, para. 97; *Rājataraṅgiṇī*, IV. 142; *Ep. Ind.*, Vol. X, p. 75; etc.

(*IE* 8-2), one of the designations often included in the *pañca-mahāśabda*, as indicated by the *Rājataraṅgiṇī*.

(*IE* 8-3), sometimes also called *Mahārāja*, *Mahāsāmanta*, *Mahāpīlupati*, *Pañcakaraṇ-oparika*, *Pāṭy-uparika*, *Purapāl-oparika*, etc., additionally.

mahāpratihāra-pīḍā (EI 12), occurs in the *Rājataraṅgiṇī*; explained as 'the office of the high chamberlain'.

mahā-pratolī (BL), main gateway; cf. *pratolī*.

Mahāpurohita (IE 8-3; CII 4), chief priest.

Mahāpurohita-ṭhakkura (IE 8-3), 'the head of the chief priests'; mentioned as a *Pātra* along with *Mahāpurohita*, *Dharmādhikaraṇika*, *Daivāgārika*, *Śaṅkhadhārin*, *Paṇḍita*, *Upādhyāya*, *Daivajña*, *Mahārthaśāsanika*, etc.

Mahāpuruṣa (BL), same as the god Viṣṇu.

(*EI* 7), official designation; probably, the same as *Mahāmanuṣya*.

Mahara (EI 1), probably a mistake for *Mahattara*, 'a village-headman' or 'a member of the village Pañcāyat'.

Mahārāja (IE 8-2; EI 30; CII 3, 4; HD), royal title first assumed by the foreign rulers of India and later adopted by indigenous rulers; originally, an imperial title; later (when the emperors assumed more dignified titles), a title of feudatories and smaller rulers; cf. Greek *Basileos Megalou* and Old Persian *Kshāyathiya vazrka*. Cf. *Ep. Ind.*, Vol. IV, p. 211.

(IE 8-2), one of the designations sometimes included in the *pañca-mahāśabda*; cf. the case of Maitraka Dhruvasena I.

(*IE* 8-3), sometimes also called *Mahāsāmanta*, *Mahāpratīhāra*, *Mahāpīlupati*, *Pañcādhikaraṇ-oparika*, *Pāṭy-uparika*, *Purapāl-oparika*, etc., additionally.

(*IE* 8-2), often used in the South even when *Mahārājādhirāja* became the popular imperial title in the North.

(*ASLV*), designation of a priest of the members of the Vallabhācārya sect. Cf. *Mahanta-mahārāja*, title of pontiffs.

Mahārāja-bappa-svāmin (IE 8-2), designation by which the father and predecessor of a ruling king is sometimes referred to.

Mahārājādhi (CII 3), abbreviation of *Mahārājādhirāja*.

Mahārājādhirāja (IE 8-2; EI 3; CII 3, 4), one of the technical titles of paramount sovereignty closely connected with *Paramabhaṭṭāraka* and *Parameśvara*; later sometimes also assumed by subordinate rulers.

Mahārājādhirāja-parameśvarī (IE 8-2), title of certain ruling queens of Orissa.

Mahārājādhirāja-pati (*Ep. Ind.*, Vol. XIX, p. 242), title.

Mahārājakula (IE 4; BL), officiald esignation of a feudatory; same as *Mahārāval* of the Rajasthan region; cf. *Rājakula*.

Mahārājakumāra, cf. *Bālaka-mahārājakumāra*.

Mahārāja-mātā (IE 8-2), epithet of the mother of a king.

Mahārājanaka (EI 21), feudatory title; cf. *Rājanaka*.

Mahārājapaṇḍita (EI9), official designation; see *Rājapaṇḍita*.

Mahārāja-pitāmahī (IE 8-2), epithet of the grandmother of a king.

Mahārāja-prayojana (SITI), probably, fees collected for the performance of police duties; same as Tamil *araśu-ppeṟu* (SITI).

Mahārājaputra (EI 26; CII 4; HD), 'son of the *Mahārāja*'; designation of a prince. See *Ep. Ind.*, Vol. II, p. 309.

Mahārājā-sāheb (BL), the same as *Mahārāja* with the Arabic honorific expression *sāhib* suffixed to it.

Mahārājātirāja (LL), imperial title; cf. *Rājātirāja*.

Mahārājñī (IE 8-2; EI 4,21; CII 4; BL; HD), designation of queens; see *Rājñī*. Cf. *Ep. Ind.*, Vol. VII, p. 91.

mahārājya (*Ep.Ind.*, Vol.XIV, p.313), 'a province'; cf. *rājya*.

Mahārāṇā (EI 21, 24; BL), derived from *Mahārāṇaka*; feudatory title; later, also a royal title. See *Rāṇā* and *Rāṇaka*.

Mahārāṇaka (EI 27; CII 4; BL; HD), title of feudatory rulers; see *Rāṇaka*. Cf. *Ind. Ant.*, Vol. XVII, p. 214.

mahārasa-karaṇa , cf. *karaṇa* (LP); the liquor department.

Mahārāṣṭrin (IE 8-3; LL), Prakrit *Mahāraṭhi*; 'ruler of a *rāṣṭra* (a district or subdivision or a group of villages)'; see *Rāṣṭrin*.

Mahārāṣṭriṇī (LL), cf. Prakrit *Mahāraṭhiṇī* (EI 7), wife of a *Mahārāṣṭrin*.

Mahāratha (EI 7), explained as 'a race' (EI 17); official designation; cf. *Mahārathin*.

Mahārathin (IE 8-3; EI 7), wrong Sanskritization of Prakrit *Mahāraṭhi* (sometimes read as *Mahārathi*) which really stands for *Mahārāṣṭrin*.

Mahārāula (EI 24; BL), same as *Mahārāvala*; derived from *Mahārājakula*; designation of a feudatory; title of nobility.

Mahārāuta (BL), designation of a feudatory; from Sanskrit *Mahārājaputra*. See *Rāuta*, *Rāvata*.

Mahārāva (BL), designation of a feudatory; from Sanskrit *Mahārāja*,

Mahārāval, *Mahārāvala* (BL), same as *Mahārāula*; designation of a fendatory; from Sanskrit *Mahārājakula*.

Mahārāya (EI 4, 24; BL), from Sanskrit *Mahārāja*.

Maharī, *Mahārī*,*Māhārī* (EI 33), same as *Meharī*, a dancing girl or *Devadāsī*.

Mahāruṇḍā, a name of the Mother-goddess (*Ep. Ind.*, Vol. XXXIII, p. 36).

Mahārtha-mahāmahattaka (CII 4), official designation; see *Mahāmahattaka*. *Mahārtha* may also be a separate official designation or an abbreviation of *Mahārthaśāsanika* (q. v.).

Mahārthaśāsanika (EI 8-3; EI 7), probably, an officer in charge of gifts; sometimes mentioned as a *Pātra*. Cf. *Mahārtha-mahāmahattaka*.

mah-āryaka (EI 8), probably, the great-grandfather; tentatively explained as 'mother's grandfather' (*Select Inscriptions*, p. 202).

mahā-śabda (IE 8-2), cf. *aśeṣa-mahāśabda* (EI 22), same as *pañca-mahāśabda* (q. v.). Cf. *paṭaha-ḍhakkā-mahāśabda* (*Ep. Ind.*, Vol. XXVI, p. 325).

mahā-sabhā (SII 1; ASLV; SITI), 'the great assembly';

meeting of the general body of the *sabhā*; meeting of the *Mahājanas* in session; body of the *Mahājanas*.

mahāsādhanabhāga (IE 12; IA 14; HD), occurring in the *Rājataraṅgiṇī*; explained as 'the office of the chief executive minister'; but cf. *Mahāsādhanika*; one of the five offices instituted by Lalitāditya of Kashmir (*Rājataraṅgiṇī*, IV. 142-43).

Mahāsādhanika (IE 8-2, 8-3; CII 4; BL; HD), official designation indicating a commander of forces; the chief military officer; one of the designations often included in the *pañca-mahāśabda* as indicated by the *Rājataraṅgiṇī*. See *Sādhanika* derived from *sādhana* or army. Cf. *Ep. Ind.*, Vol. VII, p. 91.

(*IE* 8-3), sometimes mentioned as a *Pātra*.

Mahāsāhanī (BL), cf. *Masāhaṇī* (EI 5), a military officer; the same as Sanskrit *Mahāsādhanika*.

Mahāsāhasika (IE 25), official designation; cf. *Duḥsādhya-sādhanika*.

Mahāsainyapati (EI 29; HL), commander of forces; cf. *Sainyapati* and *Mahāsenāpati*.

mahāśāli (EI 5), a kind of rice or paddy.

mahāsāṁ-karaṇa-ni (IE 8-1), abbreviation of *mahāsāndhivigrahika-karaṇa-nirīkṣita*, 'examined by the clerk of the *Mahāsāndhivigrahika*'. *Karaṇa* here may also be an abbreviation of *Adhikaraṇa* or office.

Mahāsāmanta (IE 8-2, 8-3; EI 30; CII 3, 4; BL), 'the great chieftain'; title of a feudatory of a higher rank than the *Sāmanta*; sometimes called *Mahārāja*, *Mahāpratīhāra*, *Pañcakaraṇ-oparika*, *Pāṭy-uparika*, *Purapāl-oparika*, *Senādibāhattara-niyogādhiṣṭhāyaka*, *Mahāpradhāna*, *Sarvādhikārin*, *Mahāpasāyita*, *Daṇḍanāyaka*, etc., additionally. Cf. *Ep. Ind.*, Vol. II, p. 217; Vol. IX, p. 107.

(*SITI*), a vassal chief, sometimes holding the position of a minister or governor.

(*IE* 8-2), one of the designations sometimes included in the *pañca-mahāśabda*; cf. the case of Maitraka Dhruvasena I.

(*IE* 8-3), sometimes a feudatory of a lower grade than *Rājan* and *Rājanaka*.

Mahāsāmantādhipati (IE 8-2, 8-3; EI 29, 30; CII 4; BL; HD), a feudatory title; cf. *Sāmantādhipati* (EI 16); title of feudatories who had some subordinate chiefs under them; title of a feudatory of a higher rank than the *Mahāsāmanta*;

cf. *Mahāmaṇḍaleśvara*, *Samasta-mahāsāmant-ādhipati*; sometimes also called *Mahāpradhāna*, *Bhānasavĕrgaḍĕ*, *Accupannāyadadhiṣṭhāyaka*, etc., additionally. Cf. *Ep. Ind.*, Vol. IV, p. 259. See *Mahāsāmanta*, *Mahāmaṇḍaleśvarādhipati*, etc.

Mahāsāmantarāja (EI 33), feudatory title; cf. *Mahāsāmant-ādhipati*. It may also indicate one enjoying the titles *Mahāsāmanta* and *Rājan*.

mahāsā-ni (IE 8-1), abbreviation of *mahāsāndhivigrahikanirīkṣita*, 'examined by the *Mahāsāndhivigrahika*'. See *ni*, *mahākṣa-ni*.

mahāsandhivigrah-ādhikaraṇa (EI 12; CII 4), the office or department of the *Mahāsandhivigrahika*; the department of peace and war.

Mahāsandhivigrah-ādhikaraṇa-ādhikṛta (BL), superintendent of the office of war and peace or foreign affairs. See *Sandhivigrah-ādhikaraṇ-ādhikṛta*.

Mahāsandhivigrah-ādhikṛta (CII 4; HD), same as *Mahāsāndhivigrahika*; minister of peace and war. Cf. *Ep. Ind.*, Vol. XI, p. 80; *Harṣacarita*, Parab's ed., p. 194.

Mahāsandhivigrah-ādhipati (EI 21; CII 4), same as *Mahāsāndhivigrahika*; cf. *Sandhivigrah-ādhipati*, etc.

Mahāsandhivigrah-ākṣapaṭal-ādhikṛta (EI 31), officer in charge of the accounts section of the foreign affairs department; same as *Mahāsandhivigrah-ākṣapaṭal-ādhipati*.

Mahāsāndhivigrah-ākṣapaṭal-ādhipati (*Ep. Ind.*, Vol. XXXV, p. 274), same as *Mahāsandhivigrah-akṣapaṭal-ādhikṛta*.

Mahāsandhivigrahika (BL; HD), same as *Mahāsāndhivigrahika*; designation of the minister for war and peace or of foreign affairs. Cf. *Ep. Ind.*, Vol. II, p. 309. See *Sandhivigrahika*, etc.

Mahāsāndhivigrahika (IE 8-2, 8-3; EI 30; CII 3, 4; BL; HD), same as *Mahāsandhivigrahika*; minister for peace and war or of foreign affairs; a civil or military title; one of the designations often included in the *pañca-mahāśabda* as indicated by the *Rājataraṅgiṇī*. See *Sāndhivigrahika*.

(*IE* 8-3), cf. *Gauḍa-mahāsāndhivigrahika*, etc.

Mahāsandhivigrahin (BL), designation of the minister for war and peace or of foreign affairs. See *Sandhivigrahin*, *Mahāsāndhivigrahika*, etc.

(*IE* 8-3), sometimes also called *Mahāpradhāna*, *Manĕvĕrgaḍĕ*, *Senādhipati*, *Kaḍita-vĕrgaḍĕ*, etc., additionally.

mahāsaptamī (EI 4), a *tithi*; Māgha-sudi 7; Āśvina-sudi 7.

Mahāsarvadaṇḍanāyaka (CII 3), the commander-in-chief. See *Sarvadaṇḍnāyaka* and *Daṇḍanāyaka*.

Mahāsarvādhikṛta (EI 12,28), the chief minister or administrator. Cf. *Sarvādhikṛta* and *Sarvādhikārin*.

mahā-satī (EI 31), spelt *mā-sati* in Tamil, etc.; a lady who has committeed *satī*; cf. *satī*.

Cf. mā-sati-kal, a stone raised in memory of a *satī* (*Journ. Mad. Univ.*, Vol. XXXII, p. 136).

Mahāsattrapati (EI 13), superintendent of the *sattras* (houses for free distribution of food).

Mahāsenādhipati (EI 19), commander of forces. Cf. *Mahāsenāpati*, *Senādhipati*, *Samastasenādhipati*, etc.

Mahāsenānī, commander of forces (*Ep. Ind.*, Vol. XVII, p. 156).

Mahāsenāpati (EI 30; CII 3, 4; BL; HD), 'the great commander of armies'. See *Senāpati*, *Mahāsenādhipati*. Cf. *Ep. Ind.*, Vol. VIII, p. 94.

Mahāsenāpatnī (IE 8-2; EI 20; LL), wife of a *Mahāsenāpati*.

Mahāśiraḥ-Pradhāni (ASLV), a high officer who had a seat in the Imperial Council of the Vijayanagara kings.

Mahāśramaṇa (EI 32), the Buddha.

Mahāśreṣṭhin (EI 7; CII 4; HD), 'the great banker'; the chief banker; see *Śreṣṭhin*. Cf. *Ep. Ind.*, Vol. VII, p. 91.

mahāsthāna (EI 7), a holy place.

(*EI* 24), a great temple.

Mahāsthavira (LL), Buddhist; cf. *Sthavira*, an Elder.

Mahāsvāmika (*Select Inscriptions*, p. 202), probably, 'the king'.

Mahāśvapati (BL), designation of the leader of horsemen. See *Aśvapati*.

Mahāśvasādhanika (EI 12; HD), commander of a cavalry force. Cf. *Ep. Ind.*, Vol. II, p. 309.

(*CII* 4), the great equerry.

mahāśvaśālā (EI 12; HD), explained as 'the office of the chief master of the horses'; one of the five high offices instituted by Lalitāditya of Kashmir (*Rājataraṅgiṇī*, IV. 142).

Mahāśvaśāl-ādhikṛta (IE 8-2), superintendent of the stables; one of the designations often included in the *pañca-mahāśabda* (cf. *Rājataraṅgiṇī*, IV. 142).

Mahatā (*EI* 32), the same as *Mahattaka, Mahattara* or *Mahattama*. Cf. *Mahato*.

Mahātalavara (IE 8-2, 8-3; EI 25; HD), explained by some authorities as a subordinate ruler and by others as the police magistrate of a city or the prefect of the city police. Cf. *Ep. Ind.*, Vol. XX, pp. 6, 16. See *Talavara, Talāra*, etc.

Mahātalavarī (IE 8-2; EI 20, 25), wife of a *Mahātalavara*.

mahātantra (SITI; ASLV), often mentioned in South Indian records in the sense of 'the army'; the army council; the great assembly of the army.

Mahātantrādhikṛta (IE 8-3), explained by some authorities as 'an officer in charge of judicial and charitable affairs'; but the word *tantra* also means 'administration' or 'the army'; probably 'the chief administrator'. The designation may have also indicated different functions in different localities and ages. See *Tantrapāla, Tantrapati* and *Mahātantrādhyakṣa*.

Mahātantrādhyakṣa (EI 28), official designation; same as *Mahātantrādhikṛta*.

Mahāṭhakkura (IE32;IA17), a title indicating office or rank.

Mahātīrtha (BL), epithet of a holy place or shrine. Cf. *tīrtha*.

mahātithi (EI 13), an auspicious *tithi*.

Mahātman (CII 1), a person of high rank; a rich man; explained in some cases as 'a magistrate' (cf. *Select Inscriptions*, p. 248, note 6).

māhātmya (IA 30), a eulogistic work on deities or holy places, rivers, etc.; cf. *sthala-purāṇa*.

Mahato (EI 8-3), same as *Mahattaka, Mahattara* or *Mahattama*. Cf. *Mahatā*; also *Mahto* in Wilson's Glossary.

mahātoraṇa (SITI), a variety of temple lamps ; probably the same as *makaratoraṇa*.

Mahattaka (EI 8; BL; HD), probably, a village headman or a member of the *Pañcāyat* board; same as *Mahattara*. Cf. *Ep. Ind.*, Vol. XII, p. 30 (*Mahāmahattaka*).

Mahattama (IE 8-3; EI 29; CII 4; BL; HD), probably the village headman or a member of the *Pañcāyat* board; cf. *Mahattara*. See *Ind. Ant.*, Vol. XV, p. 306; *Ep. Ind.*, Vol. III, p. 266 (*Mahattara* and *Mahattama* occur one after another, *Mahattama* being senior or superior to *Mahattara*); *Rājataraṅgiṇī*, VII. 438.

(*EI* 26), same as Gujarātī *Mahetā* or *Mehtā*.

Mahattara (IE 8-3; EI 23, 29, 30; CII 4; BL; HD), literally, 'an elder [of a town or village]'; according to Stein (*Rājataraṅgiṇī*, VII. 659); a chamberlain, a village headman or head of a family or community and a member of the village council; cf. Hindī *Mahato*; Gujaratī *Mahetā*. Cf. *Ind. Ant.*, Vol. VI, p. 114 (*rāṣṭra-grāma-mahattara*); *Daśakumāracarita*, III, p. 77 (*janapada-mahattara*).

Cf. mahattar-ādy-aṣṭakul-ādhikaraṇa (EI 31), 'office of the administrative board of the *aṣṭakula* headed by the *Mahattara*'; see *Mahattara* and *aṣṭakul-ādhikaraṇa*.

(*IE* 3-3), official guide (Beal, *Life of Hiuen Tsiang*, p. 190).

Mahattaraka (EI 23; LL), explained as 'a chamberlain'; same as *Mahattara*.

mahātrāṇa (IE 8-5), Bengali; a rent-free holding in the possession of non-Brahmanical communities, e. g. the Vaiṣṇavas).

Mahāvaḍḍavyavahārin (EI 13; SII 11-2), see *Vaḍḍavyavahārin* and *Mahāvaṇḍavyavahārin*; Sanskrit *Mahāvṛddhavyavahārin*.

Mahāvalākoṣṭhika (IE 8-3), probably a mistake for *Mahābalakoṣṭhika* (q. v.).

Mahāvaṇḍavyavahārin (EI 19; SITI), the great banker or chief merchant; head of a mercantile guild; same as *Mahāvaḍḍavyavahārin*.

mahāvāruṇī (EI 4), name of a *tithi*. See *mahāmahāvāruṇī*.

mahāvihāra (BL), Buddhist convent or monastery.

Mahāvihāra-svāmin (EI 8; CII 3; BL), designation of the builder of a Buddhist monastery and his heirs who were responsible for its maintenance; the builder or owner of a big monastery; cf. *Vihāra-svāmin*.

mahāvihār-āyatana (EI 22), a monastic establishment. Cf. *āyatana*.

Mahāvinayadhara (LL), Buddhist; cf. *Vinayadhara*, 'one who has committed the *Vinaya* texts to memory'.

Mahāvratin (EI 27; SITI), name of a Śaiva sect; followers of the said sect of Śaivism; an ascetic of the Kālāmukha sect.

mahā-vyavasthā (SITI), probably, the regulations framed by the *mahā-sabhā*.

Mahāvyūhapati (EI 19, 28, 30; HD), the chief master of battle arrays. Cf. *Ep. Ind.*, Vol. XII, p. 40.

mahāyajña (IE 7-1-2), 'five'. See *pañca-mahāyajña.*

Mahāyuvarāja (EI 32), title of a crown prince; see *Yuvarāja* and *Yuvamahārāja*.

Mahendrāditya (IE 8-2), see *āditya.*

Maheśvara (SITI), *Māheśvara,* followers of the Śaiva religion; a congregation of Śaiva devotees having a voice in the management of the affairs of a Śiva temple.

(*ASLV*), trustee of a Śaiva temple.

(*IE* 8-2), 'devotee of Maheśvara (Śiva),' epithet of a Kuṣāṇa king.

maheśvara (EI 28), the Pāśupta faith.

Maheśvara-putra (EI 33), sometimes used as an epithet of one devoted to the god Śiva.

mahī (IE 7-1-2), 'one'.

mahīdhara (IE 7-1-2), 'seven'.

Mahimada (EI 32), Indianised form of the Muhammadan name *Muḥammad* or *Mahmūd.*

Mahīmaṇḍaleśvara (BL), rare modification of the feudatory title *Mahāmaṇḍaleśvara.*

mahiṣa-kara, cf. Tamil *erumai-ppon* (SITI), tax on buffaloes.

Mahiṣī, cf. *Agaramahiṣī Agramahāmahiṣī, Mahāmahiṣī,* etc.

Mahodaya (IA 18), used in the sense of *Svāmin* or possessor.

mah-odraṅga, cf. *udraṅga.*

Mahopādhyāya (EI 6, 15), a title of teachers.

Māhut (CII 4), derived from *Mahāmātra,* an elephant-driver.

mahya (EI 28), same as *namasya.* See *Ep. Ind.,* Vol. XXVIII, pp. 77 ff.

mairā (CII 4), boundary of a field.

Maithilī, language and alphabet of Mithilā or the Tirhut region of North Bihar.

maithuna (SITI), wife's brother; elder sister's husband.

maitrī (CII 4), benevolence; one of the *bhāvanās.*

makara-saṅkramaṇa (SITI), entrance of the sun into Capricorn; commencement of the Tamil month Tai; same as *Makara-saṅkrānti.*

makara-saṅkrānti (SITI), same as *makara-saṅkramaṇa.*

makara-toraṇa (EI 29), one of the royal insignia.

(*EI* 3; SII 1, 3), an ornamental arch; an arch in the

shape of a *makara* (crocodile); gateway with figures of crocodiles. Cf. *Ep. Ind.*, Vol XXXV p. 107.

makarikā (CITD), figures of crocodiles drawn in gold dust on the cheeks and breasts of women; same as *makarikā-patra*.

(*EI* 14), cf. *mukuṭa-makarikā-marakata*.

makarikā-patra (CITD), same as *makarikā*.

makuti (CII 4), an edict addressed to the Śūdras. Cf. *Mākutika*, official designation.

māla (EI 22), an elevated ground.

Maladhāri (BL), epithet of a Jain religious teacher.

Mālākāra (LL), a florist. See *Mālin*.

malamārgaṇa (LL), cf. Gujarātī *maḷavero*; a tax to be utilised when the whole village wants to honour a particular man.

Mālava-gaṇ-āmnāta, *Mālava-gaṇa-sthiti*, *Mālava-pūrvā* (EI 23), expressions used in early records in connection with the Vikrama-saṁvat.

Mālavī, dialect of Hindī prevalent in Mālava (Malwa).

Mālavīya (EI 22), 'the king of Mālava'.

malaya (IA 14), derived from Dravidian *malai*, 'a hill'.

Malayāḷam, name of a language and alphabet.

Maleya-sāhaṇi (Naik's List, No. 264); mentioned alongwith *Peyiya-sāhaṇi*; official designation. See *Sāhaṇi*.

Mālima, same as Arabic *Mualim*, 'an instructor' (*Ep. Ind.*, Vol. XXXIV, p. 144).

Malla (CII 4), a wrestler, a match.

mallaka (EI 21) a measure.

malla-kara (HRS), found in Nepal inscriptions; tax levied as tribute to the Mallas or for defence against their attack. Cf. *turuṣka-daṇḍa*, etc. It may also be a professional tax on wrestlers.

mallaka-vundhaka, cf. *talabhedyā-ghāṇaka-mallaka-vundhaka* (IA 18); probably, a professional tax on wrestlers.

Malik, *Malika* (EI 4; BL), Muslim title of nobility; same as Arabic *Malik*; also spelt in Indian languages as *Mallika*.

Mālin (EI 9), a florist. See *Mālākāra*.

Mamátrai (IE 8-3), Greek modification of *Mahāmātra*; explained as 'commanders or rulers among Indians'.

maṁkṣūṇa, see *draṁkṣaṇa*.

māmūl-ādāya (SITI), customary payment.

man, cf. *mānayitvā* (LP) 'having accepted'; cf. Gujarātī *mānine*.

māna (CITD), Telugu-Kannaḍa; $\frac{1}{16}$th part of the measure called *tūmu*; that which can hold rice of the weight of 4 *ṭaṅkalamulu* (varying in different localities); a particular measure or weight often regarded as half of a *seru*; a measuring rod.

(*EI* 16), also called *mānaka*; name of a measure; a liquid measure (SII 11-1).

māna, *māṇa* (IE 8-6; EI 30, 31), used in medieval Orissan records in the sense of a land measure; a land measure regarded as equal to an English acre in Orissa.

māna-bhoga (SITI), enjoyment of tax-free lands.

māna-daṇḍa (SITI), measuring rod.

mānaka (EI 14, 16), name of a measure; also called *māna*.

māna-pautava (EI 30), probably, a store-house where grains were measured and stored. Cf. *mānya* (*aḻāya-mānya*).

(*IE* 8-8), scales and measures.

māna-stambha (EI 5, 8), a pillar; an elegant tall pillar with a small pinnacled *maṇṭapa* at the top erected in front of Jain temples.

manavarti, *manavartika* (EI 32), grant for maintenance; also spelt as *manovarti*, *manuvṛtti*, etc., probably derived from Sanskrit *mānya-vṛtti*.

Mānavya (EI 16), name of a *gotra* that was claimed by royal families which had originally no real Brāhmanical *gotra*.

mañca, cf. *sa-mañca-mahākaraṇa* (IE 8-5); probably, elevated platforms for official use.

maṇḍa, weight equal to 5 *māṣas* (*JNSI*, Vol. XVI, p. 46); cf. *māḍa*.

maṇḍaī (EI 23), derived from *maṇḍapikā*; same as *maṇḍī*, 'market'.

maṇḍaka (SITI), same as *maṇḍapa*.

maṇḍala (IE 8-4; EI 29, 30; CII 4), an administrative unit; a district or province.

(*SITI*), a province consisting of several *koṭṭams* or *valanāḍus*.

(*IE* 8-4), sometimes mentioned as bigger than a *viṣaya* and sometimes smaller than it; sometimes a *viṣaya* was included in a *maṇḍala*, but sometimes a *maṇḍala* was included in a *viṣaya*; sometimes *maṇḍala* and *viṣaya* are identical; sometimes a *maṇḍala* was smaller than the *vīthī* or subdivision.

(*IE* 8-4; SII 3; ASLV), sometimes used in a wider sense to indicate a country.

Cf. Kona-maṇḍala (EI 22), also called an *avani-maṇḍala* or *deśa*. Here *maṇḍala* means a kingdom or territory.

(*ASLV*), an assembled body. Cf. *mātṛ-maṇḍala*.

Maṇḍal-ācārya (EI 33, IA 14), same as *Paṭṭ-ācārya*; designation of a high priest.

(*BL*), epithet of a [Jain] religious teacher.

Maṇḍal-ādhipati (EI 25), the ruler of a *maṇḍala*; cf. *Maṇḍaleśvara Maṇḍalapati*.

Maṇḍala-gaṇin (EI 33), title; cf. *Gaṇin*.

maṇḍala-karaṇa (LP), department dealing with the administration of districts.

Maṇḍala-mudaliyār, official designation; cf. *maṇḍala-mudanmai*.

maṇḍala-mudanmai (SITI), Sanskrit-Tamil; leadership or governorship of a province, its governor or chief being known as *Maṇḍala-mudaliyār*.

Maṇḍalapati (IE 8-3; EI 26, 33), ruler or officer-in-charge of a *maṇḍala*; the governor of a district or a feudatory ruler (*Ep. Ind.*, Vol. XIX, p. 78, text line 9); same as *Maṇḍaleśa*.

Maṇḍaleśa (BL; HD), 'lord of a *maṇḍala*'; a provincial governor; same as *Maṇḍaleśvara*. See *Rājataraṅgiṇī*, VI. 73; VII. 996; VIII. 1228, 1814, 2029.

Maṇḍaleśvara (IE 8-2; BL; HD), title of a feudatory or governor lower in rank than a *Mahāmaṇḍaleśvara*; same as *Maṇḍaleśa*. Cf. *Bomb. Gaz.*, Vol. XXI, p. 354. Cf. *Mahāmaṇḍaleśvara*, 'governor of the provinces' (*Ep. Ind.*, Vol. XXXV, p. 110).

Maṇḍalika (EI 26), ruler of a *maṇḍala* or district; same as *Māṇḍalika*.

Māṇḍalika (IE 8-2; BL; CII 4), ruler of a *maṇḍala* or district; title of a feudatory chief; cf. *Maṇḍalika*, *Maṇḍalīka*.

Maṇḍalīka (IE 8-2; SII 1; SITI; BL), feudatory title; ruler of a *maṇḍala*; same as *Maṇḍalika* and *Māṇḍalika*, also called *Maṇḍaleśvara*.

maṇḍapa (IE 8-3), customs house; Marāṭhī *māṇḍavī*, from Sanskrit *maṇḍapikā*; explained by some as 'a market place'

(Hindī *maṇḍī*); but Hindī *maṇḍī* seems to be derived from the same word because the toll-stations were often situated in market-places.

(*BL*), name of a structure in front of a temple.

(*LL*), a porch or hall.

(*CII* 4), the hall in a temple.

(*CII* 4), a temple.

(*EI* 31), a temple or public building.

Cf. vaiccamudu-maṇḍapa (SITI), kitchen; same as *maḍaip-paḷḷi.*

Cf. vakkāṇikku-maṇḍapa (SITI), hall where disputations in the *śāstras* are held. Cf. *śanivāra-maṇḍapa.*

maṇḍapikā (EI 1, 3, 33), customs house; same as *śulka-maṇḍapikā* (*Ind. Ant.*, Vol. XI, p. 339 and note 31). See Ghoshal, *H.Rev. Syst.*, pp. 238-39.

(*EI* 3; CII 4); market; a market pavilion.

(*CII* 4), a small temple.

Māṇḍapika (IE 8-2), cf. Prakrit *Maṁḍavika* (EI 1), officer in charge of a *maṇḍapikā* or customs house; a collector of tolls.

maṇḍapik-ādāya (EI 23), explained as 'the market tax'; customs duties.

maṇḍapikā-karaṇa, cf. *karaṇa* (*LP*), the customs depart ment.

maṇḍapikā-paṭṭaka (LP), a contract for market-tax.

Māṇḍavī (LP), one who gets the market-tax; same as *Māṇḍapika.*

(*LP*), a tax levied on articles that are to be sold in a market-place.

(*IE* 8-3), Marāṭhī; same as *maṇḍapikā*, 'customs house'.

maṇḍavo (EI 22), market place; regarded as the same as *maṇḍapikā.*

Manĕ-vĕrgaḍĕ (IE 8-3; EI 16 ; SII 11-2), Kannaḍa; superintendent or steward of the royal household (*Ep. Ind.*, Vol. XV, p. 77); sometimes also called *Mahāpradhāna*, *Hĕri-sandhivigrahin*, *Antaḥpurādhyakṣa*, *Hĕri-Lāḷa-Kannaḍa-sandhivi-grahin*, etc., additionally.

Maneyasamastasainyādhipati (IE 8-3), leader of all the troops in the royal household. Cf. *Samastasenādhipati*, etc.

maṅgala (CII 1), a ceremony for one's good or for averting evil; cf. *kalyāṇa.*

(*SITI*), a Brāhmaṇa village; shortened form of *caturvedi-maṅgala.*

(*ASLV*), a small administrative unit.

(*IE* 7-1-2), 'eight'.

maṅgala-kalasa (CII 4), an auspicious vase. Cf. *nidrā-kalasa.*

maṅgālihā (IA 15), probably, an upper garment.

māṅgalikya (LP), some present (made in lieu of the benefit one is going to get).

māṅgalīyaka (LP), probably, a tax collected on the occasion of auspicious events in the royal family, such as the birth of a son to the king.

māṅgalya (SITI), Tamil *maṅgiliyam*; the ornament called *tāli* worn round the neck as the marriage badge by a married woman with her husband living.

maṅgaṇi, maṅgaṇī, maṅaṇī (Chamba), a tax in kind.

maṇi (IA 20), a burning glass.

māni (LP), a measure of capacity equal to about 6 maunds.

(*SII* 11-1), Kannaḍa; also spelt *Māṇi*; a bachelor; Brahmacārin.

māṇi (EI 14; Chamba), name of a measure.

maṇi-bhaṇḍalu (CITD), Sanskrit-Telugu; probably, from Sanskrit *maṇi-bhāṇḍa* or the receptacle of jewels.

maṇi-grāma (SITI), a mercantile guild.

māṇika (CITD), Telugu; a measure; $\frac{1}{4}$ of a *kuñcamu* and $\frac{1}{16}$ of a *tūmu.*

Maṇikāra (LP), a jeweller.

māṇikya-bhāṇḍāra, cf. *maṇikka-paṇḍāram-kāppār* (SITI), 'keeper of the treasury [of precious stones] in the temple or palace.'

Mānin, cf. *Māṇi* (IA 18), an Elder.

mānita (LP), accepted.

mañjāḍi (IE 8-8; EI 21, 33; SII 2, 12; SITI), Tamil; name of a weight for measuring gold and silver; about 2 or 3 *ratīs* or 4 or 5 grains; a weight equal to two *kuṉṟi-maṇi* used in weighing gold; $\frac{1}{10}$ of a *kaḻañju* and $\frac{1}{100}$ of a *śatamāna* (*JNSI*, Vol. XV, p. 141).

Mañjūra (LP), day-labourer; cf. *Majūr.*

mañjūṣā (LL), casket.

Manneya (CITD), Telugu; same as Sanskrit *Mānya*; a respectable man; a chieftain; a commander; a chief. Cf. *Mannīḍu, Manniya.*

(*SII* 11-1), ruler of a group of villages; cf. *manneya-svāmya*, tenure held by a *Manneya*.

Mannīḍu (CITD), same as *Manneya* (Sanskrit *Mānya*).

Manniya (*CITD*), same as *Manneya* (Sanskrit *Mānya*).

manohārī (LP), cf. *nija-manohāryā*, 'at one's own will'.

mano-'tireka (CII 1), eagerness; cf. *atireka*.

manovarti (EI 32), same as *manavarti* or *manuvṛtti* in the sense of *namasya-vṛitti* or *mānya*; probably derived from Sanskrit *mānya-vṛtti*.

manthana-yantraka (IA 20), a fire-producing instrument.

mantra-deva-manuja-bhūta-pitṛgaṇa (IA 15), refers to the *pañca-mahāyajña*.

Mantrapāla (EI 22), official designation; probably, a private secretary or privy councillor.

Mantrapuṣpa (IA 12), designation of a priest who repeats the *mantra* when the chief priest asks forgiveness at the conclusion of each *pūjā* at the Rāmeśvaram temple.

mantra-śakti (CII 4), the power of good counsel.

mantra-snāna (EI 4), repetition of prayers used at ablution without the actual bath.

Mantrin (EI 12, 25; CII 4; BL; HD), a minister or councillor; a counsellor; an executive officer. See *Arthaśāstra*, I. 80; *Yājñavalkyasmṛti*, I. 312; *Ep. Ind.*, Vol. IX, p. 305.

(*IE* 8-3), explained as *vyavahāra-draṣṭṛ*. Cf. *Mahāmantrin*.

(*IE* 8-3), in one case, the *Mantrin* later became a *Mahābalādhikṛta*; in another case, also a *Kumārāmātya*.

mantri-pariṣad (CII 4; ASLV), the council of ministers; same as *pariṣad*.

Manu (IE 7-1-2), 'fourteen'.

Manuṣya, cf. *Mānisi* (EI 24), a servant.

manuṣya-yajña (CII 4), reception of guests; one of the five *mahāyajñas*.

manuvṛtti (EI 32), a grant made for the maintenance of the donee; same as *manavarti*, etc.; probably derived from Sanskrit *mānya-vṛtti*.

manvādi (IA 18), name applied to certain *tithis*.

mānya (IE 8-5; EI 20, 23; ASLV), a rent-free holding, tax-free land; same as *sarva-mānya*; cf. *mānya-sthiti*, *manuvṛtti*, etc.

Cf. sthāna-mānya (CITD), an honour or glebe-land

granted by the ruler on quit-rent or on various favourable tenures.

(*EI* 13), land either liable to a trifling quit-rent or altogether exempt from tax.

Cf. aḻḻāya-mānyam (SITI), right to receive a handful of grain or the prescribed quantity of an article brought for sale in the market as charges for measuring; cf. *māna-pautava.*

Cf. guḍḍe-mānya (IA 19), a particular kind of rent-free holding.

mānya-kaṇikĕ (EI 25), a small amount of tax levied from land declared rent-free. Cf. *nikara*, *tṛṇodaka*, etc.

mānyaka-paṭṭa, a rent-free village (*Ep. Ind.*, Vol. XIX, p. 71).

mānya-sthiti, cf. *mānya*.

manyavāntara-rāṣṭra (SII 1), same as *nāḍu* or district.

mānya-vṛtti, cf. *manuvṛtti*, etc.

māppaṇam (SITI), Tamil; same as Sanskrit *mahā-paṇa*; name of a coin.

mār (IA 15), a land measure.

mara (EI 14), name of a measure.

maramakkatayam (EI 9), system of inheritance prevalent in the Malayāḷam-speaking area, according to which property is owned by females and passes from female to female.

Marāṭhī, language and people of Maharashtra.

maravaḍai (EI 17), name of a tax.

Mārga (IE 8-1), abbreviation of *Mārgaśīrṣa*, *Mārgaśira*, etc.

mārg-ādāya (EI 23; SITI), same as *vartma-daṇḍa*; levy for passage of articles of merchandise through the gift village by the village road; tolls; tolls on the articles on transit. See *mārgaka*.

mārgaka (EI 26), name of a levy; same as *mārg-ādāya*.

mārgaṇa (EI 24), a begger.

mārgaṇaka (EI 3; IA 18; CII 4; HRS), known from records like those of the Caulukyas; a levy; a kind of cess or tax; explained as 'benevolences of a general character, as distinguished from the special types called *prasthaka* and *skandhaka*'. See *mārgaṇika*.

mārgaṇika (IE 8-5), same as *mārgaṇaka*.

Mārgapa (EI 20), same as *Mārgapāla*, etc.

Mārgapāla (HD), same as *Mārgapati*, etc. See Nārada quoted in the *Mitākṣarā* on *Yājñavalkyasmṛti*, II. 71. Cf. *Dikpāla*.

Mārgapati (BL; HE), explained as 'the guardian of the frontiers or passes' (cf. *Ep. Ind.*, Vol. XX, pp. 37, 41); probably, a collector of customs duties on the roads. See *mārg-ādāya*, etc.

Mārgeśa (EI 20), same as *Mārgapati*.

marīchi, a theoretical unit of measurement (*JNSI*, Vol. XVI, p. 48).

Marjhaka (ML), title of foreign origin.

mārtaṇḍa (IE 7-1-2), 'twelve.'

maṟutu (CITD), same is *maṟuturu*.

maṟuturu (IE 8-6; CITD); also called *maṟutu*, *mattaru*, etc.; Telugu; Kannaḍa *mattar* or *mattaru*; a certain land measure of uncertain area generally used as an equvalent of *nivartana*, different kinds being mentioned as *kāl-maṟuturu*, *ghaḍa-maṟuturu*, *kommu-maṟutu*, etc.

Marvāḍī, spelt *Marwari* in English; name of the Rājasthānī dialect prevalent in Marwar.

maryādā (SITI), Tamil *mariyādi*; customary dues; manners; ways; extent; limit; also spelt in Tamil as *marjādi*, *mariśādi*, *maruśādi*, etc.

Maryādā-dhurya (BL), explained as 'the Warden of Marches.'

maryādā-parihāra (EI 22), customary exemptions of taxes. See *parihāra*.

māsa (IE 7-1-2), 'twelve.'

māṣa (EI 21, 25, 30, 33; CII 4), according to the *Kṛtyakalpataru* (Vyavahāra-kāṇḍa, ed. K.V. Rangaswami Aiyangar, p. 125), a gold coin as opposed to silver *māṣaka*; name of a weight; name of a coin; 5 *ratis* in weight; sometimes regarded as 10 *ratis* in weight and as equal to $\frac{1}{4}$ of a *śāna*. See *JNSI*, Vol. XVI, p. 41. It was sometimes regarded as $\frac{1}{20}$ of a *paṇa* of 100 *ratis* (*ibid.*, Vol. XV, p. 143). Cf. *māṣaka*, *ādya-māṣa*.

māṣaka (IE 8-8), name of a coin; cf. *māṣa* and *dināri-māṣaka*; mentioned as a silver coin (K. V. Rangaswami Aiyangar, *Kṛtyakalpataru*, Vyavahāra-kāṇḍa, p. 125).

māsārdha (IE 7-1-2), used to indicate 'six'; cf. *māsa*, 'twelve'; also *pakṣa*, 'two'.

Māśu (Chamba), one enjoying land, who does not pay rent or tax but renders service; e.g., a carpenter, etc.

masūra (ML), small-pox.

mata, cf. *guru-mata* (CII 1), 'a matter considered to be serious'.

(*LP*), a signature; cf. the use of the word with the signature as in *mataṁ mama amukasya* found copied in many copper-plate grants.

mātaṅga (IE 7-1-2), 'eight'.

mātā-pitṛ-pād-ānudhyāta (IE 8-2), 'meditating on or favoured by the feet of one's parents'; epithet of rulers; cf. *mātā-pitṛ-pād-ānudhyāna-rata.*

Mātaraḥ (CII 3), the Divine Mothers, sometimes indicated as seven in number; cf. *Mātṛ* and *Mātṛ-gaṇa.*

maṭha (EI 17, 19, 23, 31, 32; CII 3, 4; SII 1; BL; ASLV; CITD), a school or religious college; a temple; a monastery; hermitage or convent; a monastery which was a religious and educational institution. See *maṭhikā.* In Telugu records, it also means 'a bullock cart' and 'a cart load' (cf. Kannaḍa *maṭṭī*, 'a load').

(*SITI*), place where pilgrims and religious mendicants (*tapasvins*) are fed.

Maṭhādhipati (EI 25), same as *Jīyar* and *Mudaliyār*; cf. *Maṭhapati.*

Maṭhapati (EI 33), superintendent of a monastery; the chief priest of a temple.

māṭhāpatya (SITI), the office or position of a *Maṭhapati*; management of the affairs of a *maṭha* or temple.

maṭha-sthāna (EI 26), a monastery.

maṭhikā (EI 31), a hut, cottage or cell.

(*EI* 26, 32), a shrine or temple; cf. *maṭha.*

Matisaciva (IE 8-3; HD), counsellor or minister; cf. *Karma-saciva*, administrative officer. See *Ep. Ind.*, Vol. VIII, p. 44.

Mātṛ (EI 9), the Divine Mothers, often described as seven in number; cf. *mātṛ-maṇḍala*, various forms of the Mother-goddess installed around a Śiva temple.

Mātra, designation of a class of officers; cf. *Mahāmātra* in a similar sense. See *Ep. Ind.*, Vol. XVIII, p. 117 (mentioned along with *Mūlaprakṛti*; cf. *Prakṛti*).

Mātṛ-gaṇa (IA 7), the Divine Mothers, often described as seven in number. Cf. *mātṛ-maṇḍala.*

matsy-ākara, cf. *sa-matsy-ākara* (IE 8-5), 'together with the sources of fish', the fishing right belonging to the king or landlord; cf. *jala-kara.*

mātsya-nyāya (EI 4), 'the law of the fish'; anarchy.

matta (LP), a signature; corrupt form of *mata*, 'approved', written along with the signature as in *mataṁ mama amukasya*. See *mata*.

mattal (EI 16; IA 11), land measure; same as *mattar*.

mattar (EI 16, 20), Kannaḍa; land measure; same as *maṟuturu* or *nivartana*; cf. *gaṇṭi-mattar* (IA 9).

mattaru (IE 8-6; CITD), same as *mattar* or *nivartana*.

maṭṭa-skandha (LP), a layer of mud; cf. *maṭṭa-skandha-rahita* (LP), free from the layers of mud.

Maṭṭivā (IA 10), Hindī; an exorcist.

maṭṭu (CITD), Telugu; an unknown measure of land.

maukha (EI 13), same as *mukhya*; 'chief disciple'.

maulika (IE 8-5; EI 32), a tax; the principal or main tax or the perquisites of hereditary officers.

mavāḍa (CII 4), name of a tax; cf. *māvaḍai*.

māvaḍai (EI 17), name of a tax. cf. *mavāḍa*.

mayūra (CII 1), a peacock; a bird in general.

mayūṭa (HRS), probably, the contributions of fruits, fire-wood, etc., paid by villagers.

Me (Chamba), abbreviation for *Mehtā* (*Mahattaka*).

meḍhi (LP), a barn-yard, a threshing floor.

meḍhi-hāraka (LP), a special tax on the threshing-floor.

medhya, cf. *a-paśu-medhya* (IE 8-5), 'free from the obligation of supplying animals for sacrifices'.

meḍi (EI 9), also called *meli*, a kidnapper of victims for sacrifices.

meghāḍambara (SII 3), Hindusthānī; a covered *howdā*.

Meha (IA 18), abbreviation of *Mehara*.

Mehara (EI 33), village headman.

Meharī (EI 33), same as *Devādāsī*.

melāpaka (LP), a group.

meli (EI 9), same as *meḍi*. (q.v.).

Mel-śānti (SITI), Tamil-Sanskrit; chief priest in a temple.

melviṭṭiya-vaḍḍāravuḷa (IE 8-5), Kannaḍa; name of a tax; see *vaḍḍāravuḷa*.

mera (EI 6), Telugu; a fee.

Meridarkha (IE 8-3; ML), an official designation of foreign origin; same as Greek *Meridarkhes*, 'a district officer'.

Meridarkhes (IE 8-3), Greek; see *Meridarkha*.

meru (SII 3), name of a gift.

(*EI* 2; CII 4), a kind of temple.

meṣa-saṅkrānti (CII 3, etc.), the entrance of the sun into the sign Aries, regarded as the starting point of the Śaka year; see also *abdapa*.

meya (IE 8-5; EI 31; HRS), the share of grains to be paid to the king or landlord; revenue from agricultural land paid in kind; same as *bhāga*. Cf. *tulya-meya*, tax on commodities brought to market for sale.

Meykāval (ASLV), watchman in a temple.

majigiti (*Ind. Ant.*, Vol. XI, p. 242), also spelt *mijigiti*; Indianised form of Arabic *masjid*, a mosque.

mijigiti (*A.R.Ep.*, 1958-59, p. 12); see *majigiti*.

milivalita, same as Sanskrit *sammilita*, 'taken collectively' (*JAS*, Latters, Vol. XX, p. 204).

miśra (IA 18), an honorific title; cf. *Mahāmiśrapaṇḍita*.

Mīṭhika (LL), a polisher.

miti (IA 20), cf. *Saṁvat* 1384 *miti Bhādra-vadi* 3 *Guru-dine*; probably a corruption of Sanskrit *mita*, 'counted', 'calculated'.

Mleccha (EI 22), name applied to the Muhammadans and other foreigners; cf. *Mlecchesvara* (EI 32).

moci, *mocī* (EI 2; CII 4), a shoe-maker.

modala-vāḍa (IE 8-4), Kannaḍa; the chief village in a Pargana consisting of a number of villages, i.e. headquarters; sometimes called *rājadhānī*.

modati, cf. *svarge modati bhūmidaḥ*; *parasmaipada* in place of the expected *ātmanepada*.

Modina, same as Arabic *Muazzin*, 'a public crier to prayers' (*Ep. Ind.*, Vol. XXXIV, p. 144).

Mohinī (IA 19), female devils who possess men.

mokīraka (LP), a den in a mountain forest; Gujarātī *bhokaruṁ*.

mṛḍa, also called *pṛḍa* or *pruḍa* (*JNSI*, Vol. XVI, p. 40); unit of metal weight like the *mañjāḍi*.

mṛga (CII 1), a deer; an animal in general.

mṛgāṅka (IE 7-1-2), 'one'.

mṛtyuka-vṛtti (BL; HRS), land granted by the king as military pension to the heir of a person killed in a battle against the king's enemies; compensatory grant made in favour of the heir of a person who died fighting on behalf of his master. See *rakta-mānya*, etc. Cf. *vīra-śeṣā*.

mūḍā (LP), same as *mūḍaka* or *mūṭaka*; a measure of capacity equal to a hundred maunds or to 24 maunds in the Surat District.

mūḍaka (LP), same as *mūṭaka* or *mūḍā*.

Mudal, cf. *Evi-mudal* (EI 25), an official designation.

mudal (SII 3), Tamil; cost.

mudala (*Ep. Ind.*, Vol. XXXI, p. 18), used in some Orissan inscriptions in the sense of a royal order [regarding the grant of land or its execution]. Cf. *ibid.*, Vol. XXVIII, p. 305.

Mudali, Mudaliyār (SII 12; SITI), Tamil; a chief.

(*EI* 25), same as *Maṭhādhipati*.

Mudiratha (EI 33), Oḍiyā; same as *Mudrāhasta*.

muditā (CII 4), cheerfulness; one of the Buddhist *bhāvanās*.

mudrā (CII 4), the position of fingers in worship.

(*LP*), the government seal.

mūrdh-ādhikāra, cf. Tamil *mūtt-ādikāram* (SITI), supreme authority.

Mudrādhikārin (EI 30), officer in charge of the royal seal; also called *Mudr-ādhyakṣa*, etc. *Mudrādhikāri-saciva*, may be *Mudrādhikārin* and *Saciva*.

Mudr-ādhikṛta (EI 14, 15), same as *Mudr-ādhikārin*, etc.

Mudr-ādhyakṣa, same as *Mudr-ādhikārin*, etc.; cf. *Rājamudrādhikārin*. See Ghoshal, *H. Rev. Syst.*, p. 96.

Mudrāhasta (EI 33), official designation; same as Oḍiyā *Mudiratha*, designation of a class of servants in the temple of Jagannātha at Purī.

mudr-āpacāra (IE 8-8; EI 30), the crime of using counterfeit coins or the misuse of official seals.

mudrā-śaṅkha, cf. Tamil *muttirai-ccaṅgu* (SITI), a variety of conch-shell; conch-shell marked with a seal.

mudr-āvatāra, cf. Tamil *muttir-āvatāram* (SITI), an ear-ornament.

mudrā-vyāpāra (IE 8-2); 8-3; BL), 'the affairs associated with the royal seal'; often used in connection with the function of the viceroy described as conducting the said business; cf. *samasta-mudrā-vyāpārān paripanthayati, śrī-śrīkaraṇ-ādi-samasta-mudrāvyāpārān paripanthyati*. Cf. *Ep. Ind.*, Vol. XXXIII, p. 154. See also *vyāpāra*.

Muduḍa (EI 27), same as *Mutuḍa*; probably, a village headman.

muha-patti (HA), a piece of cloth held in front of the mouth by Jain monks and nuns, while they are talking, in order to avoid small living beings being destroyed by breath.

muhūrta (CII 3; IA 17), the thirtieth part of a mean day and night; equal to fortyeight minutes.

mukha (EI 22; LL), the face, the gate; a door.

Cf. dāna-mukha (ML), the principal gift.

(*EI* 16), used at the end of compounds in the sense of *mukhya*; 'head' 'heading' or 'sum'. Cf. *pañca-mukha-nagara.*

Cf. muha-patti.

mukha-kaṭṭaṇa (SITI), porch; also called *darśana-kāṇikkai*; front side of a building (SII 12).

mukha-maṇḍapa, Tamil *muga-maṇḍaka* (SITI), the front hall in a temple; cf. *mahāmaṇḍapa.*

mukha-mudrā (EI 5), same as *mauna.*

muktā (BL), epithet of a grant; a grant; possibly Arabic *mukhta.*

mukti-bhūmi (EI 27, 30), a holy place where salvation is attainable on death.

mukh-āhāra, 'principal food or meals'; same as *mukhy-āhāra.* See *Sel. Ins.*, p. 162, text line 5.

Mukhya (EI 32), city elder; member of the city council. Cf. Hindī *Mukhiyā*, a village elder.

(*CII* 1), chief officer.

(*EI* 16), see *mukha* meaning 'head', 'heading' or 'sum'.

mukhy-āhāra, cf. *mukh-āhāra.*

mūkkutti (ASLV), an ornament; the nose-screw.

mūla (SITI), original; a document regarding a title to the property or right.

(*HRS*), investment of capital which is one of the seven sources of revenue specified in the *Arthaśāstra.* See Ghoshal, *H. Rev. Syst.*, p. 26.

(*Sel. Ins.*, p. 163), seedling. Cf. *sa-mūla* (EI 13), a tree.

Mūla-bhṛtya (SITI), the chief servant; also called *Caṇḍeśvara* who was the chief servant of Śiva.

mūla-gabhāro (HA), Jain; same as *garbha-gṛha*; the sanctum where the *Mūla-nāyaka* is installed.

mūlāiṭana (EI 1), meaning doubtful.

Mūla-nāyaka (BL), epithet of a Jain Tīrthaṅkara; Mahāvīra called 'the *Mūla-nāyaka* of the Saṇḍeraka-gaccha'.

(*HA*), the main deity in the sanctum of a shrine or in a *devakulikā*; also the central Jina in a sculpture representing a group of Jinas.

mūla-pariṣad, cf. Tamil *mūla-pariṣai* (SITI), chief assembly [of a Śiva temple]; variously written in Tamil as *mūla-paraḍai*, *mūla-paruḍai*, *mūla-pariḍai*, *mūla-paruṣai*, etc.

Mūlaprakṛti (IE 7-1-2), 'one'.

(*EI* 18), probably 'the prominent subjects ' or 'landlords' or the six important officers styled *Prakṛti* (q.v.).

Mūlaratnabhaṇḍarattār (SII 2), Sanskrit *Mūlaratnabhāṇḍārastha*; treasures of the chief jewels.

Mūla-saṅgha (EI 16, 25), name of a Jain sect.

mūla-sthāna, cf. Tamil *mūla-ttānam* (SII 3; SITI; CITD), a place; the origin, base or foundation; the supreme spirit; the central shrine in a temple (SII 13); the place where the main image stands.

(*EI* 18), an important seat of monks.

mūla-vīsa (EI 6; ASLV), cf. Telugu-Kannaḍa *vīsa*, $\frac{1}{16}$ of a *haṇa* (*paṇa*); name of a tax or levy.

Mūliā (EI 31), Oḍiyā; a day-labourer; from Sanskrit *Mūlika*, possibly an abbreviation of *Pādamūlika*.

Mūḷuḍa (LL), same as *Mutuḍa* or *Muduḍa*; probably, a village headman. Cf. *Śīrṣaka*.

mūlya (CII 3), an endowment; equivalent to *akṣaya-nīvī*, a perpetual endowment.

(*HRS*), proceeds of sale of metal-ware manufactured in the government workshops, as suggested by the *Arthaśāstra*.

Mummuḍi, cf. *Mummuḍi-coḷa*, 'three times a Coḷa king'; cf. *Nūrmaḍi* and *Immaḍi*.

mummuri-daṇḍa (ASLV), name of an organisation.

mumoda (EI 13), *parasmaipada* form instead of the expected *ātmanepada*.

Mū°-nā° (PJS), contraction of *Mūla-nāyaka*, 'the principal deity in a Jain temple'; often found in medieval Jain inscriptions.

muṇḍamola (IE 8-5), cf. *khaṇḍapāla-muṇḍamola* (EI 24); name of a tax.

mundiri (EI), a land measure.

muni (SII 1; IA 30; LL), a Jain monk.

(*IE* 7-1-2), 'seven'.

murā (EI 33), a measure of capacity; cf. *muraka.*

muraka (EI 9), a measure; cf. *murā.*

mūrti (IE 7-1-2), 'three'; rarely used to indicate 'eight'; but cf. *rūpa* used in the sense of 'one'.

Muruṇḍa (EI 14, 19), Śaka title of a chief; a title or tribal name; supposed to be derived from a Scythian word meaning 'a king'.

Mūsara-vāru (CITD), Telugu; probably, goldsmiths or manufacturers of metallic objects.

muṣṭi (IE 8-6), a handful.

Cf. eka-muṣṭyā (LP), 'at the same time'.

muṭaka, mūṭaka (IE 8-5; EI 25), a measure or head-load; cf. *caṇā-satka-mūṭaka*, 'one *mūṭaka* of peas' (LP). See *Ep. Ind.*, Vol. XV, p. 303, text line 50; cf. *moṭ* (a load) in Hindī and other dialects.

mūṭaka (LP), same as *mūḍā*, a measure of capacity equal to a hundred or twentyfour maunds; a bullock's load (*Ep. Ind.*, Vol. XIV, p. 309; cf. Marāṭhī *mūṭh*, 'a bullock's pack-saddle').

mu-ṭī, abbreviation of an expression probably meaning 'a mound covered with jungle' (*Ep. Ind.*, Vol. XXX, p. 56).

mutirigai (IE 8-6), Tamil; a small land measure equal to $\frac{1}{320}$ of a *veli.*

mutkalanīya (LP), 'may be sent'; cf. Gujarātī *mokalavuṁ.*

muttāvaraṇa (EI 21), name of a tax.

Mutuḍa (EI 27), also spelt as *Muduḍa*, *Muḻuḍa*; probably, the headman of a village.

N

nabhas (IE 7-1-2), 'cypher'.

nā, cf. *nā-bhū.*

nā-bhū (IE 1), abbreviation of *nāla-bhūmi*, 'cultivated land'.

nāḍ (ASLV), same as *nāḍu*; a district; the assembly of a district; the professional association and guild of a district.

naḍa (IE 8-6), same as *nala*, a measuring rod.

Nāḍa-gauḍa, same as *Nāḍu-gauḍa*, *Nār-gāvuṇḍa*, etc.

nāḍaka, same as *nāḍuka* (IE 8-4); same as *nāḍ, nāḍu.*

Nāḍa-senabova (ASLV), officer in charge of the accounts of a *nāḍu* or district.

nāḍi (IA 7-1-2), 'three'.

nadī-kūla (IE 7-1-2), 'two'.

nadīpāla (HRS), fixed tax on villages situated upon the banks of rivers and lakes as suggested by the *Arthaśāstra*.

nadītara-sthāna (IE 8-5), ferry.

nāḍiyaka (LP), same as *aṇāḍiyaka*; a place where the carts stand to dispose of goods.

nāḍu (IE 8-4; SII 1; SITI), a country; a territorial division; a district or a subdivision; the local assembly to govern the civic affairs of the division called *nāḍu*.

(*EI* 31), a chamber.

Nāḍu-gauda (ASLV), the head of an organisation relating to a district.

nāḍuka (EI 12; ASLV), same as *nāḍu*.

naga (IE 8-1-2), 'seven'; rarely used to indicate 'eight'.

nāga (IE 7-1-2), 'eight'.

nāgadala (BL), meaning uncertain; cf. 'a race subsisting on *nāgadala*'.

nāg-āmāvāsyā, cf. *nāgara-amāvāsyā* (EI 5), name of a *tithi*.

Nagakāra (BL), wrong reading for *Taṭṭhakāra*, 'a brazier'.

nagara (IE 8-4), city; palace; cf. *navara*.

(*EI* 21; SITI), a commercial guild; guild of merchants; a mercantile town; often spelt in Kannaḍa inscriptions as *nakara* or *nakhara*; cf. *pañca-nagara*.

(*CITD*), in Telugu inscriptions, a territorial assembly like the *sabhā* and *ūr*; the merchant community in general or the organization of the merchant community of a town. In some places, the *nagara* and *ūr* carried on their functions side by side. The word is sometimes used to indicate occupational groups like *śāleyanagarattom*. Cf. K. A. Nilakanta Sastri, *The Coḷas*, Vol. II, 1st ed., p. 294.

(*EI* 4), same as Kaliṅga-nagara. Cf. *śrī-Nagara-bhukti*= *Pāṭaliputra-bhukti* (*Ep. Ind.*, Vol. XVII, p. 311).

(*IA* 17), represented in Prakrit by *nera* further corrupted to *ner* or *nar*. See *nagarī*.

Nagar-ādhikṛta (HD), the city prefect. See *Rājataraṅgiṇī*, IV. 81; VI. 70; VIII. 3334.

Nagar-ādhipa (HD), same as *Nagar-ādhikṛta*.

Nāgaraka (HD), same as *Nāgarika*; chief officer of the city; the city prefect of police. See *Arthaśāstra*, II. 36; *Kāma-*

sūtra, V. 5. 9 (the commentator explaining *Nāgaraka* as *Daṇḍa-pāśika*). Cf. *Talavara*.

Nagar-ākṣadarśa (LL), the city-judge.

Nagara-mahallaka (EI 25), the City Elder.

nagara-parivāra (ASLV), an organisation relating to a town.

Nagarapati (EI 12, 32; HD), the city prefect; ruler of a city. See *Ind. Ant.*, Vol. IV, p. 35.

Nagara-rakṣaka (IE 8-2), same as *Talāra*, *Nagararakṣin*, *Nāgarika*, etc.

Nagara-rakṣin, same as *Nagara-rakṣaka*, etc; prefect of the city police (*Ep. Ind.*, Vol. XVIII, pp. 156-57).

Nagara-śreṣṭhin (IE 8-3; EI 15, 21; BL; HD), according to some, the city banker or guild president of the town; but actually, the chairman of a board of administration like the *Pañcāyat*; same as the *Nagarseṭh* who was the chairman of the board called *Cauthiyā* in late medieval Rajasthan. See *Ep. Ind.*, Vol. XV, p. 115; *Proc. IHC*, Ahmadabad, 1954, pp. 52 ff. See *Pura-śreṣṭhin*, *Pura-pradhāna*, *Śeṭṭi*, etc.

Nagara-svāmin (SITI), headman of the merchants.

Nagarattār (EI 30), Sanskrit *Nagarastha*; leading men of the city.

(*ASLV*; SITI), members of a guild of a town; members of a mercantile guild.

Nagara-vyavahārika (IE 8-3; CII 1; HD), Prakrit *Nagala-viyohālaka*; judicial officer of a city; superintendent of the judicial affairs of a city; the city magistrate; also styled a *Mahā-mātra*. See *Paura-vyavahārika* (*Arthaśāstra*, I. 12).

nagarī (IA 17), represented in Prakrit by *nerī*; further corrupted into *nar*. See *nagara*.

Nāgarika (HD), chief of the police. See *Vikramorvaśīya*, V (after verse 4); *Daśakumāracarita*, II, pp. 58-59. The *Vaijayantī* explains the word as *Kārāpati*, the superintendent of jails.

(*ASLV*), the chief bailiff or prefect at Vijayanagara. See also Ghoshal, *H. Rev. Syst.*, pp. 95-96. Cf. *Nagara-rakṣin*, etc.

Nagar-seṭh (IE 8-3), Sanskrit *Nagara-śreṣṭhin* (q. v.); designation of the chairman of an administrative board called *Cauthiyā* in Western India. See *Śeṭṭi*.

nāga-vana (IE 8-4), an elephant-forest.

naharaṇa, a thief's weapon to dig a hole in the walls (*Journ. Or. Inst.*, Vol. X, No. 1, p. 13).

naidhānī-śilā (EI 32), a boundary pillar.

Naigama, cf. *Negama* (EI 24; LL), the inhabitant of a *nigama* (township); a merchant. See *Nigama-putra*.

naijāyamāna (LP), from *nija*; 'when they are going to get themselves separated'.

Naimittika (EI 19, 26; HD), a soothsayer or astrologer. See *Ep. Ind.*, Vol. IX, p. 305.

nairgamika (IE 8-8; EI 30), exit tax.

naivedya (EI 30), daily offerings to gods.

Naiyāmika, Naiyamika (EI 24), also called *Naiyāvika*; a law officer or judge.

Naiyogika (IE 8-3; EI 12, 24), cf. *Niyogika* (EI 8), 'an officer'; officer-in-charge of an administrative unit; same as *Niyogin*.

Naiyyoka (EI 2), a mistake for *Naiyogika*.

nakara, Kannaḍa; same as Sanskrit *nagara* (q.v.); also spelt *nakhara*.

nakha (IE 7-1-2), 'twenty'.

nakhara, Kannaḍa; same as Sanskrit *nagara* (q.v.); also spelt *nakara*.

Nākhudā Arabic; captain or commander of a ship (*Ep. Ind.* Vol. XXXIV, p. 143).

nakṣatra (CII 3), a lunar mansion.

(*IE* 7-1-2), 'twentyseven'.

nala (IE 8-6), measuring rod; same as *daṇḍa*; sometimes regarded as 12 cubits, 22 cubits, 56 cubits, etc., in length; cf. *Samataṭīya-nala*, 'the rod as used in the Samataṭa country'; *Vṛṣabhaśaṅkara-nala*, 'the rod introduced by king Vṛṣabha-śaṅkara', 'the rod of the village of Pattiyamattavura', etc. See *kol, kolu, ghaḷe*, etc.

(*IE* 8-6), cf. *aṣṭaka-navaka-nala, ṣaṭka-nala*, etc., the first probably referring to the custom of measuring the length and breadth of a plot of land by rods of different length.

(*EI* 28), used in some Orissan inscriptions in the sense of measurement of the area [of the gift land] (*Ep. Ind.*, Vol. XXXI, p. 20).

(*EI* 21), a measure.

nalā, same as *śatamāna* (q. v.).

nāla, cf. *sa-khila-nāla* (IE 8-5; EI 14); cultivated land; same as *nāla-bhūmi*.

nāla-bhūmi (IE 8-1), cultivated land; see *nāla*.

nāḷi, *nāḷi* (EI 9, 28), a grain measure; same as *nālikā*.

nālikā (IE 8-6), same as Pali *nālī* or *nāḷi*; regarded as the same as *prastha*, i.e. one-sixteenth of a *droṇa*.

nālikāvāpa (IE 8-6; EI 31), a land measure; an area of land requiring one *nālikā* measure of seed grains for sowing.

nalu, *nāluka* (EI 7; CII 4), a measure of land; same as *nalva*; 400 (or 100 or 120) square cubits.

nāma-gṛha, cf. *nāmghar* (IA 25), Assamese; a place of worship of the Vaiṣṇavas, where plays, etc., are performed.

namaka (IA 18), name applied to the first section of the *Rudrajapa*.

nāmakaraṇa (BL), naming ceremony.

nāma-liṅga (EI 15), a deity bearing the name of a person.

namas (CII 3), 'reverence'; an invocation, generally connected with the names of gods, at the commencement of inscriptions.

namasya (IE 8-5; EI 5, 13, 28), same as *mānya*, *sarva-namasya*, *namasya-vṛtti*, etc.; a rent-free tenure.

namasya-vṛtti (IE 8-5; EI 32), same as *sarva-namasya*, etc.; a tax-free holding.

nāṇā (EI 30), name of a coin; same as *nāṇaka*.

nānādeśi (EI 31; SITI; ASLV), guild of merchants coming from outside.

nāṇai (*Ep. Ind.*, Vol. XXX, p. 197, text line 18), same as Sanskrit *nāṇaka*; 'a coin.'

nāṇaka, see *nāṇai*.

naṅga (IE 8-5; EI 25), cf. *naṅge gṛhītasya yac=c=āṣṭau ṣoḍaśa vā nagara-mahallakā vicārya vadante tad=eva pranāṇam*; a word of uncertain meaning; but a fine is prescribed for a merchant's son described as *naṅge gṛhīta*.

Nāṇī (CII 4), an engraver; probably a corrution of *Vijñānin*.

nanda (IE 7-1-2), 'nine'.

nandā-dīpa, also called *nandā-dīvigĕ* (CITD); used in Telugu and Kannaḍa inscriptions in the sense of a lamp that is always kept burning before a deity in a temple; same as *akhaṇḍa-dīpa*.

nandavana, *nandāvana*, cf. *tiru-nandavanam*, etc. (SII 1); a sacred flower-garden.

nandā-viḻakku (SII 1, 2), also spelt as *nondā°*, *nundā°*; a perpetual lamp; same as *nandā-dīpa*, *akhaṇḍa-dīpa*.

nandīmukha (CII 1), a species of water-birds.

nāndī-samārohaṇa (EI 32), a ceremony.

nandīśvar-āṣṭamī (SII 11-1), same as Phālguna-sudi 8.

naptṛ (CII 1), a grandson.

(*EI* 4, 9), a great-grandson.

naptṛka, cf. *natika* (EI 22), a grandson.

Narādhipati (IA 15), royal title; same as *Narapati*.

Narapati (IE 8-2; EI 12, 19; HD; SITI), 'lord of men', 'leader of the infantry'; title borne by the Coḷa monarchs; Vijayanagara rulers, etc., in view of the large infantry they possessed; cf. the titles *Aśvapati* and *Gajapati*, and also *Aśvapati-gajapati-narapati-rāja-tray-ādhipati* which was the title of some kings. See *Ind. Ant.*, Vol. XV, p. 7; *JBORS*, Vol. V, p. 588.

Narasvāmin, probably 'a *Jāgīrdār*'; cf. *°grāme mahattama-narasvāminaḥ* (*Ep. Ind.*, Vol. XXV, p. 51).

Nār-gāvuṇḍa (EI 23, 27), village headman; also called *Nāḍa-gauḍa*; cf. *Nār-gāvuṇḍa-svāmya-bhūta*, 'being in the possession of the *Nār-gāvuṇḍas*'.

nārikela, cf. *sa-guvāka-nārikela* (EI 8-5); coconut palms [which the ordinary tenants had no right to enjoy].

Narma-saciva (EI 13), minister of amusement.

Nāsatya (IE 7-1-2), 'two'.

naṣṭa (LP), disappeared.

naṣṭabharaṭa (HRS), name of a levy; same as *naṣṭibharaṭa*; (see *Ep. Ind.*, Vol.III, note 4); may be 'compensation for losses'.

naṣṭa-rājya (IA 22), former rule of a dead king. Cf. also *vinaṣṭa-rājya*.

naṣṭibharaṭa (HRS), same as *naṣṭabharaṭa*; name of a levy (*Ep. Ind.*, Vol. III, p. 264, note 4).

Naṭa (EI 31), a dancer; sometimes mentioned in the list of officials probably indicating 'the chief dancer'.

nāṭaka-śālā (SII 3; 11-1), a theatre hall.

Nātha (*Ep. Ind.*, Vol. IX, p. 313), same as *Nāyaka*.

Naṭṭakāra (BL), mistake for *Taṭṭhakāra*, a brazier.

Nāṭṭavar (ASLV), Tamil; members of an organisation relating to a *nāḍu* or district, *nāṭya-śālā* (EI 4), dance hall.

Naubala-hasty-aśva-go-mahiṣ-āj-āvik-ādi-vyāpṛta (IE 8-3; EI 12), an officer in charge of the royal navy and cattle; looks like a combination of *Hasty-aśv-oṣṭra-naubala-vyāpṛtaka* and *Hasty-aśv-oṣṭra-go-mahiṣ-āj-āvik-ādi-vyāpṛtaka.*

naudaṇḍa, same as *naupatha* (*IHQ*, Vol. XXIII, pp. 255-56).

naukā-bandha (EI 32), a levy from the boatmen at landing places.

Nauk-ādhyakṣa (IE 8-3), officer in charge of the navy.

naukā-bhāṭaka (EI 14), charges for hiring a boat.

nau-krama (EI 19), a bridge of boats or a ferry station.

Nauvāha (*Ind. Ant.*, Vol. XI, p. 244), a ship-owner, mariner or captain.

Nauvāṭaka (EI 24), a naval officer. Cf. *Ardha-nauvāṭaka.* (*EI* 15), probably, a wall (so to say) made of a large number of boats.

Nauvittaka, leader or owner of ships (*Ep. Ind.*, Vol. XXXIV, p. 144).

nava-catuṣkikā, cf. *nava-cokī.*

nava-cokī (HA), Sanskrit *nava-catuṣkikā*; a hall (open on three sides) adjacent to and in front of the *gūḍha-maṇḍapa,* so called because it is divided into nine sections by means of the pillars supporting its ceiling.

nāvaḥ (HRS), charges for hiring royal boats; same as *nau-bhāṭaka.*

navakāra (HA), Sanskrit *namaskāra*; the chief Jain formula for worship or an obeissance to the *arhats, siddhas, ācāryas, upādhyāyas* and *sādhus.*

nava-karman, cf. Tamil *nava-karumam* (SITI); renovation; repairs. Cf. Prakrit *nava-kama* (EI 20), foundation, extension or repairs to buildings.

Navakarmapati (EI 22), an architect or the supervisor of building operations; same as *Navakarmika* and *Navakarmin.*

Navakarmika (EI 16, 23; LL), superintendent of a work (possibly of repairs); cf. *Navakamika* (EI 4, 20), an overseer of work (building or repairing operations); superintendent of building operations. Cf. *Navakarmapati.*

Navakarmin (ML), same as *Navakarmika,* the superintendent of a work. Cf. *Navakarmapati.*

nava-khaṇḍa (IE 8-4), epithet of Bhārata or Bhāratavarṣa; see *khaṇḍa*.

navamikā (EI 9), meaning uncertain.

navāṅga, cf. Pali *navaṁga* (EI 33); cf. *navāṅga-Śāstṛ-śāsana*.

nava-nidhāna, cf. *nava-nidhāna-sahita* (IA 11), epithet of gift land; see *Ind. Ant.*, Vol. VI, pp. 180 ff. (Inscriptions Nos. 4-11); explained as 'new taxes imposed for the first time'; probably 'a fresh assessment of tax' (*Ep. Ind.*, Vol. XXXIV, p. 143).

navara, Oḍiyā; same as Sanskrit *nagara*; capital city, palace.

nava-ratna (BL), the nine gems at Vikramāditya's court.

navarātra, *navarātri* (EI 11, 25; CII 4), the festival of Durgā; Āśvina-sudi 1 to 9.

navarātri-amāvāsyā (EI 5), new-moon preceding the *navarātri*; also called *mahālayā*.

navatara-bhūmī (LP), land as yet uncultivated.

navīna-pañjikā-karaṇa (LP), probably, 'to have new fences', i.e. 'to have additional land in one's possession.'

naya (EI 3), argumentation.

(*Ep. Ind.*, Vol. XVII, pp. 318 ff, text lines 26-27), a territorial division like a Pargana.

Nāyaka (EI 33; CII 4), a royal officer or ruling chief. Cf. *Ep. Ind.*, Vol. XXVII, p. 142, text line 35.

(*HD*), explained as 'the head of ten villages.' See *Artha-śāstra*, I. 12; Śukra, I. 192.

(*EI* 32; BL), title of a subordinate ruler.

(*ASLV*), one who held lands from the Vijayanagara kings on the condition of offering military service (cf. *Amara-nāyaka*).

(*EI* 7), a general.

(*Ep. Ind.*, Vol. IX, p. 313), head of a *nāḍu* or district.

(*IE* 7-1-2), 'one'.

nāyaka-naraka (CITD), Telugu-Kannaḍa; the principal hell.

Nāyakavāḍi (SITI), Sanskrit-Tamil; watchmen stationed by the State or landlord to keep watch over the crops before or during harvest time; the *inām* granted to such persons was known as *kākku-nāyaka-viḻāgam*.

nayana (IE 8-1-2), 'two'; cf. *netra*.

nāyaṅkara, *nāyaṅkāra* (EI 16; ASLV), the feudal system prevalent in the Vijayanagara kingdom, in which the *Nāyakas* enjoyed royal land on condition of offering military service; see *Nāyaka*, *Amara-nāyaka*.

Nayinār (IA 12), Tamil; the chief temple-servant.

nazrāna (EI 26), Persian; customary presents.

nell-āyam (SII 1), Tamil, revenue in paddy.

nemaka (EI 1), probably, salt.

netra (IE 7-1-2), 'two'; in some areas of Eastern India, it was used in the sense of *Hara-netra*, 'three'. The word *dṛk* seems to bear the sense of three in the Pamulavaka plates of Eastern Cālukya Vijayāditya VII (*JAHRS*, Vol. II, p. 287, text line 67).

nettara-goḍaga (ASLV), a kind of compensation.

ni (IE 8-1; EI 33), abbreviation of *nibaddha* or *nirīkṣita*, i.e. registered or approved.

(*Select Inscriptions*, pp. 238-39, 247-48), explained as an abbreviation of *nija* and as a sort of genitive suffix often with a word indicating relationship understood.

nī (LP), used for the verb *ānī*.

(*LP*), to make.

nibaddha (IE 8-1; EI 29), explained as 'registered'.

(*IA* 13), used in respect of a copper-plate grant and translated as 'prepared'.

(*IA* 15), interpreted as 'assigned'.

nibandh (*Select Inscriptions*, p. 202), to register.

nibandha (EI 7), an endowment.

(*Ghoshal, H. Rev. Syst.*, p. 49), a register.

(*SII* 2), also spelt *nivanda* or *nimanda* in Tamil; the fixed requirements of a temple; cf. *Nivandakkārar*, temple servants who attend to the *nibandha*.

(*SII* 3; SITI), expenses or arrangements; arrangement for the conduct of affairs in a temple.

nibarava (CITD), Telugu; an unknown weight used in the case of salt and paddy (unhusked rice).

nīca (CII 1), mean or low.

(*CII* 1), southern.

nīcocca-māsa (CII 3), the anomalistic month, the period in which the moon comes from perigee or apogee to the same point again; its duration is 27 days, 33 *ghaṭīs* and 16.65 *palas*, or 27 *tithis* 59 *ghaṭīs* and 33.36 *palas*; see also *kendra*.

nidāna (CITD), Telugu; same as Sanskrit *nidhāna*; a treasure; a hoard or fund; store, wealth or property.

nidhāna (HRS), explained as 'cess imposed upon agricultural land';but 'freshly assessed tax';cf. *nava-nidhāna*. cf. *sa-nidhi-nidhāna* (*Ep. Ind.*, Vol. XXXV, p. 139, text line 20), in which it is the same as *nikṣepa*; also *sa-vana-śvabhra-nidhāna*; probably, a mine.

nidhān-ālipaka (*Ep. Ind.*, Vol. III, p. 274, text line 61), probably the same as *nidhi-nikṣepa* or *nidhy-upanidhi*. But *ālipaka*, also read as *āliyaka* and often spelt as *ālīpaka*, may refer to the right on beehives and honey (see *alīpaka*).

nidhi (IE 7-1-2), 'nine'.

Cf. nidhi-nikṣepa (IE 8-5; HRS; SITI); treasure trove; a treasure-hoard; hidden treasure under the ground; one of the eight kinds of enjoyments allowed to the donees of rent-free land. Cf. *nidhāna*.

(*CITD*), a treasure; a reposistory; store; a place where anything is placed.

Cf. nidhi-nikṣepa-jala-pāṣāṇ-ārām-ādi-catuṣ-prakāra-bīravaṇa-pārikh-āya-sahita (*Ind. Ant.*, Vol. XIX, p. 247; text lines 101-02), privilege mentioned along with *aṣṭabhoga-tejassvāmya-daṇḍaśulka-yukta*.

nidhyāpti, cf. Prakrit *nijhati* (EI 2; CII 1), explanation, exhortation or argumentation; to cause understanding; cf. *anu-nidhyāpti*.

nidhyāyana, cf. *nijhati* (CII 1); the act of explaining; argumentation [in favour of a particular view]; consolation. See *nidhyāpti*.

nidrā-kalasa, a *pūrṇa-ghaṭa* kept near the head of the bed (*Matsya Purāṇa*, 265.14; *Harṣacarita*, IV).

Nigama-putra (LL), inhabitant of a *nigama* (township); a merchant; cf. *Naigama*.

nigama-sabhā (EI 7, 8), a public hall or the assembly of the town *Pañcāyat*; the city council.

nigraha (EI 27), 'reducer'. Cf. also *koṭṭa-nigraha*.

Nihelapati (IE 8-3; HD), official designation of uncertain import; probably, the governor of a territorial unit; also spelt *Nihilapati*. See Vogel, *Ant. Ch. St.*, p. 124; *CII*, Vol. III, p. 289.

Nihilapati (IE 8-3; CII 3; HD), an official title of uncertain import. See *Nihelapati*. Cf. *CII*, Vol. III, p. 289.

niḥsāra, cf. *nissāreṇa* (LP), 'in an excellent manner.'

nikara (EI 12, 33), cf. *yathādīyamāna-bhoga-bhāga-kara-nikara-ādikam*; a small tax or cess; small amount of rent fixed for a gift land; practically the same as *kara* or tax (*IHQ*, Vol. XXXIV, p. 279). Cf. *upakara*, *tṛṇodaka*, *mānya-kaṇikĕ*, etc.

nikāya (EI 7), a religious corporation.

(*EI* 18; LL), a Buddhist school or community ; a fraternity of Buddhist monks.

Cf. Kaulika-nikāya (LL), a guild of the *Kaulikas* or weavers.

(*CII* 1), a class or group.

Nikephoros (IE 8-2), Greek; royal title; 'victorious'; translated into Prakrit-Sanskrit as *Jayadhara*.

nikṣepa, cf. *nidhi-nikṣepa* (IE 8-5; HRS), deposits and finds on the soil (probably including beehives, cf. *alīpaka*, *nidhāna*); deposits; same as *upanidhi*; one of the eight kinds of enjoyment of the property allowed to the donees of rent-free land; sometimes wrongly explained as a treasure-trove (SITI). See *nidhi*.

nīla-ḍumphaka (IE 8-8), probably, one whose profession was to press indigo plants for getting blue dye; *ḍumphaka* may be Sanskrit *dṛmphaka*.

nīla-kūṭī (IE 8-8; EI 30), probably, an indigo manufactory.

nilaya (EI 9), cf. *grāma-nilaya-nāḍa-sarva-bādhā-parihāreṇa*; probably a territorial unit like a Parganā; the inhabited area of a district.

nimantraṇa (IA 20), explained as 'an invitation which admits of no refusal'.

nimitta (SII 1), a sign.

nimn-onnata (IA 16), explained as 'what is above and below'; but really, 'low and high lands'; cf. *khalla-unnata*.

nindana (LP), weeding out grass growing along with the crops; cf. Gujarātī *nindavuṁ*.

niṉṟaiṟai (EI 30), Tamil; permanent tax.

nipāna, same as *pāna*, cf. *grāma-nipāna-kūpaka* (EI 4); 'the drinking well of a village'; may also be the same as *āpāna*.

nipratiṣṭhāpita (*Ep. Ind.*, Vol. XXXIII, p. 248), same as *pratiṣṭhāpita*; established, installed.

nīra-gṛha (EI 31), 'a water-house'; same as Persian *abdār-khāna*.

nīrājana (SII 1), the waving of a lamp before an idol; same as *ārātrika*.

nirasta, *nirasti*, cf. *sarvajāta-bhoga-nirastyā* (IE 8-5), 'with all kinds of the [king's] rights renunciated'.

niravakara (EI 31), used in some Orissan inscriptions in the sense of 'the nett total after deductions'.

nirayaṇa (CII 3), destitute of precession of the equinoxes.

Nirgrantha (CII 1), a follower of the Jain religion.

Nirgranthanātha (BL), epithet of a Jain poet of the Digambara sect.

nirīkṣita (IE 8-1), same as *dṛṣṭa*, 'examined [and approved]'. See *ni*.

nirlakṣaṇa (CII 1), castration.

nīroga, the science of medicine (*Ep. Ind.*, Vol. XXXV, p. 146).

nirūdhya (LP), 'up to'.

nīru-nela, *nīr-nela* (CITD), Telugu; low lying land irrigated by water from a tank, canal, well, etc.; usually called 'wet land' and considered the most valuable. Cf. *veli-volamu* or *veli-cenu*, i.e. land on a comparatively higher level, which depends solely on rain and is called 'dry land'.

nirūpa (SITI), written order; communication from the king or other superiors.

Nirūpa (ASLV), the carrier of a royal order.

nirūpaṇa (LP), order for transfer of service; appointment.

nirūpita (LP), appointed.

nirūpita-daṇḍa (IA 18), wrongly regarded as a doubtful technical expression; actually, 'appointed as *Daṇḍa* (i.e. *Daṇḍanāyaka*)'. Cf. *niyukta-Daṇḍa*.

nirvacanīya, cf. *bhoga-sambandha-nirvacanīya* (EI 12), 'the relations [of the gift land] with the district [to which it belonged] should not be reckoned'.

nirvah, cf. *nirvahanīya* (LP), 'should be observed'.

nirvāha, cf. *vāśal-nirvāham* (SITI), same as *vāśal-kāriyam* (*kārya*).

Nirvāha (ASLV), probably, a manager.

nirvāha-sabhā (SITI), a managing or executive committee.

nirvāṇa (CII 3), annihilation of human passion; a stage in the Buddhist practices, anterior to *parinirvāṇa* or complete annihilation of personal existence by absorption into the all-pervading spirit.

(*HA*), same as *mokṣa*; liberation from all bondage including that of this earthly body; the death of the Jinas or monks who have obtained *kevala-jñāna.*

nirvāṇa-caitya (BL), name of the Buddhist memorial built at Kasia (ancient Kuśīnagara) in the Deoria District, where the Buddha obtained *mahāparinirvāṇa* (death).

nirvāpa (EI 11), dole.

nirvṛtti (ASLV), same as *viṣaya* or *koṭṭam*; an administrative division.

Niryāmaka (LP), probably, an officer who allowed licenced articles to pass.

niryātita (CII 2-1; ML), given.

niryoga-kṣema (LP), 'renouncing all claims'.

niśadam, also called *niśadi* (SII 1), supposed to be the same as *nityam.*

niśadhi (EI 28), also spelt *nisidhi*, *niṣidhi*, *niṣedhikā*, etc.; the tomb of Jain monks. Cf. *niśīdikā*, etc. (Sanskrit *niṣadyā*).

niśadi, cf. *niśadam.*

niṣadyā, cf. Prakrit *nisidiyā* (LL), a dwelling. Cf. *niśliṣṭaka.*

niṣedha (LP), same as *vyāṣedha* (q. v.).

niṣedhikā (BL), memorial on the burial ground of Jain religious teachers; cf. *nisidhi*, etc.; also *niśīdikā.*

niṣidhi, *niśidhi*, *niśīdhi* (IA 12), Jain; the tomb of Jain monks.

niṣīdī (EI 20), a Jain tomb; cf. *niṣīdhi*, etc.

niśīdikā, also spelt *niśīdigai* (SITI), the death of a Jain by fasting; the memorial set up for such a person.

nisima (ML), Prakrit; supposed to be the same as *stūpa*; cf. *nissīma.*

niṣka (IE 8-8; EI 15, 27, 30), name of a gold coin; name sometimes applied to *śatamāna*, *śāna*, *ṭaṅka*, *gaṇḍa-māḍa*, etc.; cf. *gaṇḍa-niṣka*, also called *gaṇḍa-māḍa*. See *JNSI*, Vol. XVI, pp. 41 ff.

(*IE* 8-8), a gold coin equal to sixteen silver *drammas.*

(*EI* 5), a coin equal to a half-pagoda.

(*JNSI*, Vol. XV, p. 139), a silver coin equal to one *śatamāna.*

niṣkāvala (LP), a thing on which no one has any right; cf. Sanskrit *kavala.*

niśliṣṭaka, Prakrit *nisiḍhayā* (CII 1), explained as 'a rest-house'. But the correct reading is *nisidiyā*=Sanskrit *niṣadyā* (q.v.). See *Nach. Akad. Wissen. Goetting.*, 1959, No. 4, pp. 47ff.

niśrā-nikṣepa-haṭṭa (EI 11), probably, a place in the market for storing goods to be exported.

nissīma (CII 2-1), explained as 'a piece of land outside a monastery'. See *nisima*.

niṣṭhāpita, 'caused to be completed' (*Sel. Ins.*, p. 224). Cf. *nipratiṣthāpita*, *niṣṭhita*.

(*LP*), finished.

niṣṭhita (*Select Inscriptions*, p. 203), completed. Cf. *anuṣ-ṭhita*, *niṣṭhāpita*.

nitya (EI 19), compulsory.

nivanda (SITI), allocated duties of servants in temples; temple expenses; same as Sanskrit *nibandha*.

nīva-pāta (LP), the falling of rain-water from the eaves; cf. Gujarātī *nev* or *nevāṁ*.

nivartana (IE 8-6; EI 21, 26, 28; CII 4), an area of land, which was not the same in different ages and localties. See *Ind. Ep.*, pp. 409-10; also *Matsya Purāṇa*, 283. 14-15, representing a *gocarman* as $\frac{2}{3}$ of a *nivartana* (210×210 sq. cubits).

(*CITD*), same as *maṟuturu*, the identification of the two being established by bilingual Sanskrit-Telugu inscriptions.

nivartanin (CII 4), name of a land measure, same as *nivartana*.

nivedanaka (EI 13), cf. *Vāmanasvāmi-pādānāṁ nivedanaka-nimittam*, 'in order to be presented at the feet of Vāmana-svāmin.'

nivedya (EI 15), same as *naivedya*; the food offering to a god.

niveśa (EI 28), a house-site.

niveśana (LL), a house.

niveśita (CII 1), written [on stone].

Cf. prāsādo=yaṁ niveśitaḥ (*Select Inscriptions*, p. 295, text line 19); erected.

nīvī (EI 17), a permanent endowment; same as *akṣaya-nīvī*.

nīvī-dharma (EI 15, 17; HRS), the custom regarding permanent endowments; the condition that the donee should not destroy the principal but should only enjoy the income arising from it.

nivīta, cf. *s-oṣar-āvaṣkara-sthāna-nivīta-lavaṇākara* (EI 22).

nivṛt (EI 8), a district.

niyata-bhoga (EI 30), regular offerings to gods.

niyat-āniyata (IE 8-5), regular and fixed taxes and those which were occasional.

Niyāyattār (ASLV), Tamil; Sanskrit *Nyāyastha*; a judge. Cf. *Nyāyattār*.

niyoga (EI 24; SITI), an appointment; authority; the officer bearing the same. Cf. *Niyogin*, etc.

Niyoga-niyukta (EI 23), cf. *Niyogin*, etc.

Niyogastha (*Ind. Ant.*, Vol. XVII, p. 11, text line 13), 'an officer'; same as *Niyog-niyukta*, etc.

Niyogi (ASLV), a class of Brāhmaṇas in the Telugu-speaking land.

Niyogika (IE 8-3; EI 8, 25, 32), same as *Niyogin* or *Naiyogika*, 'an officer'.

Niyogin (EI 5, 24, 30), same as *Niyogika*; 'one having a *niyoga*'. Cf. *Parameśvara-niyogin*.

Niyukta (IE 8-3; EI 12, 21, 24), official designation; same as *Niyuktaka*, *Tanniyukta*, etc.

niyukta-daṇḍa (IA 18), wrongly regarded as a doubtful technical expression; actually, 'appointed as *Daṇḍa* (i.e. *Daṇḍa-nāyaka*'). Cf. *nirūpita-daṇḍa*.

Niyuktaka (HD), probably, a subordinate officer under the *Āyuktaka*; same as *Niyukta*. See *Ep. Ind.*, Vol. XXIV, p. 84.

Niyuktak-ādhikārika (EI 33), better *Niyuktaka* and *Adhikārika*.

nṛtya-bhoga (SITI), same as Tamil *śākkai-kkāṇi*.

nṛpa (IE 7-1-2), 'sixteen'.

Nūrmaḍi (IE 8-2; SII 3), Kannaḍa, 'hundred times'; word prefixed to the names of certain kings in order to distinguish them from their predecessors bearing the same name; e.g. *Nūrmaḍi Taila*, 'one who is a hundredfold Taila'; cf. *Savāi Jayasiṁha*, 'one and one-fourth of Jayasiṁha'. See *Immaḍi* and *Mummuḍi*.

nyāya, cf. *niyāyam* (SII 2), an appointment or pledge.

(*SITI*), body or association of persons having the same duties or interests.

Cf. gardabha-cāṇḍāla-nyāyena (LP), 'like a donkey or a *Caṇḍāla*'.

Cf. khaṇḍa-badarīphala-nyāyena (LP), 'like sugar and the *badarī* fruit'.

Cf. śāka-phalaka-nyāyena (LP), 'like vegetables and fruits'.

Cf. vṛddhi-phala-bhoga-nyāya (LP), principle of enjoying the interest of a deposit; also cf. *gṛhasya bhāḍakaṁ na hi*; *drammāṇāṁ vyājaṁ na hi*; *eṣa vṛddhi-phala-bhoga-nyāyaḥ*.

Nyāya-karaṇika (EI 12), one responsible for settling disputes regarding the gift land.

(*BL*), official designation of the writer of complaints or the scribe of the law-court.

Nyāyattār (SII 12; SITI), Sanskrit *Nyāyastha*; judges; members of the court of justice; a committee of judges. Cf. *Niyāyattār*.

nyāya-vāda (LP), a judgment.

O

Oḍaya (CITD), Telugu-Kannaḍa; a king, ruler, master or leader.

Odayantrika (CII 4), correctly *Audayantrika*; a manufacturer of hydraulic machines or, more probably, a person in charge of such a machine.

Oḍiyā, spelt as *Oriya* in English; people, language and alphabet of Orissa.

ogho (HA), same as *rajo-haraṇa*; usually made of twisted woollen threads tied to a wooden handle, used by Jain monks and nuns, for removing dust particles and insects and for protecting the latter.

ohoru (IE 8-5), Oḍiyā; cf. *daṇḍoāsi-ohoru*, 'tax for the maintenance of watchmen'.

Oja (SII 11-1), same as *Ojhā*; designation derived from Sanskrit *Upādhyāya*; cf. Bengali *Ojhā*, Maithilī *Jhā*.

okapiṇḍa (IA 18; CII 1), explained as 'a fox'; probably, 'household vermin'.

olīpāta (EI 1), meaning doubtful.

om, the *praṇava* sometimes found at the commencement of inscriptions; often represented by a sign which should not be confused with the symbol standing for the auspicious word *siddham*.

oṇī (EI 27), a territorial division.

Oṇṭudāru (EI 27), Telugu; a revenue officer.

Oriya, same as *Oḍiyā*.

oṣṭha (IE 7-1-2), 'two'.

otaḍa, *otaḍā*, *otaḍī* (Chamba), dry land, unirrigable land; opposed to *kohlī* or *āli*.

P

Pa (CITD), abbreviation of the Telugu name of a certain measure of grain.

Pā (EI 32), contraction of the surname *Pāṭhin.*

pā (IE 8-1), abbreviation of *pāda.*

pabāsaṇa (HA), the seat (*āsana*) on which the figure of a Jina is placed.

pacana (LL), a cooking place.

pada (EI 33), share; quarter of the standard land measure.

(*EI* 4, 9; IA 17), a share.

(*EI* 21), a land-measure; cf. *paḍa* (*paṭa*) in *Sel. Ins.* p. 408.

Cf. sv-āṅgabhoga-pada (LP), 'under the head of personal expenditure'.

(*LL*; ML), foot-print.

pāda (IE 8-6), same as Kannaḍa *hāda*; 'one-fourth'; a measure equal to one-fourth of the standard land measure.

Cf. poā (EI 19), literally, 'one-fourth'; name of a land measure.

Cf. sa-pādika (LP), 'with one-fourth in addition'.

(*Ep. Ind.*, Vol. XXXIII, p. 248), foot-print, foot-mark.

paḍā, pāḍā (IE 8-4), corrupt forms of *pāṭaka*, 'part of a village'; often suffixed to the names of localities.

Pāda-bhakta (IE 8-2), 'devoted to the feet of'; cf. *Pād-ānudhyāta* and *Pād-ānudhyāna-rata.*

Pādacārin (CII 3), 'moving on feet'; 'personified'.

paḍaga (SITI), Tamil; name of a measure of land; cf. *pāḍaga.*

pāḍaga (IE 8-6), Tamil; same as Sanskrit *pāṭaka*; a land measure which was equal to 240 *kuḻis*, and 6¼ of which made one *veli.*

pāda-ghaṭa (IE 8-8), meaning uncertain.

Paḍaikkāṇvar (ASLV), a military class.

paḍaipaṟṟu (ASLV), a military station or cantonment.

padakā (Chamba), same as *paduka*; foot-print.

padakāra (IE 8-8), probably, a shoe-maker or a hawker (Hindī *pāukār*).

padakka (ASLV), Tamil; a chest ornament.

pāda-kula (EI 12; IA 15), probably, 'a tribe of attendants',

Pāda being the same as *Pādamūla* or *Pādamūlika*, 'an attendant'.

pada-lekhyaka (LP), the ledger in which items of income are written.

paḍalikai (SITI), Sanskrit *paṭalikā*; name of a measure of quantity.

Pādamūla (EI 12), an attendant.

(*EI* 25), foot-prints.

(*EI* 21), a sanctuary (p. 156; *Sel. Ins.*, 2nd ed., p. 512).

(*SII* 13), cf. *pādamūlattār*, temple servants.

Pādamūlika (EI 4; LL), a servant.

(*Ep. Ind.*, Vol. XVIII, p. 156), a temple attendant.

Pād-ānudhyāna-rata (IE 8-2), 'engaged in meditating on the feet of......'; cf. *Pād-ānudhyāta*.

Pād-ānudhyāta (IE 8-2; EI 2; CII 3), 'meditating on the feet or favoured by the feet of......', a technical expression for the relations of a feudatory to his paramount sovereign, of a subordinate to a chief, of a successor to his predecessor, of a son to his parents, of a nephew to his uncle, of a grandson to his grandfather, and of a younger to his elder brother; used also in respect of gods. In rare cases, the word *pāda* is omitted. Cf *Pāda-bhakta* and *Pād-ānudhyāna-rata*.

Pāda-padm-opajīvin (CII 3; IA 18), 'subsisting [like a bee] on the lotuses that are the feet of......'; a technical expression (often occurring in medieval South Indian inscriptions) for the relations of a feudatory or officer to his master; cf. *Pāda-piṇḍ-opajīvin*, *Pād-opajīvin*.

pāda-pāśa (SITI), name of a foot-ornament.

Pāda-piṇḍ-opajīvin (CII 3, etc.), 'subsisting on the food supplied by the feet of......'; a technical expression to denote the relationship of officials or subordinates to their master; same as *Pād-opajīvin* and *Pāda-padm-opajīvin*.

pāda-pīṭha (SII 2), a foot-stool.

pāda-puṣpa (SITI), same as Sanskrit-Tamil *pāda-kāṇaikkai*.

pāda-rakṣā, cf. Tamil *pāda-raṭcai* (SITI), shoes; sandals.

Pādaśaiva (IA 12), designation of a conch-blower at the Rāmeśvaram temple.

pāda-saṅghāṭa, a pair of feet (i.e. foot-prints). Cf. *Ep. Ind.*, Vol. XXXIII, p. 248.

padāti-jīvya (IE 8-5; EI 12, 29), also spelt *padāti-jīva*; tax for the maintenance of *Pāiks*; same as Oḍiyā *pāikāli*; cf. *khaṇḍa-*

pāla or *khaṇḍapālīya*.

Padātika (IE 8-3), modern *Pāik* (q. v.).

pādava-kkāṇi (SITI), Tamil; land given as wage for temple service.

padavāra (SITI), also called *paduvāra*; fee payable for exchanging landed property; transfer fee.

pādāvarta (IE 8-6; EI 4, 21, 24; CII 3), a land measure, an area of 100 *pādāvartas* being 100 feet each way, i.e. 10,000 square feet; also spelt *padāvarta*.

padavī (EI 24), 'an office'.

pāda-viṁśopaka (*viṁśaka*), see *pāvīsā*, *paisā*, *viṁśopaka*.

paḍi (EI 21), a measure.

Paḍihāra (BL), same as Sanskrit *Pratīhāra*.

pādika, cf. Telugu-Kannaḍa *pātika* (CITD); one-fourth of anything; $\frac{1}{64}$-th part of the coin termed *pagoda* (q.v).

pāḍikāval (ASLV), the right of policing, which was sometimes leased to people.

Paḍirā, cf. Oḍiyā *Sāmanta-paḍirā* (EI 32); Sanskrit *Pratirāja*; title of a feudatory or governor; cf. *Pratirājya*=*Pratirāja*.

Pādishāh (IA 20), Persian; spelt *Pādisāha*, *Pātisāha*, etc., in Indian records; a [Muhammadan] emperor.

Paḍiyāri (EI 27), Sanskrit *Pratīhārī*.

padma-bandha (CITD), a kind of artificial composition of verses, in which the syllables are arranged in the form of a lotus. Cf. *padma-vṛtta*.

padma-nidhi (IE 8-8), a sacred deposit made in the temple treasury. Cf. the coin called *padmanidhi-malla-māḍa* which was probably issued by the temples.

padma-pīṭha (SII 2), a lotus-pedestal.

padm-āsana (IA 18), used to indicate 'the sun'; cf. *padma-sadman*.

padma-sadman (IA 18), used to indicate 'the sun'; cf. *padm-āsana*.

padma-vṛtta (CITD), probably, the same as *padma-bandha*.

Pādonalakṣa (IE 8-4), name of a territory with reference to the number of villages in it; cf. *Sapādalakṣa*, *Caurāśī*.

Pād-opajīvin (IA 18), same as *Pāda-padm-opajīvin* and *Pāda-piṇḍ-opajīvin*.

padra (IE 8-4; EI 24; CII 4), 'a village'; often suffixed to the names of villages; see *padraka*. Cf. *pādrīyaka* (LP), those living in the confines of a village.

(*IE* 8-5), probably, 'inhabited area'; may also be 'common land' (cf. *padraka*); cf. *sa-padr-āraṇyaka* as an epithet of a gift village.

padraka (IE 8-4; CII 3; etc.); 'a village'; generally used as the termination of the name of a village; interpreted as 'common-land' in expressions like *Bhumbhusa-padraka* and *Śivaka-padraka*. Wilson's Glossary explains *pādar* (i.e. *padra*) as 'common-land, land adjacent to a village left uncultivated'.

paduka (Chamba, etc.), sacred foot-prints; from Sanskrit *pādukā*.

pāduka (EI 22; LL; HA), foot-prints. See *pādukā*, etc.

pādukā (*A.R.Ep*., 1958-59, p. 11), foot-prints.

pāduka-paṭṭa, *pādukā-paṭṭa* (LL), cf. Prakrit *paduka-paṭa* (EI 20), a foot-print slab.

pādukā-paṭṭī, cf. Prakrit *pājugā-paṭī* (EI 24), a slab with foot-marks.

paduvāra (SITI), same as *padavāra* (q.v.).

pāga (*bhāga* ?), cf. Kannaḍa *hāga* (EI 9), name of a coin.

(*IA* 11), same as Kannaḍa *hāga*; one-fourth [of the revenue collected]; may be Sanskrit *bhāga*.

pāghḍī, cf. *talār-ābhāvya*.

pagod, *pagoda* (EI 8-8), also called 'star pagoda'; English name of the gold coin called *hūn* (*hon*) or *varāha*; probably so called because the coins often bore the representation of a temple called *pagod* or *pagoda* by the early European travellers. The word seems to have been derived from Sanskrit *bhagavat* or *bhagavatī* meaning the deities worshipped in the temples and also often figuring on the coins. Cf. '*ṭaṅkakas* stamped with the figure of the *Bhagavat*' (Bhandarkar's List, No. 2033).

Cf. *Cīna-pagoda* (SII 12), 'the Chinese temple'; name of a Buddhist shrine at Nāgapaṭṭanam.

pāhuḍa, Sanskrit *prābhṛta*; cf. *pāhuḍa-pramāṇena* (LP), 'in proportion to the gift given by him'.

Pāik (IE 7-3; EI 33), Sanskrit *Padātika*; same as *Bhaṭa* or *Bhaṭa-manuṣya*; a footman; cf. *Piāda*.

pāikā (IE 8-5; EI 29), Oḍiyā; also called *pāikāli*; same as *padāti-jīvya*.

pāikāli, see *pāikā*.

paikamu (EI 6), Telugu; name of a coin.

pāilā (*Ep. Ind.*, Vol. XI, p. 42), a measure of capacity.

Paiṇḍapātika (LL), a Buddhist mendicant; cf. *piṇḍapāta.*

paisā, used in Hindi, Bengali, etc., for *pāvīsā* or *pāda-viṁśaka-* (*viṁśopaka*); 'a copper coin'; 'money'; also a land measure.

Paiṭakin (LL), Buddhist; a teacher of the *piṭakas.*

pāka-daṇḍa (EI 14), cf. Kannaḍa *kiṟu-kula.*

pākhī (IE 8-6), Bengali; a land measure in parts of Bengal, which is smaller than the *bīghā.*

pakhila (IA 17), apparently a mistake for *upakhila* (q.v.); cf. *sa-khilaṁ pakhilam* wrongly read or written for *sa-khil-opakhilam*; semi-waste land.

pakṣa (IE 7-1-2), 'two'; sometimes also 'fifteen'.

pakṣa-pāta, 'one who works on behalf of someone else' (*Ep. Ind.*, Vol. XXXIV, p. 250).

pakva, cf. *pakva-pura,* 'a brick-built house', same as Bengali *pākā-bāḍi.* See *Ep. Ind.*, Vol. XXXV, p. 184.

pala (EI 9, 21, 30; CII 3), name of a weight.

(*IA* 26), a weight equal to 320 *ratīs*; sometimes spelt *phala* in Pāli.

(*CITD*), in Telugu-Kannaḍa records, a weight equal to that of 10 *pagodas*; four *karṣas* or $\frac{1}{100}$ of a *tula*; the 8th part of a ser, or 3 *tolas* or rupees; 4 *tolas* or 320 *guñjās.*

(*CII* 3), the sixtieth division of a *ghaṭī*; equal to twenty-four English seconds.

pālā (LP), sheds.

(*LP*), a foot-soldier; cf. Gujarātī *pāḻo.*

pālaka (EI 3), cf. *grāmasya pālakaḥ,* 'the headman of a village'.

(*Select Inscriptions,* p. 236), escort.

pala-kāya (SITI), sundry spices as pepper, etc., used in preparing curry.

paḻampuḻḻi-māḍai (SITI), Tamil; name of an ancient coin; see *māḍai.*

Palaniyāyam (EI 21), official designation.

pālāpana (LP), cf. Gujarātī *paḻāvavuṁ,* 'to compel to obey'.

palārdha, weight equal to half of a *pala* (*JNSI,* Vol. XVI, p. 48).

Pāli, name of a language.

pālī (EI 3), embankment.

(*CII* 3), a bridge.

pāli-dhvaja (EI 30, 32; CII 4), name of the banner of certain kings or dynasties, which was their royal insignia; same as *pāli-ketana*; sometimes explained as 'flags in rows' (SII 1).

palikā, pālikā (EI 1, 11), same as *pālī*; a measure of capacity; measure of capacity for liquids (*Ep. Ind.*, Vol. XV, p. 309).

pāli-ketana (EI 29; IA 7), name of the banner of certain kings or dynasties, which was their royal insignia; also called *pāli-dhvaja*, explained as 'flags in rows' (SII 1).

pāliyā (CII 4), Gujarātī; a memorial stone.

palladikā (IA 11, 18), cf. *gṛhāṇāṁ palladikā-sametā*, an epithet of the gift land; probably, a cluster; sometimes referred to as property belonging to a deity (*Ind. Ant.*, Vol. VI, pp. 180 ff., Inscriptions Nos. 5-11). Cf. 'the entire *palladikā* belonging to the god Vakuleśvaradeva and consisting of houses facing different directions' and 'another [*palladikā*] which lay close to a two-storied temple' (*Ep. Ind.*, Vol. XXXIV, pp. 144-45).

pallava (IE 7-1-2), 'five'.

pallī (IE 8-4; EI 23), 'a hamlet'; 'a village or its part'; often suffixed to the names of localities.

paḻḻi (SII 1, 2; SITI), Tamil; often, a Jain temple; the shrine of non-Hindu communities like the Jains, Buddhists, Christians, Muhammadans, etc.; cf. *paḻḻi-ccandam*, temple land; *paḻḻi-grāma*, a village belonging to a temple.

pallī-cchanda, cf. *paḻḻi-ccanda* (EI 23, 24), 'temple land'; 'land granted to a Jain or Buddhist temple'; mentioned along with *devadāna* and *brahmadeya*; see *paḻḻi*.

palli-deva (EI 29), a village deity.

pallikā (EI 4), a village.

(*EI* 31), a habitation.

palola (IA 22), marshes or swamps.

Paṁ (IE 8-1; PJS), abbreviation of *Paṇḍita*.

(*PJS*), abbreviation of *Paṁnyāsa*.

paṇa (IE 8-8; EI 23, 24, 30; SII 11-1), same as Tamil *paṇam*, spelt in English as *fanam*; cf. *Yādavarāyan-paṇam* (SITI), name of a coin issued by the Yādavarāyas; name of a coin 80 ratis in weight; same as the copper *kārsāpaṇa*; equal to 80 cowrie-shells according to the *Līlāvatī*; copper coin $\frac{1}{16}$ of a silver *kārṣāpaṇa* according to the *Kṛtyakalpataru* (Vyavahāra-kāṇḍa, ed. K.V. Rangaswami Aiyangar, p. 125), and $\frac{1}{48}$ of a *suvarṇa* (*JNSI*, Vol. II, p. 7); also used to indicate 'money'. In Tamil, *paṇam* means a particular coin (usually, a small gold coin), or money in general, or taxes; cf. *paṇa-vargam* (SITI), a class of taxes payable in cash, same as *kāśāya-vargam*; also *paṇa-vāśi*, 'discount payable for the exchange of coins; amount payable to make up the wear in the coin'. Cf. *vil-paṇam* (SITI), sale-tax; also understood as a tax on bows or archery; *vāśal-paṇam* (SITI), door-tax or periodical payment due to the palace.

(*ASLV*), a sect or caste, eighteen in number theoretically.

(*EI* 19), a land measure.

pāṇaka (*Ep. Ind.*, Vol. XIV, p. 309), small quantity of a liquid; name of a measure.

paṇa-purāṇa (IE 8-8), a *purāṇa* [of silver] counted in *paṇas* [of copper]. Cf. *kapardaka-purāṇa*.

paṇava (EI 24), a musical instrument.

Pāṇavika, one who plays on the *paṇava* (*Ep. Ind.*, Vol. XXXIII, p. 241).

pañca (EI 22, 23), abbreviation of *pañcakula*; same as *Mahājana*; a *Pañcāyat* Board.

Pañc-ācārya (SITI), a temple priest.

pañcadhāra (CITD), the five paces of a horse called *dhorita, valgita, pluta, uttejita* and *utterita*.

Pañc-ādhikaraṇ-oparika (IE 8-2, 8-3; EI 29; BL), official designation; cf. *Pañca-karaṇ-oparika* and *Pañca-karaṇ-ādhikṛta*; the head of five departments; sometimes also called *Mahārāja, Mahāsāmanta, Mahāpratīhāra, Mahāpīlupati, Pāṭy-uparika* and *Purapāl-oparika*, additionally. See *Sapt-āmātya*.

pañca-dravya (SITI), five articles used in bathing an idol.

pañca-gavya (SITI), same as Tamil *ān-āñju*; the five products of the cow, viz., milk, butter, curds, urine and dung.

Pāñcāhaṇa, Pāñcāhaṇaṁvāru (ASLV), same as *Pāñcāḻa*.

pāñcaka (CII 3), a committee. See *pañca-maṇḍalī* and *pañcakula*.

pañcaka (CII 4), same as *Pañcāyat*.

Pañcakalpin (EI 9), same as *Pañcolī*; title and family name.

Pañcakaraṇ-ādhikṛta (EI 30), head of five departments; cf. *Pañcakaraṇ-oparika*, etc. See *Saptā-mātya*.

Pañcakaraṇ-oparika (EI 29), same as *Pañcādhikaraṇ-oparika*, etc.; head of five departments. See *Sapt-āmātya*.

pañca-karmāra, also called *pañca-kammāḻar* (SITI), the five castes of artisans, viz., goldsmith, blacksmith, brassmith, carpenter and stone-mason.

pañcaka-śālā-pratyā (LP), 'at five per cent'.

pañcakula (IE 8-3; EI 5, 25; CII 4; LP; HRS), the *Pañcāyat* Board; an assembly of administrators and arbitrators, usually consisting of five members; a board of administration charged with control of the customs house, with the deposit of property of persons dying without heirs into the royal treasury, etc.; also called *pañcapa* (EI 4); members of such a board; according to some, an officer over a certain number of villages (HD). Cf. *Ind. Ant.*, Vol. XI, p. 242. Cf. *Pañcavīra*, *Pāñcakulika*, *añjaṣṭa-sabhā*, etc.

Pāñcakulika (CII 4), the head or a member of a *pañcakula* or *Pañcāyat* board; cf. *Caturjātakīya*.

Pañcāla (EI 3; ASLV), an artisan; members of the artisan classes also called *Pāñcāḻaṁvāru*.

Pañca-laguḍika (BL), title of a warrior who could probably fight with five clubs at a time.

pañcalāṅgala (IA 18), name of a *mahādāna*.

Pañcāḻattār (ASLV), an organisation of the artisans.

Pañcālī (IA 10), same as *Pañcālikā*; a *Pañcāyat* board or its members.

pañcālī (EI 27; IA 16), territorial division.

Pañcālikā (IA 9), same as *Pañcālī*; a *Pañcāyat* board or its members.

pañca-mahāpātaka (EI 26; CII 3; CITD), the five great sins or heinous crimes, viz., killing a Brāhmaṇa, drinking intoxicating liquors, stealing gold, committing adultery with the wife of a *guru* and associating with any one guilty of these crimes. Cf. *daś-āparādha*, *pañc-ānantarya*.

pañca-mahāśabda (IE 8-2; EI 30; CII 3, 4; SITI; CITD; BL), refers to the privilege of enjoying the sounds of five musical instruments, or five titles beginning with *mahat*; five official designations or musical instruments mentioned in connection with feudatories; five official designations beginning with the word *mahā* in the North and five kinds of musical instruments in the South; in South India, it was the same as *pañca-mahāninādа*, i.e. the sounds of the five great musical instruments called the *pañca-mahāvādya* enumerated by some as a horn, a tabor, a conch-shell, a kettle-drum and a gong; in some parts of North India, the expression indicated five official designations with the prefix *mahā*.

(*CII* 3), sounds of five musical instruments, the use of which was allowed to persons of high rank and authority; usually a title of feudatories; cf. *tat-pradatta-pañcamahāśabda* (IE 8-2), used in respect of feudatory rulers who received the right of enjoying the *pañca-mahāśabda* from their overlords; rarely used in the South by independent monarchs. Cf. *pañca-vādya* (EI 4) and *pañca-mahāvādya*. See *Samadhigata-pañcamahāśabda*, etc.

Cf. pañca-māśattam (SITI), the five musical instruments, to the use of which a nobleman was entitled; sometimes enumerated as *ceṇḍai, timilai, śegaṇḍi*, cymbals and *kāhaḷam* or as *tattaḷi, maddaḷi, karaḷikai*, cymbals and *kāhaḷam*.

(*SII* 11-1), cf. grant of 40 *mattars* of land to a piper for arranging to play the five musical instruments.

pañca-mahāvādya (EI 12), enumerated as the horn, conch-shell, tambourine, trumpet and gong. See *pañca-mahāśabda*.

pañca-mahāyajña (EI 29; CII 3, 4), 'the five great sacrifices'; the five daily duties of a Brāhmaṇa enumerated as *bali, caru, vaiśvadeva, agnihotra* and *atithi*.

Pañcama-lokapāla (*Ep. Ind.*, Vol. XXXII, p. 93), epithet of certain kings; cf. *Lokapāla*.

pañca-maṇḍalī (CII 3, 4; HD), an assembly of five persons; equivalent to the modern *Pañcāit, Pañcāyat* or *Pañc*, i.e., a village jury. See *pāñcaka*.

pañca-mātṛkā, cf. Prakrit *paṁca-māluka* (EI 20), five principal texts of the Buddhists, also called *pañca-nikāya*, viz., the *Dīgha-nikāya, Majjhima-nikāya, Aṅguttara-nikāya, Khuddaka-nikāya* and *Saṁyutta-nikāya*.

pañca-mauṣṭika-loca (HA), plucking out five handfuls of hair by a would-be Jina at the time of *dīkṣā*.

pañcamī-bali (EI 11), a particular *tithi* of the year.

pañc-āmṛta (SITI), mixture of five objects for anointing idols, viz. banana, honey, sugar, ghee and grape.

pañca-mukha-nagara (LP), explained as 'a city in which there are five leading men'; cf. *pañca-mukha-nagara-viditam* (LP), 'having informed the five leading men of the city'; explained as 'the five-fold people of the town' (*Ind. Ant.*, Vol. XLI, p. 20); really 'the citizens headed by the members of the *Pañcāyat*'.

pañca-nagara, a mercantile guild (cf. *nagara*, also *pañca*); see *A.R. Ep.*, 1956-57, No. B 190.

Pañcanaikāyika (LL), Buddhist; a teacher of the five *nikāyas* (e.g. *Dīgha-nikāya*, *Majjhima-nikāya*, *Khuddaka-nikāya*, *Saṁyutta-nikaya* and *Aṅguttara-nikāya*).

pañc-ānantarya (CII 3), the five sins that entail immediate retribution. See *pañca-mahāpātaka*, *daś-āparādha*, *pañc-āparādha*.

pañcāṅga (CII 3), the Hindu almanac; in the Deccan and in some other parts, the *pañcāṅgas* are now prepared from the *Grahalāghava* and the *Tithicintāmaṇi* of *Gaṇeśa-daivajña*. The right of reading the *pañcāṅga* was sometimes granted by the rulers to individuals (ASLV).

pañcāṅga-namaskāra (HA), bowing down in such a way that five limbs of the body (viz., two hands, two knees and the head) touch the ground. Cf. *aṣṭ-āṅga-namaskāra*.

pañcāṅga-prasāda, cf. *pañcāṅga-pasāya* (*Ind. Ant.*, Vol. IX, p. 95), translated as 'five manners of gifts'; cf. *pañcāṅga-pasāya chatra sukhāsana bbalu gaddi aṅka-daṇḍa-khaṇḍane*, translated as 'gave [to that Māro-śĕṭṭi] five manners of gifts—an umbrella, a palanquin, an escort, a throne and with the faults, fines and divisions (really 'with fines and the grain share').'

pañcapa (EI 4), same as *pañcakula* (q.v.).

pañc-āparādha (HRS), known from the Gupta and other records; donee's privilege relating to the enjoyment of fines payable by persons committing five offences. Cf. *daś-āparādha*, *pañc-ānantarya*, *pañca-mahāpātaka*.

pañcaparameṣṭhi-pada (EI 2), also called °*paṭṭa*; a slab for worship containing the *oṅkāra*.

Pañcapāṭhin (EI 32), epithet or family name of Brāhmaṇas.

pañca-pātra (SITI), literally, 'a vessel made of five [metals]'; offerings of food made to a deity along with cooked rice; probably the same as *pañca-bhakṣya*.

Pañcārtha (CII 4), the Pāśupata sect of the Śaivas.

Pañcārthika, *Pāñcārthika* (CII 4; IA 18), same as *Pañcārtha*, the Pāśupata sect of the Śaivas; a follower of the Pāśupata sect.

pañca-ratna (EI 19), a group of five stanzas.

pañca-śabda (CII 4; BL), five [musical] sounds or five official designations [beginning with the word *mahā*]; same as *pañca-mahāśabda* (q.v.).

pañcāśat, see *pannasa*, *pannāsa*, etc.

pañc-āṣṭa-kula, see *añjaṣṭa-sabhai* (SITI).

Pañcastūpanikāyika (BL), epithet of a Jain religious teacher. See *Pañcanaikāyika*.

pañca-vādya (EI 4), cf. *pañca-mahāśabda*, *pañca-mahāvādya*.

pañca-vāra (EI 23), a tax; cf. *pañcavāri*, *pañcupīli*, etc.; also *pañca-vāram* (SITI), one-fifth of the produce due to the government as land-revenue.

(*SITI*), five branches in the administration of big villages, each looked after by a committee called *pañcavāra-vāriyam*.

pañcaviṁśati, see *pannavīsa*.

pañca-vīra (EI 24), also called *pañcavīra-goṣṭhī*; an administrative board of five members; cf. *pañcakula*. Also 5 deified heroes of the Vṛṣṇi clan.

pañcāyat (EI 26), a board of administration usually consisting of five members; cf. *pañcakula*, *pañcavīra*, *pañcāyati*, etc.

pañcāyati (IE 8-3), an administrative board consisting of five members; same as *pañcāyat*, *pañcakula*, etc.

pañc-āyatana (EI 28; CII 4), a type of temple 'consisting of five rooms'; a five-shrine temple.

Pañcika (EI 1), a member of the *pañcakula* or *Pañcāyat* board.

pañcīyaka-dramma (EI 1; CII 4), name of a coin. It is uncertain whether it was so called owing to its issue by some *Pañcāyat* board or because it was equal to five copper coins.

pañcolī (HD), same as *pañcakula*. Cf. *Ep. Ind.*, Vol. XXIV, p. 89.

pañcupīli (EI 24), name of a tax.

Pāṇḍā (EI 32), a temple superintendent; same as *Vārika*.

paṇḍāravāḍai (ASLV), crown lands.

pāṇḍava (IE 7-1-2), 'five'.

Paṇḍita (HD), same as *Dharmatattvavit* according to Śukra, II. 85; head of the ecclesiastical department (*Hist. Dharm.*, Vol. III, p. 115).

(*CII* 4), epithet of Brāhmaṇas.

(*IE* 8-3), the court Pandit, mentioned as *Pātra*.

pāṇḍu-lekha, *pāṇḍu-lekhya* (IE 3-5), chalk.

pāṇḍu-suta, cf. *pāṇḍava* (IE 7-1-2), 'five'.

paṅga, *pāṅga* (IE 8-5; EI 30, 33), Telugu-Kannaḍa; one-fourth of the produce sometimes collected from rent-free holdings in the possession of gods and Brāhmaṇas; a kind of tax;

sometimes used to indicate 'taxes in general'; cf. *paṅga-śulka*, *paṅga-tappu*, *paṅga-tappu-śulka*, *paṅga-parihṛta*, *paṅga-parihṛta-parihāra*, *sarva-paṅga-parihṛta*, etc. See *Ep. Ind.*, Vol. XXXIII, pp. 54 ff.

paṅga-tappu (IE 8-5), probably, interest or fine on arrears of *paṅga*.

paṅg-otkoṭa (EI 33), see *paṅga* and *utkoṭa*, names of levies.

paṅgu (EI 33), a share.

pāṇi, same as *suvarṇa* (q.v.).

Pāṇigrāhin (EI 26), Oḍiyā; Sanskrit *Pānīya-grāhin*, 'one who receives water'; the principal donee who received the water on behalf of all the other donees of a gift village; stereotyped as a family name in Orissa.

pānīya-bhājana (LL), a water-cistern.

pānīya-chāyā-maṇḍapa (EI 28), probably, a shaded hall cooled by water.

Pānīyāgārika (IE 8-3), superintendent of the water-chamber. See *Pānīyagṛhika*.

Pānīya-grāhin (EI 31), 'one who receives ceremonial water as the donee of a gift'; recipient of a grant. See *Pāṇigrāhin*.

Pānīyagṛhika (LL), superintendent of a water-house. Cf. *Pānīyāgārika*.

pānīyaka (LL), a cistern.

Pañjābī, name of the language of the Pañjāb.

paṅka (EI 33), a share; cf. *paṅga*.

paṅkti (IE 7-1-2), 'ten'.

pannasa, also spelt *pannāsa*, *pannāsu* (IE 8-6; EI 5, 12; *Ep. Ind.*, Vol. XV, p. 336, note 3), Kannaḍa; probably derived from Sanskrit *pañchāśat* in the sense of a tenure in which the donee enjoyed fifty per cent of the revenue of the donated land. Cf. *pannavīsa*. (*EI* 20), explained as 'a gift'.

pannāsa (EI 30; IA 11), Kannaḍa; same as *pannasa* (q.v.).

pannāsu (IA 10), Kannaḍa; same as *pannasa* (q.v.).

pannavīsa (*A. R. Ep.*, 1958-59, No. B. 17), Kannaḍa; Sanskrit *pañcaviṁśati*; probably a tenure in which the donee enjoyed twentyfive per cent of the revenue of the donated land. Cf. *pannāsa*, etc.

pannāya (IE 8-5; EI 27), Kannaḍa, name of a tax; cf. *pannāsa*.

Pannāyadasuṅkavĕrgaḍĕ (SII 11-2), Kannaḍa; official designation.

pāntha-śālā (CII 4), a *sarāi.*

paṇya-saṁsthā (HRS), various dues collected for the king by the superintendent of the market and the superintendent of merchandise, as suggested by the *Arthaśāstra.* See Ghoshal, *H. Rev. Syst.*, p.76.

pāpanāśinī (IA 26), the twelfth *tithi.*

Para, abbreviation of a modified form of *Purohita* (*Ep. Ind.*, Vol. XXXIV, p. 143).

para ((LL), possibly, the chief.

pāra, cf. *a-pār-āsana-carm-āṅgāra* (IE 8-5); probably, [free] ferrying of rivers [by the royal officers], which the villagers were obliged to provide.

parabrahman (IE 7-1-2), 'one'.

paradatti (SII 2), Tamil; an assembly; cf. Tamil *paraḍai*= Sanskrit *pariṣad.*

Para-deśin (SITI; CITD), an outsider; an emigrant; used along with *Sva-deśin* (i. e. native), while mentioning two classes of merchants or their respective guilds.

paraganā (Chamba, etc.), *parganā*; a territorial division; subdivision of a district, same as *pratijāgaraṇaka* of the Paramāra charters.

Parakesari-kāl (EI 30), Tamil; name of a land measure.

Parakesari-kkal (EI 30), Tamil; name of a weight.

Parakesari-nāḻi (EI 30), Tamil; name of a land measure.

Parakesari-uḻakku (EI 30), Tamil; name of a land measure.

parākhya (CII 3), a correction in time, to be applied to the mean *tithi.*

parakoṇā (EI 31), probably, the same as *parganā.*

parākram (CII 1), 'to make an effort'.

parākrama (CII 1), an effort; zealous activity.

Parama-bhāgavata (IE 8-2; EI 29, 30; CII 3), 'highly devoted to the Bhagavat (Viṣṇu)', epithet of the followers of the Bhāgavata form of Vaiṣṇavism; cf. *Paramavaiṣṇava* (highly devoted to Viṣṇu), etc. See *Atyanta-bhagavad-bhaktā.*

Parama-bhagavatī-bhakta (IE 8-2), 'a devout worshipper of the goddess Bhagavatī (Śiva's consort)'.

Paramabhaṭṭāraka (IE 8-2; EI 30; CII 3, 4), one of the technical titles of paramount sovereignty, closely connected with *Mahārājādhirāja* and *Parameśvara*; sometimes applied to a priest (generally of the Śaiva order); cf. *Paramabhaṭṭārak-ety-*

ādi-rājāvalī (IA 19); also *Paramabhaṭṭārak-etyādi-rājāvalī-tray-opeta* (IE 8-2), 'endowed with the three royal titles beginning with *Paramabhaṭṭāraka*.'

Paramabhaṭṭārikā (IE 8-2; EI 6, 7; CII 3), a title of the wives of paramount sovereigns and of ruling queens.

Parama-brahmaṇya (IE 8-2; EI 29), probably not 'highly devoted to the god Brahman', but 'highly devoted to the Brāhmaṇas'; epithet of certain Brāhmanical rulers. See *Atibrahmaṇya.*

Parama-daivata (IE 8-2; EI 28, 30; BL), 'highly devoted to the god (i. e. Viṣṇu)'; epithet of Vaiṣṇava rulers; epithet of a devotee of the Brahmanical gods. Cf. *Parama-de(dai)vat-ādhidaivata*, *Parama-guru-de(dai)vat-ādhidaivata-viśeṣa* (EI 28), epithets of pious rulers.

Parama-daivat-ādhidaivata (EI 23), same as *Parama-de(dai)-vatādhidaivata* (q. v.); epithet of pious kings.

Parama-de(dai) vat-ādhidaivata (IE 8-2; EI 23), 'one who is a great devotee of the various gods and of the supreme god'; see *Paramadaivata.*

Paramadevī (IE 8-2; CII 3), designation of the chief queen; cf. *Devī*, *Mahādevī*, etc.

Paramadīkṣita (EI 26), see *Dīkṣita.*

Param-āditya-bhakta (IE 8-2; CII 3), 'a devout worshipper of the Sun-god'; cf. *Parama-saura.*

Parama-guru (EI 31, 33), 'the supreme teacher [of the subjects]'; royal title.

Parama-guru-de(dai) vat-ādhidaivata-viśeṣa (IE 8-2), 'one who is a great teacher to his subjects and is devoted to the various gods and of the supreme deity'; see *Parama-daivata* and *Paramade(dai)vat-ādhidaivata.*

Paramahaṁsa (EI 5; BL), an ascetic; epithet of an ascetic. See *Haṁsa.*

Parama-māheśvara (IE 8-2; EI 29, 30; CII 3, 4), a devout worshipper of *Maheśvara* (Śiva)'; epithet of Śaiva rulers; see *Māheśvara.*

Parama-nārasiṁha (IE 8-2; EI 26), 'highly devoted to the man-lion incarnation of Viṣṇu'; epithet of a devotee of the man-lion form of Viṣṇu.

Parama-pāśupat-ācārya (BL), epithet of a Śaiva religious teacher.

Paramarāja (EI 31, 33), royal title. See *Paramarājādhirāja.*

Paramarājādhirāja, royal title. See *Ep. Ind.*, Vol. XXXIV, p. 219; cf. *Paramarāja*.

Parama-saugata (IE 8-2; EI 29; CII 3; BL), 'a devout worshipper of the Sugata (Buddha)'; cf. *Parama-tāthāgata*.

Parama-saura (IE 8-2), 'a devout worshipper of the Sun-god'; cf. *Param-āditya-bhakta*.

Parama-svāmin (EI 28; SII 3), epithet of deities.

(*EI* 3), title of an imperial ruler; an overlord.

Parama-tāthāgata (IE 8-2; EI 29; BL), 'a devout worshipper of the Tathāgata (Buddha)'; usually spelt *Parama-tathāgata*; cf. *Parama-saugata*.

Parama-vaiṣṇava (IE 8-2; EI 30; CII 3, 4), 'highly devoted to Viṣṇu'; epithet of Vaiṣṇava rulers; cf. *Parama-bhāgavata*, etc.

Parama-viśvāsin (IE 8-3), probably, a private secretary; same as *Rahasy-ādhikṛta*, etc.; sometimes called *Mahāpradhāna*, *Sarvādhikārin*, etc., additionally. See *Vaiśvāsika*.

parameṣṭhi-gadyāṇa (*SII*, Vol. IX, Part i, No.68), cf. *gadyāṇa*.

Parameśvara (IE 8-2; EI 29, 30; CII 3, 4), an imperial title; one of the technical titles of paramount sovereignty closely connected with *Mahārājādhirāja* and *Paramabhaṭṭāraka*.

parameśvara-hasta (SII 2), the royal cubit; cubit measured according to the length of the king's forearm. Cf. *śrīpāda-kol*.

Parameśvara-mahākoṣṭhakārin (EI 27), officer in charge of the royal treasury or store-house.

Parameśvara-niyogin (*A.R. Ep.*, 1958-59, p. 9), a special officer attached to the king. Cf. *Niyogin*.

Parameśvar-ety-ādi (IE 8-2), shortened form of *Parameśvar-ety-ādi-raj-āvalī-tray-opeta*.

Parameśvarī (EI 6), title of a queen, especially a ruling queen.

Param-opāsaka (BL; LL), epithet of a male member of the Buddhist laity; cf. *upāsaka*.

Param-opāsikā (EI 22, 32; LL; BL), epithet of a female member of the Buddhist laity; cf. *upāsikā*.

pāramparа (EI 15), same as *paramparā-balīvarda-grahaṇa*; refers to the obligation of the villagers to supply bullocks in succession for the cart of a royal agent on tour in their villages.

paramparā, cf. *a-paramparā-balīvarda* (IE 8-5); 'succession'; refers to the obligation of the villagers to supply bullocks for the cart of the touring officers visiting different villages in succession.

Pāraśava (BL), name of a community.

Pārasīka (EI 12), originally, a Persian; but used to indicate any foreigner; a Dutch in the present case.

Pārasi, *Pārasī*, *Pārasika* (EI 5; SII 1), a Persian.

Pāraśiva (SITI), probably *Pāraśava*; explained as 'one who wields a weapon; a soldier'.

parasvat (CII 1), a rhinoceros.

parata (Chamba), return, exchange, substitute, compensation; derived from Sanskrit *parivarta*; same as *badalā*.

pāratrika (CII 1), 'benefit in the other world'; merit.

para-samaya (EI 24), explained as a particular Jain doctrine; doctrines other than one's own.

parganā (EI 9, 32), a group of villages; same as *pratijāgaraṇaka* (q. v.).

Pāri (EI 31; LP; PJS), abbreviation of Gujarātī *Pārikha*, *Pārekha* (Sanskrit *Pārīkṣaka*), originally meaning 'an examiner of coins'; a surname among the Baniās of Gujarat.

paribhūta-nāman (CII 3), a nickname.

paribodha (CII 1), obstacle, fetters; being in fetters.

paricakra (LL), a circular panel.

Paricāraka (EI 31), a servant; sometimes mentioned in the list of officials.

paricchanda (*Ep. Ind.*, Vol. III, p. 16), a vessel.

pariccheda (CII 3), a territorial term meaning a group of villages.

Parichā (IE 8-3; EI 31), Oḍiyā; same as Sanskrit *Parīkṣaka*.

paridarśanā (IE 8-5; EI 29), a supervision tax probably related to division of property; may also be the same as Persian *nazrāna*.

parigha (HRS), 'door-bolt'; one of the seven sources of revenue specified in the *Arthaśāstra*.

parigraha (ML), acceptance.

parigṛhīta (IE 8-2; EI 31), 'accepted', sometimes used in place of *anudhyāta* ('meditating' or 'favoured') in passages like *tatpāda-parighṛhīta*; cf. *bappa-bhaṭṭāraka-pāda-parigṛhīta*, *bhaṭṭāraka-Mahāsena-parigṛhīta*, etc.; refers to selection or acceptance of a succession or appointment or receipt in one's favour.

Cf. *catuḥśāla-parigṛhītaṁ śaila-maṇḍapam* and *Samyaksambuddhasya dhātu-parigṛhītasya* (*Select Inscriptions*, p. 228).

parihāra (IE 8-5; EI 6; SITI), same as *maryādā-parihāra*;

exemptions from taxes and obligations granted to the donees of rent-free land; privileges of the donee of rent-free holdings; for many such privileges, see Appendix I. Cf. certain privileges in respect of a number of taxes and obligations enumerated in Tamil records as follows : *vaṭṭi-nāḻi* (payment of one *nāḻi* per *vaṭṭi*), *pudā-nāḻi* (or *pidā*°, cess on each door or tax for the maintenance of sluices), *maṉṟupādu* (fine imposed by a court of law), *ūrāṭci* (tax for running the village administration), *taragu* (tax on brokers), *kūlam* (tax on grains), *iḻam-puṭi* (tax on toddy-drawers), *nāḍu-kāval* (tax for the policing of a district), *ūḍupokku* (meaning uncertain), *uppu-kocceygai* (tax for the manufacture of salt), *nall-ā* (tax for maintaining specimen cows), *nallerudu* (tax for maintaining specimen buffaloes), *nerv-āypuvum* (meaning uncertain) and others. See *Ep. Ind.*, Vol. XVIII, p. 124.

(*IA* 17), a ring.

pārihārika (HRS), land exempted from revenue, as suggested by the *Arthaśāstra*; privileges enjoyed by the donee of a rent-free holding.

Cf. sarva-jāta-pārihārika; same as *parihāra* or the *parihāras* collectively. See *Select Inscriptions*, pp. 192, 194.

pārihīnika (HRS), damage-fee which was a branch of accidental revenue, according to the *Arthaśāstra*. See Ghoshal, *H. Rev. Syst.*, p. 28.

parikara (IE 8-5; CII 4), same as *uparikara*, occasional or minor taxes; cf. *sa-parikara* (EI 23) which is the same as *s-oparikara*.

(*SITI*), requisites of a village.

(*HA*), accessory decoration round the figure of a Jina, the motifs being taken from the Jain conception of the eight chief objects attendant upon a Jina (*aṣṭa-mahāprātihāryāṇi*, viz. the wheel of law, the caitya-tree, the lion-seat, the aureole behind the head, two attendant flywhisk-bearers, drum-beaters and pipe-players, and garland-bearers).

Parikāra (SITI), a servant.

Pārikh (EI 31), Gujaratī; Sanskrit *Pārīkṣa* ; an examiner of coins; a family name amongst the Baniās. See *Rūpa-darśaka*.

pārikh-āya (IA 19), a levy; cf. *Pārikh*, *pārīkṣika*.

parikraya (SII 1), an exchange.

parikreya (*Sel. Ins.*, p. 236), remuneration.

Parīkṣā (IE 8-3; EI 28, 31), same as Sanskrit *Parīkṣaka*; Sanskritised from Oḍiyā *Parichā*; superintendent of a department or a governor; cf. *Dvāra-parīkṣā*.

parīkṣā (IA 10), same as *divya*, an ordeal.

(*CII* 1), self-examination.

Parīkṣaka (IE 8-3), see *Parīkṣā*=Oḍiyā *Parichā*.

pārīkṣika (HRS), testing-charge for private minting of coins, according to the *Arthaśāstra*. See Ghoshal, *H. Rev. Syst.*, p. 43. Cf. *pārikhāya*.

parīkṣi-paṭṭa (IE I), meaning doubtful.

parimoṭana (EI 12), cracking.

parinirvāṇa (EI 8), the death of the Buddha.

paripanth, cf. *paripanthayati* (IE 8-2), same as *vyavaharati*; cf. *samasta-mudrā-vyāpārān paripanthayati*.

paripanthanā, 'creation of obstacles'; same as *vidhāraṇā* (EI). See *vādhā* or *bādhā*.

paripara (EI 3), a fight.

Pāripārśvika (IA 11), a servant.

paripṛcchā (CII 1), questioning.

paripūrṇa (LP), probably, 'in full youth'.

pariṣad (LL), four classes of the Buddhist order.

(*EI* 32), used in the sense of *pāriṣada*, 'a councillor'.

Cf. Tamil *paraḍai*, etc. (SII 3), an assembly.

(*CII* 1), cf. Prakrit *parisā* (EI 8), a council; the council [of ministers]; cf. *mantri-pariṣad*, 'council of ministers.'

parisara (EI 11), an area.

pariṣadā (HD), same as *sabhā*; an assembly or audience.

pariśrava (CII 1), sin.

pariśu (SII 1), probably, a contract.

parisūtra (*Hyderabad Archaeological Series*, No. 18, p. 34), explained as 'an establishment.'

parityāga (*Ep. Ind.*, Vol. XXXIV, p. 10, text line 2), donation; cf. *deyadharma-parityāga*.

Parivāra (SII 3), a servant.

Cf. *horaka-parivāra* (ML), explained as 'the following of *horakas*.'

parivār-ālaya (SII 3), surrounding verandah of a temple.

parivastra, cf. Tamil *parivaṭṭam*, *pariśaṭṭam*, *pariyaṭṭam* (SITI), literally, garment; honour done to a nobleman in a temple by tying a piece of cloth (generally, silk cloth) round his head.

Parivṛddha (EI 12), same as *Prabhu*.

parṇ-ākara, cf. *sa-parṇ-ākara* (IE 8-5), 'together with the fields producing leaves (i. e. betel-leaves).'

parṇa-śaśan (CII 1), an animal; probably, a rabbit living on leaves.

parokṣam (IA 18), 'in the absence of'; 'behind the back of'.

paṟṟu (IE 8-4), Tamil; a small territorial unit.

parṣad (LL), a congregation.

pārṣada, cf. Prakrit *pāṣaṁḍa* (CII 1), a religious community; one belonging to a *parṣad* or religious group.

pārśva (HRS), extra charge upon land over and above the king's grain-share, which was a branch of 'accidental revenue' according to the *Arthaśāstra*. See Ghoshal, *H. Rev. Syst.*, pp. 28, 38.

(*IE* 8-4), explained by some as a small territorial unit; but may be 'side'; cf. *prāveśya*.

Pārśvika (EI 9; CII 4), an aide-de-camp; also used to indicate a neighbour or one having land in the neighbourhood of the gift land (*Ep. Ind.*, Vol. XXXIII, p. 197, text line 13).

partāb (SII 1), Sanskrit *pratāpa*; a half *pagoda*.

parva-mās-otsava (EI 15), a festival.

pāruttha, a silver coin equal to 8 *drammas* of copper or billon (*JNSI*, Vol. XXII, p. 196).

parvan (IA 18), used in relation to eclipses.

Cf. Koṅkaṇa-vijaya-parvan (EI 33), festival celebrating the conquest of the Koṅkaṇ; an anniversary of the said conquest.

(*IE* 7-1-2), 'five'.

parvata (IE 7-1-2), 'seven'.

paryāya (IA 18), used in relation to an allotment.

(*CII* 1), cf. *dharma-paryāya*, 'exposition of the doctrine'; a religious text.

Cf. Pallānakāra (EI 23), Sanskrit *Paryāyakāra*, a saddler, a saddle-maker.

paryuṣita (HRS), 'outstanding revenue' which was one of the three kinds of revenue specified in the *Arthaśāstra*.

pāśa (CII 4), fetters of worldly existence.

(*IA* 18), a land measure.

(*EI* 26), a girdle.

Pasāita (EI 29, 33), also spelt *Pasāyita*; official designation; probably Sanskrit *Prasādita* in the sense of 'a fief-holder'.

pāṣāṇa (IE 8-5; SITI), one of the eight kinds of enjoyment of landed property; rocky soil and its products; mineral products; probably, stony and hilly land referring to the right of quarrying, etc.

paśānam (EI 23), a tax.

Pasāpālaka (EI 33), official designation; cf. *Pasāyita*, etc.

Pasāyati (EI 33), same as *Pasāyita* (q.v.), etc.

Pasāyita (IE 8-3;EI 33), probably Sanskrit *Prasādita* used to indicate a *Jāgīrdār*. See *Pasāita pañcāṅga-prasāda.*

pāścātya-likhita (LP), written on the back of the bond.

paśu (EI 8), animal sacrifice.

Cf. a-paśu-medhya (IE 8-5), 'free from the obligation of supplying animals for sacrifices.'

(*CII* 4), the individual soul.

Paśupāla (IA 22), nomads.

(*EI* 1), also called *Paśupālaka*; a person in charge of cattle.

pāśupata (SII 2), same as *pāśupat-āstra*; name of a weapon.

Pāśupata (*EI* 32), name of a Śaiva sect.

Pāśupat-ācārya (BL), epithet of a Śaiva religiou teachers.

Pāśupata-rājñī (BL), epithet of a Śaiva queen.

paṭa, paṭā, pāṭa (EI 28; Chamba), charter, deed; same as Sanskrit *paṭṭa* or *paṭṭaka.*

pāṭa, cf. *daṇḍapāṭa.*

pātaka (IE 8-1-2), 'five'. Cf. *pañca-mahāpātaka.*

pāṭaka (IE 8-4; EI 4, 24; IA 18), 'part of a village', a quarter; the outlying part of a village; a ḥamlet; often prefixed to the name of localities; often modified to *vāṭaka.*

(*EI* 15, 17, 28), a land measure.

(*IE* 8-6), a land measure equal to forty *droṇavāpas* or to five *kulyavāpas*; part of a village.

(*EI* 23, 24), a territorial division.

(*SITI*), portion of a field.

(*SITI*), anklet worn by women.

(*LP*), same as Gujarātī *pāḍo*, a street or the division of a town.

Paṭakāra (*Ep. Ind.*, Vol. XIII, p. 186), a weaver.

Pāṭakāra (EI 28), a splitter of wood.

Paṭakila (EI 23), village headman; same as *Paṭṭakila*, modern *Paṭel* or *Pāṭīl*; cf. *Veṭakila.*

pātāla (IE 7-1-2), sometimes used to indicare 'seven'.

Pātala-karaṇin (IA 12), official designation.

paṭalikā, cf. Tamil *paḍaligai*.

pataṅga (IA 11), a paper kite.

pātanīya (LP), 'should be left aside', i. e. 'should not be taken into account'.

(*LP*), to be kept uncultivated; see *kheḍanīya*.

Pātasāha (EI 11, 30; BL), Muslim imperial title; same as Persian *Pādshāh*. Cf. *Pātasāhi*, *Pātisāha*, *Pātusāha*.

Pātasāhi (BI), Indian modification of an imperial title of the Muhammadans; same as Persian *Pādshāh*; cf. *Pātasāha*, *Pātisāhi*, etc.

pātayiṣyāmi (LP), 'I shall deduct and thus take less.'

Paṭel, *Pāṭel* (IE 8-3; EI 7), also called *Pāṭil*; village headman; a member of the administrative board called *Cauthiyā* in Western India; cf. *Paṭṭakila*, *Paṭakila*, *Veṭakila*.

pātha (IE 8-6; IA 11), a land measure regarded as equal to 240 square feet.

pathaka (IE 8-4; EI 4, 23, 27; CII 3, 4; LP), a group of villages; a territorial division like a Parganā of later days.

Pathakīyaka (LP), explained as one who collects the road-tax [for the maintenance of the road] or the transit tax. But cf. *pathaka* also.

pāthi (IA 15), a territorial unit; same as *pathaka*.

Pāṭhin (EI3 1), epithet or family name of Brāhmaṇas.

pāṭī (IE 8-3); 'arithmetic'; cf. the designation *Pāṭy-uparika*.

pati (LL), a king; cf. *adhipati*.

(*EI* 18), same as *Kuḍipati*=Sanskrit *Grāmapati*.

Cf. *grāma-patyā* (probably the same as *grāma-jana-patitvāt*) and *nānā-patyā* (probably *nānā-grāma-jana-patitvāt*). See *JAS*, Letters, Vol. XX, pp. 203-04.

paṭi (IA 18), same as Sanskrit *prati*, but sometimes substituted for Sanskrit *pari* in Prakrit; cf. *paṭibhoga*, 'consumption [of food].'

pati-bhāga (CII 4), a share of the produce payable to the landlord.

Patihāri (EI 27), Sanskrit *Pratihārin*.

pāṭikā (CII 4), a share.

pātikā, cf. *rāja-pātikā*.

Pāṭil, see *Paṭel*, *Pāṭel*.

Pātisāha, also spelt *Pādisāha* (EI 30; BL); same as Persian *Pādshāh*; 'Muslim imperial ruler'. See *Pādishāh*.

Pātisāhi (BL), Indian modification of an imperial title of the Muslim rulers; same as Persian *Pādshāh*. See *Pātisāha*, etc.

patita (LP), uncultivated.

pātita (*Ep. Ind.*, Vol. XXXV, p. 14), 'killed in a battle'.

patra (CITD), a letter or document; a note; a written paper or deed.

(*LP*), a bond.

Cf. tāmra-patra.

Pātra (IE 8-3; EI 28, 29; BL), a minister; cf. *Mahāpurohita-ṭhakkura*, *Paṇḍita*, *Upādhyāya*, *Karaṇa-kāyastha*, etc., mentioned as *Pātra* probably meaning 'a courtier.' See *Ekapātra* and *Mahāpātra*.

pātra, probably, a document (*patra*). See *Ep. Ind.*, Vol. XXX, p. 169.

(*EI* 9), a donee.

Cf. Pātrapati.

Pātrapati, probably, the driver or owner of a horse-cart (*ṭaṅgā*). See *Ep. Ind.*, Vol. XXXIV, p. 145.

patra-samaya (*LP*), the conditions laid down in a bond.

Paṭṭa, abbreviation of *Paṭṭakila* (*A.R. Ep.*, 1958-59, No. B 296).

paṭṭa (IE 8-4; CII 3, 4), a territorial term meaning a group of villages; cf. *apara-paṭṭa* (EI 22) 'the western district'.

(*EI* 7, 9, 11; SII 1; BL), a school or spiritual line; a pontificate; a pontifical seat; the dignity of the head of a Jain school; cf. reference to a Jain religious teacher as belonging to the *paṭṭa* of another teacher and the *santāna* of a third teacher; cf., e. g., 'in the *paṭṭa* of Dharma-sūri'; also cf. '*paṭṭ-āvalī* of the Kharatara *gaccha*'.

Cf. rāja-paṭṭa, *paṭṭa-bandha*, *paṭṭ-ābhiṣeka*, etc.

(*EI* 18), a piece of land.

(*LL*), a slab; cf. Prakrit *paṭa* (EI 20), a stone slab. Cf. *yoni-paṭṭa*; *Gaurī-paṭṭa*.

(*Chamba*), also called *paṭha*; a grain measure, derived from Sanskrit *prastha*.

Same as *paṭṭaka* (q.v.); cf. *Paṭṭa-lekhin*, etc.

(*ASLV*), an account book.

(*LP*), abbreviation of *Paṭṭadhara*; probably one who has the charter for collecting government revenues; cf. *Paṭṭakila*.

Cf. Paṭṭarājñī, *Paṭṭanāyaka*, etc.

pāṭṭa, same as or a mistake for *paṭṭa*, a district. See *Ep. Ind.*, Vol. XXXIV, p. 235.

paṭṭa-bandha (EI 5, 22, 26), coronation; crowning ceremony.

Paṭṭ-ācārya (IA 14), a religious title; same as *Maṇḍal-ācārya*.

paṭṭaka (EI 30; IA 17), a passport; a charter; a copper-plate grant. Cf. *paṭṭak-ārtha-samasta-karaṇāya* (LP), 'for fulfilling all the conditions in the charter'; also Tamil *paṭṭayam* (SITI), grant inscribed on copper-plates.

paṭṭaka-dhārmika (IEZ 8-8; EI 30); probably, an authorised cess to be collected for performing a religious function; cf. *dhārmika*.

Paṭṭak-āpacārika (IE 8-3; EI 31), officer in charge of dealing with *paṭṭak-āpacāra* (crime relating to the misuse or fraud concerning grants).

Paṭṭakāra (EI 24), also called *Paṭṭalekhin*; writer of documents.

Paṭṭakila (EI 25; CII 4; HD), village headman; same as modern *Paṭel*, *Pāṭel* or *Pāṭīl*. See *Ind. Ant.*, Vol. VI, pp. 51, 53. Cf. *Veṭakila*.

paṭṭakil-ādāya (EI 21; CII 4), tax for the maintenance of the *Paṭṭakila* or village headman.

paṭṭakkārai (ASLV), neck-ring; an ornament.

paṭṭa-kūla (LP), silk cloth; cf. *pāṭoluṁ* in Gujarātī.

pattalā (EI 8-3; EI 19, 24; 26; CII 4), a territorial division; a district.

(*IA* 18; LP), same as *paṭṭa*, a royal charter; cf. *prasāda-pattalā* (LP), a deed recording the grant of rent-free land; (IA 18), cf. *prabhoḥ prasād-āvāpta-pattalayā*, explained as '[area enjoyed] under a patent obtained through the favour of the lord'.

Pattalaka (IE 8-3; EI 3, 9, 23), official designation; probably, not an officer in charge of a territorial unit called *pattalā*.

Paṭṭa-lekhin, cf. *Paṭṭakāra*.

Pattalikā (EI 9), official designation; feminine form of *Pattalaka*.

pāṭṭam (EI 21), a tax.

Paṭṭamahādevī (IE 8-2; EI 4, 20, 22; BL), designation of the chief queen; cf. *Mahādevī*.

Paṭṭamahiṣī (EI 28), a crowned queen; chief queen.

paṭṭana (HRS), duties levied upon merchants at the ports, as suggested by the *Arthaśāstra*.

(*EI* 19), same as *pattana*, a township.

pattana (IE 8-4; IP), a township; suffixed to the names of cities like *Aṇahillapura-pattana* (modern Pāṭan in the Kadi District of the former Baroda State).

Pattan-ākarasthāna-gokul-ādhikāri-puruṣa (IA 15), official designation or designations.

Paṭṭana-svāmin (ASLV), head of an organisation or a guild in a city; sometimes regarded as the same as *Mahānāḍ-prabhu*. See *Seṭṭi-Paṭṭanasvāmi*.

(*SITI*), chief or leader of the mercantile community of a town.

Paṭṭanāyaka (IE 8-3; EI 29), the chief officer or a ruling chief; same as *Puronāyaka* (cf. Tamil *Poṟṟu*). It is a family name in Orissa.

Paṭṭarājñī (IE 8-2; EI 23, 30; BL), designation of the chief queen; cf. *Rājñī*.

Paṭṭarāṇī (BL), title of a chief queen; cf. *Rāṇī*. Same as *Paṭṭarājñī*.

Paṭṭasāhanādhipati (IE 8-3; EI 15), same as *Mahāsādhanika*, etc.; see *Paṭṭasāhaṇi*.

Paṭṭasāhaṇi (EI 15), same as *Paṭṭasāhanādhipati*; see *Sāhaṇi*= Sanskrit *Sādhanika*; cf. *Kari-turaga-paṭṭasāhaṇi* (EI 5).

paṭṭa-śāla (CITD), Sanskrit °*śālā*; a reading hall; probably, 'the main hall'; in Kannaḍa, 'a silk-shop'.

(*EI* 3), name applied to the abode of certain Brāhmaṇas.

(*LP*), cf. Gujaratī *Paḍaśāla*; the first room in a house.

paṭṭ-āvalī (IA 19; SITI; BL), a list of Jain pontiffs; succession list of spiritual heads among the Jains; cf. '*paṭṭ-āvalī* of the Bṛihat-Kharatara *gaccha* [of the Jains].'

Paṭṭavārika, same as modern *Paṭvāri*; cf. *Vārika*.

Paṭṭela (EI 7), same as *Paṭṭakila*, *Paṭel* or *Pāṭil*.

paṭṭi (IE 8-6; EI 8), a measure of land; same as *nivarttana*.

paṭṭī (EI 9), a plot of land.

Same as *paṭṭa*; cf. *rāja-paṭṭī* (EI 4).

patti (SII 2), same as *nivartana*.

(*SII* 1), a sheep-fold; a square measure.

(*CII* 4), share of the produce.

(*IE* 8-3), the smallest division of the army.

pattī (IA 15), an extra land cess.

patti-bhāga (CII 4), same as *pati-bhāga*, a share of produce payable to the landlord.

Pattika (IE 8-3), leader of the *patti*, the smallest division of the army.

pattikā (CII 4), a share; same as *patti*.

paṭṭikā (EI 8, 17), same as *tāmra-paṭṭa* or *tāmra-paṭṭikā*; a copper plate or copper-plate grant.

(*EI* 3), a document.

Paṭṭikā-pālaka, same as *Pustapāla* (*Select Inscriptions*, p. 202).

paṭṭī-pada (EI 24), footprints on a slab.

Pattiyāṇaka (IA 132), official designation of doubtful import; probably, an administrator or document-writer.

paṭṭolā, cf. Tamil *paṭṭolai*.

paṭṭolai (SII 1), Tamil=Sanskrit *paṭṭolā* ; a document.

Pāṭṭolai (EI 21, 22), Tamil; official designation; cf. *paṭṭolai*, 'a document'.

paṭṭolī, 'a deed of purchase' also 'land purchased by means of a *paṭṭolī*' (*Jour. As. Soc.*, Letters, Vol. XX, p. 205). See Tamil *paṭṭolai*=*paṭṭolā*, 'a document'.

Paṭṭ-opādhyāya (HD), a writer or keeper of official documents. See *Rājataraṅgiṇī*, V. 397.

Pātusāha (BL), Indian modification of a Muslim imperial title; same as Persian *Pādshāh*.

Paṭvāri (IE 8-3), probably Sanskrit *Paṭṭavārika*; the accountant-clerk; a member of the administrative board called *Cauthiyā* in Western India.

Pāṭy-uparika (IE 8-2; 8-3; BL), official designation of uncertain implication; possibly indicating 'the head of the department of accounts'; sometimes also called *Mahārāja*, *Mahāsāmanta*, *Mahāpratīhāra*, *Mahāpīlupati*, *Pañc-ādhikaraṇ-oparika* and *Purapāl-oparika*, additionally.

pāukā (IE 8-5; EI 29), same as Oḍiyā *pāuseri*; tax on the money realised by creditors from debtors.

paüka (EI 31), misprint for Pāli *pattha*=Sanskrit *prastha*; a land measure.

pauṇḍarīka (EI 4; IA 19), name of a sacrifice.

Paurāṇika (EI 30; BL), a reciter of the Purāṇas; also probably, an astrologer. Cf. *Vyāsa.*

paura (CII 4), name of a coin.

Paura-vīthillaka, probably officers in charge of a city and a subdivision; cf. *Paura-vi(vī)thillaka-grāmakūṭa-niyuktāniyukta-pradhān-āpradhāna* (*Ep. Ind.*, Vol. XXV, p. 169, where the reading is given as *visvillaka*).

Paura-vyavahārika, cf. *Nagara-vyavahārika.* See *Hist. Dharm.*, Vol. III, pp. 112, 147.

pauṣadha (HA), Sanskrit *uposatha*; living like a Jain monk for 12 or 24 hours; the observance of fast on the eighth and fourteenth of the fortnight, the full-moon day and the day before the new moon and abstention from wicked acts, chastity, abandoment of bathing, etc., i.e. living temporarily like a monk. See *poṣadha.*

pāuseri, cf. *pāukā.*

pautava (HRS), various dues collected by the superintendent of weights and measures, as suggested by the *Arthaśāstra.*

(*EI* 30), measurement.

pauṭi (EI 29, 32), same as Sanskrit *pravarti*; a measure of capacity.

pāvāḍai (SITI), Tamil; cloth spread on the ground for persons of distinction to walk on; also food-offering on a large scale spread over a cloth in front of the deity.

pāvai (IE 8-5), same as *darśana* or *nazrāna.*

pāvaka (IE 7-1-2), 'three'.

pavana (IE 7-1-2), 'nine'.

pāvīsā (EI 33), probably, Sanskrit *pāda-viṁśaka* (*viṁśopaka*); name of a coin; regarded as equal to five cowrie-shells; same as modern *paisā.* See *lohaḍiyā* and *dramma.*

pavitra (EI 9), the *argha* vessel.

(*Ind. Ant.*, Vol. IX, p. 187), thread, 360 of which are tied round the neck of the image of Kṛṣṇa on Śrāvaṇa su-di 12.

Cf. Caitra-pavitra.

pavitraka (EI 1), meaning uncertain.

pāyalā (EI 11), also called *pāyalī*; name of a measure.

peḍā (Chamba), a grain measure; also spelt *piṭha, piḍā, pyoḍā.*

Peḍārpāla (BL), mistake for *Peḍāpāla*, 'keeper of the record-boxes'. See *Peṭapāla*.

pĕdda-gaḍyamu (CITD), Telugu; an unknown unit of measurement.

pĕjjuṅka (IE 8-5), Kannaḍa; name of a tax; same as *pĕrjuṅka*.

Pĕrgaḍĕ (IE 8-3; EI 4), Kannaḍa; a chamberlain; a superintendent or director (Sanskrit *Adhyakṣa*); see *Vĕrgaḍĕ*, *Hĕggaḍĕ*, etc.

Pĕrggāvuṇḍa (EI 26), Kannaḍa, official designation. Cf. *Gāvuṇḍa*.

pĕrjuṅka (IE 8-5), Kannaḍa; same as *pĕjjuṅka*; name of a tax or toll.

Pĕrjuṅkadapĕrgaḍĕ (EI 16), official designation.

perujuṅka (EI 28), same as *pĕrjuṅka*.

Perumān-aḍigaḻ (SITI), Tamil; a term of reverence used to indicate a god or a king. Cf. personal names like *Pramāḍi*.

perumbaḍaiyɔm (ASLV), military classes.

Peṭakapāla (EI 28, 29), keeper of the boxes containing records; record-keeper; same as *Peṭāpāla*, etc.

Peṭapāla (EI 30; BL), keeper of boxes containing official records; the record-keeper.

Peṭāpāla (EI 29), also called *Peṭakapāla*; record-keeper; same as *Peṭapāla*.

Peṭavika (EI 30), a class of officials; *Peṭavika-vārika* (IE 8-8).

peṭha (IE 8-4; CII 3), a small territorial unit; a group of villages.

Peṭṭapāla (EI 15, 28), keeper of the record-boxes; same as *Peṭāpāla*, *Peṭakapāla*, *Peḍāpāla*, etc.

Peyiya-sāhaṇi (Naik's List, No. 264), mentioned along with *Maleya-sāhaṇi*; official designation. Cf. *Sāhaṇi*.

Phā (IE 8-1), abbreviation of *Phālguna*.

phadiyā, see *phadyaka*.

phadyaka (EI 23), same as *phadiyā*; name of a coin; $\frac{1}{20}$ of a rupee and equal to 5 *dukrās* and 2 *dukānīs* (*JNSI*, Vol. XXII, p. 295).

phaiṇḍi-āyāyi (CITD), Telugu; same as *phaiṇḍivāya-maṟuturu*.

phaiṇḍivāya-maṟuturu (CITD), Telugu; a *maṟuturu* measure of land which brought an income in coin and not kind; in Telugu, *paiḍi* means gold and *āyam* income.

phala (IA 27), a Pāli form of Sanskrit *pala*.

phāla-divya (IA 17), the ordeal of taking a heated ploughshare in hand.

phalahika, cf. *sa-phalahikaṁ* (LP), with an open space round about the house; same as Gujarātī *phaliyuṁ*.

phalaka (IE 3-5), a wooden slab used as a slate.

phala-saṁskāra (CII 3), equation of the centre.

phalita, cf. *phalita-pade* (LP), also Gujarātī *huṁḍī pāke tyāre*, 'when the bill of exchange becomes due'.

phika (*LP*), a bull which is not castrated.

phuramāṇa (EI 2), Persian *farmān*; a royal order or grant.

phuṭṭa (CII 3), a Prakrit word meaning a break or damage in a construction, sometimes Sanskritised as *sphuṭita* (*Ep. Ind.*, Vol. XV, p. 144, note 3).

Piāda (IE 8-3), same as *Bhaṭa* or *Bhaṭa-manuṣya*; cf. *Pāik*.

picu, same as *suvarṇa* (q.v.).

picula, weight equal to 6 *māṣas* (*JNSI*, Vol. XVI, p. 46).

piḍā (Chamba), a grain measure; also spelt *piṭha*, *peḍā*, *pyoḍā*.

piḍāgai (ASLV), a hamlet.

Pidā-nāḻi (EI 28), name of a tax.

piḍha (LL), probably, a chair; cf. Sanskrit *pīṭha*.

piḻḻaigaḷ-tanam (SITI), Tamil; status of the prince, supposed to be an officers' cadre composed of the junior members of the royal family. Cf. *Kumār-āmātya*.

pīlu (IE 8-3), Indian form of Arabic-Persian *fīl*, an elephant.

Pīlupati (IE 8-2, 8-3; EI 13, 28; CII 4), leader of the elephant force or keeper of the elephants; cf. *Mahāpīlupati*, *pīlu*.

piñcha (IA18), bunch of feathers carried by a Jain ascetic.

piṇḍ-ādāna (EI 12), quit rent. Cf. also *piṇḍa-kara*.

piṇḍaka (*Ep. Ind.*, Vol. IV, p. 254, text line 55), same as *piṇḍ-ādāna* or *bhāga-bhoga*; cf. *samucita-kara-piṇḍak-ādi-samasta-pratyāya*; taxes assessed in a lump; cf. *piṇḍa-kara*.

(*IA* 2), same as *grāsa*; probably, a part of the produce of the fields for the maintenance of certain persons.

(*HRS*), known from Pāla records; same as *hiraṇya*, according to some.

(*LL*), probably, a slab.

piṇḍa-kara (HRS), lump assessment upon villages, as suggested by the *Arthaśāstra*. Cf. also *piṇḍ-ādāna*.

piṇḍa-pāta (EI 25), food [for the Buddhist monks].

piśāca-caturdaśī (EI 1), name of a *tithi.*

Piṣāraḍi (IA 24), Malayāḷam; the manager of a temple.

Piśunavetrika (EI 33; HD), probably, an officer who drives away undesirable persons with a cane; or, one engaged in a court for caning culprits. See *Ep. Ind.*, Vol. XI, p. 94. See *Vetrika, Yāṣṭika, Veṭakila.*

piṭaka (CII 4), a measure of capacity.

Cf. Traipiṭaka.

Pitalahāra (EI 20, 32), a brazier.

Pitāmaha (EI 24, 33), epithet of the Buddha.

(*IE* 7-1-2), 'one'; but cf. *Brahman* used to indicate 'nine'.

piṭha (Chamba), a grain measure; also spelt *piḍā, peḍā, pyoḍā.*

pīṭha (CII 4; IA 12), receptacle of a Śiva-liṅga; the ablution trough of a Śiva-liṅga; also called *Yoni-paṭṭa.*

(*SITI*), pedestal for the image of a deity.

pīṭhī (*Ep. Ind.*, Vol. III, p. 16), a pedestal or seat; same as *pīṭha* and *pīṭhikā.*

pīṭhika (ASLV), Sanskrit *pīṭhikā*; a throne; same as *rājya.*

pīṭhikā (EI 2), a platform.

Pīṭhikāvitta (IE 8-3; EI 12; HD), probably, 'those who have acquired [special] seats'; same as *Utthitāsanika.* The word occurs in such records as the Belava plate of Bhojavarmadeva (*Ep. Ind.*, Vol. XII, p. 40). Cf. *Velāvitta. Pīṭhikāvitta* is sometimes explained as the collector of state dues from pilgrims or religious institutions (Sen, *Hist.Asp. Ins. Beng.*, p. 552).

Pīṭhīpati (BL), explained as 'the lord of Magadha' in the commentary of Sandhyākaranandin's *Rāmacarita*; title of the head of the Buddhist religious institution at Bodhgayā, who was the precursor of the later *Mahant Mahārājas* of Bodhgayā. The word *pīṭhī* in this title is the same as *pīṭha* or *pīṭhikā* meaning the *vajrāsana* at Bodhgayā.

pitṛ-parvan (*Ep. Ind.*, Vol. XXXIV, p. 37), probably, *śrāddha* or *dāna* on each *amāvāsyā* day.

pitṛ-yajña (CII 4), offerings to the manes; one of the *pañca-mahāyajña.*

pla (IE 8-1), contraction of *pala*; often found in the records of the Orissa region.

pocila-bhūmi (LP), soft land.

poḍhī (LL), a cistern; cf. Sanskrit *prahi.*

Poduvāḷ (EI 18), Tamil-Malayalam; an officer supervising charitable endowments.

polācya, cf. *sa-khila-polācya* (IE 8-5); cultivated land; same as *nāla*; Hindī *polàch*, 'land constantly under cultivation.'

poṁda (Chamba), name of a tax.

poṁdī (Chamba), bottom; foot of a hill.

pon (SITI), also spelt *poṉ*; name of a gold coin also called *māḍai*. Cf. *pon-bhaṇḍāram*, 'gold-treasury'; *pon-paṇḍāra-vāśal*, 'the gate of the gold-treasury; royal gold-treasury'; *pon-vargam* (SITI), 'a class of taxes payable in gold or coin; *ponvari*, 'tax payable in gold (cash)'; also 'the fee for minting gold into coins'; probably, the same as *ponvari-māḍai.*

Cf. turai-miṉṉaṟ-pon (SITI), name of a coin.

(*IE* 8-8; EI 16), name of a coin; same as *gadyāṇa*, *hūn* or *varāha.*

poṉ (EI 24), a coin.

Poṉ-bhaṇḍāram (ASLV), a treasurer; treasury.

Pora-Pāñjīdhara-parīkṣā (EI 28), chief astrologer; cf. *puro* prefixed to certain official designations in Orissa. See *Paṭṭanāyaka*, etc.

Pora-Śrīkaraṇa (EI 28), chief secretary; cf. *puro* prefixed to certain official designations in Orissa. See *Poṟṟu.*

Poṟ-Bhaṇḍāri (EI 25), Tamil; temple officer mentioned along with *Śāsana-bhaṇḍāri* (*Ep. Ind.*, Vol. XXV, p. 132); cf. *pora* prefixed to Oḍiyā official designations like *Pora-Śrīkaraṇa*; also Tamil *Poṟṟu.*

Poṟṟu (EI 25), Tamil; official designation.

poṣadha, derived from Sanskrit *uposatha*; also called *poṣadha-vrata*; cf. *pauṣadha.*

pota (EI 9), a sacrificial victim.

potaka (LP), the government's money-bag.

(*LP*), cf. Gujarātī *potuṁ*; the amount of revenue of a village sent to the Government treasury. Cf. *pottaka.*

potra (EI 26), name of a tax. Cf. *potta.*

potta, cf. *milita-potta-drammā* (LP), collected government money. Cf. *potra.*

pottaka (LP), same as Gujarātī *potuṁ*; the amount of the revenue of a village sent to the government treasury. Cf. *potaka.*

poṭṭalikā (IE 8-8), a bundle.

pra (PJS), abbreviation of *pratimā* (especially in medieval Jain inscriptions).

(*IE* 8-1), abbreviation of *prathama*.

prabandha, name of hymnical compositions in Tamil by ancient Vaiṣṇava devotees. The contributions of hymns and prayers by the twelve *āḻvārs* in praise of Viṣṇu make up the *Nālāyiradivyaprabandham*. *Nālāyira* (four thousand) indicates the rough total number of items and *prabandham* is regarded as meaning a compilation. The first thousand is known as *Tirumoḻi* and comprises hymns of Periyāḻvār, Āṇḍāl, Kulaśekhara, etc.; the second thousand contains the hymns of Tirumaṅgai; the third comprises the compositions of the first three *āḻvārs* called *Iyaṟpā*, viz. Tirumaḻiśai, Nammāḻvar and Tirumaṅgai, and the fourth called *Tiruvāymoḻi* is entirely the work of Nammāḻvār. Nāthamunigaḷ is stated to be the compiler of this anthology. See M. S. Purnalingam Pillai, *Tamil Literature*, pp. 181 ff.

prabarha (EI 13), a worthy.

prābda (EI 16), same as *abda*, 'the year.'

prabhā (SII 2), an aureole or nimbus. Cf. *prabhā-valaya*.

prabhāṭaka (EI 24), same as *bhāṭaka* ; rent.

prabhā-valaya (*Ep. Ind.*, Vol. III, p. 16), aureole or nimbus.

prābhṛtīkṛta (EI 14), 'presented '.

Prabhu (IA 30; BL), a village official; cf. *Mahāprabhu*.

prabhujyamāna (IA 18), cf. *bhujyamāna*.

prabhu-śakti (CII 4), power derived from the royal position.

prabhu-svāmya (SII 11.1), a tenure held by a *Prabhu* (q.v.).

prabodhanī (EI 8), *prabodh-otsava* (EI 32), same as *utthāna-dvādaśī*.

pradakṣiṇa (CITD), circumambulation from left to right; paying homage to a temple, etc., by solemnly walking round it with the right hand towards it, so that the right side is always turned towards the person or object circumambulated; a reverential salutation made by walking in this manner.

pradeśa (IE 8-4), a province or district.

Prādeśika (IE 8-3; HD), cf. Prakrit *Pādesika* (EI 3), provincial governor; governor of a *pradeśa* or province. Cf. *CII*, Vol. I, pp. 4-5.

Pradeṣṭṛ (HD), a class of magistrates; the police magistrate. See Ghoshal, *H. Rev. Syst.*, p. 147; *Ep. Ind.*, Vol. XXII, p. 156; *Arthaśāstra*, I. 12; IV. 1 and 10 (last verse).

pradeya (EI 12), same as *deya*; dues.

Pradhāna (SII 1; HD; BL), an official designation sometimes indicating the chief minister or administrator also called *Pradhāna-saciva* (EI 23); cf. *pañca-Pradhānāḥ* (EI 5) 'the five ministers'. See *Ind. Ant.*, Vol. IX, p. 35 where *Mantrin*, *Amātya* and *Pradhāna* are separately mentioned.

pradhāna-maṇḍapa (LL), Buddhist; the hall for practising religious exercises.

Pradhānin (CITD), according to lexicons, a governor, minister or president; noble or courtier; etc.

(*EI* 31;ASLV), a high executive officer; same as *Pradhāna*.

(*EI* 30), a village headman.

Cf. Mahāpradhāni.

pradhāni-joḍi (SII 2; SITI), Sanskrit-Tamil; an *inām* held on a fixed quit-rent by a minister; the chief minister's quit-rent.

prādhirājya (EI 4), name of a sacrifice.

pradvāra (IA 7), a place in front of the gate; explained as 'a suburb' (EI 21); same as Gujarātī *parā*. Cf. *Valabhī-pradvāra-Homba-vāsakāt* (IA 9).

Prāḍvivāka (HD), the chief justice; a judge. See *Manusmṛti*, IX. 234.

praghaṭṭaka (EI 15), probably, a conflict.

prāghūrṇaka (LP), a present or gift.

pragrāhya (EI 12), cf. *a-kiñcit-pragrāhya*; same as *grāhya*.

prahaṇika (LL), a class of Buddhist monks.

prahara (SII 2; SITI), flaw in rubies.

prāharikya (LP), cf. Gujarātī *pahero*; a guard or custodian.

prahitaka (IA 6), doubtfully explained as 'a messenger' or 'a committee man.'

Praiṣaṇika (IE 8-3), same as *Preṣaṇika*.

prakāla (*Select Inscriptions*, p. 305, text line 15); an era; cf. *Gupta-prakālə gaṇanāṁ vidhāya*. See *kāla* in *kāl-ānuvartamāna-saṁvatsare* (ibid., p. 270, text lines 3-4), etc.

prakaraṇa (CII 1), proper occasion.

prakīrtita (EI 24), built; same as *kīrtita*.

prakrama (CII 1), an effort; zealous activity; same as *parākrama*.

prakrānta (CII 1), active or zealous.

prakraya (HRS), income from mines and salt-works, as suggested by the *Arthaśāstra.*

prakṛta, cf. *saṅgha-prakṛta.*

Prakrit, Anglicised spelling of *Prākṛta,* the name of a language.

Prākṛta, see Prakrit.

prakṛti (HD); cf. *Mahābhārata,* II. v. 23, speaking of the seven *prakṛtis* which Nīlakaṇṭha explains as referring to *Durg-ādhyakṣa* (commandant of the citadel), *Bal-ādhyakṣa* (controller general of the army), *Dharma-ādhyakṣa* (chief of the departments of charity and justice), *Camūpati* (commander of the army in the field), chaplain, physician and astrologer. The *Milindapañha* (IV. i. 36) mentions six officers, e.g., the commander-in-chief, prime minister, chief judge, chief treasurer, bearer of the sun-shade and bearer of the sword of state (cf. *Ep. Ind.,* Vol. XV, p. 77, note 6). Cf. *Mātra.*

(*EI* 16), a temple official.

(*IE* 7-1-2), 'twentyone.'

(*EI* 9), the Kṣatriya community.

Cf. sa-tantuvāya-gokuṭa-śauṇḍik-ādi-prakṛtika (IE 8-5); subjects of a king.

(*CII* 1), usage.

prakriyā (IA 18), cf. *samasta-rāja-prakriy-opeta*; prerogative.

prakṣepa (EI 13), cf. *amīṣāṁ prakṣepa-pratiṣedhau na karaṇīyau,* 'they should not be ousted [from the possession] or hindered [from their enjoyment of the gift land].'

pramadā-kula (EI 11), a host of courtesans.

pramāṇa (EI 6; SII 1; SITI), a document; a title deed.

(*Ep. Ind.,* Vol. XXVIII, p. 109), authority; witness.

(*SII* 12), cf. *mūla-pramāṇa,* original order.

pramāṇa-yaṣṭi (LL), measuring rod.

Pramātāra (HD), an officer concerned with the administration of justice, according to some (Vogel, *Ant. Ch. St.,* pp. 122-23). See *Ep. Ind.,* Vol. IV, p. 211. Cf. *Pramātṛ, Pramattavāra.*

Pramattavāra (EI 21), official designation; same as *Pramātṛ* or *Pramātāra* (q.v.); the commander of the elephant corps according to some (CII 4).

Pramātṛ (BL), same as *Pramātāra, Pramattavāra* (q.v.); a civil judge, according to some (HD); cf. *Ep. Ind.,* Vol. XVII, p. 321; literally, 'measurer [of the king's grain share]'.

Pramukha (CII 4), a member of the executive committee of a corporation.

(*EI* 28), probably the same as *Pradhānin.*

prāṇa (CII 1), living being; same as *prāṇin.*

(*IE* 7-1-2), 'five'.

Prāṇ-ācārya (EI 8), title of a physician; explained as the medical adviser of the king (HD). Cf. *Viṣṇudharmottara*, II. 24. 33-34 (for his qualifications).

prāṇa-dākṣiṇya (CII 1), gift of life.

praṇālī (CII 3), a conduit, a channel, an irrigation canal.

prāṇāntika (SITI), 'till the close of one's life'.

pranaptrika (CII 1), cf. *panatika* (EI 22), the great-grandson; but cf. *naptṛ.*

prāṇa-sameta, cf. Prakrit *praṇa-sameda* (EI 24), 'endowed with life'.

praṇaśya (LP), 'going out of sight'; cf. Gujarātī *nāśīne.*

praṇaya (IE 8-5; HRS), known from the *Arthaśāstra*, the Junagadh inscription of Rudradāman, etc.; emergency tax or benevolence; also called *praṇaya-kriyā* (IE 8-5); cf. *a-hiraṇya-dhānya-praṇaya-pradeya*, an epithet of rent-free land.

praṇaya-kriyā (EI 8), benevolence or emergency impost; same as *praṇaya.*

Prāntapāla (IE 8-3; EI 18, 29, 31), warden of the marches; also explained as the governor of a province or guardian of the frontiers (HD). Cf. Vogel, *Ant. Ch. St.*, p. 124.

prapā (EI 3; IA 18; LL), watering trough; a cistern or reservoir.

(*Ep. Ind.*, Vol. VII, p. 46, note 8), a place of distributing water gratis to travellers; a cistern.

prāpa (EI 17), 'sub-division of a district'; but see *prāpīya*, *prāveśya.*

Prapā-pūraka (IE 8-8; EI 30), a person responsible for filling the cisterns with water in a place for watering cattle or supplying water to travellers.

praparṇaka, royal order; same as Persian *parwāna* (*Select Inscriptions*, p. 248).

prapautra, cf. *pautra-prāpautrika* (CII 1); the great-grandson.

prāpīya (EI 17), same as *prāveśya*; cf. *Akṣasaraka-prāveśya* and *Akṣasaraka-prāpīya* (*Ep. Ind.*, Vol. XI, p. 109); cf. *prāpa.*

Prāpta-pañcamahāśabda (IE 8-2), same as *Samadhigata-*

pañcamahāśabda; subordinate title or epithet; sometimes applied to a crown prince. See *pañca-mahāśabda.*

prāpti (SII 2), benefit.

(*EI* 7), revenue.

(*SITI*), enjoyment; what is obtained from someone.

prārabdhi (EI 2), meaning uncertain.

prārya (EI 15), father's father or father-in-law's father. Cf. *āryaka.*

prasāda (EI 3), gift (*Ep. Ind.*, Vol. XIII, p. 162, note 2).

prāsāda (CII 4; LL), a palace or temple.

prasādaka, cf. Pali and Prakrit *pasādaka* (EI 20), one who converts some one to the Buddhist faith.

prasāda-mukta (LP), cf. Gujarātī *prasād choḍvā khāt*, 'for allowing this favour'.

prasanna (CII 1), devoted or attached.

praśasti (EI 15, 23, 24; CII 3, 4), a eulogy; a eulogistic inscription generally on stone; a copper-plate charter (with reference to the introductory section of medieval charters); rarely *praśastā* (*Ep. Ind.*, Vol. 36, p. 52), *śubhā* (Vol. 35, p. 59).

prāstarika-śreṇī (EI 23), a guild of stone-masons.

Praśāstṛ (EI 31), probably, a judge; the chief magistrate, according to some (HD); cf. *Arthaśāstra*, I. 12.

Praśiṣya (ML; SITI), the disciple's disciple.

prasṛmara (EI 13), explained as 'spreading out in some corner'.

prasṛti (EI 30), a measure; a handful.

prastha (IE 8-6; CII 4; Chamba), a measure of capacity, often regarded as one-sixteenth of a *droṇa*; cf. Pāli *pattha*, a land measure.

praṣṭha, cf. *praṣṭham* (*Sel. Ins.*, p. 236), 'immediately'.

prasthaka (HRS), known from the Gurjara-Pratihāra records; cess at the rate of a *prastha* of grain over and above the usual grain-share. Cf. *akṣapatala-prastha*, *pratihāra-prastha*, etc.

pratāpa, see *partāb*.

Pratāpa-cakravartin (IE 8-2), see *Cakravartin*.

Prathama (EI 21), prefixed to *Kāyastha* and *Kulika* to indicate representatives of certain classes as members of an administrative board of the *Pañcāyat* type.

prathama-dvādāśī (EI 12; SII 2), Āṣāḍha su-di 12.

Prathama-kāyastha (IE 8-3; EI 27; BL), representative

of the scribal class on the local council of administrators; the clerk-member of the *Pañcāyat* board (see *Ep. Ind.*, Vol. XV, p. 130); the chief scribe, according to some (HD).

Prathama-kulika (IE 8-3; BL), literally, 'the chief artisan'; designation of a member of the artisan class represented on an administrative board like the *Pañcāyat* (*Ep. Ind.*, Vol. XV, p. 130).

Prathama-pustapāla (EI 15), wrongly regarded as occurring in some epigraphs; see *Pustapāla*.

prathama-skandha (LP), the first instalment. See *skandha, skandhaka*.

prathamataram, 'at first' (*Select Inscriptions*, p. 240).

prathama-tṛtīyā (EI 7), name of a *tithi*.

Prati (LP), abbreviation of *Pratihārī*.

prati, cf. *śata-pratyā* (LP), 'per hundred'.

pratibaddha (IA 15), generally used in the sense of 'attached to' or 'belonging to' in respect of a village pertaining to a territorial unit; sometimes used in the sense of 'hailing from' or 'one whose family hails from' (cf. *vinirgata* generally used in the same sense).

pratibhāga (HRS), offerings of fruits, firewood, roots and the like payable by villagers to the king as indicated in the *Manusmṛti*.

Cf. pati-bhāga.

(*CII* 1), one's lot.

prātibhedikā (IE 8-5; EI 9, 12), an obligation or impost of uncertain meaning; may be the same as *prātivedhan'ka*.

(*Ep. Ind.*, Vol. VI, p. 298, text line 20), explained by some as 'a special right' (CII 4); but cf. *viṣṭi-prātibhedikā* (EI 14); supposed to be related to *umbara-bheda* (q.v.) and meaning a special levy on defaulters in the payment of taxes.

pratibhoga, prātibhoga (HRS), same as *pratibhāga*.

pratibodha (HA), teaching in the Jain doctrine; conversion to the Jain faith.

pratibodhita (*Ind. Ant.*, Vol. XVI, p. 132, note 3), same as *vijñāpita*.

pratibhū (EI 30), a security.

praticchanda, a model for artists (*Journ. Or. Inst.*, Vol. X, No. 1, p. 12). See *lepyakāra*.

pratidiś, cf. *bhuñjato bhojayatah kṛṣataḥ karṣayataḥ pratidiśato vā na ken=āpi paripanthanā kāryā* (*Ep. Ind.*, Vol. XXXV, p. 280, text lines 65-66); probably, 'to dispose of'.

pratiḍhakkā (EI 4, 29), a kind of drum; one of the royal insignia of certain kings of South India.

pratigaṇaka (EI 26), subdivision of a district; same as *pratijāgaraṇaka*.

pratigraha (SITI), acceptance of gifts.

Pratihāra, Pratīhāra (EI 23; BL), also called *Pratihārin* (EI 3, 23), 'a door-keeper'; but cf. *Mahāpratihāra* who was a high officer; officer in charge of the defence of the royal palace or bed-chamber or the head of the guards of the city gate; a chamberlain or inditer of grants, according to some (HD); personal attendant of a king, according to others (CII; 4). See *Ep. Ind.*, Vol.VIII, p. 73; Vol. IX, p. 192; Bṛhaspati quoted by Viśvarūpa on the *Yājñavalkyasmṛti*, I. 307 (for his qualifications); *Mahābhārata*, Ādiparvan, 85. 28-29; *Viṣṇudharmottara*, II. 24. 12; Śukra, I. 121. Cf. *Antaḥ-pratīhāra* (IE 8-3), *Rajju-pratihāra*.

pratihāra (IE 8-5), levy for the maintenance of the door-keepers of the city gates; cf. *pratihāra-prastha*.

pratihāra-prastha (HRS), tax paid by the villagers at the rate of one *prastha* of grain for payment to the *Pratihāra*; see *pratihāra*.

Pratihāra-rakṣī (IE 8-3; LL), 'a female door-keeper'; a female officer in charge of the gates of the royal harem or the personal attendant of a queen.

Pratihārin (EI 23, 30), official designation; same as *Pratihāra*.

Pratihasta, cf. Oḍiyā *Paḍihasta* (EI 28), a representative.

pratijāgaraṇaka (IE 8-4; EI 9, 32; CII 4), a territorial unit often found in Paramāra inscriptions; same as *parganā*.

pratika, cf. Prakrit *paḍika* (EI 8), see *pratikaṁ śatam*, 'one coin per cent'.

pratikara, cf. *kara*; also *a-kiñchit-pratikara* (EI 23), 'land without any yield of revenue'.

(*HRS*), compensatory allowance paid by the government to dispossessed owners of rent-fee land, as indicated by the *Rājataraṅgiṇī*.

pratikaraṇa, repairs; cf. *khaṇḍa-sphuṭita-pratikaraṇa*, same as *khaṇḍa-sphuṭita-jīrṇoddhāra* (q.v.).

(*Ep. Ind.*, Vol. XXXV, p. 114, note 2), meeting the expenses.

pratikramaṇa (LP), morning and evening prayers.

pratimā, cf. *pratimam* (SII 2), image of a human being; usually, the image of a deity.

Pratinartaka (CII 3; BL; HD), an official title; perhaps meaning 'a herald'; cf. *CII*, Vol. III, p. 190 (a person described as *tanniyukta-pratinartaka-kulaputr-āmātya*).

Pratinidhi, a representative (*Hist. Dharm.*, Vol. III, p. 150).

Pratinivāsin (EI 20), same as *Nivāsin*, a resident.

pratipad (*CII* 1), 'to follow'; same as *anuvṛt*, *anupratipad*. (*Select Inscriptions*, p. 281, text line 10); cf. *pratipādya*, 'having decided'.

pratipadā (EI 24), a slab with foot-prints. Cf. *Ep. Ind.*, Vol. XXXIII, p. 247.

pratipāditaka (EI 13), given or granted.

pratipanna, 'decided'; cf. *pratipad*.

pratipatti, cf. *pratipattau* (LP), explained as 'convincing'; but actually 'during the administration of...'.

Prātirājya (EI 3, 6), same as *Pratirāja*, 'a hostile king.'

Prātirājyika (*Ep. Ind.*, Vol. XIX, p. 71), probably, an envoy at the court of a hostile king; but cf. *Paḍirā*.

pratisamāsana (IE 8-8), refutation.

pratisāṁvatsarika-śrāddha (CII 4), the annual *śrāddha* ceremony; same as *sāṁvatsarika-śrāddha*.

Pratisaraka (IA 7), cf. *Vartmapāla-Pratisaraka-Rājasthānīya*; official designation; same as *Pratisāraka*.

Pratisāraka (EI31; HD), explained as an officer who collects tax and allows carts to go out of the *nālī* or a strip of low ground (LP); see *Pratisārin*; same as *Pratīsāraka*.

Pratīsāraka (LP), explained as 'a gate-keeper'. See *Pratisāraka*, *Pratisārin*.

Prātisāraka (HD), same as *Pratisāraka*. See *Ind. Ant.*, Vol. XV, p. 187.

Pratisārin (LP) explained as 'one who allows the merchants to go through strips of low ground'. See *Pratisāraka*.

Pratiśarīra (BI), a representative.

pratiśāsana (SII 11-1), a renewed charter.

pratiṣedha, cf. *prakṣepa*.

pratiṣiddh-āya (IA 19), same as *siddh-āya*.

pratiśraya (*Ep. Ind.*, Vol. VII, p. 46, note 8), a shelter-house for travellers. See *ucchraya*.

pratiṣṭhā (EI 11; SII 1; BL; HA), installation, consecration ; ceremony of installation or consecration (*Ep. Ind.*, Vol. XII, p. 20).

pratiṣṭhāna, cf. *yaṣṭi-pratiṣṭhāna* (CII 2-1), used in the sense of *pratiṣṭhāpana*.

pratiṣṭhāpita, cf. *a-pratiṣṭhāpita* (ML); interred.

Pratiśūraka (EI 31), probably, the superintendent of wrestling; cf. *Pratiśūrika*.

Pratiśūrika (IE 8-3), probably, the superintendent of gladitorial combats; cf. *Pratiśūraka*.

pratiṭippanaka (LP), a receipt.

Prati-vāsudeva (HA), an enemy of Vāsudeva in Jain mythology.

Prativedaka (IE 8-3; CII 1), a reporter or spy.

prativedanā (CII 1), reporting of news.

prātivedhanika (HRS), punching-fee collected from merchants at the time of the inspection of weights and measures, as indicated by the *Arthaśāstra*.

prativeśya, *prātiveśika* (CII 1), a neighbour.

prativídhāna (CII 1), supporting [with money]; gift [of money].

prativyañjana, Tamil *paḍi-viñjanam* (SITI), articles other than rice for the preparation of food-offerings in a temple, etc.

pratolī (EI 9; CII 3; BL), a gate-way; a gate-way with a flight of steps; a gate-way strongly built and considerably high. (*EI* 31), probably, a street.

pratolikā (EI 1), same as *pratolī*.

pratyabda-kāla (EI 3), an anniversary [of death].

pratyādāya (*Ep. Ind.*, Vol. XI, p. 21; Vol. XIV, p. 196; Vol. XXXV, p. 127), income or tax; cf. *pratyāya* in the same sense.

pratyaṁśa, see *agra-pratyaṁśa* (ML); a share.

pratyandhāruvā (IE 8-5; EI 12, 33), Oḍiyā; probably *pratyarthāruvā* (Sanskrit *pratyartha-rūpyaka*), name of a tax or levy of uncertain import; probably, a levy on the money realised by money-lenders from debtors. See *arthāruvā*, *pāukā*.

pratyanta (IE 8-4; CII 1), a state beyond the borders of one's territories; a land outside one's dominions; also its people; cf. *anta*.

Pratyanta-nṛpati (EI 15), ruler of a bordering state.

pratyarthāruvā (IE8-5), a tax of uncertain import; probably Sanskrit *pratyartha-rūpyaka* in the sense of a levy on amounts realised by the money lenders from debtors; also read as *pratyandhāruvā*; see *arthāruvā* and *pāukā*.

Pratyaya, probably, a lessee (*Ep. Ind.*, Vol. XXXIV, pp. 143-44).

pratyaya (EI 11, 15), a holding; sometimes also written as *pratyāya* (cf. *CII*, Vol. III, p. 170, note 5).

Cf. Prakrit *avija-pracaga saṁkara* (CII 2-1)=Sanskrit *avidyā-pratyayāḥ saṁskārāḥ*, 'in inter-connection with delusion are the *saṁkāras*', i.e. the *saṁkāras* spring from *avidyā*.

Cf. etat-pratyaye, in this matter (*Select Inscriptions*, p. 237).

pratyāya (IE 8-5; EI 29; HRS), revenue; income or tax; dues payable to the king including *bhāga-bhoga-kara* and *hiraṇya*; cf. *bhūta-vāta-pratyāya* (EI 10). See *pratyaya*.

pratyaya, pratyāya (CII 3), primarily 'income' and secondarily 'a holding, the income of which is enjoyed.' Cf. *amuka-pratyaya-amuka*.

Pratyeka-Buddha, cf. Prakrit *Pracega-Budha* (CII 2-1), Buddhist; name of certain Buddhas.

pratyupagamana (CII 1), meeting personally.

Prauḍha-pratāpa (IE 8-2), cf. *Pratāpa* and *Vīrapratāpa*.

Prauḍha-pratāpa-cakravartin (IE 8-2), see *Cakravartin*.

pravacana, exposition of texts (*Ep. Ind.*, Vol. XXXV, p. 150).

pravahaṇa (LP), same as *vāhana*; a boat.

pravahaṇa-ghoṭaka, (LP), a carriage horse.

pravaṇa (EI 1), 'excellent'.

Pravaṇi (CII 4), a banker.

pravaṇikara (EI 18, 24, 26; HRS), cf. *yathādīyamāna-bhāga-bhoga-kara-pravaṇikara-kūṭaka-prabhṛti-samast-ādaya* (IE 8-5), known from the Gāhaḍavāla records; a minor tax other than what was *bhāga-bhoga-kara*, according to some; explained by some as a tax levied from a class of merchants. See *pravaṇivāda*.

(*IA* 15), explained as *hiraṇya* or tax in cash.

pravaṇivāda (EI 21), name of a tax; cf. *pravaṇikara*.

pravara (IA 19), an invocation of ancestors at the performance of certain rites.

(*CII* 4), a member of the executive committee of a corporation.

Prāvārañcara (EI 24), supposed to be 'a licensed spy'.

pravarha (EI 13), see *prabarha.*

pravartavāpa (EI 32), also called *pravarta*; a land measure; cf. *pravarti* and *pravartikā.*

pravartamāna (IA 18,19), current [year]; cf. *atīta* or expired.

pravartana (CII 1), establishment.

pravarti, pravartikā (EI 32), a measure of capacity; cf. *pauṭi, pravarta* and *pravartavāpa.*

praveśa, prāveśa (EI 17), explained as 'a small territorial unit'; but probably refers to the assessment of the rent of a locality along with another; cf. *Siviḍi-praveśa-Kandalivāḍa-grāma* interpreted as 'Kandalivāḍa-grāma having its rent assessed along with Siviḍi' (*Ep. Ind.*, Vol XXXI, p. 59, note 1). See *prāveśya, prāpīya.*

Praveśa-bhāgika (HD), a subordinate officer of the treasury who received cash payments, according to Stein (*Rājataraṅgiṇī*, VIII, 278).

praveśaka (SITI), admission, entry.

prāveśya (EI 31), also spelt *praveśya*; explained by some as a small territorial unit; sometimes translated as 'situated in' (CII 4); but may refer to the revenure assessment of a village along with another; cf. *Ardhaṭi-prāveśya-Lavaṅgasikāyām* (*Ep. Ind.*, Vol. XV, p. 143); same as *praveśa.* Cf. *Hastiśīrṣa-prāveśya-Tāpasapottake* with *Siviḍi-praveśa-Kandalivāḍa-grāma* interpreted as 'Kandalivāḍa-grāma having its rent assessed along with Siviḍi.' Same as *prāpīya* (*Ep. Ind.*, Vol. XI, p. 109); cf. *Akṣasaraka-prāveśya* used in the sense as *Akṣasaraka-prāpīya.*

Cf. praveśa, prāveśa, prāpīya (LP), also *patra-pṛṣṭhato praveśyo dātavyaḥ*, 'should get [the sum] entered at the back of the document' (*dātavya* from *dā* 'to cut').

Cf. a-prāveśya, etc. (IE 8-5); entrance.

(*IE* 8-8; EI 30), an entry tax or levies relating to the entry of royal agents.

pravrajita (CII 1; LL), a Buddhist monk; an ascetic.

pravrajitā (LL), a Buddhist nun.

prayāṇa-daṇḍa (IE 8-5; EI 25, 26), cf. *rājasevakānāṁ vasati-daṇḍa-prayāṇa-daṇḍau na staḥ*; refers to the obligation of the villagers to provide free conveyance and carriage of loads, etc., when royal officers passed through their village. *Prayāṇa* thus seems to mean 'passage, transit', and *daṇḍa* 'levy'; cf. *rūḍhabhāroḍi.*

prayojana (LP), need; cf. *drammaiḥ hasta-prāptaiḥ prayojanaṁ jāyate* (LP), 'when there is a necessity of having the money back [before the stated time].'

Prāyopaveś-ādhikṛta (HD), officer who watched those that had resolved to fast unto death at the palace gate. See *Rājataraṅgiṇī*, VI. 14.

prayukta (IA 15), 'drawn up'.

Pregaḍā (EI 9), Kannaḍa; a minister. Cf. *Pĕrgaḍĕ*, etc.

preṣaṇa (*Ep. Ind.*, Vol. XXXI, p.9, text lines 13-14), service.

prekṣaṇaka (EI 22), a show.

Preṣaṇika (IE 8-3), officer in charge of the despatch of messengers; the dispatcher of messengers; cf. *Praiṣaṇika*, *Vaikṣepika*.

Preṣya-kula (EI 33), a batch of workers.

preta-dakṣiṇā, cf. *peta-dakkhinā* (EI 24), a gift to one's dead ancestors.

Priyadarśin (CII 1), cf. *Priyadasi* (EI 5), secondary name of the Maurya king Aśoka.

Pro, abbreviation of *Prohita*=Sanskrit *Purohita* (*Ep. Ind.*, Vol. XXX, p. 192).

Prohata, *Prohita* (Chamba, etc.) a priest; from Sanskrit *Purohita*.

Cf. Para.

pṛḍa, see *mṛḍa*.

pṛṣṭha, cf. *pṛṣṭhe hastaḥ* (LP),' hand on someone's back'; a sign of warning.

pṛthivī, cf. Prakrit *sava-puṭhaviyaṁ* (*CII*, Vol. I, p. 87, text line 7); used to indicate the dominions of the Maurya emperor Aśoka, versions other than Dhauli (Rock Edict V) having *sarvatra vijite* (i.e. 'everywhere within the dominions') in its place. Cf. *Jambudvīpa*.

pṛthvī (IE 7-1-2), 'one'.

pṛthvī-liṅga (SII 2), a Śivaliṅga made of earth.

pruḍ, see *mṛḍa*.

pu (PJS), abbreviation of *putra*, 'a son' (especially in medieval Jain inscriptions).

pūjā (CII 1; ML), an honour; the act of honouring.

Pūjāhāri (EI 33), same as *Pūjāri* (Sanskrit *pūjādhārin*); priest.

Pūjaka (SITI), one who performs worship; a temple priest.

Pūj-āmātya (IA 11), official designation; cf. 'the *Pūj-āmātya* of the province of Timbāṇaka'.

Pujāri (EI 5, 15), a priest; a temple priest; called *Pūjārī* or *Pūjāhārī* (Sanskrit *Pūjādhārin*) in the early medieval records of Orissa.

pūjā-śilā (EI 16, 22), same as *śālagrāma-śilā* (the stone emblem of Viṣṇu).

pūjā-vṛtti (SITI), tax-free land endowed to a temple for conducting worship. Cf. *tala-vṛtti*, etc.

pukkoli, *pukkolli*, *pukkūli* (IE 8-8), cf. *pukkoli-kṣetra*, explained as 'an arecanut palm plantation'. An inscription of Kadamba Mṛgeśvarman seems to suggest that it really means 'land inundated by floods' (*Ep. Ind.*, Vol. XXXV, p. 152). See *khajjana*.

pukkoli-khajjana (EI 33), a type of land; see *khajjana* and *pukkoli*.

pukkoli-kṣetra (EI 33), a type of land like *khajjana*; see *pukkoli* or *pukkoli-khajjana*.

pūlaka (CII 4), a small bundle (*Ep. Ind.*, Vol. IV, p. 309).

Punarjanman (*Ep. Ind.*, Vol. XIII, p. 290, text line 3), used in the sense of *Dvijanman* (i.e. a Brāhmaṇa).

puṇḍarīka (CII 3; BL), name of a sacrifice.

puṇyāha-vācaka (*EI* 11), a priest who officiates in a ceremony and proclaims by means of *mantras* a happy day to the ceremony and its performer.

puṇyāha-vācana (IA 14), a ceremony; cf. *puṇyāha-vācaka*.

puṇya-vācana (IA 21), a purificatory rite [in Madras]; cf. *puṇyāha-vācana*.

pura, a temple (*Ep. Ind.*, Vol. XXXV, p. 184). See *bhavana*.

pūraka (CII 3; etc.), used as a termination of the names of villages.

purāṇa (IE 8-8; EI 12, 21, 29), name of a coin; a silver coin also called *dharaṇa* and *kārṣāpaṇa* (32 or 24 *ratis*); cf. *kapardaka-purāṇa* (EI 26), meaning *purāṇa* calculated in cowrie-shells; also *paṇa-purāṇa* (i.e. *purāṇa* counted in copper *paṇas*).

(*Ep. Ind.*, Vol. XXVIII, p. 246), the Purāṇa texts, e.g. the *Āditya Purāṇa*.

purāṇa-lakṣaṇa (IE 7-1-2), 'five'.

Purapāl-oparika (IE 8-2, 8-3; BL), official designation probably indicating the governor of a city or chief amongst the governors of cities; called *Mahārāja*, *Mahāsāmanta*, *Mahāpratihāra*, *Mahāpīlupati*, *Pañcakaraṇoparika* and *Pāṭyuparika* additionally (IE 8-3). The expression may also mean two different designations, viz. *Purapāla* and *Uparika*. With *Purapāla*, cf. *Purapati*, etc.

Purapati (EI 25), mayor of a town; cf. *Pura-pradhāna*, *Puraśreṭhin*, *Nagara-śreṣṭhin*, *Purillaka*, etc.

Pura-pradhāna (CII 4), mayor of a city; cf. *Purapati*, *Puraśreṣṭhin*, *Nagara-śreṣṭhin*, *Purillaka*, etc.

Pura-śreṣṭhin (EI 25), official designation; same as *Nagara-śreṣṭhin*, *Pura-pradhāna*, *Purapati*, etc.

puratobhadra (EI 9), probably, a building with only one gate in the front side.

Purillaka (EI 29; CII 4), explained as 'the mayor of a town.' Cf. *rāja-sāmanta-viṣayapati-grāmabhogika-purillaka-cāṭa-bhaṭa-sevak-ādin* (*Ep. Ind.*, Vol. XXIX, pp. 114-15); also *Deśillaka* and *Pura-pati*, *Pura-pradhāna*, *Pura-śreṣṭhin*, *Vīthillaka*, etc.

pūrṇa (IE 7-1-2), 'cypher'.

pūrṇaghaṭaka-paṭṭa (LL), slab bearing the representation of a flower-vase.

pūrṇimānta (CII 3, etc.), the technical name for the scheme of the lunar months in Northern India, according to which the months end with the full-moon day, and the dark fortnights precede the bright; Fleet states that in astronomical works, it is always the *amānta* arrangement that is actually taken for calculations though, even in Southern India, the *pūrṇimānta* arrangement was used with the Śaka years,for the civil reckoning, up to between 804 and 866 A. D.; on the other hand, according to him, even in Northern India, it was not used with the Newar era in Nepal, though it was adopted there when the Newar era was followed by the Vikrama era in its northern variety.

Puroga (EI 23), prominent among a particular class of people; sometimes wrongly taken to be the same as *Purohita*.

Purohita (CII 4; SII 1; BL; ASLV; HD), a priest; a family priest; the royal priest; occurs in the list of functionaries in records like those of the Gāhaḍavālas (*Ep. Ind.*, Vol. IX, p. 305) and Senas (ibid., Vol. XII, p. 9). See *Hist. Dharm.*, Vol. III, pp. 111-12, 117.

Puro-nāyaka (IE 8-3; EI 28), the chief *Nāyaka*; probably the same as *Paṭṭa-nāyaka* or *Puro-Parīkṣaka*; cf. *Nāyaka*. *Puro* may really be the modification of a Dravidian word (cf. Tamil *Poṟṟu*).

Puro-parīkṣa (EI 28, 31), probably, the same as *Paṭṭa-*

parīkṣaka, 'the chief superintendent'; the chief superintendent of a department. *Puro* may really be the modification of a Dravidian word (cf. Tamil *Poṟṟu*).

Puro-pratihasta (EI 31), probably, 'the chief representative'. *Puro* may really be the modification of a Dravidian word (cf. Tamil *Poṟṟu*).

Puro-śrīkaraṇa (EI 31), probably, 'the chief secretary'. *Puro* may really be the modification of a Dravidian word (cf. Tamil *Poṟṟu*).

Puruṣa (IE 8-3), same as *Rāja-puruṣa*, 'royal officer or agent.'

(*HD*) an inferior servant (*Arthaśāstra*, II.5) or a bailiff attached to a court of justice (as in *Bṛhaspati*). See *Hist. Dharm.*, Vol. III, p. 278.

puruṣa-cchāya (EI 14), name of a measure.

puruṣ-ākāra (SITI), human form.

puruṣārika, cf. *ardha-puruṣārika*.

puruṣ-ārtha (IE 7-1-2), 'four'.

Puruṣottama-putra (EI 33), epithet of one devoted to the god Puruṣottama-Jagannātha of Purī. See *Rudra-putra*, *Durgā putra*.

puruṣa-yuga, cf. Prakrit *purisa-yuga* (EI 20); a generation.

puruṣ-āyus (IE 7-1-2), 'one hundred'.

pūrva (IE 7-1-2), sometimes used to indicate 'fourteen'.

pūrvā (IE 8-8; CII 4; ML), 'the above'; 'the aforesaid (*tithi* or *praśasti*)'; used with reference to a *tithi* and a *praśasti*; sometimes wrongly used as a synonym of a *tithi* or *praśasti*.

Cf. anupūrvī used with refrence to a *tithi*.

pūrv-ācāra (SII 3; SITI), an old usage or ancient custom. Cf. *pūrva-rīti*.

Pūrv-āgrahārika (EI 23), the former holder of an *agrahāra*.

pūrva-maryādā (ASLV), ancient constitutional usage.

pūrva-rāja (EI 17), a king of eastern countries or of early times.

pūrva-rīti (LP), old custom. Cf. *pūrv-ācāra*.

pūrva-siddh-āyatana (EI 33), epithet of a Buddhist temple; see *siddh-āyatana*.

puṣkala (IE 8-6), a measure of capacity usually regarded as equal to sixtyfour handfuls.

puṣkara (ML), a tank.

puṣpa (IE 8-8), a coin having the shape or sign of flower.

Cf. a-harītaka-śāka-puṣpa-grahaṇa (IE 8-5), flowers which

the villagers (probably, the florists) were obliged to supply to the king or landlord on occasions or to the touring officials.

puṣpaka (CII 4), a temple.

pusta (CII 4), painting.

pustaka, cf. Tamil *pottagam* (SITI); register, as of land and revenue.

Pustaka-bhāṇḍāra (EI 25), a library.

Pustakapāla (IE 8-3; EI 6, 29), record-keeper; same as *Pustapāla*; cf. *Peṭapāla*, etc.

Pustapāla (IE 8-3; EI 28; CII 4; HD), record-keeper; occurs in epigraphs like the Damodarpur plates of the Gupta age (*Ep. Ind.*, Vol. XV, p. 13; cf. Vol. XX, p. 61).

puṣya-rāga (SITI), same as *puṣpa-rāga*; a kind of gem.

puṣya-ratha (EI 3), a car. Cf. *puṣpa-ratha* or *puṣpaka-ratha*, the celestial car.

puṭi (EI 33), same as *puṭṭi* or *puṭṭidosillu*.

pūti (EI 12, 14), also read as *yūti*; cf. *tṛṇa-pūti*(or *yūti*)-*go-cara-paryanta*, epithet of a gift village. The expression *tṛṇa-pūti* or *tṛṇa-yūti* may mean 'grass-land'. The word is sometimes written as *yutī* and *yuthī* also.

putra, cf. *Nigama-putra* (LL), 'the inhabitant of a *nigama* (township).'

Cf. Durgā-putra, *Puruṣottama-putra*, etc.

(*IE* 7-1-2), probably confused with *pāṇḍu-putra* and used to indicate 'five'.

putra-sūnu (SII 2), used in the sense of *pautra*, 'son's son'.

puṭṭi (CITD), Telugu; a measure equal to twenty *tūmus*; also called *khaṇḍi* (spelt *candy* in English and found as *khaṇḍikā* in Sanskrit inscriptions) and regarded as equal to between 800 and 1000 seers. *Khaṇḍi* at Masulipatam has 3 weights, viz. 488 pounds for tobacco, 500 pounds for metals, hardware, etc., and 560 pounds for sugar, dates and other soft articles. The *puṭṭi* and its fractions also denote the area of the land that is supposed by some to produce the particular quantities of grain. According to some, it is a land measure equal to 8 acres being presumably the area which can be sown with a *puṭṭi* of grain. There were different kinds of *puṭṭis*, e.g. *gāl-puṭṭi*. Cf. also *pelle-puṭṭi* regarded as equal to 8o *kuñcas* and *Malaca-puṭṭi* or Malacca ton as equal to 300 to 240 *kuñcas*.

(*EI* 4, 27), a land and grain measure.

(*IE* 8-5), same as Telugu *puṭṭi-dosillu*, 'a fee of two handfuls from each *puṭṭi* of grain paid to the village-servants'.

puṭṭi-dosillu (EI 33), a levy; see *puṭṭi*.

pyoḍā (Chamba), a grain measure; also spelt *piṭha*, *piḍā*, *peḍā*.

R

Rā (LP), abbreviation of *Rājaputra*, *Rāuta*, etc.

rābhasya (CII 1), a crime.

rāccha-poccha (LP), Gujarātī; household furniture.

racita (CII 3; etc.), composed; a technical term used in connection with the composition of a record, as opposed to the writing on the plate or slab for facilitating the work of engraving and also to engraving. Cf. *cintita* in *Ep.Ind.*, Vol. XXXV, p.59.

rada (IE 7-1-2), 'thirtytwo'.

rādhā (EI 8), a posture of standing with the feet a span apart.

rādhānta (EI 3), same as *siddhānta*.

rāga (IE 7-1-2), 'six'.

rahāpayati (LP), 'he keeps'.

Rāhasika (IE 8-3; EI 27, 30), same as *Rahasy-ādhikṛta*, etc.; a privy councillor; a private secretary or adviser.

Rahasi-niyukta (IE 8-3), a private secretary; same as *Rahasy-ādhikṛta*, etc.

Rahasya (IE 8-3; EI 3-6, 23, 27, 30), a private secretary; same as *Rāhasika*, *Rahasy-ādhikṛta*, etc.

Rahasy-ādhikṛta (IE 8-3; EI 6, 27, 30; SITI; HD), a privy councillor or private secretary; same as *Rahasya*, *Rāhasika*, *Rahasi-niyuka*, etc.; cf. also *Vaiśvāsika*, *Paramaviśvāsin Mahāparamaviśvāsin*, etc. Cf. *Ep. Ind.*, Vol. I, p. 7; Vol. VI, p. 13; Vol. XXII, p. 298.

Rāhuta, *Rāhutta* (IE 8-2), same as *Rāvata*=Sanskrit *Rājaputra*; a title of nobility.

(*IA* 20), also called *Rāuta*; explained as 'a horseman.'

Rāhutta-rāyan (SITI), Sanskrit *Rājaputra-rājan*; title of nobility; explained as 'a cavalry officer'.

Raikvāla (Chamba), the king's personal servant.

Rāja (LP), abbreviation of *Rājaputra* (*Rājpūt*); explained as a cavalry-soldier or a *Rājpūt*. See *Ep. Ind.*, Vol. XXXIV, pp.

143-44, where it is probably an abbreviation of *Rājakula* (*Rāval*).

rāja-bhāga (LP), government revenue.

rāja-bhanḍāra (SITI, ASLV), Sanskrit *rāja-bhāṇḍāra*; royal treasury or store-house.

rāja-bhoga (EI 12), also *rāja-sambhoga*; dues enjoyed by the king or land belonging to the king's *Khās Mahāls*.

rāja-daṇḍa (SII 1), punishment imposed by the king.

rāja-datti (EI 23), a royal gift.

Rāja-dauvārika (EI 2; BL), door-keeper of the royal palace (*Ep. Ind.*, Vol. XIII, p. 115). See *Dauvārika*.

rājadhānī (EI 23), the capital; sometimes used to indicate the headquarters of a chief or governor.

Rājādhirāja (IE 8-2; EI 21, 22, 30; CII 3, 4), title of paramount sovereignty; an imperial title meaning 'the king of kings'; used in the Gupta period in some metrical passages, both alone and along with *Rājarājādhirāja*. Cf. *Adhirājarāja* (EI 9).

Rājādhyakṣa (IA 12; SII 11-2), official designation; probably the same as *Rājasthānīya*, literally, 'an officer acting for the king.'

rāja-droha (SITI), treason against the king.

rāja-dvāra (EI 32), king's court.

rāja-graha (IE 8-8); apprehension or recruitment in the king's name.

rāja-gṛha, cf. Tamil *rāja-karam* (SITI); palace (cf. *Ep. Ind.*, Vol. XXXV, p. 107) or government; officers or authorities; also the taxes due to the same. Cf. *rājakaraṅ-kāṇikkai*, 'customary presents to be made to the palace'; *rājakara-upādi*, 'tax payable to the palace or to the government officers'.

Rājaguru (EI 21, 27, 30; CII 4; BL; ASLV; HD), king's preceptor. Cf. *Bomb. Gaz.*, Vol. XXI, p. 354; *Ind. Ant.*, Vol. XII, p. 120.

rāja-huṇḍikā (LP), the royal bill of exchange.

Rājājñāprada (EI 27), probably, the same as *Ājñapti*, etc.

rājaka-daivaka (LP), calamities owing to the king or the gods; cf. *rājaka-daivaka-vaśāt* (LP).

rāja-kara, cf. *rāja-garam* (ASLV), taxes in general.

rāja-kārya (SITI), duties of the state; official work.

rājakārya-bhāṇḍāra (SITI; ASLV), a treasury related to state business; an official committee of management.

rājakīya (LP), government tax.

Cf. samasta-rājakīyānām=apraveśya (IE 8-5); same as *Rāja-puruṣa* or *Rāja-sevaka*; also *Rāja-satka*; an officer of the king.

rājakīya-māna (EI 23), same as *rāja-māna*.

Rājakula (IE 8-5; CII 3; IA 20; BL; HD), royal household; the king, royal officers and members of the royal family. Originally, 'the royal family'; then 'a member of the royal family'; and then 'a royal officer'; later, a title of nobility, same as modern *Rāval* or *Rāul*. See Bhandarkar's List, No. 324.

Cf. rājakulaṅ-kāṇi-ppaṟṟu (SITI), 'land or village in the enjoyment of the members of the royal family'. The expression occurs along with *devadāna*, *brahmadeya*, *paḻḻiccandam*, etc.

Rājakumāra (IE 8-3; LL; HD), same as *Rājaputra*; designation of a prince. Cf. *Ep. Ind.*, Vol. I, p. 5.

Rāja-lipikara (IE 8-3; EI 2; LL), king's scribe.

rāja-māna (IE 8-6; EI 12, 23, 28; SII 11-1), royal measure; the standard measure fixed or accepted by the king or government; same as *rājakīya-māna*.

rāja-māṅgalīyaka (LP), auspicious occasions for the royal family.

Rāj-āmātya (EI 26; CII 3; HD), Prakrit *Rāy-āmaca*; the king's minister. See *Ep. Ind.*, Vol. VIII, p. 91; *CII*, Vol. III, pp. 213, 216.

(*IE* 8-3), sometimes used to indicate the ministers of the feudatory rulers; see *Amātya*.

Rājamudr-ādhikārin (BL), official designation indicating the keeper of the royal seal or a governor. Cf. *Mudr-ādhikārin*, etc.

Rājan (IE 8-2, 8-3; EI 30; CII 3, 4; HD), royal title; originally used by imperial rulers; later, when emperors assumed more dignified titles, a title of feudatories and smaller rulers. Cf. Vogel, *Ant. Ch. St.*, p. 121; *Ep. Ind.*, Vol. IX, p. 297.

Rājanaka (IE 8-2, 8-3; EI 23, 29), same as *Rājānaka*, *Rājanyaka*, *Rājānika*; a feudatory; in some cases, smaller than the feudatory called *Rājan*.

Rājānaka (IE 8-2, 8-3; EI 30; BL; HD), same as *Rājanaka*, *Rājanyaka*, *Rājānika* or *Rāṇaka*; title of feudatory rulers or of the nobility; often a feudatory smaller than a *Rājan*. Cf. *Rājataraṅgiṇī*, VI. 117, 261 (title given for services to the king and surviving in the form *Rāzdān* as a family name of Kashmir Brāhmaṇas); *Ind. Ant.*, Vol. XV, pp. 304, 306.

Rājānika (EI 1), same as *Rājanaka*, *Rājānaka*, etc.

rāj-āṅka (EI 22), brand of royal animals.

Rājanya (ASLV; SITI), officers of the king.

(*IA* 22), same as *Kṣatriya*.

Rājanyaka (IE 8-2; EI 15, 23, 29; HD), same as *Rājanaka*, *Rājānaka*, *Rājānika* or *Rāṇaka*, title of subordinate rulers. Cf. *Ep. Ind.*, Vol. XII, p. 9.

Rāja-paṁ (BL), abbreviation of *Rāja-paṇḍita*.

Rāja-paṇḍita (EI 32), a court Pandit; a scholar patronised by the king.

Rāja-parameśvara (EI 4, 20), imperial title. Cf. *Rāja-rājaparameśvara*.

rāja-pāṭikā (EI 1), royal procession.

rāja-paṭṭa, cf. *rāja-paṭṭī*.

rāja-paṭṭī (EI 4; BL), royal fillet or tiara; status of a ruler or a feudatory indicated by turban. Same as *rāja-paṭṭa*.

Rājapuruṣa (IE 8-5), a royal agent or officer; same as *Rāja-sevaka* or *Rājakīya*; cf. also *Rāja-satka*.

Rāja-putra (EI 30; CII 3; 4; HD), originally 'a prince'; title of princes and subordinate rulers; but later a title of nobility especially in the modified forms *Rāvata*, *Rāuta*, etc.; sometimes also used in the sense of 'a Rājpūt' often explained as 'a horse-man'. Cf. *Ep. Ind.*, Vol. XVII, p. 321. See *Rāja-putraka*.

Rāja-putraka (EI 17), same as *Rāja-putra*; mentioned in the list of subordinates and officials addressed by the king in respect of a grant.

rāja-pradeya (SII 3), taxes.

rājaprāsāda-caityaka (LL), a small *caitya* in the royal palace.

Rājarāja (IE 8-2; LL), imperial title; cf. Greek *Basileos Besileon*.

Rājarāja-parameśvara (EI 4), imperial title. Cf. *Rājaparameśvara*.

rāj-ārghikā (IE 8-8; EI 30), name of a levy; probably, periodical offerings to the king or the king's share of articles sold in the markets.

Rājarṣi (EI 22), a sage-like king.

Rājasāmanta (EI 25), a *Rājan* and a *Sāmanta*, or one feudatory enjoying both the designations.

rāja-sambhoga (EI 12), same as *rāja-bhoga* (q.v.); land

belonging to the king's *Khās Mahāls* (*Ep. Ind.*, Vol. XXX, p. 46). Cf. *ratnatraya-sambhoga.*

Rāja-satka (IE 8-3; EI 29), literally, 'one belonging to the king', i.e. 'a servant of the king'; same as *Rāja-puruṣa* or *Rāja-sevaka.*

Rāja-sevaka (IE 8-5), same as *Rāja-puruṣa*, *Rājakīya* or *Rāja-satka.*

rāja-siddhānta (EI 24), science of polity; same as *rājanīti.*

rāja-śrāvita (EI 6; IA 19), a royal decree or proclamation.

rāj-āśraya (IA 8), the capital; same as *rājadhānī.*

Rāja-śreṣṭhin (HD), king's banker or the chief of the bankers. See Commentary on the *Yaśastilaka*, I, p. 91.

Rājasthāna, same as *Rājasthānīya* and *Rājasthān-ādhikāra* (*Ep. Ind.*, Vol. XXXV, p. 292).

Rājasthān-ādhikāra (IE 8-3), probably, the chief justice; cf. *Rājasthānīya* (a viceroy), etc.

Rājasthānī, dialect of Hindī prevalent in Rajasthan.

Rājasthānīya (IE 8-3; EI 24, 26, 30; CII 3, 4; BL; HD), 'an officer acting for the king'; generally a viceroy; probably also a subordinate ruler; but cf. *Rājasthān-ādhikāra* who was also a judge; an official title indicating a viceroy in some areas and a judge in others; an officer who carried out the object of protecting subjects, according to some (*Ind. Ant.*, Vol. V, p. 207). Cf. *CII*, Vol. III, p. 157; Vogel, *Ant. Ch. St.*, p. 112; *Ep. Ind.*, Vol. XI, p. 176 (probably, a chief justice), explained wrongly as 'an officer connected with other kings, i.e. a foreign secretary' (*Ind. Ant.*, Vol. XII, p. 122, note 76).

Rājasthān-oparika (EI 29), probably a viceroy; cf. *Rājasthānīya* and *Uparika.* See *Rājasthān-ādhikāra* and *Rājasthānīya.*

rājasūya (EI 4), name of a sacrifice.

rājasva (SITI), property belonging to the king or state [by confiscation, etc.].

Rājātirāja (IE 8-2; EI 21, 26, 30; ML), imperial title of certain foreign rulers; cf. *Basileos Basileon Megalou.*

Rāja-vaidya (IE 8-3; LL), physician to the king; the royal physician.

rāj-āvalī (EI 9; IA 30), genealogy of rulers; a list of lineal succession of kings.

(*EI* 10), royal titles; cf. *rājāvalī pūrvavat* (IE 8-2), 'the royal titles as above', often used when a repetition of the string of royal titles was avoided. Cf. *Paramabhaṭṭārak-ety-ādi-rāj-āvalī-tray-opeta* referring to the imperial titles *Paramabhaṭṭāraka, Mahārājādhirāja* and *Parameśvara.*

Rāja-vallabha (EI 6, 9, 24; CII 4), explained as 'a court-favourite'; a courtier.

rājāvarta (SII 2; SITI), a kind of gem; lapis lazuli; same as *vaiḍūrya.*

rāja-vartman (EI 22), a public road.

Rāja-veśyā-bhujaṅga (SITI), 'the lover of the courtesans of the [enemy] kings'; a title assumed by some kings after capturing the enemies' countries, probably describing *rājya-śrī* as a prostitute.

rāja-vilāsinī, king's courtesan (*Ep. Ind.*, Vol. XXXV, p. 107).

rāja-viṣaya (CII 1), a king's dominions. Cf. *Rājaviṣayādhyakṣa.*

Rājaviṣay-ādhyakṣa, explained as 'the royal superintendent of a district' (*Ep. Ind.*, Vol. XVIII, p. 234); but *rāja-viṣaya* in this case may be the king's *Khās Mahāls* so that the designation means 'the superintendent of the king's *Khās Mahāls.*'

rāja-yoga (EI 12), a particular auspicious moment.

rajjū (HRS), used in the *Arthaśāstra* probably in the sense of the cost realised by the government in connection with the expenses of land-measurement or survey.

Rajjugrāhak-āmātya (IE 8-3), same as *Rajjuka* (q.v.).

Rajjuka (IE 8-3; HD), Prakrit *Rajuka* or *Lajūka* (EI 2); an officer of the land survey and revenue department, according to some; but seems to be the governor of a district, one of whose functions was probably the survey of land with a measuring rope for the fixation of the amount of the king's share of the produce; probably the same as Greek *Agronomoi* mentioned by Megasthenes.

Rajju-pratihāra (EI 24), 'rope-jugglers or dancers'; cf. *rajju-pratihār-āpaṇa*, 'booths of rope-jugglers and dancers'; but *rajju-pratihār-āpaṇājīvika* may be a tax for maintaining surveyors and gate-keepers (toll-collectors) and from shop-keepers.

Rājñī (IE 8-2; EI 26; CII 3; HD), a queen; a title of the wives of paramount sovereigns and subordinate rulers; cf. *Mahārājñī*, etc. Cf. *Ep. Ind.*, Vol. IX, p. 305.

rajo-haraṇa (HA), same as *ogho* (q.v.).

rājya (IE 8-4; EI 19), district or province of a kingdom;

(SITI; ASLV), the biggest administrative unit of the Vijayanagara empire; same as *pīṭhika*; also means 'sovereignty'.

rājy-ābhiṣeka (IA 10), coronation.

Rājya-cintaka (EI 11; BL), a minister or the chief administrator; same as *Rājyacintākārin*.

Rājyacintākārin (EI 1), a minister or the chief administrator; same as *Rājya-cintaka*.

Rājy-ādhikṛta (EI 22, 23), chief minister; cf. *Rājyādhikārin*; also cf. *rājya*.

rākā-śaśāṅka (SII 1), same as *rākā-viṭa*; the full-moon.

rakata-paṭā (*JBORS*, Vol. XVIII, pp. 219-20), Oḍiyā; Sanskrit *rakta-paṭṭaka*, same as *rakta-mānya*; also called *sira-kaṭā tambā-paṭā* in Oḍiyā.

rākā-viṭa (SII 1), same as *rākā-śaśāṅka*; the full moon.

rakṣā (EI 17), confirmation of a former grant.

rakṣā-bhoga (EI 9), same as *rāja-bhoga*, the king's share.

(*SITI*), a fee or a share in the produce given to the village watchman.

rakṣā-maṇi (EI 15), protecting jewel.

rakṣaṇa, cf. *doṣa-vināś-āvaṣṭabdhi-rakṣaṇāya* (LP), 'for keeping it safe from the three faults, viz. *doṣa*, *vināśa* and *avaṣṭabdhi*'.

rakṣaṇīya (LP), 'to be [prepared and] maintained.'

rakta-bindu (SII 2), a flaw in diamonds.

rakta-mānya, cf. Tamil *iratta-mānya*, *iratta-kkāṇikkai* (SITI); 'blood-present'; endowment of rent-free land for the support of the descendants of warriors killed in battle; same as *mṛtyuka-vṛtti*. See *rudhira*, *rakatapaṭā*, *vīra-śeṣā*, etc. See *Ind. Arch. Rev.*, 1960-61, Section III, No. 42.

rakta-paṭṭaka, see *rakata-paṭā*.

raktikā (IA 27), same as *ratī* or *guñjā* (q.v.); a unit of measurment; about 1·825 grains or ·119 grammes in weight.

rāma (IE 7-1-2; EI 25), 'three'.

rāma-nandana (EI 7-1-2), 'two'.

rāmānuja-kūṭa (SITI), a rest-house for Vaiṣṇava travellers.

raṅgh (CII 1), 'to be eager'.

Rāṇa (EI 16, 23), same as *Rāṇaka*; see *Rāṇa-putra*, *rāṇa-kula*.

Rāṇā (IE 8-2; EI 23, 30), derived from *Rāṇaka*; title of ruling chiefs; same as *Rāṇa*, *Rāṇaka*.

Cf. Rannā.

Rāṇaka (IE 8-2; EI 23, 30; CII 4; BL; HD), derived from *Rājanaka*, *Rājānaka* or *Rājanyaka*; a feudatory title; title of feudatory rulers and, later, of the nobility. Cf. *Ep. Ind.*, Vol. XVII, p. 321.

(*EI* 9), explained as 'the chief counsellor'.

(*EI* 1), title of the great artist Śūlapāṇi described as *Vārendraka-śilpi-goṣṭhī-cūḍāmaṇi.*

Rāṇaka-cakravartin (EI 33), feudatory title; cf. *Mahā-sāmantādhipati.*

rāṇa-kula (LP), same as *rāja-kula* (q.v.).

raṇaraṇaka (LP), anxiety.

raṇa-stambha (CII 3, 4), a victory-pillar; a column in memory of the victory in a battle; same as *jaya-stambha.*

(*BL*), a memorial pillar raised for a person who died fighting for his master on the battle-field; same as *vīra-kkal* (q.v.).

Rāṇa-putra (BL), also called *Rāṇa-utra*; literally, 'the son of a subordinate king'; a title of nobility. See *Rāja-putra.*

Rāṇa-utra (BL), see *Rāṇa-putra.*

randhra (IE 7-1-2; EI 25), 'nine'; used in the sense of 'cypher' in a few late works.

Randhrapūraka (CITD), probably, a musician who played on some kind of wind instrument.

raṅga (E 1 15), abbreviation of *raṅga-bhoga.*

raṅga-bhoga (EI 17), amusement to be arranged for a deity and land granted for it; also called *śṛṅgāra-bhoga* (EI 5).

(*CITD*), enjoyment of splendour other than *aṅga-bhoga* or personal decoration; gift land received for *raṅga-bhoga.* See *aṅga-bhoga.*

raṅga-lekha (LP), 'coloured letter'; probably refers to the custom of sprinkling saffron water on the letters addressed to a king.

raṅga-maṇḍapa (SITI), inner hall of a temple; same as Tamil *tiruv-araṅgu.*

(*HA*), same as *sabhā-maṇḍapa*; main hall in a shrine.

(*EI* 9), hall in front of a shrine.

raṅg-āṅga-bhoga (EI 3), same as *aṅga-raṅga-bhoga* (i. e. *raṅga-bhoga* and *aṅga-bhoga*), etc.

raṅgat (EI 12), 'rolling'.

Rāṇī (EI 23, 33), feminine from of *Rāṇa* or *Rāṇā* (i. e. *Rāṇaka*); designation of a queen.

Rannā, name of the Sun-god's wife in West Indian mythology; probably a modification of *Rājñī.* See *Ep. Ind.*, Vol. XXXII, p. 343. The name is also spelt *Raṇṇā* or *Rāṇā.*

Ranneśa, a name of the Sun-god; cf. *Rannā.* See *Ep. Ind.*, Vol. XXXII, p. 343. The name of the Sun-god worshipped at Thanwala near Pushkar was Rannāditya (also spelt *Raṇṇāditya* and *Rāṇāditya*).

rāśi (IA 17), a sign of the zodiac.

(*IE* 7-1-2), 'twelve'.

Cf. rāśi-ppon (SITI), also called *rāśi-paṇam*; explained as 'pure gold'; probably, 'current good coin.'

Rāśi-mitra (EI 32), a friend of one, because of the birth of both under the same *rāśi.*

rāśi-paṇa, also called *rāśi-ppon* (SITI); probably 'current good coins'.

raśmi (IE 7-1-2), probably confused with *śīta-raśmi* and used to indicate 'one'.

rāṣṭra (IE 8-3, 8-4; EI 9, 23; CII 4; LL), a district or its subdivision; often the subdivision of a district; cf. *Śātavāhanīya-rāṣṭra*; also *Kona-rāṣṭra* (EI 32), variously called *deśa, maṇḍala, sīma, sthala,* etc.

Rāṣṭra-grāma-kūṭa (EI 28), i.e. *Rāṣṭrakūṭa* and *Grāmakūṭa*; cf. *Rāṣṭra-grāma-mahattara.*

Rāṣṭra-grāma-mahattara (IE 8-3; EI 6, 28), i.e. *Rāṣṭra-mahattara* and *Grāma-mahattara*; cf. *Rāṣṭra-grāma-kūṭa.*

Rāṣṭrakūṭa (EI 8-3), same as *Rāṣṭra-mahattara*; either the officer in charge of a territorial unit called *rāṣṭra* or, more probably, a member of the administrative council of a *rāṣṭra*; cf. *Grāma-kūṭa*; also *Deśakūṭa* (IA 7).

(*EI* 9), interpreted as 'the headman of a village'.

(*EI* 24), according to some, a land-holder.

(*CII* 4; HD), interpreted as 'the head of a district or subdivision'; cf. *JBBRAS*, Vol. XVI, p. 117.

Rāṣṭra-mahattara (IE 8-3), same as *Rāṣṭrakūṭa*; either the head of a territorial unit called *rāṣṭra* or, more probably, a member of the administrative council of a *rāṣṭra.*

Rāṣṭramahattar-ādhikārin (EI 25), official designation; probably, *Rāṣṭramahattara* and *Adhikārin.*

Rāṣṭrapāla (HD), head of a district, province or subdivision; same as *Rāṣṭrapati.* See *Arthaśāstra,* V. 1.

Rāṣṭrapālaka (EI 28), ruler of an administrative unit called *rāṣṭra*; same as *Rāṣṭrapati*.

Rāṣṭrapati (EI 12, 25; HD), ruler of a province, district or subdivision called *rāṣṭra*; same as *Rāṣṭrapāla*. Cf. *Ep. Ind.*, Vol. IV, pp. 278, 285; Vol. VII, p. 39.

rāṣṭra-viṣaya (IE 8-4), originally, a *rāṣṭra*, but later a *viṣaya*; cf. *Karma-rāṣṭra-viṣaya*.

Rāṣṭrika (IE 8-3; CII 1; HD; LL), Prakrit *Raṭhika* (EI 2), *Raṭṭhika* (EI 7); same as *Rāṣṭrin*; ruler of a *rāṣṭra*, i.e. a district or its subdivision; also the name of a people called 'hereditary *Rāṣṭrikas*'. Cf. *Ep. Ind.*, Vol. I, p. 5; Bhandarkar, *Aśoka*, p. 30.

(*Ep. Ind.*, Vol. XXXI, p. 78), mentioned in the list of officials addressed by the king in respect of a grant.

Rāṣṭrin (EI 7), ruler of a *rāṣṭra*; same as *Rāṣṭrika*. Cf. *Rāṣṭrapati*, *Mahārāṣṭrin*, etc.

Rāṣṭriya (IE 8-3; LL; HD), same as *Rāṣṭrika*, ruler of a district or province; a provincial governor. Cf. *Ep. Ind.*, Vol. VIII, p. 43; Pāṇini, IV. 2. 93; *Mahābhārata*, Śānti-parvan, 85.12.

Rāṣṭrīya (IE 8-3), same as *Rāṣṭriya*; a provincial governor.

Rāta (BL), modification of or mistake for *Rāvata* or *Rāuta*.

ratha, rock-cut temples at Mahābalipuram (*Journ. Mad. Univ.*, Vol. XXXII, p. 140).

Rath-ādhyakṣa (EI 18), superintendent of chariots.

Rathakāra (SITI), artisan classes; also their association.

ratha-saptamī (EI 22; CII 4; IA 17), an auspicious *tithi*; same as Māgha śu-di 7.

rath-āṣṭamī EI 29; CII 4; IA 17), same as Māgha śu-di 8.

ratha-yātrā (EI 11), a festival.

Rathika, superintendent of chariots (*Ep. Ind.*, Vol. XVIII, p. 156).

rath-otsava (EI 16), car-festival.

rathyā (EI 19), a street.

rati, *ratī* (IE 8-8; IA 19), also spelt *rattī*; a small weight; see Sanskrit *raktikā*.

rāṭi (LP), 'a cry'; cf. Gujarātī *rāḍ*.

ratna (IE 7-1-2), 'five'; sometimes also used to indicate 'nine', and rarely even 'fourteen'.

(*EI* 22; CII 4), same as the Buddhist *tri-ratna*, i.e. the Buddha, Dharma and Saṅgha.

(*ML*), a relic [of the Buddha].

ratna-dhenu (EI 13, 16, 24), name of a *mahādāna.*

ratna-gṛha (CII 3), 'the jewel-house'; the house enshrining the three *ratnas*, regarded by some as denoting a great Buddhist *stūpa.*

(*EI* 19; LL), Buddhist; a sanctuary; the sanctuary of a Buddha image.

ratn-āśva (EI 24), name of a *mahādāna.*

ratna-traya (EI 8), Jain; *samyag-darśana, samyag-jñāna* and *samyak-cāritra.*

(*EI* 27, 30, 31), Buddhist; the *tri-ratna* or trinity; a Buddhist religious establishment enshrining the three *ratnas*; rent-free land in its possession (*Ep. Ind.*, Vol. XXX, p. 46). Cf. *ratnatraya-sambhoga.*

ratnatraya-sambhoga (HRS), traced in Bengal records; rent-free holding in the possession of Buddhist religious establishments where the Buddha, Dharma and Saṅgha were worshipped; same as *ratna-traya.* Cf. *rāja-sambhoga.*

Raṭṭaguḍi (*EI* 30), same as *Raṭṭoḍī*; official designation; probably the same as *Rāṣṭrakūṭa.*

Raṭṭagul̤l̤u (EI 27), probably, the same as *Rāṣṭrakūṭa.*

rattī, see *rati.*

Raṭṭoḍi (EI 30), official designation; same as *Raṭṭaguḍi.*

Rāu (IA 18), same as *Rāva* (Sanskrit *Rājan*) or abbreviation of *Rāuta* (q.v.).

raukya-dra (LP), abbreviation of *raukya-dramma*; '*drammas* in cash'; cf. *raukya* with Gujarātī *rokaḍā.*

Rāula (EI 24, 28), derived from Sanskrit *Rājakula*; title of nobility; same as *Rāvata*, etc.

raupya-ṭaṅka, 'silver *ṭaṅka* (q.v.)'. See *JNSI*, Vol. XXII, p. 197. According to Nārada, a silver *kārṣāpaṇa* was called *raupya* in South India.

Rāuta (IE 8-2; EI 4, 28, 30, 31; CII 4; BL), same as *Rāvata*=Sanskrit *Rājaputra*; a title of feudatory rulers and noblemen.

(*IA* 20), also called *Rāhutta*; explained as 'a horseman'.

Rāutta (IE 8-2; EI 5, 30, 32), same as *Rāuta* or *Rāvata*= Sanskrit *Rājaputra*; a title of feudatories and noblemen. See *Rāuta.*

Rāva (IE 8-2; BL), spelt in English as *Rao*; title of subordinate rulers and noblemen; derived from Sanskrit *Rājan*; cf. *Rāya.*

rāva (LP), a complaint.

Rāval (BL), title of subordinate rulers and noblemen; derived from Sanskrit *Rājakula.*

Rāvala (EI 24; BL), same as *Rāval*; derived from Sanskrit *Rājakula*; title of subordinate rulers and noblemen.

rāvaṇa-bhuja (IE 7-1-2), 'twenty'.

rāvaṇa-hasta (ASLV), a musical instrument; may also indicate 'twenty' (cf. *rāvaṇa-bhuja*).

rāvaṇa-śiras (IE 7-1-2), 'ten'.

Rāvat (EI 32), a title of subordinate rulers and noblemen; same as *Rājaputra, Rāuta,* etc. See *Rāvata.*

Rāvata (IE 8-2; BL), same as *Rāvat*; derived from Sanskrit *Rājaputra*; a title of feudatories and noblemen.

ravi (IE 7-1-2), 'twelve'.

ravi-bāṇa (IE 7-1-2), 'one thousand'.

ravi-candra (IE 7-1-2), 'two'.

Rāvutu (EI 21), same as *Rāuta, Rāvata,* etc. ; derived from Sanskrit *Rājaputra*; a title of feudatories and noblemen.

Rāwa (EI 30), variant spelling of *Rāva*; derived from Sanskrit *Rājan*; title of nobility.

Rāya (IE 8-2; BL), title of nobility; derived from Sanskrit *Rājan*; cf. *Rāva.*

Rāya-rāuta (EI 31), title of nobility; derived from Sanskrit *Rāja-rājaputra.*

Rāyarāya (EI 21), title of nobility; derived from Sanskrit *Rājarāja.*

rāya-rekha (IA 15), a system of land measurement.

Rāyasa (EI 3, 17; ASLV), Kannaḍa; a secretary; an officer in the Vijayanagara administration.

rāyasa (ASLV), royal order.

(*SITI*), office of a writer; clerkship; order of the king; written orders. Cf. *Rāyasa-svāmin*, head of the *rāyasa.*

Rāyasa-svāmin (ASLV), 'the head of the *rāyasa*' (SITI); the chief secretary.

ṛddhi (EI 3), supernatural power.

ṛddhi-pāda, cf. *iddhi-pāda* (EI 5), Buddhist; four in number.

Reḍḍi (ASLV), a village official.

rekhā (EI 19), a land measure.

Cf. rekai, rekai-ppon (SITI), *irekai*; regarded as the name of a gold coin (probably bearing signs in straight lines); used in Vijayanagara inscriptions; probably, revenue income in cash.

rekhā-daṇḍa (EI 14), name of a linear measure.

reṣa (IE 8-8), meaning uncertain.

rintakāvaḍḍi (EI 33), name of a levy; cf. *antarābaḍḍi* or *āturā-baḍḍi*.

ripu (IE 7-1-2), 'six'.

ṛṣi-pañcamī (EI 23), same as Bhādrapada su-di 5.

Rītikāra (EI 32), a brazier.

rocayitavya (CII 1), 'should be liked'.

rocīka (*IE* 8-5), a tax or obligation of uncertain import.

rohaṇa (SITI), function performed at the commencement of a festival.

rohī (IA 11), Pañjābī; uplands.

roka (Chamba), cash. See *rūka* under rū.

ṛṣi (IE 7-1-2), 'seven'.

ṛtu (EI 7-1-2), 'six'.

rū (IE 8-1), abbreviation of *rūpaka* or *rūpyaka*.

(*CITD*), abbreviation of Telugu *rūka* meaning 'cash' and probably derived from Sanskrit *rūpaka*.

rūḍhabhāroḍi (HRS), system of forced carriage of loads as indicated by the *Rājataraṅgiṇī*. Cf. *prayāṇa-daṇḍa*.

rudhira, cf. Tamil *udira-paṭṭi* (SITI), literally, 'blood-land;' land given to the descendants of a person who fell fighting on the king's behalf; see also *rakta-mānya*, *mṛtyuka-vṛtti*, *rakta-paṭṭaka* and *vīra-śeṣā*.

Rudra (SITI), a Śaiva devotee.

rudra (*IE* 7-1-2), 'eleven'.

rudradāmaka, 'silver coin (*kārṣāpaṇa*) issued by Rudradāman'; name of the silver coins issued by the Śaka rulers of Western India (*JNSI*, Vol. XIII, pp. 1 7 ff.).

Rudra-gaṇa (SITI), devotees of Śiva, their managing committee looking after the affairs of a Śiva temple and being known as *Rudragaṇa-pperumakkaḷ*.

Rudra-gaṇikā (SITI), a dancing woman attached to a Śiva temple; a *devadāsī* serving in a Śiva temple.

Rudra-māheśvara (SITI; ASLV), the two classes of Śaiva devotees, known as the *Rudras* and *Māheśvaras*; designation of the authorities of a Śaiva temple.

Rudra-putra (EI 33), epithet of one devoted to the god Śiva. See *Durgā-putra, Puruṣottama-putra.*

rudr-āsya (IE 7-1-2), 'five'.

Ruṇḍā, cf. *Mahāruṇḍā.*

rundra (IA 6, 10), cf. *guṇa-rundra*, an epithet of Jinendra; also cf. *Himavad-girīndra-rundra-śikhara.*

rūpa (HRS), according to the *Arthaśāstra*, (1) a subsidiary charge in excess of the prescribed fines; (2) a charge upon mines and upon imported salt. See Ghoshal, *H. Rev. Syst.*, pp. 94, 106.

(*IE* 8-8; EI 20, 21), currency or coins; name of a silver coin; same as *rūpya* or *rūpaka.*

(*EI* 1), an animal.

(*CII* 1), a representation.

Rūpa-dakṣa, cf. Prakrit *lupa-dakha* (EI 22), a painter or sculptor. See *Ep. Ind.*, Vol. XXII, p. 30.

(*LL*), explained by some as 'a copyist'.

Rūpa-darśaka (EI 20, 21; HD), an examiner of coins. See *Arthaśāstra*, II. 5. Cf. *Pārikh.*

rūpaka (IE 8-8; EI 30; CII 4), name of a coin of silver; cf. *kṛṣṇarāja-rūpaka* (EI 25; CII 4), a silver coin issued by the Kalacuri king Kṛṣṇarāja; silver coin $\frac{1}{16}$ of the value of a gold *dīnāra* in the Gupta age (*JNSI*, Vol. II, p. 5); same as *dramma.*

Rūpakāra (EI 8; BL), a sculptor; epithet of a sculptor. See *Rūpakāraka, Rūpakārin.*

Rūpakāraka (LL), a sculptor; same as *Rūpakāra, Rūpakārin.*

Rūpakārin (EI 5), a sculptor; same as *Rūpakāra, Rūpakāraka.*

rūpa-karman (LL), carving.

rupee, Anglicised form of *rūpīa* (q.v.); derived from Sanskrit *rūpyaka.* See *JNSI*, Vol. XV, p. 142.

rūpīa (IE 8-8), same as *rūpya* or *rūpyaka.*

rūpika (HRS), tax on the sale of salt; one of the sources of revenue specified in the *Arthaśāstra.* See Ghoshal, *H. Rev. Syst.*, pp. 25, 92, 106.

rūpyaka (IE 8-8), same as *rūpaka, rūpīa, rupee.*

S

sa (IE 8-1), also written as *saṁ*; abbreviation of *saṁvatsara.*

Sā (EI 32), abbreviation of *Sādhanika* (q. v.).

(*PJS*), abbreviation of *Sāhu* or *Sādhu*, designation of a member of the mercantile community often used in medieval inscriptions.

śabda, same as *mahā-śabda*; cf. *pañca-śabda* (BL).

śābdika (BL), a grammarian.

sabhā (SII 2; SITI; ASLV), same as *mahāsabhā*; the body of the *Mahājanas*; the assembly of a Brāhmaṇa village of the Tamil-speaking area, such an assembly of a non-Brāhmaṇa village being called *ūr*; local assembly of a Brāhmaṇa village; same as Tamil *kuṟi*.

(*EI* 22), the Buddhist *saṅgha*.

sabhā-madhyama (SITI), the village common or waste land in the village belonging to the *sabhā*; also called *sabhai-ppodu*, *ūr-ppodu*, *ūr-mañjikkam*, *sabhā-mañjikkam*, etc., in Tamil.

sabhā-maṇḍapa (HA), same as *raṅga-maṇḍapa*.

sabhā-viniyoga (SITI), individual share payable to make up the expenses of the *sabhā*.

Sabrahmacārin (CII 3), a religious student of a group that follows the same *śākhā*.

sācitta (LP), probably, 'land attached to government servants as long as they serve'.

Saciva (EI 33; BL; HD), minister or counsellor. See *Hist. Dharm.*, Vol. III, p. 105, note 150.

sāda (EI 28), name of a tax.

sadaka, cf. *upari-sadaka*, explained as 'the upper region' (*Ep. Ind.*, Vol. XXXI. p. 234).

sadā-sevā, cf. Tamil *sadā-servai*, *sadā-sevai* (SII 1; SITI); constant service; permanent service.

ṣaḍaśīti (IA 19), same as *mithuna-rāśi* (Gemini).

ṣaḍ-āyatana, cf. Prakrit *ṣaḍ-ayadana* (CII 2-1), the six organs.

ṣaḍ-bhāga, cf. *dharma-ṣaḍ-bhāga* (*Sel. Ins.*, p. 348, text line 16), one-sixth of the merit for a pious work done by the subjects, which goes to the king. See ibid., p. 344, text line 3.

Sādhācārya (IA 12), assistant to the officiating priest at the Rāmeśvaram temple; also called *Adhyayana-bhaṭṭa*.

sādhana (IE 8-3; EI 24; LP), an army, cf. *sādhana-sahasra-aikam*, an army consisting of one thousand men.

(*EI* 15), an army, or money.

(*SII* 12), cf. *mūla-sādhana*, the original deed; also called *mūla-olai* in Tamil.

Sādhanika (CII 4), a general; same as *Sāhaṇi*, etc.

Sādhanin (EI 23), explained as a 'a councillor'; but really, the same as *Sādhanika* (q.v.).

sādhāra (*Ep. Ind.*, Vol. XIV, p. 177), either a mistake for *sādhāraṇa*, 'common', or means 'together with the adjacent grounds'.

sādhāraṇa (IA 20), used in the sense of *laukika*.

sadharmi-vātsalya (HA), attachment to or service of the followers of one's own faith.

sadhryagvihārin (LL), doubtful Sanskritisation of Pāli *saddhi-vihārin* (Sanskrit *sārdhaṁvihārin* under the influence of *sādhya*), companion of a Buddhist monk. Cf. Jain *Sārdhaṁcara*, *Sārdhaṁcarī* (LL).

Sādhu (EI 9), a priest.

(*HA*), a Jain monk.

(*LP*; HA), same as *Sāhu*, a merchant.

(*CII* 1), an adjective meaning 'good'.

Sādhvī (JHA), a Jain nun.

sādhya (IE 8-5; EI 15; SITI), a type of income; income from land that may be brought under cultivation in future; one of the eight kinds of enjoyment of property. See *aṣṭa-bhoga*, *siddha*.

Sādhyapāla (HD), a bailiff who summoned parties and witnesses. See *Hist. Dharm.*, Vol. III, p. 278.

sādyaskra (EI 22; CII 3; etc.), name of a sacrifice.

sagara (IE 7-1-2), confused with *sāgara* and rarely used to indicate 'seven'.

sāgara (IE 7-1-2), 'four'; used in the sense of 'seven' by some late writers (IA 19).

Sagotra (CII 3, etc.), belonging to the lineage of the person from whom the *gotra* name is derived.

Sahadeśa (IA 17), also called *Sahadeśin*, 'belonging to the same country'.

sahagamana (ASLV), self-immolation of a widow on the funeral pyre of her husband; same as *satī*.

Sahaja-kavi (*Ep. Ind.*, Vol. V, p. 231, note 1), epithet of a poet.

Sāhaṇi (IE 8-3), also called *Sāhiṇi*, etc.; derived from Sanskrit *Sādhanika*; cf. *Gaja-sāhiṇi*, etc.

(*EI* 15), see *Paṭṭa-sāhaṇi*, *Peyiya-sāhaṇi*, *Maleya-sāhaṇi*.

Sāhānī (EI 33), same as *Sādhanika*, *Sāhaṇi*, etc.

Sāhaṇia (IE 8-3), Prakrit form of *Sādhanika* from *sādhana* or army; cf. the modern family name *Sāhnī*. Same as *Sāhaṇiya*, etc.

sāhaṇikāṭi (SII 11-1), supposed to be the name of a coin.

Sāhaṇiya (EI 11), Prakrit form of *Sādhanika*; same as *Sāhaṇia*, etc.

Sāhānuṣāhi (IE 8-2; EI 19, 22, 30), title of the Kuṣāṇa kings, derived from Old Persian *Kshāyathiyānām Kshāyathiya*; same as modern Persian *Shāhān Shāh*.

śahar, Persian *shahr*, a town (*Ep. Ind.*, Vol. XXXIV, pp. 145-46).

sāhasa (CII 4), a violent crime.

Sāhasādhipati (HD), a judicial or police officer. See Śukra, I. 120.

sāhasamallāṅka (BL), epithet of a year of the Kalacuri era probably through confusion, as normally the expression would mean the Vikrama era.

sahasr-āṁśu (IE 7-1-2), 'twelve'.

sahasr-āyatana (EI 29), epithet of a temple; literally, 'having one thousand rooms or shrines'.

Sāhi, Śāhī (IE 8-2; EI 30; LL), same as Persian *Shāh*, Old Persian *Kshāyathiya*; royal title used by some Indian rulers of foreign origin.

Sāhijādā (BL), title of a prince; same as Persian *Shāhzādah*. See *Sāhiyādā*.

sahī-karī (Chamba), 'having approved; having got approved; having put the signature on'.

sāhilya (IA 23), same as *bhāṇḍāra*.

Sāhiṇi (IE 8-3; EI 32), same as Sanskrit *Sādhanika* (q.v.), interpreted as 'the master of the royal stables' (BL).

sāhitī-vidyā (EI 13), same as *sāhitya*, literature.

sāhitya, cf. *sāhitī-vidyā*.

Sāhiyādā (BL), title of a prince; same as Persian *Shāhzādah*. See *Sāhijādā*.

Sāhnī (IE 8-3), modern family name derived from Sanskrit *Sādhanika* = Prakrit *Sāhaṇia, Sāhaṇi*.

sahodara (IE 7-1-2), 'three' possibly referring to Kuntī's sons.

Sāhu (LP), same as Sanskrit *Sādhu*; a merchant.

śaibara, cf. *sa-śaibaram* (EI 17); a levy in kind according to some; but see *saivara*.

saïkā (EI 28), Sanskrit *śatikā*; a levy per one hundred articles; one payable in a hundred articles.

śaila (IE 7-1-2; EI 25), 'seven'.

śaila-devagṛha (EI 24), a stone temple.

śaila-gṛha (LL), a cave.

śaila-karman (LL), stone-work.

Śailālaka (EI 1; LL), same as *Śilālin*, an actor.

śaila-rūpakarman (LL), stone-carving.

Śaila-vardhakin (LL), cf. Prakrit *Sela-vaḍhākī* (EI 20); a stone mason.

Sainika-saṅgha-mukhya (EI 22), official designation; probably, a general.

sainya (*Ep. Ind.*, Vol. XXXI, p. 71), probably, an administrative unit.

Sainy-ādhikārin (IE 8-3), same as *Senāpati*, etc.

Sainyapati (IE 8-3), same as *Senāpati*, etc.

Śaiv-ācārya (CII 4), an ascetic of the Śaiva sect.

śaivācārya-kṣetra (SITI), tax-free land endowed to a *Śaiv-ācārya*.

śaiva-dīkṣā (EI 32), initiation into the Śaiva faith.

śaivara, a revenue term; cf. *śaibara*; a levy in kind according to Ghoshal (*H.Rev. Syst.*, p. 220); but probably the same as Marāṭhī *śerī*, 'arable land originally excluded from the village assessment' (Wilson's Glossary); may also be a tax on farm-houses (cf. *śibara*).

Śaka (EI 24), originally, the Scythians; later any foreigners including Muhammadans; used to indicate the Musalmans (*Ep. Ind.*, Vol. XII, p. 44; Bhandarkar's List, No. 926).

śaka, *śāka* (IA 9, 19), used in the sense of 'a year' or 'an era'; cf. *Vikrama-śaka* (IA 18).

śāka, cf. *a-harītaka-śāka-puṣpa-grahaṇa* (EI 8-5); vegetables which the villagers were obliged to supply to the king or land-lord on occasions or to the touring officers. Cf. *śāka-śaka*

sākā (IA 29), Rājasthānī; same as *jauhar* or *javhar*.

śākambharī-vidyā (EI 29; CII 4), name of a science, the nature of which is uncertain.

Śakānikā (CII 4), a Śaka woman. Cf. *anikā*.

śāka-paṇikā, cf. *śāka-paṇikā-nyāyena* (LP), 'like vegetables in a market'.

sakarukara, occurs in a Sātavāhana inscription probably for

Sanskrit *sa-kar-otkara* meaning the same thing as *s-odraṅga-s-oparikara*, 'with the *udraṅga* (*kara*) and *uparikara* (*utkara*) taxes'; may also be *sa-kārukara*. See *kāru-kara*.

śākhā (CII 3, 4; IA 18, 19), literally, 'a branch'; a Vedic school following any particular recension of the Vedas.

(*LL*), a section of the Jain community.

śakra (IE 7-1-2), 'fourteen'.

śakra-dhvaja, cf. *indra-daṇḍa*.

śakra-yajña (IE 7-1-2), 'one hundred'.

śakr-otthāna (EI 32), a festival, same as *śakradhvaj-otthāna*. Cf. *śakra-dhvaja*, *indra-daṇḍa*.

Sākṣin (EI 3, 23; SITI), a witness; an eye-witness.

sa-kṣīṇ-ārambha (CII 1), gentle in action.

sakta (LP), written for *satka*, 'belonging to'.

Śakti (EI 17), name of the wife of Kāmadeva.

śakti (IE 7-1-2; EI 25), 'three'; three in number (EI 6).

śakti-mukha, (SITI), cf. *śatti-mugam*; king's order; probably the same as *śrīmukha*.

śakti-traya (SII 1), the three [regal] powers.

Śākya (CII 1), a Buddhist; see *Śākya-bhikṣu*.

Śākya-bhikṣu (BL; LL), epithet of a Buddhist monk; same as *Śākya*.

Śāky-opāsikā (LL), a female member of the Buddhist laity.

śālā (EI 4; SII 1), a hall.

(*EI* 4; SITI), a school; same as *pāṭha-śālā*.

(*SII* 3), cf. *śālai* (EI 7; SITI), an alms-house; a feeding house; cf. *śālā-bhoga*.

Cf. *śālai* (EI 24), a hospital; cf. *ārogya-śālā*, *ātura-śālā*.

śālā-bhoga (SII 2; SII), same as Tamil *arac-cālā-bhogam*; land granted in favour of a feeding house (*sattra-śālā*). (EI 23), mentioned along with *devadāna* and *brahmadeya*; a rent-free holding in the possession of a *śālā* meaning an almshouse or a school.

śalākā, cf. *śalāgai* (SITI), name of a coin also called *palañ-śalāgai* (*cccu*) and *śrīyakki-palañśalāgai*.

Śālāsthāna-mukhya (EI 32), probably, officer in charge of the stables.

Salāṭa (*PJS*), Gujarātī; also called *Salāvaṭa*; a stone-cutter or mason.

Sālavī (LP), Gujarātī; a weaver.

(*PJS*), Gujarātī; a carpenter.

Śālīna (CII 4), a kind of householder.

salila-pūrvaka (IA 9), same as *udaka-pūrvam*, etc.

sallekhanā (EI 3, 6; SITI), Jain; a religious practice of the Jains; starving oneself to death; starving oneself to death in fulfilment of a vow; same as *samādhi*.

Sa-lohita (*Ep. Ind.*, Vol. XIV, p. 295), 'one having the same blood'; a relation.

śalya-traya (SII 1), the three thorns.

saṁ (IE 8-1), abbreviation of *saṁbaddha*, 'attached to', 'belonging to,' etc.; possibly also *saṁsakta*, 'relating to' (*JAS*, Letters, Vol. XX, p. 204).

(*CII* 3, 4), abbreviation of the word *saṁvatsara*, a year, or of its declensional cases that can be used in expressing a date.

Saṁ (PJS), also written *Saṁgha*; contraction of *Saṁghavī* or *Saṁghapati* in medieval Jain inscriptions; same as the modern Jain family name *Siṅghī*.

sāṁ (IE 8-1; LP), abbreviation of *sāṁvatsarika*, annual. See *sāṁ-hi*.

śam (ML) 'to prevent'.

sama, cf. *sam-ālindakam* (LP), 'with a terrace in front of the door.'

samācarya (CII 1), impartiality.

samādhi (CII 4), poetic quality of a composition.

(*EI* 33), explained as a 'granary'; probably 'an agreement'. *Cf. sallekhanā.*

Samadhigata-pañca-mahāśabda (IE 8-2; CII 3), a customary epithet of feudatory rulers, indicating that they were entitled to the privilege of the *pañca-mahāśabda* (five kinds of musical instruments), or of using five official titles beginning with the word *mahā*. There are a few instances in which the epithet is applied to paramount sovereigns in South India. The title is sometimes stated to have been conferred on a feudatory by his overlord. See *mahāśabda*, etc.

Samāhartṛ (EI 27; HD; HRS), official designation; explained as 'the collector-general'; officer in charge of the collection of various branches of revenue; compared by Ghoshal with the *Qānungo* of Mughal times (*H. Rev. Syst.*, p. 52). See *Artha-śāstra*, I. 12; II. 6; *Śabara* on *Jaimini*, XII. 1. 28; *Ep. Ind.*, Vol. VIII, p. 141; Vol. XI, p. 94.

samāja (EI 20; CII 1), a fair; a festival; a festive gathering on a particular occasion or for the celebration of an event.

Samājñapti (EI 27), same as *Ājñapti* (q.v.).

sāmaka (LP), 'collectively'; cf. Gujarātī *sāṁṭuṁ*

samakara-grāma (LP), a village for which a permanent revenue is fixed at a particular rate, not to be increased in future.

samakara-kula (LP), family on which rent is fixed once for all; farmers that have to pay revenue at a particular rate.

samākrānta (*Ep. Ind.*, Vol. XXXI, p. 20), used in some Orissan records probably in the sense of 'endowed with boundaries'.

samam (LP), 'in the same way as'.

samañjasa (SITI), conformity; resemblance.

Samañjita (SITI), accountant of a village or a village assembly.

samanta (IE 8-1), corrupt form of *saṁvat*.

Sāmanta (IE 8-2; 8-3; EI 30; CII 3, 4; BL; HD), title of feudatory rulers; a feudatory smaller than the *Rājan*; a subordinate chief; also explained as 'a minister' (SITI). See *Bomb. Gaz.*, Vol. XXI, p. 354; *Ep. Ind.*, Vol. IX, p. 297. Cf. *Mahāsāmanta*.

Sāmanta (CII 1), a neighbour; 'one who is in possession of a piece of land in the neighbourhood of the gift land' (*Ep. Ind.*, Vol. XXXIV, p. 220).

samantabhadra (*Ep. Ind.*, Vol. III, p. 199), prosperous on all sides.

Sāmant-ādhikārin (ASLV), see *Sāmanta* and *Adhikārin*.

Sāmant-ādhipati (EI 16), cf. *Mahāsāmant-ādhipati*.

Sāmanta-paḍirā (EI 32), Oḍiyā; Sanskrit *Sāmanta-pratirāja*; title of a feudatory or nobleman.

sāmantika, derived from *Sāmanta*; chiefship (*A.R.Ep.*, 1958-59, p. 12).

samanthu (IE 8-1), corrupt form of *saṁvat*.

sāmānya, cf. *traividya-sāmānya* (EI 23), *cāturvedya-sāmānya*; 'belonging to'; *Valabhī-cāturvidya-sāmānya*, 'one of the *Caturvedins* of Valabhī'; used also in the sense of *vāstavya*, 'resident of...' (*Ep. Ind.*, Vol. XXXIV, pp. 172, 176).

samāracana, repairs (*Ep. Ind.*, Vol. XXXIV, p. 144).

samāraṇa Prakrit used in Sanskrit for *samāracaṇa* (*Ep. Ind.*, Vol. XXXV, p. 59).

samarāpaṇīya (LP), to be got repaired; cf. Gujarātī *samrā-*

vavuṁ; see *samarcāpanīya*, *samāracana*.

samarāpya (LP), 'should be repaired'; cf. Gujarātī *samrāvatruṁ*; also *samāracana*.

samarcāpana (LP), repairing; cf. *samarcāpanīya* (LP), 'to be got repaired'; cf. *samarāpaṇīya*; also *samāracana*.

samasta (IE 8-1), corrupt form of *saṁvat* especially in medieval Orissan records.

Samasta-mahāsāmant-ādhipati (BL), title of a feudatory ruler of the highest rank. See *Mahāsāmant-ādhipati*.

Samasta-sen-ādhipati (EI 29, 30), 'leader of all the forces'; commander-in-chief. See *Sen-ādhipati*, *Senāpati*, *Manĕya-samasta-sainy-ādhipati*, etc.

samasta-supraśasty-upeta (IE 8-2), a royal epithet.

samasty-ety-ādi (IE 8-2), shortened form of *samasta-supraśasty-upeta*.

samasyā-pūraṇa (CII 4), completion of incomplete verses.

samat (IE 8-1), corrupt form of *saṁvat*.

samata (IE 8-1), corrupt form of *saṁvat*.

samatā (CII 1), impartiality.

samatta (IE 8-1), corrupt form of *saṁvat*.

sāma-vāda, cf. Prakrit *sama-vāyo* (CII 1), found in a rock edict of Aśoka; 'restrained speech'; same as *saṁyama* (i.e. *vāk-saṁyama*) found in one version; generally *sama-vāyo* is taken as *samavāya* or concord.

Sāmavājika (*Ep. Ind.*, Vol. VI, p. 135, note 6), probably, an officer; cf. *Sāmavāyika*, *Sāmavājin*, *Sāṁmavājin*.

Sāmavājin (EI 6), probably, an officer; cf. *Sāṁmavājin*, *Sāmavājika*.

samavasaraṇa (HA), congregation-hall believed to be built by celestials when a Tīrthaṅkara delivered his sermon.

Sāmavāyika (*Ep. Ind.*, Vol. VI, p. 135, note 6), probably, an officer; cf. *Sāmavājika*.

samaveta (IE 8-3), 'associated'; generally explained as 'assembled'; but see *samupāgata*, *upeta*, *upayāta*, etc.

samaya (EI 10), a religious system.

(*CITD*), Telugu-Kannaḍa; a sect; an assemblage, a company or congregation; established moral or ceremonial custom; cf. *samaiyam* (EI 24), a creed.

Cf. samaye (EI 19), used instead of *varṣe* in the dates after *saṁvat*.

(*SITI*), a religious mendicant; cf. *Samay-mudali*, religious head.

samay-ācāra (SITI), religious usage; established custom; supervision of the religious and social life of the people; censoring of public morals; also a class of officials called *Samayācārya* or *Dāsari*

Samayācārya (ASLV), also called *Samayācāra*; same as *Dāśari*; a censor of morals; a class of officials.

samaya-dharma (SITI), law of the *samaya* or agreement. The expression is generally used in relation to the organisation of merchants and agriculturists known respectively as *Nānādeśin* and *Citrameḷi*.

samaya-patra (SII 1; SITI; LP), an agreement; a document containing an agreement ; a deed of agreement.

sāmāyika (HA), remaining steadfast in worship or meditation (at least for 48 minutes), with the mind drawn away from attachments or ill will and abstaining from committing sins, which is the daily duty of a Jain

sambaddha (IA 15), 'belonging to' or 'connected with'.

Cf. Devadroṇī-sambaddha (IE 8-3), probably, superintendent of a temple property.

sambadhanā (LP), strong opposition.

śambala (LP), provisions.

saṁbhāla (LP), care, protection; cf. Gujarātī *saṁbal.*

sambhāra (ML), provision.

sambhoga, cf. *rāja-sambhoga*, *ratnatraya-sambhoga*; same as *bhoga*.

Sambhoga (LL), a section of the Jain community.

sambodhita (LP), advised.

sambuddha (LP), one who is no longer a minor.

saṁgrahaṇa, adultery (*Ep. Ind.*, Vol. XXV, p. 237).

ṣamhalātamaka, cf. *ṣamhalātamaka-samanvita* (EI 9), meaning uncertain; may be a name.

sāṁ-hi, abbreviation of *sāṁvatsarika-hiranya*, 'annual revenue income in cash' (*Ep.Ind.*, Vol. XXX, p. 55).

sāmīpa (CII 1), a neighbour.

samiti (EI 4), five in number.

saṁkācitaka (EI 30), cf. *poṭṭalikā-saṁkācitak-ādāna*, 'tax on bundles suspended from loops at both ends of a pole'.

saṁmat (IE 8-1), corrupt form of *saṁvat*.

sammat (ASLV), same as *samuta*; an administrative unit.

Sāṁmavājin (EI 33), same as *Sāmavājin*, *Sām vājika*.

sammukha-vāra, probably, Sunday (*Ep.Ind.*, Vol. XXXV, p. 115).

saṁmvat (EI 8-1), corrupt form of *saṁvat*.

samprāpti, cf. *sampirātti* (SITI) 'that which has been obtained'; 'an acquisition'.

Samprati (SITI), senior accountant; the manager of a temple.

sampratipatti (CII 1), proper behaviour.

Samrāṭ (EI 19, 22; CII 3,4), imperial title; a paramount sovereign.

saṁsaraṇa (CII 1), a house or road.

sāṁśayika (CII 1), 'of doubtful value'.

Saṁskṛta, see *Sanskrit*.

saṁstava (CII1), cf. *dharma-saṁstava*, 'acquaintance through *Dharma*'.

saṁsthā (HRS), king's dues derived from the market-place, as suggested by the *Arthaśāstra*.

saṁstuta (CII 1), cf. *mitra-saṁstuta-jñāti*, 'friends, acquintances and relatives'.

samta (IE 8-1), corrupt form of *saṁvat*. *Mta*=*mat*.

Samudāya (EI 25), official designation.

samudāya (ASLV), same as *gaṇa-bhoga*; a tenure in which land is enjoyed by a group of people.

(*SITI*), a village under the *gaṇa-bhoga* tenure.

(*SITI*), village common; managing committee of a temple.

samudaya-bāhya (HRS), occurs in the Damodarpur inscriptions; 'revenue-free' or 'yielding no income'.

samudāya-prāpti, *cf*. *samudāya-ppirātti* (SITI), any acquisition from the village to be enjoyed in common by the villagers.

Samudra (EI 10), an epithet of Śiva.

samudra (EI 16), same as *sapt-āmbhodhi*; name of a *mahādāna*; also means 4 (rarely 7).

samudra-ghoṣa (EI 5), name given to a musical instrument.

samūha (EI 28; CII 4), an assembly; the assembly of a corporation.

samupagata (EI 12), explained as 'assembled at'; really, 'having connection with', 'associated with'; cf. *samupagama*, 'contact'; also *samaveta*, *upeta*, *upayāta*, etc.

samupāgata (IE 8-3), 'associated'; often explained as 'assembled'; but cf. *samaveta*, *samupagata*, *upayāta*, *upeta*, etc.

samuta (ASLV), same as *sammat*; an administrative unit.

samutkrīḍā (EI 15), same as *krīḍā* or sport.

samva (IE 8-1), mistake for *saṁva* which is an abbreviation of *saṁvatsara.*

saṁva (IE 8-1) same as *saṁvat*; contraction of *saṁvatsara.*

saṁvadana (IE 8-8), submission of information.

saṁvarta-kalpa (CII 1), the aeon of destruction.

saṁvāsa, cf. *a-kūra-cullaka-vināśi-khaṭvā-saṁvāsa* (IE 8-5); same as *āvāsa*; shelter or accommodation [which the villagers were obliged to supply to the touring officers of the king].

saṁvat (IE 8-1), originally an abbreviation of *saṁvatsara* (a year) or any of its declensional cases that can be used in expressing a date; later stereotyped in the sense of 'a year' or 'an era'. It was generally regarded as indeclinable; but we have some cases of the use of forms with case-endings, e. g., *saṁvataḥ*, *saṁvatā*, *saṁvati* and *saṁvatām*. See also *saṁvate* (IE 8-1), the seventh case-ending of *saṁvata*, a corrupt form of *saṁvat*. Since the late medieval age, the word specially indicates the Vikrama era, although originally it was used with the name of any reckoning in quoting the dates of records, especially the regnal reckoning. The word is used in inscriptions in a large number of corrupt forms, e.g., *samvata*, *samvatta*, *samata*, *samanta*, *samatta*, *saṁmat*, *samasta*, *smat*, *samvatu*, *samvatū*, etc., etc.

samvat (IE 8-1), mistake for *saṁvat*, originally an abbreviation of *saṁvatsara.*

saṁvatsara (CII 3; 4; IA 17), ' a year'; 'an era', the earlier years of the Indian eras being quoted by this term (or by its abbreviations *saṁ*, *saṁvat*, etc.), without any dynastic or other appellation just as in the case of the year of a regnal reckoning.

Sāṁvatsara (HD), an astrologer. See *Viṣṇu Dh. S.*, III. 75; *Bṛhatasaṁhitā*, 2. 9; cf. *Sāṁvatsarika* (EI 5).

saṁvatsara-pratipadā, name of a *tithi.*

saṁvatsara-śrāddha (CII 4), *śrāddha* performed on the first anniversary of a person's death.

saṁvatsara-vāriya (SITI), annual committee appointed by the *sabhā*; annual committee for supervising the management of village affairs; also called *āṭṭi-vāriyam* (SITI) in Tamil.

saṁvatsara-vimokṣa-śrāddha (CII 4), same as *saṁvatsara-śrāddha* performed on the first anniversary of a person's death.

Sāṁvatsarika (HD), an astrologer. See Paiṭhīnasi quoted

in *Hist. Dharm.*, Vol. III, p. 193.

sāṁvatsarika-hiraṇya (IE 8-1), annual revenue in cash; often abbreviated as *sāṁ-hi*.

samvatta (IE 8-1), corrupt form of *saṁvat*.

samvatu, *samvatū* (IE 8-1), corrupt forms of *saṁvat*.

saṁvatuṁ (IE 8-1), corrupt form of *saṁvat*.

saṁvibhāga (CII 1), separation of one thing from another.

saṁvid (EI 32), an agreement.

sāṁvinayika, cf. *a-raṭṭha-sāṁvinayika* (EI 1), *a-rāṣṭra-sāṁvinayika* (IE 8-5); administration or control, i.e. administrative control.

Saṁvyavahārin (EI 23), an administrator; same as *Vyavahārin*; cf. *Saṁvyavahāry-ādi-kuṭumbinaḥ* (EI 24), the agriculturist householders led by the village-headman or the collector of royal dues.

sāmya (EI 23), often written for *svāmya*; cf. *teja-sāmya* standing for *tejaḥ-svāmya*.

samyak-pradhāna, cf. *sammappadhāna* (EI 5), Buddhist; four in number.

san (IA 18), Arabic; a year; an era; sometimes used in Sanskrit records; in some cases, corrupted to *sna*.

śaṇa (LP), linen.

śāṇa, name of a weight or coin; a silver coin which was $\frac{1}{8}$ of a *śatamāna* in weight and value; generally regarded as 40 *ratis* in weight, but sometimes also as 32 or 24 or 20 *ratis*; also called *niṣka*, *ṭaṅka* or *dharaṇa* or *śāṇaka*. See *JNSI*, Vol. XVI, pp. 42, 44-45. See *śāṇa-pāda*.

Śānabhoga (IE 8-3), village-accountant; same as *Senabova*, etc.

śāṇaka, see *śāṇa*.

śāṇa-pāda, same as *māṣa* (*JNSI*, Vol. p. 47).

Sanātha (IA 7), wrongly supposed to mean 'one whose father is alive' or 'a worthy'; actually, a personal name.

sañcakāra (IA 19), same as *satyakāra*; an agreement.

Sañcarantaka (HD), Prakrit; 'a spy'. See *Ep. Ind.*, Vol. I, p. 5. Kauṭilya (*Arthaśāstra*, I. 12) speaks of *Sañcāra* (wandering spies like *Tīkṣṇa*, *Rasada*, etc.). Cf. *Sañcārin*.

Sañcaratka (IE 8-3), a spy; cf. *Sañcarantaka*.

Sañcārin (EI 24), cf. *Śāsana-sañcārin* and *Ājñā-sañcārin*.

sañcarita, cf. *ājñāta* (IA 18).

ṣaṇḍa (IA 18), a bull living or wandering at liberty.

ṣaṇḍa-gula (LP), same as Gujarātī *khāṁḍ-gol*, i.e. sugar and molasses.

sandhi (EI 4; SITI), literally, 'twilight'; but actually, 'service in the temple in the morning and evening'; daily worship in temples; special worship offered in the names of persons who arrange for it by creating endowments, etc.

sandhi-pāta, emergency (*Ep. Ind.*, Vol. XXX, p. 213).

Sandhivigrah-ādhikaraṇa (CII 4), department of peace and war.

Sandhivigrah-ādhikaraṇ-ādhikṛta (EI 30; BL), official designation indicating a person in charge of the office of war and peace (i.e. foreign affairs); an officer of the ministry or the minister of foreign affairs.

Sandhivigrah-ādhikaraṇa-kāyastha, official designation of a scribe of the office of war and peace (i.e. foreign affairs).

Sandhivigrah-ādhikṛta (CII 4; BL), an officer in charge of the department or the minister of war and peace; same as *Sandhivigrahin.*

sandhi-[vigraha]-karaṇa, cf. *karaṇa* (LP); department of foreign affairs.

Sandhivigrahakārin (EI 21), same as *Sandhivigrahika.* See *Mitākṣarā* on *Yājñavalkyasmṛti*, I. 320.

sandhivigraha-ppeṟu (EI 24; SITI), Sanskrit-Tamil; a fee payable to the village *Madhyastha*; also a fee payable to document-writers; cf. *sandhivigrahi-paṇṇu.*

Sandhivigrahika (HD), minister for peace and war. See *Viṣṇudharmottara*, II. 24. 17; *Mahābhārata*, Śānti-parvan, 85. 30. See *Sāndhivigrahika.*

Sāndhivigrahika (IE 8-3; EI 30; CII 3, 4; BL; HD; LP), minister for peace and war, i.e. of foreign affairs; sometimes also called *Khādya*[*kū*]*ṭapākika*, *Kumārāmātya*, *Mahādaṇḍanāyaka*, etc., additionally; same as *Sandhivigrahika*, etc. See *Viṣṇudharmottara*, II. 24. 17; *Mitākṣarā* on *Yājñavalkyasmṛti*, I. 320; *CII*, Vol. III, p. 15.

Sandhivigrahin (IE 8-3, SITI), minister in charge of peace and war; officer in charge of the foreign relations department, who was often the writer of important documents; same as *Sandhivigrahika*, etc. Cf. *Kannaḍa-sandhivigrahin* (EI 16), *Hĕri-Lāḷa-sandhivigrahin* (EI 12), *Hĕri-sandhivigrahin* (EI 12), *Lāḷa-*

sandhivigrahin (EI 12), *Hĕri-Lāṭa-Karṇāṭa-sandhivigrahin, Hĕri-Lāṭa-sandhivigrahin,* etc.

Sandhivigrahi-paṇṇu (EI 30), name of a levy; same as *sandhivigraha-ppeṟu.*

sandhi-viḻakku (SII 1), a sacred lamp; cf. *nandā-viḻakku, sandhi-dīpa.*

sandhyā (CITD), the morning, noon and evening prayers of a Brāhmaṇa.

(*CII* 3; IA 17), a period at the commencement of each of the four Hindu ages; the *sandhyā* of the Kali-yuga lasts for 36,000 years of men, and is still running; cf. *sandhyāṁśa.*

sandhi-dīpa, cf. *sandi-viḻakku* (SITI), a twilight lamp; generally lighted in the temples in the evening, but sometimes in the morning; same as *sandhyā-dīpa.*

sandhy-āṁśa (AI 17), a period at the end of each of the four *yugas,* the *sandhy-āṁśa* of the Kali-yuga to last for 36,000 human years.

sandoha, cf. *a-puṣpa-kṣīra-sandoha* (IE 8-5), realisation or levy (cf. *a-puṣpa-kṣīra-grahaṇīya*).

Saṅgaḍi-rakṣā-pālaka (EI 6), an officer; the meaning of *saṅgaḍi* is uncertain.

saṅgam, Tamil; same as Sanskrit *saṅgha*; an assembly of ancient Tamil poets; the name given to an assembly of poets reported in tradition to have functioned in three different periods. The poets are believed to have been both literary critics and composers. Literary compositions of the age were later collected and compiled into anthologies known as *Eṭṭuttokai, Pattuppāṭṭu* and *Padineṇkīḻkaṇakku* according to their contents and size. The *saṅgam* is stated to have flourished at Kūḍal (also called Madurai in later literature) in the first and last period and at Kavāṭapuram in the middle period. The latest limit for the first two anthologies may be placed round about 700 A.D. See M. S. Purnalingam Pillai, *Tamil Literature,* pp. 14-18; S. Vaiyapuri Pillai, *History of Tamil Language and Literature,* p. 38.

saṅgha (ASLV), a social organisation.

(*BL*), a community of Buddhist monks; the Buddhist Church.

(*HA*), a Jain congregation; the Jain Church (made up of four constituents, viz. *sādhu, sādhvī, śrāvaka* and *śrāvikā*) also called *Jaina-saṅgha*; a group of pilgrims going together on pilgrimage under the leadership of a *Saṅghapati* (q.v.).

(*EI* 22), a tribe.

Cf. Tamil *saṅgam* (q.v.).

Saṅgha-pati (EI 8; BL), title of the leader of a group of Jain pilgrims to a holy place, who bears all the expenses of the whole group; same as *Saṅghaprabhu*, *Saṅghavī*, etc. Cf. the modern Jain family name *Siṅghī*.

Saṅgha-prabhu (EI 8), Jain; same as *Saṅghapati*, etc.

Saṅgha-prakṛta (LL), Buddhist; probably, a supporter of the *saṅgha*; translated as 'commissioners of the community' (Lüders, *Mathurā Inscriptions*., pp. 84 ff.).

Saṅgharāja (EI 8), Buddhist; title of the principal ecclesiastical functionary in Burma.

saṅghārāma (EI 4; ML; LL), a Buddhist monastery.

Saṅgha-sthavira (LL), an Elder of the Buddhist congregation. Cf. *Sthavira*.

saṅghāṭa, *saṅghāṭā* (*Ep. Ind.*, Vol. XXXIII, p. 248), cf. *pāda-saṅghāṭa* or *pāda-saṅghāṭā*, 'a pair of feet (i. e. foot-marks)'.

saṅghāṭī (EI 25), robe of a Buddhist monk.

Saṅghavī (BL; HA; PJS), derived from Sanskrit *Saṅgha-pati* (q.v.); designation of the leader of a *saṅgha* or group of Jains; the leader of a group of Jain pilgrims, who bears expenses of all the pilgrims going with him (cf. the Jain family name *Siṅghī*).

saṅgrahaṇa (IE 8-5), adultery.

Saṅgrahītṛ (HD), explained by some as 'a treasurer or charioteer' (*Hist. Dharm.*, Vol. III, p. 111); probably, collector of the king's grain share. Cf. Ghoshal, *H. Rev. Syst.*, p. 9.

śāni (SITI), Dravidian; wife; a term by which a Brāhmaṇa woman was referred to.

śanivāra-maṇḍapa (*A.R. Ep.*, 1958-59, p.13), name of a building attached to a temple apparently meant for some function held there on Saturdays; cf. *vaikkāṇikku-maṇḍapa* under *maṇḍapa*.

sañjāti (LP), cf. *rāja-sañjātyāṁ kartavyaḥ*, 'may be made a government property.'

Sañjīva-rāja, cf. *Sañjīvarāyar* (SITI), name of Hanumān.

saṅkācitaka (IE 8-8), a loop; same as Sanskrit *kāca*.

saṅkalpa (Chamba), also called *saṅkalpa-hast-odaka*; libation of water; donation.

saṅkara (EI 9), also called *saṅkuru*; a double sack.

śaṅkar-ākṣi (IE 7-1-2), 'three'.

saṅketa, cf. *sva-saṅketa* (LP), 'one's own special arrangement'.

śaṅkha (CII 3, etc.), conch-shell as ane mblem on seals; cf. *śaṅghu* (ASLV), the use of which was sometimes granted by kings to their favourites as a privilege.

śaṅkhadhārā, cf. *śaṁkudhāra* (CITD); Telugu; continuous blowing of the conch-shell. See *Śaṅkhadhārin*.

Śaṅkhadhārin (IE 8-3), blower of the conch-shell; sometimes mentioned as a *Pātra*.

Śaṅkhakāra (EI 28), also called *Śāṅkhika* (q.v.); maker of conch-shell bangles.

Śaṅkhika, *Śāṅkhika* (EI 24, 28), same as *Śaṅkhakāra* (q.v.), worker on conch-shells.

saṅkramaṇa (CII 3; IA 17), also called *saṅkrānti*; the entrance of the sun into a sign of the zodiac; regarded as an auspicious time for performing religiousduties.

saṅkrānti (CII 3; IA 17), same as *saṅkramaṇa* (q.v.).

(*IE* 7-1-2), 'twelve'.

ṣaṇmukha-bāhu (IE 7-1-2), 'twelve'.

sannāha (LP), armour.

Sannidhātṛ (EI 27), official in charge of the receipt of various articles into the king's treasury, according to some (HRS); superintendent of the construction of the royal treasury, store houses, etc., according to others. See *Artha-śāstra*, II. 5; cf. I.10 and 12; *Ep. Ind.*, Vol. VIII, pp. 138, 141; Vol. XI, pp. 93-94.

sannidhi, cf. *sannadi* (SII 1), presence of a deity; the front of a temple.

Sanniyuktaka (*Ind. Ant.*, Vol. XVII, p. 11, text line 14), same as *Tanniyuktaka* or a mistake for it.

Sanskrit, Anglicised form of *Saṁskṛta*, the name of the sacred language of the Indians.

santa (CITD), Telugu-Kannaḍa; a fair or market day.

(*EI* 14), name of a measure or a coin; probably, a small coin (*Ep. Ind.*, Vol. XV, p. 309).

santai (ASLV), a weekly fair.

santaka (EI 27; CII 3), Prakrit; 'belonging to'; sometimes Sanskritised as *satka*. Sometimes *santaka* (also *santika* apparently used in the same sense) has been regarded as meaning 'a territorial unit'; supposed similarly to mean 'a servant' (EI 23) or 'an officer' (EI 24).

Sāntakika (IE 8-3), official designation of uncertain import.

santāna (SITI), lineage.

(*BL*), cf. a Jain religious teacher described as belonging to the *paṭṭa* of another teacher and the *santāna* of a third teacher.

(*IA* 20), used in the sense of *āmnāya* or *kula-krama*.

(*EI* 6), same as *santānaka*, *santati*; seven in number.

santāna-śāpa (SITI), curse that prevents progeny.

Santānika-śaiva (SITI), Śaivas who belong to the line of *ācāryas* of the *santāna-kuravar*.

santati (SITI), lineage. Cf. also *sapta-santati* (EI 14) and *santānaka* (under *santāna*).

santati-praveśam (SITI), 'from generation to generation'.

Śānti, a priest in a temple; cf. Tamil-Sanskrit *Mel-śānti*; also cf. *Śāntikāra*, of which *Śānti* seems to be an abbreviation.

śānti (EI 33), a propitiatory rite; cf. *śānty-āgāra*.

santika (EI 25), proximity, presence.

Śāntikāra (SITI), a temple priest; also known as *Śāntiy-aḍigal* and *Śānti-śeyyān*.

santīraṇā, cf. *artha-santīraṇā* (CII 1), despatch of business.

Śānti-vārika (EI 12, 30, 33), priest in charge of the performance of propitiatory rites or the priest who provides for *śānti-vāri*, 'propitiatory water'.

śānty-āgāra (EI 12, 30), room wherein a bath is taken with the propitiatory water after a sacrifice; the room for performing propitiatory rites. See *Śāntyāgārika*, *Śāntyāgār-ādhikṛta*.

Śāntyāgār-ādhikṛta (EI 30), priest in charge of the room for the performance of propitiatory rites. Cf. *śānty-āgāra*, *Śānty-āgārika*.

Śāntyāgārika (EI 30), same as *Śāntyāgār-ādhikṛta*.

Shaonano Shao (EI 30), known from the legend of Kuṣāṇa coins; same as *Sāhānuṣāhī* (q.v.), Persian *Shāhān Shāh*.

Sapādalakṣa (IE 8-4), name of two territories so called with reference to the theoretical number of villages in each of them. Cf. *Pādonalakṣa*.

sapiṇḍīkaraṇa-śrāddha (CII 4), a ceremony.

sapta-kṣetra (IA 19), Jain; seven spheres of action.

Saptama-cakravartin (LP), 'the seventh emperor', i. e. the ruling monarch; according to the *Abhidhānacintāmaṇi*, the six older *Cakravartins* are: *Māndhātā Dhundhumāraś=ca Hariścandraḥ Purūravāḥ* I *Bharataḥ Kārtavīryaś=ca ṣaḍ=ete cakravartinaḥ* II

Sapta-mātṛ (EI 23), the seven Divine Mothers.

Sapt-āmātya (EI 27), an officer in charge of seven departments. Cf. *Pañca-karaṇ-ādhikṛta*, etc.

sapt-āmbhodhi (EI 16), name of a *mahādāna*; same as *sapta-sāgara*.

sapt-āṅga (CII CITD), the seven constitutent parts of a kingdom, viz., king, ministers, allies, treasury, territory, forts and forces.

sapta-sāgara (EI 24), name of a *mahādāna*; same as *sapt-āmbhodhi*.

sapta-santāna (SITI), also called *sapta-santati*; merit equal to that obtainable through progeny from their performance of seven kinds of great deeds, viz. digging of tanks, hoarding of treasure, founding of *agrahāras*, erection of temples, creation of flower gardens, getting literary works written by poets, and the establishment of Choultries. An inscription (*Ep. Ind.*, Vol. III, pp. 88 ff.) mentions the following seven meritorious acts a man ought to perform during his lifetime; viz. procreation of sons, accumulation of wealth, planting of groves, helping people (Brāhmaṇas) to marry, getting poems composed, erection of temples and excavation of tanks.

sapta-santati (SITI), same as *sapta-santāna*.

sapta-vidhi (LP), probably, seven kinds of defects.

śara (IE 7-1-2), 'five'.

sārā (EI 9; LP), care; cf. *etair=aṣṭabhir=goṣṭhikaiḥ...sārā karaṇīyā*, '[this place of worship] has to be taken care of by the following eight trustees'. Cf. also Gujarātī *sāravār*.

(*EI* 8, 11), supervision.

Śarabhaṅga (IE 8-3; 8-8; EI 23), a leader of forces; an officer of the military department; possibly, a military governor; same as Persian *Sarhang* and Hindī *Seräṅg*; also spelt *Sarabhaṅga* and *Sarobhaṅga*; Wilson's Glossary explains *Sarhang* as 'a commander' and says, "but [it is] generally applied in India to the headman of a native crew, whether on board a ship or a boat; also to the headman of a gang of natives attached to artillery, dragging guns, or to the a: my in general, as tent-pitchers, and the like, or to the head of gangs of a superior order of labourers employed in public or private works, in docks, buildings, etc.' Cf. Vogel, *Ant. Ch. St.*, pp. 123, 166 (spelt *Sarobhaṅga*), *Ind. Cult.*, Vol. VII, p. 309. Kane (*Hist. Dharm.*, Vol. III, p. 1005) is certainly wrong when he thinks that it may be connected with *śarayantra* and *Śarayantrin* (a title bestowed in Mithilā upon a very learned man who faced the ordeal of answering satisfactorily all questions on any *śāstra* put to him by learned *Ācāryas* and also the questions put by common people). See *Ep. Ind.*, Vol. XXXV, pp. 95 ff. See *Sarāṅgha*, *Sarāhang*, etc.

Sāradā, name of the alphabet which developed out of late Brāhmī and was prevalent in the Kashmir region.

Sarāhang (IA 20), also called *Sarang*, *Sarhang*, etc. See *Sarāṅgha*, *Śarabhaṅga*.

Śaraṇāgata-vajrapañjara (*Ep. Ind.*, Vol. XXXIII, p. 317), 'the impregnable shelter for one who seeks for it'; a subordinate title of the Kannaḍa-speaking area; used by the Sena kings of Bengal because they hailed from the same region.

Sarang (IA 20), also called *Sarhang*, *Sarāhang*, etc. ; see *Sarāṅgha*, *Śarabhaṅga*, etc.

Sarāṅgha (IE 8-3), Persian *Sarhang* and Indian *Śarabhaṅga*, *Serāṅg*, etc. cf. *Giligittā-sarāṅgha*, 'the chief of the army at Gilgit', in the Hatun inscription of Paṭoladeva (*Ep. Ind.*, Vol. XXX, p. 228).

Sarasvatī-bhāṇḍāra (EI 25; SITI), a library. Cf. *Sarasvatī-bhāṇḍārika*.

Sarasvatī-bhāṇḍārika (EI 25), librarian. Cf. *Sarasvatī-bhāṇḍāra*.

śarayantra, Maithilī; test [prevalent in Mithilā] of the scholarship of one who is prepared to answer any question on any *śāstra* put to him by any other scholar or by the common people. See *Proc. AIOC*, Benares, 1943; Kane, *Hist. Dharm.*, Vol. III, p. 1005.

śarayantraka (IE 3-1), same as *sūtra*; the string passing through the hole in the leaves of manuscripts for holding them together (*Vāsavadatta*, Hall's ed., p. 250).

Śarayantrin (EI 35), one who has been successful in the *śarayantra* test of Mithilā. See *śarayantra*.

sārayitvā (LP), 'having finished'; cf. Gujarātī *sārvuṁ*, 'to accomplish'.

Sārdhañcara, *Sārdhañcarī* (LL), companion of a Jain monk.

Sārdhaṁvihārin, cf. *Sādhyavihāri* (*Ep. Ind.*, Vol. XXXIV,

p. 10), Pāli *saddhivihāri*; one's fellow-priest living at the same monastery; a fellow-student. Cf. F. Edgerton, *Bud. Hyb. Sans. Gram. Dict.*, Vol. II, p. 593. See *Sadhryagvihārin.*

Sarhang (IE 8-3; IA 20), Persian; see *Śarabhaṅga*, etc.

śarīra (SITI), person; individual.

(*EI* 24; ML), corporeal relics of the Buddha.

Sarobhaṅga (IE 8-3), same as *Śarabhaṅga* or *Sarabhaṅga* (q.v.).

sarpa (IE 7-1-2), 'eight'.

sarpa-bali (IA 19), an offering in snake-worship.

sarṣapa, a small unit of measurement; sometimes specified as 'red' (*JNSI*, Vol. XVI, p. 48).

Sārthavāha (IE 8-3; EI 24, 31; BL; LL), a trader, a merchant; designation of a member of the mercantile community represented on an administrative board like the *Pañcāyat.*

Sārthavāhinī (EI 1, 24), wife of a merchant (*Sārthavāha*) or a female merchant.

sārtha-vahitra (IE 8-3), probably, a cart-load of articles for sale.

sārūpya (CITD), assimilation in the deity, one of the four states of *mukti.*

Sārvabhauma (EI 7, 27, 30, 32), title of imperial rulers.

sarv-ābhyantara-siddhi (IA 19; SII 11-1), a fiscal term denoting full and complete right of enjoyment of agricultural income or internal revenue or taxes to be paid to the village authorities; cf. *sarv-ābhyantara-siddhyā* (IA 18), also *abhyantara-siddhi.*

Sarva-daṇḍa-nāyaka (CII 3; IA 9; IA BL), official designation; 'lord of all the forces'; cf. *Samasta-sainy-ādhipati.* See *Daṇḍa-nāyaka*, *Mahādaṇḍanāyaka*, *Sarva-mahā-daṇḍanāyaka.* Cf. *Ind. Ant.*, Vol. VIII, p. 19; Vol. IX, p. 167.

Sarva-deś-ādhikārin (AI 7), chief minister; see *Deśādhikṛta*, *Sarv-ādhikārin*, etc.

Sarv-ādhikār-ādhikṛta (EI 31), chief minister or administrator; same as *Sarv-ādhikārin*, *Sarv-ādhyakṣa*, etc.

Sarv-ādhikāra-karaṇa (EI 30), probably , the office of the chief secretary, administrator or minister.

Sarv-ādhikāra-niyukta (EI 32), official designation; same as *Sarv-ādhikārin*, *Sarv-ādhyakṣa*, etc.

Sarv-ādhikārin (IE 8-3; EI 19; CII 4; HD), prime minister (cf. *Rājataraṅgiṇī*, VII. 568); minister plenipotentiary or viceroy; sometimes also called *Senāpati*, *Mahāpradhāna*, *Hiriya-bhaṇḍāgārin*, *Mahāsāmanta*, *Sen-ādi-bāhattara-niyog-ādhipati*, *Daṇḍanāyaka*, *Mahāpasāyita*, *Amātya*, *Paramaviśvāsin* or *Mahāparamaviśvāsin*, etc., additionally.

(*IE* 8-3), a governor or chief administrator (cf. 'the *Sarv-ādhikārin* of Hagaraṭage-300').

Sarv-ādhyakṣa (EI 24,27;CII 3), literally,a general superintendent; probably, the chief minister or administrator; same as *Sarv-ādhikārin*.

Sarv-ādhikṛta (HD), same as *Sarv-ādhikārin*, etc. Cf. *Ep. Ind.*, Vol. XIV, pp. 360, 362. See *Mahāsarvādhikṛta*.

sarv-āgrahāra (EI 21), same as *sarva-mānya*.

sarva-jāta, cf. *sarva-jātaa-bhoga-nirastyā* (EI 8-5), 'with all kinds of the [king's] rights renounced'.

sarva-mānya (IE 8-5, SITI; CITD), a free tenure; a rent-free holding; land exempted from taxes; lands and villages fully exempt from all taxes. This corresponds to the *iṟaiyili* class of land mentioned in the Coḻa inscriptions. Often this is associated with *aṣṭa-bhoga*, i.e. the eight forms of enjoying the land. For a discussion of this form of land tenure, see *JAHRS*, Vol. X, pp. 123-32. It is noteworthy that even the so-called tax-free (*iṟaiyili*) lands paid to the king certain dues of the nature of taxes. See K.A. Nilakanta Sastri, *The Coḻas*, 2nd ed., pp. 534-35. See *sarva-namasya*, etc.

sarva-medha (EI 4), name of a sacrifice.

sarva-namaskṛta (IA 8), same as *sarva-namasya*.

sarva-namasya (IE 8-5; EI 23; CITD), a rent-free holding; same as *sarva-mānya*, *sarva-namaskṛta*, *namasya-vṛtti*.

sarva-niyoga (EI 7), exclusive property.

Sarva-sainy-ādhikārin (IE 8-3), commander-in-chief; cf. *Maneya-samasta-sainy-ādhipati*, commander of all the soldiers in the royal household; also cf. *Sarva-daṇḍa-nāyaka*.

sarvasva-haraṇa (SITI), forfeiture of one's entire property.

Sarva-tantr-ādhikṛta (*Ep. Ind.*, Vol. XXIV pp. 144-45), a superintendent of all departments; but *tantra* is used in South Indian records in the sense of 'the army'. See *tantra*, *Tantr-ādhikārin*, etc.

sarvatobhadra (EI 9), a building having doors on all the four sides.

sarvatobhadrikā (LL; HA), quadruple image showing a Jina (or several Jinas) on each of the four faces; same as *caumukha*.

Sarvavādināyaka (EI 10), explained as 'superintendent of the intelligence department'; probably, 'the chief court Pandit.'

sarv-āya (EI 15), all the usual dues.

sarvīya (EI 13), 'good to all'.

śāsana (EI 19; IA 20), order, a royal edict; any royal record (cf. *vijaya-śāsana*).

(*IE* 8-4; EI 13, 23; CII 3; BL), a charter; land or village granted by a charter; rent-free land or village; sometimes suffixed to the names of localities which were once rent-free holdings. See also *tāmra-śāsana*, a technical term for a deed of conveyance on copper-plates.

(*EI* 9, 10), a doctrine; religion or religious faith.

Śāsana-baddha (SITI), people bound by a royal charter; original grantees of a charter.

Śāsana-bhāṇḍārin (EI 25), official designation; cf. *Śāsan-ādhikārin*, etc.

Śāsanadevī (IA 18), divine female messenger of a Jain Arhat; same as *Śāsana-sundarī*.

Śāsan-ādhikārika (*Ep. Ind.*, Vol. XII, p. 155, text line 85), same as *Śāsan-ādhikārin*, etc.; officer in charge of grants (or their writing or issue), mentioned along with *Dān-ādhikārin*, 'officer in charge of gifts'.

Śāsan-ādhikārin (EI 28, 31), officer in charge of royal grants or their issue, who was often the writer of documents; same as *Śāsan-ādhikārika*, etc.

śāsana-paṭā (Chamba, etc.), charter; same as Sanskrit *śāsana-paṭṭaka*.

śāsana-maryādā (EI 15), specification of privileges by a charter.

śāsan-ārdhika (IE 8-5; 12, 28), name of a levy; probably, the half of the cultivator's share of the produce of the land in the gift village.

Śāsayitṛ (EI 12; BL), one who is responsible for getting a royal grant executed; cf. *Dūtaka*, *Lekhayitṛ*, *Ājñāpti*.

Śāsana-sañcārin (EI 8, 24), same as *Ājñā-sañcārin*; an official messenger.

Śāsana-sundarī (IA 30), Jain; same as *Śāsanadevī*.

Śāsanika-kāyastha (EI 11), writer of a grant.

śaśāṅka (IE 7-71-2), 'one'.

ṣaṣghānī, coins issued by the Tughlaq Sulṭāns, 4 *jitals* in weight (*JNSI*, Vol. XVI, p. 44); same as *chagānī*, equal to $\frac{3}{4}$ of a *ṭaṅka* (*ibid.*, Vol. XXII, p. 198). See *śāśukāni.*

śaśin (EI 25), 'one'.

Ṣaṣṭh-ādhikṛta (IE 8-3; HD), a collector of the king's grain share which was originally one-sixth of the produce according to many authorities; cf. *Dhruvasthān-ādhikaraṇika.* See Ghoshal, *H. Rev. Syst.*, p. 246.

ṣaṣṭhatapa (IA 19), Jain; a kind of penance.

ṣaṣṭhī-amāvāsyā, cf. *caṭṭī-amavāse* (EI 5), new-moon following the *campā-ṣaṣṭhī.*

Saṣṭirātra (BL), name of a sacrifice.

śāstra (IE 7-1-2), 'six'.

śāśukāni, Indianised form of *ṣaṣghānī*; also called *śāśukāni-ṭaṅka.* See *JNSI*, Vol. XVI, 'The Śāṇa', p. 5.

śāśvatīya (SITI), perpetuity, eternity.

śata, cf. *ekādaśa-śata* (ML), 'one hundred and eleven'.

Sāta (EI 32), abbreviation of the name *Śātavāhana* or *Śātakarṇi.*

śataghnī (IA 7, 12), a gun or canon according to late works; a mechanical weapon placed at the gate of forts according to the *Vasudevahiṇḍī* (*Journ. Or. Inst.*, Vol. X, No. 1, p. 15). See *kālacakra.*

śatamāna, name of a coin; a silver coin weighing 320 *ratis* (rarely also 160 *ratis*); also called *pala, niṣka, śukti, aṣṭamikā* and *nalā*; wrongly regarded as 100 *ratis* in weight. See *JNSI*, Vol. XVI, pp. 41, 46-47. For *śatamāna* as a gold coin, see *ibid.*, Vol. XV, p. 140.

śatāṅga (EI 3), a car.

ṣaṭ-catuṣkikā, cf. *cha-cokī.*

satera, sateraka, same as Greek *stater*; regarded as equal to two *dīnāras* (*JNSI*, Vol. XV, p. 153).

satī (EI 6, 30; CII 3, 4; BL; CITD), literally, 'a chaste woman'; really 'a woman burning herself with her husband'.

(*EI* 6, 30), self-immolation of a widow usually on the funeral pyre of her husband; usually spelt *suttee* in English.

śatikā (EI 28), cf. *saïkā.*

sa-til-odaka (IA 19), cf. *sa-til-odakena vidhinā*; same as *udaka-pūrvam*, etc.

satka (EI 1, 13; IA 17), Sanskritised from Prakrit *santaka*; 'the holding of...', 'belonging to...'.

ṣaṭ-karman (SII 1), the six duties of a Brāhmaṇa.

ṣaṭpañcāśat, 'all'; cf. *ṣaṭpañcāśad-deśa*=*chappanna-deśa* (*Ep. Ind.*, Vol. V, p. 217, note 7), literally, 'fiftysix countries'; but really, 'all the world'.

ṣaṭ-paṇa, cf. *aṟuvaṇa*.

Ṣatpuruṣa (LL), a Buddhist saint.

satra (EI 10, 19, 23, 26), same as *sattra*.

sattra (SII 1; CII 3, 4), 'a charitable feeding house'; an alms-house; sometimes used to indicate one of the five *mahāyajñas*, usually called *atithi*. See *Ep. Ind.*, Vol. VII, p. 46, note 8.

(*EI* 10, 19, 23), also spelt *satra*; hospitality to guests; one of the five *mahāyajñas*.

(*IA* 15), a hall for the charitable distribution of food, etc. Cf. *satra-śālā* (*SII* 11-1), etc.

satr-āgāra (LP), a house where alms are distributed. Cf. *satra-śālā*.

satr-āgāra-karaṇa, cf. *karaṇa* (LP); department of *Dharmaśālās*.

Satrap (IA 20), Greek; same as *Khshathrapāvan*, *Kṣatrapa*, *Sertīp*.

Sattrapati (BL), priest in charge of a sacrificial session.

ṣaṭriṁśat, literally, 'thirtysix', but actually 'all' (*Ep. Ind.*, Vol. XXX, p. 115). See *aṣṭādaśa*, *ṣaṭpañcāśat*, etc.

ṣaṭtriṁśad-daṇḍ-āyudha (LP), thirtysix (really, all), kinds of weapons; sometimes enumerated as:

Cakra pāsa mogaru gadā ghana tomara tīraha ।
sakati sūla trisūla vajra kātara karaḍaṁḍha ॥
Paṭukaṭārī kaṁta sarasī ghaḍu avājī ।
kaṇīu churī khaḍga nāli golā nārājī ॥
ṣaṁḍuṁ ṣapnu muṁsala hala sīṁgani pharasī gupati gaṇi ।
niṣaṁga śāṁgi aṁkuśa guruja kuhaka bāṇa batrīsa bhaṇi ॥

Cf. *Prācīnagurjarakāvyasaṁgraha*, G.O.S., pp. 106-07.

śāttvika-dāna (SITI), gift without the pouring of water and therefore not expecting any merit in return for the donation.

Satyadharma-sthita (IE 8-2), 'adherent of the true religion'; same as *Dharma-sthita*; epithet of a Kuṣāṇa king probably pointing to his Buddhist faith.

Satya-jñāna-dariśanigaḻ (SITI), followers of a sect of Śaivism;

evidently those belonging to the lineage of Mĕykaṇḍār.

Śau, abbreviation of *Śaulkika* or *Śauṇḍika* (*A. R. Ep.*, 1953-54, No. B 117).

saudha (IA 15), used in the sense of *brahmapurī*, 'a Brāhmaṇa settlement'.

Saugandhika, cf. Prakrit *Sagandhaka* (EI 18); a dealer in scents or superintendent of the perfumery.

Saugata-parivrājaka (BL), a Buddhist medicant.

Śaulkika (IE 8-3; CII 3, 4; EI 30; HD), toll-collector or customs officer; officer in charge of collecting customs duties; superintendent of tolls or customs duties. See *Yājñavalkyasmṛti*, II. 173; *CII*, Vol. III, pp. 50, 52; Ghoshal, *H. Rev. Syst.*, p. 246.

saumya (EI 27), lunar or auspicious.

Śaunika (IE 8-3), superintendent of slaughter-houses and the sale of meat.

Śauṇḍika (IE 8-5), vintner.

Sautrika (LL), weaver.

sauvarṇa (EI 19), name of a coin; cf. *suvarṇa*.

Sauvarṇika (HD), cf. Prakrit *Sovaṇika* (EI 10), a goldsmith; the State goldsmith. See *Hist. Dharm.*, Vol. III, pp. 144-45. See *Hairaṇyika*, etc.

sauvarṇika (HRS), profits of the royal monopoly of manufacture of gold and silver articles, as indicated by the *Arthaśāstra*.

sava (IE 8-1), contraction of Prakrit *savachara*=Sanskrit *saṁvatsara*.

śāvaḍi (IE 8-4), a subdivision; same as *uśāvaḍi* or *cāvaḍi*.

savarṇa-vṛtti (SITI), profession of writing documents.

Sāvu (EI 9; CII 4), a title; same as *Sāhu* (Sanskrit *Sādhu*).

śaya (IE 3-4), derived from a Chinese word; paper.

sāyaka (IE 7-1-2), 'five'.

sāyana (CII 3), 'inclusive of precission of the equinoxes'.

śayana-pūjā (IE 8-8), a rite.

śayanīya, a cot; cf. *śayanīy-āsana-siddānnaṁ na dāpayet* (*Ep. Ind.*, Vol. XXX, p. 171).

sāyara (*PJS*), Arabic *shāher*; a tax on palm-tree juice.

Śayyāgrāhaka (HD), explained as 'the guardian of the bedchamber.' See A.S. Gadre, *Imp. Ins. Bar. St.*, p. 72. Cf. *Śayyāpāla*, *Vāsāgārika*, *Vitān-ādhipa*.

Śayyāpāla (EI 25; HD), officer in charge of the king's bed

(i. e. bed-chamber); guardian of the bed-chamber. See *Śayyāgrāhaka*, *Vāsāgārika*, *Vitān-ādhipa*.

seiā (IE 8-8), Prakrit; same as Sanskrit *setikā* (q.v.); cf. *seigā*.

seigā (IE 8-8), Prakrit; same as Sanskrit *setikā* (q.v.); cf. *seiā*.

Segāṇa (BL), official designation of uncertain import, found in the Chamba inscriptions.

śeka (EI 11), same as Sanskrit *śikya*, a loop or swing made of rope and suspended from the ends of a pole placed on one's shoulder for carrying loads, or the load itself. Cf. *saṁkācitaka*.

Sekyakāra (EI 12; BL), a brazier; secondarily, an engraver; cf. Bengali *seṅkrā*, a goldsmith.

Selahasta (EI 11), probably, the collector of the king's grain share.

senā-bhakta (HRS), contribution of oil, rice, etc., which the villagers had to pay to the royal army on march, as suggested by the *Arthaśāstra*.

Sena-bhoga, cf. *Śeṇai-bhogam* (SITI), an accountant. See *Śāṇa-bhoga*, *Senabova*.

Senabhogika (EI 18; HD), same as *Senabova*, etc.; a clerk or an accountant-clerk. Cf. *Ep. Ind.*, Vol. VI, p. 285.

Senabova (EI 5, 10; IA 18; SII 11-1), a clerk; an accountant; a village accountant; modern *Śānabhoga* or *Kuḷkarṇī*.

Sen-ādhikārika (EI 23), same as *Senāpati*, *Sen-ādhipati*, etc.; a general.

Sen-ādhipa (BL), 'leader of forces'. See *Senāpati*, etc.

Sen-ādhipati (IE 8-3; EI 23 ; SII 11-1), same as *Sen-ādhikārika*, etc.; sometimes also called *Mahāpradhāna*, *Hĕri-sandhivigrahin*, *Kaḍita-vĕrgaḍĕ*, etc., additionally. Cf. *Mahā-senādhipati*, *Senāpati*, etc.

Sen-ādi-bāhattara-niyog-ādhiṣṭhāyaka (IE 8-2; EI 5), superintendent of all appointments including those in the army.

Sena-gaṇa (SITI), a division of the Jain community; also known as *Sen-ānvaya*.

Senāgopa (LL), a general; same as *Senāpati*, etc.

sen-āṅga (IE 7-1-2), 'four'.

Senai-mudaliyār (SITI), Tamil; same as Sanskrit-Tamil *Senāpatiy-āḻvār*; name of the god Viṣvaksenai.

Senaiy-aḻṅgāḍika (SITI), a class of merchants who follow

the army with their merchandise; a class of cloth merchants.

senānī-netra (IE 7-1-2), 'twelve'.

Senāpati (IE 8-3), leader of forces; mentioned separately along with *Bal-ādhyakṣa*; probably, a subordinate of the latter; the military governor of a district, according to some (HD); commander-in-chief (ASLV), also called *Sarva-sainy-ādhikārin* and *Dalavāya*, i.e. the chief officer in charge of the military department. See *Bṛhaspati* quoted by Viśvarūpa on *Yājñavalkyasmṛti*, I. 307; *Ind. Ant.*, Vol. XV, p. 187. Puṣyamitra, the founder of the Śuṅga dynasty, was called *Senāpati* even after his accession to the Maurya throne. See *Sen-ādhipa*, etc.; cf. also *Anusenāpati* (EI 18).

(*IE* 8-3), sometimes called *Mahāpradhāna*, *Bāhattara-niyogādhiṣṭhāyaka*, *Paṭṭa-sāhan-ādhipati*, etc., additionally.

senāpati-pperuvilai (SITI), Sanskrit-Tamil; the sale of lands of a Viṣṇu temple executed in the name of Senai-mudaliyār, i. e. the god Viṣvaksenai.

Senāpatiy-āḻvār (SITI), Sanskrit-Tamil; same as *Senai-mudaliyār*, i. e. the god Viṣvaksenai.

ser (Chamba), also called *seri*; crown land; state demesne.

(*Chamba*, etc.), a weight equal to 80 *tolās*.

Seraṅg (IE), see *Śarabhaṅga*, etc.

seri (Chamba), same as *ser*; crown-land.

Sertīp (IA 20), Persian; same as Old Persian *Khshthrapāvan* and Indian *Kṣatrapa*.

śervai (ASLV), Tamil; derived from Sanskrit *sevā* (*q.v.*); a service *inām*.

śeṣa-śirṣa (IE 7-1-2), 'one thousand'.

sesi-biyyamu (CITD), Telugu-Kannaḍa; *sesi* means the remains of flowers, raw rice and other offerings made to an idol or used in a *śubha-kārya* and afterwards distributed among the worshippers and attendants. The expression probably means raw rice over which incantations have been pronounced and which is thrown on the heads of the bride and bridegroom during the marriage ceremony and in connection with similar other rites.

setikā (IE 8-5; EI 25), Prakrit *seiā*, *seigā*; a measure of weight equal to two handfuls.

Śeṭṭi (ASLV), Sanskrit *Śreṣṭhin*; the leading member of a guild. Cf. *Nagar-seṭh*, *Nagara-śreṣṭhin*.

Śeṭṭi-Pattaṇasvāmin (ASLV), designation of the president of a merchants' guild. Cf. *Nagar-seṭh*, *Nagara-śreṣṭhin*.

setu, embankment; income or taxes resulting from it (Ghoshal, *H. Rev. Syst.*, pp. 108-09).

sevā, cf. Tamil *sevai*, *śervai* (SITI); service; *inām* for services; tax-free land given to servants for enjoyment in lieu of salary.

Sevaka (SITI), a soldier; cf. *sevaka-ttevai* (SITI), expenses in connection with the supply and maintenance of retainers of chiefs and officers during their visit to a place.

śeviḍu (SITI), Tamil; a small grain measure; $\frac{1}{5}$ of an *āḷākku*.

Shāh (IE 8-2; EI 30), Persian; royal title; same as Old Persian *Khshāyathiya*. See *Sāhī*.

śibara, *sibara* (CII 4), a farm-house. But cf. *śaibara*, *śaivara*.

Siddha (CII 4), a person possessing miraculous powers; an emancipated person.

(*CII* 3), 'a perfect one'; the epithet of a class of Jain saints who are invoked in the plural.

(*LL*), a Jain saint.

(*CII* 4), cf. *siddham* (q.v.), used at the beginning of inscriptions to ensure the success of the undertaking and meaning *siddhir=astu*, 'let there be success'. Cf. *siddhi*.

(*IE* 7-1-2), 'twenty-four'.

siddha, (*IE* 8-5), income from land under cultivation. See *siddh-āya*, etc.

(*SITI*), also called *siddhi*; the right of cultivating land; one of the eight kinds of enjoying landed property; may be the same as *abbyantara-siddhi*. See *siddha*, *siddh-āya*, *ūrdhv-ādhaḥ-siddhi*.

siddha-cakra (EI 2), a *yantra* for worship.

siddham (EI30; CII 3), literally, 'success has been attained'; an invocation found in early inscriptions at the commencement of the text; used in the sense of *siddhir=astu*, 'let there be success'; sometimes confused with the *praṇava*; generally indicated in later records by a symbol having several varieties; sometimes indicated by the letter *cha*. Cf. *siddhi*

Siddhamātṛkā, name of the Indian alphabet which is derived from Late Brāhmī and from which are derived North Indian alphabets like Nāgarī; wrongly called Kuṭila, etc.

siddh-ānna (IE 8-8), cooked rice or uncooked food (cf. Hindī *sīdhā*).

siddhānta (CII 4), 'an established doctrine'; sometimes used to indicate the Śaiva doctrine or religion (SITI).

Cf. Lākula-siddhānta (EI 32), doctrine of the Śaiva teacher Lakula (Lakulīśa).

siddhānta-darśana (EI 32), philosophy.

siddha-pīṭha, see *yoga-pīṭha.*

siddha-sādhya (EI 13), present income and the income that may accrue in future.

siddha-sthāna (EI 22), the place sanctified by a holy man.

siddh-āya (EI 23; SII 11-2; ASLV), fixed income; regular income; same as Tamil *sidd-āyam*, sometimes explained as 'a tax' (EI 27); probably, agricultural income.

(*SITI*), a fixed assessment; minor taxes; minor taxes payable in cash in the days of the Vijayanagara kings; also written in Tamil as *sidd-āyam*, *sitt-āyam*. See *pratiṣiddh-āya.*

siddh-āyatana (EI 33), cf. *pūrva-siddh-āyatana* (Buddhist); temple associated with a *Siddha.*

siddhi (CII 4), emancipation; sometimes used at the beginning of documents to ensure the success of the undertaking, as *siddham* in early inscriptions, and meaning *siddhir=astu.*

(*SITI*), same as *siddham*, the right of cultivating land.

Cf. *ūrdhv-ādhaḥ-siddhi-yutā* (IA 18), together with income from horticulture and agriculture; cf. *sa-bāhy-ābhyantara-siddhi*, *siddhi* meaning 'income'. (*IE* 7-1-2), 'eight'.

śīghra-likhita, a document written in a quick hand or cursive characters (*SII*, Vol. XI, Part i, p. 29, No. 42).

siglos (IE 8-8), name of the old silver coin of the Persians (86.45 grains or 5.6 grammes).

sikāvaṇa (EI 27), name of a tax.

śikhara (SITI; CITD), top portion of the turret built over the main shrine and the gateway of a temple; the top of the *gopura* or *vimāna* of a temple.

śikhin (IE 7-1-2), 'three'.

śilā (IA 23), [an inscription on] stone.

śilā-gṛha (EI 22), a stone mansion.

śilā-guṇṭha (EI 12), Sanskrit-Telugu; a pond with a demarcation stone.

śilā-karmānta (LL), stone-work.

Śilā-kūṭa (EI 1), a stone-cutter; cf. *Śilā-kuṭṭa.*

Śilā-kuṭṭa (IA 15), a stone-cutter; cf. *Śilā-kūṭa.*

śilā-laṣṭi (CII 4), Sanskrit *śilā-yaṣṭi*; memorial pillar of stone.

śilā-lekha (IA 30; SITI), writing on a stone; an inscription on stone.

śīlana (CII 1), same as *anuśīlana*; practice.

śīla-patra (LP), certificate of good character.

śilā-prāveśa (IA 9), laying the corner-stone of a building.

śilā-śāsana (IA 30), a stone-charter; a document engraved on stone.

Śilpin (EI 4, 8; BL), epithet of an artist or artisan; generally, applied to engravers of inscriptions.

Śilpakāra (EI 32), same as *Śilpin*.

śilotara (EI 32), also called *śilotarī, śilotra, śilotrī, śilottara*; name of a tax or income; cf. *śrotaka*.

śilotarī (EI 32), see *śilotara*, etc.

śilotra (EI 32), see *śilotara*, etc.

śilotrī (EI 32), see *śilotara*, etc.

śilottara (EI 32), see *śilotara*, etc.

śilvari (EI 23), Tamil; name of a tax.

sīma (IA 18), used for 'country' in the areas on the banks of the Kṛṣṇā and the Godāvarī.

Cf. Kona-sīma (EI 32), also called a *deśa, maṇḍala, sthala*, etc.

sīmā (EI 11), five types enumerated by Nārada: *Dhvajinī matsyinī c=aiva naidhānī bhaya-varjitā| rājaśāsana-nītā ca sīmā pañca-vidhā smṛtā* (i.e. big trees or hills, rivers or tanks, underground signs and artificial marks made by men and by the king's order).

Cf. Tamil *śīrmai, śīmai* (SITI), a territorial division; also called *sīman*.

Sīmakarmakara (HD), officer in charge of boundaries or of boundary disputes. See *CII*, Vol. III, pp. 213, 216.

sīman (IE 8-4; ASLV), Kannaḍa *sīmĕ*; a small territorial unit like a Parganā; the sub-division of a district; sometimes used to indicate 'a province'.

sīmā-vivāda, cf. Tamil *śīmai-vivādam* (SITI), a boundary dispute.

Sīmĕhabbaruva (ASLV), an officer associated with the administrative unit called *sīmai*.

siṁhanikā, service rendered in lieu of taxes (Ghoshal, *H. Rev. Syst.*, p.28).

siṁha-pāda, cf. Tamil *śiṅga-pādam* (SITI), legs of a vessel or vessel-stand in the shape of lion's feet.

siṁh-āsana (EI 29), literally, 'the lion-seat'; the throne which was one of the royal insignia. Cf. *siṁha-sthāna*.

Siṁhāsan-ādhipati (EI 25), officer in charge of the king's throne.

siṁha-stambha (LL), lion-pillar.

siṁha-sthāna (LL), a lion-seat; same as *siṁh-āsana*.

sindhu (IE 7-1-2), 'four'.

sindūra (IA 19), corruption of *sindhura*, an elephant.

sīrā (IA 18), a land measure equal to four *halas*. See *hala*.

Śiraḥ-pradhānin (ASLV), cf. Tamil *Śirappradāni* (SITI), a senior minister; cf. *Pradhāni*, *Mahāpradhāni*, etc.

śiraḥ-sthāyin (IA 17), used in the description of a trial by ordeal with reference to the bearing of some sacred symbol or image on the head of the accused while undergoing it.

sira-kaṭā, cf. *sira-kaṭā tambā-paṭā* (*JBORS*, Vol. XVIII, pp. 219-20), Oḍiyā; same as *rakata-paṭā*, Sanskrit *rakta-paṭṭaka*. See also *rakta-mānya*.

siriḍika, *siriḍikā* (EI 32), name of a tax.

Śiro-rakṣika (IE 8-3), body-guard of the king.

śiro-varttanā (SII 2), top part of a Śiva-liṅga.

Śīrṣaka (EI 28), village headman; same as *Mutuḍa* or *Muḻuḍa* of South Indian inscriptions.

śirupāḍu (EI 30), Tamil; an endowment.

śiṣṣinti (IA 18), modification of *śiṣya-paṅkti*.

Śiṣya (SII 1), a pupil.

sītā (EI 31), cultivated land. Cf. *hala*.

(*HRS*), produce of the royal farms, as suggested by the *Arthaśāstra*.

sita-cāmara (EI 29), 'white chowrie'; one of the royal insignia.

Sīt-ādhayakṣa (CII 4), officer in charge of the king's *Khās Mahāl*.

sītālekhya (IA 12), chilly-powder.

śītāṁśu (IE 7-1-2), 'one'.

sitapiñcha (SII 2), a swan.

śītaraśmi (IE 7-1-2), 'one'.

śītāri (SITI), Tamil; burning of incenses.

Śithil-ācārya (IA 19), Jain; an *Ācārya* permitting laxity of observances.

sītka (EI 11), a well.

śiva (IE 7-1-2), 'eleven'.

(*SITI*), title applied to a Śaiva devotee; often *śiva*, *śambhu* etc., are used as the ending of the names of Śaiva ascetics.

śiva, cf. *śrīvijaya-śiva*-Mṛgeśavarman; used as an honorific. Cf. *śrī*, *vijaya*, *vijayaśiva*.

Śiva-bhāṇḍārin (SITI), treasury officer of a Śiva temple.

Śiva-Brāhmaṇa (EI 25; SITI), a Śaiva Brāhmaṇa; the priest of a Śiva temple; also called *Ādi-śaiva*.

śiva-dīkṣā (EI 32), same as *śaiva-dīkṣā*, *śiva-maṇḍala-dīkṣā*.

Śiva-drohin (ASLV), a sinner against the god Śiva.

śiva-māna (EI 33), a measure approved by a Śiva temple.

śivamaṇḍala-dīkṣā (EI 32), same as *śaiva-dīkṣā*, *śiva-dīkṣā*.

Śiva-pañcāyatana (EI 27), a Śiva temple consisting of five shrines.

śiva-sthala (CII 2-1), probably, the same as *dharma-sthāna*, or a Śiva shrine.

Śiva-tithi (EI 5), same as *Śiva-rātri* or *Śiva-caturdaśī*.

Śiva-yogin (SITI), a Śaiva ascetic.

skambha (LL), a post or pillar; cf. *dīpa-skambha* (LL), a lamp post. Same as Kannaḍa *kamba*, *kamma*. Cf. *stambha*.

Skandaka (HD), a petty officer; probably the head of the village administration. See *Rājataraṅgiṇī*, V. 175.

skandaka (*Ind. Ant.*, Vol. XIII, p. 69), an instalment; cf. *skandha*.

skandha (LP), an instalment; cf. *skandaka*.

skandhaka (EI 3; HRS), known from Gujara-Pratīhāra records; name of a tax; probably, a cess at a certain rate per shoulder-load.

skandhāvāra (EI 29; CII 3; BL), camp; usually called *jaya-skandhāvāra* (i. e. the victorious camp) which indicates the capital of a king in some cases. Cf. Kannaḍa *neleviḍu*=Sanskrit *sthira-śibira*.

ślo (IE 8-1), abbreviation of *śloka*.

ślotra (EI 32), same as *śilotara*, etc.; cf. *śrotaka*.

smat (IE 8-1), corrupt form of *saṁvat*.

smṛty-upasthāna, cf. *satipaṭṭhāna* (EI 5), Buddhist; four in number.

snāna-yātrā (IA 9), festival of bathing the image of Kṛṣṇa on Jyaiṣṭha su-di 15.

snāna-mahotsava (HA), bathing ceremony (i. e. birth-bath) of a Jina performed by Indra and other gods.

So (IE 8-1), abbreviation of *Soma-vāra*, Monday.

śoḍaśī, *śoḍaśikā* (SII 4), name of a coin which may have been $\frac{1}{16}$ of the standard coin in weight or value; cf. *paṇa.*

ṣoḍaśin (EI4, 22; CII 3), name of a sacrifice.

sodraṅgīkṛitya (IE 8-3), same as *udraṅgīkṛitya*; used in respect of a gift land.

śoḷaga (IE 8-6), Kannaḍa; name of a land measure.

soma (IE 7-1-2), 'one'.

soma-grahaṇa (SII 1), lunar eclipse; same as *soma-parvan.*

soma-parvan (LP), lunar eclipse; same as *soma-grahaṇa.*

Somaskanda, South Indian representation of Śiva along with Umā and Skanda.

somavatī (IA 26), same as *ba-di* 15 falling on a Monday.

soma-yāga (CII 4), name of a Vedic sacrifice.

Somayājin (SITI), one who has performed the *soma-yāga.*

sopāna (SITI), steps; stairs; a sloping roof; the base of the *garbha-gṛha* of a temple.

Soter (IE 8-2), Greek; 'saviour'; royal title; translated into Prakrit as *Tratara*=*Trātara* (Sanskrit *Trātṛ*).

śoṭī (IE 8-8; EI 30), probably, pot for measuring liquids like wine; a ladleful; name of a measure.

spārha-vihāratā, cf. Prakrit *phāsu-vihālatā* (CII 1), comfort.

spaṣṭa (CII 3), an astronomical term meaning 'apparent'; cf. *spaṣṭa-tithi*, 'an apparent *tithi*', from which the mean *tithi* has to be determined.

sphoṭana (IE 8-5), cf. *śira-sphoṭana*, 'breaking somebody's head.'

sphuram, quickly (*Select Inscriptions*, p. 240).

Śrā (IE 8-1), abbreviation of *Śrāvaṇa.*

śrāddha (CII 4), funeral rite.

śraddhā-dāna (ML), a pious gift.

śrāddh-āṅga (EI 28), gift for the merit of a deceased person.

śrāddha-kara, tax for performing *śrāddha* at Gayā (*Rājatar.*, VI. 254; VII. 1008).

śrāddha-tithi (CII 4), date on which the *śrāddha* is to be performed.

śrāhe, also spelt *śrāhi*, *srāhi*, *śrāhī*, *srāhī*, 'the year' (probably derived from Prakrit *sarahi*, Sanskrit *śaradi*, 'in the year'); the period of 12 months. Cf. *Ep. Ind.*, Vol. XV, p. 80, note 2; Vol. XXIX, p. 106; Vol. XXX, p. 161, note 12; XXXII, p. 233 and note 8.

śrāhi, *śrāhī* (IE 8-1; EI 6, 23), probably, derived from Sanskrit *śaradi*=Prakrit *sarahi*; 'in the year'; 'the year'; used sometimes in place of *saṁvat*, but sometimes side by side with it. See *srāhe*, etc.

srāhi, *srāhī*, same as *srāhe*, etc.

Śramaṇa (EI 8; CII 3; LL; BL), a Buddhist or Jain monk; an ascetic.

Śramaṇa-śrāvikā (LL), female disciple of Jain ascetics. Cf. *Śramaṇ-opāsaka*.

Śrāmaṇera (EI 25), cf. *Sāmanera* (EI 2); Buddhist; a novice monk; cf. the feminine form *Śrāmaṇerī*.

Śramaṇikā (LL), cf. *Samaṇikā* (EI 25), a Buddhist nun.

Śramaṇoddeśa (LL), Buddhist; a novice.

Śramaṇ-opāsaka (LL), lay follower of Buddhist *Śramaṇas*. Cf. *Śramaṇa-śrāvikā*.

Śrāvaka (EI 7, 8, 24; ML; LL; HA), a lay follower of Jainism or Buddhism; cf. the feminine form *Śrāvikā*, sometimes called *Śrāvikā bhaginī* in Jain records.

śrāvaka (CII 1), 'a matter relating to a declaration'.

śrāvaṇa (SITI), also called *śrāvaṇa-patra* (q.v.), sale deed; a document; cf. *śālāvaṇam* (SITI), a sale deed (*āvaṇa-śālāvaṇam*).

śrāvaṇa-patra (EI 30), a deed of declaration; a sale-deed. Cf. *śrāvaṇa*.

Śrāvikā (HA), cf. *Sāvikā* (EI 7), Jain; a female lay worshipper.

śrāvita, cf. *rāja-śrāvita* (EI 6; IA 19), decree; a proclamation.

(*EI* 28), religious instruction.

śre (PJS; LP), contraction of *Śreṣṭhin*, 'a banker' or *śreyase*, 'for the merit of...' (especially in medieval Jain inscriptions).

śreṇi, *śreṇī* (CII 3, 4; LL), Prakrit *seni* (EI 25); a corporation or guild; cf. *śreṇī-bala*, the army maintained by a guild.

śreṇi-karaṇa, cf. *karaṇa* (LP); the department of guilds.

śreṣṭhi-jīrṇa-viśvamalla-priya, wrongly read as *śreṣṭha* (LP), probably a mistake for *jīrṇa-śreṣṭhi-viśvamalla-priya*; name of a coin struck by *Śreṣṭhin* Viśvamalla. See *jīrṇa-śreṣṭhi-viśvamalla* (or *śrīmalla*)-*priya*.

Śreṣṭhin (IE 8-3; CII 4; LL), a banker or merchant or the foreman of a guild; sometimes mentioned in the list of the king's officials and subordinates addressed by him while making a grant (*Ep. Ind.*, Vol. XXIV, p. 276).

(*BL*), representative of the banker class in the council of the local administrators of a town. Cf. *Śeṭṭi*, *Nagara-śreṣṭhin.*

śrī (CII 3,etc.), honorific prefix to names often rendered variously in English; e.g., in the case of paramount sovereigns and their wives by 'glorious'; of feudatories and other ordinary persons by 'illustrious'; of priests, teachers, etc., by 'saintly'; of gods by 'holy'; sometimes *śrī* is used before consonants and *śrīmat* before vowels. The honorific *śrī* is sometimes used in South Indian records along with the words *vijaya* or *vijaya-śiva* (q.v.). Cf. *śrī-ni*, *Śrīcaraṇa*, etc.

(*IA* 17), cf. *śrī-pūrva* used for *śrī-yuta*; *śrī* is sometimes repeated for emphasis, e.g., '*śrī* 108' is written to indicate the repetition of the word for 108 times.

śrī-bali (SITI), daily offering of the *bali* service in temples; also *havir-bali*. Cf. Tamil *śrī-bali-koṭṭuvār*, a musical troupe playing on the instruments at the time of the *śrī-bali* in temples.

(*SITI*), image of the deity taken round the temple when the *bali* is offered; the procession circumambulating the temple at the time of the *bali* service.

śrī-bali-bhoga (SITI), land set apart to meet the expenses of the *śrī-bali* service in a temple; also called *śrī-bali-ppaṭṭi.*

śrī-bhāṇḍāra (EI 33; SITI), the treasury of a temple.

(*ASLV*), collective name for the trustees of a temple; same as *śrībhaṇḍāra-vāriyam.*

śrībhaṇḍāra-vāriyam (EI 33), executive body in charge of the administration of a temple. Cf. *śrī-bhāṇḍāra.*

Śrīcandana, a title of nobility in medieval Orissa (*Ep. Ind.*, Vol. XXVIII, p. 310, text lines 8-9). Cf. *Haricandana.*

Śrī-caraṇa (IE 8-1, 8-8; EI 28), literally, 'the honourable feet [of the king]'; the king; cf. *Śrī-hasta*, *Śrī-pāda*, *śrī-ni.*

śrī-dvāra (EI 6), a special type of gateway like the *makara-toraṇa.*

śrīghana (SII 1), glorious.

śrī-gośālā, cf. Tamil *tiru-kkośālai* (SITI), cow-stall of a temple.

Śrī-hasta (IE 8-1, 8-8; EI 28), literally, 'the honourable hands [of the king]'; the king; see *Śrī-caraṇa, Śrī-pāda, śrī-ni.*

śrī-jñāna, cf. Tamil *tiru-ñānam* (SITI), sacred hymns sung to the deity in a temple during worship.

śrī-kaṇṭhamaṇi, cf. *tiru-kkaṇṭamaṇi* (SITI), a kind of necklace.

śrīkāra (LP), recognition by writing.

śrīkaraṇa (IE 8-3; EI 11, 21, 31; HD), the drafting of documents; a scribe or scribe-accountant or secretary; the minister Hemādri was styled *Sarva-śrīkaraṇa-prabhu* (*Hist. Dharm.*, Vol. I, p. 356, note 849). Cf. *Karaṇa, Śrī-karaṇ-ādhipa, śrīsrīkaraṇa.*

(*EI* 23, 29, 30), record office; the record department; the department responsible for drawing up documents.

(*EI* 30; CII 4), record officer; the officer in charge of drawing documents.

Cf. Puravuvari-śrīkaraṇa-nāyaka (EI 21), official designation.

Cf. karaṇa (LP); explained as 'the income department.'

Śrīkaraṇ-ādhipa (IE 8-3; HD), superintendent of the department of records; head of all the scribes or of all the departments. See *Ep. Ind.*, Vol. XIII, p. 17. Hemādri was styled *Samasta-karaṇ-ādhīśvara* or *Samasta-karaṇ-ādhipati* (*Hist. Dharm.*, Vol. I, pp. 356-57, notes 850-51). See *śrīkaraṇa.*

Śrīkaraṇ-āgraṇī (HD), same as *Śrīkaraṇ-ādhipa*, etc.

śrīkāra-mudr-āṅkita (LP), sealed with the syllable *śrī.*

Śrīkaraṇa-prabhu (IE 8-3), same as *Śrīkaraṇ-ādhipa*, etc.

śrīkaraṇa-viditam (LP), 'having informed the records office or officer'.

Śrīkaraṇin (EI 26), same as *Śrīkaraṇ-ādhipa*, etc.

śrī-kārya (SII 2), management of a temple.

śrī-kaṭaka (LP), royal camp.

śrīkhaṇḍa (LP), also spelt *śrīṣaṇḍa*; sandal wood.

śrīkhaṇḍa-ghoḍu (LP), a kind of horse.

śrīmāḍa (EI 10), palace.

śrīmad-ādivarāha-dramma (EI 1), name of a coin, issued by king Ādivarāha (Bhoja I Pratīhāra, c. 835-85 A.D.).

Śrī-māheśvara (ASLV), a Śaiva ascetic who is one among the authorities of a Śiva temple.

śrī-malaya, cf. Tamil *tiru-malai* (SITI), literally, 'the sacred hill;' but really, the central shrine, generally of a Śiva temple.

śrī-mālikā, cf. Tamil *tiru-māḷigai-ppatti* (SITI), small shrines or niches in the *prākāra* of a temple on the inner side of the compound wall. Cf. *tiru-māḷigai-ppiḷḷai*, the temple executive.

śrī-mandira, cf. Tamil *tiru-mandiram* (SITI), a temple; also *tiru-mandira-kkoḍi*, cloth threaded round the flag-staff of a temple during festivals. See also *Tiru-mandirav-olai*, a secretary of the government; an officer entrusted with the duty of communicating the decisions of the king in writing; also *Tiru-mandirav-olai-nāyakam*, the chief secretary to the government; chief of the *tiru-mandirav-olai* department.

śrīmat (CII 3; IA 13), prefixed, like *śrī*, to names of persons and also of places; often used before names beginning with a vowel.

śrī-mukha (SII 12; SITI), royal order or charter; a letter from the king or a chief. Cf. Tamil *tiru-muga-kkāṇam*, expenses as wages, etc., paid to the person who brings the *tiru-mugam* (royal order) to the village.

śrī-nakṣatra, cf. Tamil *tiru-nakṣatra* (SITI), natal star; annual birthday; a year.

śrī-nāman, cf. Tamil *tiru-nāma-kkāṇi*, *tiru-nāmattu-kkāṇi* (SITI), literally, 'the hereditary right of enjoyment in the sacred name'; actually, land or village, generally tax-free, endowed to a Śiva temple.

śrī-nayana, cf. Tamil *tiru-nayanam* (SITI), an ornament made of gold or silver resembling the eye and put on the eyes of the idol; same as Tamil *kaṇ-malar*.

śrī-ni (IE 8-1), abbreviation of *Śrīhasta-nirīkṣita*, 'examined by the king'. See *ni* and *Śrī-hasta*, etc.

Śrīpāda (IE 8-8), used to indicate 'the king'; cf. *Śrī-caraṇa*, etc.; also Tamil *Śrīpādaṅgal* (SITI), an exalted personage; used as an expression of respect.

Cf. Tamil *śrīpadatāṅgikaḻ* (SITI), vehicle-bearers attached to a temple, as supporting the feet of the god.

śrī-paścima-mandira, cf. Tamil *tiru-meṟ-koyil* (SITI), sacred temple in the west; a Viṣṇu temple which is situated to the west of a village.

śrī-paṭṭa (EI 15), royal charter or seal.

(*EI* 2), diadem bestowed [upon a favourite] by the king.

(*Ep. Ind.*, Vol.II, p. 344), same as *rāja-paṭṭa* or *paṭṭī* (EI 4).

śrī-paṭṭikā, cf. Tamil *tiru-ppaṭṭigai* (SITI), girdle worn by the image of a deity.

śrīphala (EI 9), the *bilva* fruit.

Śrī-pṛthivī-vallabha (IE 8-2), literally, 'the husband of [the goddesses] Śrī and Pṛthivī (i.e. the god Viṣṇu)'; title assumed by some kings of the Deccan probably claiming to be incarnations of the god Viṣṇu; often abbreviated as *Śrīvallabha* or *Vallabha*.

Śrī-Rāma (ASLV), sign manual of some kings of Vijayanagara who often wrote *Śrī-Virūpākṣa* for the purpose.

śrī-raṅga, cf. Tamil *tiru-araṅgu* (SITI), same as *raṅga-maṇḍapa*.

Śrī-rudra (SITI; ASLV), also caled *Śrī-rudra-māheśvara*; a Śaiva devotee; same as *Śrī-māheśvara*.

Śrīsāmanta (EI 21, 26), sometimes a personal name (e.g. *Sandhivigrahin* Śrīsāmanta who was the writer of a royal charter) and sometimes a designation (as in *Kaṁsāra-kulaputraka-śreṣṭhin Śrīsāmanta-Svayambhū* who was the engraver of the same charter). See *Ep. Ind.*, Vol. XXV, p. 240.

śrīśrīkaraṇ-ādi-samasta-mudrā-vyāpāra, cf. *mudrā-vyāpāra*.

Śrīvallabha (IE 8-2), cf. *Śrī-pṛthivī-vallabha*.

śrīvatsa (SII 2), mole on Viṣṇu's chest; sometimes represented in the shape of a crown as found in the Hathingumpha inscription of Khāravela.

śrī-vijaya, cf. *śrī-vijaya-Nandivarman*, *śrī-vijaya-Veṅgīpura*, etc. See *The Successors of the Sātavāhanas*, p. 63. Cf. *śrī*.

śrī-vijaya-śiva, honorific prefixed to the names of a few South Indian kings; cf. *Ep. Ind.*, Vol. XXXV, p. 152, text line 4; *The Successors of the Sātavāhanas*, p. 63. Cf. *śrī*, *vijaya-śiva*, *śiva*.

śrī-vimāna (SII 2, 13), same as *vimāna*; central shrine in the temple.

Śrī-Virūpākṣa (ASLV), sign manual of the Vijayanagara kings, Virūpākṣa being their tutelary deity. Cf. *Śrī-Rāma*.

Śrī-vīthi-nāyaka, cf. Tamil *Tiru-vīdi-nāyakar* (SITI), a metallic image of the deity for being taken in procession along the streets round the temple.

śṛṅga (EI 14), mentioned in relation to a tank.

śṛṅgāra-bhoga (EI 5), same as *raṅga-bhoga* (q.v.).

śrotaka (IE 8-5; EI.32), a kind of rent; cf. *śrotra*, etc.

śrotra (IE 8-5; EI 32), probably, a tax in kind collected from farmers by a lessee of State lands; same as Marāṭhī *śilotara*, *śilotarī* or *śilotrī*; cf. *śrotaka*.

śrotriya (SITI), land or a village granted to a *Śrotriya* or Brāhmaṇa learned in the Vedas.

śruta-devatā (EI 2), the goddess of eloquence.

śruti (SII 1), a Vedic text.

(*IE* 7-1-2), 'four'.

Śrutimān (SITI), elders of a community looking after its affairs; perhaps adapted from Tamil *Keḻvi*.

śry-ājñā, cf. Tamil *śrīy-ājñai* (SITI), royal order.

śry-amṛta, cf. Tamil *tiruv-amudu* (SITI), food offering (mainly, rice) to a deity in a temple.

stambha (BL), a tower.

(*LL*), a pillar. Cf. *skambha*.

(*IE* 8-6; EI 3), same as Kannaḍa *kamma*, *kamba*, *kambha*; a land measure equal to one-hundredth of a *mattaru* or *nivartana*.

(*SITI*), lamp-stand or lamp-post.

sthā, cf. *paratra sthāpayitvā* (*LP*), 'by laying it out at interest'; *yaṣṭi-pratiṣṭhāpanaṁ sthāpayitvā*, 'besides raising the pillar' (*Select Inscriptions*, p. 136). See *sthāpayitvā*.

sthaḻ (IA 15), a standard for measuring gardens.

sthala (IE 8-4), shortened form of *deva-sthala*; sometimes suffixed to names of localities; also the subdivision of a district.

(*IE* 8-4; EI 12, 18, 24; ASLV), a small territorial unit like a Parganā; a district or its subdivision. Cf. Kona-sthala (EI 32), also called a *deśa*, *maṇḍala*, *rāṣṭra*, *sīma*, etc.

(*CITD*), a place, habitation; a holy place; a district.

Cf. *sa-jala-sthala* (IE 8-5); the land [of a village].

Cf. Tamil *sthala-kkāval* (SITI), village watch.

sthala-durga (ASLV), fort built on the plains.

Sthala-gauḍa (ASLV), officer associated with the administration of the unit called *sthala*; cf. *Sthala-karṇam*, *Gauḍa*.

sthālaka (EI 19), explained as 'a back-bone.'

Sthala-karaṇa, cf. *Sthala-karṇam* (q.v.)., a village official (*Ep. Ind.*, Vol. XVI, p. 261).

Sthala-karṇam (ASLV), an accountant-clerk associated with the administration of the unit called *sthala*. Cf. *Sthala-karaṇa*.

[*sthala*]*-patha-karaṇa*, cf. *karaṇa* (LP); the department of roadways.

sthala-purāṇa (IA 30), a eulogistic work on a holy place, river, etc. Cf. *māhātmya*.

sthala-vṛtti (EI 13), explained as 'a tenure in which payment of tax was made in kind from the produce'; cf. *tala-vṛtti* (*Ep. Ind.*, Vol. XII, p. 273).

sthalī (IE 8-4), shortened form of *deva-sthalī*; sometimes suffixed to names of localities; also the subdivision of a district (EI 11).

Sthāmya (EI 24), wrong reading of *Sthāyin* (q.v.).

sthāna (EI 8), residence.

(*IE* 8-4; SITI), literally, 'a place'; abbreviation of *deva-sthāna* or a temple; sometimes suffixed to names of localities. Cf. *bhagavato......sthāne* (Lüders, *Mathurā Ins.*, p. 62, text lines 2-3).

(*LL*), also *sthānaka*, a temple; cf. *Sthānika*, *Sthānattār.*

(*SII* 1), a shrine; cf. *mahāsthāna*, a great temple.

(*IA* 3), a *Bhūta* temple.

Cf. tāna-mānam (SITI), dignity or honour attached to a status or office.

Cf. siṁha-sthāna (LL), same as *siṁh-āsana.*

(*SII* 11-1), cf. Kannaḍa *thāna*; name of a geographical unit.

Sthāna (CII 4), a superintendent cf. *Sthānapāla*, etc.

(*EI* 9), cf. 'officer in charge of the *sthānas.*'

sthāna-bhūmi (EI 24), land belonging to a temple.

Sthān-ācārya (EI 5, 6, 16, 28), priest of a temple; the chief priest.

sthāna-dāna (LP), allowing one to stand somewhere, i.e. allotting some land to one.

sthān-ādhikāra (IA 18), office of the superintendent of a shrine.

Sthān-ādhikaraṇika (EI 3, 6, 24), officer in the administration of an outpost; see *Sthān-ādhikṛta.*

Sthān-ādhikṛta (IE 8-3; EI 24), modern *Thānādār*; officer in charge of a police or military outpost; cf. *Gaulmika.* See *Sthān-ādhipati*, *Sthānapāla*, etc.

Sthān-ādhipati (CITD), same as *Sthān-ādhyakṣa*, *Sthānapati*, etc.; a local governor; superintendent of a place; a watchman; a police officer; often also called *Sthānika-dharma-kartṛ*.

(*EI* 24), officer in charge of an outpost.

sthānaka (LL), same as *sthāna*, a temple.

sthāna-karaṇa, cf. *karaṇa* (LP); explained as 'the public works department'.

Sthānalaka (CII 4), a local officer.

Sthāna-mahājana (EI 31), same as Tamil *Sthānattār* (Sanskrit *Sthānastha*).

sthāna-mānya (CITD), probably, land granted by the ruler to his officers for their maintenance in lieu of salary.

Sthānāntarika (IE 8-3; EI 23, 28, 29), probably, superintendent of encampment or transfer of the king's residence from one camp to another.

Sthānapāla (EI 15; HD), officer in charge of a police outpost. See *Hist. Dharm.*, Vol. III, p. 149.

Sthānapati (IE 18), a civil agent kept by the *Nāyakas* at the imperial court at Vijayanagara.

(*EI* 18, 28), officer in charge of an outpost.

(*IA* 18), designation associated with a religious office; cf. *Sthān-ācārya*.

Sthānattār (SITI; ASLV), Sanskrit *Sthānastha*; managers of a temple; the temple executive.

Sthānika (IA 12; ASLV), superintendent or manager of a temple; cf. Tamil *Tānigar* (SITI), temple executive; also *Tānika-rāyar*, director of the temple ceremonies.

(*EI* 8), title of priests in Jain temples.

(*EI* 28), an officer belonging to an outpost probably serving under the *Sthānapati*, or the same as the *Sthānapati*.

(*HD*), an officer in charge of a ward of a city or a district. See *Hist. Dharm.*, Vol. III, pp. 143 and 149.

(*HRS*), according to the *Arthaśāstra*, (1) officer in charge of one-fourth of the kingdom; (2) officer in charge of one-fourth of a city.

Sthāpan-ācārya (HA), same as *Thavaṇī* (q.v.). Cf. *Sthān-ācārya*.

Sthapati (EI 4; BL; HD), a mason or architect. See *Viṣṇudharmottara*, II. 24. 39.

Sthapati-samrāj (CII 3; HD), 'the chief of architects'; the chief architect. See *CII*, Vol. III, p. 119.

sthāpayitvā, cf. Prakrit *ṭhapaïcham* (CII 2-1), literally, 'having kept'; really, 'besides', 'in addition to...'; cf. *yaṣṭi-pratiṭhanaṁ ṭhapaïchaṁ* (Sanskrit *yaṣṭi-pratiṣṭhāpanaṁ sthāpayitvā*), 'in addition to the erection of the memorial pillar'.

sthāvara, cf. *sa-sthāvara-jaṅgama* (IE 8-5); the immovable belongings of a village.

Sthavira (CII 3, etc.), a Buddhist priestly title; same as Pāli *Thera*; an Elder in the community of Buddhist monks; a senior monk. Cf. *Thaira* (EI 3), an Elder among Buddhist monks; also *Saṅgha-sthavira* (Lüders, *Mathurā Ins.*, p. 190), 'the senior of the order'.

Sthavira-kalpin (HA), a Jain *Sādhu* whose practices are not so rigorous as that of a *Jina-kalpin* and are easier to practise.

Sthavirī (LL), Buddhist; a senior nun; Pāli *Therī*.

Sthavirīya, cf. Prakrit *Therīya* (EI 33), community of the Buddhist monks called *Sthaviravādin*.

Sthāyin (wrongly read as *Sthāmin* in *Ep. Ind.*, Vol. XXIV, p. 145, text line 2), possibly, the permanent tenants of a village. See *Ep. Ind.*, Vol. XXXI, p. 234. Cf. *Āsthāyika-puruṣa*.

sthirā (*Ep. Ind.*, Vol. XXXIII, p. 181), a permanent endowment.

sthira-śibira (IA 12), same as Kannaḍa *nele-vīḍu*; 'a standing camp'; capital; cf. *jaya-skandhāvāra* of the Pāla inscriptions.

sthita (CII 1), same as *upasthita*, present.

(*BEFEO*, Vol. XLIII, p. 6, text line 15), same as *pratiṣṭhita*, installed.

sthitaka (EI 11), perpetual grant.

sthiti (EI 32), decree.

(*IE* 8-5), regulation; see *ācāra-sthiti*.

(*EI* 12), usage; practice [in respect of calculation of dates]; *Mālava-gaṇa-sthiti-vāśāt=kāla-jñānāya likhiteṣu*, '[in the years...........] written for the knowledge of time (i.e. the date of some event) according to the practice [of calculation] of the Mālava republic'; *Mālavānāṁ gaṇa-sthityā yāte śata-catuṣṭaye*, 'four hundred years...........having elapsed according to the practice [of calculation] of the Mālavas."

sthiti-pātra (IE 8-5), same as *ācāra-sthiti-pātra* (*Ep. Ind.*, Vol. XXX, p. 169); a document containing regulations; see *sthiti-vyavasthā*, etc. *Pātra* seems to be used for *patra*.

sthiti-patraka (EI 32), a record of decision.

sthitipātra-vyavasthā (IE 8-5), same as *sthiti-pātra* or *ācāra-sthithi-pātra* (*Ep. Ind.*, Vol. XXX, p. 169).

sthiti-vyavasthā (IE 8-5), same as *sthiti-pātra* or *ācāra-sthiti-pātra* (*Ep. Ind.*, Vol. XXX, p. 169).

sthūṇā (ML), a pilaster.

Stratega (IE 8-2, 8-3), Greek *Strategos* (q.v.), commander of forces.

Strategos (IE 8-2, 8-3), Greek; commander of forces, transliterated as *Stratega* (q.v.) in Indian records; a feudatory or gubernatorial title.

strī-dhana (SITI; ASLV), dowry.

Stry-adhyakṣa (IE 8-3; CII 1), superintendent of matters concerning the ladies of the royal household; cf. *Antaḥpur-ādhyakṣa*, *Stryadhyakṣa-mahāmātra*, etc.

Stryadhyakṣa-mahāmātra (HD), Prakrit *Ithijhakha-mahāmāta*, etc.; superintendent of the harem. See *CII*, Vol. I, p. 20. *Cf. Antaḥpura-mahāmātra* in the Masulipatam plates of Amma II (*Ep. Ind.*, Vol. XXIV, p. 276).

stūpa (CII 3; BL; LL), technical name of a type of Buddhist monument; a Buddhist structure enshrining relics. Sometimes the term *ratna-gṛha* (i.e. the house enshrining the three *ratnas* or the best amongst the three) seems to be used to denote a *stūpa*.

(*EI* 2), a Jain religious establishment.

(*SITI*), pinnacle of a temple.

stupī, same as *vimāna* (IA 9), q.v.

śu (IE 8-1; CII 3; LP), abbreviation of *śukla-pakṣa* or *śuddha-pakṣa* or the bright fortnight; a day of the bright half of the month; used in connection with *di* (e.g. *śu-di*), but sometimes by itself; often written as *su*. Cf. *ba-di*.

su, cf. *śu*.

subhāṣita (CII 4), a pithy saying in a stanza.

śubhra (IA 17), used to indicate the bright fortnight.

sūci (LL), *sūcī* (EI 15), a rail bar.

śu-di (IE 8-1), abbreviation of *śukla* (or *śuddha*)-*pakṣa-dina* (or *divasa*), often written as *su-di*. See *śu-ti*.

su-di (IE 8-1), mistake for *śu-di*.

śuddh-āvāsa (IA 10), Buddhist; 'pure abode' being five in number.

sudhā-karman (EI 23), white-washing.

sudhāṁśu (IE 7-1-2), 'one'.

su-divasā (IA 18; CII 1), an auspicious day.

śuka-nāsa, cf. *śukanāsi* (*Arch. Rev.*, 1960-61, Section III) literally, 'a parrot's nose' explained as 'a gargoyle or the water spout in a building' (Acharya, *Ind. Arch.*, p. 169) and 'a vestibule' (R. Narasiṁhachar, *The Keśava Temple of Somanāthapur*, p. 3); but also as 'the projection of the main body of the *śikhara* of a temple originally at the front-side' (Kramrisch, *Hindu Temple*, p. 241); also called *śuk-āṅghri*. The *Dīpārṇava* (ed. Prabhāśaṅkar O. Sompurā, p. 116) has the following stanzas on the subject :

agre kolī kapolas=tu śuka-nāsas=tu nāsikā ।
sāndhāre stambha-rekhā ca kartavyā madhya-koṣṭhake ॥
prāsādasya puro-bhāge nirvāṇa-mūla-śṛṅgakam ।
tad-agre śuka-nāśaṁ ca ek-ādi saptam=udgamam ॥
tasy=opari siṁhaḥ sthāpyo maṇḍapa-kalaśa-samaḥ ।
dvi-stambhaḥ śuka-nās-āgre vijñeyaḥ pāda-maṇḍapaḥ ॥

Sukara-kavi (*Ep. Ind.*, Vol. V, p. 231, note 1), epithet of a poet; cf. *Āśu-kavi*.

sukhā (IA 26), same as *su-di* 4.

sukhaḍi, sukhaḍī (LP), Gujarātī; also spelt *suṣaḍī*; a kind of sweetmeat; a reward.

sukhana, sukhanā (CII 1), 'causing happiness'.

sukh-āsana (*Ind. Ant.*, Vol. IX, p. 95), translated as 'a palanquin'; enumerated as one of the five *prasādas* granted by a king to a subordinate. Cf. *pañcāṅga-prasāda*.

sukha-saṅkathā-vinoda (IA 8), 'the delight of pleasing conversation'; cf. 'while he was ruling, with the delight of pleasing conversation, at the capital of Kalyāṇa'.

śukra-netra (IE 7-1-2), 'one'.

sukṛta (CII 1), a good deed.

śukti, same as *śatamāna* (q.v.).

śūla (IE 7-1-2), 'three'; cf. *triśūla*, a trident.

Śulapāla (EI 11), probably, an associate of the courtesans.

Sulatāna (BL), Indian modification of a title of the Muhammadan kings; same as Arabic *Sulṭān*. Cf. *Sulitāna*, etc.

śūlavari (EI 25), Tamil; name of a tax.

śūlin (IE 7-1-2), 'eleven'.

Sulitāna (BL), Indian modification of a title of the Muhammadan kings; same as Arabic *Sulṭān*. Cf. *Sulatāna*, etc.

śulka (IE 8-5; EI 12, 23, 25, 30; CII 4; CITD), tolls; customs duties; octroi duties; taxes particularly levied at ferries and passes and on roads, etc.; cf. *krīḍara-śulka* (EI 5), name of a tax; also *śuṅgam, śuṅkam* (SITI), customs, tolls.

(*HRS*), tax, probably identical with *bali* according to early authorities; ferry dues, tolls and transit duties according to the *Smṛtis* and lexicons; according to the *Arthaśāstra*, (1) duties levied upon articles imported into a city, (2) port-dues, (3) duty upon the sale of liquors, (4) customs collected by the ferrymen and boundary-officers, (5) duty upon mining products, (6) duty upon imported salt, and (7) duty upon animals intended for slaughter; according to Śukra, tolls and duties upon building-sites, etc. The *Amarakoṣa* explains *śulka* as *ghaṭṭ-ādi-deya* and Kṣīrasvāmin enumerates the dues as ferry duties, tolls paid at military stations or police outposts and transit duties paid by merchants.

śulk-ādhikāra, cf. *suṅk-ādhikāra* (EI 5), 'office for the collection of tolls [of the Banavāsi District]'. Same as *Śulk-ā-dhyakṣa.*

Śulkagrāha (HD), an official who collected tolls or customs duties. See Śukra, II. 128.

śulka-maṇḍapikā (EI 3, 9), customs house. See *śulka-śālā.*

(*CII* 4), explained by some as 'a market-pavilion'.

(*Ind. Ant.*, Vol. XI, p. 329 and note 31), translated as 'the rent office'.

śulka-śālā, cf. *śuṅga-śālai* (SITI), place where tolls are collected; a customs house. See *śulka-maṇḍapikā.*

śulk-ātiyātrika (IE 8-8; EI 30), boundary-crossing fee; exit tax; cf. *atiyātrika.*

Sumantra (HD), king's counsellor on matters relating to income and expenditure. See *Hist. Dharm.*, Vol. III, p. 114, note 150.

sūnā (HRS), royal dues collected by the superintendent of the slaughter-house, as suggested by the *Arthaśāstra.*

suṇḍaka (IA 19), meaning doubtful; probably, a bundle.

suṅka (EI 12), a corrupt form of *śulka* often found in South Indian inscriptions.

Suṅkapannāyadadhiṣṭhāyaka (IE 8-3), Kannaḍa-Sanskrit; superintendent of the income from tolls. See *Suṅka-vĕrgaḍĕ.*

Suṅka-vĕrgaḍĕ (EI 19), Kannaḍa; official designation; Sanskrit *Śulk-ādhyakṣa.* See *Suṅkapannāyadadhiṣṭhāyaka.*

śūnya (IE 7-1-2), 'cypher'.

śūnya-grāma, cf. 'she made a further grant of five *śūnya-grāmas*' (*Arch. Rev.*, 1960-61, Section III, No. 44).

Suṇyārā, *Suṇyārā* (Chamba), a goldsmith; from Sanskrit *Suvarṇakāra*.

Sūpakārapati (EI 13; HD), the chief cook. See *Ep. Ind.*, Vol. XIII, pp. 109, 115. Cf. *Bhānasa-vĕrgaḍĕ*, *Mahānas-ādhyakṣa*, *Ma* (*Mā*) *hānasika*, *Khādya* (*kū**)*ḷapākika*.

Suparṇa (EI 2), a class of demi-gods.

suprabhāta (IA 12), name of the morning worship at the Rāmeśvara temple.

supradārya (CII 1), 'easy to enter', 'easy to do'.

sura (IE 7-1-2), 'thirtythree'.

surabhi, see *surahī*.

surahī (HA), Sanskrit *surabhi*; inscribed stone with the representation of a cow with her calf and the sun and the moon in the upper part, the inscriptions usually recording gifts or donations or exemptions from obligations or taxes declared by kings. This indicated permanence and inviobability.

surā-karaṇa (EI 30), distillation of liquor.

Suratāṇa (IE 8-2; EI 12), same as Arabic *Sulṭān*; see *Suratrāṇa*, *Sulatāna*, etc.

Suratrāṇa (IE 8-2; EI 4, 1, 13, 32; BL), variously spelt as *Suritrāṇa*, *Suratāṇa*, etc.; Hindu adaptation of the Muslim royal title *Sulṭān*; often adopted as a personal name. Cf. *Hammīra*. See *Sulatāna*, etc.

Suravāla (EI 33), one who sets songs or musical instruments to tune.

Sūri (EI 9), title of Jain religious teachers; often used as their name-ending.

Suritrāṇa (BL), same as *Suratrāṇa*, etc.

sūrya (IE 7-1-2; EI 25), 'twelve'.

sūrya-bha (*JAHRS*, Vol. II, p. 287, text line 64), literally, 'the sun's asterism', the Hastā-nakṣatra.

sūrya-graha (EI 24), solar eclipse.

sūrya-parvan (IA 19; LP), solar eclipse.

śuśrūṣā (CII 1), obedience; cf. *dharma-śuśrūṣāṁ śuśrūṣatu*, 'one should practise obedience to morality.'

suta (IE 7-1-2), confused with *Pāṇḍu-suta* and used to indicate 'five'.

Sūta, one of the king's high functionaries (*ratna* or *ratnin*); cf. *Hist. Dharm.*, Vol. III, p. 111.

Suta-celā (BL), a pupil or disciple.

śu-ti (IE 8-1), contraction of *śukla*(or *śuddha*)-*pakṣa-tithi*.

sūtra (IA 20), a manual of religious rituals, etc.

(*HRS*), royal receipts collected by the superintendent of weaving, as suggested by the *Arthaśāstra*.

(*IE* 3-1), same as *śarayantraka*; the string holding the leaves of a manuscript together (*Vāsavadatta*, Hall's ed., p. 250).

Sūtra (PJS), abbreviation of *Sūtradhāra*, a mason.

Sūtrabhṛt (EI 33), same as *Sūtradhāra*.

Sūtradhāra (EI 24; CII 4; BL), a mason; an artisan; an epithet generally applied to the engravers of stone inscriptions of the medieval period. See *Sūtrabhṛt*, *Sūtradhṛt*, *Sūtradhārin*.

Sūtradhāra-pitāmaha, cf. *pitāmaha* (IA 19); 'the very Brahman among the masons'; title of a mason.

Sūtradhārin (EI 15), same as *Sūtradhāra*.

Sūtradhṛt (EI 31), same as *Sūtradhāra*.

Sūtrāntika (LL), a Buddhist monk versed in the *sūtra* works. See *Sūtrāntikinī*.

Sūtrāntikinī (LL), a Buddhist nun versed in the *sūtra* works. See *Sūtrāntika*.

suttee (CII 3, etc.), see *satī*.

suvarṇa (IE 8-8; EI 28; CII 3), name of a gold coin and also of a weight of gold; equal to 16 *māṣas* or 80 *ratis*; also called *akṣa*, *picu*, *pāṇi*, *kroḍa*, *binduka*, *viḍālapadaka*, *haṁsapada*, *grāsagraha* and *tola*. See *JNSI*, Vol. XVI, p. 46.

(*SII* 13), same as Tamil *kaḻañju*.

suvarṇa-daṇḍa (IE 8-5; EI 12, 28), tax on goldsmiths; same as Tamil *taṭṭar-pāṭṭam*, etc., noticed in Appendix II.

suvarṇ-ādāya (CITD), same as *suvarṇ-āya*. Cf. *hiraṇya*, etc.

Suvarṇ-ādhyakṣa (EI 24), official designation; probably the same as *Suvarṇavīthy-adhikṛta* (q.v.).

Suvarṇakāra (EI 24, BL), a goldsmith; often the epithet of the engravers of copper-plate grants.

Suvarṇavīthy-adhikṛta (EI 18), superintendent of the goldsmith's business. *Suvarṇa-vīthī* literally means 'the quarters of the goldsmiths'.

suvarṇ-āya (also called *suvarṇ-ādāya*); land revenue paid in cash. Cf. *hiraṇya*, etc.

śuvāstiyam (SITI), Tamil; right of hereditary enjoyment.

śvabhra, cf. *sa-vana-śvabhra-nidhāna*; a pit.

Svadeśin (CITD), often used with the word *Para-deśin* or *Nānādeśin* with reference to the two main communities of traders and merchants.

sva-hasta (EI 23; CII 3; IA 8), signature or sign-manual. *Cf. sva-hast-ākṣarāṇi* (LP), a receipt.

(*Ind. Ep*., p. 187, verse 77), used to indicate a grant of land because the donor's signature was required to be put on a deed of grant.

śvaḥ-śvaḥ (CII 1), daily; same as *ahar-ahaḥ*.

svalpa (EI 24), small; sometimes prefixed to the name of a locality (e.g. Svalpa-Vallūra), etc., to distinguish it from others of the same name but styled 'big' or 'medium'. Cf. *Kṣudra-Dharmagiri* and *Mahā-Dharmagiri*; *Vaḍa-Hosa* and *Maṁjhi-Hosa* (EI 35).

Svāmin (IE 8-3; EI 24; CII 3; LL), royal title probably of foreign origin, assumed by the kings of Śaka-Kuṣāṇa extraction; adopted by indigenous rulers like the Śātavāhanas.

Cf. Śāmi (SITI), the king.

Cf. Vihāra-svāmin (founder or master of a monastery), etc.

(*EI* 7), same as *Svāmi-Mahāsena*, i.e. Kārttikeya.

(*EI* 23), designation of the member of a guild.

(*EI* 5), cf. 'the 500 *Svāmins* of Aiholĕ'; probably meaning the *Māheśvaras*.

Cf. svāmi-vāram (SITI), land-lord's share; same as Tamil *mel-vāram*.

svāmi-bhoga (EI 8; SII 3), 'the master's share'; the land-lord's share.

Svāminī (CII 3), a noble lady or mistress. Cf. also *Vihāra-svāminī*.

sva-mukh-ājñā (CII 3), 'the order or command from one's own mouth'; used with reference to the king's verbal order for the preparation and issue of charters.

svāmya (SITI), ownership; right to property; cf. *ubhaya-svāmya* (EI 5), *tejaḥ-svāmya*; also *manneya-svāmya* (SII 11-1), tenure held by a *Manneya*.

svara (IE 7-1-2), 'seven'.

Svaratrāṇa (BL), same as *Suratrāṇa*, etc.

svarga (IE 7-1-2), 'twentyone'.

svarṇa, cf. *śoṇa-vari* (SITI), *svarṇa-vari*, explained as 'tax payable in gold'; same as Tamil *pŏn-vari*; but cf. also *suvarṇa-daṇḍa*, profession-tax payable by the goldsmiths.

Svarṇa-bhāṇḍārin, cf. *Poṉ-paṇḍārigaḷ* (EI 33), members of the administrative council of a temple.

svarṇ-ādāya (SII 1; SITI), 'revenue in gold'; taxes payable in coin. Cf. *hiraṇya*, *suvarṇ-ādāya*, etc.

svarṇa-daṇḍa, see *suvarṇa-daṇḍa*.

Svarṇakāra (EI 24), a goldsmith.

svarṇa-kṣmā (EI 16), name of a *mahādāna*.

svarṇa-meru (EI 24), name of a *mahādāna*.

svarūpa (SITI), an estate of the Nambūdris, royal personages, etc., of Malai-nāḍu.

sva-samaya (EI 24), explained as a Jain doctrine; the doctrines of one's own religion.

svasti (CII 3, 4), welfare; auspicious word used at the beginning of some inscriptions to ensure success of the undertaking; an exclamation used at the commencement of inscriptions. Sometimes used as a neuter noun, with *astu* in the *maṅgala* at the end of documents.

svastika-paṭṭa (LL), slab with the representation of a *svastika* symbol.

svastyayana (EI 31), rite for averting evil.

sva-tala (EI 11), surface of the ground [of the gift land].

svatantra (SITI), a share; a customary fee; emoluments.

svayaṁvara (EI 8), the bride's selection of her husband.

śveta-cchatra (EI 29), 'the white umbrella'; one of the royal insignia; same as *śvet-ātapatra*.

śveta-garut (SII 2), swan.

śvetāmbara (IA 7), a Jain sect; same as *Śvetapaṭa*.

Śvetapaṭa (IA 7), same as *Śvetāmbara*.

śvet-ātapatra (EI 29), 'the white umbrella', one of the royal insignia; same as *śveta-cchatra*.

svolikā-pāta, *svolī-pāta* (EI 1), meaning doubtful. *Svo*=*kho* ?

syādvāda (EI 3; SII 1), Jain; also called *syādvāda-mata*, *syādvāda-vidyā*; scepticism.

Syāramallika (EI 33), probably Persian *Sair Malik* (i.e. *Malik-us-Sai*), collector or taxes, *Sair* meaning 'tax'.

T

tabu (IA 20, 29), a taboo.

Tad-āniyuktaka (IE 8-3; EI 23), official designation; same as *Tad-āyuktaka*.

tadātva (CII 1), the present time; the time being.

Tad-āyuktaka (IE 8-3; EI 6, 23), an officer who was a subordinate to the *Āyuktaka*; mentioned along with *Viniyuktaka*; cf. *Tad-āniyuktaka*, *Tan-niyuktaka*, *Tad-viniyuktaka*, etc.

Tādāyuktaka (EI 15), same as *Tad-āyuktaka*.

tad-bhava (IA 7), a word in Prakrit or the regional languages, which is modified from a Sanskrit word.

Tad-viniyuktaka (IE 8-3), same as *Tad-āyuktaka* or *Tan-niyuktaka*.

Tagarapati (EI 13), mistake for *Nagarapati*.

taila, oils; a branch of revenue according to the *Artha-śāstra*. See Ghoshal, *H. Rev. Syst.*, p. 90.

tail-ābhyaṅga (IA 22), cf. *abhyaṅga*.

taila-ghāṇaka (EI 19), oil mill.

taila-parṇikā (EI 24), explained as 'leaves producing oil'.

Tailika-rāja (EI 23), 'chief of a guild of oilmen'; designation of the chairman of the oilmen's guild.

Tairthika (EI 32), same as *Tīrthika*, a priest [of the non-Buddhists].

(*IE* 8-3), cf. *Tūthika* (*EI* 1; LL), ferry-officer or officer in charge of the places of pilgrimage.

Tājika Tajjika (EI 23, 32), *Tājiya*, *Tāyika*; an Arab.

ṭākā, Bengali form of *ṭaṅka*, meaning a silver coin (rupee) and also money.

ṭhākorkhānā (HA), same as *balānaka*.

takṣ-āçārya, cf. Tamil *tacc-ācāriyam* (SITI), the status of the master carpenter; chief of the carpenters. Cf. *tacc-ācāriya-kkāṇi*, the right of officiating as the chief carpenter, as also the stone-mason of a temple; the land set apart for the enjoyment of the holder of that office.

takṣan (IE 7-1-2), 'eight'.

tala, cf. *sa-tala* (IE 8-5); surface of the ground.

tāla (IE 8-5), a palmyra palm; cf. *sa-tālaka* as an epithet of a gift village referring to the right of enjoying the trees by privileged tenants in some areas.

tāla (SII 2), Tamil; a dish.

(*EI* 21; SITI), Tamil; the treasury

tala-bhedyā (IA 18), word of uncertain implication; mentioned with *ghāṇaka, mallaka, vundhaka* etc. (IA 18); cf. *talabhedyā-ghāṇaka-mallaka-vundhaka-daṇḍadoṣa-prāpt-ādāya* (*Ind. Ant.*, Vol. XVIII, p. 83, text lines 19-20), epithet of gift village. See *tala-bhoga.*

tala-bhoga (IA 7; SII 11-1), explained as 'the enjoyment of sites of land'; really, 'land granted for the maintenance of a temple at the time of its consecration'; same as *tala-vāṭaka, tala-vṛtti,* and probably also *tala-bhedyā.*

Tāladhvaja (BL), official designation of the governor of a territory; same as Gujarātī *Tāḻājā.*

Talaivan (SII 1), Tamil; a chief.

Talaiyāṟi (SII 1), Tamil; same as Kannaḍa *Talāri*; a watchman. See *Talavara.*

talaka (LP), 'on the spot'.

(*EI* 23), a territorial division.

taḻāka (EI 14), same as *taṭāka, taḍāga*; a tank.

tala-pada (HRS), known from Caulukya records; lands fully assessed for revenue, as distinguished from estates which were held on condition of service or for a reduced lump assessment; explained as Gujarātī *talpat,* 'land paying rent to the government' (IA 11).

tala-pāṭa (SITI), Tamil; an army; armaments.

tāla-patra, Tamil *olai* (SITI); literally, 'palmyra-leaf'; an order from the king or a person in authority. Cf. *olai-ccādanam,* 'a document written on palm-leaf'; *olai-ccampaḍam,* 'wages paid to the messenger who brings the *olai* to meet his expenses on the way'; also written as *olai-ccambaḻam, olai-ccammāḍam,* etc.; same as *nirūpa-ccambaḍam*; cf. *olai-nāyaka,* 'the chief secretary or the senior officer looking after correspondence.'

tāla-paṭṭa (IA 15), probably the same as *tāla-patra,* meaning 'an ear-ornament'.

Talaprahārin (EI 6), official designation; probably the same as *Talārī* or *Kotwāl.*

Talāra (IE 8-2; EI 22; LP; BL; HD), administrator of a city or prefect of the city police; same as *Talavara, Talārī* or *Kotwāl. Talavara* of early South Indian inscriptions means a *Rājasthāniya* (a Duke or a viceroy) according to some commentators and the *Kotwāl* or a city magistrate according to others. A subdivision of high class Khatris of the Punjab is called *Tālwār*. Cf. *Tala-rakṣa* or *Tal-ārakṣa*; also called *Ārakṣika* and *Daṇḍapāśika*. See Bhandarkar's List, No. 579; *IHQ*, 1960, p. 266.

talār-ābhāvya (EI 11), tax for payment to the *Talāra*; according to some, *Talāra* is the *Kotwāl* and *bhāvya* or *ābhāvya* is what is called *sambhāvanā*, i. e. *pāghḍī*, and *talār-ābhāvya* is the *pāghḍī* money given to the *Kotwāl* (LP).

Talārī (IE 8-2), Telugu-Kannaḍa; 'a village watchman'; same as *Talāra*.

talārika (ASLV), the office of the *Talāra*.

Tal-ārakṣa (EI 22), same as *Talavara*.

Talāṭī (*Ind. Ant.*, Vol. XII, p. 165, noted 38), a stipendiary (i.e. not hereditary) village accountant in the Kannaḍa- and Marāṭhī-speaking areas.

Talavara (IE 8-2; EI 20, 28), a title of the nobility or of subordinate rulers in some cases (a *Rājasthānīya* according to Vinayavijaya's *Subodhikā* commentary on the Jain *Kalpasūtra*); but the designation of the administrator of a city or of the police officer in charge of a city, according to some sources (Hemacandra explaining *Talāra* as *Nagara-rakṣaka*); cf. *Talāra*, *Talārī*, etc.; also *Mahātalavara*.

(*Ep. Ind.*, Vol. XXXI, p. 78), cf. *Talavara* mentioned in the list of royal officials.

Talavargika (EI 3), official designation.

talavārikā, cf. Kannaḍa *taḻavārikā* (EI 1), the village-watchman's quit-rent; cf. *Taḻavāra* or *Talāri* (Tamil *Talaiyāri*), 'a village-watchman'.

Tālāvārika (IA 12), official designation; same as either *Talārī* or *Talāṭī* (a stipendiary village-accountant in the Marāṭhī- and Kannaḍa-speaking areas).

tala-vāṭaka (EI 31), same as *tala-pāṭaka* or *tala-vṛtti*. But cf. *tala-vāṭaka* in *tala-vāṭaka-vāstunā saha kṣetram*, 'a piece of land together with suburbs, gardens and homestead land' (*Select Inscriptions*, p. 349, text line 18). The meaning here may also be 'adjoining land' which was probably the original implication of the expression.

Talāvāṭaka (*CII*, Vol. III, p. 216; also p. 217 and note), possibly the superintendent of temple property (cf. *tala-vāṭaka*);

same as Gujarātī *Talāṭī* (a petty revenue officer), according to some (HD).

tala-vṛtti (EI 13, 15, 21, 33; IA 7; SII 11-1; SITI), 'endowment of the adjoining land'; land granted for the maintenance of a temple or deity at the time of its consecration; same as *tala-bhoga*, *tala-vāṭaka*, *tala-pāṭaka*.

tāli, *tālī* (EI 1), a measure of liquor.

(*SII* 3), the marriage badge; cf. *māṅgalya*.

tallaja (SII 1), excellent.

ṭaṁ (Chamba, etc.), abbreviation of *ṭaṁkā*.

Tāmbūladān-ādhikṛta (EI 19), officer supplying betel *bīḍās* to the king. Cf. *Vārgulika*, etc.

Tāmbūlaka-vāhaka (EI 28), bearer of the king's betel-box; same as Oḍiyā *Vāguli*. See *Tāmbūladān-ādhikṛta*, etc.

Tāmbulika (EI 28), producer and seller of betel leaves.

tambūru (ASLV), a musical instrument.

Tamil, name of an alphabet and language.

Tammaḍi (CITD), Telugu; also called *Tammaḻa*, *Tāṁbaḻi*, *Taṁbala-vāḍu* and *Taṁbiga*; a Śaiva priest.

tāmra (IE; EI 8, 23), same as *tāmra-śāsana*; a copper-plate grant; also land granted by means of such charters.

Tāmrahāra, cf. *Tāmerā* (EI 16), a coppersmith.

tāmraka (IE; EI 1, 4), same as *tāmra-paṭṭa*; a copper-plate grant; also gift land.

tāmra-patra (EI 23), also called *tāmra-paṭṭa*, *tāmra-paṭṭaka*; same as *tāmra-śāsana*.

tāmra-paṭṭa (EI 19, 23, 24; CII 4; Chamba), a copper-plate charter; gift land. Cf. *tāmra-patra*, *tāmra-paṭṭaka*.

tāmra-paṭṭaka (EI 4, 23), same as *tāmra-paṭṭa*.

tāmra-phalī (EI 22), a copper plate. Cf. *triphalī-tāmra-śāsana*.

tāmra-praśasti (CII 4), eulogy written on copper plates; a copper-plate charter.

tāmra-śāsana (IE; EI 23; CII 3), a copper-charter; a technical term for a deed of conveyance written on copper plates; also gift land. See *śāsana*.

tāna (IE 7-1-2), 'fortynine'; but sometimes used to indicate 'thirtyfour'.

tanaya-prāpta (CII 3), 'an adopted son'.

tāṇḍava (CII 4), name of the dance of Śiva.

taṇḍula, unit of measurement; half of a *dhānya-māṣa* (*JNSI*, Vol. XVI, p. 48).

taṇḍula-parvata (IA 9), name of a gift.

ṭāṅk (IA 26), also called *tāṅkī*, etc.; same as *ṭaṅka*.

ṭaṅka (EI 9,20; CII 4; ML), name of a coin; cf. *Vijayarāja-ṭaṅka*, *ṭaṅka* issued by Vijayarāja; spelt often as *ṭaṅkā* and in old Bengali as *taṅkā*; same as *śāna* also called *dharaṇa*; a coin in general; regarded as equal to 4 silver *fanams*; name applied to both gold and silver issues 80 *ratis* in weight (*JNSI*, Vol. XXII, pp. 197-98); silver coins of the Delhi Sulṭāns—96 or 100 *ratis* in weight. See *JNSI*, Vol. XVI, pp. 42-49. Cf. *śāśukāni-ṭaṅka*, *hema-ṭaṅka*, *raupya-ṭaṅka*; also *ṭaṅka* (LP), a copper coin equal to half of a pice.

(*Chamba*), a copper coin equal to $\frac{1}{20}$ of a Rupee.

ṭaṅkaka (EI 19; CII 4; BL), name of a coin; a silver coin. Cf. '*ṭaṅkakas* stamped with the figure of the *Bhagavat*' (Bhandarkar's List, No. 2033).

ṭaṅka-śālā, cf. Tamil *iṭaṅka-śālai* (SITI), a mint.

ṭaṅka-śālā-karaṇa, cf. *karaṇa* (LP); the department of minting coins.

tanmātra (IE 7-1-2), 'five'.

Tan-niyuktaka (IE 8-3); an officer probably under the *Āyukta*; same as *Tad-āyuktaka* or *Tad-viniyuktaka*.

tantali (IE 8-5), a tamarind tree; cf. *sa-tantalika*, epithet of a gift village referring to the right to enjoy such trees by privileged tenants in some areas.

tantra (ASLV), army, government; cf. *Tantrin* in South Indian inscriptions.

(*SITI*), army, mainly the infantry; cf. *Tantrin* in South Indian inscriptions.

(*CII* 4), explained as 'Home Affairs'.

(*LP*), cf. *tantre nirūpita*, 'officially sent'.

(*IHQ*, Vol. XXXIV, p. 277), cf. *Tantr-ādhikārin*, 'officer in charge of administration', in the Bhāturiyā inscription of Rājyapāla. In this case, a person was at first a *Mantrin*, then a *Saciva* and finally a *Tantr-ādhikārin*.

Cf. Sarva-tantr-ādhikṛta (EI 24), superintendent of all departments.

Tantr-ādhikārin (EI 33), also called *Tantr-ādhyakṣa*, *Tantrapāla*, etc.; probably, officer in charge of administration. See

Sarvatantr-ādhikṛta.

Tantr-ādhipa (EI 25, 29; CII 4), same as *Tantr-ādhikārin*, etc.; minister for home affairs, according to some. See *Sarvatantr-ādhikṛta.*

Tantr-ādhyakṣa (EI 33), same as *Tantr-ādhikārin*, etc. See *Sarvatantr-ādhikṛta*, *Tantrapati*, etc.

tantra-karaṇa, cf. *karaṇa* (LP); explained as 'the political department'.

Tantra-nāyaka (ASLV), official designation associated with *tantra* meaning the army or government. See *Tantr-ādhikārin*, etc.

Tantrapāla (SITI), chief of the army.

(*IE* 8-3; EI 33), probably, officer in charge of administration; cf. *Mahātantr-ādhyakṣa*, *Sarva-tantr-ādhikṛta*, *Tantrapati* and *Mahātantr-ādhikṛta*, etc.

(*HD*), an officer like the *Chargé-d' Affaires*, according to some; cf. *Tantrapāla-Mahāsāmanta-Mahādaṇḍanāyaka* (*Ep. Ind.*, Vol. XIV, p. 185; cf. Vol. V, p. 77).

(*Hyderabad Archaeological Series*, No. 18, p. 34), explained as 'an officer of the king's bodyguard or royal retinue.'

(*Ep. Ind.*, Vol. XV, p. 77), explained as 'a councillor.'

(*SII* 11-2), cf. *Tantrapālaradhiṣṭhāyaka*; also *Tantrapāladadhiṣṭhāyaka* (*A. R. Ep.*, 1958-59, p. 12).

Tantrapati (IE 8-3); HD), occurs in the *Rājataraṅgiṇī*, VIII. 2322; explained as *Dharm-ādhikārin*, 'officer in charge of the department of justice and charity'; see *Bṛhattantrapati*. Cf. the Muslim official designations *Ṣadrus-Ṣudūr*, etc., explained as 'the chief judge and officer in charge of the king's charities' (*Journ. As. Soc. Pak.*, Vol. IV, pp. 53-54).

Tantravāya (EI 24), a weaver. Cf. *tunnavāya*=a tailor.

Tantrin (SITI; ASLV), a soldier; a trooper; a leader of the army; a temple priest; a weaver. It has been supposed that the Tamil words *Kaikkoḷar* and *Aṭavi* came to signify both a soldier and a weaver on the analogy of the word *Tantrin* used in both the senses. Cf. *Tantrimār*, members of the army corps; a class of persons who perform worship in temples; a priest.

tanu (IE 7-1-2), 'one'; rarely used to indicate 'eight'.

(*Select Inscriptions*, pp. 241, 245); one's own; see *tanuvaka*.

tanuvaka (CII 2-1), Prakrit; used in the sense of *svakīya*; see *tanu*.

tapana (IE 7-1-2), 'three' with reference to *Agni*; but

'twelve' with reference to 'the sun'.

tapasvin (SITI), an ascetic; a recluse; a religious mendicant.

tāpa-traya (SII 1), the three kinds of pain.

tāpita (EI 23, 24), 'heated' [for affixing the seal to a copper-plate grant].

Tapodhana (CITD), in Telugu-Kannaḍa records, often used to indicate Jain monks; in Orissan records, a Śaiva ascetic.

tār (SII 1), name of a silver coin, equal to 1/6 of a gold *fanam*.

tara (EI 9), same as *nilaya*; the family aggregate of dwellings with some of them meant for servants and artisans; also a street or a hamlet.

(*HRS*), same as *tara-deya*, ferry dues, as indicated by the *Arthaśāstra*. See *tārya*.

Cf. taram (EI 7), revenue.

tara-deya, ferry dues. See Ghoshal, *H. Rev. Syst.*, pp. 78, 227.

tarapaṇī (HA), a wooden water-vessel used by Jain monks.

Tarapati (IE 8-3; CII 4; HD), officer in charge of the ferries; superintendent of the ferries; cf. *Tarika* and *Tairthika*; but see *Ep. Ind.*, Vol. XVII, p. 321, where *Tarika* and *Tarapatika* are separately mentioned, and *Ep. Ind.*, Vol. XVIII, p. 306, text line 35 where *Tarapati* is likewise mentioned separately from *Tarika*.

Taravara (EI 20, 25), same as *Talavara* (q.v.); official designation.

Taravu-śāttu (SITI), an officer of the Coḻa kings, possibly associated with *taravu*.

Tarika (IE 8-3; HD), a ferry officer or one in charge of a ferry service. Cf. *Ep. Ind.*, Vol. XVII, p. 321.

tarika (HRS), same as *tara*; ferry dues.

tarka (IE 7-1-2; EI 25), 'six'.

(*CII* 4), logic.

Tarkuka (*Ep. Ind.*, Vol. VIII, p. 34, note 7), a supplicant; a beggar.

tārya (HRS), same as *tara*; ferry dues.

tata (IE 7-1-2), probably confused with *tattva* and used to indicate 'five'.

taṭāka-mātṛka (*Ep. Ind.*, Vol. XVI, p. 98), 'tank-nourished [land].'

tāt-āmbā (*Ep. Ind.*, Vol. XXXIII, p. 261), the mother, step-mother or aunt of one's father.

tāṭaṅka (EI 16), an ear-ornament.

tathā-jñātīya (EI 8), used for *taj-jñātīya* (*taj-jātīya*; cf. *jñātīya*).

tat-pāda-parigṛhīta (IE 8-2), see *parigṛhīta.*

tatsama (IA 7), a Sanskrit word used in the regional languages without change or with slight change.

Taṭṭār (SII 1), goldsmith; cf. *Taṭṭhakāra.*

Taṭṭhakāra (EI 15, 28; BL), a brazier, cf. *Ṭhaṭhara, Ṭhaṭherā.*

tattva (IE 7-1-2; EI 8), 'twentyfive'; rarely also used to indicate 'five.'

tauṇḍika (IE 8-8), 'biting of crops with the mouth'; cf. *gavāṁ tauṇḍike.*

tejaḥ (EI 12), abbreviation of *tejaḥ-svāmya.*

tejaḥ-svāmya (IE 8-5; EI 16), cf. *aṣṭabhoga-tejaḥsvāmya*; *tejaḥsvāmya* is *tejo-yukta-svāmya*, 'ownership endowed with full authority', which resulted from the eight (i.e. all or various) kinds of enjoyment. See *tejo-mānya.*

tejaskara (EI 24), polisher.

tejī (LP), fine.

tejo-liṅga (SII 2), the Śivaliṅga of light.

tejo-mānya, cf. *teja-mānyam* (SITI), the ownership of landed property with the *aṣṭa-bhoga* or eight (various or all) kinds of enjoyment; also called *tejaḥ-svāmyam.*

Tĕlugu, also spelt *Tĕnugu*, name of a language and alphabet.

Tĕlugu-Kannaḍa, also called Kannaḍa-Tĕlugu; name of the medieval alphabet prevalent in the Telugu- and Kannaḍa-speaking areas.

Ṭha (IE 8-1; LP; PJS), abbreviation of *Ṭhakkura.*

Ṭhā (PJS), contraction of *Ṭhākura*, a modification of *Ṭhakkura.*

thaḍa (LP), stem or trunk of a tree; a tree.

ṭhaka, cf. *ṭhakka* (IA 6); *ṭhaka-purisa* is explained as 'a trader', and associated with *ṭhag*, 'a cheat'.

thākamāna (LP), remainder; what remains to be paid up; cf. *thakalelī bākī* in Marāṭhī. See also *apūryamāṇa-thākamāna-drammāḥ*, i.e. *drammas* (coins) which are not completely paid off and are still to be paid.

Ṭhakkura (IE 8-3; EI 23, 30; CII 4; HD), supposed to be a title derived from a Turkish word (*Tegin*); occurs as a title in the *Rājataraṅgiṇī*, VII. 290, 706, 738; probably, a fief-holder; sometimes mentioned in the list of subordinates; generally used as a title of particular persons indicating their rank or office. The significance of the word possibly varied in different localities and ages. Its foreign origin is supported by its unpopularity in the South. Cf. *Ep. Ind.*, Vol. XIII, p. 297; Vol. XIX, p. 243.

(*IE* 8-3), probably a fief-holder; mentioned as *Pātra.*

(*EI* 9), explained as 'the lord-in-waiting'.

Ṭhakkurājñī (EI 8; CII 4; IA 16), title of the wife of a *Ṭhakkura*; same as *Ṭhākurāṇī* in some dialects.

Ṭhākri (CII 4), same as *Ṭhākur.*

Ṭhakura, *Ṭhākura* (EI 23, 33; CII 4), same as *Ṭhakkura.*

Ṭhākura (LP), Gujarātī ; ofte . a member of the Koli caste of Gujarat, who generally tries to detect thieves, etc.

(*LP*), Gujarātī *Ṭhākor*, the chief among certain tribes of Rajputs; a small chieftain.

ṭhāmi (LP), a kind of earthern pot.

Thānāpati (EI 30), same as *Sthānapati*; officer in charge of an outpost.

Thaṭhara, *Thaṭhāra* (Chamba), a brazier or coppersmith; same as *Taṭṭhakāra.*

thavaṇī (HA), a wooden stand used as a symbol for the teacher or the Tīrthaṅkara, a religious text or certain prescribed small objects being placed on it and worshipped by Jain monks; same as *sthāpan-ācārya.*

ṭheka (LP), special restraint.

ti (IE 8-1), abbreviation of *tithi.*

ṭi (IE 8-1), abbreviation of *ṭīkar* or *ṭikkara*, 'a mound'.

tigula-daṇḍa (IE 8-5), name of a tax; see *turuṣka-daṇḍa* and *āndhra-daṇḍa*. *Tigula* is the same as *Tamiḻ*. *Tigula-daṇḍa* may also be 'the Tamilian measuring rod'.

ṭīkara (IE 8-1), same as *ṭikkara*; a mound.

tikharā (EI 1), meaning doubtful.

ṭikkara (EI 28), same as *ṭīkara*; a mound.

tilamaka (CII 3; IA 9), a water-course; probably, a channel leading the waters from the hillside over the terraced fields.

Tila-piṣaka (CII 4; LL), an oil-miller.

tīmmira (EI 11), a land measure; cf. *timpira*, etc.

timpīra (IE 8-6; EI 23, 24, 29), also spelt *timpira*, *ṭimpira*, etc.; a land measure mentioned in Orissan records.

ṭippanaka (LP), a certificate.

tirama (EI 24), Tamil form of *dramma*.

Tīrṇa-daṇḍa (CII 1), 'one who has been convicted'.

tīrtha (IE 8-3, 8-4; EI 3; SII 1; CII 4; LL), a place of pilgrimage; a holy place or holy waters; a bathing place; a flight of steps for descent into a river; a ferry; sometimes suffixed to the names of localities.

Tīrthakara (BL), epithet of the Jinas; same as *Tīrthaṅkara* (q.v.).

Tīrthaṅkara (CII 3; EI 9); epithet of the 24 great leaders of the Jain faith; propagator of the Jain faith or *tīrtha*; creator of the four sections, viz. monk, nun, layman and laywoman (*sādhu*, *sādhvī*, *śrāvaka* and *śrāvikā*); same as Jina; sometimes spelt *Tīrthakara*; also called *Ādikartṛ*.

Tīrthika (EI 9), Buddhist; teacher of a religion other than one's own; a non-Buddhist (especially, Śaiva) teacher.

(*EI* 32), same as *Tairthika*, 'a priest'.

Tīrth-opādhyāya (BL), title of a family priest at Jagannātha-kṣetra (Purī).

Tirumeni-kāval (ASLV), watchman in a temple.

tiruviḍaiyāṭṭam (EI 30), Tamil; a gift.

tithi (CII 3; IA 17), a lunar day; one mean *tithi* is equal to 0.9843529572 of a mean solar day and night; the mean *tithis* in a solar year are 371, and 3 *ghaṭīs* and 53.4 *palas*; generally the term *tithi* means the end of a *tithi*, not its beginning or duration, and the week-day of a *tithi* is the week-day on which that *tithi* ends; the *tithis* given in the *Pañcāṅgas* are apparent, not mean, and they are intended to be given from apparent sunrise.

Cf. Tamil *tiyadi*, *tedi* (SITI), a date.

(*IE* 7-1-2), 'fifteen'.

(*EI* 16), same as *mahā-tithi*, an auspicious *tithi*; cf. *saptamī* called the *tithi* of the sun-god and *aṣṭamī* that of the god Śiva (*Ep. Ind.*, Vol. V, p. 168, note 4).

tithi-bhoga (CII 3; IA 16), duration of a *tithi*.

tithi-dhruva (CII 3; IA 16), constant of a *tithi*; a term denoting the number of complete *tithis* that elapse from the commencement of Caitra upto the *tithi* during which the *Meṣa-saṁkrānti* occurs. See *tithi-śudhi.*

tithi-kendra (CII3), anomaly of a *tithi*, expressed in *tithis*; an annual variation in the *tithi-kendra* is 7 *tithis*, 9 *ghaṭīs* and 42 *palas*. See *kendra.*

tithi-spaṣṭa-kendra (IA 16), the apparent anomaly of a *tithi.*

tithi-śuddhi (CII 3), the subtraction of *tithis*; a term denoting the number of *tithis* that elapse from the commencement of Caitra up to the time of the *Meṣa-saṁkrānti.* See *tithi-dhruva.*

tola, tolā, cf. Telugu-Kannaḍa *tulā* (CITD), weight of a rupee, taken as the unit of the system of weights; fixed at 180 grains troy by the British; also called *suvarṇa* (*JNSI*, Vol. XVI, p. 46).

tolaka, same as *tola*; equal to 2 *śānas* or 80 *ratis*; also called *kola, draṅkṣaṇa, badara, kṣudraka, vaṭaka*, etc. (*JNSI*, Vol. XVI, pp. 41, 44).

torai (SITI), Tamil; a standard linear measure of four fingers' breadth.

toraṇa (CII 4; LL; CITD), an arch; a gateway; an arched doorway; a portal; a temporary ornamental arch; also a garland in Telugu-Kannaḍa.

Cf. toraṇa-kkāṇikkai (SITI), tax on gates or presents for decorating the village with arches.

Traipiṭaka, cf. *Trepiṭaka* (EI 9), one versed in the three *piṭakas*, i. e. the three classes of Buddhist religious literature.

Traipiṭak-opādhyāya (LL), Buddhist; teacher of the three *piṭakas.*

Traipuruṣa (*Hyderabad Archaeological Series*, No. 18, pp. 34-35), same as the composite god Tripuruṣa.

trairājya (EI 19), a group of three realms.

trairājya-sthiti (EI 27), cf. *trairājya-sthitim=ātmasāt=kṛtavataḥ*, 'of one who has obtained steadiness in the three realms.'

Traividya (LL), Buddhist; teacher of the three *piṭakas*. (*EI* 16), cf. *Trivedin.*

Traividya-sāmānya (EIZ23), same as *Trivedin*; cf. *Cāturvidya-sāmānya=Caturvedin.*

trāsa (SII 2), flaw in a ruby.

Trātṛ (IE 8-2; LL), same as Prakrit *Trātara*, 'the saviour'; royal title of foreign origin; Greek *Soter.*

trayī (SII 1), the three Vedas.

trayodaśama (EI 15), same as *trayodaśa.*

Tri (EI 32), abbreviation of *Trivedin.*

tri (IE 7-1-2), 'three'.

tribhāg-ābhyantara-siddhi (IE 8-5), generally spelt *tribhog-ābhyantara-siddhi*; the right to enjoy one-third of the revenue, the other two parts going in equal shares to gods and Brāhmaṇas. Cf. *abhyantara-siddhi, bāhy-ābhyantara-siddhi, tribhoga.*

tri-bhaṅga (EI 17), pose in standing images with bends in three limbs, viz. the neck, the wrists and the knees.

tri-bhaṅgi, cf. *tri-bhaṅga*; see *Ep. Ind.*, Vol. XXXIV, p. 65.

tri-bhoga (EI 16; IA 19), a joint tenure enjoyed by a private person, a god (or gods) and the Brāhmaṇas (cf. *Ind. Ant.*, Vol. XIX, p. 271). See *tribhāg-ābhyantara-siddhi*, etc.

tribhog-ābhyantara (EI 15), same as *tribhog-ābhyantara-siddhi, tribhāg-ābhyantara-siddhi, tribhoga.*

tribhogya (*Ep. Ind.*, Vol. XIV, p. 313), cf. *gaṇa-bhogya.*

tribhuvana-vijaya-stambha (SII 1), a pillar commemorating the conquest of 'the three worlds', the conventional claim of a hero.

tri-cīvara (EI 25), complete robe of a Buddhist monk.

tri-daṇḍa, cf. *Tridaṇḍin* (IA 10); tree staves tied together as borne by Brāhmaṇa mendicants.

tridaśa (IE 7-1-2), 'thirtythree'.

tridīnārikya (EI 15), same as *traidīnārikya*, 'priced at three *dīnāras*.'

tri-gata (IE 7-1-2), 'three'.

tri-guṇa (IE 7-1-2), 'three'.

tri-jagat (IE 7-1-2), 'three'; but *jagat* sometimes also means 'fourteen'.

trika (HA), a group of three figures of the *Tīrthaṅkaras.*

tri-kāla (SII 1; SITI), the three parts of the day, viz. morning, noon and evening [when worship is offered in temples].

(*IE* 7-1-2, 'three'.

trikūṭa (EI 3), a junction of three villages (*Ep. Ind.*, Vol. XIII, p. 34, note 3); same as *trikuṭa* or *trikuṭṭa*. Cf. *tri-sandhi*; also Telugu *muggaḍa*, 'a junction of three or more villages'.

tri-lakṣaṇa (EI 3), three qualities.

tṛṇa, cf. *a-tṛṇa-kāṣṭha-grahaṇa* (IE 8-5); grass which the villagers were obliged to supply to the king or landlord on occasions or to the touring officers.

tṛṇa-yūti, cf. *yūti*.

tṛṇa-yūti (or *puti*)-*gocara* (EI 17),grass-fields and pasturelands.

tṛṇ-odaka (IE 8-5; EI 12, 28), name of a tax or cess; the grazing tax.

trinetra (IE 7-1-2), 'three'.

tripada (LP), the three chief account books, viz. *rojmol*, *khātā-vahī* and *pāvtī-vahī*.

tripada-lekhyaka (LP), accounts book and receipt book.

Tripāṭhin (EI 4, 31), same as *Trivedin*; epithet or family-name of Brāhmaṇas.

triphalī-tāmraśāsana (EI 3), a grant engraved on three copper plates.

tri-piḍi-dāna (*Ind. Ant.*, Vol. XIX, p. 271), a grant to be enjoyed by three generations.

Tripuruṣa (EI 33), a composite deity (*tri-mūrti*); a combined image of Brahman, Viṣṇu (represented as Sūryanārāyaṇa in Gujarat) and Śiva.

trisahasra (EI 31), also called *trisahasra-vidyā*; certain sciences.

tri-sandhi (*Ep. Ind.*, Vol. XII, p. 34, note 3), a junction of three villages; cf. *trikūṭa* or *trikuṭṭa*; also Telugu *muggaḍa*, 'the junction of three or more villages'.

triśara (SII 2), name of an ornament.

trisparśā (IA 26), the twelfth *tithi*.

tri-sthalī (EI 21), the three holy places, viz. Gayā, Prayāga and Kāśī.

triṣṭubh (IE 7-1-2), 'eleven'.

triśūla, cf. *tiriśūlam* (SITI), trident; same as *śūla*.

tri-tīrthī (HA), an image showing figures of three Jinas, usually one Jina standing or sitting in the centre as the main deity of the group and two others sitting or standing on the two sides.

tri-varga (SII 1), the three objects of human life.

Trivedin (EI 4), same as *Tripāṭhin*; epithet of Brāhmaṇas later stereotyped as family name.

Trividha-kṣitīśa-cūḍāmaṇi (IE 8-2), epithet of a king probably referring to the *Aśvapati*, *Gajapati* and *Narapati* types of rulers, i. e. those who were strong in elephants, cavalry and infantry respectively.

troḍanikā (IE 8-5), same as *troṭana*; cf. *karṇa-troḍanikā*, 'cutting somebody's ears.'

troṭana (IE 8-5), cf. *karṇa-troṭana*, same as *karṇa-troḍanikā*.

tryakṣa-mukha (IE 7-1-2), 'five'.

tuḍavu (SITI), Tamil; a liquid measure.

tukkhāra (CII 4), a Tokharian horse; cf. *Tuḥkhāra* people of the Purāṇas.

tulā (IA 26), a weight [of silver].

(*CITD*), Telugu-Kannaḍa; same as Sanskrit *tola* or *tolaka*; the weight of one rupee or 30 canteroy fanams; $\frac{1}{3}$ of a *navaṭāku*; a measure or weight of gold and silver, being 100 *palas* or about 145 ounces troy. The *tulā* varied a great deal according to the age and locality.

tulā-bhāra (EI 4, 17, 26; SITI), name of a *mahādāna*; same as *tulāpuruṣa*; weighing a king or an exalted personage against gold or other precious metals and stones and distributing the same to temples, etc.

tul-ādhiroha (EI 3), same as *tulā-puruṣa*.

tulā-puruṣa (EI 29; CII 4), name of a *mahādāna*; same as *tulā-bhāra*.

tulasī-vivāha (EI 32), name of a ceremony.

Tulu, name of a language which is written in Malayāḷam eharacters.

tulya (SITI), literally, 'equal'; a true copy.

tulya-meya (EI 7, 10; HRS), 'what is to be weighed and measured'; same as *meya* in *deya-meya*; known from records like those of Harṣavardhana, in which it may be epithet of *bhāga-bhoga* or a separate item (*Ind. Ep.*, p. 394).

tūmbu (SITI), Tamil, a measure of capacity; cf. *tūmu*.

tūmu (EI 27), a grain measure; cf. *tūmbu*.

tūnk (HA), Jain; top of a mountain or hill on which there is a shrine or several shrines.

turaga (IE 7-1-2), 'seven'.

Turaga-sādhanika (EI 25), the leader of cavalry. Cf. *Sādhanika*, etc.

Turaka (EI 32), same as *Turuka* and *Turuṣka*; a Turk or Turkish Muhammadan; a Muhammadan.

turaṅgama (IE 7-1-2), 'seven.'

Turīya-janman (EI 24; CII 4), same as *Śūdra.*

Turuka (EI 32), cf. *Turaka* and *Turuṣka.*

Turuṣka (EI 5, 17, 32), originally, a Turk or a Turkish Muhammadan; later, Muhammadans in general.

turuṣka-daṇḍa (HRS; *Ep. Ind.*, Vol. XIV, p. 196, Vol. XI, p. 21), name of a tax collected by the Gāhaḍavāla kings from their Muhammadan subjects or for defending their kingdom from Muhammadan attacks; cf. the *danegeld* in early English history. See *andhra-daṇḍa, tiguḷa-daṇḍa, bhoṭṭa-viṣṭi.*

turya (IE 7-1-2), 'four'.

Tyāgī-ācārya (IA 19), Jain; an *Ācārya* who does not permit laxity of observances.

U

u (IE 8-1), abbreviation of the land measure called *udāna* (q. v.).

ubhaya, cf. *ubhaiyam* (SII 1), an offering.

Cf. ubhaya-paliśai (SITI), interest in two ways, i.e. in money and in kind.

(*SITI*), a tax payable in gold; probably the same as *ubhaya-mārga* or the tolls collected on the highways in both the directions, i. e. inward and outward.

(*SII*, Vol. III, p. 209), a gift to a temple or monastery in Tamil records.

ubhaya-mukhī (*Ep. Ind.*, Vol. XIII, p. 15, note 4), a cow in the act of giving birth to a calf; sometimes explained as 'a pregnant cow' (EI 6).

ubhayamukhī-dakṣiṇā (CITD), some special kind of religious present or fee; the gift of a cow at the point of giving birth to a calf (cf. *ubhayamukhī*).

Ubhaya-nānā-deśi (SITI), the two divisions of the *Nānādeśi* oiganisation, e. g., the *Nānādeśi* and the *Citrameḷi.*

(*CITD*), explained as the entire merchant community, *i. e.* including both the *Sva-deśi* and *Para-deśi.*

ubhaya-svāmya, cf. *ubhaya-sāmya* (EI 5), probably, two kinds of ownership.

ucaṭa (LP), impatience, anxiety; cf. Gujarātī *uchāṭ.*

ucc-āvaca (CII 1), 'more or less', 'of various kinds'.

ucchanna (CII 3), corruption of *utsanna*; found in Sanskrit inscriptions. See *JAS*, Letters, Vol. XX, 1954, p. 204.

ucchīrṇa (IA 19), a loan.

ucchraya (*Ep. Ind.*, Vol. VIII, p. 46, note 3), a shelter; same as *pratiśraya*.

ucchṛṅkhala (LP), free from a burden.

uchālaka-bhṛta (LP), loaded with *uchālaka* (Gujarātī *ucāḻo*), i. e. household furniture that can be easily moved about.

uḍa (IE 7-1-2), 'twentyseven'.

udag-ayana (EI2 3), the winter solstice; same as *uttarāyaṇa*.

udagayana-parvan (EI 20), cf. *udag-ayana*.

Uḍaiyār (SITI), Tamil; literally, a possessor; a king or lord; the chief deity of a temple. Cf. *uḍaiyār-śālai*, the feeding house attached to a temple.

udaka-bandha (EI 3), a sluice.

udaka-dhārā, cf. *udaka-dārai* (SITI), [a gift given] with the libation of water; also referred to in Tamil as *udakañśeydu* and *udakaṁ paṇṇi*. See *udaka-pūrvam*, etc.

udaka-pūrvam (IA 7), also expressed as *udak-ātisargeṇa*, 'with libations of water'; refers to the custom of pouring water in the hand of the donee while making the ceremonial gift of an object which cannot be placed in the latter's hands. Cf. *Dravyasya nāma gṛhṇīyād=dadān=īti tathā vadet* । *toyaṁ dadyāt=tato haste dāne vidhir=ayaṁ smṛtaḥ* ॥ (*Agni Purāṇa*, Ch. 209, verses 49-50).

udaka-sarga (IA 8), same as *udak-ātisarga* (cf. *udaka-pūrvam*).

udak-āsīhāra-kullaka, cf. *sa-vanaspaty-udak-āsīhāra-kullaka-pānīya-sametā* (IE 8-5), translated as 'together with the fruit-trees and with the water-courses and channels' (with the omission of the doubtful words).

udamāna (IE 8-6; EI 29), a small land measure; probably the same as *unmāna* and *udāna*.

udāna, see *udamāna*.

udapāna (CII 1; LL), a well or reservoir.

udāra (CII 1), a person of high rank; a rich man.

udara-bandhana (SII) 2), a waist-band; name of an ornament.

udaram-bharīṇa (IA 17), same as *udaram-bharin*, 'filling the belly.'

udarcis (IE 7-1-2), 'three'.

udāsīna, cf. *udāsīna-vāriyam* (SITI), a committee which is neutral to both the parties; same as *madhyastha* or the arbitration committee.

udaya (EI 24), 'the produce [of a field]'.

Udaya-giri (IA 22), the mythical Sun-rise mountain.

udbali, cf. *umbaḻi* (EI 13), *umbaḻam*, *umbaḻikkai*, *umbaḻika* (SITI), rent-free gift of land; land granted rent-free for the performance of service; same as *mānya*. See *udbalika*.

udbalika (IE 8-5; CII 1), free from taxes; free from the obligation of paying *bali* probably meaning land tax payable in addition to the king's share of grains.

uddāman (EI 9), same as *uddāma*.

uddātavya, 'to be repaid' (*Select Inscriptions*, p. 239); 'to be handed over' (*ibid.*, p. 246).

uddeśa (CII 4), a territorial division.

(*EI* 14), cf. *s-oddeśa* (IE 8-5); space above the ground; same as *ūrdhva*.

uddha (IA 19), explained as 'deserted'. Cf. *uddha-grāma*.

uddha-grāma (LP), the village of which the revenue is fixed in a lump sum.

uddha-khila-bhūmi (LP), table land which is uncultivated (*khila*). But cf. *uddha-grāma*.

uddhāra (LP), borrowed on trust or credit; cf. *udhār*.

(*IE* 8-5), same as *udraṅga*; cf. Tamil *uttāra*.

uddhāra-proddhāra (LP), taking on credit ; cf. Marāṭhī *udhār-pādhār*.

uddhārya (*LP*), 'may be debited'; cf. Gujarātī *udhāravuṁ*.

uddhārya-vyavahāra (LP), the business of lending money.

uddyotita (EI 13), literally, 'caused to shine'; actually 'with repairs effected.'

udgaṇaka (LP), a revenue chart.

udgaṇanīya (LP), cf. Gujarātī *gaṇī āpavuṁ*, 'the charge should be handed over.'

udghāṭita (*Ep. Ind.*, Vol. XXXI, p. 20), same as *utkīrṇa*.

udgrāh, cf. *udgrāhayiṣyāmi* (LP), 'I shall get the revenue collected [from the country in this way]'; also *udgrāhita* (LP), 'taxed'; *udgrāhyamāṇa* (LP), cf. Gujarātī *ughrāvayuṁ*.

udgrantha (IE 8-5), same as *udraṅga.*

udharita (IA 18), meaning uncertain.

Udīcīpati (BL), literally, 'the ruler of the north (i.e. the northern province of an empire)'; title of a viceroy.

udraṅga (IE 8-3; 8-5; EI 22; CII 3, 4; HRS), explained as 'the fixed tax', 'the land tax', 'the principal tax' or 'the tax on the permanent tenants'; generally mentioned along with *uparikara,* i. e. minor taxes or the tax on temporary tenants; same as *kḷpta. Udraṅga* may have been paid in grains at least in some regions since the *Audraṅgika* (collector of *udraṅga*) is sometimes separately mentioned together with the *Hiraṇyasāmudāyika* (collector of revenue in cash). In one case, the land is said to have been granted after making it *udraṅga,* i. e. *s-odraṅga.* See *s-odraṅga* (IA 10), *draṅga, uttāra.* Cf. *mah-odraṅga* in *pravartita-mahodraṅg-ādi-dāna-vyasan-ānupajāta-santoṣa* (*Ep. Ind.*, Vol. XXII, p. 118, text line 40).

udraṅgīkṛtya (IE 8-3), same as *s-odraṅgīkṛtya*; used in respect of a gift land. Cf. *udraṅga.*

udrava (EI 27), name of a tax.

udumbara (LP), 'threshold'; cf. *gṛh-odumbara-madhye,* 'into the house'; cf. *umbara-bheda.*

udvasa, cf. *udvasa-kuṭumbika* (LP), cultivators who have come from outside and settled.

udvāta (EI 13), tempest; cf. *bhūta-vāta-pratyāya.*

udyāma (CII 1), used in the sense of *udyama* or exertion.

udyāna (CII 1), march; a garden.

ukka, ukkā (Chamba), the total sum; a lump sum.

ukkoḍa, a kind of levy; probably, periodical presents; same as *utkoṭa.* See *Ep. Ind.*, Vol. XXXIII, p. 56.

ukkoṭa-bhaṅga, same as *khoṭa-bhaṅga* (q.v.) according to the *Abhidhānarājendra,* s.v. *parihāra*; cf. *utkoṭa* and *ukkoḍa,* periodical presents (*Ep. Ind.*, Vol. XXXIII, p. 56).

ukkuṭṭhī (IE 8-8), Prakrit; see *utkṛṣṭi.*

ukta-niyoga (EI 33), doubtful expression probably indicating an official designation. Cf. *uttara-niyoga.*

ukthya, (EI 22; CII 3), name of a sacrifice.

ullanbana (IE 8-8), a crime, the real nature of which is uncertain.

ullekha, 'high-flashing' (*Ep. Ind.*, Vol. XVI, p. 36).

Ullekhaka, engraver (*Ep. Ind.*, Vol. XXXIV, p. 203 and note 11). See *Vilekhaka*.

ulluñcana (LP), cleaning.

Umarāva (EI 26; BL), title of a feudatory ruler; same as the Muhammadan title *Umrah*.

umbaḻi (ASLV), Tamil; same as Sanskrit *udbali* (q.v.).

umbara (IE 8-8), same as Prakrit *ummara*; threshold or door; cf. *umbara-bheda*, also *udumbara* and *unmara*.

umbara-bheda (IE 8-5; EI 25), 'violation of the closed door'; the right of royal officers to enter into a house with doors closed for realising taxes. This probably related to the houses of merchants who were away from their home-towns in the course of their business; cf. *unmara* or *umbara*; also *prātibhedikā*.

umura-bheda (CII 4), mistake for *umbara-bheda* (q.v.); forcible entry into a house. Cf. *unmara*.

ūnābdika-śrāddha (CII 4), a rite.

uñcha, cf. *uñcha-kara-bhar-ādi-vivarjita*; tolls (*Ep. Ind.*, Vol. XXXIII, p. 89); may be collection of small quantities of crops (cf. *prastha*).

uṇbaḻi (SII 11-1), same as Sanskrit *udbali*.

uñchamanna (EI 26), used along with *maṟumanna*; a privilege of the donee of rent-free land; see *uñcha*.

uñcha-vṛtti (EI 24), a gleaner of corn.

unmāna (IE 8-6; EI 15, 21, 29), name of a small land measure; same as *udāna* or *udamāna* (q.v.).

unmara (EI 30), Sanskritised form of Prakrit *ummara* (cf. *umbara*); threshold. Merchants, who were often absent from home for a long time, were sometimes made free from *unmara-bheda* (entry into their house) by royal officers probably because they paid their dues on their return from business tours. Cf. *prātibhedikā*.

unnata (IE 8-5), high land.

unnīti, 'adopted daughter' (*Select Inscriptions*, p. 237).

upa-dhā (CII 1), cf. *hita-sukham=upadadhyuḥ*; to bring [welfare and happiness to the people].

upādhi (SII 1), probably, a condition.

Cf. opādi (SII 2), dues.

Upādhyāya (CII 4), a teacher; epithet of Brāhmaṇas.

(*IA* 19), Jain; an *Ācārya* who has the right of reading the sacred text, but not of explaining it.

(*IE* 8-3; EI 7), epithet of teachers; mentioned as a *Pātra*. (*CII* 3), a sub-teacher who is the instructor in only a part of the Veda, or in grammar and the other *Vedāṅgas*.

Upādhyāyinī (LL), a female teacher; the wife of an *Upādhyāya*.

upaga (CII 1), suitable; cf. *manuṣy-opaga*, 'beneficial to men'.

upagata (CII 1), same as *saṅgata*, intimately associated; see *upeta*, etc. See *Ind. Ep.*, pp. 161 ff.

upagatā (LP), a receipt.

upa-han (CII 1), to harm; cf. *upaghāta*, injury.

upakara (*Ep. Ind.*, Vol. XXXIV, p. 106, note 5), cf. *nikara* and *upaskara*.

upakārikā, probably, a territorial unit around the headquarters of an administrative unit (*Ep. Ind.*, Vol. XV, p. 286).

upakhila, cf. *sa-khil-opakhila* (Chamba), 'together with fallow (*khila*) and partially fallow (*upakhila*) land'. See *pakhila*.

upakḷpta (EI 15; CII 3, 4), a levy; probably, the tax on temporary tenants or the unfixed taxes or minor income; cf. *sa-kḷpt-opakḷpta* (IE 8-5), also *kḷpta*, *kḷpta-kara*, *udraṅga* and *uparikara*.

upakrama-karaṇa, cf. *karaṇa* (LP); the department of new undertakings.

upakṣaya (LP), expense; 'other expenses'; cf. *s-opakṣaya*, *sañjāt-opakṣaya*, 'expenses incurred'.

upakṣiti (IE 8-5; EI 33), probably, tax on inferior land; may also be the same as *upakṣaya*.

upalakṣita (*Select Inscriptions*, p. 202), 'examined'.

upāna (SITI), the first moulding above the plinth, in the construction of temples.

upanidhi (IE 8-5; EI 12), same as *nikṣepa*; cf. *nidhi*.

upanipātaka (CII 3), same as *upapātaka*.

upapātaka (CII 3), sins of the second degree.

upapīṭha (SII 2), a lower pedestal; cf. *pīṭha*; also *upapīṭhattukaṇḍappaḍai*, the lower tier of the basement of a temple.

Upapradhānin (ASLV), an executive officer lower in rank than the *Pradhānin*.

Uparahiṇḍīya (LP), a tax-inspector.

uparakṣita (LL), explained as 'kept in custody'.

Uparika (IE 8-3; CII 3; BL; HD), a viceroy; the governor of a province. An *Uparika* was appointed by the emperor and he himself appointed the governor of the district (cf. *Ep. Ind.*, Vol. XV, p. 130). He is sometimes styled *Mahārāja* and *Rājaputra*. Viśvarūpa on the *Yājñavalkyasmṛti*, I. 307, quotes a prose passage from *Bṛhaspati* where the requisite qualities of an *Uparika* are set out. See Vogel, *Ant. Ch. St.*, p. 123. The word literally means 'one placed at the top'.

(*IE* 8-3), cf. *Auparika*, a viceroy.

Cf. Bṛhad-uparika (IE 8-3).

Uparika-mahārāja (IE 8-3), an *Uparika* enjoying the title *Mahārāja*.

uparikara (IE 8-5; CII 3, 4; HRS), explained as 'additional taxes', 'unfixed taxes', 'minor taxes', or 'tax paid by the temporary tenants'; cf. *s-oparikara* (IA 10), sometimes called *parikara* (cf. *sa-parikara* in place of *s-opakriara*). See *upri*.

upa-riṅkh (EI 12), to spread.

Upāsaka (EI 3, 8, 27; CII 3), a Buddhist lay worshipper; a lay follower of the Buddha; cf. *Upāsikā*.

(*SII* 13), a temple servant.

upasampadā (EI 9; IA 22), the initiation of a Buddhist monk.

upasandhi (SITI), intermediary service of worship in a temple, between the morning and the midday service.

Upāsanin (EI 32), title or family name of Brāhmaṇas.

upasanna, cf. *kṛt-opasannā* (EI 30); word of doubtful import.

Upāsikā (CII 3, 4), feminine form of *Upāsaka* (q.v.); a female lay-follower of the Buddha.

upaskara (HRS), known from the Kamauli plate of Vaidyadeva; probably meaning *upakara* (q.v.) or the appurtenance to a tax (*kara*).

Cf. nikara.

upāśraya (LL), a shelter.

upasthāna (LL), reception room.

(*HRS*), a group of royal receipts arising from underhand methods of collection of the contributions in kind, as suggested by the *Arthaśāstra*.

upasthāna-śālā (LL), hall of reception.

upatalpa (EI 8), the upper story [of a house].

upāli (SITI), Tamil; also spelt *opādi*; Sanskrit *upādhi*; literally, obstruction; dues; anything payable as a debt or obligation.

upātta, cf. *sa-bhūt-opātta-pratyāya* (EI 23), 'together with the income derived on account of changes in the natural phenomena.'

upāya (EI 6, 25), four in number; 'four'. Cf. *catur-upāya* (SII 1).

(*SITI*), probably, minor taxes.

upayāta (EI 33), same as *opeta*, *upagata*, 'closely associated'. See *samupagata*, *samaveta*, etc.

Upayukta (HD), same as *Upayuktaka*, 'a subordinate officer'. See *Arthaśāstra*, II. 5; *Ep. Ind.*, Vol. IV, p. 285.

Upayuktaka (IE 8-3; HD), probably the same as *Niyuktaka*, *Viniyuktaka*, *Tad-viniyuktaka*, etc. See *Upayukta*; cf. *Yuktak-Opayukta* (*Ep. Ind.*, Vol. VII, p. 40).

Upayuktika (EI 23), official designation; probably the same as *Upayuktaka*.

upekṣā (CII 4), Buddhist; indifference; one of the *bhāvanās*.

upeta (CII 1), same as *saṅgata*; 'intimately associated'; cf. *upagata*, *upayāta*, *samupagata*, *samaveta*, etc.

upoda (Chamba), name of a tax.

uposath-āgāra (EI 23), 'the *uposatha* hall'. See *poṣadha*, *pauṣadha*

upri (IE 8-5), Marāṭhī; same as *uparikara* (q.v.), tax on temporary tenants, according to some.

ūr (ASLV), the assembly of a non-Brāhmaṇa village, that of a Brāhmaṇa village being called *sabhā* or *mahāsabhā*.

urandara (LP), delay.

ūrdhva, cf. *s-ādha-ūrdhva* (IE 8-5), '[what is] above the surface of the ground'; same as *uddeśa*.

Cf. *ūrdhva-dina-pāṭikāyām* (LP), 'for the series of days afterwards.'

ūrdhv-ādhaḥ (IA 16), explained as 'what is above and below [in the gift land]'; cf. *ūrdhv-ādhaḥ-siddhi-yutā* (IA 18), 'with income from the produce above and below the surface of the ground'; same as *s-ādha-ūrdhva*, epithet of the gift land.

ūrdhva-paṭṭa (LL), an upright slab.

ūrdhvayita, cf. Prakrit *ubhayita* (EI 20), raised. See *ūrdhvita.*

ūrdhvita, Prakrit *ubhayita* (*Sel. Ins.*, p. 222), raised, contributed. See *ūrdhvayita.*

Ur-gāmuṇḍa (IA 12), Kannaḍa; official designation; cf. *Gāmuṇḍa.*

ūrṇa (EI 8), a mark between the brows of the Buddha.

ūrṇa-sthāna (IE 8-3), a wool factory. Cf. *Aurṇasthānika*, officer in charge of the *ūrṇā-sthānas* (*Select Inscriptions*, p. 360, text line 4).

Uroḍĕ (IA 8), Kannaḍa; the village headman; cf. *Uroḍĕya.*

Uroḍĕya (IA 12), Kannaḍa; official designation; cf. *Uroḍĕ.*

ūr-paddinkāḍi (EI 28), name of a rural tax.

urvarā (IE 7-1-2), 'one'.

uṣara, cf *sa-gartt-oṣara* (IE 8-5); a saline spot or barren land.

uśāvaḍi (IE 8-4; SITI), a subdivision of the district; same as *śāvaḍi* or *cāvaḍi.*

ūṣmala (EI 12), glowing.

uṣṇīṣa, cf. Prakrit *uṁnisa* (EI 20; LL), a coping stone. (*EI* 8), protuberance of the Buddha's skull.

utkalita, cf. *kaṭakam=utkalitam* (IA 14, 30), 'the camp was pitched'.

utkara (IE 8-5), probably, minor taxes; but see *kāru-kara.* Cf. *upakara*, *nikara*, etc. But see also Ghoshal, *H. Rev. Syst.*, p. 47.

utkarṇita (LP), frightened.

utkarṣa (CII 1), used in the sense of *utkṛṣṭa.*

Utkhātakārmaṇa (EI 15), epithet of a donee.

utkheṭana (EI 32; HRS), known from certain records from Assam; explained as an impost levied upon the villagers on specified occasions; probably, the trouble of free labour. Cf. *Utkheṭayitā*, *Autkheṭika.*

Utkheṭayitā (EI 12; BL; HRS), known from certain Assam records; explained as a tax-collector; officer in charge of *utkheṭana* (q.v.); same as *Autkheṭika.*

utkīrṇa (CII 3), 'engraved'; a technical expression for the actual engraving of an inscription on copper or stone; sometimes indicated by the word *udghāṭita* (*Ep. Ind.*, Vol. XXXI, p. 20) and *ghaṭita* (*Ind. Ant.*, Vol. XII, p. 121). See *Ullekhaka*, *likhita.*

utkoṭa (IE 8-5, 8-8; EI 33), Prakrit *ukkoḍa*; a levy; customary presents to be made on occasions to the king or landlord and others. See *Ep. Ind.*, Vol. XXXIII, p. 56.

ut-kṝ, 'to engrave'; cf. Prakrit *kaṇḍāra*, used in some Kannaḍa inscriptions (*Bul. Dec. Col. Res. Inst.*, Vol. XI, 1950, pp. 170-71). Cf. *utkīrṇa*, *udghāṭita*, *Ullekhaka*, *Vilekhaka*.

utkṛṣṭi (IE 8-8; EI 30), same as Prakrit *ukkuṭṭhī* (q.v.), Sanskrit *utkrośa*; wailing.

utkrośa (IE 8-8), see *utkṛṣṭi*.

utkṛti (IE 7-1-2), 'twentysix'; rarely 'twentyone'.

utpadyamāna-viṣṭika (CII 4), 'with the right to unpaid labour as occasion may arise'; a privilege attached to gift lands.

utpanna, decided or acertained (*Select Inscriptions*, pp. 284, 286); same as *pratipanna*; cf. *pratipad*.

ut-pāṭ (LP), Gujarātī *upāḍavuṁ*; cf. *Vaidyanātha-patram=utpāṭayati*, 'takes a *bilva-patra* of the god Vaidyanātha (Śiva)', i. e. swears.

utpāta (EI 33), unusual phenomenon.

utpaṭṭa, cf. *upaṭṭa* (EI 13), abundance; exuberance or overflowing [expecially of rich dishes at a feast].

utpatti (EI 12), cf. *samast-otpatti-sahita*, 'together with all the produce (or income)'.

utsāha (*Ep. Ind.*, Vol. XIV, p. 189), generous gift, bounty.

utsāha-śakti (CII 4), personal energy.

utsaṅga (HRS), extra cess levied upon villagers and citizens on occasions of festival events, such as the birth of a prince, as suggested by the *Arthaśāstra*.

utsarpaṇa, cf. *pañca-mahāyajña-kriy-otsarpaṇ-ārtham* (*Ep. Ind.*, Vol. XXXV, p. 279, text lines 64-65).

utsarpita (CII 1), erected.

utsṛta (CII 1)=*ucchrita*, man of a high position; a rich man.

utta (LP), modification of Sanskrit *putra*.

uttama-dāni (SITI), a gift made without expecting any merit for the same; a superior kind of gift.

uttama-gosāsa (IA 11), meaning uncertain.

uttam-ottama (EI 25), a type of temple.

uttāna-dvādaśi (SITI), twelfth day of the bright fortnight in the month of Kārttigai when the god Viṣṇu is believed to wake up from his sleep; see *utthāna-dvādaśī*.

uttara, cf. *uttarāṇi* (LP), same as *uttar-ākṣarāṇi*. See *akṣara*.

uttāra (SITI), a regular fixed payment; same as *uddhāra*.

Uttarakulika (EI 30), a class of officials.

Uttarakulika-vārika (IE 8-8), an official designation of uncertain import. See *Vārika*.

Uttara-mantrin (EI 8; SITI), the chief minister.

uttara-niyoga (EI 32), 'subsequent assignment'; cf. *ukta-niyoga*.

uttara-sabhā (EI 19), the supreme assembly.

uttara-vāda (SITI), a guarantee; responsibility.

uttar-āyaṇa (IA 17; SII 1), the winter solstice; the period during which the sun gradually moves from south to north; cf. *dakṣiṇ-āyana*.

utthāna (CII 1), exerting oneself.

utthāna-dvādaśī (*Ep. Ind.*, Vol. XVIII, pp. 163, 167, 169), name of a *tithi* (EI 9); twelfth day of the bright fortnight in the month of Kārttigai when the god Viṣṇu is believed to wake up from his sleep (SITI).

utthāya, 'of one's own accord' (*Select Inscriptions*, p. 248).

Utthit-āsanin (IE 8-3); see *Autthitāsanika*.

uttiram (SII 2), the projecting part of a wall.

uvaṭaka (EI 1), probably, a verandah, porch or vestibule; cf. Marāṭhī *oṭī*.

V

va (IE 8-1), abbreviation of *vaḍḍavāra* (Saturday or Thursday).

va (CII 3; IA 8-1), an abbreviation of *vadya* or 'the dark fortnight' or else a substitute for *ba* (abbreviation of *bahula*) used in connection with *di*; see *ba-di*, *va-di*.

va, *vā* (IE 8-1), abbreviation of Prakrit *vassa* or *vāsa*-Sanskrit *varṣā*, the rainy season.

vā (IE 8-1), abbreviation of *vāra*.

Cf. vā-bhū, *vā-ṭī*.

(*LP*), abbreviation of *Vāṇija*, a merchant.

vā-bhū (IE 8-1), abbreviation of *vāstu-bhūmi*, 'homestead land.'

Vācaka (LL), a Jain preacher.

vacana (IE 7-1-2), 'three'.

Vacanakāra (EI 23), an author of *vacanas* or sayings; cf. *subhāṣita*.

vācanika, cf. *rāja-vāchanika* (CII 1), a royal order.

vaco-gupti (CII 1), restraint in the matter of speech.

vāḍa (CITD), Telugu-Kannaḍa; a street, a range of houses.

(*EI* 11), a ward.

(*IA* 7), also *vāḍi*; often suffixed to geographical names.

(*CII* 4), name of a tax.

vāḍa, vāḍā (IE 8-4), corrupt forms of *pāṭaka*, 'part of a village'; in some dialects, also 'a village'; often suffixed to the names of localities.

Vaḍaharaka (EI 11), same as Marvāḍī (Marwari) *Baḍero*; an old man.

Vaḍḍ-ācārya (SII 11-1), Sanskrit *Vṛddh-ācārya* or *Bṛhad-ācārya*; designation of a Jain teacher.

vaḍḍa-vāra (EI 13; CITD), Telugu-Kannaḍa; Saturday or Thursday (A. Venkatasubbiah, *Some Śaka Dates in Inscriptions*, pp. 57. ff.); same as *bṛha-vāra*. The word in the Telugu part of an inscription is explained as *śanaiścara-vāra* in the Sanskrit portion of the said record; sometimes wrongly supposed to stand for some other day, e.g. Friday (IA 23) or Sunday (Venkatasubbiah, *op. cit.*, p. 58). Cf. *Ep. Ind.*, Vol. XII, p. 147; XIII, p. 16; Vol. XXXI, p. 100, note 1; Vol. XXXIII, p. 1, note 2; *Ind. Ant.*, Vol. XXII, pp. 111, 251-52; XXIII, p. 168. *Vaḍḍa*=*vṛddha* or *bṛhat*.

Vaḍḍa-vyavahāri (SITI; ASLV), the leader of a merchant guild; a banker; the principal money-changer; chief of the *Nānādeśi* (non-local) merchants. Cf. *Mahāvaḍḍavyavahāri*.

Vaḍavā (EI 22, 27), Marāṭhī; record-keeper.

vādha (EI 16), land measure.

vādhā, cf. *bādhā*.

vāḍhaḍhā (IA 15), a doubtful word probably meaning 'a drum'.

vadhri-kukkuṭa (IA 18, CII 1), Prakrit *vadhi-kukuṭa*; a capon; also Sanskritised as *vṛddhi-kukkuṭa*.

vadhū, one's own wife; one's son's wife. (*putra-vadhū*)

va-di (IE 8-1), abbreviation of *vadya-pakṣa-dina* or a mistake for *ba-di* (q.v.).

vāḍi (IA 7), same as *vāḍa*; often suffixed to geographical names.

vādya (SITI), a musical instrument.

Vādya-mahārāja, cf. Tamil *Vācciya-mārāyaṉ* (SITI), the head musician or the chief *Meḻakāraṉ* of a temple or palace; title conferred by the king on an expert in instrumental music.

vagaira (IA 20), Persian; 'and so forth'.

Vāgulī (EI 28), Oḍiyā ; also written *Bāgulī*; the king's betel-bearer; same as *Vārgulika*, etc.

Vāgulika, Vāgūlika (CII 4; BL), explained by some as 'a seller of betel-leaves'; the bearer of the betel-box of an Orissan ruler; same as *Vārgulika*, etc.

Vāguṇi (EI 24), mistake for *Vāguli*.

vaha, cf. *a-vaha* (IE 8-5); [free] carrying of loads [which the villagers had to provide for the touring officers of the king or land-lord]; may also be a horse for the use of the officers.

(*EI* 31; IA 18; CII 4), a streamlet; a water-channel.

(*Ep. Ind.*, Vol. XIV, p. 177), a common highway.

vāha, cf. *Vāha-nāyaka*.

Vāhaka (EI 3), probably, a driver or attendant of cattle.

vāhalā (EI 3), a water course.

Vāhali (BL), official designation explained as 'the lord of horses'.

vahamāna (LP), cf. *vahamāna-hala-balīvarda*, 'bullocks used in ploughing land'; *vahamāna-samakara-bhūmi* in which *vahamāna* means '[the land that is] being ploughed'.

(*LP*), travelling.

vāhana (LP), a load-carrier; a cart, ship, etc. See *vahitra*.

Vāha-nāyaka (EI 23), official designation; probably, 'the officer in charge of the king's *Khās Mahāls*' (from *vāha*, a plough); may also be the superintendent of transport. See *vāhoṭaka*.

vahikā (LP), an account book.

Vāhinīpati (EI 28; IA 10), leader of forces; a general; cf. *Senāpati*, etc.

vahaṇi (IA 18), meaning uncertain.

vahitra (IE 8-5, 8-8; EI 30), boat or any large carrier like a cart; see *vāhana*. Cf. *sārtha-vahitreṣu praveśe nirgame ca pratyekaṁ rūpakaḥ devasya yātr-otsave dātavyaḥ* (*Ep. Ind.*, Vol. XXV, p. 232).

(*IE* 8-8),cf. *bhāṇḍa-bhṛta-vahitra*,'a wagon full of pots or jars'.

vahni (IE 7-1-2, 'three'.

vāhoṭaka (LP), either Gujarātī *vighoṭi*, an assessment of land collected per *vighā* (*bīghā*), or the plough tax (i.e. land tax) from *vāha*, a plough.

vāhyāli (BL), explained as 'stables'; cf. *bāhy-āli*. (*EI* 6), explained as 'a camp'.

vahni (EI 33), 'three'.

vaibhoga, cf. *aṅga-raṅga-vaibhoga* (EI 3; SII 1; SITI); same as *bhoga*.

vaidarveyaka, cf. *vedaveyaka* (IA 18; CII 1), an eel.

vaidharaṇa (HRS), a compensation fee levied upon the sale of liquors, royal merchandise, mining products and imported salt, as suggested by the *Arthaśāstra*.

vaidila (CII 3), a word of uncertain import.

Vaidya (EI 9, 30; BL), a physician; member of the physician community.

vaidya-bhāga (SII 2), same as *vaidya-bhoga*, *vaidya-vṛtti*.

vaidya-bhoga (SITI), also called *vaidya-bhāga*, *vaidya-vṛtti*; land set apart for the maintenance of the physician.

Vaidya-paricāraka, cf. Tamil *Vaijya-paricārakar* (EI 24), medical attendants.

vaidya-vṛtti (SII 1), land enjoyed by the Vaidyas for their maintenance ; cf. *vaidya-bhāga*, *vaidya-bhoga*.

Vaijaka (EI 26), official designation; probably *Vaidyaka*.

vaijayika, carrying victory; cf. *Ep. Ind.*, XXXII, p. 88. See *vijaya-vaijayika*.

vaijayika-dharmasthāna (EI 22), 'the victorious office of justice'.

Vaikṣepika (EI 8-3; EI 26), probably, the dispatcher of messengers; same as *Preṣaṇika*. Cf. *Ep. Ind.*, Vol. XXVI, p. 206. See also *vikṣepa*.

Vailabdhika (EI 8-3; EI 30), officer in charge of *vilabdhi* (q.v.); probably, the custodian of recovered stolen property.

Vaidāntika (BL), an exponent of the *Vedānta*.

vaira (IA 18), blood-money.

Vairāgi (SITI), an ascetic serving in a temple.

vaiśāradya cf. *vesārajja* (EI 5), Buddhist; four in number.

Vaiṣayika (EI 7), probably, the ruler of a *viṣaya* or district.

vaiśvadeva (EI 10, 14, 23; CII 3, 4), offerings to gods; one of the five *mahāyajñas*; sometimes called *vaiśvānara*.

vaiśvānara (IE 7-1-2), 'three'.

Cf. vaiśvadeva.

Vaiśvāsika (IE 8-3; EI 9, 28, 29), probably the same as *Rahasyādhikṛta*, etc.; cf. *Paramaviśvāsin*, *Viśvāsa*, *Viśvāsika*; the privy councillor or private secretary.

(*EI* 3), mentioned a'ong with *Antaraṅga.*

vaiśy-āgrahāra (IE 8-5; EI 30, 33), a privileged holding created in favour of members of the mercantile community; see *agrahāra.*

vaiśya-vāṇiya-nagarattār (SITI), ASLV), Sanskrit *vaiśya-vāṇija-nagarastha*; a corporation of the merchants; the guild of a class of merchants.

vājapeya (EI 22; CII 4; BL), name of a Vedic sacrifice.

vājin (IE 7-1-2), 'seven'.

Vāji-vaidya (BL), explained as 'a veterinary physician'; literally, 'a physician for horses'.

vajra (HA), thunderbolt.

Cf. vaccira-ppaḍai (SITI), the lower or foundation tier of the wall of a temple.

vajrāsana (LL), name of the seat on which the Buddha sat for meditation for the attainment of supreme knowledge (*bodhi*).

vāk-pāruṣya (EI 30), use of abusive language.

vākṣa (Chamba), tax in cash; same as *bācha.*

valadī (*Ind. Ant.*, Vol. XVIII, p. 17, text line 21), correctly *baladī* derived from *balīvarda*; same as *vara-balīvarda*, etc.

vāḻa-giri (SITI), abbreviation of the name of the mythical mountain called *cakravāla-giri.*

vaḻanāḍu (IE 8-4; EI 25), Tamil ; a province; a district consisting of sub-divisions called *kuṟṟam* or *nāḍu.*

valakṣa (IA 17), used to indicate the bright fortnight.

vālanīya (LP), see *valiṣyati.*

Valatkauṣan (CII 3), official designation of uncertain import; probably, a mistake for *Bala-kauṣṭhika*, officer-in-charge of the treasury of the military department. Cf. *Mahavalākoṣṭhika.*

Valākoṣṭhika, probably, a mistake for *Balakoṣṭhika*; cf. *Valatkauṣan*, *Mahāvalākoṣṭhika.*

valaya (CITD), a ring; a bracelet; in Telugu-Kannaḍa, also an enclosure, a boundary.

vala-yaṣṭi (CII 4), mistake for *bala-yaṣṭi*, memorial pillar.

valaya-yaṣṭi (EI 33; CII 3), wrong emendation of *bala-yaṣṭi* and supposed to mean 'a boundary-pillar'. See *bala-yaṣṭi.*

vālayitvā (LP), Gujarātī *vāḻine.*

valhoḍīya (LP), rams.

vāḻi (SII 2), ear-ring.

valiṣyati (LP), cf. Gujarātī *vāḻi levāmāṁ āvaśe*; see *vālanīya.*

valita, vaḻita (E 12; SITI), same as *vaṇita*; a small territorial unit; a district or its subdivision.

valita-patra-vidhi (LP), cf. Gujarātī *vaḻat-dān-khat.*

valīvarda, variant spelling of *balīvarda* (q.v.); cf. *a-paramparā-valīvarda*, etc. (IE 8-5); a pair of bullocks [which the villagers were obliged to provide for the cart of the royal officers when they were camping or touring in the village].

valla (IE 8-8), name of a weight equal to 3 *ratis*; see *dvi-vallakya.*

Vallabha (IE 8-3; EI 12, 26), the king's favourite or a courtier; same as *Rājavallabha.*

(*IE* 8-2), same as *Vallabharāja*; a shortened form of the title *Śrī-pṛthivī-vallabha* assumed by certain imperial rulers of the Kannaḍa-speaking area.

vallakya, cf. *dvi-vallakya.*

Vallava (IE 8-3; 27; LL), official designation; officer in charge of the king's cattle; same as Sanskrit *Vallabha*, a herdsman.

vāmana-mudrā (SITI), figures of *śaṅkha* and *cakra* marked on the boundary stones set up to demarcate the lands of a Viṣṇu temple. Cf. *Vāmana-kkal*, boundary stone of land granted for religious purposes.

vāṁphaya, cf. *niddhi-vāṁphaya-sahita* (EI 12), wrong reading of *nidhi-nikṣepa-sahita.*

vaṁśadhara (EI 24), a palanquin-bearer.

Vaṁśakara (LL), a bamboo-worker.

Vaṁś-āvalī (IA 30), a genealogical list; called *kula-pañjī* or *kula-pañjikā* in Bengal.

Vāṁśika (EI 33), a flute-player.

vaṁśya, same as *dhvaṁśī* (q.v.).

vana, a source of income. See Ghoshal, *H. Rev. Syst.*, pp. 109-10. Cf. *nāga-vana* (IE 8-4), an elephant-forest.

vanacara (EI 12), an animal.

vanadhi (IE 7-1-2), used in the sense of *vāridhi* to indicate 'four.'

vana-durga (ASLV), fort built in the midst of forests.

Vaṇajāraka, also spelt *Vaṇijāraka* (EI 11), same as the *Vanjārī* of Rājasthān, whose hereditary calling is to carry grains on pack-bullocks; cf. *Vaṇijjāraka*.

vandāpanā (IE 8-5; EI 12, 33), Oḍiyā; presents to be made on meeting the king or landlord; same as Persian *nazrāna*; cf. *vijaya-vandāpanā*.

Vaṅgālī, see *Bengali* which is its Anglicised spelling.

Vāṇija, *Vāṇijaka* (EI 15; LL), a merchant.

Vaṇijjāraka (BL), probably, merchants or traders of caravans; cf. *Vaṇajāraka*.

Vaṇik (IE 8-3; BL), merchant or a member of the merchantile community.

vaṇik-patha, 'trade-route'; a revenue term. See Ghoshal, *H. Rev. Syst.*, pp. 79-80.

vaṇik-sthāna (EI 23), an association of merchants.

Vaṇik-suvarṇakāra (BL), probably, 'one who is a banker and a goldsmith'; cf. the Suvarṇa-vaṇik community of Bengal.

vaṇiṅ-koṭṭa (CII 4), 'the traders' fortress'.

Vaṇiṅ-nagara (CII 4), 'a town of merchants'.

vaṇita (IE 8-4; SITI), Kannaḍa; same as *vaḻita*; a small territorial unit like a Parganā.

vañjulī (IA 26), the twelfth *tithi*.

vanniā (IE 8-8), Prakrit; same as Sanskrit *varṇikā* (q.v.).

vaṇṭaka (EI 9, 13), a share.

vaṇṭya (EI 12), a district; cf. *vĕṇṭhĕ*, *vĕṇṭhĕya*.

vāpa (*Ep. Ind.*, Vol. XV, p. 310, note 4), explained as a handcast or handful; but really, the same as *vapa*, sowing [seed grains apparently by handcast].

(*EI* 15), cf. *kulyavāpa* (area requiring one *kulya* measure of seeds to be sown by handcast); see *vāpa-gatyā*, etc.

(*EI* 3), a land measure.

vāpa-gatyā, cf. *vauge* (EI 10), grain sown broadcast.

vāpī (EI 13), step-well; an irrigation well; same as *vāpikā*.

(*Ep. Ind.*, Vol. VII, p. 46, note 8), a well with a flight of stairs; cf. *kūpa* which is an ordinary well.

(*EI* 22), a reservoir of water.

vāpikā (CCI 3), a step-well, an irrigation well; same as *vāpī*.

vappaka (EI 23), a land measure. Same as *vapyaka*, *vāpa*.

vapyaka (EI 3), a land measure; same as *vappaka*, *vāpa*.

vāra (BL), a board of administrators [formed by the *śreṣṭhins*, *sārthavāhas* and others].

(*IA* 16), the solar day.

(*SITI*), method of reciting the Vedas.

(*Ep. Ind.*, Vol. III, p. 17, note 1), probably, a week.

(*EI* 30; SITI), a share of the produce.

(*EI* 24), a multitude. Cf. also *vāra-Nāka-Lokta-Gāñik-ādīnāṁ*, 'belonging to Nāka, Lokta and Gāñika collectively' (*JAS*, Letters, Vol. XX, pp. 202, 204).

(*CII* 1), cf. *vārataḥ*, 'in consequence of an occasion.'

(*EI* 23), same as *vāra-goṣṭhī*; a committee; cf. *vāra-pramukha*. *Vāra* is the same as Tamil *vāriyam*.

(*IE* 7-1-2), 'seven'.

Cf. bāre (Chamba), 'during or in the time of'.

vara-balīvarda (EI 12, 33), tax on choice bullocks for bull-fights; cf. *valadī*, *yamalikambali*, etc.

varada-mudrā (HA), the gift-bestowing attitude of the right hand with palm outwards and fingers pointing downwards.

vāra-goṣṭhī (EI 5, 23), a committee's assembly.

vara-grāma (SITI), village given as a gift to a temple or *maṭha* or a Brāhmaṇa.

vāra-gṛha (EI 19), outside houses ; cf. Sanskrit *bahir-gṛha*.

varāha (IE 8-8; EI 25; SITI; SII 1), also called *hūn* or *hon*; name of a gold coin called *pagoda* or 'star *pagoda*' in English; Cf. *doḍḍa-varāha* (EI 20), *varāha-paṇam* (SITI), *varāhanpuḻḻi-kuḻigai* (SITI), *parumuḻai-varāhan* (SITI); etc.

varāha-gadyāṇa (EI 8, 27), same as *varāha* or *gadyāṇa*; i.e. a *pagoda*.

varāhakīya-viṁśopaka (EI 1), name of a coin which was one-twentieth of a *varāha* in value.

varāha-mudrā, cf. *varāha-muddirai* (SITI), the seal or emblem bearing the figure of a boar, being the crest of certain kings like those of Vijayanagara.

varāka (CII 1), distressed.

Vārakṛta (EI 23), official designation.

varaṇa (SITI), the selection or election of a person to a committee.

varaṇḍikā-vṛta (LP), 'surrounded by a verandah'.

Vāra-pramukha (EI 5), the head of a committee.

vāra-siddhi, cf. *a-vāra-siddhika* (EI 8-5); probably refers to the supply of unpaid labour by the villagers in turn.

varaṭakā (EI 1), 'cowrie-shell used as a coin'; same as *varāṭikā*.

varāṭikā, 'a cowrie-shell used as a coin'; money. See *Gaurī-varāṭikā*, *varaṭakā*, *barāḍ*.

varavajhe (*Ind. Ant.*, Vol. XIV, p. 103, text line 12), doubtful name of a tax; same as *vara-balīvarda*, *baladī*, etc.

vara-yātrā (IE 8-8; EI 30), probably, the procession of a bride-groom to the bride's place for marriage.

Vardhaki (LL), a carpenter; cf. *Śaila-vardhaki*, a mason or sculptor.

vardhamāna (LP), 'when cut down.'

vārdhi (EI 25), 'seven'.

varga (CII 1), a group or cadre of officers.

Vārgulika (IE 8-3; EI 28; BL), same as Oḍiyā *Bāguli*, *Vāguli*; the bearer of the king's betel-box. Cf. *Veṭakila*.

vari (SITI), Tamil; tax; revenue register; order of the king and his officers fixing the revenue. Cf. *vari-ppotta-gam*, tax register; an officer maintaining the same; also *Vari-ppottaga-nāyakam*, the head office of the revenue accounts; the chief officer of the same office.

vāridhi (IE 7-1-2), 'four'.

Vāriga (EI 33), corruption of *Vārika*.

vāri-gṛha-karaṇa, cf. *karaṇa* (LP); explained as 'the department of water works'.

Vārika (IE 8-8; EI 30, 32), a class of officials; the priest or superintendent of a temple like a *Pāṇḍā* of modern times; cf. *Deva-vārika* (EI 27), superintendent of a temple; also cf. Tamil *Vāriyan* (SITI), a supervisor.

Cf. *Mahāgandhakuṭī-vārika* (LL), 'superintendent of the great *gandhakūṭī* (q.v.).' The official designation *Pāṭvāri* seems to be derived from *Paṭṭavārika*.

Cf. Tamil *vāriyaṁ* (SITI), an executive committee; appointment as a member of that body; an office of superivision; cf. *śrībhaṇḍāra-vāriyam* (EI 33). See *SII*, Vol. III, p. 151, note.

Cf. *bārika* (EI 5, 19), a village official; one entrusted with putting an official seal or stamp to a document; cf. *bārika-jana-hasta*.

vārinidhi (IE 7-1-2), 'four'.

varkara (IA 19), a goat; cf. *botkaṭa*, etc.

varṇa (IE 7-1-2), 'four'.

(*Select Inscriptions*, p. 187, text line 6), same as *varṇanā*, a description or list.

varṇana (*Select Inscriptions*, p. 202), a written order.

varṇikā (IE 8-8; EI 30), same a Prakrit *vanniā*, a sample; sometimes, a small measure of capacity (*Ep. Ind.*, Vol. XIV, p. 302, verse 69).

varṣa (CII 3, 4; IA 17), a year; used for *saṁvatsara* or its abbreviations.

(*EI* 23), the rainy season.

Cf. varṣe (IA 19), used in the dates after the quotation of *saṁvat*; sometimes abbreviated to *va*. Cf. *samaye* used in the same sense.

Cf. Tamil *varuṣa-kāṇikkai* (SITI), annual presents.

(*IE* 7-1-2), 'nine'; cf. the nine divisions of Jambu-dvīpa.

varṣa-granthi (EI 8), an anniversary.

varṣa-paryuṣita (IE 8-8; EI 30), probably, 'camping for the rainy season only'; used in connection with merchants.

varṣa-vartamānī, the annual Durbar (*Journ. Or. Inst.*, Vol. X, p. 15).

varṣa-vṛddhi, probably 'birthday anniversary' (*JAS*, Letters, Vol. XX, p. 206).

Vārta, Vartta (CII 4; IA 14), same as *Vṛtti-bhuj*, 'one who enjoys a grant or the share of a grant'; a person in possession of a *vṛtti*.

vartamāna (HRS), 'running revenue', as suggested by the *Arthaśāstra*.

vartamāna-bhaviṣyat (IE 8-3), 'of the present and future'; used with reference to the officers associated with a gift land.

vartanā (SITI), perquisites due to an office; periodical presents to be offered to an officer of rank by his subordinates and the people. Cf. *vartanī*.

vartanī (HRS), transit duties collected by the ferrymen, the superintendent of tolls and the boundary officer, as suggested by the *Arthaśāstra*. Cf. *vartanā*.

(*IA* 18), a district; often found suffixed to the names of districts in the Kaliṅga region.

(*Ep. Ind.*, Vol. XXXIV, p. 174), a road.

Vārt-ānukarṣaka (IA 6), official designation of doubtful meaning; probably, a spy; mentioned in the *Mahābhārata.*

vartma-daṇḍa (IE 8-5), tolls collected on the roads for the passage of articles of merchandise through a village. Cf. Tamil *vaḻiy-āyam* (SITI), 'tolls on the roadway'.

Vartmapāla (IE 8-3), superintendent of roads or the collector of the *vartma-daṇḍa.*

vāru-ghoṭaka (LP), a riding horse; cf. Marāṭhī *vāru.*

vāruṇī, cf. *mahāmahāvāruṇī*, *mahāvāruṇī* (EI 25); name of a *tithi.*

Va-sā (PJS), probably, an abbreviation of *Vaṇik-sādhu*, 'a merchant'.

vasad-bhoga-maryādā (IA 5), explained as 'the condition that the gift villages should be enjoyed only by those residing therein'; the custom relating to the enjoyment of the gift land yb the donee by residing therein; but see *vasad-bhogya-maryādā.*

vasad-bhogya-maryādā (EI 24), interpreted as 'with the tenants' occupancy rights assured'; same as *vasad-bhoga-maryādā.*

vasadi (EI 10), Sanskrit *vasati*; a Jain temple; cf. *vasahī.*

Vāsāgārika (IE 8-3; EI 30), officer in charge of the king's bed-chamber. See *Vitān-ādhipa*, *Śayyāpāla*, *Śayyāgrāhaka.*

vasahī (HA), Sanskrit *vasati*; a Jain temple; cf. *vasadi.*

vāsaka (EI 3, 14, 23, 30; IA 13), royal residence whence the copper-plate grants were often issued; the camp or capital of a king.

vāsa-kṣepa (HA), scattering of powder; also the powder itself.

Vāśal (ASLV), same as *Vāśal-kāriyam*; chief guard of the palace.

Vāśal-kāriyam (ASLV), also called *Vāśal*; chief guard of the palace.

vāśal-paṇam (SII 1), the door-money.

vāsanikā (EI 23), a dwelling.

vasantagaruvu (ASLV), a rest house.

vasanta-maṇḍapa (SITI), *maṇḍapa* in the midst of a pleasure garden where the spring-festival of a deity is celebrated.

vasant-otsava (BL), spring festival.

Vāsāpaka (EI 6, 12; CII 4; IA 12, 13), explained as 'officials whose duty was to assign places of residence to strangers'; also spelt *Vāsāvaka*; cf. also the tax called *vāsāvakī* (EI 33). Cf. *Ind. Ant.*, Vol. XIII, p. 69, note 11.

Vāsāvaka (CII 4), same as *Vāsāpaka*.

vasāvakī (EI 33), name of a tax; cf. the official designation *Vāsāpaka* or *Vāsāvaka*.

vasati, modified to *basadi* (EI 10), *baṣahi* (HA), *pasti*, *basti* (SITI), etc.; a Jain temple.

vasati-daṇḍa (EI 25), obligation of the villagers to supply food to the royal officers camping in their village; explained by some as 'the tax for the lodging of touring royal officers' (CII 4); but probably refers to an obligation and not a tax.

Vāsela-kuṭuṁbika (LP), resident farmers; cf. Gujarātī *Vasṇārā-kaṇbī*.

Vāstavya (EI 16), a community of the *Kāyasthas*.

(*Ep. Ind.*, Vol. XXXIV, p. 172, note 3), rarely also called *sāmānya*; 'resident'.

vāstu (EI 15, 32), homestead land.

vāstu-bhūmi (IE 8-1), homestead land.

vāstuka, a building site. See Ghoshal, *H. Rev. Syst.*, pp. 97-98.

vāstu-kṛtya (SITI), building work.

vāstu-parivāra (SITI), vacant site attached to a house.

vastu-prābhṛtaka, cf. *vastu-prābhṛtakena* (LP), 'in exchange for a present'.

vasu (IE 7-1-2; EI 15), 'eight'.

vāsu (E*p* 11), a ward.

vasudhā (IE 7-1-2), 'one'.

vasundharā (IE 7-1-2), 'one'.

vasu-patra-padma (IA 9), eight-petalled lotus.

vāta (IE 8-5; EI 15; CII 3), cf. *sa-bhūta-vāta-pratyāya*, etc.; probably, storms (cf. *udvāta*); also called *āvāta*.

vāt-ādeya (EI 32), 'income resulting from storms'; same as *vāta-pratyāya*.

vāṭaka (LL), a garden.

(*IE* 8-4; EI 15; IA 7), corrupt form of *pāṭaka*; 'part of a village'; often suffixed to names of localities.

Cf. the second component in *Talla-vāṭaka*, meaning modern *vāḍa*, spelt in English as *wara*.

vaṭaka, same as *tolaka* (q.v.).

vāta-pratyāya (EI 32; CII 4), explained by some as 'octroi duty', but actually, 'income resulting from storms'; same as *vāt-ādeya*. See *bhūta-vāta-pratyāya*, etc.

va-ti (IE 8-1), contraction of *vadya-pakṣa-tithi*, though *va* may be a mistake for *ba* (*bahula*).

vāṭi, *vāṭī* (IE 8-6; EI 28, 30), also called *vāṭikā* (q. v.); land measure equal to twenty *māṇas* in Orissa.

vā-ṭī, abbreviation of *vāstu-ṭīkara*, 'a mound containing land suitable for building houses.' See *Ep. Ind.*, Vol. XXX, p. 56.

vāṭikā (EI 15; SITI), same as *nilam* or *veḷi*, defined in the *Mayamata* as 5120 square *daṇḍas*, the length of the *daṇḍa* being 4 cubits; 4. 48 acres.

(*EI* 30), a land measure equal to twenty *māṇas* in Orissa; same as *vāṭi*, *vāṭī*; equal to 20 acres.

(*EI* 27), a hamlet.

vāt-ottara (IE 8-5), 'resulting from storms'; cf. *vāt-ādeya*, etc.

vaṭṭa-grāma (EI 24), subsidiary village.

vaṭṭam (SITI), money-changer's commission; trade discount.

Vaṭṭeḻuttu, name of an alphabet prevalent in medieval times in the southern part of the Tamil-speaking area and the land to its west.

vāva (IE 8-2), one's uncle or a relation of one's father's generation; cf. *vāva-pād-ānudhyāta*, 'meditating on (or, favoured by) the feet of the uncle (or a relation of one's father's generation).'

Vāy-kkeḻvi, *Vāy-kkeḻviyār* (SITI), an officer who received the king's oral orders; an officer in attendance on the king, acting as the intermediary between the king and his subjects; the king's order. Cf. *Ājñapti*.

vāyu (IE 7-1-2), 'fortynine'.

veda (IE 7-1-2), 'four' (the four Vedas being *Ṛk*, *Yajus*, *Sāman* and *Atharvan*); rarely used to indicate 'three' (cf. *trayī*) in late records (IE 7-1-2; IA 9).

veda-maṭha (ASLV), school for teaching the Vedas.. There was such a school at Kāñcīpuram. Cf. *śālā*, *khaṇḍikā*, *Ṛgveda-khaṇḍikā*.

Veda-pārāyaṇa (IA 12), priest who repeats the Veda at the Rāmeśvaram temple.

vedaveyaka (CII 1), Prakrit; see *vaidarveyaka*.

veda-vṛtti (SITI), tax-free land set apart for meeting the expenses of reciting the Vedas.

vedi (EI 32), a seat; also a raised platform (cf. *vedikā*).

See *JBRS*, Vol. XXXIX, Parts 1-2, pp. 43-44, 47; *Ep. Ind.*, Vol. XXXV, p. 192.

vedikā (LL), a rail; also, a raised platform (cf. *vedi*). See *Ep. Ind.*, Vol. XXXV, p. 192.

Vĕggaḍĕ (IE 8-3), same as *Vĕrgaḍĕ, Pĕggaḍĕ, Pĕrgaḍĕ, Hĕggaḍĕ*, etc. (q.v.).

Velā-durga-pāla (SITI), a port officer.

Veḻai-kkārar (SITI), Tamil; trusted warriors even prepared to lay down their lives in the service of their master.

velākula, velākūla (IE 8-4; EI 31; LP), a harbour.

velākula-karaṇa, cf. *karaṇa* (LP); the harbour department.

velāpura, cf. *velāura* (IA 10, 14), a harbour; same as *velākūla*.

Velāvitta (HD), meaning uncertain. See *Rājataraṅgiṇī*, V. 226; VI. 73, 106, 126. Cf. *Pīṭhikāvitta*.

veḻi (IE 8-6; EI 25), Tamil; a big land measure. See *vāṭikā*.

veli-cenu (CITD), Telugu; usually, a field on a high level depending on rain water.

veli-polamu (CITD), Telugu; see *veli-volamu*.

veli-volamu (CITD), Telugu; also called *veli-polamu*; similar to *veli-cenu*.

veḻḻi (EI 15), name of a coin.

venā (EI 31), a kind of grass.

veṇī (IA 17), a stream or river.

veṅkaṭa-vilāsa-maṇṭapa (ASLV), hall in which the royal council met at Vijayanagara.

vĕṇṭhĕ (EI 16; ASLV), same as *viṣaya, nirvṛtti, koṭṭam*, etc.; an administrative division; also called *vĕṇṭhĕya, vaṇṭya, vĕṭha, vĕṭa*.

vĕṇṭhĕya (EI 16), a sub-division or district; same as *vĕṇṭhĕ*.

Vĕrgaḍĕ (IE 8-3), Kannaḍa; same as *Vĕggaḍĕ, Pĕrgaḍĕ, Hĕggaḍĕ*, etc.; also Sanskrit *Adhyakṣa, Adhikārin* (a superintendent or governor).

veśya (CII 4), explained as 'situated in...'. Cf. *prāveśya*.

vĕṭa (IE 8-4), same as *vĕṇṭhĕ*, etc.

Veṭakila (IE 8-3); HD), probably 'the bearer of *vīṭikā* (betel *bīḍā*)'. See Vogel. *Ant. Ch. St.*, p. 128. Cf. *Vārgulika*; also *Paṭṭakila*.

vetana, vetanā (SITI), wages (used along with *veṭṭi*, i.e.

Sanskrit *viṣṭi* or unpaid labour); probably wages for the labourers in the public works of the village.

vĕṭha (IE 8-4), Kannaḍa; same as *vĕṇṭhĕ*, *vĕṭa*, etc.; a small territorial unit.

Vetrika (EI 9; CII 4), explained by some as 'the chamberlain'; cf. *Yāṣṭika*, *Piśuna-vetrika*.

vi (CITD), abbreviation of Telugu *vinnapamulu*, representation or saying. It may stand for *visālu* (*visā* or *vīsa*) also.

vibhāga (HRS), king's share of the output of mines; as suggested by the *Arthaśāstra*, rent from mines and from the private manufacturers of salt.

vibhava (IA 14), used in the sense of *nirvāṇa* (q.v.).

vibheda (IE 8-4), subdivision of a *khaṇḍa* of Bhārata or Bhārata-varsa.

vibhoga (EI 16), holy ashes; same as *vibhūti* (q.v.).

vibhūti (IA 12), holy ashes; same as *vibhoga*.

(*SITI*), also called *vibhūti-kāṇikkai* in Tamil inscriptions; originally, voluntary contribution to a temple by the devotees while receiving the sacred ashes; later, it was collected as a tax.

Vicārakartṛ, (EI 8), a supervisor.

vicitra-kavitva (CITD), probably, a class of poetry like *citra-kavitva*, abounding in all kinds of highly artificial verses displaying the pedantry and verbal jugglery of the composer.

viḍālapadaka, same as *vivarṇa* (q.v.).

vidha (SITI), variety, kind.

vidhāraṇā (EI 1), same as *paripanthanā*, 'creating obstacles'.

vidhi-patra (LP), a judgement.

vidhu (IE 7-1-2), 'one'.

viḍūra-sāra (EI 3), same as *vaiḍūrya*.

vidvaj-jana (SITI), a body of learned men.

vidyā (CII 4), the right knowledge.

(*IE* 7-1-2), 'fourteen'.

vidyā-bhoga (EI 18), same as *vidy-ānubhoga* and *vidyā-dhana*.

vidyā-cāraṇa, see *cāraṇa* (EI 3).

vidyā-dhana (HRS), explained as land assigned as a reward for learning; same as *vidyā-bhoga* and *vidy-ānubhoga*.

vidyādhara-toraṇa (SII 2), an ornamental arch probably depicting Vidyādharas; cf. *makara-toraṇa*.

Vidy-ādhikārin (EI 11, 25; HD), officer in charge of a school or of schools; the director of education. Cf. *Ep. Ind.*, Vol. XI, p. 314.

vidy-ānubhoga (SITI), an endowment of land to a school for the encouragement of learning.

Vidyārthin (SITI), a student.

vidyā-sthāna (EI 2; SII 2; SITI), an educational institution for higher studies; a college.

vigrahadramma-visovaka (EI 1), name of a coin; the latter part of the name (i.e. *visovaka=viṁśopaka*) suggests that it was one-twentieth of the *vigraha-dramma* in value.

vigrahapāla-dramma (EI 1), name of a coin; same as *vigrahapāla-satka-dramma, vigrahapālīya-dramma.*

vigrahapāla-satka-dramma (EI 1), see *vigrahapālīya-dramma*, etc.

vigrahapālīya-dramma (EI 1; CII 4), name of a coin apparently so called after a king named Vigrahapāla.

vigrahatuṅgīya-dramma (EI 1; CII 4), name of a coin apparently so called after a king named Vigrahatuṅga.

vihāra (EI 22, 25; CII 3, 4; BL), a Buddhist or Jain monastery or temple or convent (EI 35).

(*HA*), wandering of a Jain monk; also a Jain temple.

Vihārakāraka, cf. Prakrit *Viharakarahvaa* (CII 2-1), 'one who builds a monastery'; same as *Vihārasvāmin*; explained by some as 'the superintendent of monastery' (ML).

Viharamāṇa-Jina (HA), a Jina at present living in other *kṣetras*.

Vihārapāla, 'the manager of a monastery' (*Select Inscriptions*, p. 345).

Vihārasvāmin (EI 8, 33; CII 3; BL; LL), 'the master of a monastery'; the builder or owner of a monastery. Cf. *Vihārakāraka*.

Vihārasvāminī (CII 3; IA 11), the feminine form of *Vihārasvāmin*; wife of a *Vihārasvāmin* or the female owner of a *vihāra*.

vihāra-yātrā (CII 1), a pleasure-tour.

vihārikā (EI 23, 27), derived from *vihāra, vihāraka*; a small *vihāra* or monastery.

vihiṁsā (CII 1), hurting, injuring.

vihita (CII 1), established; settled.

vihṛtayati, '[he] wastes' (*Select Inscriptions*, p. 245).

vijālayitavya, to be untied (*Select Inscriptions*, p. 238).

Vijāṭin (IA 11), cf. *Vijāṭi-vidyādhara*, 'a *Vidyādhara* unwinding his head-dress'.

vijaya, used in Kannaḍa inscriptions in the sense of 'going in state, going in a triumpal procession, making a state procession, making a state progress through one's dominions' (*Ep. Ind.*, Vol. V, p. 223, note 6; Vol. VI, p. 51, note 5).

(*Ep. Ind.*, Vol. XXXI, p. 18), Oḍiyā, etc.; used in Oḍiyā inscriptions in the sense of 'stay'.

(*IA* 7), cf. *vijaya-rājya-saṁvatsara*, *vijaya-saṁvatsara*, *vijaya-kaṭaka*, *vijaya-skandhāvāra*, etc. Cf. *śrī-vijaya* and *śrī-vijaya-śiva*.

vijayā (IA 26), same as *su-di* 11 or the eleventh *tithi*.

vijay-ābhiṣeka (SITI), being crowned as a victor; same as *vīr-ābhiṣeka*.

vijaya-candra (SII 2), name of an ornament.

vijayā-daśamī (EI 31), Āśvina-sudi 10.

vijayaka (LP), same as *vijaya*, victory.

vijaya-kaṭaka (EI 2; LP), 'the victorious camp'; the royal camp or capital.

vijaya-lekha (EI 9), a royal record.

vijayarāja-ṭaṅka (CII 4), name of a coin apparently so called after a ruler named Vijayarāja who was its issuer.

vijaya-saptamī (EI 3), name of a *tithi*.

vijaya-śāsana (EI 33), any royal record (cf. *śāsana*); sometimes the same as *dharma-vijaya-śāsana* (q.v.).

vijaya-śiva, cf. *śrī-vijaya-śiva-Mṛgeśavarman*, etc. (*The Successors of the Sātavāhanas*, pp. 261 ff.); an honorific prefixed to royal names. See *śrī*, *vijaya*, *śiva*.

vijaya-stambha (SITI), pillar of victory.

vijaya-vaijayika, victory; sometimes used as an adjective qualifying the regnal date (*Ep. Ind.*, Vol. XXXV, p. 152, text line 5; cf. ibid., Vol. XXXII, p. 88).

vijaya-vandāpanā (IE 8-5; EI 12), Oḍiyā; a levy; presents to be offered to the king or landlord on the occasion of his victorious return from a campaign or for the preparation of a campaign; cf. *vandāpanā*.

vijaya-vikṣepa (IA 13), epithet of a place where a king was staying. See *vikṣepa*.

vijita (CII 1), dominions.

Vijñānin (EI 20, 32), an artisan; same as *Śilpin*; epithet of an artisan who is usually the engraver of an inscription.

vijñāpanā (IA 10), also called *vijñapti*; an application; a request; cf. Kannaḍa *binna-vattaḷĕ*=Sanskrit *vijñāpana-patra* (SII 11-1).

Vijñapti (EI 29), official designation. Cf. *Ājñapti*, etc.

vijñapti (SITI), sometimes also spelt *vijñāpti*; petitioning to the king (cf. *vijñāpanā*); an officer who brings the petition of the subjects to the king's notice.

(*EI* 23; SII 2), also called *vijñāpya*, an application or petition.

vi-jñāpi (CII 3, etc.), verb used in connection with the making of a grant by the king at the request, or on the advice, of someone who was the real donor.

vijñāpya (EI 23), cf. Tamil *viṇṇappam* (SII 1), a petition; also called *vijñapti*.

vikara, cf. *vikara-padāni* (LP), a small present, a bonus; cf. Gujarātī *pān-sopārī*.

(*LP*), cf. *vikara-pada* explained as 'miscellaneous expenses'.

vikaraṇa-paṭṭaka (LP), a merket-tax contract.

Vikramāditya (IE 8-2), see *āditya*.

vikṛti (IE 7-1-2), 'twentythree'.

vikṣepa (IA 7, 13), cf. *vijaya-vikṣepa* used as an epithet of the place whence a royal charter was issued; cf. *vijaya-vikṣepāt Bharukaccha-vāsakāt*; wrongly interpreted as 'a camp or cantonment' (IA 17). See also *Vaikṣepika*.

vilabdhi (IE 8-3; EI 30), used in the *Rājataraṅgiṇī*, probably in the sense of presents offered to the king or the stolen property recovered; explained as 'an assignment'. See *Vailabdhika*.

vilahaṇā (LP), probably, an escort; suite.

Vilāsinī (EI 33), same as *Devadāsī*; also called *Gaṇikā*, etc.

Vilekhaka (EI 22), an engraver. Cf. *Ullekhaka*, *utkṛ*.

vi-lok, cf. *vilokyante* (LP), 'are being searched for', used in respect of one who is in search of money in times of difficulty.

vimāna (SITI), the pinnacle or upper structure over the sanctum of a temple; the central shrine of a temple (SII 3); also called *śrī-vimāna* (SII 13); same as *garbha-gṛha*.

(*EI* 3, 23), a shrine.

(*IA* 9), the steeple tower over a shrine; also called *stupi*.

viṁśatika, regarded as equal to 20 *māṣas* (*JNSI*, Vol. XVI, p. 52); cf. *viṁśopaka*.

viṁsatima (CII 3), used for *viṁśatitama*, twentieth.

viṁsopaka (EI 1), corrupt form of *viṁśopaka*, a copper coin which was $\frac{1}{20}$ of the standard silver coin in value.

viṁśopaka (IE 8-6, 8-8; EI 29, 30; CII 4), a copper coin which was one-twentieth of the standard silver coin in value; cf. *Viśālapriya-viṁśopaka* (IE 8-8); *Varāhakīya-viṁśopaka* (EI 1); *Vṛṣa-viṁśopaka* (q.v.); a land measure equal to one twentieth of the standard land measure. See *vīsa*, *viṁsopaka*, *vīsovā*, *visovaka*.

Cf. *viśopaka* (LP), supposed to be the same as *vighā*, a measure of land equal to 20 *vasas* [in Gujarat].

vīṇā (ASLV), a musical instrument. Cf. *vīṇai-kkāṇi* (SITI), right of playing on the *vīṇā* before the god in a temple during worship.

vinamu (CITD), Telugu; an unknown weight greater than a *cinna* or *cinnamu*, otherwise called *sinna*.

vināśa (LP), 'not doing anything at all'.

vināśin, cf. *a-kūra-chullaka-vināśi-khaṭvā-vāsa* (IE 8-5), an attendant, or fuel. The villagers were obliged to supply it to the touring officers of the king.

vinaṣṭa-rājya (IE), same as *gata-rājya* or *atīta-rājya*, someone's sovereignty that was a thing of the past.

vinaya (IE 8-8; EI 30), fines.

(*EI* 13), same as *indriya-jaya*.

Vinayadhara (LL), Buddhist; one who has learnt the *Vinaya* texts by heart.

Vināyaka (LL), a teacher of the *vinaya* texts; a name of the god Gaṇeśa.

Vināyaka-homa (EI 26), a rite; same as *Gaṇeśa-homa*.

vindu (EI 7-1-2), also spelt *bindu*; 'cypher'.

(*SII* 2), a flaw in diamonds.

Vinibaddhakāra, see *Vinibandhakāra*.

Vinibandhakāra (EI 8), same as *Vinibaddhakāra*; explained as 'one who registers [a document]'; really, 'one who cancels the registration [of a document]' (*Select Inscriptions*, p. 202).

vinirgata (EI 7), cf. *Pāṭaliputra-bhaṭṭāgrahāra-vinirgata* (*Ep. Ind.*, Vol. XXXII, p. 122, text line 16); 'hailing from', or more suitably 'one whose family hails from'. When a locality called Aṭṭamūla is described as *vinirgata* from Bṛhad-dhaṭṭa, it seems to mean that the former was originally a part of the latter (*ibid.*, Vol. XXXIII, p. 151).

viniyoga (SITI), an employment; use; expenditure.

(*EI* 24), a tax; cf. Tamil *vāśal-viniyogam* (SITI), same as *vāśal-paṇam*; also *sabhā-viniyoga* (SII 13).

Viniyukta (HD), an officer probably under the *Āyuktaka*; same as *Viniyuktaka* (q.v.), etc. Cf. *Ep. Ind.*, Vol. XV, p. 256.

Viniyuktaka (CII 3, 4), an official title meaning a smaller administrative officer serving under a higher officer; an official probably under the *Āyuktaka*; same as *Viniyukta*. Cf. *Ep. Ind.*, Vol. XI, pp. 80, 83.

(*IE* 8-3), mentioned along with *Tadāyuktaka*. Cf. *Tad-viniyuktaka*.

Vipra-vinodin (SITI), a class of Brāhmaṇas who were adepts in jugglery and magical practices.

vīra (IE 8-2), sometimes prefixed to the names of kings and even treated as almost an integral part of the name; cf. *pratāpa*, *vīra-pratāpa*, etc.

(*EI* 3), Jain; same as *Mahāvīra*.

Cf. vīra-kaḻ (SITI), also written *vīra-kkaḻ*, *vīra-gaḻ*; a hero-stone; an inscribed or uninscribed stone pillar raised in honour of a person who died in fighting for a good cause.

Vīrabhadra (SITI), also called *Vīramuṣṭi*; member of a militant class of temple servants who diligently protected the properties and rights of the temples. Cf. *Vīrakośa*.

vīr-ābhiṣeka (EI 18; SITI), 'anointment as a hero'.

vīra-bhoga (SITI), land assigned for the maintenance of a warrior.

vīra-gaḻ (CII 4), also written *vīra-kkaḻ*. See *vīra*.

vīra-kkaḻ (CII 4), also written *vīra-gaḻ*, a stone pillar raised in memory of heroes. See *vīra*.

Vīrakośa, official designation (*The Successor of the Sāta-vāhanas*, p. 110, note 2); mentioned along with *Hastikośa* as an officer related to a district; probably, an officer in charge of the local soldiers or infantry men. Cf. *Vīrabhadra*, etc.

Virakta (SITI), an ascetic; a man free from worldly attachment; a recluse of the Śaiva order.

viral-ariśi (ASLV), rice provided for goldsmiths for amputating the last two fingers of the wives of farmers.

vīra-mālā, cf. *vīra-mālai* (SITI), a poem in praise of a warrior.

Vīramuṣṭi (SITI), same as *Vīrabhadra*.

vīra-paṭṭa (SII 2; SITI), an ornament; a front plate, probably a plate worn on the forehead by distinguished warriors.

vīra-paṭṭaṇa (SITI), also called *eṟi-vīra-paṭṭaṇam*; a mercantile town inhabited by the *eṟi-vīrar*.

Vīra-pratāpa (IE 8-2), cf. *Vīra* and *Pratāpa*.

vīra-śāsana (SITI), CITD) explained by some as the same as *vīrakal*, 'a hero stone', established for commemorating the death of soldiers on the battle-field; a grant made by the king in recognition of the heroic activity of a person; a charter recording the grant of land or other property to a warrior.

vīra-śeṣa, cf. *vīra-śeṣai* (SITI); probably, the provision made for the descendants of dead warriors; sometimes explained as a tax (EI 22). Cf. *mṛtyuka-vṛtti*, *rakta-mānya*, etc.

vīra-siṁhāsana (SII 1), the throne of heroes.

Vīra-yātrika (IA 17; HD), an official designation; probably, the leader of an expedition; a person taking part in a military expedition. See Vogel, *Ant.Ch.St.*, p. 129.

Virūpākṣa-pati, cf. Prakrit *Virūpakha-pati* (EI 20), epithet of the god Mahāsena or Kārttikeya, Virūpākṣa probably being the name of a host of which the god was conceived as the leader.

vīsa (IE 8-8; EI 5), name of a coin (*JNSI*, Vol. XXVI, pp. 127ff.); cf. *lokkiya-vīsa*, probably meaning 'a *vīsa* minted at Lokkiguṇḍi'; Sanskrit *viṁśa*, *viṁśaka*, *viṁśatika*, or *viṁśopaka*.

(*Ep. Ind.*, Vol. VI, p. 232, note 6), Telugu-Kannaḍa; $\frac{1}{16}$ of a *haṇa* (*paṇa*); but $\frac{1}{20}$ of the standard coin in value essentially.

(*CITD*), also called *visā*, *visya*, *visāmu*; Telugu-Kannaḍa; the fraction $\frac{1}{16}$; gold equal in weight to one grain of rice; $\frac{1}{256}$ of a *Hun* or *Pagoda*; 40 *palas*; a measure of land equal nearly to 2 acres.

visā, also spelt *visāmu* (CITD), see *vīsa*.

viṣahara-bhoga (SITI), also called *viṣa-vṛtti*; land set apart for the support of a poison-doctor.

vīsala-priya-dramma, also called *vīsala-prī-dramma*; cf. *jīrṇa-viśvamalla-priya*, etc. (*A.R.Ep.*, 1957-58, Nos. B 490-92).

visaṁsthula (LP), agitated, unsteady.

visatiaṭhū-prastha (IA 18), a levy; probably *viṁśatisatka-prastha*, 'one out of 20 *prasthas*.'

viṣa-vṛtti (SITI), same as *viṣahara-bhoga*.

viṣaya (EI 8-4), a district; often a kingdom or territory; sometimes a *viṣaya* was included in a *maṇḍala*; but, in some cases, a *maṇḍala* was included in a *viṣaya*; at times *maṇḍala* and *viṣaya* were synonymous.

(*IE* 8-5; EI 30; CII 3, 4; BL; SITI), a district; cf. *viṣaya-suṅka* (EI 24), the tax of a district; *Viṣaya-vyavahārin*, officer in the service of a district.

(*ASLV*), same as *nirvṛtti* or *koṭṭam*; an administrative division.

(*IE* 8-4; CII 4), sometimes used in a wider sense to indicate 'a country'.

(*IE* 7-1-2), 'five'.

visaya (CITD), same as Telugu *visā*, *visāmu*.

Viṣaya-bhogika (EI 28), probably, the *ināmdār* or *ināmdārs* of a district.

Viṣaya-bhūbhuj (IA 15), explained as 'a native ruler' as opposed to a 'foreign con queror.'

viṣaya-dāna (HRS), name of a tax (*Ep. Ind.*, Vol. XI, p. 21; Vol. XIV, p. 196), probably, a regional tax or taxes realisable from a particular district ; known from Gāhaḍavāla records; cf. *viṣayālī*.

Viṣaya-dānika (EI 7; CII 4), collector of the levy called *viṣaya-dāna*; or a district officer in charge of gifts or an officer in charge of gift lands in a district; or the collector of the revenue of a district.

Viṣay-ādhikaraṇa (EI 23, 31), administrative officer of a district; the district administrator's office.

Viṣay-ādhipati, same as *Viṣayapati* (*Ep. Ind.*, Vol. XXXIV, p. 219).

Viṣaya-karaṇa (EI 32), probably, the chief scribe at the office of the administrators of a district.

viṣayālī (EI 33), name of a tax; probably the same as *viṣaya-dāna*.

Viṣay-āmātya (EI 27, 30), governor of a district; an *Amātya* in charge of a *viṣaya* or an *Amātya* under the *Viṣayapati*. See *Ep. Ind.*, Vol. XXX, p. 64.

viṣayaṇa (EI 1), meaning doubtful.

Viṣayapāla (EI 28), same as *Viṣayapati*.

Viṣayapati (IE 8-3; CII 3, 4; BL; HD), governor of a district called *viṣaya*; distinguished from *Viṣaya-vyāpṛtaka*; same as *Viṣay-ādhipati*. Cf. *Ind. Ant.*, Vol. V, p. 114. See *Viṣayeśa*, *Viṣayeśvara*, etc.

Viṣaya-vyāpṛtaka (IE 8-3), sometimes distinguished from the *Viṣayapati*; an officer associated with the administration of a district (cf. *Viṣaya-vyavahārin*).

Viṣaya-vyavahārin (IE 8-3), an administrative officer in a district or a member of the district council. Cf. *Viṣaya-vyavahārin*, *Viṣayika*, *Viṣayin*.

Viṣayeśa (HD), same as *Viṣayapati*, etc.

Viṣayeśvara (EI 26), same as *Viṣayapati*, etc.

Viṣayika (EI 24), same as *Viṣaya-vyavahārin*; cf. *Viṣayin*.

Viṣayik-ādhikārika (EI 32), taken to be a single official designation; probably *Viṣayika* and *Ādhikārika*.

Viṣayin (EI 24, 32), possibly, the same as *Viṣaya-vyavahārin*; cf. *Viṣayika*.

viseṇima, *viseṇimā* (CII 4), a tax, also called *viseṇim-ādāya* (EI 21).

viśeṣ-ādāya (SITI), also called *viśeṣ-āya*; a special group of taxes.

viśeṣ-āya (SITI), same as *viśeṣ-ādāya* (q.v.).

viśikha (BL), name of a kind of building.

viśīrṇa, wearing out, worn out part of a building ; cf. *bhagna-viśīrṇa-samāracana* (*Ep. Ind.*, Vol. XXXIV, p. 144).

Viśiṣa (IE 8-3; EI 1, 30), probably, the governor or commander of a fort; a word of uncertain derivation.

viṣṇu-bāhu, see *hari-bāhu* (IE 7-1-2), 'four'.

viṣṇu-gṛha (SITI), a Viṣṇu temple.

viṣṇu-pada (IE 7-1-2), 'cypher'.

viṣṇu-tithi (IA 19), same as Jyaiṣṭha-sudi 11.

viṣṇu-śrādha (*Ep. Ind.*, Vol. XXXIV, p. 37), an expression of doubtful meaning.

vīsovā (CII 4), name of a coin; a land measure; same as *viṁśopaka*.

visovaka (EI 1), corrupt form of *viṁśopaka* (q.v.).

viṣṭapa (IE 7-1-2), 'three'.

vistaraṇa (EI 1), meaning doubtful.

viṣṭi (IE 8-5; CII 4; HRS), labour which the villagers were obliged to provide to the king or landlord on occasions; unpaid labour; forced labour.

Cf. veṭṭi (SITI), unpaid labour for public works in the village without time or other limits; usually mentioned along with *vetana* as *veṭṭi-vetanai*. Cf. *veṭṭi-ccoṟu*, the obligation of feeding *veṭṭi* labourers free of cost; also cf. Tamil *veṭṭi-pāṭṭam* (EI 24), explained as 'a kind of tax'; tax in lieu of *viṣṭi*.

viśuddhi, cf. *viśuddhiṁ yāvat* (LP), 'till the account is clear'.

viṣuva (CII 4; SII 1), the autumnal or vernal equinox; also called *viṣuvat* (q.v.).

viṣuvat (IE 7-1-2), 'two'.

Cf. viṣuva.

viśva (IE 7-1-2), same as *viśvedevāḥ*, 'thirteen.'

viśvacakra (EI 24), name of a *mahādāna*.

viśvedevāḥ (IE 7-1-2), 'thirteen'; same as *viśva*.

viṣvag-devā (LL), Jain; a quardruple image.

Viśvakarman (LL), an architect.

Viśvāla (EI 31), Oḍiyā; a village watchman.

Viśvāsa (EI 24), official designation; same as *Vaiśvāsika*; cf. the titles *Viśvāsa-Khāna*, *Viśvāsa-rāya*, etc., conferred by the Muslim rulers especially in the Bengal region.

viśvāsana (CII 1), 'being inspired with faith'.

viśva-sattā (IA 14), wrong Sanskritisation of Prakrit *vasasata* (Sanskrit *varṣa-śata*); translated as 'universal rule'. See *Ep. Ind.*, Vol. XXXIV, p. 241, note 1.

Viśvāsika (EI 24), same as *Vaiśvāsika* (q.v.), etc.

Viśvaviśvopaka (IA 19), Jain; explained as 'one whose body and soul exhibit marks of an *ācārya*'.

vitāna (SII 13), probably, a canopy.

Vitān-ādhipa (*Ep. Ind.*, Vol. XIII, p. 325, note 3), supposed to be 'an officer in charge of the king's bed-chamber'. Cf. *Vāsāgārika*, *Śayyāpāla*, etc.

viṭapa (IE 8-5), a bush; used in *sa-jhāṭa-viṭapa*; a branch. Cf. *Ep. Ind.*, Vol. V, p. 183.

viṭha-vigāra (Chamba), unpaid labour; from Sanskrit *viṣṭi* and Persian *begār*.

vīthi, *vīthī* (SII 1), a street.

(*EI* 24, 30; CII 4), a shop; a stall or shop in a market.

(*EI* 21, 23, 29, 30), a territorial unit; the subdivision of a district.

(*IE* 8-4), sometimes a subdivision forming part of a *maṇḍala*, but sometimes a district forming part of a *bhukti* or province.

Vīthī-mahattara (HD), headman of the territorial unit called *vīthī*. Cf. *IHQ*, Vol. XIX, pp. 16, 21.

vīthy-adhikaraṇa (EI 31), administrative office of a subdivision called *vīthī*.

vitta-bandha (CII 4), mortage.

viṭṭolla-kara (HRS), known from Maitraka records; explained as the contribution in forced labour.

Vivāha (EI 12), 'one whose vehicle is the bird'; i.e. Viṣṇu.

vivāha (CII 1), marriage of a daughter; cf. *āvāha* which means the marriage of a son.

vivāha-kara, cf. Tamil *kaṇṇāla-kkāṇan* (EI 28), the marriage fee; cf. *vivāha-ppaṇam*.

vivāha-paṇa, cf. *vivāha-ppaṇam* (SITI), same as *kaṇṇāla-kkāṇam*; a tax on marriage.

vivīta (HRS), royal dues collected by the superintendent of pastures, as suggested by the *Arthaśāstra*.

Vivīt-ādhyakṣa (EI 28), known from the *Arthaśāstra*; officer in charge of the pasture land. Cf. *Vrajabhūmika*.

viyat (IE 7-1-2), 'cypher'.

vodā (IE 8-5; EI 29), a kind of levy in Oḍiyā records; same as Oḍiyā *vadāi*, 'the obligation of offering uncooked food.'

voḍī, *voḍrī* (EI 23), $\frac{1}{4}$ *paṇa*; 20 cowrie-shells; cf. *kapardaka-voḍī*, '*voḍī* counted in cowrie-shells'.

volāpana, see *volāpika*, *vulāvi*.

Volāpika (LP), an officer in charge of collecting the tax called *volāpana* or *vulāvī*. It is supposed that a *Volāpaka* or the men under him accompanied the merchants in their journey for the safety of their goods and the *volāpana* tax was collected from the merchants for safeguarding their goods.

voṭa, cf. *boṭa*.

vraja, see *Vraja-bhūmika*. Cf. Ghoshal, *H. Rev. Syst.*, p. 110.

vraja-bhūmi (IE 8-4), grazing land.

Vrajabhūmika (CII 1; EI 2; HD), Prakrit *Vacabhūmika*; superintendent of cowpens; officer in charge of the royal cattle and pasture lands. Cf. *Vivīt-ādhyakṣa*.

vrata (CITD), religious vow; a self-imposed task; a religious act of devotion or austerity; vowed observance; a vow in general. There are many *vratas* mentioned in the different *Purāṇas*. But new *vratas* crop up in different parts of the country.

(*EI* 4), five in number.

vrīhi-kara, cf. Tamil *arisi-kkāṇam* (SITI), a levy for husking paddy into rice.

vṛddha (LP), participle of *vṛdh*, 'to cut'.

Cf. Vṛddha-Gaṇeśa (IA 19), 'the senior Gaṇeśa'.

Vṛddha-dhānuṣka (IE 8-3), senior archer; the chief archer.

Vṛddharāja (EI 3; LL), 'prosperous king'; title of a pious king.

vṛddhi (EI 28), a super tax or the interest on arrears of taxes; also interest.

vṛddhi-kukkuṭa (CII 1), Prakrit *vadhi-kukuṭa*; a cock that has been caponed; also Sanskritised as *vadhri-kukkuṭa*.

vṛṣatāpa-śāsana (EI 13), same as *tāmra-śāsana*.

vṛṣa-viṁśopaka (*Ep. Ind.*, Vol. XV, p. 39), name of a coin (probably bearing the figure of a bull); cf. *viṁśopaka*.

vṛtti (SITI), means; livelihood, occupation; grant of land for one's livelihood.

(*SII* 3), land granted for service.

(*EI* 17, 31; CITD), share; share in a village granted to a Brāhmaṇa as a free gift.

Vuḍhā-leṅkā (EI 28), Oḍiyā; official designation; cf. *Leṅkā*.

vulāpikā (LP), tax for the maintenance of the camp-followers; cf. Gujarātī *vaḷāmaṇ vulāyiyā*; also *volāpika*, *vulāviyā* (q.v.).

vulāvī (LP), same as *volāpana*; a tax.

Vulāviyā (LP), a camp-follower; cf. Gujarātī *Vuḷāviyā*. See *vulāpikā* and *Volāpika*.

vuṁvaka (EI 14), name of a measure.

Cf. '*rūpakas* to be levied on each *vuṁvaka* of the distillers' (*Ep. Ind.*, Vol. XIV, p. 309).

Vya (PJS), abbreviation of *Vyavahārin*, especially in medieval Jain inscriptions.

Vyā (PJS), abbreviation of *Vyāpārin* (merchant) or *Vyāsa* (exponent or reciter of epic and Puranic texts) especially in medieval Jain inscriptions. Cf. *vyā-bhū*.

vyā-bhū (IE 8-1), abbreviation of *vyāmiśra-bhūmi*; 'mixed land'; land containing different categories such as cultivable, fallow, homestead, etc.

vyācaraṇa (EI 15), meaning uncertain; probably, commerce.

vyāghra-carman (IE 8-5; EI 12, 28), tiger's skin [which was the king's monopoly]; tax probably payable by hunters in tiger's skin; refers to the right to keep tiger's skins without surrendering them to the king.

vyāja, *vyājaka* (LP), interest; cf. *dvika-śata-vyājena*, 'at 2 per cent interest'. See *vyājī*.

vyājī (HRS), as suggested by the *Arthaśāstra*, (1) compensation fee levied upon the sale of liquors, royal merchandise, mining products, salt and sugar; (2) charge paid for minting coins; (3) subsidiary charge over and above the regular fines. See *vyāja*.

vyākaraṇa-dāna-maṇḍapa (SITI), hall in the Śiva temple at Tiruvoṟṟiyūr, where Sanskrit grammar is taught with the belief that the *Māheśvara-sūtras*, on which Sanskrit grammar is founded, were composed by the god Śiva.

vyākhyā-vṛtti (SITI), land set apart to meet the expenses of expounding the Purāṇas and other *śāstras*.

vyakta (CII 1), experienced.

vyāmiśra-bhūmi (IE 8-1), an area consisting of different kinds of land such as cultivated land, homestead land, fallow land, etc. See *vyā-bhū*.

vyañjana, cf. *vĕñjanam*, *viñjanam* (SITI), condiment; vegetable relish; condiments and curry in food offerings; cf. *vĕñjana-bhaṇḍāram*.

(*CII* 1), a letter or an implication.

vyāpādita (LP), 'much harassed'.

vyāpāra (SII 1), a trade.

(*Ep. Ind.*, Vol. XXXVI, p. 20), administration. Cf. *mudrā-vyāpāra*.

vyāpāra-karaṇa, cf. *karaṇa* (LP), the department of commerce.

Vyāpārin (EI 22; SII 1), a merchant.

Vyāpṛta (IE 8-3; EI 6), cf. *Vāpata* (EI 9), a governor; a superintendent; cf. also official designations like *Hasty-aśva-naubala-vyāpṛta* or °*vyāpṛtaka*, etc.

Vyāsa (EI 11; PJS), a reciter or exponent; a Brāhmaṇa

who recites or expounds the epics and Purāṇas in public. Cf. *Paurāṇika.*

vyasana (CII 1), misfortune.

vyāṣedha (LP), *vyāṣedhaḥ kāritaḥ* or *niṣedhaḥ kāritaḥ*, 'proved the countrary [in the court that it was his own land and not *ḍohalikā* land'] ; *vahamāna-bhūmi-vyāṣedha*, 'no one should stop him when he is ploughing his own piece of land'.

(*LP*), seizure; confiscation as government property.

vyatikara (LP), 'in connection with'.

vyatīpāta (IA 19), used in relation to eclipses.

Vyava (LP), abbreviation of *Vyavahārika* in the sense of a dealer, a money-lender, a merchant.

vyavacchinna, fixed (*Select Inscriptions*, p. 237); demarcated.

vyavahāra, cf. *vyavahāra-pade* (LP), 'as a tax from merchants'.

Vyavahār-ābhilekhitaka (EI 30), the clerk who writes down the statements of cases in a court of law.

vyavaharamāṇa (LP), current.

vyavaharaṇa (EI 11), administration.

vyavahāra-patra (LP), a deed relating to a loan or debt.

vyavahāra-samatā (CII 1), impartiality in judicial proceedings.

Vyavahārika (EI 7, 32), an administrator; same as *Vyavahārin* (q.v.) or *Vyavahartṛ*; see also *Vyava.*

Vyavahārin (EI 19, 24, 28, 29; BL; LL; HD), an administrator; sometimes explained as 'a controlling officer'; same as *Vyavahārika.* Cf. *Ep. Ind.*, Vol. XVIII, pp. 60, 63.

(*LL*), a merchant. See also *Vyava.*

vyavasthā, cf. *vyavasthai* (EI 24; SITI), regulations; rules of proper conduct; a settlement or arrangement; a deed of agreement.

(*EI* 22; SII 2), a resolution; a declaration.

(*EI* 32), an agreement.

(*SII* 3), conditions.

vyaya (*HRS*), government expenditure; cf. Tamil *viyāyam* (SITI), expenditure, as opposed to *āyam* or income.

(*IE* 7-1-2), 'twelve'.

vyaya-karaṇa, cf. *karaṇa* (LP), the department of expenditure.

vyoman (IE 7-1-2; EI 33), 'cypher'.

vyūha (IE 7-1-2), 'four'.

Vyuṣita (Prakrit *Vivutha*), sometimes taken to be *Vyuṣṭa* (CII 1); 'one who is away from his residence'. See *IHQ*, 1962, pp. 222 ff.

Y

yāga (EI 31), a ceremony.

Yakṣa (CII 4; HA), a semi-divine being; a demi-god belonging to the class of *vyantara-devatās* according to Jain mythology.

yajña-vidyā (EI 8), knowledge regarding the performance of sacrifice.

yadā tad=āpi (LP), 'only'.

Yādava-cakravartin (IE 8-2), title assumed by kings of the Yādava dynasty; see *Cakravartin*.

yāga-maṇḍapa (SITI), sacrificial hall in a temple; same as *yāga-śālā*.

yāga-śālā (SITI), same as *yāga-maṇḍapa* (q.v.).

yakṣa-dvāra, gateway adorned with Yakṣa figures (*Ep. Ind.*, Vol. XXXV, p. 107).

yama (IE 7-1-2), 'two'.

yāma (EI 7-1-2), 'eight'.

yamala (IE 7-1-2), 'two'.

yamala-patra (LP), treaty of alliance.

yamalikāmali (EI 24), a tax probably on a pair of prize bullocks (*yamala-kambalin*; cf. *varabalīvarda*); also spelt *yamalikambali*, *yamalikāmbali*. See *valadī*.

yamalikambali (IE 8-5), name of a tax; also spelt *yamalikāmbali*, *yamalikāmali* (q.v.).

yamalikāmbali (HRS), a tax known from the Gāhaḍavāla records; also spelt *yamalikamabali*, *yamalikāmali* (q.v.).

yānaka (*Ep. Ind.*, Vol. IV, p. 253, note 4), probably a cart-road.

yānikā, same as *yānaka*, probably, a cart road (*Ep. Ind.*, Vol. IV. p. 253, note 4).

yantra (SITI), a mechanical contrivance, as for diverting water.

(*HA*), a mystic diagram.

yantra-kuṭī (IE 8-8; EI 30), an oil mill or manufactory.

yaśas (CII 1), glory in this life; cf. *yaśo vā kīrtir=vā.* See *kīrti.*

yaṣṭi (EI 33; CII 4; ML), a memorial pillar; a relic pillar raised in memory of the dead.

Cf. jaṣṭi (EI 19), a land measure.

Cf. laṣṭi (EI 16), a memorial pillar.

Cf. śilā-yaṣṭi (LL), a stone pillar.

Yāṣṭika (HD), staff bearer; an attendant on the king. See *Rājataraṅgiṇī*, VI 203; Pāṇini, IV. 4. 59. See *Vetrika, Piśuna-vetrika.*

Yaṣṭi-prātiṣṭhānaka (ML), the erection of a pillar; same as Sanskrit *yaṣṭi-pratiṣṭhāpana.*

yathākāla-bhāvin (IE 8-3), same as *vartamāna-bhaviṣyat, yathāsambadhyamānaka*; also written as *yathā-kāl-ādhyāsin* (q.v.).

yathākāl-ādhyāsin (EI 4, 23), 'one who may be employed [in the area including the gift land] from time to time'; one who may be associated with the area about the gift land in different periods of time; same as *yathākāla-bhāvin, vartamāna-bhaviṣyat, yathā-sambadhyamānaka.*

yathā-sambadhyamānaka (IA 9), same as *yathākāla-bhāvin, vartamāna-bhaviṣyat, yathākāl-ādhyāsin.*

yaṭhi (CII 4), Prakrit; same as Sanskrit *yaṣṭi* (q.v.); a memorial pillar.

Yati (BL), a monk.

yātrā (EI 11; CII 4), festival; the festival of a deity; same as *yātr-otsava.*

yātrā-dāna (EI 27), gift or levy for running a festival.

(*SITI*), propitiatory gift made before starting on an expedition of conquest by the king.

yātr-otsava (IE 8-5; EI 3, 9), same as *yātrā* (q.v.); the festival of a deity; festival in honour of a deity.

yauta (CII 1), a respite; cf. *yautaka.*

yava, one-fifteenth of a *māṣa* (*JNSI*, Vol. XVI, p. 45); equal to 2 *dhānyamāṣas* (*ibid.*, p. 48); $\frac{1}{8}$ of a *rati.*

Yāvadeka-pātra (*Ep. Ind.*, Vol. XXVII, p. 122, text lines 4-5), official designation. See *Pātra.*

Yavana (EI 26; CII 1), originally, an Ionian Greek; then, people of Greek nationality; ultimately, any foreigner.

Yavuga (EI 14), royal title of foreign origin.

yoga (CII 4), meditation; a philosophical system.

(*EI* 18), a council or corporation.

(*CII* 3; IA 17), addition of the longitudes of the sun and moon; an astrological element.

Cf. yogaṁ yuñjantām, 'let them obtain the association [of the gods]'. See *Ep. Ind.*, Vol. XXXI, p. 208. Cf. *yuj*.

yoga-kṣema (IA 7; LP), death; cf. *jāta-yoga-kṣema*, dead.

yoga-paṭṭa (EI 14), band used by the ascetics to keep their limbs in a position of rigidity.

yoga-paṭṭaka, cf. *joga-vaṭṭigĕ* (IA 14), explained as 'a garment worn during contemplation'; same as *yoga-paṭṭa* (q.v.).

yoga-pīṭha (IA 10), a holy place where an ascetic obtained perfection (*siddhi*) by his austerities; also called *siddha-pīṭha*.

yogin, cf. *yogīndra* (SII 1) a [Jain] ascetic.

yojana (CII 1, 4), name of a measure of distance; a distance of about nine miles.

yoni-paṭṭa, same as *gaurī-paṭṭa*; see *pīṭha*.

yuddhita,'onewho died fighting' (*Ep. Ind.*, XXXI, p. 324).

yudhya (EI 4), name of a sacrifice.

yuga (IE 7-1-2), 'four'; rarely, 2 or 12.

yuga, *yugā* (EI 1), meaning doubtful; cf. *yugā* in the sense of 'a voucher'.

yugā (CII 4), a voucher.

yug-ādi (CII 4; IA 18), name applied to certain *tithis*; day of the commencement of a *yuga*; e.g. Vaiśākha-sudi 3, regarded as the commencement of the Kṛta-yuga.

yugādi-tithi (EI 13), see *yug-ādi*.

Yugādi-parvan (EI 14), name of an auspicious time; same as *yugādi-tithi*.

yugala (IE 7-1-2), 'two'.

yugandharī (EI 11), same as *javār* (*jawār*), millet.

yugma (IE 7-1-2), 'two'.

Yugyacarya (CII 1), a charioteer.

yuj (CII 1), cf. *vṛddhir=yujyatām*, 'should devote themselves for an increase'; *śāśvataṁ samayam=[etad]=yuñjyuḥ*, 'they may strive for this at all times'. Cf. *yoga*.

Yukta (EI 8-3; HD), an officer in general; also an official designation (*CII*, Vol. 1, p. 4); the word used in Rock Edict III of Aśoka is explained by some scholars as the designation of a class of officers, although there also the word may be understood in the sense of 'an officer'; but it is an official designation in passages like *yukta-niyukta-vāsāvak-ādhikārika* (*Ep. Ind.*, Vol. XXI, p. 144) where it may be the same as *Āyuktaka*.

Cf. Yuktaka, *Āyukta*, etc.

Yuktaka (IE 8-3; HD), same as *Yukta*, *Āyukta* or *Āyuktaka*. See *Ep. Ind.*, Vol. VII, pp. 26, 39-40.

yūpa (EI 2, 24, 33), sacrificial pillar; it was sometimes made of stone and inscribed.

yūthī, also spelt *yūtī* (IA 17), generally written as *yūti* or *pūti*; cf. *tṛṇa-yūti* (or *pūti*)*-gocara-paryanta*, 'as far as grass land and pasture land'.

yūti, cf. *sva-sīmā-tṛṇa-yūti-gocara-paryanta* (IE 8-5); also written as *pūti*; a word of uncertain import; probably, '[land] reserved [for growing grass, etc.]' Cf. *go-yūti*, *tṛṇa-yūti*, *kāṣṭha -yūti*.

Yuvamahārāja (IE 8-2; EI 3, 20, 24), modification of *Yuvarāja*; designation of the heir-apparent or crown-prince; same as *Mahāyuvarāja*.

Yuvarāja (IE 8-2, CII 3, 4; HD; ASLV), designation of the heir-apparent or crown-prince. See *Arthaśāstra*, I. 12 (mentioned among the 18 *tīrthas*); cf. *CII*, Vol. II, Part i, p. 40.

Cf. Tamil *Tuvarāśaṉ* (EI 4), also *Duvarāja*.

Cf. Mahāyuvarāja (EI 32), same as *Yuvamahārāja* (q.v.).

Appendix I

PRIVILEGES ATTACHED TO FREE HOLDINGS

a-bhaṭa-cchātra-prāvśeya (EI 26, 27; CII 3), same as *a-cāṭa-bhaṭa-prāveśya*, *Chātra* (literally, 'the umbrella-bearer') being used for *Cāṭa* probably meaning 'the leader of a group of *Bhaṭas* (i. e. *Pāiks* or *Piādas*)'; same as *a-prāveśya*, etc.

a-bhaṭa-prāveśya, same as *a-prāveśya*, etc. Cf. Prakrit *a-bhaḍa-papesa* (*Select Inscriptions*, p. 435).

a-bhṛita-praveśya (EI 24), same as *a-bhaṭa-prāveśya*; cf. *a-prāveśya*, etc.

abhyantara-siddhi (EI 22), same as *abhyantara-siddhyā*, *abhyantara-siddhika*; refers to internal revenue income or taxes to be paid to local authorities; cf. *sa-bāhy-ābhyantar-ādāya*.

abhyantara-siddhika, (EI 20) same as *abhyantara-siddhi*.

abhyantara-siddhi-sahita (EI 27),same as *abhyantara-siddhi*, etc.

abhyantara-siddhyā, 'together with the internal income or taxes to be paid to the local authorities'; cf. *abhyantara-siddhika* and *sa-bāhy-ābhyantar-ādāya*. Cf. *Ind. Ep.*, p. 398.

ā-candr-āditya-kālīya(IE),'to be enjoyed as long as the moon and sun endure' (i.e. permanently); epithet of the gift land.

ā-candr-ārka-kṣiti-sama-kālam, 'as long as the moon, the sun and the earth exist' (i.e. permanently).

ā-candr-ārka (IE; SITI), 'in perpetuity.'

ā-candr-ārk-ārṇava-kṣiti-sthiti-sama-kālīna (EI), 'to last as long as the moon, the sun, the seas and the earth endure' (i.e. permanently); cf. *Ep. Ind.*, Vol. XXXII, p. 134.

ā-candr-ārk-ārṇava-kṣiti-sarit-parvata-sama-kālīna, 'to be enjoyed as long as the moon, the sun, the seas, the earth, the rivers and hills exist (i.e. permanently)'; cf. *Ep. Ind.*, Vol. XXXIII, p. 134.

ā-candra-tārakam, 'as long as the moon and stars endure' (*Ep. Ind.*, Vol. XXXV, p. 149, text line 12), i.e. permanently.

a-cār-āsana-carm-āṅgāra (IE;EI 27), refers to the freedom of the gift village from the obligation to supply conveyance, accommodation, hide (i.e. hide-seats) and charcoal free of charges to the touring officers on their visit. The word *cāra* meaning 'passage or conveyance' is sometimes substituted by *pāra* meaning 'ferrying'.

a-cāra-siddhika (EI 26), explained by some as 'without grazing right for the royal cattle'. Cf. *a-vāra-siddhika.*

a-carm-āṅgāraka, refers to the freedom of the gift village from the obligation to supply hide-seats and charcoal to the king or landlord on occasions or to the touring royal officers on their visit. Cf. Prakrit *a-camm-aṅgālaka* (*Select Inscriptions,* p. 409).

a-cāṭa-bhaṭa-gocara (EI 22), same as *a-cāṭa-bhaṭa-praveśa,* etc.

a-cāṭa-bhaṭa-praveśa (EI 27, 29; CII 3), refers to the freedom of the gift village from the entry of the *Cāṭas* (leaders of groups of *Pāiks* and *Piādas*) and the *Bhaṭas* (*Pāiks* and *Piādas*); cf. *a-bhaṭa-praveśa, a-bhaṭa-chātra-prāveśya, a-bhṛta-praveśa,* etc.

a-cāṭa-bhaṭa-prāveśya (CII 3, 4), same as *a-cāṭa-bhaṭa-praveśa;* refers to the freedom of the gift land from being entered by the *Bhaṭas* (the king's *Pāiks* and *Piādas*) and the *Cāṭa* (the leader of a group of *Pāiks* and *Piādas*); cf. *Chātra* in place of *Cāṭa* in *a-bhaṭa-cchātra-prāveśya;* also *Bhṛta* for *Bhaṭa* in *a-bhṛta-praveśya.*

a-caṭṭa-bhaṭṭa-praveśa (EI 27), same as *a-cāṭa-bhaṭa-praveśa.*

a-cullaka-kūra-khaṭvā-grahaṇa, similar to *a-kūra-chullaka-vināśi-khaṭv-āvāsa,* etc. See *Ep. Ind.,* Vol. XXXI, p. 5.

a-dugdha-dadhi-grahaṇa, refers to the freedom of the gift village from the obligation of supplying milk and curds to the king or landlord on occasions or to the touring officials on their visit. Cf. Prakrit *a-dudha-dadhi-gahaṇa* (*Select Inscriptions,* p. 439).

a-harītaka-śāka-puṣpa-grahaṇa, refers to the freedom of the gift land from the supply of myrobalan, vegetables and flowers to the king or landlord on occasions or to the touring officers on their visit. Cf. Prakrit *a-haritaka-sāka-pupha-gahaṇa* (*Select Inscriptions,* p. 439).

a-harīta-parṇa-śāka-puṣpa-phala-dugdha-dadhi-ghṛta-takra-grahaṇa, similar to *a-harītaka-śāka-puṣpa-grahaṇa* and *a-dugdha-dadhi-grahaṇa,* etc. See *Ep. Ind.,* Vol. XXXI, p. 5.

a-hasta-prakṣepaṇīya (EI 11, 23), same as a *a-bhaṭa-praveśa,* etc. Cf. *samasta-rājakīyānām=a-hasta-prakṣepaṇīya.*

a-hiraṇya-dhānya-praṇaya-pradeya (EI 26), refers to the freedom of the gift land from the payment of revenue in cash, the king's grain share and the benevolence or emergency imposts. Cf. Prakrit *a-hiraṇṇa-dhaṇṇa-ppaṇaya-ppadeya* (*Select-Inscriptions,* pp. 408-09).

a-karada (EI 26), refers to the freedom of the donee of the gift land from paying taxes in general.

a-karadāyin (EI 26, 27), same as *a-karada*.

a-kara-vāt-ottara (IE; EI 32), sometimes with *āvāta*, *vāt-ādeya*, *bhūt-opātta-pratyāya*, etc., in place of *vāt-ottara*; cf. *sa-bhūta-vāta-* (or *pāta*)*-pratyāya*, etc;. 'free from the collections resulting from storms (e.g. uprooted trees, fruits, etc.).'

a-kara-viṣṭi-koñjalla (IE), refers to the freedom of the donee of the gift land from the payment of taxes and the obligation to supply free labour and *koñjalla* (*kāñji*) to the king's labourers. Cf. *Select Inscriptions*, p. 439.

a-khaṭvā-cullaka-vaināśika, cf. Prakrit *a-khaṭṭa-collaka-veṇesika* (EI 26), refers to the freedom of the gift village from the obligation to supply cots, food and attendant or fuel to the touring royal officers on their visit or to the king or landlord on occasions. Cf. *a-kūra-cullaka-vināśi-khaṭv-āvāsa*, etc.

a-kiñcit-kara, 'not to pay even a small amount as rent or tax'; epithet of gift land; same as *a-kiñcit-pragrāhya*. It has to be noted that sometimes a small amount of tax was fixed for the gift lands. Cf. *kara-śāsana*.

a-kiñcit-kara-grāhya (EI 27), same as *a-kiñcit-kara*, etc.

a-kiñcit-pragrāhya (EI 29), refers to the freedom of the gift land from the payment of taxes and the obligation of supplying articles to the king or landlord on occasions and to the touring officers on their visit; same as *a-kiñcit-kara*, etc.

a-kiñcit-pratikara (EI 23), '[land] free from any yield of revenue'; cf. *utpratikarā*. But *pratikara* also means 'compensation'.

a-kūra-cullaka-vaināśi-khaṭv-āvāsa (or °*saṁvāsa*), cf. *a-kūra-yollaka-venesi-khaṭṭ-āvāsa* (EI 26); refers to the freedom of the gift village from the obligation of supplying boiled or unboiled rice, pots or fire-places for cooking, attendant or fuel, cot and shelter to the king or landlord on occasions or to the touring officers on their visit; same as *a-kūra-cullaka-vināśi-khaṭvā-saṁvāsa*, etc. See *sāmant-āmātya-dūtānām=anyeṣām c=ābhyupāgame śayanīy-āsana-siddh-ānnaṁ na dāpayet* (*Ep. Ind.*, Vol. XXX, p. 171).

a-lavaṇa-guḍa-kṣobha (EI 26), same as *a-lavaṇa-khātaka*, *guḍa* or sugar being added to *lavaṇa* or salt; cf. *a-lavaṇa-klinna-khātaka*.

a-lavaṇa-khātaka, cf. Prakrit *a-loṇa-khādaka* (EI 7), refers to the freedom of the gift land from being dug out or its trees being pierced for salt.

a-lavaṇa-klinna-khanaka (EI 26), same as *a-lavaṇa-klinna-kreṇi-khanaka.*

a-lavaṇa-klinna-khātaka, same as *a-lavaṇa-khātaka, klinna,* sometimes wrongly spelt *kliṇva,* probably, 'toddy, sugar, etc.' being added to *lavaṇa* or salt. Cf. *a-lavaṇa-guḍa-kṣobha, a-lavaṇa-klinna-kreṇi-khanaka,* etc. Cf. *Select Inscriptions,* p. 408.

a-lavaṇa-kliṇva(nna)-kreṇi-khanaka (EI 26, 27), same as *a-lavaṇa-klinna-khātaka.*

a-lavaṇa-kreṇi-khanaka (EI 23), same as *a-lavaṇa-klinna-khātaka.*

a-lekhanī-praveśatayā (EI 29), probably refers to the absence of the right to re-grant the gift land to any other party on the part of the king and to alienate the gift land on the part of the donee; *lekhanī-praveśa* may mean that the gift land should not be made the subject of another document.

anācchedya (*Ep. Ind.*, Vol. XII, p. 267, note), 'unresumable'; but since *anāhāra,* 'unresumable', is sometimes used in the same context, probably, 'uncurtailable'; epithet of gift land.

anādeśya (EI 12), same as *anirdeśya.*

anāhāra, 'unresumable' (*Ind. Ep.*, p. 395), cf. *anācchedya.*

anaṅguli-prakṣepaṇīya (EI 23), also called *anaṅguli-prekṣaṇīya* same as *a-bhaṭa-praveśa,* etc.

anaṅguli-prekṣaṇīya (EI 23), same as *anaṅguli-prakṣepaṇīya, a-bhaṭa-praveśa,* etc.

anāsedhya (*Ep. Ind.*, Vol. II, p. 267, note 4), refers to the freedom of the people associated with the gift land from legal restraints.

anavamarśya, refers to the freedom of the gift land from troubles associated with the visit of royal agents. Cf. Prakrit *anomasa* (*Select Inscriptions*, pp. 192, 194).

a-pārampara, same as *a-paramparā-balīvarda* or *a-paraṁparā-balīvarda-grahaṇa,* a privilege of the donee of rent-free land (*Ep. Ind.*, Vol. XV, p. 42).

a-paramparā-balīvarda (SITI), refers to the freedom of the gift village from the supply of bullocks primarily for the conveyance of royal officers on tour.

a-paramparā-balīvarda-grahaṇa (EI 26), same as *a-pārampara,* etc.

a-paramparā-go-balīvarda (EI 22, 26, 27), same as *a-pāram-para*, etc., in which *go* (cow) has been added to *balīvarda* (bullock).

a-paripanthya, 'without opposition'; cf. *Ind. Ep.*, p. 394.

a-paśu-medhya (*Select Inscriptions*, p. 414), refers to the freedom from the supply of animals for sacrifice.

a-prāveśya, refers to the freedom of the gift land from the entry of royal agents; same as *a-bhaṭa-praveśa*, etc. Cf. Prakrit *a-pāvesa* (*Select Inscriptions*, pp. 192, 194).

a-puṣpa-kṣīra-grahaṇa (EI 26), same as *a-puṣpa-kṣīra-san-doha*, etc.

a-puṣpa-kṣīra-grahaṇīya, refers to the freedom of the gift land from the supply of flowers and milk to the king or land-lord on occasions or to the touring officers on their visit; same as *a-puṣpa-kṣīra-sandoha*, etc. Cf. Prakrit *a-puppha-kkhīra-gahaṇi* (*Select Inscriptions*, p. 409).

a-puṣpa-kṣīra-sandoha (EI 26, 27), same as *a-puṣpa-kṣīra-grahaṇīya*, etc.

aputra-dhanaṁ nāsti, 'there is no confiscation, by the king, of the property of persons dying without a son'; cf. *aputrā-sahita*, etc. Cf. *Ep. Ind.*, Vol. XXV, p. 237

aputrā-sahita (IE), 'together with the right to confiscate the property of persons dying without leaving any son'; epithet of gift village. Cf. *aputra-dhanaṁ nāsti*.

a-rāṣṭra-sāṁvinayika (EI 26), refers to the freedom of the gift land from the administrative control to which the district in which it was situated was subject. Cf. Prakrit *a-raṭha-saṁ-vinayika* (*Select Inscriptions*, pp. 92, 94). See *bhoga-sambandha-nirvacanīya*, *grāma-nilaya-nāḍa-sarva-bādhā-parihāreṇa*, etc.

asan-nara-pravṛtti-vinivṛtt-ācāra (*Ind. Ant.*, Vol. XI p. 113, text lines 36-37), translated as 'the established customs [of the gift land] are withheld from [injury by] the enterprise of wicked men.'

aṣṭa-bhāgika, 'paying one-eighth of the produce [in place of the usual one-sixth]'. Cf. Prakrit *aṭha-bhāgiya* (*Select Ins-criptions*, p. 70).

aṣṭabhoga-tejaḥsvāmya-daṇḍaśulka-yukta (*Ind. Ant.*, Vol XIX, p. 247, text line 102), mentioned along with *nidhi-nikṣepa pāṣāṇ-ārām-ādi-catuṣprakāra-bīravaṇa-pārikh-āya-sahita*. See *aṣṭa-bhoga*, *tejaḥ-svāmya*, etc.

aṣṭādaśa-jāti-parihāra, the eighteen (i.e. all or various) kinds of exemptions [usually enjoyed by rent-free holdings]. Cf. Prakrit *aṭṭhārasa-jāti-parihāra* (*Select Inscriptions.*, pp. 439-40).

a-triṇa-kāṣṭha-grahaṇa (EI 26), refers to the freedom of the donee of the gift village from the supply of grass and fuel to the king or landlord on occasions or to the touring officers on their visit.

a-vaha (EI 26), refers to the freedom of the gift village from the obligation of carrying loads of the touring officers, etc., or of supplying a horse to them free of charges.

a-vāra-siddhika (IE), refers to the freedom of the gift village from the obligation to supply unpaid labour in turn. Cf. *a-cāra-siddhika.*

bhāga-bhoga-paśu-hiraṇya-kara-śulka (EI 20), 'together with [the right to] the share of the produce, periodical offerings, cattle or animals [for sacrificial purposes], tax in cash, tax in kind and tolls'.

bhāviṣyat-kara-rahita (*EI* 24), 'without all the taxes to be levied in future.'

bhogasambandha-nirvacanīya (EI 12), 'the relations [of the gift land] with the administrative unit (i.e. *bhoga,* to which it belonged) should not be reckoned [since the land is granted after separating it from the district] (*bhogād=uddhṛtya*)'. Cf. *a-rāṣṭra-sāṁvinayika, grāma-nilaya-nā ḍa-sarva-bādhā-parihāreṇa.*

bhūmi-cchidra-nāyena or °*cchidra-pidhāna-vyāyena*, 'in accordance with the principle of cultivating the land for the first time and enjoying it free of taxes as a result'. The word *chidra* in the first means 'cultivation' and *chidra-pidhāna* in the second 'reclamation of uncultivable land for the first time.' Sometimes *vidhāna* is wrongly used for *pidhāna*. See *Ind. Ep.*, pp. 397-98.

bhūta-bhaviṣyad-vartamāna-niḥśeṣ-ādātya-sahita, 'together with the arrears of taxes and with the present and future taxes in their entirety'; epithet of gift village. Cf. *Ind. Ep.*, p. 395.

candr-ārka-kālikaṁ śulkam=ādeyaṁ samasta-rājye n=āsti, 'there is no collection of tolls in the whole kingdom as long as the moon and the sun exist'. Cf. *Ep. Ind.*, Vol. XXV, p. 237.

candr-ārka-sthiti-kālaṁ yāvat, 'as long as the moon and sun endure (*Ep. Ind.*, Vol. XXXV, p. 135, text lines 21-22); sometimes *candr-ārka-ksiti*°, *candr-ārk-ārṇāva-kṣiti-sarit-parvata*°, etc.

catuḥ-sīm-āvacchinna, same as *sva-sīm-āvachinna, catur-aghāṭa-viśuddha*, etc. Cf. Majumdar, *Ins. Beng.*, Vol. III, p. 125.

catuḥ-sīmā yāvat, same as *catuḥ-sīmā-paryanta*, etc. Cf. *Ind. Ep.*, p. 402.

catur-āghāṭa-viśuddha, 'with the boundaries well demarcated'; same as *catuḥ-sīm-āvacchina*, etc. Cf *Ind. Ep.*, p. 396.

catur-āghāṭ-āntarvarti-jala-pāṣāṇa-nidhi-nikṣepa - śulk - ādi- sarva-tejaḥsvāmya-sahita (*Ep. Ind.*, Vol. XXXIV, p. 40, text lines 37-38). See *tejaḥ-svāmya*, etc.

catuṣ-kaṇṭaka-viśuddha (EI 23), cf. *catur-āghāṭa-viśuddha*; probably refers to the custom of demarcating a plot of land by planting thorny shrubs on the borders.

caura-varjam, also quoted as *cora-varjam*, *cora-daṇḍa-varjam*, *cora-rājāpathyakāri-varjam*, etc.; according to some 'with immunity from the police tax', while others take it to be related to *a-cāṭa-bhaṭa-praveśa* and think that the policemen were prohibited from entering a gift village except in connection with the apprehension of criminals; may also mean 'without any right to inflict punishment of thieves, etc., or to levy fines from thieves, etc.' See *CII*, Vol. III, p. 109.

cora-daṇḍa-varja (EI 27), same as *caura-varja*, etc.

cora-varja (IE), 'without the right to punish the thieves and to realise stolen articles'; cf. *sa-caur-oddharaṇa*. But see also *cauravarjam.*

deśa-maryād-āruvaṇ-ānvita (*Ind. Ant.* Vol. XIX, p. 247, text line 103), refers to the right to levy the tax called *āruvaṇa* (Sanskrit *ṣaṭ-paṇa*) according to the local custom.

deva-Brāhmaṇa-bhukti-varja (EI 23, 30), 'excluding the property of the gods (i.e. temples) and Brāhmaṇas'.

devakula-puṣkariṇy-ādhikaṁ kārayitvā, refers to the right of the donee to build temples and excavate tanks in the gift land without the permission of the king or landlord as was necessary in the case of ordinary tenants. Cf. Majumdar, *Ins. Beng.*, Vol. III, p. 125.

go-gauḍa-sameta, 'together with the cattle and herdsmen [of state farms] or with the grazing tax'; epithet of gift village. *Go-gauḍa* may be the same as *go-kara*. Cf. *Ind. Ep.*, p. 402.

grāma-nilaya-nāḍa-sarva-bādhā-parihāreṇa (EI 9), 'with the exemption of all troubles connected with [the administration of] the village, subdivision (literally, habitation) and d strict [in which the gift land is situated]'. Cf. *a-rāṣṭra-sāṁvinayika*, etc.

gṛh-āvataraṇa - harita-pakva-sasy-ekṣu-cāraṇa-lavan-opamardana-rocikā-ciṭolā-grahaṇa-pīṭhaka-pīṭhikā-khaṭv-āpaharaṇa - kāṣṭh-endhana-

ghāsa-bus-ādikaṁ na kenacit=[*kartavyaṁ*] *pragrāhyaṁ* [*ca*], 'no one should enter into the donee's house, should graze one's cattle on the green crops in his fields, should harvest the ripe crops in his fields, should crush his sugar-cane, should accept *rocikā* and *ciṭolā* from him, should take stools, seats and cots from him and should take wood, fuel, grass, chaff, etc., from him'. For *gṛh-āvataraṇa*, see *umbara-bheda*. Words like *rocikā*, *ciṭolā*, etc., are not intelligible, although they certainly refer to certain obligations or levies. Cf. *Ind. Ep*., p. 394.

guvāka-nārikel-ādikaṁ laggāvayitvā, refers to the right of planting arecanut and coconut palms in the gift land without the permission of the king or landlord as was necessary in the case of ordinary tenants; cf. *sa-guvāka-nārikela*. Cf. Majumdar, *Ins. Beng*., Vol. III, p. 125.

hastidaṇḍa-varabalīvarda-coṭāla-andhā (*rthā* ?)*ruvā-pratyandhā-* (*rthā* ?)*ruvā-adattā-padātijīva-ahidaṇḍa-ānta* (*tu* ?)*rāvaḍḍi-bandha-daṇḍa-vijayavandāpanā-mārgaṇika-prabhṛti-bhaviṣyat-kara-sahita*, refers to the donee's right to enjoy various taxes the nature of some of which is doubtful. These include the tax for keeping elephants and prize bullocks, tax for the maintenance of the king's *Padātis* (footmen or *Pāiks*), tax on the professional snake-charmers, ransom in lieu of imprisonment, presents to be made to the king on his return from a victorious campaign and tax to be paid for using the road in the gift village for the transit of articles of merchandise. See the expressions separately as noticed above. See also *suvarṇa-daṇḍa-ahidaṇḍa*.........below. Cf. *Ind. Ep*., p. 401.

jana-dhana-sahita (*Ep. Ind*., Vol. XXXV, p. 135), 'together with the tenants and revenue income [of the village]'; some as *sa-jana-dhana*.

kuśa-latā-pūta-hast-odakena, cf. *udaka-pūrvam*, etc. See *Ind. Ep*., p. 395

mahādoṣa-vivarjita (EI 23), 'excluding fines for great crimes'; cf. *doṣa* and *daṇḍa-doṣa* (fines) noticed above.

mukt-oparikara (EI 29), free from minor taxes or without freedom from them. Cf. *s-oparikara*.

nānā-vṛkṣa-sameta, 'together with the various trees'; epithet of gift village. Some of the trees not to be enjoyed by unprivileged tenants were mango, *madhūka*, jack, coconut, arecanut, palmyra palm, sīsu, tamarind tree, etc. But the group was different in different parts of the country. Cf. *Ind. Ep*., p. 402.

nava-nidhāna-sahita (IA 11), probably,'with the taxes fixed afresh', though *nidhāna* is often the same as *nikṣepa* (q.v.).

nidhi-nikṣepa-pāṣāṇ-ārām-ādi-catuṣprakāra - bīravaṇa-pārikh-āya-sahita (*Ind. Int.*, Vol. XIX, p. 247), mentioned along with *aṣṭabhoga-tejassvāmy-daṇḍaśulka-yukta.* See the expressions as separately noticed above.

nidhi-nikṣep-āputrakadhana-daṇḍ-opajātaka-sahita, 'together with the right to enjoy treasure-trove and the occasional finds and accumulations on the land and to confiscate the property of persons dying without leaving any son, and to enjoy the right to appropriate the income derived from fines'; epithet of gift village. Cf. *Ind. Ep.*, 406.

nidhi-nikṣepa-sahita, see *sa-vṛkṣamālā-nidhi-nikṣepa-sahita.*

nidhy-upanidhi-hastidanta - vyāghracarma - nānāvanacara-sameta, refers to the right of the donee to treasure-troves, occasional finds or accumulations on the ground, elephants' tusks, tiger's skin and certain prized animals without surrendering them to the king as ordinary tenants had to do; epithet of the gift village. Cf. *Ind. Ep.*, p. 402.

niṣiddha-cāṭa-bhaṭa-praveśa (EI 22), same as *a-praveśa*, etc.

parihṛta-paṅg-otkoṭa (EI 33), 'exempted from the levies called *paṅga* and *utkoṭa*'. See the words as saparately noticed.

parihṛta-sarva-pīḍa (EI 27, 29), 'free from all troubles'; same as *sarva-pīḍā-varjita, sarva-bādhā-vivarjita,* etc.

phalaratika (*Ep. Ind.*, Vol. XXXV, p. 135), refers probably to the right to enjoy all kinds of fruits in the gift land without special permission that was necessary for ordinary tenants.

prasiddha-catuḥ-sīm-āvacchinna, 'demarcated by the well-known boundaries on all the sides'; epithet of the gift land. Cf. *catur-āghāṭa-viśuddha*, etc. Cf. *Ind. Ep.*, p. 402.

pratiṣiddha-cāṭa-bhaṭa-praveśa (EI 23, 27), same as *a-praveśa*, etc.

pratiṣiddha-cāṭ-ādi-praveśa (*I.E.*, p.395), same as *a-praveśa*, etc.

pūrva-bhujyamāna-deva-brāhmaṇa-kṣetra-khaṇḍalakaṁ varjayitvā (or *vihāya*), see *Ep. Ind.*, Vol. XXXV, p. 135; same as *deva-brāhmaṇa-bhukti-varja*, etc. Cf. *Ind. Ep.*, p. 398.

pūrva-bhuktaka-bhujyamāna-deva-brahma-dāya-varjita (EI 23), same as *deva-brāhmaṇa-bhukti-varja*, etc.

pūrva-pratta-deva-brahma-deya-rahita, sometimes with *dāya* in place of *deya*; refers to the absence of the donee's right to have any control over that land in the gift village which was already a rent-free holding in the possession of gods or Brāhmaṇas; same as *deva-brahmaṇa-bhukti-varja*, etc. Cf. *Ind. Ep.*, p. 398.

putra-pautrādi-santati-krameṇa, same as *putra-pautr-ānvaya-kram-opabhogya*, etc. Cf. *Ind. Ep.*, p. 399.

putra-pautr-ādy-anvay-opabhogā, °*ānugaminī*, etc.; same as *putra-pautr-ānugamaka*. Cf. *Ind. Ep.*, pp. 394-95.

putra-pautr-ānugamaka, 'the donee's right of enjoying the gift land should pass on to his sons and grandsons'; epithet of gift land; same as *putra-pautr-ānvaya-kram-opabhogya*, etc. Cf. *Ind. Ep.*, p.392.

putra-pautr-ānvaya-kram-opabhogya, refers to the permanent nature of a gift of land to be enjoyed by the donee as well as his descendants; same as *putra-putr-ānugamaka* (*I.E.*, p. 398).

rāja-bhāvya-sarva-pratyāya-sameta (EI 23), *bhāvya* being often changed to *ābhāvya*; same as *a-kiñcit-pragrāhya*, etc.

rāja-grāhya-samasta-pratyāya-samanvita (EI 22), same as *a-kiñcit-pragrāhya*, etc.

rāja-rājapuruṣair=apy=anaṅguli-nirdeśyam, same as *srava-rāja-kīyānām=a-hasta-prakṣepaṇīyaḥ*, etc. Cf. *Ind. Ep.*, p. 400.

rājasevakānāṁ vasatidaṇḍa-prayāṇadaṇḍau na staḥ, refers to the freedom of the gift village from the obligation to provide accommodation and conveyance, etc., to the royal officers on tour; cf. *a-kūra-chullaka-vināśi-khaṭv-āvāsa*, *a-paramparā-balīvarda*, etc. See *CII*, Vol. III, p. 98, note 2.

rājñā rājapuruṣair=apy=anaṅguli-prakṣepaṇīya (*Ind. Ant.*, Vol. XIX, p. 247, text lines 103-04), same as *sarva-rājakīyānām=a-hasta-prakṣepaṇīyaḥ*, etc.

ramya (*Ep. Ind.*, Vol. XXXV, p. 135), refers to the fact that the gift land had nothing unpleasant about it.

ṛṇ-ādāy-ādi-sambandha-varjita (EI 23), refers to the freedom of the gift land from confiscation for the realisation of debts incurred by the donee.

sa-bāhy-ābhyantar-ādāya, 'together with the external and internal income or taxes to be paid to the state and to the village authorities'; epithet of the gift village; cf. *abhyantara-siddhyā*, etc. Cf. *Ind. Ep.*, p. 395.

sa-bhoga (EI 27; IA 9), 'together with the *aṣṭa-bhoga*'.

sa-bhūta-pāta-pratyāya (CII 3), refers to the income from the gift land as a result of some action of nature's agencies. Sometimes *vāta* and *āvāta* are found for *pāta* probably in the sense of 'a storm' (cf. *udvāta*) and also *upātta*, 'realised'.

sa-bhūta-vāta-pratyāya (EI 23), with *pāta* sometimes in place of *vāta*; 'together with the income arising out of a change of the natural phenomena (such as due to earthquakes, storms, etc.)'; epithet of gift land.

sa-bhūt-opātta-pratyāya (EI 23), same as *sa-bhūta-vāta-pratyāya*, etc. The word *upātta* means 'realised'.

sa-caur-oddharaṇa (EI 12, 23, 29), 'together with the right to punish thieves and recover stolen property or fines'; epithet of gift villages. Cf. *caura-varja*, etc.

sa-daṇḍa-doṣa (EI 23), 'together with [the right to] levy fines for crimes'; the meaning of *doṣa* is really doubtful in the context.

sa-daṇḍa-nigraha (EI 24), refers to the king's power to punish [culprits] by fines or corporal punishment.

sa-daś-āpacāra, same as *sa-daś-āparādha*; cf. *Ind. Ep.*, p. 397.

sa-daś-āparādha (EI 27), also quoted as *sa-daś-āpacāra*; 'together with the right to punish and realise fines for the ten offences (murder, theft, etc.)'; epithet of gift village; cf. *sahya-daś-āparādha* probably meaning that the crimes committed in the gift village should not be punished by the king.

sa-deya-meya (EI 7), same as *sa-dhānya-hiraṇy-ādeya*, etc.

sa-dhānya-hiraṇy-ādeya (EI 11, 12, 23; IA 9), 'together with the king's grain share and taxes in cash'.

s-ādha-ūrdhva, 'together with what is [produced or found] below and above the ground'; epithet of gift land. Cf. *Ind. Ep.*, p. 395.

s-āgama-nirama-praveśa, 'together with approaches, ingress and egress'; epithet of gift land. Cf. *Ind. Ep.*, p. 394.

sa-gart-āvaskara (*Ep. Ind.*, Vol. XXXV, p. 135), mentioned along with *s-oṣara*. The word *avaskara* (also *avakara*) probably means 'a mound'.

sa-gart-oṣara (EI 27, 29), 'together with pits and saline spots or barren lands'; epithet of gift village.

sa-giri-gahana-nidhāna (EI 24), 'together with hills, forests and deposits'. See also *nidhāna* noticed above.

sa-gokula, 'together with the cowpens'; epithet of gift village. Cf. *Ind. Ep.*, p. 395.

sa-gopracāra (EI 12), 'together with the pasture lands'.

sa-gulma-latā (EI 12), same as *sa-gulma-latāka*, etc.

sa-gulma-latāka, 'together with shrubs and creepers'; epithet of the gift land. Cf. *Ind. Ep.*, p. 402.

sa-guvāka-nārikera (EI 12), sometimes with *nālikela* in place of *nārikera*; 'together with the arecanut and coconut palms'; epithet of gift land; see *guvāka-nārikel-ādikaṁ laggāvayitvā.*

sa-haṭṭa-ghaṭṭa-sa-tara (EI 22), 'together with market-places and ferries (or passes) and with ferry-dues'.

sa-hiraṇya-bhāga-bhoga (EI 23), same as *sa-deya-meya*, etc. See the words as separately noticed.

sa-hiraṇya-bhāga-bhog-oparikara-sarv-ādāya-sameta (EI 23), 'together with all levies such as *hiraṇya*, *bhāga*, *bhoga* and *uparikara*'. See the various words as noticed separately.

sa-hiraṇy-ādāna (EI 26), 'together with levies in cash'; privilege of the donee of rent-free and.

sahya-daś-āparādha (IE), see *sa-daś-āparādha.*

sa-jala-sthala (EI 12, 27, 29), 'together with land and waters [of the gift village]'.

sa-jala-sthal-āraṇya (EI 23), 'together with the land, waters and jungles [of the gift village]'.

sa-jala-sthala-sahita (EI 23), same as *sa-jala-sthala.*

sa-jana-dhana (*Ep. Ind.*, Vol. XXXV, p. 139), same as *jana-dhana-sahita.* Cf. *sa-jana* (*ibid.*, Vol. V, p. 185).

sa-jāṅgal-ānūpa (EI 12), 'together with arid and marshy lands'.

sa-jhāṭa-viṭapa, 'together with bushes and shrubs (or branches)'.

sa-kar-otkara=Prakrit *sa-kar-ukara* (EI 7); refers to a piece of land granted with the donee's right to enjoy major and minor taxes; cf. *s-odraṅga-s-oparikara* and *sa-kḷpt-opakḷpta*, etc. See *kar-otkara* as noticed separately above; also cf. *kāru-kara.*

sa-khalla-unnata=*sa-khall-onnata* (EI 12), 'together with low and high lands'; epithet of gift land. *Khalla* is Oḍiyā *khāl* 'low land'. Cf. *sa-nimn-onnata.*

sa-khaṇḍapālīya, 'together with the tax for the maintenance of the swordsmen'; epithet of gift village; cf. *padāti-jīvya*, tax for the maintenance of *Pāiks* or footmen. Cf. *Ind. Ep.*, p. 402.

sa-khaṭa-viṭapa (EI 12), mistake for *sa-jhāṭa-vitapa* or *sa-kheṭa-viṭapa.*

sa-kheṭa-ghaṭṭa-naditara-sthān-ādi-gulmaka (EI 29), 'together with the military, police or customs outposts in the hamlets, landing places on the banks of rivers (or passes in the hilly tracts) and ferrying stations'; epithet of gift village.

sa-kheṭa-viṭapa, 'together with outposts and bushes'; epithet of gift village. Cf. *Ind. Ep.*, p. 402.

sa-khila-nāla, 'together with the fallow and cultivated lands'; epithet of gift village; same as *sa-khila-polācya.* See Majumdar, *Ins. Beng.*, Vol. III, p. 125.

sa-khila-polācya, 'together with fallow and cultivated land'; same as *sa-khila-nāla.* Cf. *Ind. Ep.*, p. 394.

sa-khil-opakhila, 'together with land which is fallow and partially fallow'. *Pakhila* in the same context is a mistake for *upakhila.*

sa-kḷpta (EI 24), 'together with the tax on permanent tenants or the fixed revenue'; same as *s-odraṅga.*

sa-kḷpt-opakḷptaka (EI 24, 27), refers to the freedom of the gift land from the payment of fixed taxes on permanent tenants as well as occassional taxes or taxes on temporary tenants; same as *s-odraṅga-s-oparikara.*

sa-kṛta-prānta, cf. Prakrit *sa-kutu-ppanta* (EI 26), 'together with the demarcated boundaries'; epithet of the gift land.

sa-lavaṇa (EI 12), 'together with salt (i.e. the right to enjoy salt produced in the land). Cf. *a-lavaṇa-khātaka*, etc.

sa-lavaṇ-ākara (EI 12), 'together with the salt pits'. Cf. *a-lavaṇa-khātaka*, etc.

sa-loh-ādy-ākara, together with the mines of metals, etc.'; epithet of gift village. Cf. *Ind. Ep.*, p. 395.

sa-loha-lavaṇ-ākara (EI 23, 26), 'together with the mines and salt-pits', epithet of gift land. Cf. *sa-loh-ādy-ākara, a-lavaṇa-khātaka*, etc.

sa-madhūka-cūta-vana-vāṭikā-viṭapa-tṛṇa-yūti-gocara-paryanta, 'together with the *madhūka* and mango trees, forests, gardens, bushes (or, branches), grass *yūti* (grass land) and including the pasture land'; cf. *Ind. Ep.*, p. 396. It is better to take *sa-madhūka-cūta-vana-vāṭikā-viṭapa* and *tṛṇayūti-gocara-paryanta* separately.

sa-madhūk-āmra-vana-vāṭikā-viṭapa-tṛṇa-yūti-gocara-paryanta (EI 24), 'together with the *madhuka* and mango trees, forests, gardens, shrubs and as far as and the grass *yuti* (grass land) and pasture lands'. See *sa-madhūka-cūta......*, above.

sa-mandira-prākāra, 'together with temples and walls'; epithet of gift village. Cf. *Ind. Ep.*, p. 395.

trees and areas covered by jungles (or areas covered with mango and *madhūka* plantations)'; see *Ind. Ep.*, p. 402

sa-mañca-mahākaraṇa (EI 26), 'together with *mañca* (probably, platforms for the collection of tolls) and *mahākaraṇa* (official documents)'; epithet of the gift land.

sāmant-āmātya-dūtānām=anyeṣām=c=ābhyupāgame śayanīy-āsana-siddhānnaṁ na dāpayet, refers to the obligation of the people to supply beds, seats and boiled or unboiled rice to feudatory rulers, ministers, messengers and others encamped in a village; see *a-kūra-cullaka-vināśi-khaṭv-āvāsa*, etc. See *Ep. Ind.*, Vol. XXX, p. 171.

samasta-bhāga-bhoga-kara-hiraṇy-ādi-pratyāya-sameta, 'together with all incomes including the king's grain share, the periodical offerings to be made to the king or landlord and to the touring officers, taxes in grains, taxes in cash, etc.'; epithet of gift land; same as *sa-hiraṇya-bhāga-bhoga*, etc. See *Ind. Ep.*, p. 397.

samasta-bhāga-bhoga-kara-hiraṇy-ādāya-sameta (EI 23), same as *sa-hiraṇya-bhāga-bhoga*, etc.

samasta-rājakīyānām=apraveśya, same as *a-bhaṭa-praveśa*, *a-cāṭa-bhaṭa-praveśya*, *a-bhaṭa-cchātra-prāveśya*, etc. (*Ind. Ep.*, p. 398).

samasta-rājakīyānam=ahasta-prakṣepaṇīya (CII 3), same as *ā-bhaṭa-praveśa*, etc.

samasta-rājapratyādāya-sameta (*Ep. Ind.*, Vol. XXXV, p. 129), same as *sa-hiraṇya-bhāga-bhoga*, etc.

samast-otpatti-sahita (EI 12), 'together with all the produce or income'.

samast-otpatti-śulk-otpatti-sahita (EI 23), 'together with all the produce of the land and the income arising from tolls'.

sa-matsya-kacchapa (EI 12), 'together with the right to catch fish and tortoises'; epithet of gift village.

sa-matsy-ākara (EI 24), 26), 'together with the sources of fish (e.g., rivers, tanks, etc)'; epithet of gift village.

samhalātamaka-samanvita (EI 9), the reading is apparently wrong; meaning uncertain.

sa-mīna-toya (EI 24), 'together with fish and the waters' or 'together with the waters containing fish.'

s-āmra-madhūka (IE; EI 12, 27, 29), 'together with the mango and *madhūka* trees'.

s-āmra-madhu-vana (EI 12), same as *s-āmra-madhū-van-ākīrṇa*.

s-āmra-madhu-van-ākīrṇa, see *Ind. Ep.*, p. 402.

s-āmra-panasa (EI 12), 'together with mango and jack trees'.

samuchita-deya-bhāga-bhoga-kara-hiraṇy-ādi (EI 23), same as *sa-hiraṇya-bhāga-bhoga*, etc.

samudayabāhy-ādyastamba (EI 23), '[land] covered with original shrubs (i.e. never cultivated) and not yielding any revenue [to the State].'

sa-mūla (EI 13), 'together with the root crops'.

nidhān-ālīpaka-kumārīsāhas-āputrādhana-pradhān-āpradhāna-doṣa-samanvita (*Ep. Ind.*, Vol. III, p. 274), see the words as noticed separately above. The word *doṣa* here means 'fines'.

sa-nidhi (EI 27), refers to the freedom of the donee of the gift land from the obligation of surrendering to the king underground treasures in the land on their discovery.

sa-nidhi-nidhāna (*Ep. Ind.*, Vol. XXXV, p. 139), same as *sa-nidhi-nikṣepa*, etc.

sa-nidhi-nikṣepa, see *nidhi*, *nikṣepa*, *nidhāna*, *ālipaka*, etc., as noticed separately. Cf. *Ind. Ep.*, p. 396.

sa-nidhy-upanidhi (EI 26), same as *sa-nidhi-nikṣepa*, etc.

sa-nimn-onnata (IA 16), same as *sa-khall-onnata*.

sa-nirgama-praveśa (EI 12), 'together with ingress and egress'.

s-ānūpa-jāṅgala (*Ind. Ant.*, Vol. XVIII, p. 34, text line 5), same as *sa-jāṅgal-ānūpa*.

sa-padr-āraṇya (EI 23, 24), same as *sa-padr-āraṇyaka*.

sa-padr-āraṇyaka (EI 12), 'together with habitations and jungles'; epithet of gift land.

sa-pallika (*Ep. Ind.*, Vol. XXXV, p. 135), 'together with its hamlets'.

sa-parikara (EI 23), same as or a mistake for *s-oparikara*.

sa-parṇ-ākara (EI 26), 'together with the fields growing betel leaves'; epithet of gift village.

sa-pratīhāra, 'together with the tax for the maintenance of the watchmen of the city gates'; cf. *Ind. Ep.*, p. 401.

sarva-bādhā-parihāra (EI 23, 24), same as *parihṛta-sarva-pīḍa*, etc.

sarva-bādhā-vivarjita (EI 24), same as *parihṛta-sarva-pīḍa*, etc.

sarv-ābhyantara-siddhi (EI 20; IA 19), 'together with the entire internal revenue income or all the taxes to be paid to local authorities'.

sarv-ābhyantara-siddhyā (IA 18), same as *sarv-ābhyantara-siddhi*.

sarv-ādāna-ditya-viṣṭi-prātibhedikā-parihīna (CII 4), 'free from all levies, *ditya*, forced labour and *prātibhedikā*'. See *ditya* and *prātibhedikā* as noticed above.

sarv-ādāna-saṅgrāhya (6II 4), 'with the right to levy all the dues'; same as *sarv-ādāya-sameta*.

sarv-ādāna-viṣṭi-prātibhedikā-parihīna (CII 4), 'free from the payment of all imposts and the obligation regarding unpaid labour and *prātibhedikā*'; epithet of gift village. See *prātibhedikā* as noticed above.

sarv-ādāya-sameta (EI 23), same as *sarv-ādāna-saṅgrāhya*, etc.

sarv-ādeya-viśuddha (CII 4), 'with all kinds of taxes fixed'; same as *sarv-ādāya-sameta* (cf. *sarv-āya-viśuddha*).

sarva-ditya-viṣṭi-jemaka-kara-bhara-parihīna (CII 4), 'free from the burden of all the *ditya*, forced labour, *jemaka* and taxes'. See *ditya* and *jemaka* as noticed above.

sarva-ditya-viṣṭi-prātibhedikā-parihīna (EI 9; CII 4), 'free from all kinds of *ditya*, forced labour and *prātibhedikā*'. See the words as noticed separately.

sarva-ditya-viṣṭi-prātibhedikā-parihṛta (*Ep. Ind.*, Vol. VI, p. 298, text lines 201-21), same as *sarva-ditya-viṣṭi-prātibhedikā-parihīna*. See the words as noticed above.

sarva-jāta-bhoga-nirasta, refers to a grant of land with all kinds of royal rights abrogated. Cf. *Ind. Ep.*, p. 390.

sarva-jāta-bhoga (EI 24), 'together with all kinds of privileges to be enjoyed.'

sarva-jāta-pārihārika, cf. Prakrit *sava-jāta-pārihārika* (*Select Inscriptions*, pp. 92, 94),'endowed with all kinds of exemptions.'

sarva-kara-parihāra (EI 23, 27), 'exemption from all taxes.'

sarva-kara-sameta (EI EI 23, 27), 'together with all taxes.'

sarva-paṅga-parihṛta (EI 33), 'free from all levies falling in the category of *paṅga*'. See *paṅga* noticed above.

sarva-parihāra-kārudeya (EI 24), refers to all kinds of exemptions including the dues from artisans.

sarva-pīḍā-parihṛta (EI 23), same as *sarva-pīḍā-varjita*, *sarva-pīḍā-vivarjita*, etc.

sarva-pīḍā-varjita (EI 23), same as *parihṛta-sarva-pīḍa*, *sarva-bādhā-vivarjita*, etc.

sarva-pīḍā-vivarjita (EI 27), same as *parihṛta-sarva-pīḍa*, etc.

sarva-rājakīyānām=a-hasta-prakṣepaṇīyaḥ (CII 3), same as

a-bhaṭa-praveśa, a-cāṭa-bhaṭa-prāveśya, a-bhaṭa-cchātra-prāveśya, etc.

sarva-vādhā-vivarjita, with *vādhā* in the place of *bādhā*; same as *parihṛta-sarva-pīḍa, sarva-pīḍā-varjita*, etc. Cf. *Ind. Ep.*, p. 401.

sarva-viṣṭi-parihāra-parihṛta (EI 23, 24, 26), 'endowed with the exemptions from all kinds of unpaid labour'; epithet of the gift village.

sarv-āya-sahita (*Ind.Ant.*, Vol. XIX, p. 247, text line 203), 'together with the entire income.'

sarv-āya-viśuddha (EI 23),'having fixed and regular income.'

sarv-opadrava-varjita (EI 24), same as *parihṛta-sarva-pīḍa*, etc.

sarv-oparikar-ādāna-sahita, 'together with the right to levy all minor taxes or taxes on temporary tenants'; epithet of gift village. Cf. *Ind. Ep.*, p. 401.

sarv-oparikara-kar-ādāna-sameta (EI 23), 'together with all the levies falling in the categories of *uparikara* and *kara*'. See *kara* and *uparikara* as noticed above.

sarv-otpatti-sahita (EI 23), 'together with whatever is produced (i.e. crops or income).'

sarv-eṣṭi-parihāra-parihṛta (EI 27), *sarv-eṣṭi* may be a mistake for *sarva-viṣṭi*.

sa-saibara (EI 17), also written *sa-śaivara*; 'together with unassessed arable lands or the tax on farm-houses'; cf. *śaivara* and *saibara* noticed above.

sa-sarva-pallika (*Ep. Ind.*, Vol. XXXV, p. 129), 'together with all the hamlets'.

sa-sarv-āśan-ekṣu-karpāsa-śaṇ-āmra-madhūk-ādi-bhūruha, 'together with *aśana* (*pītaśāla*), sugarcane, cotton-plants, hemp-plants, mango, *madhūka* and other trees'; epithet of gift land. Cf. *Ind. Ep.*, p. 395.

sa-sāṭa-viṭapa (EI 12), mistake or wrong reading of *sa-jhāṭa-viṭapa* (q.v.).

s-āṣṭādaśa-prakṛty=opeta (EI 2), 'together with the eighteen (i.e. all) kinds of tenants (i.e. tenants belonging to all the communities)'.

sa-sthāvara-jaṅgama, 'together with the immovable and movable belongings [of the gift village]'. Cf. *Ind. Ep.*, p. 395.

sa-tala (EI 12, 29), 'together with the surface of the ground'.

sa-tālaka (EI 12), 'together with palmyra palms'; epithet of gift village.

sa-tantalika (EI 12), 'together with tamarind trees'.

sa-tantuvāya-gokuṭa-śauṇḍik-ādi-prakṛtika, 'together with such tenants as the weavers, cowherds or milkmen and vintners'; epithet of gift village. Cf. *Ind. Ep.*, p. 393.

sa-tara (EI 22), see *sa-haṭṭa-ghaṭṭa-sa-tara.*

s-āṭavi-viṭapa-samanvita (EI 23), 'together with forests and shrubs'.

sa-tṛṇa-kāṣṭh-odak-opeta (EI 24), 'together with the grass, fuel and waters [of the gift village]'.

sa-vanaspaty-udak-āsīhāra-kullaka-pānīya-sameta 'together with the fruit-trees and various kinds of water courses'; epithet of gift land. Cf. *Ind. Ep.*, p. 394.

sa-vana-śvabhra-nidhāna, 'together with forests, pits and mines'; epithet of gift village. Cf. *Ind. Ep.*, p. 395.

sa-vāta-bhūta-pratyāya (EI 11; IA 9), same as *sa-bhūta-vāta-pratyāya*, etc.

sa-viṭapa-latā (EI 24), 'together with shrubs and creepers'.

sa-viṭap-āraṇya, 'together with bushes and jungles'; epithet of gift village.

sa-vṛkṣamālā-kula (EI 23; IA 11), 'together with various gardens or plantations'. See *nānā-vṛkṣa-sameta.*

sa-vṛkṣamālā-nidhi-nikṣepa-sahita (EI 23), see *sa-vṛkṣamālā-kula* and *sa-nidhi-nikṣepa.*

sīm-āntargata-vastu-sahita, 'together with [all] things within the boundaries'; cf. *Ind. Ep.*, p. 395.

sīsū-madhūka-tāla-prabhṛti-nānā-vṛkṣa-sameta, refers to the right to use various trees in the gift village without the king's permission which was necessary for the ordinary tenants. See *nānā-vṛkṣa-sameta*, etc. Cf. *Ind. Ep.* p. 401.

s-oddeśa (EI 12, 29), 'together with the space above the surface of the ground'; epithet of gift land.

s-odraṅga (EI 12, 27, 29), 'together with the tax called *udraṅga*'. *Udraṅga* is=*uddhāra*, Tamil *uttāra*, fixed taxes.

s-opajāt-ānya-vastuka (EI 26), 'together with all the articles that may be produced [in the gift land] other than those ment'oned.'

s-opanidhi (EI 12, 27), refers to the freedom of the donee of the gift land from the obligation of surrendering to the king any valuables found on it; cf. *niṣepa* in *sa-nidhi-nikṣepa.*

s-oparikara (EI 12, 27, 29), sometimes quoted as *sa-pari-kara*; 'together with minor taxes or taxes realisable from temporary tenants'; epithet of gift village.

s-oparikara-daṇḍa (EI 27), 'together with minor taxes (or the tax on temporary tenants) and fines.'

s-ordhv-ādhaḥ (EI 23), same as *s-ādha-ūrdhva* (q.v.).

s-ordhv-ādhaś=catur-āghāṭa viśuddha (EI 24), see *s-ordhv-ādhaḥ* and *catur-āghāṭa-viśuddha*. *Āghāṭa* is often writtten *āghāṭana*.

s-oṣara (*Ep. Ind.*, Vol. XXXV, p. 135), 'together with barren lands (or saline spots)'.

s-oṣar-āvaskara-sthāna-nivāta-lavaṇ-ākara (EI 22), see the various words as noticed above. *Nivāta=āvāta.*

s-otpadhyamāna-viṣṭi (EI 11), same as *s-otpadyamāna-viṣṭika* (q.v.).

s-otpadhyamāna-viṣṭika (EI 23, IA 11), 'together with the right to get unpaid labour whenever that may be due from the tenants'; epithet of gift land.

su-kṛṣṭa (*Ep. Ind.*, Vol. XXXV, p. 135), 'well-cultivated'.

śulka - daṇḍa - dāṇa - kāruka - maulika-śrotra-nidhi-nikṣepa-jala-paṣāṇa-tejaḥ-svāmyam=ity-ādy-aṣṭa-bhoga-sahitam, 'together with right to the enjoyment of the gift land in eight ways such as the rights to tolls, fines (or obligations), customs duties, taxes on artisans, fixed revenue, rent of public buildings, treasure-trove, occasional finds or deposits, fishing, quarrying and *tejaḥ-svāmya* (full authority arising out of ownership).' See the various words as noticed above. Cf. *Ind. Ep.*, Vol. XXXII, p. 42.

su-pallik-āpeta (*Ep. Ind.*, Vol. XXXV, p. 139), same as *sa-pallika.*

suvarṇadaṇḍa-ahidaṇḍa-vartmadaṇḍa-vandāpanā-vijayandāpanā-tṛṇodaka-śāsanārdhika-cara (*vara* ?) *balīvarad-ārthāruvā-pratyarthāruvā-padātijīvya-ādattā-āturāvaḍḍi-bhaviṣyat-kar-ādi-sahita*, refers to the right of the donee to levy various taxes, the nature of some of which is uncertain (see the different expressions as noticed above). These include tax on the goldsmiths and snake-charmers, tolls to be collected for using the road passing through the gift village for the transit of articles of merchandise, presents to be made to the king or landlord on occasions, especially on his return from a victorious campaign, etc. See *hastidaṇḍa-varabalīvarda*...... above. Cf. *Ind. Ep.*, p. 402.

svacchand-opabhogen=opabhoktum, refers to the right of the donee to enjoy the gift land according to his own free will. Cf. *Ind. Ep.*, p. 399.

sva-sīmā-paryanta (EI 23), 'as far as its boundaries'; epithet of gift land.

sva-sīmā-tṛṇa-gocara-goyūti-paryanta (EI 23), 'as far as the grass land on the boundaries as well as the pasture lands and *goyūti*'. *Goyūti* may be an enclosure for cattle.

sva-sīmā-tṛṇa-kāṣṭha-yūti-gocara-paryanta (EI 23), 'as far as the *yūti* (preserve) of grass and wood as well as the pasture lands on the boundaries'.

sva-sīmā-tṛṇayūti-gocara-paryanta (EI 23), 'as far as the preserve of grass as well as the pasture lands on the boundaries'.

sva-sīmā-tṛṇa-goyūthī-gocara-paryanta, same as *sva-sīmā-tṛṇa-yūti-gocara-paryanta*, *yūthī* being a synonym of *yūti* (also spelt *pūti*), probably meaning 'a preserve'. See *sva-sīmā-tṛṇa-gocara-goyūti-paryanta*, etc. Cf. *Ind. Ep.*, p. 394.

sva-sīmā-tṛṇa-yūti-gocara-paryanta, 'as far as its boundaries, the *yūti* of grass and pasture land'; cf. *Ind. Ep.*, p. 397.

sva-sīm-āvacchinna, 'with its boundaries demarcated'; epithet of gift village. Cf. *Ind. Ep.*, p. 395.

talabhedyā-ghāṇaka-mallaka-vundaka-daṇḍadoṣa-prāpt-ādāya (*Ind. Ant.*, Vol. XVIII, p. 83, text lines 19-20), see the words as noticed separately above.

talabhedyā-govāṭikā-śākamuṣṭi-tailapalikā-kumbhapūrak-ākāśot-pati-pātāla-nidhi-nikṣhpa-devāyatan-odyāna-taḍāga-vāpī-kup-ādi-sahita (*Ep. Ind.*, Vol. XXXII, p. 155).

tila-darbh-odaka-pavitra-pāṇinā (*Ep. Ind.*, Vol. XXXV, p. 135, text line 23), cf. *udaka-pūrvam*, etc.

tṛṇa-kāṣṭh-odak-opeta (EI 23), 'together with grass and fuel and the waters'.

tṛṇa-pūti (or *yūti*)-*gocara-paryanta* (EI 12), epithet of gift land; see *sva-sīmā-tṛṇa-yūti* (or *pūti*)-*gocara-paryanta*, etc.

udaka-pūrvam, cf. *udak-ātisargeṇa*, *udakena*, *tila-darbh-odaka-pavitra-pāṇinā*, *kuśa-lalā-pūta-hast-odakena*, etc.

udakena, cf. *udaka-pūrvam*, etc. Cf. *Ind. Ep.*, pp. 136-37.

udbalika, 'free from land tax'; cf. *utpratikara*. Cf. Prakrit *ubalika* (*Select Inscriptions*, p. 70).

umbara-bhedaḥ rājapuruṣāṇām=āvāsako jemakaś=ca n=āsti, 'there is no entry of royal officers into a house with its door closed (referring especially to the houses of merchants away from home on business tours abroad) nor should there be any provision for their accommodation and meals'. See *Ep. Ind.*, Vol. XXV, p. 232-33.

uñcha-kara-bhar-ādi-vivarjita (*Ep. Ind.*, Vol. XXXIII, p. 89); see *uñcha*, etc., as noticed separately above.

urdhv-ādhaḥ-siddhi-yuta (IA 18), 'together with the income from fruits and roots.'

utpratikara (EI 23), same as *a-kiñcit-pratikara*; cf. *udbalika.*

vana-vāṭikā-tṛṇa-jantu-gocara-paryanta (*Ep. Ind.*, Vol. XXIII p. 229), 'including forests, gardens, grass fields and pasture lands for cattle and animals.'

vāstu-kṣetra-jalādhāra-gartā-mārga-samanvita (EI 22), 'together with homestead lands, tanks, pits, pathways and roads'.

vātoḍarīya (EI 22), epithet of gift land; probably a corruption of *vāt-ottarīya*; cf. *sa-bhūta-vāt-ādeya*, etc.

yathādīyamāna-bhāgabhogakara-paravaṇikara-kūṭaka-prabhṛti-samast-ādāya, sometimes with *turuṣka-daṇḍa* and *kumāra-gadyāṇaka* in place of *kūṭaka*, and *hiraṇya*, *jalakara*, *gokara*, *nidhi-nikṣepa*, *yamali-kambali*, etc., added to the list. *Bhāga-bhoga-kara* means 'taxes in general together with the king's share of grains and the periodical offerings payable to him.' For *pravaṇi-kara*, *kūṭaka* and *yamalikambali*, see the words as noticed above. *Turuṣkadaṇḍa* was a tax levied from the Muhammadan subjects or for the defence of the kingdom from Muhammadan attacks and *Kumāra-gadyāṇa* may be a tax of one *gadyāṇa* levied on the occasion of a prince's birth. *Hiraṇya* is 'tax in cash', *jala-kara* fishing tax, *go-kara* grazing tax, *nidhi* treasure-trove and *nikṣepa* valuables found or accumulated on the land. Cf. *Ind. Ep.*, p. 397.

yathā-pradīyamāna-bhāga-bhoga-hiraṇy-ādika (EI 23), 'whatever is payable as *bhāga-bhoga*, *hiraṇya*, etc.' See the words as noticed separately; also *yathā-samucita-bhāga-bhoga-kara-hiraṇy-ādi-sarva-rāja-bhāvya-pratyāya* (*Ind. Ep.*, p. 394).

yath-otpadyamāna-bhāga-bhog-ādika (EI 23), 'with the power to realise *bhāga*, *bhoga*, etc., whenever they become due.' See the words as noticed separately above.

APPENDIX II

TAX NAMES IN DRAVIDIAN LANGUAGES

abhiṣeka-kkāṇikkai (SITI), Sanskrit-Tamil; presents offered to a king at the time of his coronation.

ācārya-pūjanai (SITI), honorarium payable to priests.

accu-taṟi, accu-ttaṟi (SITI), Tamil; a variety of loom; tax payable on looms.

accu-vari (SITI), Tamil; probably, the same as *pŏn-vari*; duty payable for minting gold or metal into coins; cf. *akkaśālai-vari.*

adhikāra-ppeṟu (SITI), Sanskrit-Tamil; probably, presents offered to an officer.

adhikāra-varttanai (SITI), customary payments made to an officer at stipulated periods.

aḍimai-kkāśu (SITI), Tamil; fee collected from temple servants.

aḍi-kkāśu (SITI), Tamil; tax collected from stall-keepers in markets.

āḍi-ppaccai (SITI), Tamil; probably, perquisities payable in grain in the month of *Āḍi* after the harvest.

ādirai-ppāṭṭam (SITI), Tamil; tax on cattle; cf. *attiṟai-pāṭṭam.*

āḍukkalai-ppuṟam (SITI), Tamil; an enowment for the kitchen expenses of a temple.

akkaśālai-vari (SITI), Tamil; tax payable to the mint for minting coins; cf. *accu-vari.*

āḻ-amañji (SII 12), a levy; explained as 'workmen pressed into service without wages' (SITI); Sanskrit *viṣṭi.*

aḻḻāya-mānyam (SITI), Tamil-Sanskrit; probably, the right to receive a handful of grain or a prescribed quantity of an article sold in the market as wages for measuring.

āḻ-nĕl, āṇĕl (SITI), Tamil; a tax payable in paddy.

alpamirai (SITI), Tamil; a minor tax payable in grains.

aḻu (SITI), Tamil; a variety of market dues; probably, the same as *aḻḻu* and *aḻḻāya-mānyam.*

aḻugal-śarakku (SITI), Tamil; the right of collecting the refuse and waste thrown in the village.

āḻ-vari (SII 12; SITI), Tamil; poll-tax. See *per-kkaḍamai, per-vāśi.*

āṇai-ccālai (SITI), Tamil; 'an elephant stable'; tax payable for the maintenance of the elephant stable.

āṇḍ-eḻuttu-ttevai (SITI), Tamil, a tax of uncertain import.

aṅgāḍi-kkūli, aṅgāḍi-ppāṭṭam (SITI), Tamil; tax on bazars, shops, etc.

anniyāya-vāva-daṇḍa-iṟai (SITI), Tamil-Sanskrit; penal tax imposed on some unauthorised item of occupation or enjoyment.

antara-viniyogam (SITI), Sanskrit; individual share to make up the shortage in the total revenue occasioned by the grant of exemptions of *antar-āyam* or *uḻ-vari.*

antar-āyam (SITI), Sanskrit; internal revenue; taxes levied by a local body; also called *uḻ-vari.*

antarāya-kkāśu; *antarāya-ppāṭṭam* (SITI), Sanskrit-Tamil; internal taxes; minor taxes like the profession tax, etc., payable to the village assembly.

anuvarttanai (SITI), a class of contingent dues which come under the head *varttanai.*

arakkal (SITI), Tamil; an instalment of land-tax.

arandai (EI 18), name of a tax.

araśu-ppeṟu (SITI), Tamil; same as *mahārāja-prayojana*; probably, fees collected for payment for the performance of police duties in the rural areas.

ārāycci, kāriyav-ārāycci (SITI), Tamil; cess paid for the superintendence of transactions.

arcanā-bhoga , *arcanā-vṛtti* (SITI), Sanskrit ; land set apart for meeting the expenses of worship (*arcanā*) in the village temple.

arikoḻi, ariśi-ttuṇḍam (SITI); taxes of uncertain import.

arikūli (SITI), Tamil; dues payable in handfuls of the stalks harvested.

arimukkai (SII 12), a levy.

arippadikkāval (SII 12), a levy.

ariśi-kkāṇam (SITI), Tamil; tax for husking paddy into rice.

āṟṟaṅkarai-ttevai (SITI), Tamil; tax for keeping the river-bund in repair.

āṟṟu-kkulai (SITI), Tamil; 'river-bund'; tax to repair breaches in the river-bund.

āṟṟukkāl-amañji (SITI), Tamil; unpaid labour to keep the channel from the river in good repair.

aruntoḍu (SITI), Tamil; 'eating-plate'; a tax payable according to the number of eating plates in feeding houses.

āśuvikaḻ-kāsu, *āśuva-kkāśu*, *āśuva-kkaḍamai* (SITI), Tamil; tax payable by the Ājīvakas or for maintaing Ājīvaka monks.

āṭci-ppāṭṭam (SITI), Tamil; probably, a succession tax.

ātirai (SITI), Tamil; probably, the expenses for the *ārdrā* festival in the month of Mārgaḻi.

aṭiyuṟai (SITI), Tamil; offerings made at the feet of a high personage; written differently as *aḍiyiṟai*, *aḍiyaṟai*, etc.

āṭṭai-kkāṇikkai (SITI), Tamil; annual contribution or presents.

attiṟai-ppāṭṭam (SITI), Tamil; tax on cattle; cf. *ādiraipāṭṭam*.

aṭṭaṇaikkāl (SITI), Tamil; a kind of stand or pedestal (probably of eight legs).

āṭṭukk-iṟai, *āṭṭiṟai* (SITI) Tamil; tax on sheep; also called *āṭṭu-vari*.

aṭṭukkiṟai (SITI), Tamil; tax on charities.

āvaṇam (SITI), Tamil; a document; generally, a sale-deed; also called *villaiy-āvaṇam*; cf. *āvaṇa-kkaḷari* (SITI), place where documents like the sale-deeds, etc., are registered; a registration office.

avasara-varttanai (SITI), presents payable to an *Avasara*, an officer of the royal household having the duty of bringing to the notice of the king anything that demanded his immediate attention.

āyam (SITI); 'income'; tax in general.

baṇṇigitĕre, Kannaḍa; a kind of levy (*A. R. Ep.*, 1958-59, p.12).

bilkoḍĕ (EI 28), Kannaḍa; tolls.

birāḍa (EI 24), name of a tax.

baṇṇigĕ (EI 28), name of a tax.

bhatt-āya (SII 11-1), same as Sanskrit *bhakt-āya*.

biṭṭi (SII 11-1), same as Sanskrit *viṣṭi*.

bittu-kaṭṭĕ, Kannaḍa; same as *bittu-vaṭṭa*.

bittu-vaṭṭa, a portion of the produce from the land irrigated by a tank, granted to a person who excavated or repaired the tank (*A. R. Ep.*, 1958-59, p. 10).

brāhmaṇa-rāśa (*rāja*)*-kkāṇam* (SITI), Sanskrit-Tamil; tax payable by the Brāhmaṇa (*purohita*) to the king.

cakra-kāṇikkai (SITI), Sanskrit-Tamil; profession-tax paid by the potters; also called *tirigai-āyam*.

daṇḍa-kāṇam (SII 13), fines.

daśabandha (SITI), Sanskrit; tax or cess levied to keep the sources of water supply, like the tank, etc., in good repair.

dhāny-ādāya (SITI), Sanskrit; tax payable in grains.

dhānya-varga, cf. *tāniya-varakkam*.

eraḍu dogarāca-ppaṇṇu (EI 30), name of a tax.

eccoṟu (SII 13), a tax or the obligation of free feeding.

eḍai-vari (SITI), Tamil; tax on weights.

eḍuttu-kkoṭṭai (SITI), Tamil; a tax of uncertain import.

eḍuttukkoṭṭi (SII 12), a levy.

elavai (SITI), also spelt *ĕlavai*; Tamil; death-duty; fee for creamatorium.

ĕḻuttu-viniyogam (SITI), Tamil-Sanskrit; dues payable as *ĕḻuttu* for the village-accountant to be apportioned among the villagers.

eṇi-kkāṇam (SITI), Tamil; ladder tax evidently levied on toddy-drawers.

ĕṇṇĕy (SITI), Tamil; tax levied on the oil-trade; obligation for the supply of oil.

eraḍu-bilkodĕ (IE 8-5), Kannaḍa; name of a tax.

eri-āyam (SITI), Tamil-Sanskrit; income from fishing in the tank, etc.; amount payable by the owners of the fields irrigated by the tank for its upkeep.

eri-īvu (SITI), Tamil; share in the expenses of the maintenance of the tank.

er-kkaḍamai (SITI), Tamil; tax on ploughs.

er-ppŏn (SITI), Tamil; tax to be paid in cash for each plough; also called *er-kkaṇikkai*, etc.

erumai-ppŏn (SITI), Tamil; tax payable on buffaloes.

erikkāḍi (SII 12), tank cess of one *kāḍi* of paddy per field.

eri-mīṉ-pāṭṭam (SII 12), a tax; income from fish in the tank.

hĕjjuṅka, same as *pĕrjuṅka*, Kannaḍa; name of tax.

iḍaṅgai-vari (SITI), Tamil; tax paid by the members of the *iḍaṅgai* community or the left-hand classes.

iḍai-ppāṭṭam, also called *iḍai-ppūṭci* (SITI), Tanmil; tax on herdsmen or cattle-breeders.

iḍaitturai, also spelt *iḍatorai* (SITI), Tamil; a tax of uncertain import.

iḍaiyar-vari (SITI), Tamil; tax on shepherds.

ilaivāṇiya-ppāṭṭam (SITI), tax on the sellers of betel-leaves.

iḍatorai, see *iḍaitturai*.

ilakkulam (SII, 13), a tax.

īlam-puñjai, *īlam-puṭci* (SITI), Tamil; tax for toddy-drawing.

ilāñjanai-pperu, also called *lāñjinai-pperu*, *lāñjanai-pperu* (SITI), Tamil; fee for affixing the royal seal; *ilāñjanai*=Sanskrit *lāñchana*.

ilvari (SITI), Tamil; house-tax; cf. *manai-ppaṇam,manav-irai*.

inavari (SII 12), *inavari-kkāśu* (SITI), Tamil; communal tax.

irai (SII 13; SITI), Tamil; a general term denoting revenue income and the taxes to be paid to government; land tax.

irai-dravyam (SITI), Tamil-Sanskrit; explained as a lump sum paid in lieu of land tax; amount payable in commutation of the taxes payable on landed property.

irai-kāval (SITI), Tamil; amount of deposit which yielded interest per annum equal to the tax due on the land; sometimes regarded as a tax for police duties.

iraiyili-mudal (SII 13), same as *irai-dravyam*.

iraiyili-kkāśu (SITI), Tamil; amount paid for compounding taxes in order to make the land tax-free; also regarded as the amount payable to meet the shortage in the revenue occasioned by the grant of exemption from tax on certain lands.

īraṅkolli, *īraṅkolli* (SITI), Tamil; 'a washerman'; tax payable by washermen.

iravu (EI 30), Tamil; royal dues.

iruppu-kkaṭṭi (SITI), Tamil; probably, the cake of the Mahua seeds after the extraction of oil, largely used as soap; tax for the manufacture and sale of such cakes.

iśai-kkiḍāy (SITI), Tamil; 'beautiful ram'; dues to be paid for the ram kept for show; cf. *aḷag-erudu-kkāśu*.

joḍi, also spelt *śoḍi* (SITI), Tamil; name of a small quit-rent.

koḍai-vaḍaikkāy (SITI), Tamil; tax on arecanuts brought for sale.

kaḍamai (SITI), Tamil; revenue, tax to be paid to the government in kind.

kadir-kkāṇam (SITI), Tamil; tax paid in sheaves of corn.

kāḍu-kāval (SITI), Tamil; tax for the preservation and maintenance of forests.

kaṇakka-mikudi (SII 12), a tax.

kaḻḻavalika (EI 28), name of a tax.

kānika, Kannaḍa; also called *kāṇika-kanĕ*.

kanikĕ-kappa, *kappa-kānikĕ*, etc.; customary presents; presents from inferior to superior (EI 33).

kāṇikkai (EI 17, 21; SITI), Tamil; presents or customary payment as offerings to the king and other high officials.

kaṇṇāla-kkāṇam (SII 13; EI 28), marriage fee; collected by the village assembly; same as *vivāha-ppaṇam*; cf. *ugappār-pŏn*.

kaṇṇār-iṟai (SITI), Tamil; profession tax payable by a brazier.

kānuka (CITD), same as *kāṇika*, etc.

kappa (EI 33), Kannaḍa; tolls;

karaṇikka-joḍi (SII 2; SITI), quit-rent of the *Karaṇam* or *Karṇam* (village-accountant or *Paṭvārī*).

kārāṇmai (SITI), Tamil; a tenure with the hereditary right of enjoyment; cultivation right; tax for the same; also known as *kārāṇkiḻamai*.

kāriya-ppeṟu (SITI), Tamil; probably, the same as *kāriya-vārāycci*, *ārāycci*.

kāriya-vārāycci (SITI), Tamil; cess paid for the superintendence of transactions; same as *ārāycci*.

kāṟ-kaḍamai (SII 12), a tax.

karppūra-vilai (SITI), Sanskrit-Tamil; sale-price paid for temple lands; price paid for cultivation rights of temple lands and in commutation of the taxes thereon.

kārttigai-kkāśu, *kārttigai-kkāṇi*, *kārttigai-ppaccai*, *kārttigaiy-ariśi* (SITI), Tamil; payments in kind in the month of Kārttigai, i.e. during the harvest; cf. *āḍi-ppaccai*.

karuvi-paṇam, *karivi-ppaṇam* (SITI), Tamil; tax on the implements in cash, probably paid by the barbers.

karuvūla-vari (SITI), Tamil; fee for the safe-custody of precious articles in the treasury; or fee for the watch of the treasury.

kāś-āyam (SITI), *kāśu-āyam*; Tamil-Sanskrit; tax and

dues payable in coin; also called *kāśāya-vargam, kāśu-vargam* and *kāśu-kaḍamai.*

kāśu-kaḍamai (SITI), Tamil; tax payable in coin.

kāṭci (SITI), Tamil; presents offered to a highly superior person at the time of meeting.

kāṭciy-eradu-kkāśu (SITI), Tamil; tax probably on bulls kept for show.

kāṭṭāḷ-kāśu (SITI), Tamil; tax of uncertain import.

kaṭṭaṇam (SITI), Tamil; periodical presents made to superiors by their subordinates.

kaṭṭ-āyam (SITI), Tamil-Sanskrit; consolidated amount payable for the minor taxes; also written as *kaṇḍ-āyam*; sometimes taken as the compulsory payment of certain dues.

kattigai-ppaccai (SII 12), see *kārtigai-kkāśu,* etc.

katti-kkāṇam (SITI), Tamil; tax on weapons like sword, etc., or tax on the manufacture of swords or arms.

kaṭṭu-kkuttagai (SITI), Tamil; rent fixed at the time of farming out the land; payment of consolidated rent.

kaṭṭumukkai (SITI) Tamil; 'three handfuls in the bundle'; a contribution of three handfuls for every bundle of paddy stalks harvested, which were payable to the temples; cf. *arimukkai.*

kāval-peṟu (SII 12), name of a tax; cf. *kāval-kāni,* the right to guard temples.

kīḻ-iṟai (SITI; SII 12), Tamil; minor taxes, or tax fixed at a lower rate.

kīḻ-iṟai-ppāṭṭam (SITI), Tamil; small cesses and taxes like *mīn-pāṭṭam,* etc.

kiṟṟu-vari (SITI), Tamil; tax on thatched sheds.

kirukula (SITI), Tamil; commercial tax or tolls on retail articles; also called *kirukūla-viśeṣam*; cf. *kūlam.*

kŏḍi-kkaḍami (SITI), Tamil; explained as a tax for the cultivation of the medicinal plant *kŏḍi-veli,* otherwise known as *citra-mūlam*; probably, the same as *kodi-kkaḍamai,* tax on new cloth; cf. *tiru-ppudiyidu.*

kol-kūli (SITI), Tamil; tax for measuring or weighing.

kol-niṟai-kūli (SITI), Tamil; tax on articles measured by weight.

kŏḻmuṟai-ppāḍu (SITI), Tamil; customary dues.

kŏḻu (SITI), Tamil; tax on ploughshares.

kŏḻvari (SITI), Tamil; tax in kind.

ko-murai (SITI), Tamil; revenue due to the king.

ko-pada-vāram (SITI), Tamil-Sanskrit; tax due to the king.

koṭṭai-kkūli (SITI); 'wages on nuts'; probably, charges for the upkeep of forts; cf. *koṭṭai-magamai.*

koṭṭai-magamai (SITI), Tamil; tax for the maintenance of forts.

koyil-vāśi (SITI), Tamil; minor taxes payable to the palace.

kuḍi-kkāṇam (SITI), Tamil; fee paid by the tenants; probably, the same as *kuḍi-kkāśu* and *kuḍi-ppaṇam.*

kuḍimai (SII 12; SITI), Tamil; taxes in general (with the exception of land revenue) payable to the state for the protection of the civil rights it offers; tenancy tax.

kudirai-māṟṟu (SITI), Tamil; tax on horses.

kudirai-ppandi (SITI, Tamil; 'a stable'; tax for the same.

kudirai-vari (SITI), Tamil; tax on horses; also known as *kudirai-māṟṟu, kudiraiv-ilāḍam*; probably the same as *kudirai-ppandi.*

kudiraiv-ilāḍam (SITI), Tamil; 'horse-shoe'; fee for shoeing horses; probably connected with *kudirai-ppandi.*

kuḻavaḍai (EI 17), tax for the enjoyment of the tank and its income.

kūlam (SITI), Tamil; tax on grains and pulses; cf. *kirukulam.*

kumara-kaccāṇam (SITI), Tamil; explained as a tax payable in coin for the maintenance of the temple of Kumāra or Subrahamaṇya; but same as *kumāra-gadyāṇa* (q. v.).

kūṟṟariśi (SITI), Tamil; obligation of husking paddy belonging to the temple into rice and the charges to be met for the same.

kuṟṟu-nĕl, kūṟṟu-nĕllu (SITI), Tamil; tax for husking paddy payable to king.

kuśa-kkāṇam (SITI), Tamil; tax on potters; also known as *tirigaiāyam, śakkara-kkāṇikkai.*

lañjanai-pperu, lañjinai-ppeṟu, see *ilañjanai-ppeṟu.*

māḍai-kkūli (SITI), Tamil; tax for minting gold into coins.

mādā-ppaḍi (SITI), Tamil; allowances payable monthly; also called *mādārikka, mādan* and *mādārikkai.*

māḍu-kāṇikkai (SITI), Tamil; obligation of supplying draught cattle to the visting nobles by the tenants.

magamai, *maganmai*, *magaṇamai* (SITI), Tamil; small portion of the income or of the value of articles of merchandise collected as voluntary contribution by the merchants from among themselves for the maintenance of temples, etc.

maganmai (SITI), Tamil; poll-tax.

makkaḷ-peṟu (SITI), Tamil; one's obligations as a citizen; probably, dues payable to a temple, or poll-tax.

mallāyi-maghamai (SITI), Tamil; probably a customary collection in the market.

māmagam (SITI), Tamil; tax payable in cash probably for the great Māgha (Mahāmāgha) festival; or, a mistake for *mārgam*.

manai-meyppān-koḷḷum-iṟai, tax for the supervisor of houses or the building-supervisor; cf. *meyppān* (SITI), Tamil; 'shepherd; grazier;' a supervisor; probably related to *kaṇkāṇi*.

manai-ppaṇam (SITI), Tamil; house tax; also called *manai-vari*. Cf. *ilvari*.

maṉaiy-iṟai (SITI), Tamil; house-tax.

mandai-ppaṇam (SITI), Tamil; tax on cattle grazing in the village common.

maṇḍala-mudanmai-ppeṟu (SITI), Sanskrit-Tamil; fee for presents offered to the rulers of the *maṇḍala* or district.

maṇ-madil (SITI), Tamil; 'high wall or rampart made of mud'; tax for the erection and upkeep of such a wall.

māppadakku (SITI), Tamil; payment at the rate of one *padakku* or two *kuruṇi* for every *mā*.

māppaṇam (SITI), Tamil; a tax payable at the rate of one *paṇam* for every *mā*.

māppaṭṭaḍai (SITI), Tamil; tax probably for the penning of cattle; may also be *mara-ppaṭṭaḍai*, 'a timber depot'; tax payable for the same.

mara-kkaḍamai (SITI), Tamil; tax payable for trees.

mara-mañjāḍi (SITI), Tamil; tax of one *mañjāḍi* for every tree.

mārg-ādāyam (SITI), Sanskrit; tolls on the articles in transit.

mariyādi (SITI), Tamil; customary dues; also spelt *mar-jādi*, *mariśādi*, *maruśādi*, etc., and used in the sense of manner, way, extent, limit.

māṭṭukkaṟai (SITI), Tamil; probably, a tax on cattle (cows and buffaloes).

māvinda-kkaḍamai (SITI), Tamil, tax payable to the king.

melaḍi (SITI), Tamil; taxes paid in kind.

melviṭṭiya-vaḍḍāravuḷa, cf. *vaḍḍāravuḷa*.

mel-vĕṭṭa-pperu (SITI), land set apart for meeting expenses of public works (*vĕṭṭi*).

meṇi-ppŏn (SITI), Tamil; poll-tax; tax on individuals.

merai (SITI), Tamil; portion of the crop given at the threshing floor to certain village officers and servants as perquisite.

mer-pāḍi-kāval (SITI), Tamil; policing duty over the *nāḍu*. See *nāḍu-kāval.*

meṭṭu-nilam (SITI), Tamil; 'high land'; tax payable for the cultivation of such land.

miḷagu-taragu (SITI), Tamil; brokerage on pepper trade.

monampāṭṭam (SITI), Tamil; a tax of uncertain import.

mudaṟṟiraman, mudal-tiramam (SITI), Tamil; tax (payable in cash) of uncertain import; *tiramam* is the coin called *dramma* (from Greek *drachma*).

muḷḷaḍiśinnam (SII 12; SITI), Tamil; a tax of uncertain import; probably, payment for clue in detection.

mūṅgil-vari (SITI), Tamil; tax on bamboos.

muttāvaṇam (SITI), Tamil; a tax probably on the sale of pearls.

nāḍu-kāval (SITI), Tamil; 'policing duty of the *nāḍu*'; tax payable by the residents in the division for the same.

nāḍu-talaiyārikkam (SITI), Tamil; police-tax of the *nāḍu*; same as *nāḍu-kāval.*

nal-kiḍā, naṟ-kiḍā (SITI), Tamil; cess for the upkeep of the show-ram; or, tax for show-rams.

nall-ĕrudu (SII 12; SITI), Tamil; cess for the maintenance of a model bull, which was probably also used for breeding purposes; cf. *aḻagerudu-kkāśu, kāṭci-ĕrudu-kkāśu*, etc.

nall-erumai (SITI), tax for the maintenance of specimen buffaloes.

naṟ-kiḍā (SII 12), a tax.

nāṭṭu-kkaṇakku-vari (SITI), Tamil; tax payable for the maintenance of the revenue accounts of the *nāḍu* or the country as a whole.

nāṭu-kkāṇikkai (SITI), Tamil; presents payable to or by the assembly of the *nāḍu.*

nāṭṭupāti (SITI), Tamil, *nāḍu-upādi*; the obligations to be met and taxes payable to the local assembly of the *nāḍu.*

nāṭṭu-viniyogam (SITI), Tamil-Sanskrit; individual share payable to make up the shortage in the total revenue by the grant of exemptions by the assembly of the *nāḍu.*

nĕll-āyam (SITI), Tamil-Sanskrit; tax payable in paddy; also known as *nĕṟ-kaḍamai.*

nĕy (SITI), Tamil; tax on the traders in ghee; same as *nĕy-vilai*; cf. also *eṇṇĕy.*

nilattiṟappu-kaḍamai (SII 12), a tax.

nīrāṇikka-vari (SITI), Tamil; tax for the supervision of the regulation of water supply in a village.

nīr-kkāṇam (SITI), Tamil; water-cess; also known as *nīr-vilai.*

nīr-nilai-kkāśu (SITI), Tamil; tank-cess.

niruṇi-suṅka (SII 11-1), water tax.

nīr-vilai (SITI), Tamil; water-cess.

nūl-āyam (SITI), Tamil-Sanskrit; tax on cotton thread for weaving cloth.

oḻi-vaṇṇāṟ-pāṟai (SITI), Tamil; tax payable by the washerman calculated on the number of washing stones.

paccai-ppaṇam (SITI), Tamil; payment in cash towards the obligation of *paccai* payable in kind; also referred to as *paccai-ppāṭṭam.* Cf. *Kārttigai-paccai,* etc.

paḍai-ppaṇam (SITI), Tamil-Sanskrit; tax for the maintenance of an army unit or fee from the army; also known as *paḍai-kkāṇikkai.*

paḍan-kaḻi (SITI), Tamil; an obligation of uncertain import.

pāḍavari (SITI), Tamil; tax probably on metallic mirrors.

padavāram, also spelt *paduvāram* (SITI), Tamil; fee payable for exchanging landed property; transfer fee.

pāḍikkāval (SITI), Tamil; 'watch or the police duties of the village'; contribution for the same.

paduvāram, cf. *padavāram.*

paḻanel (SII 13), a tax.

pālikka-ppāṭṭam (SII 12), a tax.

paṇa-vargam (SITI), Sanskrit; class of taxes payable in cash; same as *kāśāya-vargam*; cf. *paṇam,* coin, money.

paṇa-vāśi (SITI), Sanskrit-Tamil; discount payable for the exchange of coins; amount payable to make up the wear in the coin.

pañca-vārav-ūr-iḍu-vari (SITI), Sanskrit-Tamil; levied by the *pañca-vāriyam* (the five committees) of the local assembly (*ūr*).

pañcu-ppīli (SITI; EI 24), Tamil; tax on cotton; also referred to as *pāñjupili*.

paṇḍa-vĕṭṭi (SITI), Tamil; a variety of *vĕṭṭi*, probably for the temple lands.

pāṇḍivari (SITI), Tamil; probably tax on carts drawn by bulls.

paṇi-kkŏttu (SITI), Tamil; 'village servants'; cess collected for their maintenance.

paṉ-kuṟuṇi (SITI), Tamil; cess payable at the rate of one *kuṟuṇi* of the produce for each field.

pannāya (IE 8-5; EI 27), Kannaḍa; name of a tax.

pāṟai-kkāṇam (SITI), Tamil; tax on washing stone payable by washermen; sometimes explained as the tax on quarries.

paṟai-ttaṟi (SII 12; SITI), Tamil; a variety of handloom; the tax for the same.

paṟaiy-iṟai (SITI), Tamil; a tax [payable in cash] probably for tomtoms.

paśānam (EI 23), name of a tax.

pāśi-ppāṭṭam (SITI), Tamil; tax on fishing; same as *mīn-pāṭṭam*.

paṭṭāḍai-āyam (SITI), Tamil-Sanskrit; tax on silk cloth.

paṭṭāḍai-nūl-āyam (SITI), Tamil-Sanskrit ; tax on silk thread used for weaving cloth.

paṭṭaḍai-vari (SITI), Tamil; tax probably for the use of the threshing floor.

pāṭṭam (SITI, EI 21), Tamil; tax or rent; payable probably for an industry or a profession.

pāṭṭa-nĕl (SITI), Tamil; paddy to be paid by the tenant to the landlord as per terms of lease.

paṭṭaya-kkāṇikkai (SITI), Tamil; fee for the issue of royal charters.

paṭṭi-kkāḍi (SITI), Tamil; tax payable in grain at the rate of one *kāḍi* for each *paṭṭi* of land.

paṭṭi-kkāl (SITI), Tamil; tax payable in cash at the rate of one fourth (probably of *paṇam*) for each *paṭṭi* of land.

paṭṭigai-kkāṇam (SITI), Tamil; obligation to pay at the rate of one *kāṇam* for each *paṭṭi* of land; probably, the same as *paṭṭaya-kkāṇikkai*.

paṭṭi-ppŏn (SITI), Tamil; tax payable in coin.

paṭṭi-ttaṇḍam (SITI); Tamil; probably, punitive tax of a village.

pāvai (EI 8-5), similar to Persian *nazarāna*.

pĕjjuṅka (EI 8-5), Kannaḍa; name of tax; also spelt *pĕrjuṅka*, *pĕrujuṇka*, *hĕjjuṅka*; probably derived from *piriya-suṅka*=Sanskrit *bṛhac-chulka*.

pĕrjuṅka, cf. *pĕjjuṅka*.

pĕr-kkaḍamai (SII 12; SITI), Tamil; explained as poll tax, the same as *āḻvari*; (also called *pervāśi*); but may be a payment to be made on the occasion of the naming ceremony of a child.

pĕrujuṅka, cf. *pĕjjuṅka*.

perum-pāḍi-kāval (SII 12; SITI), Tamil; police duties of a larger area, as distinct from the *śiṟu-pāḍi-kāval* for the village.

pidā-nāḻi (EI 28), Tamil; same as *pudā-nāḻi*.

pŏṉ-vari (SII 12), a tax.

pracaṇḍa-kāṇikkai (SITI), Sanskrit-Tamil; a variety of military cess; this is found mentioned along with other military cessess like *paḍai-ppaṇam*, etc.

pradhāni-joḍi (SII 2; SITI), the chief minister's quit-rent.

puḍā-naḻi (SITI), Tamil; probably, a local cess on each door or gate or house; also, mentioned as *pidā-nāḻi*.

pulavari (SITI), Tamil; 'tax on a *pulam* (piece of land)'; probably to be corrected as *pulvari* meaning 'tax on grass.'

pullavari (SITI), tax payable for grazing cattle.

pullandi (SITI), Tamil; an obligation probably connected with the pasture land in the form of fine on stray cattle.

puḻugu-kaḍamai (SITI), Tamil; fee for meeting the expenses of coating the image of gods with civet; also known as *puḻuguvari*.

puṟa-kkaḍamai (SITI), Tamil; external taxes, i.e., taxes and fees payable to the state.

puṟav-āyam (SITI), Tamil; revenue from external sources, collected mainly in cash.

puṟavĕṭṭi (SITI), Tamil; a variety of *vĕṭṭi* for public work, probably outside the area in question.

puravu (SITI), Tamil; land revenue.

puravu-nĕl (SITI), Tamil; revenue paid in paddy.

puravu-pŏn (SITI), Tamil; revenue paid in gold.

śakkara-kkāṇikkai (SITI), Tamil; tax on potters; also known as *tirigai-āyam*; cf. *kuśa-kkāṇam*.

śaṇḍāla-ppeṟu (SITI), Tamil; a local cess or tax collected from or for the *Caṇḍālaṣ*.

sandhivigraha-ppeṟu (SITI), Sanskrit-Tamil; fee payable to the village *madhyastha*; also a fee payable to the document writers.

śaṭṭu-vari (SITI), Tamil; tax for the grazing ground in the village.

śavai-kkaḍamai (SITI), Tamil; taxes payable to the *sabhā*.

śekk-āyam (SITI), Tamil-Sanskrit; tax on oil-presses; also called *śekk-iṟai* and *śekku-kkaḍamai* (SII 12).

śekku-kaḍamai (SII 12), same as *śekk-āyam*.

śekku-maṉṟāḍi (SITI), Tamil; a tax or cess; probably related to *śekku*.

seṅkŏḍi-kkāṇam (SITI), Tamil; explained as 'the tax on the cultivation of the medicinal plant known variously as *śeṅgŏḍi*, *kŏḍiveli* and *citramūlam*'; see also *kŏḍi-kkāṇam*.

śeṭṭiyār-magamai (SITI), Tamil; voluntary contribution (*magamai*) of the merchants.

śeṭṭiy-iṟai (SITI), Tamil; tax on merchants; also known as *śeṭṭ-iṟai*.

śevaka-kkāśu (SITI), Tamil; fee for the maintenance of the soldiers; or, tax levied on the soldier.

śil-kuḍimai (SITI), minor taxes and cesses payable to the local authority.

śill-antar-āyam (SITI), Tamil-Sanskrit; minor taxes which fall in the group of *antar-āyam* or *uḷ-vari*.

śil-āyam (SITI), Tamil-Sanskrit; same as *śill-irai*, *śil-vari*.

śill-iṟai (SITI), Tamil; same as *sil-āyam*, *śil-vari*.

śil-vari (SITI; EI 27), Tamil; minor taxes; same as *śil-āyam*, *śil-iṟai*.

śiṟṟ-āyam (SITI), Tamil; minor taxes.

śiṟu-ppāḍi-kāval (SII 12), a levy.

śiru-śuṅgam (SITI), Tamil; minor tolls.

śoḍi, see *joḍi*.

śŏṇa-vari (SITI), Tamil; same as *pŏn-vari*; explained as 'tax payable in gold'; but may be professional tax payable by the goldsmiths; cf. *suvarṇa-daṇḍa*.

śuḍu-kāṭṭu-ppāṭṭam (SITI), Tamil; fee payable by a prostitute, especiallly those accompanying the army.

śūla-vari (EI 25; SITI), Sanskrit-Tamil; a tax payable for the unkeep probably of a Śiva temple.

suṅka (EI 12), same as Sanskrit *śulka*, tolls.

śuṟṟ-āya-kkāśu (SII 12), a tax.

svarṇ-ādāyam (SITI), Sanskrit; revenue in gold; taxes payable in coin; or, prefession tax payable by the goldsmiths.

śaḍa-kkaḍamai (SITI), Tamil; tax on shepherds.

taḷai-kkāṇam (SITI), Tamil; fee or tax on the *taḷai* or foot-binding used by toddy-tappers.

talaiyārikkam (SITI), Tamil; tax payable for the maintenance of the village watchman; same as *talaiyāri-kkāṇi*.

taṇḍaliṟ-kaḍamai, taṇḍaṟ-kaḍamai (SITI), Tamil; fee payable for the maintenance of tax-collectors; or, tax on bill-collectors.

taṇḍa-kkāṇam, taṇḍa-kkuṟam, etc. (SITI), in which *taṇḍa* is punitive tax and *kuṟṟam* fines for crimes committed.

taṇiyāḷ (SII 12), a tax.

tāniya-varakkam, dhānya-varga (SITI), Sanskrit; 'the grain group'; class of taxes payable in grains.

taṇṇīr-kkāṇam (SITI), Tamil; water-cess.

taragi-pāṭṭam (SII 12), brokerage fee.

tarav-iḍu-nĕl (SITI), Tamil; paddy given in lieu of wages.

taravu (SITI), Tamil; 'that which has been given'; collection of debt or tax on pressure; also a dun; also used in the sense of 'order or instruction'.

taravu-kŏḷḷudal (SITI), Tamil; 'to obtain a receipt for anything given'; collection of tax exercising pressure.

taṟi-akkave (SII 13), same as *taṟi-ppuḍavai*.

taṟi-irai (SII 12, 13), same as *taṟi-ppuḍavai*.

taṟi-kkaḍamai (SII 12), same as *taṟi-ppuḍavai*.

taṟi-kkuṟai (SITI), same as *taṟi-ppuḍavai*.

taṟi-ppuḍavai (SITI), Tamil; tax on looms payable in the shape of cloth.

taṟi-taḷai (SITI), Tamil; tax on looms; probably, the same as *taṟi-kkaḍamai*.

taṭṭār-pāṭṭam, taṭṭāra-ppāṭṭam (SII 12; SITI), Tamil; tax on goldsmiths. Cf. *suvarṇa-daṇḍa* noticed above.

taṭṭ-ŏli (SITI), Tamil; mentioned along with *taṭṭār-pāṭṭam*; probably, tax on the smiths or the workshop of the artisans like the blacksmiths.

taṭṭu-kkāṇam (SITI), Tamil; same as *taṭṭār-pāṭṭam*; 'fee for hammering'; probably also the same as *taṭṭukk-āyam*.

tevai (SII 12), a levy.

tiṅgaḻ-kāśu (SITI), Tamil; tax payable every month; cf. *tiṅgaṭ-coṟu, tiṅgaḻ-nĕy, tiṅgaḻ-mogam*, etc. Cf. also *māda-ppaḍi*.

tirigai-āyam (SITI), tax payable by the potter for his trade; cf. *tirigai*, a potter's wheel.

tiru-muga-kkāṇam (SITI), Tamil; expenses as wages, etc., payable to the person who brings the *tiru-mugam* (royal order) to a village.

tivuḷ-desa (EI 30), Tamil; name of a tax.

tīyeṟi-śoṟu (SII 13), Tamil; literally, 'offering in fire'; supposed to be the name of a tax.

tol-ŏṭṭu (SITI), Tamil; a fee probably connected with hides and skins.

toni-kkaḍamai (SITI), Tamil; tax on boats.

toraṇa-kkāṇikkai (SITI), Tamil; presents for decorating the village with arches, etc.; or tax on gates.

toṭṭa-ppuravu (SITI), Tamil; tax on garden lands.

tulā-kkūli (SITI), Sanskrit-Tamil; fee for weighing in balance.

tūśaka-ttaṟi (SITI), Tamil; tax probably on looms weaving tent-materials.

ugappār-pŏn (SITI), Tamil; tax payable in gold on joyous occasions like marriage; probably the same as *kaṇṇāla-kkāṇam*.

ulavu-kāṭci (SITI), Tamil; probably, presents offered to the king or other exalted persons when going in procession round the village.

ulgu (SITI), Tamil; customs duties; tolls.

ulliya-kkūli (SITI), Tamil; probably, water-fee for irrigation from wells; tax or wages for well-digging.

uluppai (SITI), Tamil; presents of fruits, articles of food, etc., offered to great personages; free supplies made by the people or subordinates to officials on tour.

uḷ-vari (SITI), Tamil; internal revenued; taxes levie

by the local body; same as *antar-āyam*; orders issued by the government fixing the amount of such taxes.

uppu-kkāśu (SITI), Tamil; salt-tax.

ural-vari (SITI), Tamil; tax or fee for the maintenance of the mortar for husking paddy.

ūr-ĕṭṭu (SITI), Tamil; 'committee of eight members of the village assembly (*ūr*)'; taxes payable for the expenses of the committee.

ūr-iḍu-varippāḍu (SII 13; SITI), Tamil; tax levied by the village assembly (*ūr*).

ūr-kkaḍamai (SITI), Tamil; obligations and taxes payable to the village assembly (*ūr*).

ūr-ttaniśu (SII 13), a tax.

ūśi-vāśi (SITI), Tamil; tax probably connected with tailoring.

uvacca-vari (SITI), Tamil; tax payable by or for the maintenance of the *uvaccar* (drummers in temple service).

uvacca-kkāṇi (SITI), Tamil; rent-free land given to the *uvaccaṉ* for serving as drummer in a temple.

vaḍḍarāvuḷa, vaḍḍāravuḷa (EI 19, 28; IE 8-8), Kannaḍa; name of a tax.

vagainda-kāśu (SITI), Tamil; tax payable in cash for marking the details, as of land; fees for subdivision of land; also the fee for settlement, as of a dispute.

vāla-mañjāḍi (SITI), Tamil; probably the same as *vāla-vari* and *vāla-kkāṇam*; tax of a *mañjāḍi* on the units of measurement in the length of a house-site.

valaṅgai-iḍaṅgai-maganmai (SITI), Tamil; tax on the right-hand and left-hand castes, to be paid by all able-bodied men capable of bearing arms.

vaḻinaḍaikk-iḍum-paṇam (SITI), Tamil; road cess.

vaḻiy-āyam (SITI), Tamil-Sanskrit; tolls on the roadways.

vaḻudiy-accu-vargam (SITI), Tamil-Sanskrit; group of taxes payable in Pāṇḍya coins.

vaṇṇār-vari, vaṇṇāra-ppāṟai (SITI), Tamil; tax on washermen.

vaṉ-pāṭṭam (SITI), Tamil; fixed rent in kind due under a lease-deed which does not provide for any relief against loss due to drought.

vari (SITI), Tamil; tax, revenue register, order of the

king and his officer fixing the revenue; cf. *vari-ppŏttagam*, tax register; officer maintaining the same; also *Vari-kkūṟu-śeyvār*, *Varrikkukkūṟu-śeyvār* (SITI), Tamil; officers grading the cultivable land and fixing the tax payable thereon.

variśai (SITI), Tamil; village dues; cess payable by or to the local authority.

vāśalil-ponda-kuḍimai (SITI), Tamil; 'burden of citizenship dues at the gate'; taxes, probably other than the land revenue, payable to the state.

vāśal-kāṇikkai, (SITI) Tamil; presents offered to the palace, probably annually.

vāśal-kuḻi-ppaṇam (SITI), Tamil-Sanskrit; probably, door-tax, i.e., house-tax based on the main doorways.

vāśal-paṇam (SITI), Tamil-Sanskrit; periodical payment due to the palace; door-tax.

vāśal-tiramam (SITI), Tamil; door-tax; *tiramam* is the same as *dramma*.

vāśal-viniyogam (SITI), Tamil-Sanskrit; same as *vāśal-paṇam*, etc.

vaṭṭam (SITI), money-changers' commission; trade discount.

vaṭṭi-nāḻi (SITI), Tamil; probably, a tax payable at the rate of one *nāḻi* for each *vaṭṭi*.

vāykkāl-pāṭṭam (SITI), Tamil; channel cess; fee for keeping the channels in good repairs.

veli-kkāśu (SITI), Tamil; tax (payable in cash) of uncertain import; cf. *veli-kkuḻi-ppaṇam*.

veli-ppayaru (SII 12; SITI), same as *veli-kkāśu*

veḷḷān-iṟai (SITI), Tamil; cultivation tax.

veṇḍugoḷ, *veṇḍukoḷ* (SII 12; SITI), Tamil; supplication; petition; fee for the same; also known as *veṇḍukoḷ-vari*.

vĕṭṭi (SII 12, 13), same as Sanskrit *viṣṭi*, 'unpaid labour'.

vĕṭṭi-vedinai (SII 13), explained as a tax.

veyadi-kāṇam (SITI), Tamil; tax payable in grains, probably on thatched sheds; or, may be related to *veynĕl* (collection of bamboo-grain from forests).

vibhūti-kāṇikkai (SITI), Sanskrit-Tamil; contribution paid voluntarily to a temple by its devotees while receiving the sacred ashes, later collected as compulsory dues.

viḍai-pper, *viḍai-ppeṟu* (SITI), Tamil; perquisites payable on the receipt of a reply to a petition to the king.

vil-paṇam (SITI), Tamil-Sanskrit; sale-tax; also explained as a tax on bows or on archery.

vipravinodi-vari (SITI), Sanskrit-Tamil; tax from or for the maintenance of the *Vipravinodins* (Brāhmaṇa magicians).

vīra-śeṣai (SITI); EI 22), sometimes supposed to be the name of a tax; but see *vīra-śeṣa*.

viṟ-paṇam (SITI), *vil-paṇam*; Tamil-Sanskrit; tax on bows and arrows; may also be a tax on sales.

viruttu-ppaṭṭigai (SITI), Tamil; tax probably on profits and the income from interest.

viśa-kkāṇam (SITI), Tamil; tax or share in the produce as remuneration due to a *Viyavaṉ* or village headman.

viśeṣ-āyam, *viśeṣ-ādāyam* (SITI), Sanskrit; a special group of taxes.

vivāha-ppaṇam (SITI), Sanskrit-Tamil; marriage fee; cf. *kaṇṇāla-kkāṇam*.

Appendix III

NAMES OF COINS, METAL WEIGHTS, etc.

accu, Tamil; name of a coin; money; tax or income.

āchu, same as *āsu*; cf. *accu*.

āḍa, also spelt *aḍḍa*; name of a coin; half of a *fanam*; cf. *aḍḍaga* and *aḍḍuga*.

aḍatālīsa-gānī, 6 *aṭha-gānīs* or *ṭaṅkas*.

aḍḍa, same as *aḍa* (q.v.).

aḍḍa-cinna, cf. *āḍa* or *aḍḍa* and *cinna* or *sinna*.

aḍḍaga, also spelt *aḍḍuga*; same as *āḍa*, *aḍḍa*.

aḍḍuga, same as *aḍḍaga*.

aḍi-kkāśu, 'tax collected from the stall-keepers in the market'; see *kāśu*.

aḍimai-kkāśu, 'fee collected from the temple servants (or for their maintenance)'; see *kāśu*.

ādivarāha-dramma, 'a *dramma* issued by Ādivarāha (Patīhāra Bhoja I, c. 836-85 A.D.)'; same as *śrīmad-ādivarāha-dramma*; see *dramma*.

ādya-māṣa, the original *māṣa* of 5 *ratis* as opposed to the later *māṣa* of various weights upto 10 *ratis*. Cf. *māṣa*.

ājīvaka-kāśu, same as Tamil *āśuva-kkāśu*; 'tax collected from the *Ājivakas* (or for the maintenance of the Ājīvaka monks)'; see *kāśu*.

akkam, one-twelfth of a *kāśu* (q.v.).

akṣa, same as *suvarṇa* (q.v.).

aḻag-accu, see *accu*.

ambili-gadyāṇa, see *gadyāṇa*.

amudan-accu, see *accu*.

anai-accu, see *accu*.

āṇaka, Sanskritized form of Muhammadan *āna*=English *anna*.

aṇḍika, *aṇḍikā*, $\frac{1}{4}$ of a *māṣa*; also regarded as the same as *paṇa* which was $\frac{1}{12}$ or $\frac{1}{16}$ of a *dīnāra* or *suvarṇa* in value.

aṅka-gadyāṇa, see *gadyāṇa*.

anna, Anglicised form of Muhammadan *āna*; $\frac{1}{16}$ of *rupee*, property, etc.

ardha-kakinī, half of a *kākinī* (q.v.).

arṇikā, equal to 2 *māṣas*.

aṣṭamikā, same as *śatamāna*.

āsu, cf. *accu*.

āśuva-kkāśu, same as *ājīvaka-kāśu* (q.v.); see *kāśu*.

aṭha-gānī, same as *ṭaṅka*.

aureus, Roman gold coin (124 grains); same as the gold *denareus* (q.v.).

badara, same as *tola* or *tolaka*.

baḍi-māḍuvulu, see *māḍa*.

balotra, name applied to an Indian silver coin by the Muslim chroniclers of the early medieval period.

barāḍ, modified form of *varāṭaka* (q.v.).

bārah-gānī, 1½ *aṭha-gānīs* or *ṭaṅkas*.

beḻḻiya-dramma, Kannaḍa; 'silver *dramma*'; see *dramma*.

bhāga, see *hāga*, *pāga*.

bhairava-gadyāṇa 'a *gadyāṇa* minted by a goldsmith named Bhairava'; cf. *bṛhat-bhairava-gadyāṇa*; see *gadyāṇa*.

bhīmapriya-dramma, 'a *dramma* minted by a goldsmith named Bhīma'; see *dramma*.

bhujabala-māḍai, 'a *māḍai* issued by a ruler named or entitled Bhujabala'; see *māḍa*, *māḍai*.

binduka, same as *suvarṇa* (q.v.).

bṛihat-bhairava-gadyāṇa, 'the bigger *bhairava-gadyāṇa* (q.v.)'; see *gadyāṇa*.

buḍ̤ī, Bengali name for a unit equal to 5 *gaṇḍās*; cf. *voḍī*, *voḍrī*, *kapardaka-voḍī*; also *kākinī*.

cāmara, also called *cāmara-māḍa*; probably 'a *māḍa* bearing the figure of a fly-whisk'; see *māḍa*.

cāmara-māḍa, see *cāmara* and *māḍa*.

carsam (*karṣa* ?), equal to 4 *māḍas*; see *māḍa*.

cash, Anglicised spelling of *kāśu*.

'*cast*', see '*die-struck*' and '*punch-marked*'.

caubīsa-gānī, 3 *aṭha-gānīs* or *ṭaṅkas*.

cau-gānī, ½ of an *aṭha-gānī* or *ṭaṅka*.

cavala, also spelt *cavela*; ⅛ of a *pagoda* (q.v.).

cavela, same as *cavala*.

cha-gānī, ¾ of an *aṭha-gānī* or *ṭaṅka*.

cīna-kkanakkam, Tamil; 'Chinese gold coin'.

cinna, also spelt *sinna*; same as *fanam* (q.v.); ⅛ of a *pagoda* (q.v.)

ciravida, Telugu; supposed to be a kind of *gadyāṇa* (q.v.).

dām, derivative of *dramma* (q.v.); copper coin, $\frac{1}{40}$ of a Mughal *rupee* (q.v.).

dama, same as *dāma* or *dramma* (q.v.).

dāma, same as *dām* or *dramma* (q.v.).

damma, same as *dramma* (q.v.).

ḍāṅg, corrupt form of *ṭanka* (q.v.); cf. *dāṅk*.

dāṅk, corrupt form of *ṭaṅka* (q.v.); cf. *ḍāṅg*.

daric, gold coin of ancient Iran (about 133 grains); double *daric*=Greek *stater* or *tetradrachma*, four times the *drachma* in weight.

dāya-dramma, 'tax or money to be paid'; see *dramma*.

dehlīwāl, see *jītal*.

denarius, name of the Roman silver (also gold) coin; equal to Greek *drachma*; origin of the Indian coin name *dīnāra*, etc.

dhānaka, same as *māṣa*; cf. *hemadhānyaka*; same as *dhānika* (q.v.); also called *aṇḍika* and regarded as equal to 4 *kārṣāpaṇas* or $\frac{1}{12}$ of *suvarṇa* (*JNSI*, Vol. II, p. 8).

dhānika, equal to 4 *kārṣāpaṇas* or 64 *paṇas* according to the *Kṛtyakalpataru*.

dhānya-māṣa, $\frac{1}{2}$ of *yava*.

dharaṇa, old silver coin of 32 *ratis* (about 58 grains); also called *kārṣāpaṇa* and *purāṇa*; 24 (actually about 20) *ratis* in weight and half of *gadyāṇa* in value according to medieval authorities; otherwise called *dramma*, *śāna* or *ṭaṅka*; sometimes regarded as a gold coin or weight equal to ten *palas* or 40 *suvarṇas* or *niṣkas* (3200 *ratis*); cf. *śatamāna* (*silver*)=10 *dharaṇas* (320 *ratis*).

dhvaṁśi, same as *vaṁśya*; a minute unit of measurement.

didrachma, 'two-drachma', 'double drachma'; see *drachma*.

'*die-struck*', coins on which the symbols and legends were impressed by means of an anvil and a single punch, both bearing negative representations, by placing a blank on the socket in the anvil and striking the punch placed on it by a hammer; see *punch-marked*.

dinära, also spelt *dinnāra*; generally spelt *dīnāra* (q.v.); a cowrie-shell according to the Kashmir chronicle.

dīnāra, derived from Roman *denarius* (124 grains); name of a gold coin equal to 16 silver coins called *rūpaka*, etc. (about 20 *ratis*); a silver coin according to the *Kṛtyakalpataru*; sometimes called *kāśu* in Tamil, etc.; sometimes regarded as half of *satera* or *sateraka* (Greek *stater*); see *dināra*.

dināri, generally spelt as *dīnāra*; local modification of the Roman *denarius* prevalent in the Ikṣvāku kingdom in the Krishna-Guntur region.

dināri-māṣaka, same as *dināri*, or one-sixteenth of a *dināri* or *dīnāra* in weight or value.

dinnāra, see *dināra*.

diramam, Tamil form of *dramma*.

doḍḍa-varāha, see *varāha*.

do-gānī, $\frac{1}{4}$ of an *aṭha-gānī* or *ṭaṅka*.

dra, abbreviation of *dramma*.

drachma, Greek silver coin; equal to 6 *obols*; Attic standard 67 grains, but the Indo-Greek standard was soon modified, their coins of 37 or 38 grains being called *drachma* or *hemi-drachma* by different scholars; origin of the Indian coin name *dramma* (q.v.).

drakṣaṇa, same as *draṁkṣana* or *tola*; equal to 8 *māṣas* (80 *ratis*); cf. *drakṣuṇa*.

drakṣuṇa, same as *drakṣaṇa* or *tola*.

draṁkṣaṇa, same as *tola*.

drama, same as *dramma*.

dramma, Indian form of Greek *drachma*; a silver coin $\frac{1}{16}$ of a gold *niṣka* according to the *Līlāvatī*; name applied to the Śaka-type silver *purāṇa*, *dharaṇa* or *kārṣāpaṇa* (about 20 *ratis*, also called *rūpaka*); copper coin (*dām*) regarded as $\frac{1}{40}$ of a Mughal *rupee*; money in general; the name first occurs on the Yaudheya coins.

dramm-ārdha, half of *dramma* (q.v.).

dramma-tribhāga, one-third of *dramma* (q.v.).

draṅga, variant of *dramma* (q.v.).

du-gānī, same as *do-gānī*.

dukra, $\frac{1}{5}$ of a *phadiyā*.

dukānī, $\frac{1}{2}$ of a *phadiyā*.

fadiyā, see *phadiyā*.

fanam, Anglicised form of Tamil *paṇam* (q.v.); Sanskrit *paṇa* (q.v.); a gold coin equal to $\frac{1}{20}$ of a *varāha*.

ga, abbreviation of *gadyāṇa*.

gadhaiyā, same as *gadhiyā*.

gadhaiyā-paisā, same as *ghadhiyā*.

gadiāṇaka, cf. *kumāra-gadiāṇaka*, name of a tax; same as *gadyāṇa*.

gadhiyā, also spelt *gadhaiyā*; copper coin imitated from old Sasanian issues.

gadhiyā-paisā, same as *gadhiyā* (q.v.).

gadiyāṇa, same as *gadyāṇa*.

gadyā, abbreviation of *gadyāṇa*.

gadyāna, same as *gadyāṇa*.

gadyāṇa, a gold coin or weight; generally regarded as 48 *ratis* (about 88 grains) in weight; sometimes called 'the gold *gadyāṇa*'; sometimes regarded as a coin like a farthing, equal to $\frac{1}{4}$ or $\frac{1}{5}$ of the *paikamu* (q.v.); regarded in some places as equal to 20 *vals*, 8 *māṣas* or $\frac{1}{2}$ *tola*.

gadyānaka, same as *gadyāṇaka* or *gadyāṇa* (q.v.).

gadyāṇaka, same as *gadyāṇa*.

gadyāṇa-ponnu, '*gadyāṇa* of gold'; same as *pon-gadyāṇa*; see *gadyāṇa*.

gaṇḍā, equal to 4 cowrie-shells; $\frac{1}{20}$ of a *paṇa*; cf. *gaṇḍaka*.

gaṇḍagopālaṉ-māḍai, '*māḍa* issued or minted by Gaṇḍagopāla'; see *māḍai*.

gaṇḍaka, same as *gaṇḍā*. Cf. *kākinī*.

gaṇḍa-māḍa, probably '*māḍa* bearing the figure of a rhinoceros' or an abbreviation of *Gaṇḍagopālan-māḍai* (q.v.); sometimes characterised by the epithet 'small'; sometimes also called *kārṣāpaṇa*, *niṣka* and *gaṇḍa-niṣka*; see *māḍa*.

gaṇḍa-niṣka, same as *gaṇḍa*; see *māḍa* and *niṣka*.

gandhashasti-māḍa, same as *gandhavāraṇa-māḍa*; probably, '*māḍa* bearing the figure of an elephant in rut'; see *māḍa*.

gānī, cf. *aṭha-gānī*, equal to a *ṭaṅka* and weighing a *tola*.

gara-dramma, see *dramma*.

gāva-gadyāṇa, see *gadyāṇa*.

ghaṭita-hīna-drammāḥ, '*drammas* (money) that are wanting'; see *dramma*.

golakā, same as *gulikā*, etc.

goḷakkai, Tamil; same as *golakā* (*gulikā*).

grāsagraha, same as *suvarṇa* (q.v.).

gulikā, same as *golakā*, etc.; a small coin apparently globular or circular in shape; supposed to be a coin issued by the Śambhuvarāya chiefs and also by the Pāṇḍyas; cf. *vīra-champan-kuḷigai* and *vaḷḷāl-vaḻi-tiṟantāṉ-guḷikai*.

guñjā, same as *rati* or *raktikā* (1·83 or about $1\frac{3}{4}$ grains).

hāga, Kannaḍa; same as Sanskrit *bhāga*; probably $\frac{1}{4}$ of the standard coin; see *pāga*.

haṁsapada, same as *suvarṇa* (q.v.).

hema, same as *māṣa*; cf. *hema-dhānyaka*.

hema-dhānyaka, same as *māṣa*; see *hema* and *dhānaka*.

hema-ṭaṅka, 'a gold *ṭaṅka* (q.v.).'

hemi-drachma, Greek; same as Sanskrit *dramm-ārdha* (q.v.); see *drachma*, *dramma*, etc.

hon, variant spelling of *hūn*; same as *varāha*, *gadyāṇa* (gold *gadyāṇa*) and *pagoda* (star *pagoda*); cf. *suvarṇa*.

hūn, same as *hon* or *varāha* (q.v.), etc.

iḻa-kkaruṅ-kāśu, 'Ceylonese coin'; see *kāśu*.

iḻa-kkāśu, 'Ceylonese coin'; see *kāśu*.

inavari-kkāśu, 'communual tax in cash'; see *kāśu*

jagadaḷaṁ-gadyāṇa, see *gadyāṇa*.

jaithala, same as *jītal* (q.v.).

jīrna-śreṣṭhi-śrīmalla-priya, possibly, 'an old coin of the mint of *Śreṣṭhin* Śrīmalla'.

jīrṇa-śreṣṭhi-viśvamalla-priya, same as *jīrṇa-viśvamalla-priya*; possibly, 'an old coin of the mint of *Śreṣṭhin* Viśvamalla'.

jītal, a copper coin, $\frac{1}{48}$ of a silver *ṭanka* of the Delhi Sulṭāns; also called *delhīwāl*; $\frac{1}{8}$ of a silver *tār* which was itself $\frac{1}{8}$ of a *fanam*.

jīrṇa-viśvamalla-priya, same as *jīrṇa-śreṣṭhi-viśvamalla-priya*, possibly, 'an old coin of the mint of Viśvamalla'; cf. *vīsala-priya-dramma*.

kaḍā, Bengali, etc; cowrie-shell regarded as coin; $\frac{1}{4}$ of *gaṇḍā* and $\frac{1}{80}$ of *paṇa* in some areas. Cf. *kapardaka*, etc.

kāhaṇa, Bengali, etc; also spelt *kahāṇa* and *kāhāṇa*; same as *kāhāpaṇa*=*kārṣāpaṇa*.

kahāṇa, same as *kāhaṇa*=*kārṣāpaṇa*.

kāhāṇa, same as *kāhaṇa*=*kārṣāpaṇa*.

kāhāpaṇa, same as Sanskrit *kārṣāpaṇa* and modern *kāhaṇ*, etc.

kāka, same as *kākinī*.

kākanikā, same as *kakanī*, *kakinī* (q.v.).

kakinī, equal to 20 cowrie-shells according to the *Līlāvatī*; $\frac{1}{4}$ of a *paṇa*; same as *buḍī*. Cf. *gaṇḍā*

kaḷañju, Tamil; name of a weight or coin weighing 10 *mañjāḍis* (32 *ratis* theoretically); sometimes called *suvarṇa* (q.v.).

kāṇam, Tamil; name of a coin; a gold coin or weight.

kāṇikĕ, also spelt *kāṇiki*; $\frac{1}{64}$ part of a coin; money or tolls.

kāṇiki, same as *kāṇikĕ* (q.v.).

kaparda, same as *kapardaka*, etc.; cowrie-shell used as coin.

kapardaka, also called *kaparda*, *kapardikā*, *kapardī*, etc.; cowrie-shell used as coin. Cf. *kaḍā*.

kapardaka-purāṇa, 'a *purāṇa* (q.v.) counted in *kapardakas*'.

kapardaka-voḍī, 'a *voḍī* counted in *kapardakas*'; cf. *buḍī* and *voḍī*.

kapardī, same as *kapardikā*, *kapardaka*, etc.

kapardikā, same as *kapardī*, *kapardaka*, etc.

karṣa, name of a weight equal to 80 *ratis* or about 146 grains; sometimes regarded 100 *ratis* or about 183 grains; sometimes also regarded as 120 *ratis* in weight; a coin (cf. *kārṣāpaṇa*).

kārṣāpaṇa, silver coin weighing 32 *ratis* (about 58 grains), also called *purāṇa* or *dharaṇa*; copper coin of 80 *ratis* or about 146 grains (sometimes 100 *ratis* or about 183 grains), also called *paṇa*; Śaka-type silver coin of about 20 ratis, also called *rūpaka*, *dramma*, etc.; gold coin of 80 *ratis* (cf. *suvarṇa*); name applied to *gaṇḍa māḍa* (probably $\frac{1}{2}$ *tola* in weight), also called *niṣka* (q.v.); same as *kāhaṇa*, etc.; cf *karṣa* of 120 *ratis*.

karṣ-ārdha, 'half of a *karṣa* (q.v.).'

karuṅ-kāśu, 'Ceylonese coin'; see *kāśu*, *īḻa-kkāśu*, etc.

kāśu, Tamil; spelt in English as *cash*; name of a copper coin, $\frac{1}{100}$ of a *fanam*; sometimes called *dīnāra*; money; tax; cf. *kāśu-kaḍamai*, 'tax in coins'; also Sanskrit *karṣa*.

kaṭhāri-aṅkuśa-gadyāṇa, probably, 'a *gadyāṇa* bearing the representation of a dagger and a goad'; see *gadyāṇa*.

kola, same as *tola*; equal to 2 *śāṇas*.

koḻakkai, Tamil; same as *golakā*, etc.

komarina-gadyāṇa, same as *kumāra-gadyāṇa*; name of a tax; see *gadyāṇa*.

kovai, Tamil; name of a gold coin.

kroḍa, same as *suvarṇa* (q.v.).

kṛṣṇala, same as *rati* or *guñjā* (about $1\frac{3}{4}$ grains); regarded as equal to 3 *ratis* by the *Kṛtyalalpataru* which seems to confuse *rati* with *yava*.

kṛṣṇarāja-rūpaka, '*rūpaka* issued by Kṛṣṇarāja (Kalacuri Kṛṣṇa, sixth century A.D.)'; see *rūpaka*.

kṣudraka, same as *draṁkṣaṇa* or *tola* (q.v.); cf. *kṣudrama*.

kṣudrama, variant of *kṣudraka*; same as *tola* (q.v).

kumāra-gadyāṇaka, name of a tax; see *gadyāṇa*; cf. *komarina-gadyāṇa* and *kumara-kaccāṇam.*

kumara-kaccāṇam, Tamil; same as *kumāra-gadyāṇaka.*

kuḻigai, same as *gulikā*, etc.

kulottuṅga-māḍa, '*māḍa* issued by Kulottuṅgá (i.e. Coḻa-Cālukya Kulottuṅga I, 1070-1120 A.D.)'; see *māḍa.*

lāgi-drammāḥ, 'expenses incurred'; see *dramma.*

lohaḍiyā, equal to 20 *pāvīsās* or 100 cowrie-shells.

lohitaka, equal to 3 *māṣas* (30 *ratis*).

lokki-gadyāṇa, '*gadyāṇa* minted at Lokki (modern Lakkundi in the Dharwar District, Mysore State)'; see *gadyāṇa.*

māḍa, Telugu; gold or silver coin, 40 *ratis* (about 73 grains) in weight; half of a *dīnāra*; half of a *pagoda*, or tenth of a *paṇa* (*fanam*) in value; same as *māḍha*, *māḍhā*, *māḍai*; 50 per cent; cf. *gaṇḍa-māḍa* also called *kārṣāpaṇa* and *gaṇḍa-niṣka*; Tamil modification of Sanskrit *māṣa.*

māḍa-badipātuka, fraction of a *māḍa*; see *māḍa.*

māḍai, Tamil; same as *māḍa*, etc.

māḍha, Oḍiyā; also spelt *māḍhā*; same as *māḍa*, etc.

mahāpaṇa, cf. *māppaṇam.*

malla-nandi-māḍa, probably, '*māḍa* bearing the figure of a wrestler and a bull', or '*māḍa* minted by Mallanandin'; see *māḍa.*

malla-māḍa, possibly, '*māḍa* bearing the figure of a wrestler', or an abbreviation of *malla-nandi-māḍa*; see *māḍa.*

maṁkṣuṇa, equal to 7 *māṣas* (70 *ratis*).

maṇḍa, equal to 5 *māṣas* (50 *ratis*); cf. *māḍa.*

mañjāḍi, $\frac{1}{10}$ of a *kaḻañju*, $\frac{1}{100}$ of a *śatamāna*; sometimes regarded as 5½ grains in weight, but may be about 4 grains also.

māppaṇam, same as Sanskrit *mahāpaṇa*; may be also 'tax of one *paṇa* per *mā* measure of grains'.

marīci, a minute unit of measurement.

māṣa, name of a weight or a coin weighing 5 *ratis* originally; later regarded as 10 *ratis* in weight; $\frac{1}{4}$ of a *śāna* and $\frac{1}{8}$ of a *śatamāna*; sometimes regarded as $\frac{1}{20}$ of a *paṇa* of 100 *ratis* (i.e. 5 *ratis*); a gold coin (as opposed to the silver *māṣaka*) according to the *Kṛtyakalpataru*; cf. *ādya-māṣa*, *māḍa.*

māṣaka, same as *māṣa*; according to the *Kṛtyakalpataru*, a silver coin as opposed to the gold *māṣa*

mṛḍa, name of a weight like *māñjāḍi* (q.v.). Cf. *pṛḍa*, *pruḍ.*

mudal-tiramam, *mudaṟṟiramam*, Tamil; 'tax payable in cash'; cf. *tiramam=dramma* (q.v.).

nalā, same as *śatamāna* (q.v.).

nal-kāśu, see *kāśu*.

nall-ānai-accu, see *accu*.

nānā, same as *nāṇaka*; cf. Kuṣāṇa coins bearing the representation of the West Asian mother-goddess Nana.

nāṇai, same as *nāṇaka*, *nānā*.

nāṇaka, a coin; see *nāṇai*, *nānā*.

nat-kāśu, see *kāsu*.

nellūr-māḍai, 'the Nellore *māḍai*'; see *māḍa*, *māḍai*.

niṣka, gold coin or weight equal to one *karṣa* (80 *ratis* or about 146 grains) of 16 *māṣas* or to 4 or 108 or 150 *suvarṇas* (q.v.); silver coin equal to one *śatamāna* (320 *ratis*); sometimes identified with *māḍa* (q.v.).

obol, Greek coin; $\frac{1}{6}$ of *drachma* (q.v.).

pāda-viṁśopaka, 'one-fourth of a *viṁśopaka* (q.v.)'; cf. *pāvīsā* which is the same as *paisā*.

padmanidhi-malla-māḍa, probably, '*maḍa* bearing the figure of a wrestler meant for depositing in a temple treasury'; but cf. *malla-māḍa*, etc.; see *māḍa*.

paduccalāgai-accu, see *accu*.

pāga, same as Kannaḍa *hāga*; $\frac{1}{4}$ of the standard coin; probably the same as Sanskrit *bhāga*.

pagoda, also called 'star *pagoda*'; Anglicised form of the name of the gold coin called *gadyāṇa*, *hūn* (*hon*) or *varāha*; since the word *pagoda* also meant 'a temple', the coin seems to have been so named owing to the representation of a temple or a deity on it; *pagoda* may be a corruption of *bhagavatī* meaning 'the mother-goddess'.

paikamu, Telugu; supposed to be a small coin equal to $\frac{1}{4}$ or $\frac{1}{5}$ of a *gadyāṇa* (q.v.).

paisā, $\frac{1}{64}$ or $\frac{1}{100}$ of a *rupee*; same as *pāvīsā*=Sanskrit *pāda-viṁśaka* (°*viṁśatika* or °*viṁśopaka*).

pala, weight of 320 *ratis* (cf. *śatamāna*); equal to 4 or 5 *suvarṇas* according to the *Yājñavalkyasmṛti*.

paḻamudal-ānai-accu, same as *palañśalāgai*; see *accu*.

paḻam-puḻḻi-māḍai, see *māḍa*, *māḍai*, etc.

paḻañjalāgai-accu, same as *palañśalāgai*; see *accu*.

palaṅ-kāśu, see *kāśu*.

paḷañ-śalāgai, Tamil; a kind of coin (*accu*) probably of the shape of a *śalākā*. Cf. *śrī-yakki-paḷañ-śalāgai*.

pal-ārdha, $\frac{1}{2}$ of a *pala* (q.v.).

paṇa, same as the copper *kārṣāpaṇa*, 80 *ratis* in weight according to Manu, etc.; equal to 80 cowrie-shells according to the *Līlāvatī*; regarded in East India during the late medieval period as equal to 80 cowrie-shells and $\frac{1}{16}$ of a *kāhaṇ* = *kārṣāpaṇa* (q.v.); $\frac{1}{16}$ of a *suvarṇa* according to some; $\frac{1}{48}$ of a *kārṣāpaṇa* according to the *Kṛtyakalpataru*; same as Tamil *paṇam* (q.v.)

paṇam, Tamil; spelt *fanam* in English; same as Sanskrit *paṇa* (q.v.); but in Tamil, a small gold coin or money in general; cf. *paṇa-vargam*, 'taxes in cash', also called *kāś-āya-vargam* (literally, 'taxes payable in *kāśu*, i.e. cash or money').

paṇa-purāṇa, '*purāṇa* (q.v.) counted in *paṇas* (q.v.)'; cf. *kapardaka-purāṇa* and *kapardaka-voḍī*.

paṇa-vāśi, Tamil; 'discount for the exchange of coins'; see *paṇam*.

paṇcālav-accu, see *accu*.

pañciyaka-drama, probably, '*dramma* minted by the *pañca* or *pañcakula* i.e. the *Pañcāyat* Board'; or '*dramma* equal to five copper coins'; see *dramma*.

pāṇi, same as *suvarṇa* (q.v.).

parameṣṭhi-gadyāṇa, see *gadyāṇa*.

partāb, name of a gold coin; a half *pagoda* (q.v.).

parumuḷai-varāhan, see *varāha*.

pāruttha, a silver coin equal to 8 *drammas* of copper or billon; cf. *poruttha-dramma*.

paura, cf. *purāṇa*.

pāvīsā, $\frac{1}{20}$ of a *lohaḍiyā*; same as Sanskrit *pāda-viṁśaka* (°*viṁśatika* or °*viṁśopaka*) and modern *paisā* (q.v.).

phadiyā, same as *phadyaka*; a copper coin about two annas in value.

phadyaka, same as *phadiyā* (q.v.).

picu, same as *suvarṇa* (q.v.).

picula, equal to 6 *maṣas* (60 *ratis*).

pon, also spelt *poṉ* in Tamil; same as *hon* (i.e. *hūn* or *varāha*); same as 'gold' *māḍai*, *gadyāṇa*, etc.; money. Cf. Tamil *pon-bhaṇḍāram*, *pon-paṇḍāra-vāśal*; also *pon-vargam*, *pon-vari*, etc., meaning 'taxes payable in gold or coins'.

poṉ, Tamil; see *pon.*

pon-gadyāṇa, 'gold *gadyāṇa*'; same as *gadyāṇa-ponnu*; see *gadyāṇa.*

poruttha-dramma, see *dramma*; cf. *pāruttha.*

pratāpa, same as *partāb.*

pṛḍa, a variant of *mṛḍa* (q.v.). Cf. *pruḍ.*

priyaśrāha-gajamalla-gadyāṇa, probably, *gadyāṇa* minted by Priyaśrāha and Gajamalla (or Gajamalla of Priyaśrāha); see *gadyāṇa.*

pruḍ, a variant of *mṛḍa* (q.v.). Cf. *pṛḍa.*

puḻḻi-guḻikai-varāhan, see *gulikā* and *varāha.*

'*punch-marked*', name applied to old Indian coins of copper and silver, on which the symbols were punched by different punches as was not the case with the die-struck and cast coins. Similar coins were sometimes cast from dies also.

purāṇa, a silver coin also called *dharaṇa* and *kārṣāpaṇa*, 32 *ratis* (about 58 grains) in weight; name applied to the silver punch-marked coins and also to the Śaka-type silver coins weighing about 20 *ratis.*

rājarāja-māḍa, Telugu; '*māḍa* or *māḍai* issued by king Rājarāja (Coḻa Rājarāja I, 985-1016 A.D.)'; see *māḍa.*

rājarājan-māḍai, Tamil; same as *rājarāja-māḍa.*

rajendracoḻa-māḍa, '*māḍa* issued by king Rājendra-coḻa (Rājendra I, 1016-43 A.D.)'; see *māḍa.*

raktikā, modern *rati*; a little above $1\frac{3}{4}$ grains.

rāśi-paṇam, 'current good coins'; also called *rāśi-ppon.*

rāśi-ppon, same as *rāśi-paṇam* (q.v.).

rati, same as *raktikā*; a little above $1\frac{3}{4}$ grains.

raupya-ṭaṅka, 'a silver *ṭaṅka* (q.v.)'; a silver *kārṣāpaṇa* so called in South India according to Nārada.

rekai-ppon, regarded as the name of a gold coin of the Vijayanagara times so called probably for bearing linear marks (*rekhā*); may be 'revenue income in cash'.

rekhā, cf. *rekai-ppon.*

rudradāmaka, '*kārṣāpaṇa* issued by Rudradāman'; name applied to the silver coins issued by the Śaka rulers of Western India; its later imitations were called *rūpaka*, *dramma*, etc.

rūpa, same as *rūpaka* or *rūpyaka* (q.v.).

rūpaka, silver coin; silver coin $\frac{1}{16}$ (about 20 *ratis*) of a gold *dīnāra*, etc.; also called *dramma*, *purāṇa*, *kārṣāpaṇa*, etc.; same as modern *rupee*; cf. *kṛṣṇarāja-rūpaka.*

rupee, English form of *rūpīya* (q.v.); silver coin equal to 16 *annas* and 64 *paisās*.

rūpīya (*rūpīah*), Muhammadan name of *rūpya*, *rūpaka* or *rūpyaka* (q.v.); same as modern *rupee*.

rūpya, same as *rūpaka* or *rūpyaka* (q.v.); same as modern *rupee*.

śāhaṇikāṭi, supposed to be the name of a coin.

śalāgai, Tamil; name of a coin also called *paḻañśalāgai* (*accu*); probably had the shape of a *śalākā*.

śalākā, same as Tamil *śalāgai*.

sambiraṇippalaṅ-gāśu, see *kāśu*.

śāṇa, name of a weight or a coin 40 *ratis* in weight; equal to 4 *māṣas*; sometimes regarded as 32 *ratis* and called *niṣka* and *ṭaṅka*; rarely also regarded as equal to 24 or 20 *ratis*.

śāna-pāda, same as *māṣa* (q.v.).

śānaka, same as *śāna* (q.v.).

sarṣapa, sometimes called 'red *sarṣapa*'; a small unit of measurement.

śāśukāni, also called *śāśukāni-ṭaṅka*; same as *ṣaṣghānī*.

śāśukāni-ṭanka, same as *śāśukāni* or *ṣaṣghāṇī*.

ṣaṣghānī, Tughluk coin, 4 *jītals* in weight and value.

śatamāna, the weight of 320 *ratis*; literally, 'a hundred units of measurement', the unit probably being the *mañjāḍi* (q.v.); also called *pala* and *niṣka* (320 *ratis* of gold or silver); during the medieval period, sometimes regarded as 160 *ratis*; name sometimes applied to an ancient gold coin.

satera, also spelt *sateraka*; probably the same as Greek *stater*; regarded as equal to 2 *dīnāras*.

sateraka, same as *satera* (q.v.).

sauvarṇa, same as *suvarṇa* (q.v.).

śenapaka-kkuḻigai, see *kuḻigai*, *gulikā*, etc.

siglos, name of the silver coin (86.45 grains) of ancient Irān.

sinna, same as *cinna* (q.v.).

ṣoḍaśī, also called *ṣoḍaśikā*; probably, one-sixteenth of the standard silver coin in weight or value; cf. *paṇa*.

soḍaśikā, same as *ṣoḍaśī* (q.v.).

śoḻiya-kkāśu, 'the *Coḻa kāśu* (copper coin)'; see *kāśu*.

śreṣṭhi-jīrṇa-viśvamalla-priya, probably a mistake for *jīrṇa-śreṣṭhi-viśvamalla-priya*, 'old coin minted by *Śreṣṭhin* Viśvamalla'.

śrīmad-ādivarāha-dramma, '*dramma* issued by *śrīmad*-Ādivarāha'; cf. *ādivarāha-dramma*; see *dramma*.

śrī-yakki-pa̱lañ-śalāgai, cf. *yakki-accu*, *pa̱lañ-śalāgai*, *śalākā*.

stater, Greek silver and gold coin; silver stater was also called *tetradrachma*; gold stater had the same weight as Persian double *daric* (265 grains).

śukti, same as *śatamāna* (q.v.).

surabhi-māḍa, probably, '*māḍa* bearing the figure of a cow'; see *māḍa*.

suvarṇa, weight of 16 *māṣas* or 80 *ratis* (about 146 grains); 16 *kārṣāpaṇas* or *rūpakas* or 48 *paṇas* according to different authorities; called *picu*, *pāṇi*, *kroḍa*, *binduka*, *viḍālapadaka*, *haṁsapada*, *grāsagraha* and *tola*; also called *niṣka*; $\frac{1}{4}$ of *pala*; gold coin weighing 80 *ratis*; name applied to Tamil *ka̱lañju* (about 32 *ratis* or 58 grains theoretically).

suvarṇa-gadyāṇa, 'gold *gadyāṇa*'; see *gadyāṇa*.

ṭākā, modern Bengali form of *ṭaṇkā* (from *ṭaṅkaka*); silver coin; money; written in old Bengali as *taṅkā*; see *ṭaṅka*.

ṭaṁ, abbreviation of *ṭaṅka*.

taṇḍula, $\frac{1}{2}$ of a *dhānya-māṣa*.

tāṅk, also called *tāṅkī*; same as *ṭanka*.

ṭaṇka, a coin in general; a silver coin (often one *tola* in weight); same as *śāna*; equal to 4 silver *fanams*, silver coin of the Delhi Sulṯāns, 96 or 100 *ratis* in weight; same as *aṭha-gānī* (q.v.); a small copper coin; $\frac{1}{2}$ of a *rupee*. There were gold and copper *taṅkas*; see *hema-ṭaṅka* and *raupya-ṭaṅka*. Cf. *ṭāṅk*, etc.

ṭaṅkaka, same as *ṭaṅka* (q.v.); name of a silver coin; sometimes mentioned as bearing the figure of the *Bhagavat*.

ṭāṅkī, same as *ṭaṅka*.

tār, name of a silver coin, equal to $\frac{1}{6}$ of a gold *fanam*.

tetradrachma, 'four-drachma'; quadruple drachma; see *drachma*.

tirama, Tamil form of *dramma*.

tola, also spelt *tolaka*; 80 *ratis* in weight; same as *suvarṇa*.

tolaka, same as *kola* or *tola*; 80 *ratis* in weight.

triśūla-kāśu, probably, '*kāśu* bearing the representation of a trident'; possibly issued by the authorities of a Śiva temple; see *kāśu*.

tu̱lai-ppon, Tamil; 'correct weight' or 'good current coin'.

turai-miṉṉar-pon, a kind of *pon* (i.e. *hon*, *gadyāṇa* or *varāha*).

uṇḍi-accu, see *accu*.

uppu-kkāśu, 'salt money'; name of a tax; see *kāśu*.

ūr-kaḻañjū, see *kaḻañju*.

ūr-kāśu, see *kāśu*.

uttama-gaṇḍa-māḍa, probably 'good (i.e. new) *gaṇḍamāḍa*' or '*gaṇḍa-māḍa* issued by king Uttama (i.e. Uttama-coḻa, 980-85 A.D.); see *māḍa*.

vagainda-kāśu, name of a tax; see *kāśu*.

val, sometimes regarded as $\frac{1}{20}$ of a *gadyāṇa*.

valla, equal to 3 *ratis*.

vaḷāl-vaḻi-tiṟantāṉ-guḷikai, Pāṇḍya coin supposed to be issued by Jaṭāvarman Sundara-pāṇḍya I; see *gulikā*, etc.

vaḷudiy-accu-vargam, see *accu*.

varāha, a gold coin; same as *hūn* or *hon* (q.v.); also called *pagoda* (q.v.) or 'star *pagoda*'.

varāha-gadyāṇa, same as *varāha* (q.v.), *gadyāṇa* or *pagoda* (q.v.).

varāha-paṇam, probably 'money calculated in *varāha* (q.v.).'

varāha-viṁśopaka, $\frac{1}{20}$ of a *varāha*; see *varāha* and *viṁśopaka*.

varāhan-puḷḷi-kuḷigai, see *varāha* and *gulikā*, etc.

varāṭakā, same as *varāṭaka* or *varāṭikā*.

varāṭikā, cowrie-shell used as a coin; money.

vāśal-paṇam, 'door-tax'; periodical payment due to the palace; same as *vāśal-tiramam*; see *paṇa*.

vāśal-tiramam, 'door-tax'; same as *vāśal-paṇam*; see *dramma*.

vaṭaka, same as *draṁkṣaṇa* or *tola*.

veḷḷi, name of a coin.

veli-kkāśu, same as *veli-ppayaṟu*; name of a tax; see *kāśu*.

veli-ppayaṟu, same as *veli-kkāśu* (q.v.).

viḍālapadaka, same as *suvarṇa* (q.v.).

vigraha-dramma, '*dramma* issued or minted by Vigraha'; same as *vigrahapāla-dramma*, etc.; see *dramma*.

vigraha-dramma-visvovaka, '$\frac{1}{20}$ of the *vigraha-dramma*'; see *dramma* and *viṁśopaka*.

vigrahapāla-dramma, '*dramma* issued or minted by Vigrahapāla'; same as *vigraha-dramma* (q.v.), etc.; see *dramma*.

vigrahapāla-satka-dramma, same as *vigrahapāla-dramma* (q.v.), etc.; see *dramma*.

vigrahapālīya-dramma, '*dramma* issued or minted by Vigrahapāla'; same as *vigraha-dramma* (q.v.), etc.

vigrahatuṅgīya-dramma, '*dramma* issued or minted by Vigrahatuṅga'; cf. *vigraha-dramma*, etc.; see *dramma*.

vijayarāja-ṭaṅka, '*ṭaṅka* issued by Vijayarāja'; see *ṭaṅka*.

vil-paṇam, 'sales tax', or 'tax on bows or archery'; see *paṇa*.

viṁśatika, regarded as equal to 20 *māṣas*; cf. *viṁśopaka*.

viṁsopaka, corruption of *viṁśopaka*.

viṁśopaka, $\frac{1}{20}$ of the standard silver coin of about 20 *ratis*; same as *visvovaka*, *visopaka*, *vīsovā*, etc.

vīracampan-guḻigai, *gulikā* of the Śambhuvarāya king Vīracampa; see *gulikā*, etc.

vīrapañcālan-kāśu, see *kāśu*.

vīsala-priya-dramma, also called *vīsala-prī-dramma*; cf. *jīrṇa-viśvamalla-priya*, *Vīsala* being the same as *Viśvamalla*.

visopaka, corruption of *viṁśopaka*.

vīsovā, corruption of *viṁśopaka*.

visvovaka, corruption of *viṁśopaka*.

voḍī, also called *voḍikā* and *voḍrī*; sometimes regarded as a cowrie-shell used as coin; but really, the unit equal to 5 *gaṇḍās* =20 cowries. Cf. *buḍḍī*, *kapardaka-voḍī* (q.v.).

voḍikā, same as *voḍī*. Cf. *buḍḍī* and *kapardaka-voḍī* (q.v.).

voḍrī, same as *voḍī*.

vṛiṣa-viṁśopaka, 'a *viṁśopaka* bearing the figure of a bull'; see *viṁśopaka*.

yādavarāyan-paṇam, 'coin issued by the Yādavarāyas'; see *paṇa*.

yakki-accu, '*accu* bearing the figure of a *Yakṣī* (a village goddess)'; see *accu*.

yava, $\frac{1}{18}$ of *māṣa*; $\frac{1}{3}$ of *rati*.

INDEX

A

ā-candr-ārk-ārṇava-kṣiti-sthiti-sama-kālīna 388
ā-candra-tārakam 388
ācāra 3
ācaraṇa 67
ācāra-pātra 4
a-cār-āsana-carm-āṅgāra 29, 66, 388
a-cāra-siddhika 389, 393
ācāra-sthiti 324
ācāra-sthiti-pātra 4, 324-25
Ācāri 4
Ācariya 4
a-carm-āṅgāraka 20, 67, 389
Ācārya 4, 112, 213, 299, 301, 314, 332, 346, 350, 379
ācāryakula 4, 89
ācārya-pīṭha 4
ācārya-pūjana, ācārya-pūjanai 4, 409
a-cāṭa-bhaṭa-gocara 389
a-cāṭa-bhaṭa-praveśa 389, 394
a-cāṭa-bhaṭa-prāveśya 67, 73, 388-89, 401, 404
a-cāṭa-bhaṭa-prāveśyaṁ cora-drohaka-varjam 67
a-caṭṭa-bhaṭṭa-praveśa 51, 68, 389
ācchanna 4
accu 4-5, 16, 34, 428-29, 436-37, 439, 441-42
accu-pannāya 4
Accupannāyadadhiṣṭhāyaka 4, 181, 183, 188
accu-taṟi, accu-ttaṟi 409
accuvari 5, 409
āchu 5, 34, 428
acita 5
a-cullaka-kūra-khaṭvā-grahaṇa 389
āḍa 5, 428
ādāna 5
āḍāṇaka 5
āḍānake muktā 5
aḍatālīsa-gānī, aḍatālīs-gānī 35, 428
aḍattā, ādatta, ādattā 5
ādāya 2, 5, 14, 22-23, 31
adbhuta 5
adbhutadharma 5
adbhuta-śānti 5
aḍḍa 5, 428
aḍḍa-cinna 5, 428
aḍḍaga 5, 428
aḍḍāṇaka 5
addhika 27
aḍḍuga 5, 428
Ādeśakārin 5
Ādeśa-naibandhika 5
ādeya 5, 90
āḍha, āḍhā 5
adhaḥ 5
āḍhaka 5-6, 101
āḍhakavāpa 6
ādhāna 6
ādhau dattam 6
ādhau kṛtam 6
ādhau muktam 6
āḍhavāpa 5-6
Adhi 6
Ādhi
adhika 6
āḍhika 5
adhik-ākṣara 6
adhika-paḍi 6
Adhikāra 6
adhikāra-mel-eḻuttu 6
adhikaraṇa 6-8, 145, 187
adhikaraṇa-daṇḍa 6
Adhikaraṇa-lekhaka 6
adhikaraṇ-āvadhāraṇā 6, 38
Adhikaraṇika, Ādhikaraṇika 6-7
adhikāra-ppeṟu 7, 409
adhikāra-ppŏn 7
adhikāra-varttanā, adhikāra-vartanai 7, 409
Adhikārika, Ādhikārika 7, 221, 308, 378
Adhikāri-mukhya 7
Adhikārin 6, 121, 277, 289, 369
Adhikṛta 7, 14
Adhimahārāja 7

C

H

K

L

N

O

P

Q

R

V

76, 203, 275, 281, 427
vīra-siṁhāsana 376
Vīra-yātrika 376
viṟ-paṇam 427
viruda 60
Virūpakha-pati 376
Virūpākṣa-pati 376
viruttu-ppaṭṭigai 427
visa 159
visā 370, 376-77
vīsa 206, 370, 374, 376
viṣahara-bhoga 376-77
viśa-kkāṇam 427
Vīsala 442
vīsala-prī-dramma 376, 442
vīsalapriya-dramma 135, 376, 433, 442
viśālapriya-viṁśopaka 374
visālu 370
visaṁsthula 377
visāmu 376-77
visatiaṭhū-prastha 377
viṣa-vṛtti 376-77
viṣaya 12, 57, 161, 194-95, 219, 359, 369, 377-78
Viṣaya-bhogika 377
Viṣaya-bhūbhuj 377
viṣaya-dāna 377
Viṣaya-dānika 377
Viṣay-ādhikaraṇa 377
Viṣay-ādhipati 377
Viṣaya-karaṇa 377
viṣayālī 377
viṣaya-māna 63
Viṣay-āmātya 377
viṣayaṇa 378
Viṣayapāla 378
Viṣayapati 60, 377-78
viṣaya-suṅka 377
Viṣaya-vyāpṛtaka 378
Viṣaya-vyavahārin 377-78
Viṣayeśa 378
Viṣayika 378
Viṣayik-ādhikārika 378
Viṣayin 60, 378
viseṇima, viseṇimā 378
viseṇim-ādāya 5, 378
viśeṣ-ādāya, viśeṣ-ādāyam 378, 427
viśeṣ-āya, viśeṣ-āyam 378, 427
viśikha 378
viśīrṇa 378
Viśiṣa 378
Viṣṇu 66, 70
viṣṇu-bāhu 378
viṣṇu-gṛha 378
viṣṇu-pada 378
viṣṇu-śrāddha 378
viṣṇu-tithi 378
viśopaka 373
visovā 412
vīsovā 378
visovaka 371, 374, 378, 442
viṣṭapa 378
vistaraṇa 378
viṣṭi 131, 370, 379, 409, 411, 426
viṣṭi-prātibhedikā 258
viśuddh-ākṣarāṇi 15
viśuddhi 379
viśuddhiṁ yāvat 379
viṣuva 379
viṣuvat 379
viśva 379
viśvacakra 379
viṣvag-devā 379
Viśvakarman 379
Viṣvaksenai 308, 309
Viśvāla 379
Viśvamalla 442
Viśvāsa 360, 379
Viśvāsa-Khāna 379
viśvāsana 379
Viśvāsa-rāya 379
viśva-sattā 379
Viśvāsika 182, 360, 379
Viśvaviśvopaka 379
viśvedevāḥ 379
visvillaka 248
visvovaka 442
visya 376
vitāna 379
Vitān-ādhipa 307-08, 366, 379
viṭapa 379

Addenda et Corrigenda

N.B.—Misprints that may be more or less easily corrected by the readers include (1) a few cases of *ṛ* written as *ṛi* (e.g., p. 388—*bhṛta*, p. 393—*tṛṇa*) and *cha* written for *ca* (p. 324, line 3); (2) wrong use of capital and small letters at the beginning of entries meant for indicating persons and objects respectively; (3) entries put away from their proper places (e.g., p. 10—*agahara*, p. 49—*bhamāti* and *Bhāṇaka*, p. 211—*naṅga* and *Nāṇī*, p. 257—*prāstarika-śreṇī*, p. 412—*aradu dogarāca-ppaṇṇu*, p. 433—*jīrṇa-viśvamalla-priya*), and (4) occasional omission of diacritical marks in *ā*, *ĕ*, ŏ, *ḍ*, *ṇ*, *ś*, *ṭ*, etc.

Page 5, line 26—*Read*—mortgaged

„ 9— Add—*ādya-stamba*, 'covered with original shrubs', i.e. yielding no revenue income, never cultivated.

„ 11, line 17—Read—*āgrahāyanī*

„ 16 — Add—*ā-mā*, abbreviation of *ādya-māṣa* (i.e. the original *māṣa* of 5 *ratis*).

„ 26, line 27—Read—*Ārakṣ-ādhikṛta*.

„ 28, line 12—Read—*Arhad-āyatana*.

„ 35, line 14—*Add*—Cf. *Bṛhad-aśvavāra*.

„ „ line 23—*Add*—RE XIII of Aśoka seems to speak of the *Aṭavī* or foresters as habitually criminal.

„ „ lines 29ff.—Read—*aṭha-gānī*, a billon coin equal to 8 copper *jitals* and to ⅛ of a silver *ṭaṅka*.

„ 40, line 26—*Add*—Cf. also *nivāta*.

„ 44, line 13—*Add*—See *vāhyāli*.

„ 45 — Add—*Balisādhaka*, tax-collector (Ghoshal, *Ag. Syst.*, p. 25).

„ 47, line 35—*Add*—Cf. *pāga*.

„ 48, line 13—*Add*—In *bhoga-bhāga-dhānya-hiraṇya* of the Kurud plates (*Ep. Ind.*, Vol. XXXI, p. 264), we have probably to understand *dhānya-hiraṇya* realised as *bhoga-bhāga*.

„ „ line 36—*Add*—See *pagoda*.

Page 61 line 34—*Adā*—tenure of $\frac{1}{20}$ of the revenue of an area granted to the Brāhmaṇas.

„ 62 — Add—*Bṛhad-aśvavara*, a cavalry officer (Tripathi, *History of Kanauj*, p. 137).

„ 64, line 35—*Read*—$\frac{1}{20}$ of a rupee.

„ 71, line 8—Read—*Cau.*

„ 77— Add—*daivaka*; see *rājaka-daivaka.*

„ 80, line 4—*Add*—May also be *Dāṇḍa* (*Dāṇḍanāyaka*) and *Bhogika.*

„ 88— Add—*deva-hala*, same as *deva-bhoga-hala*; cf. *hala-nyāya*, *bhikṣu-hala*. See *Suc. Sat.*, pp. 84, etc.

„ 91, line 7—Add—*Bhoga-bhāga-dhānya-hiranya* of the Kurud plates (*Ep. Ind.*, Vol. XXXI, p. 264) probably means *dhānya-hiranya* realised as *bhoga-bhāga.*

„ „ line 38—Read—*dhārā-datta.*

„ 97— Add—*Digvijayin*, 'the conqueror of the quarters'; title of some rulers conventionally claiming to have conquered the *cakravarti-kṣetra* (q.v.).

„ „ line 13—*Add*—It normally means 'the conquest of the quarters', conventional claim of a type of Indian rulers.

„ 101, line 2—Read—collection of revenue (cf. *Rājatar.*, VII. 2010)

„ „ line 12—*Read*—watch-station for the collection of tolls

„ „ line 15—Read—*Audraṅgika.*

„ —Add—*dukra*, $\frac{1}{8}$ of a *phadiyā.*

„ 111, line 12—*Read*—EI 9.

„ „ line 34-35—Read—*gānī*, cf. *aṭha-gānī*, a billon coin equal to 8 copper *jitals* and to $\frac{1}{6}$ of a silver *ṭaṅka.*

„ 115, line 22—Read—*ghaṭikā-sthāna.*

„ 119, line 29—Read—*go-yuthī.*

„ 125 — Add—*hala-nyāya*, custom followed in granting rent-free holdings; same as *brahmadeya-maryādā*, etc.

Page 129, last line—*Add*—Also cf. *suvarṇ-ādāya, svarṇ-āya.*
„ 131, line 16—Read—*indr-āsana.*
„ „ line 28—*Add*—Cf. *Mahābhārata*, XII, 103.2:*atr=āpy=udāharant=imam=itihāsaṁ purātanam Bṛhaspateś=ca saṁvādam=Indrasya ca Yudhiṣṭhira* ||
„ 138, line 17—Add—*Kaivarta-bhoga* and *Kaivarta-vṛtti* really mean the land enjoyed by the fishermen for their service, e.g., ferrying, supply of fish and boats, etc.
„ 144, line 30—*Add*—Note that *boḍi* or *voḍi* is also the same as Bengali *buḍi* which is ¼ of a *paṇa* and is equal to 20 cowrie-shells.
„ 150, line 31—*Add*—probably derived from Sanskrit *karṣa.*
„ „ line 36—Read—*nat-kāśu.*
„ 151, line 38—*Add*—explained as 'a commander of the elephant force' (Tripathi, *History of Kanauj*, p. 137).
„ 158, line Add—*kedāra*, coin of the Kidāra-Kuṣāṇas (Bhandarkar, *Carm. Lect.*, 1921, p. 205).
„ „ line 12—Read—*kliṇva-kreṇi* (for *klinna-kreṇi*)
„ 164, line 34—*Add*—Same as *Senabova* (q. v.).
„ 165, line 6—Read—*Kulavārika.*
„ 166, line 39—*Read*—occurs, *for*—occury.
„ 170— Add—*laṅkā*, islet in a river (*Kākatīya-saṁcika*, No. 31).
„ 182, line 18—Read—*Pañcāyat* board.
„ 190, line 19—*Read*—IE 8-2
„ 197, line 6—Read—*maṅgalikā.*
„ 200, line 5—Read—*marīci.*
„ 216— Add—*Nigrāhaka*, tax-collector (Ghoshal, *Ag. Syst.*, p. 25). cf. *Koṭṭa-nigraha.*
„ 220— Add—*nivāta*; see *s-oṣar-āvaskara-sthāna-nivāta-lavaṇ-ākara* (EI 22); same as *āvāta.*
„ 228, line 3—*Add*—The expression *pāli-ddhaya* in Apabhraṁśa is explained as 'small flags' (*Bhār. Vid.*, Vol. XXV, p. 34).
„ 230, line 23—*Add*—Bengali *pāñcālī* is a kind of versified composition so called probably because it was originally sung either before the

members of the Pañcāyat board or at puppet shows.

Page 232 Add—*pañcāṅgula*, impression the palm with outstretched fingers dipped in sandal paste or any such thing; also called *Pañcāṅgulika.*

„ 242, line 19—Read—religious teachers.

„ 244, Add—*Pāṭīpati* (Tripathi, *History of Kanauj*, p. 137); cf. *Pāṭyuparika.*

„ 245, line 14—*Read*—IE 8-8.

„ 256, line 12—Read—*Pranapṭṛka*

„ 257 — Add—*prasūti-śālā*, maternity home (*Kākatiyasaṁcika*, No. 31).

„ 266, line 4—Read—*Puraśreṣṭhin.*

„ 268 — Add—*putra*, cf. *Kerala-putra*, king of the Keralas; *Guhila-putra*, descendant of Guhila.

„ 305, lines 3ff.—Read—*ṣaṣghānī*, billon coin of the Tughluq Sulṭāns, equal to six copper *jitals* and to $\frac{1}{8}$ of a silver *ṭaṅka*; same as *cha-gānī* and *śāśukāni.*

„ 308, last line—Read—*Senaiy-aṅgādikaḷ*

„ 310, line 28—Read—*abhyantara-siddhi.*

„ 312 — Add—*siṁhakara*, 'lion-tax' (Ghoshal, *HRS*, p. 232).

„ 331, last line—Read—*Malik-us-Sair.*

„ 340, line 31—Read—*ṭī.*

„ 342, line 3—Read—*tīthi-śūdhi*

„ „ line 38—*Read*—EI 23.

„ 355— Add—*utpratikara*, same as *apratikara* (*Ep. Ind.*, Vol. XIX, p. 54, line 10).

„ 356— Add—*utthāpita*, dedicated (*E.I.*, 16, p. 15).

„ 359, line 1—Read—*vahni* (IE 7-1-2, EI 33), 'three'.

„ „ line 7—*Omit.*

„ 362, line 38—*Read*—CII 3

„ 371, line 3—Add—explained as 'the chief court Pandit' (Sarma, *Reḍḍi Kingdoms*, pp. 466-67).

„ 381— Add—*vṛndāvana*, see *bṛndāvana.*

„ 382— Add—*Vyantara*, see *Yakṣa.*

„ 384— Add—*Yāma-ceṭī* (Tripathi, *History of Kanauj*, p. 137), probably, a female attendant to the *ghaṭī-yantra* (q.v.); cf. *Yāmakinī.*

Page 384 — Add—*Yāmakinī*; cf. *Yāma-ceṭī*.

„ 407, line 26—Read—*nidhi-nikṣepa-devāyatan-odyāna*.

„ 411, line 24—Read—*vilaiy-āvaṇam*.

„ 412, line 26—Read—*eraḍu-bilkoḍe*.

„ 415, line 6—Read—*kāṭciy-erudu-kkāśu*.

„ 417, line 1—Read—*magaṇmai*, for—*magaṇamai*.

„ 418, line 16—Read—*mudaṟṟiramam*.

„ 421, line 9—Read—*pĕrujuṅka*, for—*pĕrujuṇka*.

„ 422, line 7—*Read*—Caṇḍālas.

„ 428, line 7—Read—*aḍatālīsa-gānī*, billon coin equal to the silver *ṭaṅka* and to 48 copper *jitals*.

„ 429, line 5—Read—*aṭha-gānī*, billon coin equal to 8 *jitals* and to $\frac{1}{8}$ of a silver *ṭaṅka*.

„ „ 13—Read—*bārah-gānī*, billon coin equal to 12 copper *jitals* and to $\frac{1}{4}$ of the silver *ṭaṅka*.

„ „ line 33—Read—*caubīsa-gānī*, billon coin equal to 24 copper *jitals* and to $\frac{1}{2}$ of a silver *ṭaṅka*.

„ „ line 34—Read—*cau-gānī*, billon coin equal to 4 copper *jitals* and to $\frac{1}{12}$ of a silver *ṭaṅka*.

„ „ line 37—Read—*cha-gānī*, billon coin equal 6 copper *jitals* and to $\frac{1}{8}$ of a silver *ṭaṅka*; same as *ṣaṣghānī* and *śāśukāni*.

„ 431, line 9—Read—*do-gānī*, billon coin equal to 2 copper *jitals* and to $\frac{1}{24}$ of a silver *ṭaṅka*; same as *du-gānī*.

„ „ line 29—Read—*du-gānī*, billon coin equal to 2 copper *jitals* and to $\frac{1}{24}$ of silver *ṭaṅka*; same as *do-gānī*.

„ 432, line 25—Read—*gānī*, cf. *aṭha-gānī*, billon coin equal to 8 copper *jitals* and to $\frac{1}{8}$ of a silver *ṭaṅka*.

„ 439— Add—*ṣaḍ-voḍḍika-dramma* (*JUPHS*, Vol. XVIII, p. 200), copper *dramma* equal to 6 *voḍḍikas* or 120 cowrie-shells.

„ 440, lines 24-25—*Omit*—same as *aṭha-gānī* (q.v.).